SOCIOLOGY

ANTHONY GIDDENS

Polity Press

Copyright © Anthony Giddens 1989

First published 1989 by Polity Press in association with Basil Blackwell
Reprinted 1989, 1990 (twice)

Editorial office:
Polity Press, 65 Bridge Street, Cambridge CB2 1UR, UK

Marketing and production:
Basil Blackwell Ltd
108 Cowley Road, Oxford OX4 1JF, UK

British Library Cataloguing in Publication Data

Giddens, Anthony
Sociology.
1. Sociology
I. Title
301
ISBN 0-7456-0545-1
ISBN 0-7456-0546-X Pbk

Typeset in 11 on 12½pt Palatino by Gecko Limited, Bicester, Oxon
Printed in Great Britain by Butler and Tanner Ltd, Frome

SOCIOLOGY

Contents

xxii   *Contents*

Acknowledgements

Many people have helped me in the preparation of this book. Special mention must be made of Graham McCann, who was involved in the project from the beginning, and who gathered together material I was able directly to utilize in the work, as well as assisting in numerous other ways. I owe an enormous debt to Don Fusting, of Norton Inc., New York, whose detailed comments on earlier drafts have been of vital importance. Among those whose help and encouragement have also been invaluable, and to whom I would like to give especial thanks here, are: Pip Hurd, Claire Robinson, Gill Motley, Helen Pilgrim, David Held, Michael Hay, John Thompson, Silvana Dean and Claire Andrews. Avril Symonds was extraordinarily efficient in typing and retyping different versions of the manuscript. Harriet Barry did a marvellous job of copy-editing the book, making many suggestions for alterations, and contributing in important ways to its final form.

I am indebted to a variety of individuals for having taken the time to read and comment on various chapters of the book. They have materially influenced the final product. Particular thanks are due to: Andy Webster, Kevin Bonnett, Dede Boden, Abigail Buckle, Michelle Stanworth, James Slevin, Teresa Brennan, Phil Manning, Sam Hollick and Michele Giddens.

I am grateful to the following for their permission to reproduce previously published material: Aldine de Gruyter for figure 1 from *Man the Hunter*, eds Richard B. Lee and Irven DeVore, copyright © 1968 by the Wenneren Foundation for Anthropological Research, Inc.; Philip Allan Publishers Ltd for tables 8 and 9 from *Social Studies Review*, March 1987; American Anthropologist Association for an extract on pages 38–9 from 'Body ritual among the Nacirema', *American Anthropologist*, 58, 1956; Ballantine Books, a division of Random House, Inc., for the extract on pages 577–8 from *The Population Bomb* by Paul R. Ehrlich, 1971; Basil Blackwell Ltd and Polity Press for table 10 from *Space Weapons: Deterrence or Delusion* by Rip Bulkeley and Graham Spinardi, 1987; figure 8 from *Survival and Change in the Third World* by Ben Crow and Mary Thorpe,

1988; figure 20 from *Unemployment: Economic Theory and Evidence* by Peter Sinclair, 1987; the Bodley Head Ltd for an extract on pages 345–6 from *War* by Gwynne Dyer, 1985; John Calder (Publishers) Ltd for an extract on page 486 from *The Assembly Line* by Robert Linhart, 1981; Century Hutchinson Publishing Group Ltd for an extract on page 262 from *There Ain't No Black in the Union Jack* by Paul Gilroy, 1987, p. 181; Collins Publishers for an extract on pages 42–3 from *Cannibals and Kings: The Origins of Culture* by Marvin Harris, 1978; the Daily Telegraph plc for figure 10 from the 14 June 1987 issue of the *Sunday Telegraph*; Gower Publishing Company Ltd for figure 9 from *Britain's Black Population* by the Runnymeed Trust and the Radical Statistics Race Group, Heinemann Education, 1980; Haper and Row, Publishers, Inc. for figure 22 from *Global Shift* b Peter Dicken, copyright © 1986 by Peter Dicken; and an extract on page 157 from *The Dynamics of Sex and Gender*, 2nd edn, by Lauren Walum Richardson, copyright © 1981 by Houghton Mifflin Co.; the Controller of Her Majesty's Stationery Office for figures 12, 17, 18, 19, 23, 24, tables 3, 11 and data on page 681 from Crown copyright material; the Illustrated London News Picture Library for an adapted extract on pages 266–7 from 'Britain now' by L. Taylor, *Illustrated London News*, October 1987; Lescher and Lescher Ltd for an extract on page 164 from '. . . and then the prince knelt down and tried to put the glass slipper on Cinderella's foot' from *If I Were in Charge of the World* by Judith Viorst, 1987; Macmillan Publishing Company for tables 13, 14 from *The Other World: Issues and Politics in the Third World* by Joseph Weatherby, Jr, Dianne Long, William Alexander et al., tables 2.1, 3.2, copyright © 1986 by Macmillan Publishing Company; Macmillan Publishers Ltd for table 2 from *Women and the Economy* by A. T. Maillier and M. J. Rosser, 1987; table 4 from *Values and Social Change in Britain* by Mark Abrams, David Garrard and Noel Timms, 1986; figure 2 from *Introduction to the Sociology of Development* by Andrew Webster, 1986; and tables 5, 6 from *The Upper Classes: Property and Privilege in Britain* by John Scott, 1982; Methuen and Co. for an extract on page 65 from *The Magic Years: Understanding and Handling the Problems of Early Childhood* by Selma Fraiberg, Scribners, 1959; Jo Nesbitt for cartoon on page 158 from *Daughters and Sons* by June Statham, 1986, drawn by Jo Nesbitt; the New Yorker Magazine, Inc. for cartoons on pages 13, 36, 292, 376, 399; Open University Press for table 1 and figure 5 from *Crime and Punishment: Intrepreting the Data* by A. Bottomley and K. Pease, 1986, table 1.2 and figure 1.1; Oxford University Press, Inc. for figure 16 from *The World Crisis in Education: The View of the Eighties* by Philip H. Coombs, copyright © 1985 by Philip H. Coombs; Penguin Books Ltd and Editions Gallimard for the plate on page 295 from *Discipline and Punish* by Michel Foucault, translated by Alan Sheridan, Penguin Books, 1977, copyright © 1977 Alan Sheridan; Time, Inc. for table 12 from *Fortune Magazine* 3 August 1987, p.18, copyright © 1988 Time, Inc.; Thames and Hudson Ltd for table 15 from *Private Opinions, Public Polls* from Leslie Watkins and Robert M. Worcester, 1986; Unwin Hyman Ltd for figure 21 from

The Developing World by Andrew Reed, Bell and Hyman 1979; figure 4 from *Time Resources, Society and Ecology: On the Capacity for Human Interaction in Space and Time* by T. Carlstein, Allen and Unwin, 1982; and extracts on page 285 from *Japan in the Passing Line* by Stoshi Kamata, Allen and Unwin, 1982; John Wiley and Sons, Inc. for an extract on pages 185–6 from *Understanding the Rape Victim* by S. Katz and M. A. Mazur, 1979, p. 307; World Priorities for table 7 and figure 11 from *World Military and Social Expenditures 1983* by Ruth Leger Sivard, copyright © 1983 by World Priorities.

Preface: About This Book

This book is written in the belief that sociology has a key role to play in modern intellectual culture and a central place within the social sciences. After teaching at all levels of sociology for some while, I became convinced of the need to filter some of the discipline's current advances and developments into an elementary introduction to the field. This book is not just an attempt to write yet another introductory text, but represents an endeavour to reframe some of the main perspectives and concerns of the subject.

My aim has been to write a work that combines some originality with an analysis of all the basic issues of interest to sociologists today. Although many of my previous writings have been concerned with theory, I have never believed that theoretical debates have much interest for their own sake. Theoretical reasoning is only valuable if it helps illuminate empirical issues. In this text, I have tried to cover the background to the important advances in theoretical thinking happening at the present time. But the best way of mastering the connections between theory and research is by the active attempt to understand social institutions. Therefore I have emphasized the study of distinct problems and fields within sociology. The book does not try to introduce overly sophisticated notions; nevertheless, ideas and findings drawn from the cutting edge of the discipline are incorporated throughout. I hope it is not in any way a partisan treatment, but covers the major available perspectives in sociology in a judicious way.

Basic themes

The book is constructed around a number of basic themes, each of which is relevant to what I hope is the distinctive character of the work. One theme is the relation between the *social* and the *personal*. Sociological thinking is a vital help to self-understanding, which in turn can be focused back upon an improved understanding of the social world. Studying sociology should be a liberating experience: sociology enlarges our sympathies and imagination, opens up new perspectives on the sources of our own behaviour, and deepens a sense of cultural settings different from our own. In so far as sociological work challenges dogma, teaches appreciation of cultural variety and allows us insight into the working of social institutions, the practice of sociology enhances the possibilities of human freedom.

A second theme is that of the *world in change*. Sociology was born of the transformations which wrenched the industrializing social order of the West away from the forms of life characteristic of pre-existing societies. The world which has thus been created is the dominant object of concern of sociological analysis. The pace of social change has continued to accelerate, and it is possible that we stand on the threshold of transitions as fundamental as those which occurred in the late eighteenth and nineteenth centuries. Sociology has prime responsibility for charting out the transformations which have taken place in the past, and for grasping the major lines of development taking place today.

Third, the book takes a strongly *comparative* stance. The study of sociology cannot be taught solely through understanding the institutions of any particular society. While I have of course slanted the discussion especially towards Britain, such discussion is always balanced by a rich variety of materials drawn from other societies or cultures. These include researches carried out in other Western countries, but I have also referred frequently to material concerned with the Soviet Union and the East European societies. The industrialized societies, however, can no longer be studied independently of the Third World, and this book includes much more material on Third World countries than has been usual hitherto in introductions to sociology. In addition, I strongly emphasize the connections of sociology and anthropology, whose concerns overlap comprehensively. Given the close connections which now mesh societies across the world with one another, and the virtual disappearance of many forms of traditional social system, sociology and anthropology increasingly become indistinguishable.

Fourth, the book recognizes the necessity of taking an *historical orientation* to sociology. This involves far more than just filling in the 'historical context' within which events occur. Some such information is certainly necessary, given that students' knowledge even of relatively recent history may be limited. But one of the most important developments in sociology over the past few years has been the resurgence of historical analysis. This should not be understood solely as a matter of applying a sociological outlook to the past, but as contributing in a basic way to our understanding of institutions in the present. Recent work in historical sociology is used widely in the book, and provides a framework for the interpretations offered within most of the separate chapters.

Fifth, particular attention is given throughout the text to *issues of gender*. The study of gender is ordinarily regarded as a specific field within sociology as a whole – and this volume contains a chapter devoted to thinking and research on the issue (chapter 6). However, questions of gender relations are so fundamental to sociological analysis that they cannot simply be relegated to one particular subdivision of the subject. Thus many of the following chapters contain sections concerned with issues of gender.

Sixth, a major theme of the book is the *globalizing of social life*. For far too long, sociology has been dominated by the view that societies can be studied as independent unities. This was never truly the case even in the past. In current times we can see a clear acceleration in processes of global integration. This is obvious, for example, in the expansion of international trade across state boundaries. But even in the technical literature of sociology, the implications of rapidly increasing globalization have not yet fully been explored, and on the introductory level they are usually ignored altogether. The emphasis on globalization in this book also connects closely with the weight given to the interdependence of First, Second and Third Worlds today.

The organization of the book

There is no abstract discussion of basic sociological concepts at the beginning of this book. Instead, concepts are explained when they are introduced in the relevant chapters, and I have sought throughout to illustrate ideas, concepts and theories by means of concrete examples. While these are usually taken from sociological research, I have quite often used material from other sources (such as newspaper reports) for illustrative purposes. I have tried to keep the writing style as simple and direct as possible, while endeavouring to make the book lively and 'full of surprises'. If taught appropriately, no subject in the academic curriculum is more absorbing, illuminating and challenging than sociology.

The chapters follow a sequence designed to help the student achieve a progressive mastery of the different fields of sociology, but I have taken care to ensure that the book can be used flexibly, and is easy to adapt to needs of particular courses. Chapters can be missed out, or studied in a different order, without much loss. Each chapter has been written as a fairly autonomous unit, with cross-referencing to other chapters at relevant points.

The six parts of the book provide a comprehensive coverage of the major areas of sociology. Part 1, consisting of a single chapter, outlines the basic concerns of the subject. Part 2 concentrates on culture, society and the individual, analysing the interplay between social influences and personal experience, with gender a major theme. The chapters included here cover culture, the development of different types of human society, socialization, everyday social interaction, conformity and crime. In Part 3, the themes of inequality, power and ideology are explored. Several core areas of sociology are discussed here: stratification, ethnicity and race, groups and organizations, politics and the state, and war and the military. Part 4 deals with basic social institutions, analysing their influence upon key areas of human behaviour. The chapters in this part are concerned with marriage and the family, education and the media, work and economic life. Part 5 groups together chapters in which the theme of *change* is developed with special emphasis, analysing globalization, modern urbanism, population, health and ageing, revolution and social movements. It concludes with a discussion of social change in general.

Finally, in Part 6, the major research methods and theoretical perspectives employed in sociology are discussed. Although this material has been placed at the end of the book it can be read at any point.

Chapter summaries and glossary

Each chapter has been carefully structured to make the learning process as entertaining, yet systematic, as possible. Every chapter is followed by a concise summary, plus a list of basic concepts and important terms which it introduces. All these concepts and terms are included in the glossary at the end of the book, which provides a very extensive reference source. Whenever a new term is first mentioned in the text itself, it is printed in **bold**.

Further research: reading and libraries

Libraries contain abundant sources of information which students can use to follow up, or expand upon, issues discussed here. References are given throughout the text and listed fully in the Bibliography at the end. Moreover, every chapter concludes with a list of recommended readings and I have included a short Appendix which provides a guide to library resources and how to use them.

For students: how to use this book

Treat the book as a friend, not an enemy! It is long because it is comprehensive. There is no need to fear that you have to read every chapter, or that they must be tackled in the sequence in which they are set out. Each chapter can be treated more or less as a self-contained unit. If you are reading the book in conjunction with a taught course, tailor the chapters you study to the ordering used by the teacher.

Use Part 6 ('Methods and Theories in Sociology') as a resource to help expand upon the material provided in the rest of the chapters. If you wish, you can read this part last of all, as it appears in the text. Anyone with no knowledge of sociology before opening the book is recommended to follow this strategy. For those who come to the book with some previous understanding of the subject, it might be rewarding to read chapters 21 and 22 *early on* – perhaps even immediately after chapter 1. This will allow you to use an initial grasp of methods and theories to illuminate your reading of the other chapters.

PART I

Introduction to Sociology

Sociology offers a distinct and highly illuminating perspective on human behaviour. Learning sociology means taking a step back from our own personal interpretations of the world, to look at the social influences which shape our lives. Sociology does not deny or diminish the reality of individual experience. Rather, we obtain a richer awareness of our own individual characteristics, and those of others, by developing a sensitivity towards the wider universe of social activity in which we are all involved.

In the first part of this book we look at the basic concerns of sociology, discussing its relationship to other subjects in the social sciences. Learning sociology is in part a process of self-exploration. No one can study sociology without having to confront challenges to some of their own deeply held views.

1

Sociology: Problems and Perspectives

We live today – in the late twentieth century – in a world which is intensely worrying, yet full of the most extraordinary promise for the future. It is a world awash with change, marked by the terrifying possibility of nuclear war and by the destructive onslaught of modern technology on the natural environment. Yet we have possibilities of controlling our destiny, and shaping our lives for the better, which would have been quite unimaginable to earlier generations. How did this world come about? Why are our conditions of life so different from those of our forebears? What directions will change take in the future? These questions are the prime concern of sociology, a discipline which consequently has a fundamental role to play in modern intellectual culture.

Sociology is the study of human social life, groups and societies. It is a dazzling and compelling enterprise, having as its subject-matter our own behaviour as social beings. The scope of sociology is extremely wide, ranging from the analysis of passing encounters between individuals in the street up to the investigation of global social processes. A few examples will provide an initial taste of its nature and objectives.

What is sociology about? Some examples

Love and marriage

Why do people fall in love and get married? The answer at first sight seems obvious. Love expresses a mutual physical and personal attachment two individuals feel for one another. These days, many of us might be sceptical of the idea that love 'is for ever', but 'falling in love', we tend to think, derives from universal human sentiments and emotions. It seems entirely natural for a couple who fall in love to want to set up house together, and to seek personal and sexual fulfilment in their relationship.

Yet this view, which seems so self-evident, is in fact quite unusual. Falling in love is not an experience most human beings have, and it is rarely associated with marriage. The idea of romantic love did not become widespread until fairly recently in the West, and has never existed in most other cultures. It is only in modern times that love, marriage and sexuality have been regarded as closely bound up with one another. In the Middle Ages, and for centuries afterwards, people married mainly in order to perpetuate the ownership of a title or property in the hands of family, or to raise children to work the family farm. Once married, they may sometimes have become close companions; this happened after marriage, however, rather than before. There were sexual liaisons outside marriage, but these involved few of the sentiments we connect with love. Love was regarded 'as at best a necessary weakness and at worst a kind of sickness' (Monter, 1977, p. 123).

Romantic love first made its appearance in courtly circles, as a characteristic of extra-marital sexual adventures indulged in by members of the aristocracy. Until about two centuries ago, it was wholly confined to such circles, and kept specifically separated from marriage. Relations between husband and wife among aristocratic groups were often cool and distant – certainly compared to our expectations of marriage today. The wealthy lived in large houses, each spouse having his or her own bedroom and servants; they may rarely have seen each other in private. Sexual compatibility was a matter of hazard, and was not considered relevant to marriage. Among both rich and poor, the decision to marry was taken by family and kin, not by the individuals concerned, who had little or no say in the matter. (This remains true in many non-Western cultures in current times.)

Neither romantic love then, nor its association with marriage, can be understood as 'given' features of human life, but are shaped by broad social influences. These are the influences sociologists study – and which make themselves felt even in seemingly purely personal experiences. Most of us see the world in terms of familiar features of our own lives. Sociology demonstrates the need to take a much wider view of why we act as we do.

Health and illness

We normally think of health and illness as matters concerned only with the physical condition of the body. A person feels aches and pains, or gets feverish. How could this have anything to do with wider influences of a social kind? In fact, social factors have a profound effect upon both the experience and the occurrence of illness, as well as upon how we react to being ill. Our very concept of 'illness', as involving physical malfunctioning of the body, is not shared by people in all societies. Sickness, and even death, are thought of in some other cultures as produced by evil spells, not by treatable physical causes (Evans-Pritchard, 1950). In our society, Christian Scientists reject much orthodox thinking about illness, believing that we are really spiritual and perfect in the image of God, sickness coming from a misunderstanding of reality, 'letting error in'.

How long one can expect to live, and the chances of contracting serious diseases such as heart troubles, cancer or pneumonia, are all strongly influenced by social characteristics. The more affluent the background people are from, the less likely they will be to suffer from a serious illness at any point in their lives. In addition, there are strongly defined social rules about how we are expected to behave when we become ill. A person who is ill is excused from many or all of the normal duties of everyday life, but the sickness has to be acknowledged as 'serious enough' to be able to claim these benefits without criticism or rebuke. Someone who is thought to be suffering only from a relatively mild form of infirmity, or whose illness has not been precisely identified, is likely to be seen as a 'malingerer' – as not really having the right to escape from daily obligations (Segal, 1976; Cockerham, 1986).

A further example: crime and punishment

The following horrific description concerns the final hours of a man put to death in 1757, having been accused of plotting to assassinate the King of France. The unfortunate individual was condemned to have flesh torn from his chest, arms and legs, and a mixture of boiling oil, wax and sulphur spread over the wounds. His body was then to be drawn and quartered by four horses, the dismembered parts subsequently burnt. An officer of the watch left an account of the proceedings:

> The executioner dipped an iron in the pot containing the boiling potion, which he poured liberally over each wound. Then the ropes that were to

> be harnessed to the horses were attached with cords to the condemned man's body; the horses were then harnessed and placed alongside the arms and legs, one at each limb . . . The horses tugged hard, each pulling straight on a limb, each horse held by an executioner. After a quarter of an hour, the same ceremony was repeated and finally, after several attempts, the direction of the horses had to be changed, thus: those at the thighs towards the arms, which broke the arms at the joints. This was repeated several times without success.
>
> After two or three attempts, the executioner Samson and he who had used the pincers each drew out a knife from his pocket and cut the body at the thighs instead of severing the legs at the joints; the four horses gave a tug and carried off the two thighs after them, namely, that of the right side first, the other following; then the same was done to the arms, the shoulders, and the four limbs; the flesh had to be cut almost to the bone. The horses, pulling hard, carried off the right arm first and the other afterwards. (Foucault, 1979, pp. 4–5)

The victim was alive until the final severance of his limbs from his torso.

Before modern times, punishments like this were not uncommon. As John Lofland has written, describing traditional forms of execution:

> Early historic executions were calculated to maximise the condemned's period of dying and his consciousness during it. Pressing to death by a progressively heavy weight placed upon the chest, breaking upon the wheel, crucifixion, strangling, burning at the stake, cutting off strips of flesh, stabbing non-vital parts of the body, drawing and quartering, and other techniques all consumed rather prolonged periods of time. Even hanging was a slow-working technique for most of its history. When the cart was merely driven from beneath the condemned or the trapdoor merely opened, the condemned slowly strangled, writhing for many minutes before succumbing . . . to shorten this struggle, the executioner sometimes went beneath the scaffold to pull the condemned's legs. (Lofland, 1977, p. 311)

Executions were often carried out in front of large audiences – a practice that persisted well into the eighteenth century in some countries. Those who were to be done to death would be drawn through the streets in an open cart, to meet their end as part of a well-publicized spectacle, at which crowds would cheer or hiss, according to their attitude towards the particular victim. Hangmen were public celebrities, having something of the fame and following conferred on film stars in modern times.

Today, we find such modes of punishment completely repellent. Few of us could imagine actively gaining enjoyment from watching someone being tortured or violently put to death, whatever crimes they might have committed. Our penal system is based on imprisonment, rather than the inflicting of physical pain, and in most Western countries the death penalty has been abolished altogether. Why did things change? Why did prison sentences replace the older, more violent forms of punishment?

It is tempting to suppose that in the past people were simply more brutal, while we have become humane. But to a sociologist, such an explanation is unconvincing. The public use of violence as a means of punishment had been established in Europe for centuries. People did not suddenly come to change their attitudes towards such practices 'out of the blue'; there were wider social influences at work, connected with major processes of change occurring in that period. The European societies then were becoming *industrialized* and *urbanized*. The old, rural order was being rapidly replaced by one in which more and more people worked in factories and workshops, moving to the rapidly expanding urban areas. Social control over urban-based populations could not be maintained by older forms of punishment, which, relying on setting a fearful example, were only appropriate in quite tightly knit, small communities where the numbers of cases were few.

Prisons developed as part of a general trend towards the establishing of organizations in which individuals are kept 'locked away' from the outside world – as a means of controlling and disciplining their behaviour. Those kept locked away at first included not only criminals, but vagabonds, the sick, unemployed people, the feeble-minded and the insane. Prisons only gradually came to be separated from asylums and hospitals for the physically ill. In prisons, criminals were supposed to be 'rehabilitated' to become good citizens. Punishment for crime became oriented towards creating the obedient citizen, rather than publicly displaying to others the terrible consequences which follow from wrong-doing. What we now see as more humane attitudes towards punishment tended to *follow on* from these changes, rather than causing them in the first place. Changes in the treatment of criminals were part of processes which swept away traditional orders which people had accepted for centuries. These processes created the societies in which we live today.

Implications: the nature of sociology

At this point we can take stock of the examples discussed so far. In each of the three cases – love, marriage and sexuality, health and illness, and punishment for crime – we have seen that what might be seen to be 'naturally given' human sentiments and feelings are in fact pervasively influenced by social factors. An understanding of the subtle, yet complex and profound, ways in which our lives reflect the contexts of our social experience is basic to the sociological outlook. Sociology focuses in particular upon social life in the *modern world* – the world brought into being by the sweeping changes in human societies which have occurred over the past two centuries or so.

Change in the modern world

The changes in human ways of life in the last two hundred years have been very far-reaching. We have become accustomed, for example, to the fact that most of the population do not work on the land, living in towns and cities rather than in small rural communities. But this was *never* the case until the modern era. For virtually all of human history, the vast majority of people have had to produce their own means of subsistence, living in tiny groups or small village communities. Even at the height of the most developed traditional civilizations – like ancient Rome or traditional China – less than 10 per cent of the population lived in urban areas, everyone else being engaged in food production. Today, in most of the industrialized societies, these proportions have become almost completely reversed: generally more than 90 per cent of people live in urban areas, and only 2–3 per cent of the population work in agricultural production.

It is not only the outer aspects of our lives that have changed; these transformations have radically altered, and continue to alter, the most personal and intimate aspects of our daily existence. To extend a previous example, the spread of ideals of romantic love was strongly conditioned by the transition from a rural to an urban, industrialized society. As people moved into urban areas, and began to work in industrial production, marriage was no longer prompted mainly by economic motives – by the need to control the inheritance of land and to work the land as a family unit. 'Arranged' marriages – fixed through the negotiations of parents and relatives – became less and less common. Individuals increasingly came to initiate marriage relationships on the basis of emotional attraction, and in order to seek personal fulfilment. The idea of 'falling in love' as a basis for contracting a marriage tie, was formed in this context. (For further discussion, see chapter 12 : 'Kinship, Marriage and the Family'.)

Similarly, before the rise of modern medicine, European views of health and illness resembled those found in many non-Western countries. Modern methods of diagnosis and treatment, together with an awareness of the importance of hygiene in preventing infectious disease, only date from the early nineteenth century. Our current views of health and sickness emerged as part of wider social transformations influencing many aspects of people's beliefs about biology and nature.

Sociology had its beginnings in the attempts of thinkers to understand the initial impact of the transformations which accompanied industrialization in the West, and remains the basic discipline concerned with analysing their nature. Our world today is radically different from that of former ages; it is the task of sociology to help us understand this world and its likely future.

Sociology and 'common sense'

The practice of sociology involves gaining knowledge about ourselves, the societies in which we live, and other societies distinct from ours

"Dearly beloved, we are gathered here yet again . . ."

Drawing by Opie; © 1980 The New Yorker Magazine, Inc.

in space and time. Sociological findings both *disturb* and *contribute to* our **common-sense beliefs** about ourselves and others. Consider the following list of statements:

1 Romantic love is a natural part of human experience, and is therefore found in all societies, in close connection with marriage.
2 How long people live is dependent upon their biological make-up and cannot be strongly influenced by social differences.
3 In previous times the family was a stable unit, but today there is a great increase in the proportion of 'broken homes'.
4 In all societies some people will be unhappy or depressed; therefore rates of suicide will tend to be the same throughout the world.
5 Most people everywhere value material wealth, and will try to get ahead if there are opportunities to do so.
6 Wars have been fought throughout human history. If we face the threat of nuclear war today, this is because of the fact that human beings have aggressive instincts that will always find an outlet.
7 The spread of computers and automation in industrial production will greatly reduce the average working day of most of the population.

Each of these assertions is wrong or questionable, and seeing why will help us to understand the questions sociologists ask – and try to answer – in their work. (These points will be analysed in greater detail in later chapters.)

1 As we have seen, the idea that marriage ties should be based on romantic love is a recent one, not found either in the earlier history of Western societies, or in other cultures. Romantic love is actually unknown in most societies.
2 How long people live is very definitely affected by social influences. This is because modes of social life act as 'filters' for biological factors that cause illness, infirmity or death. The poor are less healthy on average than the rich, for example, because they usually have worse diets, live a more physically demanding existence, and have access to inferior medical facilities.
3 If we look back to the early 1800s, the proportion of children living in homes with only one natural parent was probably as high as at present, because many more people died young, particularly women in childbirth. Separation and divorce are today the main cause of 'broken homes', but the overall level is not very different.
4 Suicide rates are certainly not the same in all societies. Even if we only look at Western countries, we find that suicide rates vary considerably. The suicide rate of the United Kingdom, for example, is four times as high as that of Spain, but only a third of the rate in Hungary. Suicide rates increased quite sharply during the main period of industrialization of the Western societies, in the nineteenth and early twentieth centuries.

5 The value which many people in modern societies put upon wealth and 'getting ahead' is for the most part a recent development. It is associated with the rise of 'individualism' in the West – the stress which we tend to put on individual achievement. In many other cultures, individuals are expected to put the good of the community above their own wishes and inclinations. Material wealth often is not highly prized compared to other values, such as religious ones.

6 Far from having an aggressive instinct, human beings do not have instincts at all, if 'instinct' means a fixed and inherited pattern of behaviour. Moreover, throughout most of human history, when people lived in small tribal groups, warfare did not exist in the form it came to have subsequently. Although some such groups were aggressive, many were not. There were no armies, and when skirmishes occurred casualties would often be deliberately avoided or limited. The threat of nuclear war today is bound up with a process of the 'industrialization of war' that is a major aspect of industrialization in general.

7 This assumption is rather different from the others, because it refers to the future. There is good reason to be at least cautious about the idea. The fully automated industries are still fairly few and far between, and jobs eliminated by automation might be replaced by new ones created elsewhere. We cannot yet be sure. One of the tasks of sociology is to take a hard look at the actual evidence available on such issues.

Obviously sociological findings do not always contradict common-sense views. Common-sense ideas often provide sources of insight about social behaviour. What needs emphasizing, however, is that the sociologist must be prepared to ask of any of our beliefs about ourselves – no matter how cherished – *is this really so?* By doing this, sociology also helps to *contribute* to whatever 'common sense' is at any time and place. Much of what we regard as common sense, 'what everyone knows' – for example, that divorce rates have risen greatly over the period since the Second World War – is based on the work of sociologists and other social scientists. Much research, of a regular kind, is necessary to produce material from year to year on patterns of marriage and divorce. The same is true of very many other areas of our 'common-sense' knowledge.

Sociological questions: factual, comparative, developmental and theoretical

Factual questions

Some of the questions sociologists ask, and try to answer, are largely **factual**. As we are members of a society, we all already have a certain amount of factual knowledge about it. For example, everyone in Britain is aware that there are laws which they are supposed to observe, and that to go against these is to risk criminal punishment. But the knowledge possessed by the average individual of the legal system, and of the nature and types of criminal activity, is likely to be sketchy and incomplete. Many aspects of crime and justice need direct and systematic sociological investigation. Thus we might ask: what forms of crime are most common? What proportion of people who engage in criminal behaviour are caught by the police? How many of these are in the end found guilty and imprisoned? Factual questions are often much more complicated and difficult to answer than one might think. For instance, official statistics on crime are of dubious value in indicating the real level of criminal activity.

Comparative questions

Factual information about one society, of course, will not tell us how far we are dealing with an unusual case rather than a very general set of influences. Sociologists often want to ask **comparative questions**, relating one social context within a society to another, or contrasting examples drawn from different societies. For instance, there are significant differences between the legal systems of Britain and the Soviet Union. A typical comparative question might be: how far do patterns of criminal behaviour and policing vary between the two countries? (Some important differences are in fact found between them.)

Developmental questions

In sociology we need to look not only at existing societies in relation to one another, but also to compare present and past. The questions sociologists ask here are **developmental**. To understand the nature of the modern world, we have to look at pre-existing forms of society, and also study the main direction processes of change have taken. Thus we can investigate, for example, how the first prisons originated – an issue touched upon earlier.

Theoretical questions

Factual – or what sociologists usually prefer to call **empirical** – investigations concern *how* things occur. Yet sociology does not consist of just collecting facts, however important and interesting they may be. We also want to know *why* things happen, and to do so we have to learn to pose theoretical questions, to enable us to interpret facts correctly in grasping the causes of whatever is the focus of a particular study. We know that industrialization has had a major influence upon the emergence of modern societies. But what are the origins and preconditions of industrialization? Why do we find differences between societies in their industrialization processes? Why is industrialization associated with changes in modes of criminal punishment, or in family and marriage systems? To respond to such questions, we have to develop **theoretical** thinking. Theories involve constructing abstract interpretations which can be used to explain a wide variety of empirical situations. A theory about industrialization, for example, would be concerned to identify the main features that processes of industrial development have in common, and would try to show which are most important in explaining such development. Of course, factual and theoretical questions can never completely be separated. We can only develop valid theoretical approaches if we are able to test them by means of empirical study.

We need theories to help us make sense of facts. Contrary to popular assertion, facts do not speak for themselves. Many sociologists work primarily on empirical questions, but unless they are guided in research by some knowledge of theory, their work is unlikely to be illuminating. This is true even of research carried out with strictly practical objectives.

'Practical people' tend to be suspicious of theorists, and may like to see themselves as too down-to-earth to need to pay attention to more abstract ideas, but all practical decisions have some theoretical assumptions lying behind them. Someone running a business, for example, might have scant regard for 'theory'. None the less, every approach to business activity involves theoretical assumptions, even if these often remain unstated. Thus he or she might assume that employees are motivated to work hard above all according to the level of wages they receive. This is not only a theoretical interpretation of human behaviour – it is also a mistaken one, as research in industrial sociology tends to demonstrate.

Intended and unintended consequences of human action

Sociologists draw an important distinction between the purposes of our behaviour – what we intend to do – and the **unintended consequences** which it brings about. The purposes for which we do things may be very different from the consequences they produce. We can understand much about societies in this way. Schools are set up, for example, for the purpose of teaching skills of reading and writing and to allow children to acquire new knowledge. Yet the existence of schools also has consequences that are not so plainly recognized or intended. Schools keep children out of the job market until they are of a certain age. The school system also tends to reinforce inequalities, by channelling students towards different jobs according to their academic ability.

Most of the major changes in history are probably unintended. Before the 1917 Russian Revolution, various political groups were trying to overthrow the existing regime. None of these, however – including the Bolshevik party which eventually came to power – anticipated the process of revolution that in fact occurred. A series of minor tensions and clashes produced a process of social transformation much more radical than anyone initially tried to bring about (Skocpol, 1979).

Sometimes behaviour undertaken with a particular aim in view actually has consequences that *prevent* the achievement of that aim. Some years ago, laws were introduced in New York City compelling the owners of deteriorating buildings in low-income areas to bring them up to a minimum standard. The intention was to improve the basic level of housing available to poorer sections of the community. The result was in fact the opposite. Owners of run-down buildings abandoned them altogether, or put them to other uses, so that there was a greater shortage of satisfactory accommodation than before (Sieber, 1981, p. 64). We can find a comparable example by returning to the case of prisons and asylums. Over the past few years, in Britain and some other Western countries, the process of shutting people away from the community has been partly reversed. In an effort to create 'community care' for offenders and for the mentally ill, some of the inmates of prisons and mental hospitals have been released to live in the outside world. The results have, however, rebounded to some extent on the hopes of the liberal reformers who supported the innovation. Many erstwhile mental patients have found themselves living in acute poverty, unable to cope with the new environment into which they have been plunged. The consequences for them have been disastrous.

Both continuity and change in social life have to be understood in terms of a 'mix' of intended and unintended consequences of people's actions. Sociology has the task of examining the resulting balance between **social reproduction** and **transformation**. Social reproduction refers to how societies 'keep going' over time, transformation to the changes they undergo. A society is not a mechanical device like a clock or an engine, which 'keep going' because they have a momentum of forces built into them. Social reproduction occurs because there is continuity in what people do from day to day and year to year, and in the social practices they follow. Changes occur partly because people intend them to occur, and partly – as the example of the Russian Revolution indicates – because of consequences that no one either foresees or intends.

What can sociology show us about our own actions?

As individuals, all of us know a great deal about ourselves and about the societies in which we live. We tend to think we have a good understanding of why we act as we do, without needing sociologists to tell us! And to some degree this is true. Many of the things we do in our day-to-day lives we engage in because we understand the social conventions involved. Yet there are definite boundaries to such self-knowledge, and it is one of the main tasks of sociology to show what these are.

On the basis of the discussion so far, we can illuminate the nature of these boundaries quite easily. As we saw earlier, people make many common-sense judgements about themselves and others which turn out to be wrong, partial or ill-informed. Sociological research both helps to identify the limitations of our social judgements and at the same time 'feeds back' into our knowledge of ourselves and the social environment. Another essential contribution of sociology lies in showing that, although all of us understand much of what we do, and why, often we have little knowledge of the consequences of our actions. The unintended, and unforeseen, consequences of actions affect all aspects and contexts of social life. Sociological analysis explores the delicate and subtle connections between intentional and unintentional features of the social world.

Social structure and human action

An important concept that helps us understand these connections is that of **social structure**. The social environments in which we exist do not just consist of random assortments of events or actions. There are underlying regularities, or patternings, in how people behave and in the relationships in which they stand with one another. It is these regularities to which the concept of social structure refers. To some degree it is helpful to picture the structural characteristics of societies as resembling the structure of a building. A building has walls, a floor and a roof, which together give it a particular 'shape' or form. But the metaphor can be a very misleading one if applied too strictly. Social structures are made up of human actions and relationships: what gives these their patterning is their *repetition* across periods of time and distances of space. Thus the ideas of social reproduction and social structure are very closely related to one another in sociological analysis. We should understand human societies to be *like buildings that are at every moment being reconstructed by the very bricks that compose them*. The actions of all of us are influenced by the structural characteristics of the societies in which we are brought up and live; at the same time, we recreate (and also to some extent alter) those structural characteristics in our actions.

Developing a sociological outlook

Learning to think sociologically means cultivating powers of the imagination. Studying sociology *cannot* be just a routine process of acquiring knowledge. A sociologist is someone who is able to break free from the immediacy of personal circumstances. Sociological work depends upon what C. Wright Mills, in a famous phrase, called the **sociological imagination** (Mills, 1970). Most textbooks in sociology, in fact, draw attention to the term. But – unlike Mills himself – they usually employ it quite unimaginatively!

The sociological imagination necessitates, above all, *being able to 'think ourselves away' from the familiar routines of our daily lives in order to look at them anew.* Consider the simple act of drinking a cup of coffee. What could we find to say, from a sociological point of view, about such an apparently uninteresting piece of behaviour? The answer is – an enormous amount.

We could point out first of all that coffee is not just a drink which helps maintain the liquid intake of the individual. It has *symbolic value* as part of day-to-day social rituals. Often the ritual associated with coffee-drinking is much more important than the act of consuming the drink itself. For example, two people who arrange 'to have coffee' together are probably more interested in meeting and chatting than in what they drink. Drinking and eating are in all societies occasions for social interaction and the enactment of rituals – and these offer a rich subject-matter for sociological study.

Second, coffee is a *drug*, containing caffeine, which has a stimu-lating effect on the brain. Coffee-addicts are not regarded by most people in Western culture as 'drug users'. Why this should be is an interesting sociological question. Like alcohol, coffee is a 'socially acceptable' drug whereas, for instance, marijuana is not. Yet there are cultures which tolerate the consumption of marijuana, but disfavour both coffee and alcohol. (For further discussion of these issues, see chapter 5: 'Conformity and Deviance'.)

Third, an individual sipping a cup of coffee is caught up in an extremely complicated set of *social and economic relationships* stretch-ing world-wide. The production, transport and distribution of coffee requires continuous transactions between many people thousands of miles away from the coffee-drinker. Studying such global transactions forms an important task of sociology, since many aspects of our lives are now affected by world-wide trading exchanges and communications.

Finally, the act of sipping a cup of coffee presumes a whole process of *past social and economic development.* Along with many other now familiar items of Western diets – like tea, bananas, potatoes and white sugar – coffee only became widely consumed from the nineteenth century onwards. Although coffee originated in the Middle East, its mass consumption dates from the period of Western colonial expansion about a century and half ago. Virtually all the coffee we drink in the Western countries today comes from areas (South America and Africa) that were colonized by the Europeans.

Developing the sociological imagination means using materials from **anthropology** (the study of traditional societies) and history as well as from sociology itself. The *anthropological* dimension of the sociological imagination is vital, because it allows us to see what a kaleidoscope of different forms of human social life exist. In contrasting these with our own, we learn more about the distinctiveness of our specific patterns of behaviour. The *historical* dimension of the sociological imagination is equally fundamental: we can only grasp the distinctive nature of our world today if we are able to compare it with the past. The past is a mirror which the sociologist must hold up to understand the present. Each of these tasks involves 'thinking ourselves away' from our own customs and habits – in order to develop a more profound understanding of them.

There is yet another aspect of the sociological imagination – the one upon which, in fact, Mills laid most emphasis. This concerns *our possibilities for the future*. Sociology helps us not only to analyse existing patterns of social life, but to see some of the 'possible futures' open to us. The imaginative pursuit of sociological work can show us not just what *is the case*, but what *could become the case* should we seek to make it so. Unless they are based on an informed sociological understanding of current trends, our attempts to influence future developments will be ineffective or frustrated.

Is sociology a science?

Sociology occupies a prime position among a group of disciplines (including also anthropology, economics and political science) which are usually termed the *social sciences*. But can we really study human social life in a 'scientific' way? To answer this question, we have first of all to understand the main characteristics of science as a form of intellectual endeavour. What is **science**?

Science is the use of systematic methods of investigation, theoretical thinking, and the logical assessment of arguments, to develop a body of knowledge about a particular subject-matter. Scientific work depends upon a mixture of boldly innovative thought and the careful marshalling of evidence to support or disconfirm hypotheses and theories. Information and insights accumulated through scientific study and debate are always to some degree *tentative* – open to being revised, or even completely discarded, in the light of new evidence or arguments.

When we ask, 'is sociology a science?', we mean two things: 'Can the discipline be closely modelled upon the procedures of natural science?' and 'Can sociology hope to achieve the same kind of precise, well-founded knowledge that natural scientists have developed in respect of the physical world?' These issues have always been to some degree controversial, but for a long period most sociologists answered them in the affirmative. They held that sociology can, and should, resemble natural science both in its procedures and the character of its findings (a perspective sometimes known as **positivism**).

This view has come to be seen as naïve. Like the other social 'sciences', sociology *is* a scientific discipline in the sense that it involves systematic methods of investigation, the analysis of data, and the assessment of theories in the light of evidence and logical argument. Studying human beings, however, is different from observing events in the physical world, and neither the logical framework nor the findings of sociology can adequately be understood simply in terms of comparisons with natural science. In investigating social life we deal with activities that are **meaningful** to the people who engage in them. Unlike objects in nature, humans are self-aware beings, who confer sense and purpose on what they do. We cannot even describe social life accurately unless we first of all grasp the meanings which people apply to their behaviour. For instance, to describe a death as a 'suicide' necessitates learning something about what the person in question was intending when he or she was killed. 'Suicide' can only occur where an individual actively intends self-destruction. A person who accidentally steps in front of a car and is killed cannot be said to have committed suicide; the death was not willed by that person.

The fact that we cannot study human beings in exactly the same way as objects in nature is in some ways an advantage to sociology; in other respects it creates difficulties not encountered by natural scientists. Sociological researchers profit from being able to pose questions directly to those they study – other human beings. On the other hand, people who know their activities are being scrutinized frequently will not behave in the same way as they do normally. For example, when individuals answer questionnaires, they may consciously or unconsciously give a view of themselves which differs from their usual attitudes. They may even try to 'assist' the researcher by giving the responses they believe he or she wants.

Objectivity

Sociologists strive to be detached in their research and theoretical thinking, trying to study the social world in an open-minded way. A good sociologist will seek to put aside prejudices that might prevent ideas or evidence being assessed in a fair-minded manner. But nobody is completely open-minded on all topics, and the degree to which anyone can succeed in developing such attitudes towards contentious issues is bound to be limited. However, **objectivity** does not depend solely, or even primarily, upon the outlook of specific researchers. It has to do with methods of observation and argument. Here the *public character* of the discipline is of major importance. Because findings and reports of research are available for scrutiny – published in articles, monographs or books – others can check the conclusions. Claims made on the basis of research findings can be critically assessed and personal inclinations discounted by others.

Objectivity in sociology is thus achieved substantially through the effects of mutual *criticism* by members of the sociological community.

Many of the subjects studied in sociology are controversial, because they directly concern disputes and struggles in society itself. But through public debate, the examination of evidence and the logical structure of argument, such issues can be fruitfully and effectively analysed (Habermas, 1979).

The practical significance of sociology

Understanding social situations

Sociology has many practical implications for our lives. Sociological thinking and research contribute to practical policy-making and social reform in several obvious ways. The most direct is simply through providing *clearer or more adequate understanding* of a social situation than existed before. This can be either on the level of factual knowledge, or through gaining an improved grasp of *why* something is happening (in other words, by means of theoretical understanding). For instance, research may disclose that a far greater proportion of the population is living in poverty than was previously believed. Any attempt to foster improved living standards would obviously stand more chance of success if based on accurate rather than faulty information. The more we understand about why poverty remains widespread, however, the more likely it is that successful policies can be implemented to counter it.

Awareness of cultural differences

A second way in which sociology aids in practical policy-making is through helping to foster greater *cultural awareness* on the part of different groups in society. Sociological research provides a means of seeing the social world from a diversity of cultural perspectives, thereby helping to dispel prejudices which groups hold towards one another. No one can be an enlightened policy-maker who does not have a cultivated awareness of varying cultural values. Practical policies which are not based on an informed awareness of the ways of life of those they affect have little chance of success. Thus a white social worker operating in a West Indian community in a British city will not gain the confidence of its members without developing a sensitivity to the cultural differences which often separate white and black in Britain.

Assessment of the effects of policies

Third, sociological research has practical implications in terms of *assessing the results of policy initiatives*. A programme of practical reform may simply fail to achieve what its designers sought, or bring in its train a series of unintended consequences of an unpalatable kind. For instance, in the years following the Second World War, large public housing blocks were built in city centres in many countries. These were planned to provide high standards of accommodation for low-income groups from slum areas, and offered shopping amenities and other civic services close at hand. However, research showed that many of those moved from their previous dwellings to large apartment blocks felt isolated and unhappy. High-rise buildings and shopping malls often rapidly became dilapidated, and provided breeding-grounds for mugging and other violent crimes.

The increase of self-knowledge

Fourth, and in some ways most important of all, sociology can provide **self-enlightenment** – increased self-understanding – to groups in society. The more people know about the conditions of their own action, and about the overall workings of their society, the more they are likely to be able to influence the circumstances of their own lives. We must not picture the practical role of sociology only as assisting policy-makers – that is, powerful groups – to take informed decisions. Those in power cannot be assumed always to have in mind the interests of the less powerful or underprivileged in the policies they pursue. Self-enlightened groups can respond in an effective way to policies pursued by government officials or other authorities, and can also form policy initiatives of their own. Self-help groups (like Alcoholics Anonymous) and social movements (like women's movements) are examples of social associations which directly seek to bring about practical reforms (see chapter 9: 'Groups and Organizations').

The sociologist's role in society

Should sociologists themselves actively advocate, and agitate for, practical programmes of reform or social change? Some argue that sociology can preserve its objectivity only if practitioners of the subject are studiously neutral in moral and political controversies, but there is no reason to think that scholars who remain aloof from current debates are necessarily more impartial in their assessment of sociological issues than others. There is bound to be a connection between studying sociology and the promptings of social conscience. No sociologically sophisticated person can be unaware of the inequalities that exist in the world today, the lack of social justice in many social situations or the deprivations suffered by millions of people. It would be strange if sociologists did not take sides on practical issues, and it would be illogical as well as impractical to try to ban them from drawing on their sociological expertise in so doing.

Concluding comments

In this chapter we have seen sociology as a discipline in which we set aside our personal view of the world to look more carefully at the influences that shape our lives and those of others. Sociology emerged as a distinct intellectual endeavour with the early development of modern industrialized societies, and the study of such societies remains its principal concern. But sociologists are also preoccupied with a broad range of issues concerning the nature of social interaction and human societies in general. In the following chapter, we shall investigate the diversity of human culture, looking at the enormous contrasts between customs and habits followed by different peoples. To do so, we need to embark on a voyage of cultural exploration around the world. We have to retrace, on an intellectual level, the travels which Christopher Columbus, Captain Cook and other adventurers undertook when they set off on their perilous journeys across the globe. As sociologists, however, we cannot look at these only from the explorers' point of view – as voyages of 'discovery', for these expeditions initiated a process of Western expansion which had a dramatic impact on other cultures, and on subsequent world social development.

Summary

1 Sociology can be identified as the systematic study of human societies, giving special emphasis to modern, industrialized systems.

2 Sociology came into being as an attempt to understand the far-reaching changes that have occurred in human societies over the past two or three centuries. Industrialization, urbanism and new types of political system are among the important features of the modern social world.

3 The changes involved were not just large-scale ones. Major shifts have also occurred in the most intimate and personal characteristics of people's lives. The development of a stress on romantic love as a basis for marriage is an example of this.

4 Sociologists investigate social life by posing distinct questions and trying to find the answers to these by systematic research. These questions may be factual, comparative, developmental or theoretical. In sociological research it is important to distinguish between intended and unintended results of human action.

5 The practice of sociology involves the ability to think imaginatively and to detach oneself from preconceived ideas about social relationships.

6 Sociology has close ties with other social sciences. All the social sciences are concerned with human behaviour, but concentrate on different aspects of it. The connections between sociology, anthropology and history are particularly important.

7   Sociology is a *science* in the sense that it involves systematic methods of investigation and the evaluation of theories in the light of evidence and logical argument. But it cannot be modelled directly upon the natural sciences, because studying human behaviour is in fundamental ways different from studying the world of nature.

8   Sociologists attempt to be objective in their studies of the social world, approaching their work in an open-minded way. Objectivity depends not only upon the attitudes of the researcher, but upon the public evaluation of research and theory which is an essential part of sociology as a scholarly discipline.

9   Sociology is a subject with important practical implications. It can contribute to social criticism and practical social reform in several ways. First, the improved understanding of a given set of social circumstances often gives us all a better chance of controlling them. Second, sociology provides the means of increasing our cultural sensitivities, allowing policies to be based on an awareness of divergent cultural values. Third, we can investigate the consequences (intended and unintended) of the adoption of particular policy programmes. Finally, and perhaps most important, sociology provides self-enlightenment, offering groups and individuals an increased opportunity to alter the conditions of their own lives.

Basic concepts

sociology	science
social structure	objectivity

Important terms

common-sense beliefs	social reproduction
factual questions	social transformation
comparative questions	sociological imagination
developmental questions	anthropology
empirical investigation	positivism
theoretical questions	meaningful activities
unintended consequences	self-enlightenment

PART II

Culture, the Individual and Social Interaction

In this part of the book, we start our exploration of the diverse field of sociology by looking at the interconnections between individual development and culture, analysing the major types of society within which human beings live today or have lived in the past. Our personalities and outlooks are strongly influenced by the culture and society in which each of us happens to exist. At the same time, in our day-to-day behaviour we actively re-create and reshape the cultural and social contexts in which our activities occur.

In the first chapter of this part (chapter 2), we examine the unity and the diversity of human culture. We consider in what ways human beings resemble, and differ from, the animals, and analyse the range of variations found between different human cultures. The extent of human cultural variability has only come to be studied as a result of changes which have in fact altered or destroyed many cultures in which people lived before modern times. These changes are outlined, and the main types of society which dominate the world today are contrasted to those which preceded them.

The following chapter (chapter 3) discusses socialization, concentrating on the process by which the human infant develops into a social being. To some degree, socialization continues throughout the individual's life, so studying socialization also involves analysing the 'cycle of the generations' – the changing relationships between young, middle-aged and older people.

In chapter 4 we examine how people interact with each other in everyday life, looking at the delicate, yet profoundly important, mechanisms whereby individuals interpret what others say and do in their face-to-face encounters. The study of social interaction can tell us much about the larger social environments in which we live.

Chapter 5 moves on to look at wider social processes, beginning with the study of deviance and crime. We can learn much about the way the majority of a population behaves by studying the exceptions – people whose behaviour deviates from generally accepted patterns.

The last chapter in this part (chapter 6) discusses problems of gender, analysing how changing social conditions have affected the position of women and men in modern societies. This chapter also includes an examination of the nature of sexuality, looking at the main influences governing patterns of sexual behaviour.

2

Culture and Society

The meeting of cultures

About half a century ago, some islanders in the Western Pacific began constructing elaborate large wooden models of aeroplanes. Hours of patient labour went into their construction, although no one there had ever seen a plane at close range. The models were not designed to fly; they were central to religious movements led by local prophets. The religious leaders proclaimed that if certain rites were performed, 'cargo' would arrive from the skies. Cargo consisted of the goods Westerners had been seen to bring into the islands for themselves. The whites would then disappear and the ancestors of the native peoples would return. The islanders believed that as a result of faithful observation of certain rites, a new era would arrive, in which they would enjoy the material wealth of the white intruders while otherwise continuing their traditional ways of life (Worsley, 1970).

Why did these 'cargo cults' come into being? They originated in the clash between the traditional ideas and customs of the islanders and modes of life introduced through Western influence. The wealth and power of the whites were plain to see, and the islanders assumed that the mysterious flying objects which delivered the riches enjoyed by the interlopers were the very source of such wealth. From the islanders' point of view, it was logical to attempt to bring the aeroplanes under their own control by religious and ritual means. At the same time, they were seeking to protect and preserve their own customs threatened by the arrival of the newcomers.

The islanders' knowledge of Western patterns of behaviour and technology was relatively slight; they interpreted the activities of the Europeans in terms of their own beliefs about, and outlook upon, the world. In this respect, their reactions were similar to those found almost everywhere before modern times. Even people in the great civilizations of previous ages had only a vague awareness of the ways of life of other peoples. When Western adventurers and merchants sailed off into remote parts of the globe in the sixteenth and seventeenth centuries, they regarded those with whom they came into contact as 'barbarians' or 'savages'.

Early contacts with other cultures

The Europeans who travelled to the Americas in the 1500s went looking for giants, amazons and pygmies, the Fountain of Eternal Youth, women whose bodies never aged and men who lived for several hundred years. The familiar images of traditional European myths helped guide the voyages undertaken. The American Indians were initially regarded as wild creatures, having more affinity with animals than with human beings. Paracelsus, the sixteenth-century medical writer, pictured North America as a continent peopled with creatures that were half-man, half-beast. Nymphs, satyrs, pygmies and wild men were thought to be soulless beings created spontaneously from the earth. The Bishop of Santa Marta in Colombia, South America, described the local Indians as 'not men with rational souls but wild men of the woods, for which reason they could retain no Christian doctrine, no virtue nor any kind of learning' (Pagden, 1982, p. 23).

Conversely, the Europeans who established contact with the Chinese Empire during the seventeenth and eighteenth centuries were treated with disdain by its rulers. In 1793, King George III of England sent a trade mission to China to foster commercial exchange. The 'barbarian' visitors were allowed to set up some trading outposts in China, and to benefit from the luxuries that country could provide. The Chinese themselves, the visitors were told, were quite uninterested in anything the Europeans had to offer: 'Our Celestial Empire possesses all things in prolific abundance and lacks no products within its borders. There is therefore no need to import the manufactures of outside barbarians in exchange for our own produce.' A request for permission to send Western missionaries to China met with the answer: 'The distinction between Chinese and barbarians is most strict, and your Ambassador's request that barbarians shall be given full liberty to disseminate their religion is utterly unreasonable' (Worsley, 1967, p. 2).

The gulf between East and West was so great that each held the most bizarre beliefs about the other. For example, even as late as the end of the nineteenth century it was widely believed in China that foreigners, particularly the English, would die of constipation if deprived of rhubarb. Until two centuries ago, no one had the 'overall view' of the world that we now take for granted.

One of the most dramatic first contacts between Westerners and other cultures occurred as late as 1818. An English naval expedition looking for a passage to Russia between Baffin Island and Greenland, within the Arctic Circle, had a chance encounter with the polar Eskimos. Until that day the Eskimos had thought they were the only people in the world! (Oswalt, 1972, p. 23).

The concept of culture

In this chapter we shall look at the unity and diversity of human life and culture. The concept of **culture**, together with that of **society**, is one of the most widely used notions in sociology. Culture consists of the **values** the members of a given group hold, the **norms** they follow, and the *material goods* they create. Values are abstract ideals, while norms are definite principles or rules which people are expected to observe. Norms represent the 'dos' and 'don'ts' of social life. Thus monogamy – being faithful to a single marriage partner – is a prominent value in most Western societies. In many other cultures, a person is permitted to have several wives or husbands simultaneously. Norms of behaviour in marriage include, for example, how husbands and wives are supposed to behave towards their in-laws. In some societies, a husband or wife is expected to develop a close relationship with parents-in-law; in others they are expected to keep a clear distance from one another.

When we use the term in ordinary daily conversation, we often think of 'culture' as equivalent to the 'higher things of the mind' – art, literature, music and painting. As sociologists use it, the concept includes such activities, but also far more. Culture refers to the whole way of life of the members of a society. It includes how they dress, their marriage customs and family life, their patterns of work, religious ceremonies and leisure pursuits. It covers also the goods they create and which become meaningful for them – bows and arrows, ploughs, factories and machines, computers, books, dwellings.

'Culture' can be conceptually distinguished from 'society', but there are very close connections between these notions. 'Culture' concerns the *way of life* of the members of a given society – their habits and customs, together with the material goods they produce. 'Society' refers to the *system of interrelationships* which connects together the individuals who share a common culture. No culture could exist without a society. But, equally, no society could exist without culture. Without culture, we would not be 'human' at all, in the sense in which we usually understand that term. We would have no language in which to express ourselves, no sense of self-consciousness, and our ability to think or reason would be severely limited – as we shall show in this chapter and in chapter 3 ('Socialization and the Life-Cycle').

The chief theme of both the current chapter and the next, in fact, is the biological versus the cultural inheritance of humankind. The relevant questions are: What distinguishes human beings from the animals? Where do our distinctively 'human' characteristics come from? What is the nature of human nature? These questions are crucial to sociology, because they set the foundation for the whole field of study. To answer them, we shall analyse both what human beings share and how cultures differ.

Cultural variations between human beings are linked to differing types of society, and we shall compare the main forms of society that can be identified from past and present. Throughout the chapter, attention will be concentrated on how social change has affected human cultural development – particularly since the time when Europeans began to spread their ways of life across the world.

The human species

In spite of the clashes and misunderstandings which occurred, the increasing intrusion of Westerners into other parts of the globe gradually made it possible to understand what human beings share as a species, as well as the variabilities of human culture (Hirst and Woolley, 1982). Charles Darwin, an ordained minister of the Church of England, published his book *On the Origin of Species* in 1859, after two journeys around the world on HMS *Beagle*. Painstakingly amassing observations of the different animal species, Darwin set out a view of the development of human beings and animals quite different from any previously held.

As we have seen, it was not uncommon for people at that time to believe in beings that are half-beast, half-human, but with Darwin's findings, such possibilities were completely swept away. Darwin claimed to find a continuity of development from animals to human beings. Our characteristics as humans, according to him, have emerged from a process of biological change which can be traced back to the initial origins of life on earth, more than three billion years ago. Darwin's view of humans and animals was for many even harder to accept than that of half-beast, half-human, creatures. He set in motion one of the most debated, yet persuasive, theories in modern science – the theory of **evolution**.

Evolution

According to Darwin, the development of the human species has come about as a result of a *random* process. In many religions, including Christianity, animals and human beings are seen as created by divine intervention. Evolutionary theory, by contrast, regards the development of the animal and human species as devoid of purpose. Evolution is a result of what Darwin called *natural selection*. The idea of natural selection is simple. All organic beings need food and other resources, such as protection from climatic extremes, in order to survive, but not enough resources exist to support all the types of animal that exist at any given point in time, because they produce far more offspring than the environment can provide food for. Those best adapted to their environment survive, while others, less well able to cope with its demands, perish. Some animals are more intelligent, faster, or have superior eyesight to others. In the struggle for survival, they have advantages over those less well endowed. They live longer, and are able to breed, passing on their characteristics to subsequent generations. They are 'selected' to survive and reproduce.

There is a continuous process of natural selection, because of the biological mechanism of **mutation**. A mutation is a random genetic change, altering the biological characteristics of some individuals in a species. Most mutations are either harmful or useless in terms of survival value, but some give an animal a competitive advantage over others: individuals possessing the mutant genes will then tend to survive at the expense of those without them. This process explains both minor changes within species and major changes leading to the disappearance of entire species. For example, many millions of years ago giant reptiles flourished in various regions of the world. Their size became a handicap as mutations occurring in other, smaller, species gave them superior adaptive capabilities. The early ancestors of humans were among these more adaptable species.

Although the theory of evolution has been refined since Darwin's day, the essentials of Darwin's account are still widely accepted. Evolutionary theory allows us to piece together a clear understanding of the emergence of different species, and their relation to one another.

Human beings and the apes

The evolution of life, it is now generally agreed, began in the oceans. About four hundred million years ago, the first land-based creatures emerged. Some of these gradually evolved into the large reptiles, who

were later displaced by mammals. Mammals are warm-blooded creatures who reproduce through sexual intercourse. Although the mammals were much smaller in bodily size than the giant reptiles, they
were more intelligent and manoeuvrable. Mammals have a greater capacity to learn from experience than other animals, and this capacity
has reached its highest development in the human species. Human
beings are part of a group of higher mammals, the *primates*, which
originated some seventy million years ago.

Our closest relatives among animal species are the chimpanzee,
gorilla and orang-utan. On learning about Darwin's account of evolution, the wife of the Bishop of Worcester is said to have remarked:
'Descended from monkeys? My dear, let us hope that it is not true.
But if it is true, let us hope that it does not become widely known.' Like
many others since, the lady misunderstood what evolution involves.
Human beings are not descended from the apes; humans and apes
all trace their evolution from much more primitive groups of ancestor
species living many millions of years ago.

The ancestors of human beings were primates who walked erect, and
were about the size of modern pygmies. Their bodies were probably fairly
hairless, but in other respects they looked more like apes than humans.
Various other types of hominid (beings belonging to the human family)
existed between this period and the emergence of the human species as
it is found today. Human beings recognizably identical in all respects
to ourselves appeared about fifty thousand years ago. There is good
evidence that cultural development preceded, and probably shaped, the
evolution of the human species. The use of tools and the development
of fairly elaborate forms of communication, together with the formation
of social communities, almost certainly played a major part in the evolutionary process. They offered greater survival value for the ancestors
of the human species than was available to other animals. Groups which
possessed them were able to master their environment much more
effectively than those which did not. However, with the emergence of
the human species proper, cultural development became intensified.

Because of their parallel lines of development, the human species
shares a number of characteristics with other primates. The physical
structure of the human body is similar in most respects to that of the
apes. Like human beings, the apes tend to live in social groups, have
large brains compared to their body size, and have a long period
during which the young are dependent on their elders.

In some ways, however, human beings differ appreciably from their
nearest relatives. Human beings stand erect, while apes crouch. The
human foot differs strikingly from the hand, while in most apes these
are more similar. The human brain is distinctly larger, in relation to
body size, than the brain of even the most intelligent of the apes.
While the period of infant dependency among the higher animals is
two years or less, among human beings it is some seven to eight years.

Nature and nurture

Sociobiology

Although they recognized the evolutionary continuity between the animals and human beings, until recently most biologists tended to emphasize the distinctive qualities of the human species. This position has been challenged by the work of *sociobiologists,* who see close parallels between human behaviour and that of the animals. The term **sociobiology** derives from the writings of the American Edward Wilson (Wilson, 1975, 1978). It refers to the application of biological principles in explaining the social activities of all social animals, including human beings. According to Wilson, many aspects of human social life are grounded in our genetic make-up. For example, some species of animals have elaborate courtship rituals, whereby sexual union and reproduction are achieved. Human courtship and sexual behaviour, according to sociobiologists, generally involve similar rituals, based also on inborn characteristics. In most animal species, to take a second example, males are larger and more aggressive than females, and tend to dominate the 'weaker sex'. Perhaps genetic factors explain why, in all human societies we know of, men tend to hold positions of greater authority than women. According to Wilson and his followers, by demonstrating that many such aspects of human behaviour are genetically programmed, sociobiology will increasingly be able to absorb sociology and anthropology into a single, biologically based, discipline.

The major issues thus raised have been extensively debated over recent years (Sahlins, 1976; Caplan, 1978; Montagu, 1980; Wiegele, 1982; Kitcher, 1985). They remain highly controversial. Scholars tend to fall into two camps, depending to some degree on their educational background. Authors sympathetic to the sociobiological viewpoint are mostly trained in biology, rather than the social sciences, while the large majority of sociologists and anthropologists tend to be sceptical of sociobiology's claims. Probably they know rather little about the genetic foundations of human life, and biologists have similarly limited knowledge of sociological or anthropological research. Each side finds it difficult to fully understand the force of the arguments advanced by the other.

Some of the passions generated early on by Wilson's work have now abated, and it seems possible to produce a reasonably clear assessment. Sociobiology is important – but more for what it has shown about the life of the animals than for what it has demonstrated about human behaviour. Combined with the studies of ethologists (biologists who carry out 'field work' among animal groups, rather than studying animals in artificial circumstances in zoos or laboratories), sociobiologists have been able to demonstrate that many animal species are more 'social' than was previously thought. Animal groups have a considerable influence over the behaviour of individual members of the species. On the other hand, little evidence has been found to demonstrate that genetic inheritance controls complex forms of human activity. The ideas of the sociobiologists about human social life are thus at best no more than speculative. Our behaviour, of course, is genetically *influenced*, but our genetic endowment, as members of the human species, probably conditions only the potentialities and limits of our actions, not the actual content of what we do.

Instincts

Most biologists and sociologists agree that human beings do not have any 'instincts'. Such a statement runs contrary not only to the hypotheses of sociobiology, but to what most ordinary people believe. Aren't there many things we do 'instinctively'? If someone throws a punch, don't we instinctively blink or shy away? In fact, this is not an example of an instinct when the term **instinct** is used precisely. As understood in biology and sociology, an instinct is a *complex* pattern of behaviour that is genetically determined. The courtship rituals of many of the lower animals are instinctive in this sense. The stickleback (a small fresh-water fish), for example, has an extremely complicated set of rituals which have to be followed by both male and female if mating is to occur (Tinbergen, 1974). Each fish produces an elaborate array

"Evolution's been good to you, Sid."

Drawing by Lorenz; © 1980 The New Yorker Magazine, Inc.

of movements, to which the other responds, creating an elaborate 'mating dance'. This is genetically patterned for the whole species. A spontaneous blinking of the eye, or movement away of the head, in the face of an anticipated blow, is a *reflex act* rather than an instinct. It is a single, simple response, not an elaborate behaviour pattern. To speak of this as 'instinctive' in the technical sense is thus mistaken.

Human beings are born with a number of basic reflexes similar to the eye-blink reaction, most of which seem to have some evolutionary survival value. Very young human infants, for example, will suck when presented with a nipple, or a nipple-like object. A young child will throw up its arms, to catch at support, when suddenly losing its balance, and pull its hand back sharply if it touches a very hot surface. Each of these reactions is obviously useful in coping with the environment.

Human beings also have a number of biological given *needs*. There is an organic basis to our needs for food, drink, sex and the maintenance of certain levels of body temperature. But the ways in which these needs are satisfied or coped with vary widely between – and within – different cultures.

For example, all cultures tend to have some kind of standardized courtship behaviour. This is obviously related to the universal nature of sexual needs, but their expression in different cultures – even including the sexual act itself – varies enormously. The normal position for the sexual act in Western culture involves the woman lying on her back, and the man on top of her. This position is seen as absurd by people in some other societies, who usually have intercourse lying side by side, with the man facing the woman's back, with the woman on top of the man, or in other positions. The ways in which people seek to satisfy their sexual needs thus seem to be culturally learned, not genetically implanted.

Moreover, humans can override their biological needs in ways which appear to have no parallel among the animals. Religious mystics may fast for very long periods. Individuals may choose to remain celibate for some part or all of their lives. All animals, including human beings, have a drive towards self-preservation, but unlike other animals humans are able deliberately to go against that drive, risking their lives in mountaineering or other hazardous pursuits, and even committing suicide.

Cultural diversity

The diversity of human culture is remarkable. Values and norms of behaviour vary widely from culture to culture, often contrasting in a radical way with what people from Western societies consider 'normal'. For example, in the modern West we regard the deliberate killing of infants or young children as one of the worst of all crimes. Yet in traditional Chinese culture, female children were frequently strangled at birth, because they were regarded as a liability rather than an asset to the family.

In the West, we eat oysters, but we do not eat kittens or puppy dogs, both of which are regarded as delicacies in some parts of the world. Jews do not eat pork, while Hindus eat pork but avoid beef. Westerners regard kissing as a normal part of sexual behaviour, but in many other cultures the practice is either unknown or regarded as disgusting. All these different traits of behaviour are aspects of broad cultural differences which distinguish societies from one another.

Small societies (like the 'hunting and gathering' societies, which will be discussed later in the chapter) tend to be culturally uniform, but industrialized societies are themselves culturally diverse, involving numerous different **sub-cultures**. In modern cities, for example, there are many sub-cultural communities living side by side. Gerald Suttles carried out a field-work study of a slum area in Chicago's West Side. In just this one neighbourhood, he found many different sub-cultural groupings: Puerto Ricans, blacks, Greeks, Jews, gypsies, Italians, Mexicans, and Southern whites. All of these groups had their own 'territories' and ways of life (Suttles, 1968).

Cultural identity and ethnocentrism

Every culture contains its own unique patterns of behaviour, which seem alien to people from other cultural backgrounds. As an example, we can take the Nacirema, a group described in a celebrated research investigation by Horace Miner (1956). Miner concentrated his attention on the elaborate body-rituals in which the Nacirema engage, rituals which have strange and exotic characteristics. His discussion is worth quoting at length:

> The fundamental belief underlying the whole system appears to be that the human body is ugly and that its natural tendency is to debility and disease. Incarcerated in such a body, man's only hope is to avert these characteristics through the use of the powerful influences of ritual and ceremony. Every household has one or more shrines devoted to this purpose. . . . The focal point of the shrine is a box or chest which is built into the wall. In this chest are kept the many charms and magical potions without which no native believes he could live. These preparations are secured from a variety of specialized practitioners. The most powerful of these are the medicine men, whose assistance must be rewarded with substantial gifts. However, the medicine men do not provide the curative potions for their clients, but decide what the ingredients should be and then write them down in an ancient and secret language. This writing is understood only by the medicine men and by the herbalists who, for another gift, provide the required charm. . . .
> The Nacirema have an almost pathological horror of and fascination with the mouth, the condition of which is believed to have a supernatural influence on all social relationships. Were it not for the rituals of the mouth, they believe that their teeth would fall out, their gums

bleed, their jaws shrink, their friends desert them, and their lovers reject them. They also believe that a strong relationship exists between oral and moral characteristics. For example, there is a ritual ablution of the mouth for children which is supposed to improve their moral fibre.

The daily body ritual performed by everyone includes a mouth-rite. Despite the fact that these people are so punctilious about care of the mouth, this rite involves a practice which strikes the uninitiated stranger as revolting. It was reported to me that the ritual consists of inserting a small bundle of hog hairs into the mouth, along with certain magical powders, and then moving the bundle in a highly formalized series of gestures. (Miner, 1956, pp.503–4)

Who are the Nacirema, and in which part of the world do they live? You will be able to answer these questions for yourself, as well as identifying the nature of the body rituals described, simply by spelling 'Nacirema' backwards. Almost any familiar activity will seem strange if described out of context, rather than being seen as part of the whole way of life of a people. Western cleanliness rituals are no more, or less, bizarre than the customs of some Pacific groups who knock out their front teeth to beautify themselves, or of certain South American tribal groups who place discs inside their lips to make them protrude, believing that this enhances their attractiveness.

We cannot understand these practices and beliefs separately from the wider cultures of which they are part. A culture has to be studied in terms of its own meanings and values – a key presupposition of sociology. Sociologists endeavour as far as possible to avoid **ethnocentrism**, which is judging other cultures by comparison with one's own. Since human cultures vary so widely, it is not surprising that people coming from one culture frequently find it difficult to sympathize with the ideas or behaviour of those from a different culture. The 'cargo cult' example that opened this chapter illustrated one culture's difficulty in dealing with another. In sociology, we have to ensure that we remove our own cultural blinkers in order to see the ways of life of different peoples in an unbiased light.

Cultural universals

Amid the diversity of human cultural behaviour there are some common features. Where these are found in all, or virtually all, societies they are called **cultural universals** (Oswalt, 1972; Friedl, 1981; Hiebert, 1976). There is no known culture without a grammatically complex *language*. All cultures have some recognizable form of *family system*, in which there are values and norms associated with the care of children. The institution of *marriage* is a cultural universal, as are *religious rituals* and *property rights*. All cultures, also, have some form of *incest prohibition* – the banning of sexual relations between close relatives, such as father and daughter, mother and son, or brother and sister. A variety of other cultural universals have been identified by anthropologists – including the existence of art, dancing, bodily adornment, games, gift-giving, joking and rules of hygiene (Murdock, 1945).

Yet rather less is universal than would appear from this list, because there are so many variations within each category. Consider, for example, the prohibition against incest. What is defined as incest in different cultures varies considerably. Most often, incest is regarded as sexual relations between members of the immediate family, but among many peoples it includes cousins, even in some instances all people bearing the same family name. There have also been societies in which at least a small proportion of the population have been permitted to engage in incestuous practices. This was the case within, for instance, the ruling class of ancient Egypt.

Language

No one disputes that possession of language is one of the most distinctive of all human cultural attributes, shared by all cultures (although many thousands of different languages are spoken in the world). Animals can communicate with one another, yet no animal species possesses a developed language. Some of the higher primates can be taught linguistic skills – but only in a highly rudimentary way. One of the most famous chimpanzees known to sociology, called Washoe, was taught a vocabulary of well over a hundred words using the American Sign Language for the Deaf (Gardner and Gardner, 1969, 1975). Washoe was also able to put together a few rudimentary sentences. For example, she could communicate 'Come hug-love sorry sorry', meaning that she wanted to apologize after acting in a way she knew was disapproved of.

The experiments with Washoe were much more successful than similar ones done with other chimpanzees – hence Washoe's fame in the sociological literature. But Washoe was not able to master any rules of grammar and could not teach other chimps what she knew. Even after having been trained for several years, her linguistic capacity was far below that of the average human child of two. Every competent adult human language speaker has a vocabulary of thousands of words, and is able to combine them according to rules so complex that linguists spend their entire careers trying to find out what they are (Linden, 1976; Seidenberg et al., 1979).

Speech and writing

All societies use speech as a vehicle of language. However, there are of course other ways of 'carrying' or expressing language – most notably, writing. The invention of writing marked a major transition in human history. It first began as the drawing up of lists. Marks would be made on wood, clay or stone to keep records about significant events, objects or people. For example, a mark, or sometimes a picture, might be drawn to represent each field possessed by a particular family or set of families (Gelb, 1952). Writing began as a means of storing information, and as such was closely linked to the administrative needs of the early states and civilizations (this will be discussed in more detail later in the chapter). A society which possesses writing can 'locate itself' in time and space. Documents can be accumulated which record the past, and information can be gathered about present-day events and activities.

Writing is not just the transfer of speech to paper or some other durable material. It is a phenomenon of interest in its own right. Written documents or texts have qualities in some ways quite distinct from the spoken word. The impact of speech is always by definition limited to the particular contexts in which words are uttered. Ideas and experiences can be passed down the generations in cultures without writing, but only if they are regularly repeated and transmitted by word of mouth. Texts, on the other hand, can endure for thousands of years, and through them those from past ages can in a certain sense 'address' us directly. This is, of course, why documentary research is so important to historians. Through interpreting the texts left behind by dead generations, historians can reconstruct what their lives were like. The biblical texts, for example, have formed an enduring part of the history of the West for the past two thousand years. We can still read and admire the plays of the great dramatists of ancient Greece.

Semiotics and material culture

The symbols expressed in speech and writing are the chief ways in which cultural meanings are formed and expressed, but they are not the only ways. Both *material objects* and *aspects of behaviour* can be used to generate meanings. A 'signifier' is any carrier of meaning – any set of elements used to convey communication. The sounds made in speech are signifiers, as are the marks made on paper or other materials in writing. Other signifiers, however, include dress, pictures or visual signs, modes of eating, forms of building or architecture, and many other material features of culture (Hawkes, 1977). Styles of dress, for example, normally help signify differences between the sexes. In our culture, until relatively recently, all women used to wear skirts and all men trousers. In other cultures, this is reversed: women wear trousers and men skirts (Leach, 1976).

The analysis of *semiotic systems* – non-verbal cultural meanings – opens up a fascinating field for sociology and anthropology. **Semiotic** analysis can be very useful in comparing one culture with another. Given that cultural meanings are symbolic, it allows us to contrast the ways in which different cultures are structured. For example, the buildings in cities are not simply places in which people live and work. They often have a symbolic character. In traditional cities, the main temple or church was usually placed on high ground in or near the city centre. It symbolized the all-powerful influence which religion was supposed to have over the lives of the people.

Of course, material culture is not simply symbolic, but is vital to catering for physical needs – in the shape of the tools or technology used to acquire food, make weaponry, construct dwellings and so forth. Variations in material culture provide the main means of classifying different types of society in history, because how people organize to meet their basic needs influences most other aspects of their culture. We now turn to a comparison of the varying forms of human society.

Types of pre-modern society

The explorers, traders and missionaries sent out during Europe's great age of discovery met with many different peoples. As the anthropologist Marvin Harris has written:

> In some regions – Australia, the Arctic, the southern tips of South America and Africa – they found groups still living much like Europe's own long-forgotten stone age ancestors: bands of twenty or thirty people, sprinkled across vast territories, constantly on the move, living entirely by hunting animals and collecting wild plants. These hunter-collectors appeared to be members of a rare and endangered species. In other regions – the forests of eastern North America, the jungles of South America, and East Asia – they found denser populations, inhabiting more or less permanent villages, based on farming and consisting of perhaps one or two large communal structures, but here too the weapons and tools were relics of prehistory.
>
> Elsewhere, of course, the explorers encountered fully developed states and empires, headed by despots and ruling classes, and defended by standing armies. It was these great empires, with their cities, monuments, palaces, temples and treasures, that had lured all the Marco Polos and Columbuses across the oceans and deserts in the first place. There was China – the greatest empire in the world, a vast, sophisticated realm whose leaders scorned the 'red-faced barbarians', supplicants from puny kingdoms beyond the pale of the civilised world. And there was India – a land where cows were venerated and the unequal burdens of life were apportioned according to what each soul had merited in its previous incarnation. And then there were the native American states and empires, worlds unto themselves, each with its distinctive arts and religions: the Incas, with their great stone fortresses, suspension bridges, over-worked granaries, and state-controlled economy; and the Aztecs, with their bloodthirsty gods fed from human hearts and their incessant search for fresh sacrifices. (Harris, 1978, pp. 13–14)

This seemingly unlimited variety of pre-modern societies can actually be grouped into three main types, each of which is referred to in Harris's description: hunters and gatherers (Harris's 'hunters and collectors'); larger agrarian or pastoral societies (involving agriculture or the tending of domesticated animals); and non-industrial civilizations or traditional states. We shall look at the main characteristics of these in turn.

Hunters and gatherers

For all but a tiny part of our existence on this planet, human beings have lived in small groups or tribes, often numbering no more than thirty or forty people. The earliest type of human society consisted of **hunters and gatherers**. Rather than growing crops, or tending animals, these groups gained their livelihood from hunting, fishing and gathering edible plants growing in the wild. Hunting and gathering cultures continue to exist today in some parts of the world, such as the jungles of Brazil or New Guinea, but most have been destroyed or absorbed by the global spread of Western culture, and those that remain are unlikely to stay intact for much longer (Wolf, 1983). Currently, less than a quarter of a million people in the world support themselves chiefly through hunting and gathering – only 0.001 per cent of the total global population.

Research by anthropologists over the past fifty years has provided much information about hunting and gathering societies. Given the diversity of human culture, we have to be careful in generalizing even about one type of society, but some common characteristics of hunting and gathering communities do set them apart from other types (Bicchieri, 1972; Diamond, 1974; Schrire, 1984).

Compared to larger societies – particularly modern industrial systems – little inequality is found in hunting and gathering groups. Hunters and gatherers move about a good deal; since they are without animal or mechanical means of transport, they can take few goods or possessions with them. The material goods they need are limited to weapons for hunting, tools for digging and building, traps and cooking utensils. Thus there is little difference among members of the society in the number or kind of material possessions. Differences of position or rank tend to be limited to age and sex. Males seem virtually everywhere to be the hunters, while women gather wild crops, cook and bring up the children. The 'elders' – the oldest and most experienced men in the community – usually have an important say in major decisions affecting the group. But just as there is little variation in wealth among members of a community, differences of power are much less than in larger types of society. Hunting and gathering societies are usually 'participatory' – all adult male members tend to assemble together when important decisions are taken or crises faced.

Hunters and gatherers do not just move about in a completely erratic way. Most have fixed territories, around which they migrate regularly from year to year. Many hunting and gathering communities do not have a stable membership; people often move between different camps, or groups split up and join others within the same overall territory.

The Mbuti pygmies

Of the hundreds of descriptions of hunting and gathering societies that have been written, we shall look at just one, to illustrate their way of life: the society of the Mbuti (pronounced 'Mubooti') pygmies, who live in an area of Zaire, in Central Africa (Turnbull, 1983; Mair, 1974). The Mbuti inhabit a heavily forested area, difficult for outsiders to penetrate. They themselves know the forest intimately, and move about in it as they please. There is plenty of water, edible wild plants and animals to be hunted. The houses of the Mbuti are not permanent dwellings, but are made of leaves on a framework of branches. They can be set up in a matter of hours, and abandoned when the Mbuti move on – as they do continuously, never staying more than a month at any one site.

The Mbuti live in small bands, made up of four or five families. The bands have a fairly permanent membership, but there is nothing to stop either an individual or a family leaving one group and joining another. Nobody 'runs' any band – there are no chiefs. Older men have a duty, however, to quiet 'noise' – bickering or quarrelling – which the pygmies believe displeases the spirits of the forest. If a conflict gets too severe, the members of a band split up and go to join others.

The Mbuti were first studied in the 1960s, when their traditional way of life remained intact. Since then, it has come under increasing strain. The outside world has encroached more and more on the forest, and the Mbuti are becoming drawn into the money economy of the villages around the forest's perimeters. I have presented the account of their way of life in the present tense, but it is now on the verge of extinction. Much the same is true of the examples of other types of small traditional society which are given later in the chapter.

The original 'affluent societies'?

Unlike the Mbuti, most hunting and gathering societies remaining in existence today are confined to inhospitable areas. Such groups may live close to starvation level, because the environment is too harsh to provide more than a minimal living. Hunters and gatherers have mostly long since been driven out of the more fertile areas of the world, and the fact that they now live in circumstances where survival is a perennial struggle has led many scholars to assume that all such peoples lived in conditions of material deprivation. This was probably not in fact the case in the past. A prominent anthropologist, Marshall Sahlins, has called hunter-gatherers the 'original affluent societies' – because they had more than enough to provide for their wants (Sahlins, 1972). Past hunters and gatherers living in the more hospitable regions of the world did not have to spend most of the day working, 'engaged in production'. Many may have worked for a shorter average number of hours per day than the modern factory or office employee.

Hunters and gatherers have little interest in developing material wealth beyond what is needed to cater for their basic wants. Their main preoccupations are normally with religious values, and with ceremonial and ritual activities. Many hunters and gatherers participate regularly

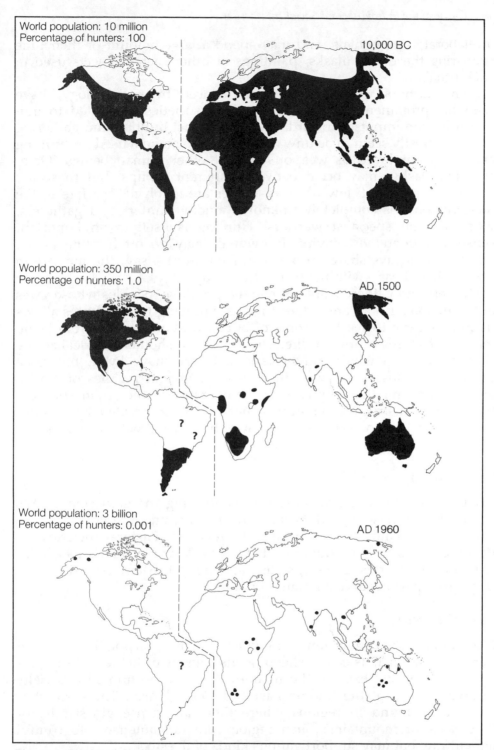

Figure 1 The decline of hunting and gathering societies in relation to world population growth
Source: Richard B. Lee and Irven De Vore (eds), *Man the Hunter* (Chicago: Aldine Press, 1968), frontispiece.

in elaborate ceremonials, and may spend a large amount of their time preparing the dress, masks, paintings or other sacred objects used in such rituals.

Some authors, especially those influenced by sociobiology, have seen the prominence of hunting in these societies as related to universal human impulses towards war, but in fact hunting and gathering societies mostly seem to be unwarlike. The implements used for hunting are rarely employed as weapons against other human beings. Occasionally, clashes may occur between different groups, but these are usually very limited: few or no casualties are involved. Warfare in the modern sense is completely unknown among hunters and gatherers, who have no specialist warriors. Hunting is itself in an important sense a co-operative activity. Individuals may go off hunting alone, but almost always share the results of the hunt – say, the meat from a wild pig or boar – with the rest of the group.

Hunters and gatherers are not merely 'primitive' peoples whose ways of life no longer hold any interest for us. Studying their cultures allows us more clearly to see that some of our institutions are far from being 'natural' features of human life. Of course, we should not idealize the circumstances in which hunters and gatherers have lived, but none the less, the absence of war, the lack of major inequalities of wealth and power, and the emphasis on co-operation rather than competition, are all instructive reminders that the world created by modern industrial civilization is not necessarily to be equated with 'progress'.

Pastoral and agrarian societies

About twenty thousand years ago, some hunting and gathering groups turned to the raising of domesticated animals, and the cultivation of fixed plots of land, as their means of livelihood. **Pastoral societies** are those relying mainly on domesticated livestock, while **agrarian societies** are those that grow crops (practise agriculture). Many societies have had mixed pastoral and agrarian economies.

Pastoral societies

Depending on the environment in which they live, pastoralists rear and herd animals such as cattle, sheep, goats, camels or horses. Many pastoral societies still exist in the modern world, concentrated especially in areas of Africa, the Middle East and Central Asia. These societies are usually found in regions where there are dense grasslands, or in deserts or mountains. Such regions are not amenable to fruitful agriculture, but may support various kinds of livestock.

Pastoral societies usually migrate between different areas according to seasonal changes. Because they have animal transport, they move across much larger distances than the hunting and gathering peoples. Given their nomadic habits, people in pastoral societies do not normally accumulate many material possessions, although their way of life is more complex in material terms than that of hunters and gatherers. Since the domestication of animals permits a regular supply of food, these societies are usually much larger than hunting and gathering communities. Some pastoral societies number a quarter of a million people or more.

Ranging as they often do over large tracts of territory, pastoralists regularly come into contact with other groups. They frequently engage in trade – and also in warfare. Many pastoral cultures have been peaceful, wishing only to tend to their livestock and engage in community ritual and ceremonial. Others have been highly warlike, deriving their livelihood from conquest and pillage as well as from the herding of animals. Pastoral societies display greater inequalities of wealth and power than hunting and gathering communities. In particular, chiefs, tribal leaders or warlords often wield considerable personal power.

A classic description of a pastoral society was given by E. E. Evans-Pritchard, who studied the Nuer, a society in the Southern Sudan in Africa (Evans-Pritchard, 1940). The livelihood of the Nuer depends mainly on the raising of cattle, although they also grow some crops as well. The people live in villages situated from five to twenty miles apart from one another. In the 1930s, when Evans-Pritchard carried out his study, the Nuer numbered about 200,000 people. They all speak the same language and follow similar customs, but there is no central political authority or form of government. The Nuer are divided into tribes, which sometimes collaborate with one another, but mostly live separately.

Each tribe has its own area of land, the divisions mostly being marked by water-courses. The Nuer attach no particular significance to land, however, except in so far as it provides a place to graze their cattle. Part of the year, during the dry season, they move to live in camps near water-holes. Much of the life of the Nuer is bound up with their cattle, which are in many ways central to their culture. They have a profound contempt for neighbouring peoples having few or no cattle. Every major phase of life – birth, entering adulthood, marriage and death – is marked by rituals to do with cattle. Men are often addressed by the names of their favourite oxen and women their favourites among the cows they milk.

The Nuer tribes quite often wage war on one another, and also sometimes form an alliance to fight outsiders. Just as they live for their cattle, so they fight wars for them – for instance, raiding the nearby Dinka, another pastoral society, to steal their herds. A Nuer saying goes: 'more people have died for the sake of a cow than for any other cause.'

Agrarian societies

Agrarian societies seem to have originated at about the same date as pastoral ones. At some point, hunting and gathering groups began to sow their own crops rather than simply collecting those growing in the wild. This practice first developed as what is usually called 'horticulture', in which small gardens are cultivated by the use of simple hoes or digging instruments. Many peoples in the world still rely primarily on horticulture for their livelihood.

Like pastoralism, horticulture provides for a more assured supply of food than is possible by hunting and gathering, and therefore can support much larger communities. Since they are not on the move, cultures gaining a livelihood from horticulture can develop larger stocks of material possessions than can either pastoral or hunting and gathering communities. Once groups are settled in particular places, regular trading and political ties can be developed between separate villages. Warlike behaviour is common in horticultural societies, although the level of violence tends to be less pronounced than among some pastoral groups. Those who grow crops are not ordinarily practised in arts of combat; nomadic pastoral tribesmen, on the other hand, can mass together as marauding armies.

The Gururumba are a New Guinea tribe of just over a thousand people living in six villages (Newman, 1965). In each village there are several gardens, fenced off from one another. Plots are owned by different families within these fenced areas. Everyone, adults and children, is involved in tending the plots, although men and women are responsible for separate types of fruit and vegetables. Each family has more than one plot, and cultivates different plants at certain times of the year, thus providing a consistent food supply. Gururumba culture involves a complicated system of ceremonial gift exchanges that families carry on with one another, through which prestige in the community can be achieved. The people thus have gardens in which they grow crops to cater for their day-to-day needs, and other plots in which they cultivate 'prestige' crops. 'Prestige' crops are given far more care than those relating to ordinary needs.

The Gururumba also raise pigs, which are not kept mainly for food but again as items of gift exchange designed to achieve status in the community. Every few years a massive pig feast is held in which hundred of pigs are killed, cooked and given as gifts. As in pastoral groups, among the Gururumba there is more inequality than in hunting and gathering cultures. Chiefs and tribal leaders play a prominent role, and there are substantial differences in the material wealth people possess.

Non-industrial civilizations or traditional states

From about 6000 BC onwards we find evidence of larger societies than ever existed before, contrasting in distinct ways with earlier types (Burns and Ralph, 1974). These societies were based on the development of cities, showed very pronounced inequalities of wealth and power, and were associated with the rule of the kings or emperors. Because they involved the use of writing, and a flourishing of science and art, they are often called *civilizations*. However, since they developed more co-ordinated government than other forms of society, the term **traditional states** is also often used to refer to them.

Most traditional states were also *empires*; they achieved the size they did through the conquest and incorporation of other peoples (Eisenstadt, 1963; Claessen and Skalnik, 1978; Kautsky, 1982). This was true, for instance, of traditional China and Rome. At its height, in the first century AD, the Roman Empire stretched from Britain in North-west Europe to beyond the Middle East. The Chinese Empire, which lasted for more than two thousand years, up to the threshold of the present century, covered most of the massive region of Eastern Asia now occupied by modern China. No traditional states still exist in the world today. Although some, like China and Japan, remained more or less intact up to the start of the twentieth century, all have now been destroyed or dissolved into more modern systems.

The earliest traditional states developed in the Middle East, usually in fertile river areas (Kramer, 1959). The Chinese Empire originated in about 2000 BC, at which time powerful states were also found in what is now India and Pakistan. A number of large traditional states existed in Mexico and Latin America, such as the Aztecs of the Mexican peninsula and the Inca of Peru. The Inca state had been established for about a century before the arrival of the Spanish adventurer, Pizarro, who landed in South America in 1535 with only a small force of soldiers. Yet by building alliances with other native tribes hostile to the Inca, he was able rapidly to bring about the downfall of the Inca state and claim the area for Spain. His was one of the first of a series of encounters between Western influences and traditional states that was eventually to lead to their complete disappearance.

The Maya

As an example of a traditional state we shall look at a third American civilization, that of the Maya, who lived in the Yucatan Peninsula, by the Mexican Gulf. Maya civilization flourished from AD 300 to 800. The Maya built elaborate religious centres, surrounding them with their dwellings, all built in stone. The religious shrines took the form of large pyramids, at the top of each of which was a temple. At Tikal, the biggest of the pyramids, the surrounding city held some 40,000 inhabitants. It was the main administrative centre – effectively the capital city – of the Maya State.

Maya society was ruled by an aristocratic class of warrior-priests. They were the highest religious dignitaries in the society, but were also military leaders, and fought continuous wars with surrounding groups. The majority of the population were peasant farmers, all of whom were required to give up a proportion of their production to their aristocratic rulers, who lived in conditions of some luxury.

It is not known for certain why Maya civilization collapsed, but it was probably conquered by neighbouring tribes. By the time the Spanish arrived, the Maya state had long since disappeared.

Features of the traditional state

The traditional state was the only type of society in history, before the emergence of modern industrialism, in which a significant proportion of the population was not directly engaged in the production of food. In hunting and gathering communities, and in pastoral and agrarian societies, there was a fairly simple **division of labour.** The most important separation of tasks was between men and women. In traditional states, by contrast, a more complicated occupational system existed. There was still strict division of labour by sex, the activities of women being mainly confined to the household and the fields. However, among men we see the emergence of specialized trades, such as those of merchant, courtier, government administrator and soldier.

There was also a basic division of classes between aristocratic groups and the remainder of the population. The ruler was at the head of a 'ruling class' that maintained the exclusive right to hold the higher social positions. The members of this class usually lived in considerable material comfort or luxury. The condition of the mass of the population, on the other hand, was frequently very hard. Slave-owning was a common feature of these societies.

A few traditional states were mainly built up through trade, and were ruled by merchants, but most were either established through military conquest or involved a substantial build-up of armed forces (McNeill, 1983; Mann, 1986). Traditional states saw the development of professional armies, anticipating modern types of military organization. The Roman army, for example, was a highly disciplined and intensively trained body of men and was the foundation on which the expansion of the Roman Empire was built. We also find in traditional states the beginning of the mechanization of war. The swords, spears, shields and siege equipment carried by the Roman army were manufactured by specialized craftsmen. In the wars conducted between traditional states, and between these states and 'barbarian' tribes, casualties were far higher than they had ever been before.

Societies in the modern world

Traditional states have now completely disappeared from the face of the earth. Although hunting and gathering, agrarian and pastoral societies continue to exist in some regions, they are only to be found in relatively isolated territories – and, in most cases, even these last surviving examples are disintegrating. What has happened to destroy the forms of society which dominated the whole of history up to two centuries ago? The answer, in a word, is *industrialization* – the emergence of machine production, based on the use of inanimate power resources (like steam or electricity). The *industrialized societies* are utterly different in many respects from any previous type of social order, and their development has had consequences stretching far beyond their European origins.

The industrialized societies

Modern industrialization first came into being in England, as a result of the 'Industrial Revolution' initiated in the eighteenth century. This is really a short-hand name for a complex set of technological changes affecting the means whereby people gain their livelihood. These changes involved the invention of new machines (like the spinning jenny, for weaving yarn), the harnessing of power resources (especially water and steam) to production, and the use of science to improve production methods. Since discoveries and inventions in one field lead to more in others, the pace of technological innovation in the industrialized societies is extremely rapid, compared to traditional forms of social system.

A prime distinguishing feature of industrialized societies is that the large majority of the employed population works in factories or offices, rather than in agriculture. In even the most advanced of traditional states, only a tiny proportion of the population were not engaged in working on the land. The relatively rudimentary level of technological development simply did not permit more than a small minority to be freed from the chores of agricultural production. In industrialized societies, by contrast, only some 2 to 5 per cent of the population works in agriculture, their efforts providing food for the rest.

Industrialized societies are also much more highly urbanized than any type of traditional social system. In some industrialized countries, well over 90 per cent of people live in towns and cities, where most jobs are to be found and new job opportunities are continually created. The size of the largest cities is vastly greater than the urban settlements found in traditional civilizations. In these new urban areas, social life becomes more impersonal and anonymous than before, many day-to-day encounters being with strangers rather than with individuals known to one another on a personal basis. Large-scale organizations, such as business corporations or government agencies, come to influence the lives of virtually everyone.

A further characteristic of industrialized societies concerns their political systems, which are much more developed and intensive than forms of government in traditional states. In traditional civilizations, the political authorities (monarchs and emperors) had little direct influence on the customs and habits of most of their subjects, who lived in fairly self-contained local villages. With industrialization, transport and communications became much more rapid, making for a more integrated 'national' community. The industrialized societies were the first **nation-states** to come into existence. Nation-states are political communities with clearly delimited 'borders' dividing them from each other, rather than the vague 'frontier areas' which used to separate traditional states. In nation-states, governments have extensive powers over many aspects of citizens' lives, framing laws which have universal application to those living within their borders.

Industrial technology has been by no means limited in its application to peaceful processes of economic development. From the earliest phases of industrialization, modern production processes have been put to military use, and this has radically altered modes of waging war, creating weaponry and modes of military organization greatly in advance of those possessed by non-industrial cultures. Superior economic strength, political cohesion and military might underlie the seemingly irresistible spread of Western ways of life across the world over the past two centuries.

If large numbers of traditional societies and cultures have now disappeared, this is not because their ways of life were 'inferior'. It is because they were unable to resist the impact of the combination of industrial and military *power* which the Western countries developed. The concept of **power** – and a closely associated notion, that of **ideology** – are of great importance in sociology. By power is meant the ability of individuals or groups to make their own concerns or interests count, even where others resist. Power sometimes involves the direct use of force, but is almost always also accompanied by the development of ideas (ideologies) which *justify* the actions of the powerful. In the case of Western expansion, the intruders justified their activities by seeing themselves as 'civilizing' the 'heathen' peoples with whom they came into contact.

The three 'Worlds'

From the seventeenth to the early twentieth centuries, the Western countries established colonies in many areas previously occupied by traditional societies, using their superior military strength where necessary. Although virtually all these colonies have now attained their independence, the process of **colonialism** reshaped the social and cultural map of the globe. In some regions, like North America, Australia and New Zealand, which were only thinly populated by hunting and gathering communities, the Europeans became the majority population. In other areas, including much of Asia, Africa and South America, the local populations remained in the majority. Societies of the first of these types, such as the United States, have become industrialized. Those in

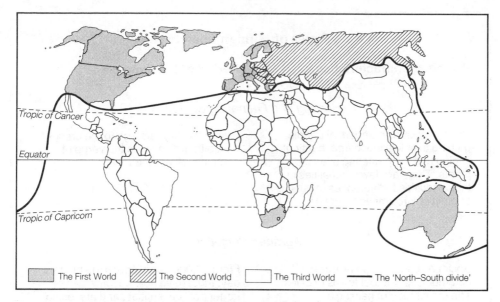

Figure 2 The three 'Worlds' and the 'North–South divide'
Source: Andrew Webster, *Introduction to the Sociology of Development* (London: Macmillan, 1986), p. 5.

the second category are mostly at a much lower level of industrial development, and are often referred to today as **Third World** societies.

Third World societies

Third World societies include China, India, most of the African countries (such as Nigeria, Ghana or Algeria) and those in South America (for example Brazil, Peru or Venezuela).

In Third World countries there is only a low level of industrialization, and the large majority of the population is engaged in agricultural production. Since many of these societies are situated south of the USA and Europe, they are sometimes referred to collectively as 'the South', and contrasted to the wealthier, industrialized 'North'. While they may include peoples living in traditional fashion, Third World countries are very different from pre-existing forms of traditional culture. They have political systems derived from, or modelled on, those established first of all in the Western societies – that is to say, they are nation-states. While most of the population still lives in rural areas, many of these societies are experiencing a very rapid process of urbanization. Although agriculture remains the dominant form of economic activity, crops are often produced for sale on world markets rather than for local consumption. Third World countries are not merely societies that have 'lagged behind' the more industrialized areas. The conditions in which billions of people now live in the Third World have been in large part brought about by contact with the West, undermining earlier, more traditional, systems.

Types of Human Society

Principal Characteristics	Period of Existence

Hunting and Gathering Societies

Consist of small numbers of people, gaining their livelihood from hunting, fishing and the gathering of edible plants. There are few inequalities in these societies; differences of rank or position are limited to age and sex.

From 50,000 years ago to the present day, although now on the verge of complete disappearance.

Agrarian Societies

Societies based on small rural communities, without towns or cities. The main mode of gaining a livelihood is through agriculture, often supplemented by hunting and gathering. These societies are marked by stronger inequalities than among hunters and gatherers, and are ruled over by chiefs.

From 12,000 years ago to the present day. Most have now become part of larger political entities, and are losing their distinct identity.

Pastoral Societies

Societies which depend on the tending of domesticated animals for their material subsistence. Their size ranges from a few hundred people up to many thousands. Pastoral societies are usually marked by distinct inequalities, and are ruled by chiefs or warrior kings.

The same span of time as agrarian societies. Pastoral societies are also today mostly part of larger states, and their traditional ways of life are becoming undermined.

Traditional States or Civilizations

In these societies, agriculture is still the main basis of the economic system, but cities exist, in which trade and manufacture are concentrated. Traditional states can sometimes be very large, numbering millions of people, although most were small compared to the larger industrialized societies today. Traditional states possess a distinct apparatus of government (hence their name), headed by a king or emperor. Major inequalities exist between different classes.

From about 6000 BC until the nineteenth century. All traditional states have now disappeared.

First World Societies

Societies based on industrial production, with a considerable role allowed to free enterprise. Only a tiny proportion of the population works in agriculture, and the majority of people live in towns and cities. Major class inequalities exist, although these are less pronounced than in traditional states. These societies form distinct political communities or nation-states.	From the eighteenth century to the present day.

Second World Societies

Societies which have an industrial base, but where the economic system is centrally planned. Only a fairly small proportion of the population works in agriculture, and most people live in towns and cities. Major class inequalities exist, although the aim of the Marxist governments of these societies is to create a 'classless' system. Like First World countries, Second World countries form distinct political communities or nation-states.	From the early twentieth century (following the Russian Revolution of 1917) to the present day.

Third World Societies

Societies in which the majority of the population works in agriculture, and lives in rural areas, mostly using traditional methods of production. Some of the agricultural produce, however, is sold on world markets. Some Third World countries have free enterprise systems, while others are centrally planned. Third World societies, like those of the First and Second Worlds, are distinct political communities or nation-states.	From the eighteenth century (as colonized areas) to the present day.

First and Second World societies

The term **First World** refers to the industrialized countries of Europe, the United States, Australasia and Japan. First World countries nearly all have multi-party, parliamentary systems of government. **Second World** societies are industrialized societies ruled by governments affiliated to Communism. These include the Soviet Union, together with East European societies such as Czechoslovakia, Poland or Hungary.

There are significant differences between First and Second World societies on an economic as well as a political level. Whereas the economic systems of the First World countries are based on market principles – allowing a major role for free enterprise – those of Second World states are centrally planned. But the greatest contrasts are between the industrialized societies as a whole, on the one side, and the Third World countries on the other. By comparison with the industrialized nations, the Third World societies are mostly very poor. Many of them have experienced massive rates of population growth, placing extreme strain on their ability to generate sufficient resources to provide even a minimally adequate standard of living for their citizens.

In chapter 1, it was pointed out that the chief focus of sociology is the study of the industrialized societies – the First and Second Worlds. As sociologists, can we thus safely ignore the Third World, leaving this as the domain of anthropology? We certainly cannot. The three Worlds have developed in *interconnection* with one another, and are today more closely related than ever before. Those of us living in the industrialized societies depend on many raw materials and manufactured products coming from Third World countries to sustain our lives. Conversely, the economies of most Third World states depend on trading networks that bind them to the industrialized countries. We can only fully understand the industrialized order against the backdrop of the Third World societies – in which, in fact, by far the greater proportion of the world's population lives. (For further discussion, see chapter 16: 'The Globalizing of Social Life'.)

Conclusion

First, Second and Third World societies are all different from the traditional types of social order which dominated the world for thousands of years, until some two centuries ago. The explorations which Western travellers undertook across the globe set off processes of change that have destroyed many pre-modern cultures. There remains enormous cultural diversity, however, both within and between societies. As human beings, we all share major traits in common – but we are all also strongly influenced by the cultural values and habits of the societies in which we exist. In the following chapter, we shall look at some of the processes which affect our individual development from infancy through to the later phases of life.

Summary

1   *Culture* consists of the *values* held by a given group, the *norms* they follow and the *material goods* they create.

2   The human species emerged as a result of a long process of biological *evolution*. Human beings are part of groups of higher mammals, the

primates. There seems strong evidence that cultural development preceded, and probably shaped, the evolution of the human species.

3 *Sociobiology* is important primarily for its insights concerning animal behaviour; the ideas of the sociobiologists about human social life are highly speculative. Our behaviour is genetically influenced, but our genetic endowment probably conditions only the potentialities of our behaviour, not the actual content of our activities.

4 Human beings have no *instincts* in the sense of complex patterns of unlearned behaviour. A set of simple reflexes, plus a range of organic needs, are innate characteristics of the human individual.

5 Forms of behaviour found in all, or virtually all, cultures are called *cultural universals*. Language, the prohibition against incest, institutions of marriage, the family, religion and property are the main types of cultural universals – but within these general categories there are many variations in values and modes of behaviour between different societies.

6 Several types of pre-modern society can be distinguished. In *hunting and gathering* societies, people do not grow crops or keep livestock, but live by gathering plants and hunting animals. *Pastoral* societies are those in which the raising of domesticated animals provides a major source of livelihood. *Agrarian* societies depend on the cultivation of fixed plots of land. Larger, more developed agrarian societies form *traditional states* or *civilizations*.

7 The development and expansion of the West led to the conquest of many parts of the world, radically changing long-established social systems and cultures.

8 In industrialized societies, industrial production (whose techniques are also used in the production of food) becomes the main basis of the economy. *First World* industrialized countries include the nations of the 'West', plus Japan, Australia and New Zealand. *Second World* countries are industrialized societies ruled by communist governments. *Third World* countries, in which most of the world's population live, were almost all formerly colonized areas. The majority of the population works in agricultural production, some of which is geared to world markets.

Basic concepts

culture	norms
society	power
values	ideology

Important terms

evolution	pastoral societies
mutation	agrarian societies
sociobiology	traditional states
instinct	division of labour
sub-culture	nation-states
ethnocentrism	colonialism
cultural universals	Third World
semiotics	First World
hunting and gathering societies	Second World

Further reading

Ruth Benedict, *Patterns of Culture* (New York: Mentor Books, 1946) — a classic study of cultural differences; still worth reading.

Kenneth Bock, *Human Nature and History: A Response to Sociobiology* (New York: Columbia University Press, 1980) — a critique of the aspirations of sociobiology.

Jack Goody, *The Domestication of the Savage Mind* (Cambridge: Cambridge University Press, 1977) — an analysis of the impact of writing and literacy on cultural development.

Edmund Leach, *Culture and Communication: The Logic by which Symbols are Connected* (Cambridge: Cambridge University Press, 1976) — a discussion of the nature of cultural symbolism.

Raymond Williams, *Culture* (Glasgow: Fontana, 1981) — a useful general discussion of the concept of culture.

Peter Worsley, *The Three Worlds: Culture and World Development* (London: Weidenfeld and Nicolson, 1984) — an analysis of the connections between the First, Second and Third Worlds.

3

Socialization and the Life-Cycle

Animals low down on the evolutionary scale, such as most species of insects, are capable of fending for themselves very soon after they are born, with little or no help from adults. There are no generations among the lower animals, because the behaviour of the 'young' is more or less identical to that of 'adults'. As we go up the evolutionary scale, however, these observations apply less and less; the higher animals have to *learn* appropriate ways of behaviour. Among the mammals, the young are quite often completely helpless at birth and have to be cared for by their elders, and the human infant is most helpless of all. A human child cannot survive unaided for at least the first four or five years of life.

Socialization is the process whereby the helpless infant gradually becomes a self-aware, knowledgeable person, skilled in the ways of the culture into which she or he is born. Socialization is not a kind of 'cultural programming', in which the child absorbs passively the influences with which he or she comes into contact. Even the most recent new-born infant has needs or demands that affect the behaviour of those responsible for its care.

Socialization connects the different generations to one another (Turnbull, 1984). The birth of a child alters the lives of those who are responsible for its upbringing – who themselves therefore undergo new learning experiences. Parenting usually ties the activities of adults to children for the remainder of the lives of both. Older people still remain parents when they become grandparents, of course, thus forging another set of relationships connecting different generations with each other. Although the process of cultural learning is much more intense in infancy and early childhood than later, learning and adjustment go on through the whole life-cycle.

In the sections to follow, we shall continue the theme of 'nature' versus 'nurture' introduced in the previous chapter. We shall first analyse the development of the human individual from infancy to early childhood, identifying the main stages of change involved. A number of theoretical interpretations have been put forward by different writers about how and why children develop as they do, and we will describe and compare these. Finally, we shall move on to discuss the main groups and social contexts which influence socialization during the various phases of individuals' lives.

'Unsocialized' children

What would children be like if, somehow, they were raised without the influence of human adults? Obviously no humane person could bring up a child away from human influence as an experiment. There have been, however, a number of much-discussed cases of children who spent their early years away from normal human contact. We shall begin the chapter by looking at two of these cases, before moving on to study more orthodox patterns of child development.

The 'wild boy of Aveyron'

On 9 January 1800 a strange creature emerged from the woods near the village of Saint-Serin in southern France. In spite of walking erect, he looked more animal than human, although he was soon identified as a boy of about eleven or twelve. He spoke only in shrill, strange-sounding cries. The boy apparently had no sense of personal hygiene, and relieved himself where and when he chose. He was brought to the attention of the local police and taken to a nearby orphanage. At first he tried constantly to escape, only being recaptured with some difficulty, and refused to tolerate wearing clothes, tearing them off as soon as they were put on him. No parents ever came forward to claim him.

The child was subjected to a thorough medical examination, which turned up no abnormalities of a major kind. On being shown a mirror, he seems to have seen the image, but did not recognize himself. On one occasion he tried to reach through the mirror to seize a potato he saw in it. (The potato was in fact being held behind his head.) After several attempts, without turning his head, he took the potato by reaching back over his shoulder. A priest who was observing the boy from day to day, and who described the potato incident, wrote:

> All these little details, and many others we could add prove that this child is not totally without intelligence, reflection, and reasoning power. However, we are obliged to say that, in every case not concerned with his natural needs or satisfying his appetite, one can perceive in him only animal behaviour. If he has sensations, they give birth to no idea. He cannot even compare them with one another. One would think that there is no connection between his soul or mind and his body . . . (Shattuck, 1980, p. 69; see also Lane, 1976)

Later the boy was moved to Paris and a systematic attempt was made to change him 'from beast to human'. The endeavour was only partly successful. He was toilet-trained, accepted wearing clothes and learned to dress himself. Yet he was uninterested in toys or games, and was never able to master more than a few words. So far as we can tell, on the basis of detailed descriptions of his behaviour and reactions, this was not because he was mentally retarded. He seemed either unwilling or unable fully to master human speech. He made little further progress, and died in 1828, aged about forty.

Genie

It cannot be proved how long the 'wild boy of Aveyron' lived on his own in the woods, or whether or not he suffered from some congenital defect that made it impossible for him to develop like a normal human being. However, there are examples from current times which reinforce some of the observations made about his behaviour. A very recent case is provided by the life of Genie, a California girl who was locked in a room from the age of about one and a half until she was over thirteen (Curtiss, 1977). Genie's father kept his wife, who was going blind, more or less completely confined to the house. The main connection between the family and the outside world was through a teenage son, who attended school and did the shopping.

Genie had a hip defect from birth which stopped her learning to walk properly, and her father frequently beat her. When Genie was twenty months old, he apparently decided she was retarded and 'put her away' in a closed room with the curtains drawn and the door shut. She stayed in that room for the next eleven years, seeing the other members of the family only when they came to feed her. Genie had not been toilet-trained, and spent part of her time harnessed, naked, to an infant's potty seat. Sometimes at night she was removed, only to be put into another restraining garment, a sleeping bag within which her arms were imprisoned. Tied up in this way, she was also enclosed in an infant's cot with wire mesh sides and a mesh cover overhead. Somehow in these appalling circumstances she endured the hours, days and years of her life. She had almost no opportunity to overhear any conversation between others in the house. If she attempted to make a noise, or to attract attention, her father would beat her. He never spoke to her, but instead made barking, animal-like sounds if she did anything to annoy him. She had no proper toys or other objects with which to occupy her time.

In 1970 her mother escaped from the house, taking Genie with her. The condition of the girl came to the notice of a social worker, and she was placed in the rehabilitation ward of a children's hospital. When she was first admitted to the hospital, she could not stand erect, run, jump or climb, and was only able to walk in a shuffling, clumsy way. She was described by a psychiatrist as 'unsocialized, primitive, hardly human'. Once in a rehabilitation ward, however, Genie made fairly rapid progress. She learned to eat quite normally, was toilet-trained, and tolerated being dressed like other children. Yet she was silent almost all of the time, except when she laughed, her laugh being high-pitched and 'unreal'. She masturbated constantly, in public situations, refusing to abandon the habit. Later she lived as a foster child in the home of one of the doctors from the hospital, and gradually developed a fairly wide vocabulary, enough to make a limited number of basic utterances. Yet her mastery of language never progressed beyond that of a three- or four-year-old.

Genie's behaviour was studied intensively and she was given a variety of tests over a period of some seven years. These seemed to indicate that she was neither feeble-minded nor suffered from any other congenital defects. What seems to have happened to Genie, as to the 'wild boy of Aveyron', is that by the time she came into close human contact, she had got beyond the age at which the learning of language and other human skills is readily accomplished by children. There is probably a 'critical period' for the learning of language and other complex accomplishments, after which it is too late to master them fully. The 'wild boy' and Genie provide some sense of what an 'unsocialized' child would be like. Each retained many 'non-human' responses, yet, in spite of the deprivations they suffered, neither displayed any lasting viciousness. They responded quickly to others who treated them sympathetically, and were able to acquire a minimum level of ordinary human abilities.

Of course, we have to be cautious about interpreting cases of this sort. In each of these examples, it is possible that a mental abnormality had remained undiagnosed. Alternatively, the experiences to which the children were subjected may have inflicted psychological damage that prevented them from mastering the skills most children acquire at a much earlier age. Yet there is sufficient similarity between these two case histories, and others that have been recorded, to suggest how limited our faculties would be in the absence of an extended period of early socialization.

Let us now look directly at the early phases of child development. In so doing, we will be able to understand in a more comprehensive way the processes by which the infant becomes recognizably 'human'.

The early development of the infant

Perceptual development

All human infants are born with the capacity to make certain perceptual distinctions and respond to them (Richards and Light, 1986). It used to be thought that the new-born infant was swamped by a mass of sensation among which it had no way of differentiating. In a famous observation, the psychologist and philosopher William James wrote: 'The baby, assailed by eyes, ears, nose, skin and entrails all at once, feels it all as one great blooming, buzzing confusion' (James, 1890). This is no longer seen as an accurate portrayal by most students of infant behaviour – even new-born infants react selectively to their environment.

From the age of one week, a patterned surface (stripes, concentric circles or a face-like picture) is looked at more often than even a brightly coloured plain surface. Under the age of one month, these perceptual capacities are still weak, and images more than about a foot away are blurred. Thereafter, visual and auditory abilities increase rapidly. By the age of about four months a baby will keep in sight a person moving about the room. Sensitivity to touch, and pleasure in warmth, are present from birth.

Crying and smiling

Just as infants selectively respond to the environment, adults discriminate among the patterns of behaviour of the baby, assuming that these give clues to what she or he wants or needs. Crying is seen to indicate hunger or discomfort, smiling or certain other facial expressions to mean contentment. This very recognition treats these responses as social actions on the part of the infant. Cultural assumptions are deeply involved in this process, however. Crying is a good example. In Western culture, the baby is physically separate from the mother for most of the day, in a cot, pram or play-area. Crying here tends to be a signal that the infant needs attention. In many other cultures, the new-born infant spends much of the day, for a period of many months, in direct contact with the mother's body, carried in a sling. Where this is the practice, a mother may pay attention only to extreme bouts of crying, which are treated as emergencies. Squirming movements of the infant are taken as the main signal that it needs food or some special treatment (Liederman, Tulkin and Rosenfeld, 1977).

Cultural differences have also been demonstrated in the interpretation of smiling. All normal babies smile, in certain circumstances, after about a month or six weeks. An infant will smile if presented with a face-like shape simply containing two dots in place of eyes. It will also smile at a human face if the mouth is hidden just as readily as when it is not. Smiling seems to be an inborn response, not learned, or even triggered, by seeing another smiling face. One reason why we can be sure of this is that children born blind begin smiling at the same age as sighted children, although they have had no chance to copy others doing so. The situations in which smiling is regarded as appropriate, however, vary between cultures, and this is related to the early reactions adults give to the smiling response of infants. Infants do not have to learn to smile, but they have to learn when and where it is thought proper to do so. Thus the Chinese, for example, smile less often in 'public' settings than Westerners do – say, when greeting a stranger.

Infants and mothers

An infant is able to distinguish its mother from other people by three months of age (Schaffer, 1970). The baby still does not recognize the mother as a *person*; rather, it responds to certain characteristics, probably the eyes, voice and manner in which it is held. Recognition of the mother is shown in reactions such as stopping crying only when she (rather than anyone else) picks the infant up, smiling more at her than at other people, lifting the arms or clapping to mark the mother's appearance in the room, or, once the child is mobile, crawling to be close to her. Cultural differences influence which reactions tend regularly to appear. In a study of a Ugandan culture, Ainsworth found that embracing, hugging and kissing between mothers and infants was rare, while clapping hands to express pleasure, on the part of both mother and child, was much more common than is usually found in Western families (Ainsworth, 1977).

The infant's attachment to its mother only becomes firm after about the first seven months of life. Before this time, separation from the mother will not produce any specific protest and other caretaking agents will be accepted without any change in usual levels of responsiveness. At about the same age, children will start to smile only at some individuals rather than indiscriminately. It is also at this stage that an infant begins to get an understanding of the mother as a distinct person. The child recognizes that the mother exists even when she is absent from his or her immediate presence, and can hold some sort of image of her in mind. This also implies the beginning of the experience of time, because the child has both a memory of the mother and anticipation of her return. Infants of eight or nine months are able to look for hidden objects, beginning to understand that objects have an independent existence, regardless of whether or not they are in view at any particular moment.

Selma Fraiberg has illustrated this phase of the infant's behaviour brilliantly in the course of a work designed to inform parents about children's growth.

> Have you a six- or seven-month-old baby who snatches the glasses off your nose? If you do, you hardly need this piece of advice. Remove the glasses when the baby reaches for them, slip them in a pocket or behind a sofa pillow (and don't forget where *you* hid them!). Don't trouble to be sneaky about it, let the baby see you hide them. He will not go in search of them. He will stare at the place he last saw them – on your nose – then lose interest in the problem. He does not search for the glasses because he cannot imagine that they have an existence when he does not see them.
>
> When the baby is around nine months old, don't rely on the old tricks. If he sees you remove your glasses and slip them behind a sofa pillow he will move the pillow and pounce on your glasses. He has learned that an object can be hidden from sight, yet can still exist! He can follow its movements in your hand to the place of hiding and actively search for it there. This is a tremendous step in learning and one that is unlikely to be overlooked by the parents whose glasses, earrings, pipes, fountain pens and key-cases are now not only lifted from their persons, but defy safekeeping. Parents who have babies in this stage of development are little interested in the theoretical aspects of the problem as posed here, but a theory can always bring some practical benefits. We still have some tricks up our sleeve. Let's try this: let the baby see you slip your glasses behind the pillow. Let him find them, persuade him to give them to you, then hide the glasses under a second pillow. Now he is confused. He will search for the glasses under the *first* pillow, in the first hiding place, but he will not search for them in the second hiding place. This means that the baby can conceive of the glasses having an existence when hidden, but only in one place, the first hiding place where his search had earlier been successful. When the baby does not find the glasses under the first pillow, he continues to search for them there, but it does not occur to him to search for them in the second hiding place or anywhere else. An object can still vanish. In a few weeks he will extend his search from the first hiding place to the second one and he is on his way to the discovery that an object can be moved from place to place and still have a permanent existence. (Fraiberg, 1959, pp. 49–50)

The early months of a child's life are also a period of learning for the mother. Mothers (and other caretaking agents, like fathers or older children) learn to grasp the communications conveyed by the infant's behaviour and to respond to them appropriately. Some mothers are much more sensitive to these cues than others, and different cues tend to be emphasized, and reacted to, in varying cultural settings. The 'readings' mothers make of their children's behaviour strongly influence the pattern of interaction that develops between them. For instance, one mother might see a child's restlessness as indicating fatigue and put the infant to bed. Another might interpret the same behaviour as meaning that the child wants to be entertained. Mothers often project their own characteristics on to their babies, so one who finds it hard to maintain a stable caring relationship with her child might perceive the infant as aggressive and rejecting towards herself.

The forming of attachments to specific individuals marks a fundamental threshold in socialization. The primary relationship, usually between infant and mother, becomes one in which strong feelings are invested, and on the basis of which complex social learning processes start to occur.

The development of social responses

The relationship between child, mother, and other caretaking agents alters around the end of the baby's first year of life. Not only does the child then begin to speak, but he or she is able to stand – most children are able to walk alone at about fourteen months. In their second and third years, children develop an increasing capacity to understand the interactions and emotions of other family members. The child learns how to comfort, as well as how to annoy, others. Children of two years old show distress if one parent gets angry with the other, and may hug one or the other if that person is visibly upset. A child of the same age is also able to tease a brother or sister, or a parent.

From about the age of one onwards, play starts to occupy much of the child's life. At first, a child will mainly play alone, but increasingly demands someone else to play with. Through play, children further improve their bodily co-ordination and start to expand their knowledge of the adult world. They try out new skills, and they imitate the behaviour of grown-ups.

In an early study, Mildred Parten set out some categories of the development of play which are still generally accepted today (Parten, 1932). Young children first of all engage in *solitary independent play*. Even when in the company of other children, they play alone, making no reference to what the others are doing. This is followed by *parallel activity*, in which a child copies what the others are doing, but does not try to intervene in their activities. Subsequently (at age three or thereabouts), children engage more and more in *associative play*, in which they relate their own behaviour to that of others. Each child still acts as he or she wishes, but takes notice of and responds to what the others do. Later, at around age four, children take up *co-operative play* – activities which demand that each child collaborates with the other (as in playing at 'mummies and daddies').

Over the period from age one to four or five, the child is also learning discipline and self-regulation. One thing this means is learning to control bodily needs and deal with them appropriately. Children become toilet-trained (a difficult and extended process), and learn how to eat their food in a polite way. They also learn to 'behave themselves' in the various contexts of their activity, particularly when interacting with adults.

By about five, the child has become a fairly autonomous being. He or she is no longer just a baby, but almost independent in the elementary routines of life at home – and ready to venture further into the outside world. For the first time, the developing individual is able to spend long hours away from the parents without too much worry.

Attachment and loss

No child could reach this stage without the years of care and protection provided by the parents or other caretaking agents. As was mentioned earlier, the relation between child and mother is usually of overriding importance during the early phases of a child's life. Research suggests that if this relationship is in any way impaired, serious consequences can occur. Some thirty years ago the psychologist John Bowlby carried out research which indicated that a young child who did not experience a close and loving relationship with its mother would suffer major personality disturbances in later life (Bowlby, 1951). A child whose mother dies shortly after its birth, for example, Bowlby claimed, would be affected by anxieties that would have a long-term impact on her or his subsequent character. This became known as the theory of **maternal deprivation**, and has since given rise to a large number of further investigations into child behaviour. The results claimed by Bowlby also received support from studies of some of the higher primates.

Isolated monkeys

Harry Harlow carried out some celebrated experiments rearing Rhesus monkeys away from their mothers, in order to explore the ideas put forward by Bowlby. Apart from being isolated from contact with others, the material needs of the monkeys were carefully provided for. The results were very striking: the monkeys brought up in isolation showed an extreme level of behaviour disturbance. When introduced to other, normal, adult monkeys they were either fearful or hostile, refusing to interact with them. They would spend much of their time sitting huddled in the corner of the cage, resembling in their posture human beings suffering from schizophrenic withdrawal. They were unable to mate with other monkeys, and in most cases could not be taught to do so. Females who were artificially impregnated devoted little or no attention to their young.

In order to see whether it was absence of the mother that produced these abnormalities, Harlow brought up some young monkeys in the company of others of the same age. These animals showed no sign of disturbance in their later behaviour. Harlow concluded that what matters for normal development is that the monkey has the opportunity to form attachments to another or others, regardless of whether these include the mother herself (Harlow and Zimmerman, 1959; Harlow and Harlow, 1962; Novak, 1979).

Deprivation in human infants

It cannot be assumed that what happens with monkeys will occur in the same way among human infants (Harlow didn't suggest that his results demonstrated anything conclusively about human experience). Nevertheless, research on human children suggests parallels with the observations Harlow was able to make, although demonstrating long-term consequences of deprivation in infancy is obviously difficult (since experimentation would be unthinkable). Studies of human infants tend to bear out the conclusion that what matters for the security of a child is the development of consistent patterns of early emotional attachment. These need not be with the mother herself, and therefore the term 'maternal deprivation' is somewhat misconceived. It is the opportunity to form stable, emotionally close, relations with at least one other human being in infancy and early childhood which matters. The immediate effects of deprivation of such ties upon young children have been well documented. Research on children admitted to hospital has shown that emotional distress is most pronounced for children of between six months and four years of age. Older children tend to suffer less severely and in a less prolonged way. The reactions of young children are not just due to the effects of being placed in a strange environment; the same consequences are not found if the mother or other well-known caretaking agents are continuously present in the hospital.

Long-term influences

While the evidence about long-term influences is more ambiguous, in general it seems that deprivation of close early attachments often does produce behaviour disturbances of a lasting kind. Only in rare cases, such as those of the 'wild boy of Aveyron' and Genie, are human children more or less completely isolated from other people. So we would not expect to find a clear demonstration of the profound disturbances which affected Harlow's animals. However, there is considerable evidence to show that children without stable attachments in infancy show linguistic and intellectual retardation, as well as experiencing difficulties later in forming close and lasting relationships with others. Reversal of these characteristics becomes progressively more difficult after the age of about six to eight.

The socialization of the infant

Bowlby's original claim that 'mother-love in infancy and childhood is as important for mental health as are vitamins and proteins for physical health' (Bowlby, 1951, p. 62) has been in some part disconfirmed. It is not contact with the *mother* that is decisive, nor is what is involved simply the absence of love. The security provided by regular contact with a familiar person is also important. Yet we can conclude that human social development depends in a fundamental way on the early formation of lasting bonds with other people. This is a key aspect of socialization for the majority of people in every culture, although its precise nature and consequences are culturally variable.

General theories of child development

Bowlby's work concentrated on limited aspects of child development, above all the importance of emotional bonds between infants and those who care for them. How should we understand other features of children's growth, especially the emergence of a sense of self – the awareness that the individual has a distinct identity, separate from others? During the first months of its life, the infant possesses little or no understanding of differences between human beings and material objects in its environment, and has no awareness of self. Children do not begin to use concepts like 'I', 'me' and 'you' until the age of two or after. Only gradually do they then come to understand that others have distinct identities, consciousness and needs separate from their own.

The problem of the emergence of self is a much-debated one, and is viewed rather differently in contrasting theoretical perspectives. To some extent, this is because the most prominent theories about child development emphasize different aspects of socialization. The work of the great psychologist and founder of psychoanalysis, Sigmund Freud, concentrates above all on how the infant controls anxieties, and on the emotional aspects of child development. The American philosopher and sociologist, George Herbert Mead, gives attention mainly to how children learn to use the concepts of 'I' and 'me'. The Swiss student of child behaviour, Jean Piaget, worked on many aspects of child development, but his most well-known writings concern **cognition** – the ways in which children learn to *think* about themselves and their environment.

Freud and psychoanalysis

Sigmund Freud, a Viennese physician who lived from 1856 to 1939, not only strongly influenced the formation of modern psychology; he was one of the major intellectual figures of the twentieth century. The impact of his ideas has been felt in art, literature and philosophy, as well as in the human social sciences. Freud was not simply an academic student of human behaviour, but concerned himself with the treatment of neurotic patients. **Psychoanalysis,** the technique of therapy he invented, involves getting patients to talk freely about their lives, particularly about what they can remember of their very early experiences. Freud came to the view that much of what governs our behaviour is **unconscious**, and involves the persistence into adulthood of modes of coping with anxieties developed very early on in life. Most of these early childhood experiences are lost to our conscious memory, although they are the basis on which our **self-consciousness** is established.

Personality development

According to Freud, the infant is a demanding being, with energy it cannot control because of its essential helplessness. A baby has to learn that its needs or desires cannot always be satisfied immediately – a painful process. In Freud's view, infants have needs not just for food and drink, but for erotic satisfaction. Freud did not mean that infants have sexual desires in the same way as older children or adults do. The 'erotic' refers to a general need for close and pleasurable bodily contact with others. (The idea is not so distant from what emerges from Harlow's experiments and the literature on child attachments. Infants do indeed have a need for close contact with others, including cuddling and caressing.)

As Freud describes it, human psychological development is a process involving major tensions. The infant learns progressively to control his or her drives, but these remain as powerful motives in the unconscious. Freud distinguishes several typical stages in the development of the abilities of the infant and young child. He gives particular attention to the phase – at around age four to five – at which most children are able to relinquish the constant company of their parents and enter a wider social world. Freud calls this phase the *Oedipal* stage. The early attachments which infants and young children form to their parents have a defined erotic element, in the sense noted above. If such attachments were allowed to continue and develop further, as a child matured physically she or he would become sexually involved with the parent of the opposite sex. This does not happen because children learn to repress erotic desires towards their parents.

Little boys learn that they cannot continue to be 'tied to their mother's apron strings'. According to Freud, the young boy experiences intense antagonism towards his father, because the father has sexual possession of the mother. This is the basis of the **Oedipus complex**. The Oedipus complex is overcome when the child represses both his erotic attachments to his mother, and his antagonism towards his father (most of this happens on the unconscious level). This marks a major stage in the development of an autonomous self, because the child has detached himself from his early dependence upon his parents, particularly his mother.

Freud's portrayal of female development is much less well worked out and obscure. He believes that something of a reverse process occurs to that found in boys. The little girl represses her erotic desires for the father and overcomes her unconscious rejection of her mother by striving to become like her – to become 'feminine'. In Freud's view, how children cope with the Oedipus complex strongly influences later relationships, especially sexual relationships, into which the individual enters.

Criticisms

Freud's theories have been widely criticized and have often met with very hostile responses. Some have rejected the idea that infants have erotic wishes, as well as the thesis that what happens in infancy and early childhood establishes unconscious modes of coping with anxiety that endure throughout life. Feminist critics have seen Freud's theory as directed too much towards male experience, giving too little attention to female psychology. Yet Freud's ideas continue to exert a powerful influence. Even if we do not accept Freud's ideas in their entirety, some of them are very probably valid. There almost certainly are unconscious aspects to human behaviour, resting upon modes of coping with anxiety established first of all in infancy.

The theory of G. H. Mead

The background and intellectual career of G. H. Mead (1863–1931) was in most respects quite different from that of Freud. Mead was primarily a philosopher, who spent most of his life teaching at the University of Chicago. He wrote rather little, and the publication for which he is best known, *Mind, Self and Society* (1934), was in fact put together by his students on the basis of their lecture notes and other sources. Since they form the main basis of a general tradition of theoretical thinking, **symbolic interactionism**, Mead's ideas have had a very broad impact in sociology. (For further discussion of symbolic interactionism see chapter 22: 'The Development of Sociological Theory'.) But Mead's work provides in addition an interpretation of the main phases of child development, giving particular attention to the emergence of a sense of self.

There are some interesting similarities between Mead's views and those of Freud, although Mead sees the human personality as less racked by tension. According to Mead, infants and young children first of all develop as social beings by imitating the actions of those around them. Play is one way in which this takes place. In their play, as has been noted above, small children often imitate what adults do. A small child will make mud pies, having seen an adult cooking, or dig with a spoon having observed someone gardening. Children's play evolves from simple imitation to more complicated games in which a child of four or five will act out an adult role. Mead calls this *taking the role of the other* – learning what it is like to be in the shoes of another person. It is only at this stage that children acquire a developed sense of self. Children achieve an understanding of themselves as separate agents – as a 'me' – by seeing themselves through the eyes of others.

We achieve self-awareness, according to Mead, when we learn to distinguish the 'me' from the 'I'. The 'I' is the unsocialized infant, a bundle of spontaneous wants and desires. The 'me', as Mead uses the term, is the **social self**. Individuals develop *self-consciousness*, Mead argues, by coming to see themselves as others see them. Both Freud and Mead see the child becoming an autonomous agent, capable of self-understanding, and able to operate outside the context of the immediate family, at about age five. For Freud, this is the outcome of the Oedipal phase, while for Mead it is the result of a developed capacity of self-awareness.

A further stage of child development, according to Mead, occurs when the child is about eight or nine. This is the age at which children tend to take part in organized games, rather than unsystematic 'play'. It is not until this period that children begin to understand the overall *values and morality* according to which social life is conducted. To learn organized games, one must understand the rules of play, and notions of fairness and equal participation. The child at this stage learns to grasp what Mead terms the **generalized other** – the general values and moral rules involved in the culture in which he or she is developing. This is placed at somewhat later age by Mead than by Freud, but once more there are clear similarities between their ideas on this point.

Mead's views are less controversial than those of Freud. They do not contain so many startling ideas, and they do not depend on the theory of an unconscious basis to personality. Mead's theory of the development of self-consciousness has deservedly been very influential. On the other hand, Mead's views were never published in a comprehensive form and are useful as suggestive insights rather than as providing a general interpretation of child development.

Piaget: cognitive development

The influence of Jean Piaget's work has been not far short of that of Freud. Born in Switzerland in 1896, Piaget spent most of his life directing an institute of child development in Geneva. He published an extraordinary number of books and scientific papers, not just on child development, but on education, the history of thought, philosophy and logic. He continued his prodigious output right up to his death in 1980.

Although Freud gave so much importance to infancy, he never studied children directly. His theory was developed on the basis of observations made in the course of treating his adult patients in psychotherapy. Mead did not study children's behaviour either, working out his ideas in the context of philosophical discussion. Piaget, by contrast, spent most of his life observing the behaviour of infants, young children and adolescents. He based much of his work on the detailed observation of limited numbers of individuals, rather than studying large samples. None the less, he claimed his major findings to be valid for child development in all cultures.

The stages of cognitive development

Piaget places great emphasis on the child's ability actively to make sense of the world. Children do not passively soak up information, but select and interpret what they see, hear and feel in the world around them. From his observations of children, and the numerous experiments he conducted into their ways of thinking, he concluded that human beings go through several distinct stages of cognitive development, i.e. learning to *think* about themselves, and their environment. Each stage involves the acquisition of new skills and depends on the successful completion of the preceding one.

The first stage is the **sensorimotor,** which lasts from birth up to about age two. Until aged about four months, an infant cannot differentiate itself from the environment. For example, the child will not realize that its own movements cause the sides of its crib to rattle. Objects are not differentiated from persons, and the infant is unaware that anything exists outside the range of its vision. As research we have already looked at shows, infants gradually learn to distinguish people from objects, coming to see that both have an existence independent of their immediate perceptions. Piaget calls this early stage *sensorimotor* because infants learn mainly by touching objects, manipulating them and physically exploring their environment. The main accomplishment of this stage is that by its close the child understands its environment to have distinctive and stable properties.

The next phase, called the **pre-operational** stage, is the one to which Piaget devoted the bulk of his research. This stage lasts from ages two to seven, when children acquire a mastery of language and become able to use words to represent objects and images in a symbolic fashion. A four-year-old might use a sweeping hand, for example, to represent the concept 'aeroplane'. Piaget terms the stage pre-operational because children are not yet able to use their developing mental capabilities systematically. Children in this stage are **egocentric**. As Piaget uses it, this concept does not refer to selfishness, but to the tendency of the child to interpret the world exclusively in terms of its own position. She or he does not understand, for instance, that others see objects from a different perspective to his or her own. Holding a book upright, the child may ask about a picture in it, not realizing that the person sitting opposite can only see the back of the book.

Children at the pre-operational stage are not able to hold connected conversations with another. In egocentric speech, what each child says is more or less unrelated to what the previous speakers said. Children talk together, but not *to* one another in the same sense as adults. During this phase of development, children have no general understanding of categories of thought that adults tend to take for granted: concepts such as causality, speed, weight or number. Even if the child sees water poured from a tall, thin container into a shorter, wider one, he or she will not understand that the volume of water remains the same – concluding there is less water, because the water-level is lower.

A third stage, the **concrete operational** period, lasts from ages seven to eleven. During this phase, children master abstract, logical notions. They are able to handle ideas such as causality without much difficulty. A child at this stage of development will recognize the false reasoning involved in the idea that the wide container holds less water than the thin, narrow one, even though the water-levels are different. She or he becomes capable of carrying out the mathematical operations of multiplying, dividing and subtracting. Children by this stage are much less egocentric. In the pre-operational stage, if a girl is asked 'How many sisters have you?', she may correctly answer 'one'. But if asked, 'How many sisters does your sister have?' she will probably answer 'none', because she cannot see herself from the point of view of her sister. The concrete operational child is able to answer such a question correctly with ease.

The years from eleven to fifteen cover what Piaget calls the **formal operational** period. During adolescence, the developing child becomes able to grasp highly abstract and hypothetical ideas. When faced with a problem, children at this stage are able to review all the possible ways of solving it and go through them theoretically in order to reach a solution. The young person at the formal operational stage is able to understand why some sorts of questions are trick ones. To the question 'What creatures are both poodles and dogs?', the child might or might not be able to give the correct reply (the answer is 'poodles'), but he or she will understand why this answer is right and appreciate the humour in it.

According to Piaget, the first three stages of development are universal; but not all adults reach the formal operational stage. The development of formal operational thought depends in part upon processes of schooling. Adults of limited educational attainment tend to continue to think in more concrete terms and retain large traces of egocentrism.

Criticisms

Margaret Donaldson has questioned Piaget's view that children are highly egocentric, compared to adults (Donaldson, 1979). The tasks which Piaget set the children he studied, according to her, were presented from an adult standpoint, rather than in terms that were understandable to them. Egocentrism is equally characteristic of adult behaviour – in some situations. To make the point, she quoted a passage from the autobiography of the British poet, Laurie Lee, describing his first day at school as a small boy.

> I spent that first day picking holes in paper, then went home in a smouldering temper.
> 'What's the matter, Love? Didn't he like it at school then?'
> 'They never gave me a present.'
> 'Present? What present?'
> 'They said they'd give me a present.'
> 'Well now, I'm sure they didn't.'
> 'They did! They said, "You're Laurie Lee, aren't you? Well; just you sit there for the present." I sat there all day but I never got it. I ain't going back there again.' (Lee, 1965, p. 50)

As adults we tend to think that the child has misunderstood, in a comic way, the instructions of the teacher. Yet on a deeper level, Donaldson points out, the adult has failed to understand the child, not recognizing the ambiguity in the phrase 'sit there for the present.' The adult, not the boy, is guilty of egocentrism.

Piaget's work has also been much criticized on grounds of his methods. How can we generalize from findings based on observations of small numbers of children all living in one city? Yet for the most part Piaget's ideas have stood up well in the light of the enormous amount of subsequent research they have helped to generate. The stages of development he identifies are probably less clear-cut than he claimed, but many of his ideas are now generally accepted.

Connections between the theories

There are major differences between the perspectives of Freud, Mead and Piaget; yet it is possible to suggest a picture of child development which draws upon them all.

All three authors accept that, in the early months of infancy, a baby has no distinct understanding of the nature of objects or persons in its environment, or of its own separate identity. Throughout the first two or so years of life, before the mastery of developed linguistic skills, most of the child's learning is unconscious because she or he has as yet no awareness of self. Freud was probably right to claim that ways of coping with anxiety established during this early period – related, in particular, to interaction with mother and father – remain important in later personality development.

It is likely that children learn to become self-aware beings through the process suggested by Mead – the differentiating of an 'I' and a 'me'. Children who have acquired a sense of self retain egocentric modes of thinking, however, as Piaget indicated. The development of the child's autonomy probably involves greater emotional difficulties than either Mead or Piaget seemed to recognize – which is where Freud's ideas are particularly relevant. Being able to cope with early anxieties may well influence how far a child is later able to move successfully through the stages of cognition distinguished by Piaget.

Taken together, these theories explain a great deal about how we become social beings, having an awareness of self and able to interact with others in a regular way. However, they concentrate upon socialization in infancy and childhood, and none of the authors provides an account of the social contexts in which socialization takes place – a task to which we now turn.

Agencies of socialization

We can refer to the groups or social contexts within which significant processes of socialization occur as **agencies of socialization**. In all cultures, **the family** is the main socializing agency of the child during infancy. But at later stages of an individual's life, many other socializing agencies come into play.

The family

Since family systems vary widely, the range of contacts which the infant experiences is by no means standard across cultures. The mother is everywhere normally the most important individual in the child's early life, but, as has been pointed out, the nature of the relationships established between mothers and their children is influenced by the form and regularity of their contact. This is, in turn, conditioned by the character of family institutions and their relation to other groupings in society.

In modern societies, most early socialization occurs within a small-scale family context. The majority of British children spend their early years within a domestic unit containing mother, father and perhaps one or two other children. In many other cultures, by contrast, aunts, uncles and grandchildren are often part of a single household and serve as caretakers even for very young infants. Yet within British society there are many variations in the nature of family contexts. Some infants are brought up in single-parent households; some are cared for by two mothering and fathering agents (divorced parents and step-parents). A high proportion of women with families are now employed outside the home and return to their paid work relatively soon after the births of their children. In spite of these variations, the family normally remains a major agency of socialization from infancy to adolescence and beyond – in a sequence of development connecting the generations.

Families have varying 'locations' within the overall institutions of a society. In most traditional societies, the family into which a person is born largely determines the individual's social position for the rest of his or her life. In modern Western societies, social position is not inherited at birth in this way. Yet the region and social class of the family into which an individual is born affect patterns of socialization quite sharply. Children pick up ways of behaviour characteristic of their parents or others in their neighbourhood or community.

Varying patterns of child-rearing and discipline, together with con-trasting values and expectations, are found in different sectors of large-scale societies. It is easy to understand the influence of dif-ferent types of family background if we think of what life is like, say, for a child growing up in a poor black family living in a run-down city neighbourhood, compared to one born into an affluent white family in a white suburb. Many sociological studies have been carried out allowing us to detail these differences more precisely.

Of course, few if any children simply take over in an unquestioning way the outlook of their parents. This is especially true in the con-temporary world, in which change is so pervasive. Moreover, the very existence of a diversity of socializing agencies leads to many divergencies between the outlooks of children, adolescents and the parental generation.

Peer relationships

Another socializing agency is the **peer group.** Peer groups are friendship groups of children of a similar age. In some cultures, particularly small traditional societies, peer groups are formalized as **age-grades.** Each generation has certain rights and responsibilities, which alter as its members grow older. (Age-grade systems are normally confined to males.) There are often specific ceremonies or rites which mark the transition of individuals from one age-grade to another. Those within a particular age-set generally maintain close and friendly con-nections throughout their lives. A typical set of age-grades consists of childhood, junior warriorhood, senior warriorhood, junior elderhood and senior elderhood. Men do not move through these grades as individuals, but as whole groups.

The family's importance in socialization is quite obvious, since the experience of the infant and very young child is shaped more or less exclusively within it. It is less apparent, especially to those of us living in Western societies, how significant peer groups are. Yet, even without formal age-grades, children over four or five usually spend a great deal of time in the company of friends of the same age. Given the high proportion of women now in the workforce, whose young children are together in day-care centres, peer relations are even more important today than before, and schools are of course a major influence here. The theories of Mead and Piaget each rightly stress the importance of peer relations. Piaget lays particular emphasis on the fact that peer relations are more 'democratic' than those between a child and its parents. The word 'peer' means 'equal', and friendship relations established between young children do tend to be reasonably egalitarian. A forceful, or physically strong, child may to some extent try to dominate others. Yet since peer relations are founded on mutual consent, rather than the dependence inherent in the family situation, there has to be a large amount of give and take. Piaget points out that, because of their power, parents are able (in varying degrees) to enforce codes of conduct upon their children. In peer groups, by contrast, a child discovers a different context of interaction, within which rules of conduct can be tested out and explored.

Peer relationships often remain important throughout a person's life. Particularly in areas in which there is not much mobility, individuals may be members of the same informal clique, or keep the same group of friends, for most or all of their lives. Even where they do not, peer relations are likely to have a significant impact beyond childhood and adolescence. Informal groups of people of similar ages at work, and in other contexts, are usually of enduring importance in shaping individuals' attitudes and behaviour.

Schools

Schooling is a formal process: there is a definite curriculum of subjects studied. Yet schools are agencies of socialization in more subtle respects too. Alongside the formal curriculum there is what some sociologists have called a **hidden curriculum** conditioning children's learning (see chapter 13: 'Education, Communication and Media'). Children are expected to learn to be quiet in class, punctual at lessons and observe rules of school discipline. They are called upon to accept and respond to the authority of the teaching staff. Reactions of teachers also affect the expectations children have of themselves. These, in turn, become linked to their job experience when they leave school. Peer groups are often formed at school, and the system of keeping children in classes related to age reinforces their impact.

The mass media

Newspapers, periodicals and journals flourished in the West from the end of the eighteenth century onwards, but were confined to a fairly small readership. It was not until a century afterwards that such printed materials became part of the day-to-day experience of millions of people – influencing their attitudes and opinions. The spread of **mass media** involving printed documents was soon accompanied by electronic communication. British children spend the equivalent of almost a hundred school days per year watching television. Adults watch almost as often. A research study showed that, if a news report on television differs from a newspaper account, more than twice as many people will believe the televised version as the newspaper one (Roper Organization, 1977, p. 4).

A vast amount of research work has been carried out trying to analyse the influence of particular television programmes, or types of programmes, on the attitudes of children and adults. Most of this research is not conclusive in its implications. It is still not agreed, for example, how far the portrayal of violence promotes aggressive behaviour among children. But it cannot be doubted that the media profoundly influence people's attitudes and outlooks. They convey a whole variety of information which individuals would not otherwise acquire. Newspapers, books, radio, television, films, recorded music and popular magazines bring us into close contact with experiences of which we would otherwise have little awareness.

There are few societies in current times, even among the more traditional cultures, which remain completely untouched by the mass media. Electronic communication is accessible even to those who are completely illiterate, and in the most isolated areas of Third World countries it is common to find people owning radios, or even television sets.

Other socializing agencies

As many other socializing agencies exist, besides those mentioned, as there are groups, or social contexts, in which individuals spend large parts of their lives. *Work* is in all cultures an important setting within which socialization processes operate, although it is only in industrial societies that large numbers of people go 'out to work' – that is, go each day to places of work quite separate from the home. In traditional communities many people till the land close to where they live, or have workshops in their dwellings. 'Work' in such communities is not so clearly distinct from other activities as it is for most members of the workforce in the modern West. In the industrialized countries, going 'out to work' for the first time usually marks a much greater transition in an individual's life than entering work activity in traditional societies. The work environment often poses unfamiliar demands, perhaps calling for major adjustments in the person's outlook or behaviour. Although the local community usually influences socialization much less in modern societies than in other types of social order, it has not become wholly irrelevant. Even within large cities there are quite often strongly developed neighbourhood groups and organizations – such as voluntary associations, clubs or churches – which powerfully affect the ideas and activities of those who become involved in them.

Resocialization

In some conditions, adult individuals may experience **resocialization,** marked by the disruption of previously accepted values and patterns of behaviour, followed by the adoption of radically different ones. One type of circumstance in which this may happen is when an individual enters a **carceral organization** – a mental hospital, prison, barracks, or other setting in which he or she is separated from the outside world and subjected to rigorous new disciplines and demands. In situations of extreme stress, the changes in outlook and personality involved may be quite dramatic. From the study of such **critical situations,** in fact, we get considerable insight into orthodox processes of socialization.

Behaviour in the concentration camp

The psychologist Bruno Bettelheim has provided a famous description of resocialization among people put in concentration camps in Germany by the Nazis in the late 1930s and 1940s. The account was partly based on his own experiences when interned for periods in two of the most notorious camps, Dachau and Buchenwald. The conditions of camp life were appalling. The prisoners faced physical torture, constant verbal abuse, severe scarcity of food and other elementary provisions for the sustenance of life. As a practising psychotherapist, Bettelheim was used to seeing people alter their outlook and behaviour in fairly fundamental ways, as they responded to treatment. But the change the prisoners experienced under the enormous strains of camp life were much more radical and rapid. In the camps, Bettelheim wrote, 'I . . . saw fast changes taking place and not only in behaviour but personality also; incredibly faster and often much more radical changes than any that were possible by psychoanalytic treatment' (Bettelheim, 1986, p. 14).

According to Bettelheim, all the prisoners underwent changes in personality, which followed a definite sequence. The very process of initial imprisonment was shocking, for people were ruthlessly torn away from family and friends, and often subjected to torture during their journey to the camps. Most new prisoners tried to resist the impact of camp conditions, seeking to maintain the modes of conduct associated with their previous lives, but this proved impossible. Fear, deprivation and uncertainty caused the prisoners' personalities to crumble. Some prisoners became what the rest called *Muselmänner*, 'walking corpses', apparently devoid of will, initiative or any interest in their own fate.

These men and women soon died. Others became childlike in their behaviour, losing a sense of time and an ability to 'think ahead', and having marked swings of mood in response to apparently trivial events.

Most of those who had been in the camps for more than a year or so – the 'old prisoners' – behaved quite differently. The old prisoners had experienced a process of resocialization, by means of which they coped with the brutalities of camp life. They were often unable to recall names, places and events in their previous lives. The reconstructed personalities of the old prisoners developed by imitation of the outlook and behaviour of the very individuals they had found so repugnant when they first came into the camps – the camp guards themselves. They aped the guards' behaviour and even used tattered pieces of cloth to attempt to imitate their uniforms.

Bettelheim writes:

> Old prisoners felt great satisfaction if, during the twice daily counting of prisoners, they really had stood well at attention or given a snappy salute. They prided themselves on being as tough, or tougher, than the SS. In their identification they went so far as to copy SS leisure-time activities. One of the games played by the guards was to find out who could stand being hit the longest without uttering a complaint. This game was copied by old prisoners, as if they were not hit often enough without repeating the experience as a game. (Bettelheim, 1986, p. 158)

'Brainwashing'

Parallel responses and changes have been noted in other critical situations – for example, in the behaviour of individuals subjected to forced interrogation or 'brainwashing'. In the initial stages of such interrogation, the individual attempts to resist the pressures imposed. After this, he or she seems to regress to a childlike stage. Resocialization takes place when new traits of behaviour are developed, modelled on the authority figure in the situation – the interrogator. As William Sargant, who has studied numerous types of critical situation, notes: 'One of the more horrible consequences of these ruthless interrogations, as described by the victims, is that they suddenly begin to feel affection for the examiner who has been treating them harshly . . .' (Sargant, 1959, p. 192).

What seems to happen in critical situations is that the socialization process is 'thrown into reverse'. Socialized responses are stripped away, and the individual experiences similar anxieties to those of a young child removed from parental protection. The individual's personality is then effectively restructured. The radical changes in personality and behaviour noted in critical situations represent an extreme case of normal characteristics of socialization in other settings. People's personality, values and outlook are never simply 'fixed', but alter in relation to their experiences throughout the life-cycle.

An illustration from fairly recent times is the experience of the young American men sent to fight in Vietnam in the 1960s and early 1970s. Under the extreme pressure of fighting in an unfamiliar jungle environment, against a determined and resourceful enemy, many soldiers underwent personality changes resembling those identified by Bettelheim and Sargant. They became resocialized into the harsh and brutal situation in which they found themselves. On their return to the United States after the war, the combat veterans found that they faced a new process of resocialization – back into the peacetime world for which they were now ill-suited.

The life course

The various transitions through which individuals pass during their lives seem at first sight to be biologically fixed – from childhood to adulthood and eventually to death. Things are much more complicated than this, however. The stages of the human life course are social as well as biological in nature. They are influenced by cultural differences, and also by the material circumstances in which people live in given types of society. For example, in the modern West death is usually thought of in relation to old age, because most people enjoy a life-span of seventy years or more. In traditional societies, however, more people died in younger age-groups than survived to old age.

Childhood

To those living in modern societies, *childhood* is a clear and distinct stage of life. 'Children' are distinct from 'babies' or 'toddlers'. Childhood intervenes between infancy and the onset of adolescence. Yet the concept of childhood, like so many other aspects of our social life today, has only come into being over the past two or three centuries. In traditional societies, the young moved directly from a lengthy infancy into working roles within the community. The French historian, Philippe Ariès, has argued that 'childhood', as a separate phase of development, did not exist in mediaeval times (Ariès, 1973). In the paintings of mediaeval Europe, children were portrayed as 'little adults', having mature faces and the same style of dress as their elders. Children took part in the same work and play activities as adults and did not have the distinct toys or games that we now take for granted.

Right up to the start of the twentieth century, in Britain and most other Western countries, children were put to work at what now seems a very early age. There are many countries in the world today, in fact, in which young children are engaged in full-time work, often in physically demanding circumstances (coal-mines for example) (UNICEF, 1987). The idea that children have distinctive rights, and the notion that the use of child labour is morally repugnant, are quite recent developments.

Some historians, developing the view suggested by Ariès, have suggested that in mediaeval Europe most people were indifferent, or even hostile, to their children. This view has been rejected by others, however, and is not borne out by what we know of traditional cultures still existing today. Most parents, particularly mothers, almost certainly formed the same kinds of attachments to their children as are usual now. However, because of the long period of 'childhood' which we recognize today, societies are in some respects more 'child-centred' than traditional ones. Both parenting and childhood have become more clearly distinct from other stages than was true of traditional communities.

It seems possible that, as a result of changes currently occurring in modern societies, 'childhood' is again becoming eroded as a distinct status. Some observers have suggested that children now 'grow up so fast' that the separate character of childhood is diminishing once more (Suransky, 1982; Winn, 1983). For example, even quite small children might watch the same television programmes that adults do, becoming much more familiar early on with the 'adult world' than preceding generations.

Adolescence

The existence of 'teenagers' is a concept specific to modern societies. The biological changes involved in puberty (the point at which a person becomes capable of adult sexual activity and reproduction) are universal. Yet in many cultures these do not produce the degree of turmoil and uncertainty often found among young people in the modern West. When there is an age-grade system, for example, coupled with distinct rites that signal the person's transition to adulthood, the process of psycho-sexual development generally seems easier to accomplish. Adolescents in traditional societies have less to 'unlearn' than their counterparts in modern ones, since the pace of change is slower. There is a time at which our children are required to be children no longer: to put away their toys and break with childish pursuits. In traditional cultures, where children are already working alongside adults, this process of 'unlearning' is normally much less severe.

The distinctiveness of being a 'teenager' in Western societies is related both to the general extension of child rights and to the process of formal education. Teenagers often try to follow adult ways, but are treated in law as children. They may wish to be in work, but are constrained to stay in school. Teenagers are 'in between' childhood and adulthood, growing up in a society subject to continuous change (Elkind, 1984).

Adulthood

Most young adults in the West today can look forward to a life stretching right through to old age. In pre-modern times, few could expect such a future with much confidence. Death through sickness, plague or injury was much more frequent among all age-groups than it is today, and women in particular were at great risk because of the high rate of mortality in childbirth.

On the other hand, some of the strains we experience were less pronounced in previous times. People usually maintained a closer connection with their parents and other kin than in today's more mobile populations, and the routines of work they followed were the same as those of their forebears. In current times, major uncertainties have to be resolved in marriage, family life and other social contexts. We have to 'make' our own lives more than people did in the past. The creation of sexual and marital ties, for instance, now depends upon individual initiative and selection, rather than being fixed by parents. This represents greater freedom for the individual, but the responsibility can also impose strains and difficulties.

Keeping a 'forward-looking outlook' in middle age has a particular importance in modern societies. Most people do not expect to be 'doing the same thing all their lives' – as was usually the case for the majority of the population in traditional cultures. Men or women who have spent their lives in one career might find the level they have reached in middle age unsatisfying and further opportunities blocked. Women who spent their early adulthood raising a family, and whose children have left home, may feel themselves to be without useful social value. The phenomenon of a 'mid-life crisis' is very real for many middle-aged people. A person may feel he or she has thrown away the opportunities that life had to offer, or will never attain goals cherished since childhood. Yet there is no reason why the transitions involved should lead to resignation or bleak despair; a release from childhood dreams can be liberating.

Old age

In traditional societies, older people were normally accorded a great deal of respect. Among cultures which had age-grades, the 'elders' usually had a major, often the final, say over matters of importance to the community as a whole. Within families, the authority of both men and women often increased with age. In industrialized societies, by contrast, older people tend to lack authority within either the family or the wider social community. Having retired from the labour-force, they may be poorer than ever before in their lives. At the same time, there has been a great increase in the proportion of the population aged over sixty-five. Only one in thirty people in Britain in 1900 was over sixty-five; the proportion today is one in five. The same sort of change is found in all the industrially advanced countries (see chapter 18: 'Population, Health and Ageing').

Transition to the age-grade of elder in a traditional culture often marked the pinnacle of the status an individual – at least a male – could achieve. In the industrialized societies, retirement tends to bring the very opposite consequences. No longer living with their children and ejected from the economic arena, it is not easy for older people to make the final period of their life rewarding. It used to be thought that those who successfully cope with old age do so by turning to their inner resources, becoming less interested in the external rewards social life has to offer. While this may no doubt often be true, it seems likely that, in a society in which many are physically healthy in old age, an 'outward-looking' view will come more and more to the fore. Those in retirement might find renewal in what has been called the 'Third Age' (following childhood and adulthood), in which a new phase of education begins.

Death and the succession of the generations

In mediaeval Europe, death was much more visible than it is today. In the modern world most people die in the enclosed environments of hospitals, removed from contact with their relatives or friends. Death is seen by many people in the West today as the end of an individual life, not as part of the process of the renewal of the generations. The weakening of religious beliefs has also altered our attitudes towards death. For us death tends to be a subject that goes undiscussed. It is taken for granted that people are frightened of dying, and thus doctors or relatives quite commonly hide from a mortally ill person the news that they will shortly die.

According to Elisabeth Kübler-Ross, the process of adjusting to the imminence of death is a compressed process of socialization that involves several stages (Kübler-Ross, 1975). The first is *denial* – the individual refuses to accept what is happening. The second stage is *anger*, particularly among those dying relatively young, who feel resentful at being robbed of the full span of life. This is followed by a stage of *bargaining*. The individual concludes a deal with fate, or with the deity, to die peacefully if allowed to live to see some particular event of significance, such as a family marriage or birthday. Subsequently, the individual frequently lapses into *depression*. Finally, if this state can be overcome, she or he might move towards a phase of *acceptance*, in which an attitude of peace is achieved in the face of approaching death.

Kübler-Ross notes that when she asks her lecture audiences what they fear most about dying, the majority of people say they are afraid of the unknown, pain, separation from loved ones or unfinished projects. According to her, these things are really only the tip of the iceberg. Most of what we associate with death is unconscious, and this has to be brought to light if we are to be able to die in an accepting way. Unconsciously, people cannot conceive of their own death except as a malicious entity come to punish them – which is how they also unconsciously think of serious illness. If they can see that this association is an irrational one – that, for example, being terminally ill is not a punishment for wrongdoing – the process is eased (Kübler-Ross, 1987).

In traditional cultures, in which children, parents and grandparents often live in the same household, there is usually a clear awareness of the connection of death with the succession of the generations. Individuals feel themselves to be part of a family, and a community, which endures indefinitely, regardless of the transience of personal existence. In such circumstances, death may perhaps be looked upon with less anxiety than in the more rapidly changing, individualistic social circumstances of the industrialized world.

Socialization and individual freedom

Since the cultural settings in which we are born and come to maturity so influence our behaviour, it might appear that we are robbed of any individuality or free will. We might seem to be merely stamped into pre-set moulds which society has prepared for us. Some sociologists do tend to write about socialization – and even about sociology more generally! – as though this were the case, but such a view is fundamentally mistaken. The fact that from birth to death we are involved in interaction with others certainly conditions our personalities, the values we hold, and the behaviour in which we engage. Yet socialization is also at the origin of our very individuality and freedom. In the course of socialization each of us develops a sense of self-identity, and the capacity for independent thought and action.

This point is easily illustrated by the example of learning language. None of us invents the language we learn as a child, and we are all constrained by fixed rules of linguistic usage. At the same time, however, understanding a language is one of the basic factors making possible our self-awareness and creativity. Without language, we would not be self-conscious beings, and we would live more or less wholly in the here-and-now. Mastery of language is necessary for the symbolic richness of human life, for awareness of our distinctive individual characteristics and for our practical mastery of the environment.

Summary

1   Socialization is the process whereby, through contact with other human beings, the helpless infant gradually becomes a self-aware, knowledge-able human being, skilled in the ways of the given culture and environment.

2   The work of Sigmund Freud suggests that the young child learns to become an autonomous being only as she or he learns to balance the demands of the environment with pressing desires coming from the unconscious. Our ability to be self-aware is built, painfully, upon the repression of unconscious drives.

3   According to G. H. Mead, the child achieves an understanding of being a separate agent by seeing others behave towards him or her in regular ways. At a later stage, entering into organized games, learning the rules of play, the child comes to understand 'the generalized other' – general values and cultural rules.

4   Jean Piaget distinguishes several main stages in the development of the child's ability to make sense of the world. Each stage involves the acquisition of new cognitive skills and depends upon the successful completion of the preceding one. According to Piaget these stages of cognitive development are universal features of socialization.

5   Agencies of socialization are structured groups or contexts within which significant processes of socialization occur. In all cultures, the family is the principal socializing agency of the child during infancy. Other influences include peer groups, schools and the mass media.

6   Recognition of the need for formal schooling diminishes the control that family and peer relations exert over socialization processes. To educate means deliberately to teach skills or values. The school also educates in more subtle ways, instilling attitudes and norms via the 'hidden curriculum'.

7   The development of mass communications has enlarged the range of socializing agencies. The spread of mass printed media was later accompanied by the use of electronic communication. Television exerts a particularly powerful influence, reaching people of all ages at regular intervals every day.

8   In some circumstances, involving a marked alteration in the social environment of an individual or group, people may undergo processes of resocialization. Resocialization refers to a restructuring of personality and attitudes, consequent upon situations of great turmoil or stress.

9   Socialization continues throughout the life-cycle. At each distinct phase of life there are transitions to be made or crises to be overcome. This includes facing up to death, as the termination of personal existence.

Basic concepts

socialization   self-consciousness
the unconscious

Important terms

maternal deprivation   formal operational period
cognition   agencies of socialization
psychoanalysis   family
Oedipus complex   peer group
symbolic interaction   age-grades
social self   hidden curriculum
generalized other   mass media
sensorimotor stage   resocialization
pre-operational stage   carceral organization
egocentrism   critical situations
concrete operational stage

Further reading

Philippe Ariès, *Centuries of Childhood* (Harmondsworth: Penguin, 1973) — a
    classical – although controversial – discussion of the historical emergence
    of 'childhood' as a distinct phase of human development.
N. Dickson (ed.), *Living in the 80s: What Prospects for the Elderly?* (Mitcham:
    Age Concern, 1980) — a general survey of problems faced by older people in
    modern societies.
C. Jenks (ed.), *The Sociology of Childhood* (London: Batsford, 1982) — a useful
    general survey of childhood from a sociological perspective.
Elisabeth Kübler-Ross, *Living with Death and Dying* (London: Souvenir Press,
    1987) — a sensitive account of attitudes to death.
Martin Richards and Paul Light (eds), *Children of Social Worlds* (Cambridge:
    Polity Press, 1986) — a collection of articles discussing research on the social
    contexts of child development.

4

Social Interaction and Everyday Life

Two people pass one another on a city pavement. Both briefly exchange glances, rapidly scanning the other's face and style of dress. As they get close and pass by, each looks away, avoiding the other's eyes. What is happening here goes on millions of times a day in the towns and cities of the world.

When passers-by quickly glance at one another, then look away again when they come close, they demonstrate what Erving Goffman (1967, 1971) calls the **civil inattention** we require of one another in many situations. Civil inattention is not at all the same as merely ignoring another person. Each individual indicates to the other recognition of that person's presence, but avoids any gesture that might be taken as too intrusive. According civil inattention to others is something we do more or less unconsciously, but it is of fundamental importance in our day-to-day lives. By it, people imply to one another that they have no reason to suspect others' intentions, be hostile to them or in any other way specifically avoid them (Goffman, 1963).

The best way to see the importance of this is by thinking of examples where it doesn't apply. On some occasions a person may stare fixedly at another, allowing her or his face openly to express a particular emotion. This will normally only occur between lovers, family members or close friends, or where one person is angry with another. Strangers, or chance acquaintances, whether encountered on the street, at work or at a party, virtually never hold the gaze of another in this way. To look fixedly at another person may easily be taken as an indication of hostile intent. It is only where two groups are strongly antagonistic to one another that strangers might indulge in such a practice. Thus Southern whites in the US have been known to give a 'hate stare' to blacks walking past.

Even friends in close conversation have to be careful about how they look at one another (Goodwin, 1981). Each individual demonstrates attention and involvement in the conversation by regularly looking at the eyes of the other, but not *staring* into them. To look too intently at someone might be taken to be a sign of mistrust about, or at least failure to understand, what the other is saying. Yet if each party to the conversation does not engage the eyes of the other at all, he or she is likely to be thought evasive, shifty or otherwise odd.

The study of day-to-day social life

Why should anyone concern themselves with seemingly trivial aspects of social behaviour? Passing someone on the street, or exchanging a few words with a friend, seem minor and uninteresting activities, things we do countless times a day without needing to give them any thought. In fact, the study of such apparently insignificant forms of social interaction is of major importance in sociology – and, far from being uninteresting, is one of the most absorbing of all areas of sociological investigation. There are two reasons why studying day-to-day social interaction is so important.

(1) The routines of daily life, which involve us in more or less constant face-to-face interaction with others, make up the bulk of our social activities. Our lives are organized around the repetition of similar patterns of behaviour from day to day, week to week, month to month, and even year to year. Think of what you did yesterday, for example, and the day before that. If they were both weekdays, in all probability you got up at about the 'same time as usual' (an important routine in itself). You may have gone off to class fairly early in the morning, involving a journey from home to school or college which you make

on virtually all weekdays. You perhaps usually meet some friends for lunch, returning to classes or private study in the afternoons. Later, you retrace your steps back home, possibly going out later in the evening with other friends. Of course, the routines we follow from day to day are not identical, and our patterns of activity at weekends usually contrast with those on weekdays. If a major change occurs in a person's life – like leaving college to take up a job – major alterations in daily routines usually have to be made. Normally, however, a new and fairly regular set of habits is established. Our day-to-day routines, then, and the interactions in which they involve us with others, give structure and form to what we do. We can learn a great deal about ourselves as social beings, and about social life itself, from studying them.

(2) Studying social interaction in everyday life sheds light on larger social systems and institutions. All large-scale social systems, in fact, depend on the patterns of social interaction we engage in during the course of our daily lives. This is easy to demonstrate. Consider again the case of two strangers passing on the street, the most transient type of social interaction one could imagine. When we take such an event on its own, it perhaps has little direct relevance to large-scale, more permanent, forms of social organization. But when we take into account many such interactions, this is no longer so. Extremely wide-ranging features of social life are sustained through civil inattention and other interactional devices whereby we relate to strangers. In modern societies, most people live in towns and cities, and constantly interact with others whom they do not know on a personal basis. Civil inattention is one among other mechanisms which gives city life, with its bustling crowds, and many fleeting, impersonal contacts, the character it has.

We will return to this point at the end of the chapter, but first we must look at the nature of social interaction in day-to-day life and discuss the non-verbal cues (facial expressions and bodily gestures) which all of us use when interacting with each other. We will then move on to analyse everyday speech or talk – how we use language to communicate to others the meanings we wish to get across. After this, we shall focus on the ways in which our lives are structured by daily routines, giving particular attention to how we co-ordinate what we do across space and time.

Non-verbal communication

Social interaction involves numerous forms of **non-verbal communication** – the exchange of information and meaning through facial expressions, gestures or movements of the body. Non-verbal communication is sometimes referred to as 'body language', but this is misleading, because we characteristically use such non-verbal cues to eliminate, amplify or expand upon what is said in words.

The face and emotion

One major aspect of non-verbal communication is the facial expression of emotion. Paul Ekman and his colleagues have developed what they call the Facial Action Coding System (FACS) for describing movements of the facial muscles that give rise to particular expressions (Ekman and Friesen, 1978). By this means they have tried to inject some precision into an area notoriously open to inconsistent or contradictory interpretations – for there is little agreement about how emotions are to be identified and classified. Charles Darwin, the originator of evolutionary theory, claimed that basic modes of emotional expression are the same among all human beings. Although some have disputed the claim, Ekman's researches among people from widely different cultural backgrounds seem to confirm this. Ekman and Friesen carried out a study of an isolated community in New Guinea, whose members had previously had virtually no contact with Westerners (Ekman and Friesen, 1971). Facial expressions of six emotions (happiness, sadness, anger, disgust, fear, surprise) shown in other studies to be recognized among many different peoples were also found among the members of this culture.

The judgements made by the New Guinea community of different emotions, as shown in pictures of facial expressions, conformed fairly closely to those found in other research work. According to Ekman, such results support the view that the facial expression of emotion, and its interpretation, are innate in human beings. However, he acknowledges that his evidence does not conclusively demonstrate this, and it may be that widely shared cultural learning experiences are involved. However, Ekman's conclusions are supported by other types of research. Eibl-Eibesfeldt studied six children born deaf and blind to see how far their facial expressions were the same as those of normal individuals in particular emotional situations (Eibl-Eibesfeldt, 1972). It was found that the children smiled when engaged in obviously pleasurable activities, raised the eyebrows in surprise when sniffing at an object with an unaccustomed smell, and frowned when repeatedly offered a disliked object. Since they could not have seen others behaving in these ways, it seems that these responses must have been innately determined.

Using the FACS system, Ekman and Friesen identified a number of the discrete facial muscle-actions in new-born infants which are also found in the adult expression of emotion. Infants seem, for example, to produce facial expressions similar to the adult expression of disgust (pursing the lips and frowning) in response to sour tastes. But although the facial expression of emotion seems to have innate aspects, individual and cultural factors influence exactly what form facial movements take, and the contexts in which they are deemed appropriate. How people smile, for example, the precise movement of the lips and other facial muscles, and how fleeting the smile is, all vary widely between cultures (Birdwhistell, 1971).

There are no gestures or aspects of bodily posture which have been shown to characterize all, or even most, cultures. In some societies, for instance, people nod when they mean 'no', the opposite to our practice. Gestures which we tend to use a great deal, such as pointing, seem not to exist among certain peoples (Bull, 1983). Other gestures employed frequently elsewhere are unknown in Anglo-American culture. A gesture called the cheek-screw, where a straightened forefinger is placed in the centre of the cheek and rotated is used in parts of Italy as a gesture of praise. It appears to be unknown in other parts of Europe.

Like facial expressions, gestures and bodily posture are continually used to 'fill out' utterances, as well as conveying meanings when nothing is actually said. The non-verbal impressions which we 'give off' – convey inadvertently – often indicate that what we say is not quite what we really mean. Blushing is perhaps the most obvious example, but there are innumerable more subtle indicators that can be picked up by others. Genuine facial expressions tend to evaporate after four or five seconds, and a smile or display of surprise which lasts longer could very well indicate deceit. Like any of the forms of talk and activity around which our daily lives are built, facial expression, gestures or body posture can be used to joke, show irony or scepticism. A facial expression of surprise which lasts too long, for example, may deliberately be used as a parody – to show that the individual is not in fact surprised after all by a given event or happening, even though he or she might have reason to be.

'Face' and culture

We can speak of 'face' in a broader sense than we have done thus far, referring to the *esteem* in which an individual is held by others. In daily social life, we normally give a good deal of attention to protecting or 'saving' each other's 'face'. Much of what we usually call 'politeness' or 'etiquette' in social gatherings consists of disregarding aspects of behaviour that might otherwise lead to a 'loss of face'. Episodes in an individual's past, or personal characteristics that might produce embarrassment if mentioned, are not commented on or referred to. Jokes about baldness are avoided if it is realized a person is wearing a hair-piece – unless those concerned are very well known to one another (Goffman, 1969, p. 228). Tact is a sort of protective device which each party involved employs in the expectation that, in return, their own weaknesses will not be deliberately exposed to general view. Our day-to-day lives, therefore, do not just 'happen'. Without realizing it most of the time, all of us skilfully maintain a close and continuous control over facial expression, body posture and gesture in the interaction we carry on with others.

Some people are 'specialists' in the control of facial expression and the tactful organizing of interaction with others. The skills of diplomats, for example, involve just such a specialism. A good diplomat has to be able – giving every appearance of ease and comfort – to interact with others with whose views he or she might disagree, or even find repellant. The degree to which this is managed successfully can affect the fate of whole nations. Skilful diplomacy, for instance, can defuse tensions between nations and prevent a war.

Social rules, conversations and talk

Although there are many non-verbal cues we routinely use in our own behaviour, and in making sense of that of others, much of our interaction is carried through **talk** or **conversation**. It has always been accepted by sociologists that language is fundamental to social life. Recently, however, an approach has been developed that is specifically concerned with how people *use* language in the ordinary contexts of everyday life. Most language-use is in fact talk – casual verbal exchange – carried on in informal conversations with others. The study of conversations has been strongly influenced by Goffman's work, and Goffman wrote on the topic directly. But the most important figure influencing this type of research is Harold Garfinkel, the founder of **ethnomethodology** (Garfinkel, 1984).

Ethnomethodology is the study of the 'ethno-methods' – the folk or lay methods – people use to make sense of what others do, and particularly what they say. All of us apply methods of *making sense* in our interaction with others, which we normally employ without having to give any conscious attention to them. We can only make sense of what is said in conversation by means of knowledge of the social context that does not appear in the words themselves. Take the following conversation (Heritage, 1984, p. 237):

    A: I have a fourteen year old son.
    B: Well, that's all right.
    A: I also have a dog.
    B: Oh, I'm sorry.

What do you think is happening here? What is the relation between the contributors to the conversation? We can understand what was said, and why, quite easily as soon as we guess or are told that it is a conversation between a prospective tenant and landlord. The conversation then becomes sensible and 'obvious'. Yet without knowing the social context, the responses of individual B seem to bear no relation to the statements of A. *Part* of the sense is in the words, and *part* is in the way in which the social context emerges from the talk. In context the conversation becomes quite sensible and its meaning obvious.

Shared understandings

The most inconsequential forms of daily talk presume complicated, shared knowledge 'brought into play' by those involved. We take this for granted, but even our small talk is so complex that it has so far proved impossible to programme even the most sophisticated computers to converse with human beings as we do among ourselves. The words used in ordinary talk do not have precise meanings, and we 'fix' what we want to say, or our understanding of what is said, through the unstated assumptions that back it up. If one person asks another: 'What did you do yesterday?' there is no obvious answer provided by the words in the question themselves. A day is a long time, and it would be logical for someone to answer: 'Well, at seven sixteen, I woke up. At seven eighteen I got out of bed, went to the bathroom and started to brush my teeth. At seven nineteen I turned on the shower . . .' We understand the type of response the question calls for by knowing who the individual is asking it, what sort of activities we normally carry on together, what the person usually does on a particular day of the week, and many other things.

Garfinkel's experiments

The 'background expectancies' with which we organize ordinary conversations were highlighted by some experiments Garfinkel undertook with student volunteers. The students were asked to engage a friend or relative in conversation, insisting that the sense of any commonplace remarks made be clarified. Casual remarks, or general comments, were not just to be left, but actively pursued to make their meaning precise. If someone said 'Have a nice day', they were to respond, 'Nice in what sense, exactly?; 'Which part of the day do you mean?', and so forth. One of the transcripts of the exchanges that resulted ran as follows:

> (*S waved his hand cheerily.*)
> S: How are you?
> E: How am I in regard to what? My health, my finance, my school work, my peace of mind, my . . .
> S: (*red in the face and suddenly out of control*) Look! I was just trying to be polite. Frankly, I don't give a damn how you are.
>
> (Garfinkel, 1963, p. 222)

Why do people get so upset when apparently minor conventions of talk are not followed? The answer is that the stability and meaningfulness of our daily social life depend on the sharing of unstated cultural assumptions about what is said and why. If we were not able to take these for granted, meaningful communication would be impossible. Any question or contribution to a conversation would have to be followed by a massive 'search procedure' of the sort Garfinkel's subjects were told to initiate in response to everyday remarks, and interaction would simply break down. What seem at first sight to be unimportant conventions of talk, therefore, turn out to be fundamental to the very fabric of social life, which is why their breach is so serious.

We should note that in everyday life people on occasion deliberately feign ignorance of the unstated knowledge involved in interpreting a statement, remark or question. This may be done to rebuff the other, poke fun at them, cause embarrassment, or call attention to a double meaning in what was said. Consider, for example, this classic exchange between parent and teenager:

P: Where are you going?
T: Out.
P: What are you going to do?
T: Nothing.

The responses of the teenager are effectively the opposite of those of the volunteers in Garfinkel's experiments. Rather than pursuing enquiries where this is not normally done, the teenager declines to provide appropriate answers at all – effectively saying, 'Mind your own business!' The initial question might get quite a different response from another person in another context, viz:

A: Where are you going?
B: I'm going quietly round the bend.

B deliberately 'misreads' A's question in order ironically to convey worry or frustration. Comedy, joking and wit thrive on such deliberate misunderstandings of the unstated assumptions involved in talk. There is nothing threatening about this so long as the parties concerned recognize the intent to provoke laughter.

Forms of talk

It is a sobering experience to hear a tape-recording, or read a transcript, of a conversation to which one has contributed. Conversations are much more fractured, hesitant and ungrammatical than most people realize. When we take part in everyday talk, we tend to think that what is said has a polished character, because we unconsciously 'fill in' the background to the actual words exchanged, but real conversations are quite different from fictional accounts of conversations in novels, in which characters speak in well-formed and grammatical sentences.

Look at the following sequence, which is entirely characteristic of most real-life conversation (Heritage, 1984, p. 236).

E: Oh *ho*ney that was a lovely *l*uncheon I shoulda *ca*:lled
you s:soo ⌐ ner but *I* ⌐ : lo:ved it. It w's just deli:ghtfu ⌐ :l ⌐
M: └   Oh::: ┘   └Well ┘

M: I w's gla⌐ d you ⌐(came).
E: └'nd yer f:┘ *friends* 're so da:rl:ng, =

M: =*Oh*::: ⌐ : it w'z: ⌐
E: └ e–that P–┘a:t isn' she a do: ⌐ :ll? ⌐
M: i Ye– h └*isn's*┘ she pretty,

    (.)

E: *Oh*: she's a beautiful girl. =

M: =Yeh *I* think she's a pretty gir–l.

Key
[] One speaker is talking at the same time as the other.
ho Italic type represents a stress upon a particular utterance, word or phrase, such as a change in the pitch of the voice or in its degree of loudness.
= Indicates that speech carries on without a gap, even though one person takes over talking from another.
: Indicates very slight pause, with change of stress or intonation, within a word.
( ) Indicates slightly longer gap than usual between utterances.

Neither party to this conversation finishes a sentence. Each interrupts the other, talks across the other, or leaves words 'hanging in the air'.

As in the case of Goffman's work on civil inattention, it might easily be presumed that the analysis of ordinary conversations is rather marginal to the main concerns of sociology; indeed many sociologists have been severely critical of ethnomethodological research for just this reason. Yet some of the arguments used to show why Goffman's work is so important to sociology also apply to ethnomethodology. Studying everyday talk has shown how complicated is the mastery of language that ordinary people command. The immense difficulties involved in programming computers to do what human speakers are able to carry out without effort drives home the level of this complexity. In addition, talk is an essential element of every realm of social life. The Watergate tapes of President Nixon and his advisers were nothing more or less than a transcript of conversation, but they were part of the exercise of political power at the highest levels (Molotch and Boden, 1985).

Lapses of body and tongue

Response cries

Some kinds of utterances are not talk, but consist of muttered exclamations, or what Goffman has called **response cries** (Goffman, 1981). Consider someone saying 'Oops!' after knocking over or dropping something. 'Oops!' seems to be merely an uninteresting reflex response to a mishap, rather like blinking the eye when a person moves a hand sharply towards another's face. It is not, however, an involuntary response of this type at all, and lends itself to detailed analysis which illuminates general characteristics of our actions as human beings. That 'Oops!' is not an involuntary reaction to misadventure is shown by the fact that people do not usually make the exclamation when alone. 'Oops!' is normally directed towards *others* present. The exclamation demonstrates to those witnessing a mishap that the lapse is only minor and momentary, not something which should cast doubt on the individual's command of his or her actions.

'Oops!' is only used in situations of minor failure, rather than in major accidents or calamities – which also demonstrates that the exclamation is part of our controlled management of the details of social life. Moreover, the exclamation may be offered by someone observing the lapse, rather than the individual experiencing it. The 'Oops!' may be used to sound a warning to another at the same time as conveying the assurance that the mishap is not being treated as indicating incompetence on the part of the person responsible for it. 'Oops!' is normally a curt sound, but the 'oo' in it may be prolonged in some situations. Thus someone might extend the sound to cover a critical moment in performing a task; or a parent may utter an extended 'Oops!' or 'Oopsadaisy!' when playfully tossing a child in the air. The sound covers the brief phase when the child may feel a loss of control, reassuring it, and probably at the same time developing its understanding of response cries.

This may all sound very contrived and exaggerated. Why bother to analyse such an inconsequential utterance in this detail? Surely we do not pay as much deliberate attention to all aspects of what we say, and how we act, as this example suggests? Of course we don't – on a conscious level. The crucial point, however, is that we *take for granted*, in ourselves and others, an immensely complicated, continuous control of our appearance and actions. In situations of interaction we are never expected just to be 'present' on the scene. Others expect, and we expect of others, that they display what Goffman calls 'controlled alertness'. A fundamental part of 'being human' is continually demonstrating to others our competence and ability in the routines of daily life.

Slips of the tongue

'Oops' is a response to a minor bodily mishap. We all also make mistakes in speech and pronunciation in the course of conversations, lectures, speeches and other situations of talk. In his investigations into the 'psychopathology of everyday life', Freud analysed numerous examples of such lapses of the tongue (Freud, 1975). According to Freud, no mistakes in speaking, including mispronounced or misplaced words, stammering or stuttering, are in fact accidental. All are symptoms of inner conflicts, associated with ways in which our unconscious influences what we consciously say and do. Slips of the tongue are unconsciously motivated – by motives or feelings that we feel on an unconscious level, but which are repressed from our conscious minds – or which we try consciously but unsuccessfully to suppress. These often, but by no means always, involve sexual associations. Thus one may try to say 'organism', but instead say 'orgasm'. Or, in an example Freud gives, someone is asked, 'What regiment is your son with?' She answers, 'With the 42nd Murderers' (*Mörder* in German, rather than the word she intended to say, *Mörser*, 'Mortars').

As in other cases of the misunderstanding of actions or talk, slips of the tongue are often humorous, and could pass as jokes. The difference lies simply in whether or not the speaker consciously intended the words to come out as they did. Slips of the tongue shade over into other types of 'inappropriate' speech, which Freud also believes are often unconsciously motivated – as when a person fails to see that something he or she says has a clear double meaning. These again can be taken as jokes if deliberately intended – but are otherwise lapses in the controlled production of talk which we expect people to sustain.

One of the best ways of illustrating these points is to look at lapses in the talk of radio and television announcers. Announcers' speech is not like ordinary talk, because it is not spontaneous but scripted. It is also expected to be more nearly 'perfect' than ordinary talk – delivered with fewer hesitations and more clearly articulated. Hence when announcers, such as news-readers, 'fluff' what they have to say, or make 'bloopers', they are much more visible and obvious than in casual conversations. Yet announcers do, of course, make slips of the tongue, and many are funny or have the 'only too true' nature to which Freud called attention. Here are some examples of mispronunciations of this type (Goffman, 1981):

In closing our TV Church of the Air, let me remind all of our listeners that time wounds all heals.

This is the Dominion network of the Canadian Broad Corping Castration.

Viceroys – if you want a good choke.

Beat the egg yolk and then add the milk, then slowly blend in the sifted flour. As you do you can see how the mixture is sickening.

Other examples come into the category of 'inappropriate speech', where a double meaning that should have been spotted comes through:

Ladies who care to drive by and drop off their clothes will receive prompt attention.

Folks, try our comfortable beds. I personally stand behind every bed we sell.

The loot and the car were listed as stolen by the Los Angeles Police Department.

And here in Hollywood it is rumoured that the former movie starlet is expecting her fifth child in a month.

We tend to laugh more at verbal mistakes when announcers (or teachers in lectures) make them than when they occur in ordinary conversation. Broadcasters and teachers are supposed to be specialists in the production of faultless talk. The humour does not only reside in what is said, or mis-said, but in the discomfiture which the broadcaster might show at delivering a less than perfect performance. We temporarily see behind the mask of cool professionalism to the 'ordinary individual' behind.

Face, body and speech in interaction

Let us summarize at this point where we have got to so far. Everyday interaction depends on subtle relationships between what we convey with our faces and bodies and what we convey in words. We use the facial expressions and bodily gestures of others to expand on what they communicate verbally, and to check how far they are sincere in what they say. Mostly without realizing it, each of us keeps a tight and continuous control over facial expression, bodily posture and movement in the course of our daily interaction with others.

Sometimes, however, we make verbal slips which, as Freud's example of the 'murderers' indicates, briefly reveal what – consciously or unconsciously – we wish to keep concealed. Lots of verbal slips have an 'only too true' quality – like 'the mixture is sickening' in the example of the cake mix, which the announcer probably thinks is quite unappetizing: verbal slips often inadvertently display our true feelings.

Face, bodily management and speech, then, are used to convey certain meanings and to hide others. We also organize our activities in the *contexts* of social life to achieve the same ends – as we shall now go on to show.

Encounters

In many social situations, we engage in what Goffman calls **unfocused interaction** with others. Unfocused interaction takes place whenever individuals in a given setting exhibit mutual awareness of one another's presence. This is usually the case in any circumstance in which large numbers of people are assembled together, as on a busy street, in a theatre crowd or at a party. When individuals are in the presence of others, even if they do not directly talk to them, they continually engage in non-verbal communication. In their bodily appearance, movement and position, facial and physical gestures, they convey certain impressions to others.

Focused interaction occurs when individuals directly attend to what each other says or does. Save when an individual is standing alone, say at a party, all interaction when individuals are co-present with one another involves both focused and unfocused exchanges. Goffman calls a unit of focused interaction an **encounter**, and much of our day-to-day life consists of continuous encounters with other individuals – family, friends, workmates – frequently occurring against the background of unfocused interaction with others present on the scene. Small-talk, formal discussion, games and routine face-to-face contacts (with ticket clerks, waiters, shop assistants and so forth) are all examples of encounters.

Encounters always need 'openings', demonstrating the discarding of civil inattention. Where strangers meet and begin to talk – for example, at a party – the moment of ceasing civil inattention is always risky, since misunderstandings can easily occur about the nature of the encounter being established (Goffman, 1971, pp. 214–21). Hence, the joining of eye contact may first of all be ambiguous and tentative. A person can then act as though no direct move were intended, if the overture is not accepted. In focused interaction, each individual communicates as much by facial expression and gesture as by the words actually exchanged. Goffman distinguishes in this context between the expressions individuals 'give' and those they 'give off'. The first are the words and facial expressions by means of which people try to produce certain impressions upon others. The second concerns other clues that may be used to check a person's sincerity or truthfulness. For instance, a restaurant-owner listens with a polite smile to the statements of customers that they much enjoyed the food they were served. At the same time, she or he would be noting how pleased they seemed to be while eating the food, whether a lot was left over, and the tone of voice in which they expressed their satisfaction.

Contexts and locations

Daily social life takes place as a series of encounters with others in varying contexts and locations. Most of us meet and talk to a variety of others in the course of the average day. A woman gets up, breakfasts with her family, and perhaps accompanies her children to school, stopping briefly to exchange pleasantries with a friend at the school gates. She drives to work, probably listening to the radio. During the course of the working day, she enters into many interchanges with colleagues and visitors, ranging from transitory conversations to formal meetings. Each of these encounters is likely to be separated by 'markers', or what Goffman calls *brackets*, which distinguish each episode of focused interaction from the one before and from unfocused interaction going on in the background (Goffman, 1974).

Where others are close at hand, or at a party, those holding a conversation will tend to position themselves, and control their voice levels, so as to create a 'huddle' separate from others. They may stand facing one another, for example, effectively making it difficult for others to intrude until they decide to break up, or 'soften the edges', of their focused interaction by moving to different positions in the room. On more formal occasions, recognized cueing devices are often used to signal the opening and ending of a particular encounter or phase of interaction. To signal the opening of a play, for instance, a bell rings, the lights go down and the curtain is raised. At the end of the act or performance the auditorium lights go on again and the curtain falls.

Markers are generally particularly important either when an encounter is especially divergent from the ordinary conventions of daily life, or where there might be ambiguity about 'what is going on'. Where an individual poses naked in front of an art class, he or she does not usually undress in the presence of the group, or dress again in their presence at the end of the encounter. Undressing and dressing in private allows the body to be suddenly exposed and hidden. This both marks the boundaries of the episode, and conveys that it is devoid of the sexual meanings that otherwise might be involved.

In very confined spaces, such as lifts, it is difficult or impossible to mark off a unit of focused interaction. Nor can others present, as they will do in other situations, easily display that they are 'not listening' to – not a part of – whatever conversation is carried on. It is also difficult for strangers not to be seen 'looking at' others more directly than the norms of civil attention allow. Thus in lifts people often adopt an exaggerated 'not listening' and 'not looking' pose, staring into space or at the elevator buttons – anywhere but at their fellow passengers! Conversation is usually suspended or confined to brief exchanges. Similarly, if several people are sitting talking to one another, and one is interrupted to take a phone call, the others cannot readily show complete inattention, and may carry on a sort of hesitant, limp conversation (Goffman, 1963, p. 156).

Impression management

Goffman and other writers on social interaction often use notions from the theatre in analysing social interaction. The concept of **social role**, widely used for this purpose (and also more generally) in sociology, originated in a theatrical setting. Roles are socially defined expectations which a person in a given *status* or **social position** follows. To be a teacher, for example, is to hold a specific position; the teacher's role consists of acting in specified ways towards her or his pupils. In the **dramaturgical model** Goffman employs, social life is seen as though played out by actors on a stage – or on many stages, because how we act depends on the roles we are playing at a particular time. People are very sensitive to how they are seen by others, and use many forms of *impression management* to ensure that others react to them in the ways they wish. Although this may sometimes be done in a calculated way, usually it is among the many things we do without conscious attention. A person will dress and behave quite differently when attending a business meeting than when relaxing with friends at a football match.

Front and back regions

Much of social life, Goffman suggested, can be divided up into **front regions** and **back regions**. Front regions are social occasions or encounters in which individuals act out formal or stylized roles – they are 'on-stage performances'. The back regions are where they assemble the props and prepare themselves for interaction in the more formal settings. Back regions resemble the 'backstage' of a theatre, or the 'off-camera' activities of filming. When they are safely 'behind the scenes', people can relax, and give vent to feelings and styles of behaviour they keep in check when on 'front stage'. Thus a waitress may be the soul of quiet courtesy when serving a customer in the dining room of a restaurant, but become loud and aggressive once behind the swing-doors of the kitchen. There are probably very few restaurants in which customers would like to eat if they could see all that goes on in the kitchens.

Back regions permit 'profanity, open sexual remarks, elaborate griping . . . rough informal dress, "sloppy" sitting and standing posture, use of dialect or substandard speech, mumbling and shouting, playful aggressivity and "kidding", inconsiderateness for the other in minor but potentially symbolic acts, minor self-involvements such as humming, whistling, chewing, nibbling, belching and flatulence' (Goffman, 1969, p. 128).

Team-work is often involved in creating and preserving front-region performances. Thus, two prominent politicians in the same party might put on an elaborate show of unity and friendship before the television cameras, even though each cordially detests the other. A wife and husband may take care to conceal their quarrels from their children, preserving a front of harmony, only to fight bitterly once the children are safely tucked up in bed.

Adopting roles: intimate examinations

James Henslin and Mae Briggs studied a very specific, and highly delicate, type of encounter – what happens when a woman visits a doctor for a gynaecological examination (Henslin and Briggs, 1971). Most such pelvic examinations are carried out by male doctors. The experience is fraught with potential ambiguities and embarrassment for both parties. Men and women in Western culture are socialized to think of the genitals as the most private part of the body, and seeing, and particularly feeling, the genitals of another person is ordinarily associated with intimate sexual encounters. Many women feel so worried by the prospect of a pelvic examination that they refuse to visit the doctor even when they suspect there is a strong medical reason to do so.

Henslin and Briggs analysed material collected by Briggs, a trained nurse, from a large number of gynaecological examinations. They interpreted what they found as having several typical stages. Adopting the dramaturgical metaphor, they suggested that each phase can be treated as a distinct 'scene', in which the parts the actors play alter as the episode unfolds. The 'prologue' is where the woman enters the waiting-room preparing to assume the role of patient, temporarily discarding her outside identity. Called into the consulting room, she adopts the 'patient' role and the first scene opens. The doctor takes up a businesslike, professional manner, but treats the patient as a proper and competent person, maintaining eye contact and listening politely to what she has to say. If he decides an examination is called for, he tells the patient so, and leaves the room; 'scene one' is over.

As he leaves, the nurse comes in. She is an important 'stagehand' in the main scene shortly to begin. She soothes any worries that the patient might have, acting as both a confidante – knowing some of the 'things women have to put up with' – and a collaborator in what is to follow. Crucially, the nurse helps alter the patient from a 'person' to a 'non-person' for the vital scene – a body of which part is to be scrutinized, rather than a complete human being. The nurse not only supervises the patient's undressing, but takes over aspects which normally the individual would control. Thus, she takes the patient's clothes and folds them. Most women wish their underwear to be out of sight when the doctor returns, and the nurse makes sure that this is so. She guides the patient to the examining table, and covers most of her body with a sheet before the physician comes back into the room.

The central scene now opens, with nurse as well as doctor present. The presence of the nurse helps ensure that the interaction between doctor and patient is free of sexual overtones, and also provides a legal witness should the physician be charged with unprofessional conduct. The examination proceeds as though the personality of the patient were absent – the sheet across her separates the genital area from the rest of the body, and her position does not allow her to see the procedures of the examination itself. Save for any specific medical queries, the doctor ignores her, sitting on a low stool, out of sight of her face. The patient collaborates in becoming a temporary 'non-person', not initiating conversation and keeping any movements to a minimum.

In the 'interval' between this and the final scene, the nurse again plays the role of stagehand, helping the patient to become a 'full person' once more. At this juncture, the two may again engage in conversation, the patient expressing relief that the examination is over. Having dressed and regroomed herself, the patient is ready to face the concluding scene. The doctor re-enters, and in recounting the results of the examination again treats the patient as a complete and responsible person. Resuming his polite, professional manner, he conveys that his reactions to her are in no way altered by the intimate contact with her body which he has been permitted. The 'epilogue' is played out when she leaves the physician's office, taking up again her identity in the outside world.

Encounters and personal space

In Western culture, on most occasions, people maintain a distance of at least three feet when engaged in focused interaction with others. When standing side by side, even if not within the same encounter, they may stand more closely together. There are cultural differences in the definition of **personal space**. In the Middle East, for example, people often stand closer to one another than is thought acceptable in the West. Westerners visiting that part of the world are likely to find themselves disconcerted by this unexpected physical proximity.

Edward T. Hall, who has worked extensively on non-verbal communication, distinguishes four zones of private space. *Intimate distance*, of up to one and a half feet, is reserved for very few social contacts. Only those involved in relationships in which regular bodily touching is permitted – such as parents and children, or lovers – operate within this zone of private space. *Personal distance* (from one and half to four feet) is the normal spacing for encounters with friends and reasonably close acquaintances. Some intimacy of contact is permitted, but this tends to be strictly limited. *Social distance*, from four feet to twelve feet, is the zone usually maintained in formal settings of interaction, as in interviews. The fourth zone is that of *public distance*, of beyond twelve feet, preserved by those who are performing to a watching audience.

In ordinary interaction, the most fraught zones are those of intimate and personal distance. If these spaces are 'invaded', people try to recapture their space. A stare might convey to the other 'move away!' or the individual might elbow the intruder aside. In cases where people are forced into proximity closer than they deem desirable, some kind of physical boundary might be established, as when a reader at a crowded library desk physically demarcates a private space by stacking books around its edges (Hall, 1959, 1966).

Interaction in time and space

Seeing how activities are distributed in space – and time as well – is fundamental to analysing encounters, and also to understanding basic aspects of social life in general. All interaction, of course, is *situated* – it occurs in a particular place, and has a specific duration in time. Our actions over the course of a day tend to be 'zoned' in time as well as in space. Thus, for example, people who go out to work spend a 'zone' – say, from 9 a.m. to 5 p.m. – of their daily time working. Their weekly time is also zoned: they are likely to work on weekdays, and spend weekends at home, altering the pattern of their activities on the weekend days. Time spent at work normally means spatial movement as well – a person journeying between home and work may take a bus from one area of a city to another, for example, or perhaps commute in from the suburbs. When we analyse the contexts in which social interaction goes on, therefore, it is often useful to analyse people's movements across *time-space*. As we move through the temporal zones of the day, we are also often moving across space as well.

Social geographers have introduced the useful and intriguing notion of **time–space convergence** to analyse how social development and technological change affect patterns of social activity. Time–space convergence refers to the way in which, with improved transport systems, distances 'shrink'. Thus the time taken to travel from the east to the west coast of the United States can be calculated in terms of the varying rates of mobility which become possible with advances in transport methods. On foot, the journey takes more than two years; on horseback, eight months; by stage-coach, four months; by rail in 1910, four days; by car today, two and a half days; by regular air services five hours; by the fastest available jet transport just over two hours; by space shuttle, a few minutes (Janelle, 1968; Carlstein et al., 1978). Modes of social life become radically reorganized with increasing time–space convergence, affecting the lives of us all. Many of the goods we use, and much of the food we eat, for instance, are transported over large distances, even from the other side of the world. This has helped to produce much greater global interdependence (see chapter 16: 'The Globalizing of Social Life').

We can understand how social activities are organized in time and space by means of the concept of **regionalization**, which refers to how social life is zoned in time-space. Take the example of a private house. A modern house is regionalized into rooms, hall-ways and floors if there is more than one storey. These various spaces of the house are not just physically separate areas, but are zoned in time as well as space. The living rooms and kitchen are used most in the daylight hours, the bedrooms at night. The interaction which occurs in these various 'regions' is bounded by both spatial and temporal divisions. Some areas of the house form 'back regions', with 'performances' being put on in the others. The whole house, at a given period of the week, can become a back region, as can paths across time and space traced outside. Once again these matters are beautifully captured by Goffman:

> Of a Sunday morning, a whole household can use the wall around its domestic establishment to conceal a relaxing slovenliness in dress and civil endeavour, extending to all rooms the informality that is usually restricted to kitchen and bedrooms. So, too, in American middle-class neighbourhoods, on afternoons the line between children's playground and home may be defined as backstage by mothers, who pass along it wearing jeans, loafers and a minimum of make-up . . . And, of course, a region that is thoroughly established as a front region for the regular performance of a particular routine often functions as a back region before and after each performance, for at these times the permanent fixtures may undergo repairs, restoration, and rearrangement, or the performers may hold dress rehearsals. To see this we need only glance into a restaurant, or store, or home, a few minutes before these establishments are opened to us for the day. (Goffman, 1969, p. 127)

Clock time

In modern societies, the zoning of our activities is very strongly influenced by the experience of clocks and **clock time**. Without clocks, and the precise timing of activities – and thereby their co-ordination across space – industrialized societies could not exist (Wright, 1968; Mumford, 1973). The measuring of time by clocks is today standardized across the globe – making possible the complex international transport systems and communications on which our lives now depend. World standard time was not introduced until 1884, at a conference of nations held in Washington. The globe was then partitioned into twenty-four time zones, each one hour apart, and an exact beginning of the universal day was fixed (Zerubavel, 1982).

Monasteries were the first organizations to try to schedule the activities of their inmates precisely across the day and week, a practice originating as early as the fourteenth century. Today there is virtually no group or organization which does not do so – the greater the number of people and resources involved, the more precise the scheduling has to be. Eviatar Zerubavel (1979) demonstrated this in his study of the temporal structure of a large modern hospital. A hospital has to operate on a twenty-four-hour basis, and co-ordinating the staff and resources is a highly complex matter. For instance, the majority of nurses work for set periods on different wards, moving around the different sectors of the hospital, and they are also called upon to alternate between day and night shift work. All these individuals, and the resources they need, have to be integrated together both in time and in space.

Time geography

An illuminating way of analysing activities across time and space has been developed by the Swedish social geographer Torsten Hägerstrand (Hägerstrand, 1973; Carlstein et al., 1978). Hägerstrand calls his approach **time geography**, but it actually deals with movements in time–space. The time-geographic approach looks at the physical environment (streets, buildings, roads, neighbourhoods) in which social activities are carried on, tracing how this influences – and is influenced by – the daily and weekly movements of individuals and groups. We can map the daily paths which individuals trace – what people do, at which parts of the day, and where – in the course of a typical day or week.

A very simple example can be given. Two individuals, let us say A and B, live in different neighbourhoods in a city. Their time–space paths in the course of the day bring them into contact with one another at point X for a certain period – perhaps they meet in a coffee-shop or restaurant, and share a conversation – after which their paths diverge, as each moves off to other activities in separate places. By recording the typical activities, it is quite easy to construct a 'time–space picture' of their lives. In this way, we can portray the mosaic of activities in time and space which compose the life of urban neighbourhoods and communities (see figure 3).

Time–space constraints

We can understand some of the factors influencing the patterning of urban life by identifying simple, yet basic, characteristics of human activity which affect how time–space is organized. Three kinds of constraint set limits to the unfolding of day-to-day activities, in terms of their location in time and space.

Capability constraints are limits set by the physical constitution of individuals. For instance, all human beings have needs for food and sleep, which have to be catered for in the time–space zoning of their activities. Those who work in one area have to be transported,

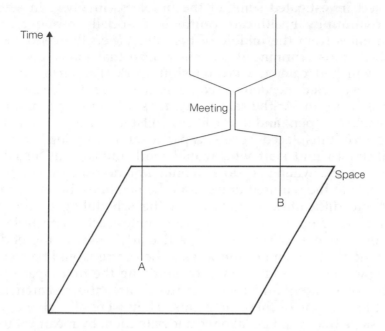

Figure 3 Individual paths in time and space: A and B move to meet each other, spend some time together and then go their separate ways

or transport themselves, back to the homes in which they prepare their food and rest for the night.

Coupling constraints are limits set by the abilities of people to come together in particular places to interact with one another. Where (as in cluttered traditional cities) there are few roadways providing easy access from one area to another, most forms of interaction are necessarily confined to distances that can easily be covered on foot. Moreover, all physical settings have what Hägerstrand calls a 'packing capacity' – a limit to the numbers of persons who can occupy a particular space for the purposes of a given type of activity. The rush hour is a graphic example of this. There are absolute limits to the volume of traffic streets can carry; at peak times, no one in fact gets anywhere in a 'rush' but usually at a slow crawl.

Authority constraints concern limits set by the system of power in a community or broader society. How much power people have to live where they want, for example, is limited by their financial resources. Most people might want to live in neighbourhoods of elegant and luxurious homes, but only relatively few have the resources to do so. Planning regulations also often limit the sorts of dwellings that can be constructed in different areas.

As an illustration of how these concepts help inform empirical study, we can take a research project conducted from a time-geographic perspective in the city of Newcastle in New South Wales, Australia.

The project investigated some of the problems involved in setting up a new community health-care centre in a socially mixed area about fourteen miles from the middle of the city. When the centre was first established, those running it did not realize that many people in the area for which it catered were on shift work. Far more clients than had been expected needed to come into the centre either before 7 a.m. or after 5 p.m. At the same time, most of the clients assumed the centre would be open, and its facilities available, during normal hours.

The centre thus faced severe capacity and coupling problems. It was difficult to find staff who would work outside the usual hours; those who were willing to do so could not necessarily get transport into the area at the required times from the neighbourhoods where they lived. Acute difficulties were faced in the scheduling of the centre's services: some periods of the day were quite slack, with little for the staff to do, while at other times – particularly towards the end of the day, and right at the end of the week – the centre would be so jammed with people that it couldn't cope. By studying the time–space paths of a number of workers and clients at the centre, the researchers could pinpoint the origins of these problems. They were also able to suggest positive steps that could be taken to alleviate them by means of the more systematic allocation of resources (Parkes and Thrift, 1980, pp. 271–2).

Zoning

The distribution of activities in time–space over the past century or so – particularly in quite recent times – has been influenced by what has been called the *colonization of time*. Processes of spatial migration to, and within, cities have been accompanied by a 'migration' into the time-zones of evening and night. As Murray Melbin observes:

> The last great frontier of human immigration is occurring in time: a spreading of wakeful activity throughout the twenty-four hours of the day. There is more multiple shift factory work, more police coverage, more use of the telephone at all hours. There are more hospitals, pharmacies, aeroplane flights, hostels, always-open restaurants, car rental and gasoline and auto repair stations, bowling alleys, and radio stations always active. There are more emergency services such as auto-touring, locksmiths, bail bondsmen, drug and poison and suicide and gambling 'hot lines' available incessantly. Although different individuals participate in these events in shifts, the organisations involved are continually active. (Melbin, 1978, p. 100)

Melbin estimates that after midnight in the USA there are some thirty million people active, excluding those getting ready to go to sleep. Even during the 'depths of the night' – 3 a.m. to 5 a.m. – well over ten million people are up and about.

These changes, of course, always have spatial implications, and are affected by the various types of constraint influencing time–space zoning. The night-time activities of one area demand corresponding processes during the day in other regions. For instance, a plane travelling overnight might arrive very early in the morning at its destination, requiring the mobilizing of airport facilities and transport links. The organizations which cater for the increased level of activity in evening and night-time hours face the sort of coupling constraints mentioned in the research on the Newcastle community health-care centre.

One researcher studied the time–space organization of areas in central Boston in the United States. Cycles of neighbourhood use can be described in four ways.

1 *Continuous use*: incessant areas.
2 *Evacuation*: empty at night.
3 *Invasion*: active especially at night.
4 *Displacement*: shifting from day to night.

Some areas, like certain residential neighbourhoods near the city centre, are in more or less constant use by large numbers of people, although what they are doing there alters at different phases of the daily cycle. The business area is largely evacuated at night. The entertainment areas are invaded in the evenings and early hours, but may be largely empty during the day. Various fringe areas which contain both businesses and entertainments experience a displacement of one population by another at the end of the day (Lynch, 1976).

Everyday life in cultural and historical perspective

Some of the mechanisms of social interaction analysed by Goffman, Garfinkel and others seem to be universal; but many are not. The providing of 'markers' to signal the opening and closing of encounters, for example, is no doubt characteristic of human interaction everywhere. Various means used to organize encounters are also found in all gatherings of human beings – such as keeping the body turned away from others when forming a conversational 'knot'. Yet in many respects our day-to-day lives in modern Western societies are very different from those of people in other cultures. For instance, some aspects of civil inattention are irrelevant to the behaviour of members of very small societies, where there are no strangers and few, if any, settings in which more than a handful of people are together at any one time. Much of Goffman's discussion of civil inattention, and other aspects of interaction, primarily concerns societies in which contact with strangers is commonplace.

Our daily lives have been shaped in fundamental ways by the changes associated with industrialism, urbanism and the development of modern states. An example will help to demonstrate some of the contrasts between social interaction in modern and traditional societies. One of the least developed cultures in terms of technology remaining in the world is that of the !Kung (also sometimes known as the Bushmen), who live in the Kalahari desert area of Botswana and Namibia, in Southern Africa (Lee, 1968, 1969) (the exclamation mark refers to a click sound made before the name is pronounced). Their way of life is changing, because of outside influences, but we'll discuss their traditional patterns.

The !Kung live in groups of some thirty or forty people, in temporary settlements near to water-holes. Food is scarce in their environment, and they must walk far and wide to find it. Such roaming takes up most of the average day. Women and children often stay back in the camp, but equally often the whole group may spend the day walking. Members of the community will sometimes fan out over an area of up to 100 square miles in the course of a day, returning to the camp at night to eat and sleep. The men in particular may be alone, or in twos and threes, for much of the day. There is one period of the year, however, when the routines of their daily activities change: the winter rainy season, when water is abundant and food much easier to come by. The everyday life of the !Kung during this period is centred around ritual and ceremonial activities, preparation for and enactment of which is very time-consuming.

The members of most !Kung groups never see anyone they do not know reasonably well. Until contacts with the outside became more common over recent years, they had no word for 'stranger'. While the !Kung, particularly the males, may spend long periods of the day out of contact with others, in the community itself there is little or no opportunity for privacy. Families sleep in flimsy, open dwellings, with virtually all activities open to public view. No one has studied the !Kung with Goffman's observations on everyday life in mind, but it is easy to see that some aspects of his work have limited application to !Kung social life. There are few opportunities, for example, to create front and back regions. The 'closing off' of different gatherings and encounters by the walls of rooms, separate buildings of many kinds, and the different neighbourhoods of cities – these aspects of day-to-day life in modern societies are remote from the activities of the !Kung.

Tommy Carlstein has analysed aspects of !Kung social life using the concepts of time-geography (Carlstein, 1983). Like all hunters and gatherers, he argued, the !Kung face a time–space conflict between food storage and social mobility, which affects the nature of their daily lives. The more food they try to store, to protect against lean times, the more they are pinned down in one place. But if they should concentrate their activities in a fixed settlement, their sources of food would become limited, because they would not be able to travel

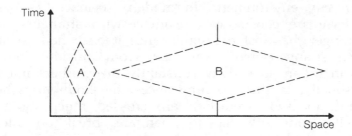

Figure 4 The possible range of mobility through space in the course of a day. Prism A denotes a culture dependent on walking for physical mobility. Prism B denotes a culture that has domesticated transport animals
Source: T. Carlstein, *Time Resources, Society and Ecology: On the Capacity for Human Interaction in Space and Time* (London: Allen and Unwin, 1983), p. 75.

far enough afield to find the food they need in the first place. The !Kung cope with this dilemma in a way that gives their mode of life its shape. They simply move camp when necessary.

We can represent the possible range of mobility through space in the course of a day in the shape of a prism (see figure 4). If, say, the !Kung had lived in the desert regions of North Africa, where camels provide much greater mobility, the prism would be greatly extended laterally. An increase in spatial mobility can have drastic consequences for the way of life of a people. For instance, the introduction of horses among the American Indians in the plains allowed them to catch up with the bison herds. This altered their material way of life, which, in turn, caused changes in some of their main habits and customs.

Microsociology and macrosociology

The study of everyday behaviour in situations of face-to-face interaction is usually called **microsociology**. **Macrosociology** is the analysis of large-scale social systems, such as a business firm, the political system or the economic order. Macrosociology also includes the analysis of long-term processes of change – such as the development of industrialism. At first sight it might seem as though micro and macro analyses are quite distant from one another. In fact the two are closely connected (Knorr-Cetina and Cicourel, 1981; Giddens, 1984), as this chapter has tried to demonstrate.

Macro analysis is essential if we are to understand the institutional background of day-to-day life. The ways in which people live their everyday lives are greatly affected by the broader institutional framework within which they exist, as is obvious when the daily cycle of activities of a culture like that of the !Kung is compared to life in a Western city environment. In modern societies, as has been pointed out, we are constantly in contact with strangers. Indeed, the term 'stranger' has lost the significance it once had. A stranger was literally a 'strange person' who came from 'outside'. Individuals who live in an urban area today constantly meet others not known to them personally. In these circumstances, the boundaries between unfocused and focused interaction are crossed much more often. The city-dweller constantly has to open and break off interaction with others he or she has not previously met.

Micro studies are in their turn necessary for illuminating broad institutional patterns. Face-to-face interaction is clearly the main basis of all forms of social organization, no matter how large in scale. Suppose we are studying a business corporation. Many of the activities of the firm could be studied in terms of face-to-face behaviour. We could analyse, for example, the interaction of directors in the boardroom, people working in the various offices or the workers on the shop-floor. We would not by this means build up a picture of the whole corporation, since many of the ties involved do not put people in face-to-face contact. Through printed materials, letters, the telephone and computers, many connections transcend the immediacies of personal interaction. Yet we could certainly contribute significantly to understanding how the organization works.

Summary

1   Many apparently trivial aspects of our day-to-day behaviour turn out on close examination to be both complex and important aspects of *social interaction*. An example is the gaze – looking at other people. In most interaction, eye-contact is fairly fleeting. To stare at another person could be taken as a sign of hostility – or, on some occasions, of love. The study of social interaction is a fundamental area in sociology, illuminating many aspects of social life.

2   Many different expressions are conveyed by the human face. It is widely held that basic aspects of the facial expression of emotion are innate. Cross-cultural studies demonstrate quite close similarities between the members of different cultures both in facial expression and the interpretation of emotions registered on the human face.

3   'Face' can also be understood in a broader sense to refer to the esteem in which an individual is held by others. Generally, in their interaction with other people, we are concerned to 'save face' – protect our self-esteem.

4   The study of ordinary *talk* and *conversation* has come to be called *ethnomethodology*, a term first coined by Harold Garfinkel. Ethnomethodology is the analysis of the ways in which we actively – although usually in a taken-for-granted way – make sense of what others mean by what they say and do.

5   We can learn a great deal about the nature of talk by 'response cries' (exclamations) and studying slips of the tongue (what happens when people mispronounce or misapply words and phrases). Slips of the tongue are often humorous, and are in fact closely connected psychologically to wit and joking.

6   *Unfocused interaction* is the mutual awareness individuals have of one another in large gatherings, when not directly in conversation with one another. *Focused interaction*, which can be divided up into distinct *encounters* – or episodes of interaction – occurs where two or more individuals are directly attending to what the other or others are saying and doing.

7   Social interaction can often be studied in an illuminating way by applying the *dramaturgical model* – studying social interaction as if those involved were actors on a stage, having a set and props. As in the theatre, in the various contexts of social life there tend to be clear distinctions between *front regions* (the stage itself) and *back regions*, where the actors prepare themselves for the performance and relax afterwards.

8   All social interaction is situated in time and space. We can analyse how our daily lives are 'zoned' in time and space combined, by looking at how activities occur during definite periods and at the same time involve spatial movement. *Time geography* provides one means of documenting this.

9   The study of face-to-face interaction is usually called *microsociology* – as contrasted to *macrosociology*, which studies larger groups, institutions and social systems. Micro and macro analysis are in fact very closely related and each complements the other.

Basic concepts

encounter	social position
social role	

Important terms

civil inattention	front region
non-verbal communication	back region
talk	personal space
conversation	time–space convergence
ethnomethodology	regionalization
response cries	clock time
unfocused interaction	time geography
focused interaction	microsociology
dramaturgical model	macrosociology

Further reading

Paul Drew and Anthony Wootton, *Erving Goffman: Exploring the Interaction Order* (Cambridge: Polity Press, 1988) — a collection of articles discussing major aspects of Goffman's work.

Erving Goffman, *The Presentation of Self in Everyday Life* (Harmondsworth: Penguin, 1969) — one of Goffman's main works, in which he discusses how individuals organize their interaction with others to foster particular views of themselves.

Erving Goffman, *Behaviour in Public Places* (New York: Free Press, 1963) — an analysis of the rituals enacted by individuals in public settings of interaction.

'Symposium on Erving Goffman', *Theory, Culture and Society*, vol. 2, no. 1 (Winter 1983) — a set of articles critically analysing Goffman's work.

Henri Lefebvre, *Everyday Life in the Modern World* (London: Allen Lane, 1971) — a discussion of how social change in modern times has affected the nature of daily life.

E. Livingstone, *Making Sense of Ethnomethodology* (London: Routledge and Kegan Paul, 1987) — a useful general account of ethnomethodology, setting out clearly the basic ideas involved.

E. P. Thompson, 'Time, work discipline and industrial capitalism', *Past and Present*, 38 (1967) — a celebrated analysis of the connections between modern industry and the regulation of time.

5

Conformity and Deviance

As we have seen from previous chapters, human social life is governed by norms or rules. Our activities would collapse into chaos if we did not stick to rules which define some kinds of behaviour as appropriate in given contexts, and others as inappropriate. Orderly behaviour on the highway, for example, would be impossible if drivers did not observe the rule of driving on the left and other traffic conventions. The norms we follow in our actions give the social world its orderly and predictable character, and much of sociology is concerned with showing how social order is achieved. But there is another side to the story. Not everyone conforms to social expectations all of the time. Drivers sometimes disregard the rules of traffic behaviour, even if the lives of others are thereby endangered. When in a great hurry, or under the influence of drink, a person might drive recklessly, perhaps even taking a short cut up a one-way street. People quite often *deviate* from the rules they are expected to follow.

The study of deviant behaviour is one of the most fascinating tasks of sociology. It is a complex area of analysis because there are as many types of rule-violation as there are social norms and values. Since norms vary between different cultures, and between differing sub-cultures within the same society, what is normal in one cultural setting is deviant in another. Smoking marijuana is a deviant activity in British culture while drinking alcohol is not. Exactly the reverse is the case in some Middle Eastern societies.

What is deviance?

Deviance may be defined as non-conformity to a given norm, or set of norms, which are accepted by a significant number of people in a community or society. No society can be divided up in a simple way between those who deviate from norms and those who conform to them. Most of us on some occasions transgress generally accepted rules of behaviour. Many people have at some point committed minor acts of theft, like taking something from a shop without paying for it, or appropriating small items from work – such as office notepaper – and putting them to private use. Large numbers of individuals have smoked marijuana, purchased alcohol while under age, used illegal drugs, or taken part in prohibited sexual practices.

The scope of the concept of deviance is very wide, as some examples will illustrate. The American billionaire Howard Hughes was a highly successful businessman who built up his massive fortune through a mixture of hard work, inventive ideas and shrewd decisions. In terms of his drive to individual success, his activities in business conformed to some of the key values in Western societies – values emphasizing the desirability of material rewards and individual achievement. On the other hand, in some areas his behaviour deviated sharply from orthodox norms. He lived the last few years of his life almost completely isolated from the outside world, hardly even coming out of the hotel suite which he had made his home. He let his hair grow very long and cultivated a long straggly beard, making him look more like a biblical prophet than a successful businessman.

Hughes was both highly successful and highly deviant in his behaviour. As a contrasting example we might take the career of Ted Bundy. Bundy's way of life, on the face of things, conformed to the norms of behaviour of a good citizen. Bundy led what seemed on the surface to be not only a normal life, but a most worthy one. For example, he played an active role in the Samaritans, an association which organizes a twenty-four-hour phone-in service for people who are distressed or suicidal. Yet Bundy had also carried out a series of horrific murders. Before sentencing him to death, the judge at his trial praised Bundy for his abilities (he had prepared his own defence), but finished by noting what a waste he had made of his life. Bundy's career shows that a person can seem entirely normal while secretly engaging in acts of extreme deviance.

Deviance does not just refer to individual behaviour, but concerns the activities of groups as well. An illustration is the Hare Krishna cult, a religious group whose beliefs and mode of life are quite different from those of the majority of people living in the United Kingdom. The cult was established in New York in 1965, when Sril Prabhupada came from India to spread the word of Krishna consciousness to the West. He aimed his message particularly at young people who were drug-users, proclaiming that one could 'stay high all the time, discover eternal bliss', by following his teachings (Rockford, 1985). The Hare Krishnas became a familiar sight to many, dancing and chanting in the streets. They were regarded in a tolerant light by most of the population, even if their beliefs seemed eccentric.

The Hare Krishnas represent an example of a **deviant sub-culture**. Although their membership today has declined, they have been able to survive fairly easily within the wider society. The organization is wealthy, financed by donations given by members and sympathizers. Their position diverges from that of another deviant sub-culture which might be mentioned here by way of contrast: the homeless. People who are 'down and out' live on the streets by day, spending their time in parks or in public buildings (like libraries). They may sleep outside as well, or find refuge in dosshouses. Many of the homeless manage to eke out only a miserable existence on the fringes of the wider society.

Norms and sanctions

We most often follow social rules or norms because, as a result of socialization, it has become habitual for us to do so. Take, for example, the rules involved in language. Using language means knowing a variety of rules of grammar and speech. Most of the time, we simply utilize these without having to give them any thought, since we learned them in early childhood. It is only when we try later to master a foreign language that we recognize how many rules have to be learned even to be able to speak simple sentences correctly. The norms governing interaction in social encounters, discussed by Goffman (see chapter 4: 'Social Interaction and Everyday Life') provide another illustration.

Maintaining attitudes of civil inattention towards strangers, using tact in our conversations with friends, or following the procedures establishing 'markers' between encounters – all these we usually do without even realizing that distinct rules of procedure are involved.

Other types of norm we follow more in the conscious belief that the behaviour they involve is justified. This is true, for instance, of the norms of traffic behaviour mentioned earlier. Drivers accept that they have to observe rules like driving on the correct side of the road or stopping when the traffic light is red because if the majority of drivers did not abide by such rules most of the time, the roads would become vastly more dangerous even than they are at present.

Less agreement is found about some other aspects of road behaviour – like speed limits. No doubt the majority of drivers accept that speed limits of some type are necessary to protect each other, cyclists and pedestrians. But few motorists rigorously respect the limits. They are likely to drive within them if they know or suspect that there is a police car nearby, but once they are confident that there are no police to be seen, many drivers will speed up to well beyond the legal maximum.

This example directs our attention towards some very important aspects of conformity and deviance. All social norms are accompanied by **sanctions** which protect against non-**conformity**. A sanction is any reaction from others to the behaviour of an individual or group which has the aim of ensuring that a given norm is complied with. Sanctions may be positive (the offering of rewards for conformity) or negative (punishment for behaviour which does not conform). They can also be formal or informal. A formal sanction exists where there is a definite body of people or an agency whose task it is to ensure that a particular set of norms is followed. Informal sanctions are less organized, and more spontaneous, reactions to non-conformity.

The main types of formal sanction in modern societies are those involved in the system of punishment represented by the courts and prisons. The police, of course, are the agency charged with bringing offenders to trial and possible imprisonment. Most motoring offences are punished with fines or loss of licence, but these are sufficient punishments to ensure that drivers who knowingly depart from the traffic regulations keep a watchful eye open for the police. Fines, imprisonment, or execution are all types of formal *negative* sanctions. Not many formal *positive* sanctions exist to reward traffic behaviour – although sometimes 'road proficiency' or 'good driving' awards are offered to stimulate obedience. Formal positive sanctions are found in many other areas of social life, however – for instance, the presentation of medals for bravery in combat, degrees or diplomas to mark academic success, or awards for performances in sports events.

Informal sanctions, positive and negative, are commonplace features of all contexts of social activity. Those of a positive type include saying 'well done' to someone, or giving the person an appreciative smile or a pat on the back. Examples of negative informal sanctions are speaking insultingly to, scolding, or physically shunning a given individual. Although formal sanctions are usually more dramatic and visible than informal ones, informal sanctions are of fundamental importance in ensuring conformity to norms. Wanting to secure the approval of family, friends and colleagues, or wishing to avoid being ridiculed, shamed or rejected, often influences people's behaviour more than formal rewards or punishments.

Laws, crimes and punishment

Laws are norms defined by governments as principles that their citizens must follow, formal sanctions being used by those authorities against people who do not conform. Where there are laws, there are also **crimes**, since crime can most simply be defined as any mode of behaviour which breaks a law. The nature of behaviour regarded as criminal, the relative seriousness of different crimes, and the ways in which criminal activities are punished by state authorities – each of these has changed significantly over the past two or three centuries. As was mentioned in chapter 1 ('Sociology: Problems and Perspectives'), the reasons for this can be traced to the replacement of traditional societies, based on the local village community, by industrialized social systems, in which most people live in the more anonymous locations of towns and cities.

Crimes in pre-industrial times

In pre-industrial Europe the most serious crimes, those which received the highest penalties, were religious in nature, or were crimes against the property of the ruler or the aristocracy. The transgressions involved are either not treated as crimes at all today, or are thought of as minor offences. Heresy (the proclaiming of religious doctrines other than Christianity), sacrilege (stealing or damaging church property) and even blasphemy (taking God's name in vain, or speaking negatively about religious matters) were for a long time punishable by death in many parts of Europe. Hunting or fishing, the cutting down of trees or bushes, or picking fruit, on the lands of the king or aristocracy by the common people were also capital offences (although the death penalty was not always actually enforced).

The murder of one commoner by another was not generally seen to be as serious as these other crimes; the culprit could often atone for the crime simply by paying a certain amount of money to the relatives of the victim. However, the victim's family would sometimes take justice into their own hands, by killing the murderer. One problem with this mode of punishment – often known as the *blood feud* – was that the family of the original killer might then respond in kind, leading to a pattern of multiple killings. In a few areas, like Southern Italy, the practice of the blood feud has persisted into the twentieth century (and still is used as a mode of dispensing 'justice' between rival 'crime families' in the United States today).

Changes in modes of punishment

Before the early nineteenth century, imprisonment was rarely used to punish crime, either in Europe or the United States. Most towns of any size had a local gaol, but these were normally very small, and were not capable of holding more than three or four prisoners at any time. They were used to 'cool off' drunks for the night, or occasionally as places where accused persons awaited trial. In the bigger European cities, there were prisons of some size; most of the people interned in these were convicted criminals awaiting execution. These institutions were very different from the prisons that were built in great numbers from the turn of the nineteenth century onwards. Prison discipline was lax or non-existent. Sometimes those who were to be executed were plunged into dungeons, and saw only the gaoler before being taken to execution, but more often the prison atmosphere was amazingly free and easy by modern standards.

Jonathon Atholl, a historian of crime, has described life in Newgate, one of the early London prisons. It was a bustling, lively place, full of visitors at most times of the day. In 1790 one of the condemned men held a ball at the prison, apparently not an uncommon event:

> Tea was served at 4 p.m. to the music of violins and flutes, after which the company danced until 8 p.m. when a cold supper was produced. The party broke up at 9 o'clock, the usual hour for closing the prison. (Atholl, 1954, p. 66)

The main forms of punishment for crime until the nineteenth century were putting people in the stocks, whipping, branding with hot irons or hanging. These were usually carried out publicly, and were well attended. Some executions attracted thousands of people. Those about to be hanged might make speeches, justifying their actions or proclaiming themselves innocent. The crowd would cheer, boo or hiss, according to their assessment of the accused's claims.

Prisons and asylums

Modern prisons have their origins, not in the gaols and dungeons of former times, but in workhouses (also known as 'hospitals'). Workhouses date from the seventeenth century in most European countries, being established during the period when feudalism was breaking down and many peasant workers could not get work on the land, and so became vagrants. In the workhouses they were provided with food, but forced to spend most of their time in the institution, and made to work extremely hard. The workhouses also, however, became places in which other groups were interned if no one was prepared to care for them outside: the sick, aged, feeble-minded and mentally ill.

During the eighteenth century, prisons, asylums and hospitals gradually became distinct from one another (Ignatieff, 1978; Doerner, 1981; McConville, 1981). Reformers came to object to traditional punishments, seeing deprivation of liberty as a more effective way of coping with criminal activities. Murder became recognized as the most serious crime, as rights of individual freedom developed within the wider political system, for to kill another person is the ultimate attack on that individual's rights. Since prisons were supposed to have the effect of training criminals in sober habits of discipline and conformity, the idea of punishing people in public progressively dropped away. Executions, for example, were hidden from public view, rather than put on display. (During the twentieth century, most Western countries have abolished the death penalty altogether – some states of the United States being exceptions in this respect.)

The behaviour of the mad increasingly came to be seen as evidence of a type of sickness; the concept of **mental illness** first made its appearance in the late eighteenth century (Scull, 1979), and firmly established in the nineteenth century. Madness became *medicalized* – taken over by the medical profession. Since insanity was henceforth recognized as a disease (rather than, as previously, a variant of feeble-mindedness or as possession of the mind by demons), it was regarded as something which only doctors were qualified to treat. People could still be placed in asylums against their will, but a doctor's certificate was now needed.

Explaining deviance

The nature and content of deviant behaviour vary widely both from the past to the present and from one society to another. This is something we must seek to explain. In the following sections, we shall discuss some of the leading theories of deviance, giving particular attention to theories of crime. None of the theories provides a comprehensive explanation of crime as a whole, let alone all deviance. But they overlap in some ways, and can be combined together in others, to provide a reasonable understanding of major aspects of deviant behaviour.

Biological and psychological theories of crime and deviance

The argument from biology

Some of the first attempts to explain crime and other forms of deviance were essentially biological in character. Broca, an early

French anthropologist, claimed to discern peculiarities in the skulls and brains of criminals which distinguished them from the law-abiding population. The Italian criminologist Cesare Lombroso, working in the 1870s, claimed that certain people were born with criminal tendencies, throw-backs to a more primitive type of human being (Lombroso, 1911). Criminal types, he believed, could be identified by the shape of the skull. He accepted that social learning could influence the development of criminal behaviour, but regarded most criminals as biologically degenerate or defective.

These ideas became thoroughly discredited, but the thesis that criminality is influenced by biological make-up has repeatedly been suggested in various guises (Eysenck, 1977; Mednick et al., 1987). At one time a popular method of trying to demonstrate the likely influence of heredity on criminal tendencies was to study family trees. Richard Dugdale investigated the Dukes family in the United States, which included 140 criminals among its 1,200 members (Dugdale, 1877). He compared the Dukes with the descendants of Jonathan Edwards, a well-known preacher in colonial America. The Edwards family included no criminals, but more than one President of the United States, together with high-ranking justices, writers and religious leaders. Comparison with the Dukes was supposed to show the difference in genetic inclinations to criminality (Estabrook, 1916). As a demonstration of its case, however, the research was less than convincing, because Jonathan Edwards's *forebears* included people who had been convicted of crimes! If criminality were indeed an inherited trait, some of his descendants therefore should have been criminals too. Studies of family histories demonstrate virtually nothing about the influence of heredity, because it is impossible to disentangle inherited and environmental influences. The conditions under which children in the Edwards family were raised contrasted with those of the Dukes, who grew up among thieves. No one can say from this type of evidence where the causal influences lie.

The idea of a connection between biological make-up and criminality was revived in the work of William A. Sheldon in the 1940s. Sheldon distinguished three main types of human physique, claiming one to be directly associated with delinquency. Muscular, active types (*mesomorphs*), he proposed, are more likely to become delinquent than those of thin physique (*ectomorphs*), or more fleshy people (*endomorphs*). Subsequent studies carried out by other researchers claimed rather similar findings (Sheldon et al., 1949; Glueck and Glueck, 1956). However, while views of this sort still have their advocates, such research has been widely criticized. Even if there were an overall relationship between bodily type and delinquency, this would show nothing about the influence of heredity. People of the muscular type of physique Sheldon associated with delinquency may be drawn towards gang activities because these offer opportunities for the physical display of athleticism. Moreover, nearly all studies in this field have been restricted to delinquents in borstals. If there is any link with body build, it may be that the tougher, athletic-looking delinquents are more liable to be 'put away' than fragile-looking, skinny ones.

More recently, some researchers have tried to link criminal tendencies to a particular set of chromosomes in genetic inheritance (Cowen, 1979). It has been claimed that criminals, particularly those guilty of violent crimes, include a disproportionately high number of men who had an extra Y chromosome. Some studies in maximum security prisons indicated that one in a hundred of the male inmates have the abnormality, compared to one in a thousand men in the population as a whole. Subsequent research along these lines, however, proved inconclusive and contradictory. Observers soon realized that the inconsistent findings resulted from the small size of the samples being investigated. Research with a large representative population indicated that XYY men are not more likely to be involved in violent crime than are XY males (Mednick et al., 1982).

It remains possible that biological factors may have some remote influence upon certain types of crime. For instance, some individuals might have a genetic make-up that inclines them towards irritability and aggressiveness. This could be reflected, in some contexts, in crimes of physical assault on others (Delgard and Kringlen, 1976, pp. 71–4). Yet there is no decisive evidence that any traits of personality are inherited in this way, and even if they were, their connection to criminality would at most be only a distant one.

Crime and psychopathic personality: the psychological view

Like biological interpretations, psychological theories of crime associate criminality with particular types of personality. Freud's ideas have had some influence on psychological interpretations of crime, although Freud himself wrote little or nothing in the field of criminology. Later authors have drawn upon his ideas, however, to suggest that, in a minority of individuals, an 'amoral' or *psychopathic* personality develops. According to Freud, much of our sense of morality derives from the self-restraints we learn as young children during the Oedipal phase of development (explained in chapter 3). Because of the nature of their relationships with their parents, some children never come to develop these restraints, and therefore lack an underlying sense of morality. **Psychopaths** are said to be withdrawn, 'emotionless' characters, who delight in violence for its own sake.

Individuals who have psychopathic traits do sometimes commit violent crimes (Taylor, 1982), but there are major problems with the concept of psychopathy. It is not at all clear that the notion is valuable at all, let alone whether the traits involved are inevitably criminal. Nearly all studies of individuals said to possess psychopathic characteristics have been of convicted prisoners, and these characteristics almost inevitably tend to be presented in a negative way. If we describe the traits supposedly involved positively, the personality type sounds quite different, and there seems no particular reason why people of this sort should be inherently criminal. Should we be looking for non-institutionalized psychopathic individuals for a research study, we might place the following ad:

ARE YOU ADVENTUROUS?
Researcher wishes to contact adventurous, carefree people who've led exciting impulsive lives. If you're the kind of person who'd do almost anything for a dare, call 337-XXXX any time.

(Widom and Newman, 1985, p. 58)

Such people might be explorers, heroes, gamblers or just those who get bored with the routines of day-to-day life. They might be prepared to contemplate criminal adventures, but would seem just as likely to look for challenges in socially respectable avenues.

Whether derived from Freud or from other perspectives in psychology, psychological theories of criminality can at best only explain aspects of crime. While a small minority of criminals may have personality characteristics distinct from the remainder of the population, it is highly unlikely that the majority do so. There are many different types of crime, and it is implausible to suppose that those who commit them share some specific psychological characteristics.

Even if we confine ourselves to one distinct category of crime, such as crimes of violence, many different circumstances are involved. Some such crimes are carried out by lone individuals, while others involve organized groups. It is not likely that the psychological make-up of those who are 'loners' will have much in common with the members of a close-knit gang. If consistent differences could be linked to forms of criminality, we still could not be sure which way the line of causality would run. It might easily be that becoming involved with groups in which criminal activity is common influences the attitudes and outlooks of individuals, rather than these actually stimulating criminal behaviour in the first place.

Society and crime: sociological theories

A satisfactory account of the nature of crime must be sociological, for what crime is depends upon the social institutions of a society. One of the most important aspects of sociological thinking about crime is an emphasis on the interconnections between conformity and deviance in different social contexts. Modern societies contain many different sub-cultures, and behaviour that conforms to the norms of a particular sub-cultural setting may be regarded as deviant outside it. For instance, there may be strong pressure upon a member of a boy's gang to 'prove himself' by stealing a car. Moreover, there are wide divergencies of wealth and power in society, which greatly influence opportunities open to different groups. Crimes like theft and burglary, not surprisingly, are carried out mainly by people from the poorer segments of the population. Other crimes, like embezzling or tax-evasion, are by definition limited to persons in positions of some affluence (Box, 1983, chapter 2).

Differential association

Edwin H. Sutherland (a member of the 'Chicago School' of American sociology, called thus because of their association with the University of Chicago), linked crime to what he called **differential association** (Sutherland, 1949). The idea of a differential association is a very simple one. In a society which contains many different sub-cultures, some social environments tend to encourage illegal activities, whereas others do not. Individuals become delinquent or criminal through associating with others who are the carriers of *criminal norms*. For the most part, according to Sutherland, criminal behaviour is learned within primary groups, particularly peer groups. This theory is very different from the view that there are some psychological differences which separate criminals from other people. It sees criminal activities as learned in much the same way as law-abiding ones, and in general directed towards the same needs and values. Thieves try to make money in much the same way as people in orthodox jobs, but they choose illegal modes of doing so. (For a review see Gibbons, 1979, chapter 3.)

Anomie as a cause of crime

Robert K. Merton's interpretation of crime, which links criminality to other types of deviant behaviour, similarly emphasizes the normality of the criminal (Merton, 1957). Merton drew upon the concept of **anomie** – first introduced by Emile Durkheim (1858–1917), one of the founders of sociology – to develop a highly influential theory of deviance. Durkheim developed the notion of anomie to refer to the thesis that in modern societies traditional norms and standards become undermined, without being replaced by new ones. Anomie exists when there are no clear standards to guide behaviour in a given area of social life. In these circumstances, Durkheim believed, people feel disoriented and anxious; anomie is therefore one of the social factors influencing dispositions to suicide.

Merton modified the concept of anomie to refer to the strain put on individuals' behaviour when accepted norms conflict with social reality. In American society – and to some degree in all modern Western societies – generally held values emphasize 'getting ahead', 'making money', etc: material success. The means of achieving these are supposed to be self-discipline and hard work. According to these beliefs, people who really work hard can succeed, no matter what their starting-point in life. This is not in fact valid because most of the disadvantaged have very limited opportunities for advancement.

Yet those who do not 'succeed' find themselves condemned for their apparent inability to make material progress. In this situation, there is great pressure to try to 'get on' by any means, legitimate or illegitimate.

Merton identifies five possible reactions to the tensions between socially endorsed values and the limited means of achieving them. *Conformists* accept both generally held values and the conventional means of trying to realize them, no matter whether or not they meet with success. The majority of the population falls into this category. *Innovators* are those who continue to accept socially approved values, but use illegitimate or illegal means to try to follow them. Criminals concerned to acquire wealth through illegal activities exemplify this type of response.

Ritualism characterizes those who go on conforming to socially accepted standards although they have lost sight of the values that originally prompted their activity. The rules are followed for their own sake, without a wider end in view, in a compulsive way. A ritualist would be someone who dedicates himself or herself to a boring job, even though it has no career prospects and provides few rewards. *Retreatists* are people who have abandoned the competitive outlook altogether, thus rejecting both the dominant values and the approved means of achieving them. An example would be the members of a self-supporting commune. Finally, *rebellion* is the reaction of individuals who reject both the existing values and the normative means, but wish actively to substitute new ones and reconstruct the social system. The members of radical political groups fall into this category.

Anomie and association: delinquent sub-cultures

Merton wrote rather little about criminal activity as such. He also provided few suggestions as to why some reactions to anomie are chosen over others. These gaps were filled by later researchers, who linked Sutherland's idea of differential association (the idea that the group of people with whom individuals associate influences them for or against crime) to Merton's definitions. Richard A. Cloward and Lloyd E. Ohlin studied delinquent boys' **gangs** (Cloward and Ohlin, 1960). They argued that such gangs arise in sub-cultural communities where the chances of achieving success legitimately are small – such as communities of deprived ethnic minorities. The members of the gangs accept some aspects of the desirability of material success, but these values are filtered through local community sub-cultures. In neighbourhoods where established criminal networks exist, gang sub-cultures help lead individuals from petty acts of theft into an adult life of crime. In areas where such networks are not found, gang delinquency tends to take the form of fighting and vandalism, as there is little opportunity for gang members to become part of criminal networks. Those who cannot cope either with the legitimate social order or the gang sub-cultures tend to withdraw into the retreatism of drug addiction.

Cloward and Ohlin's work has close parallels with a somewhat earlier study of delinquent sub-cultures by Albert Cohen (1955). Cohen identified 'delinquency neighbourhoods' in the larger American cities, within which gang culture has become a way of life. According to him, rather than being interested in material gain, gang members tend to steal for much the same reasons as they might engage in fighting and vandalism. All these activities express a rejection of 'respectable' society. Recognizing their deprived position within the social order, the gangs create oppositional values of their own.

Evaluation

The studies of Cloward and Ohlin, and Cohen, are important because they emphasize connections between conformity and deviance – lack of opportunity for success in the terms of the dominant society being the main differentiating factor between those who engage in criminal behaviour and those who do not. Yet there is in fact little evidence to support the thesis that people in poorer communities accept the same level of aspiration to 'success' as those in more affluent social settings. On the contrary, most tend to adjust their aspirations to what they see as the reality of their situation. It is also mistaken to suppose that discrepancies between aspirations and opportunities are confined to the less privileged. It might be suggested that there are pressures towards criminal activity – and perhaps some of the other types of deviance suggested by Merton – whenever there is a major gap between aspirations and opportunities. Such a gap may be relevant, for example, to the so-called 'white-collar' crimes of embezzlement, fraud or tax-evasion.

Labelling theory

One of the most important approaches to the understanding of criminality has come to be called **labelling theory** – although this term itself is a label for a cluster of related ideas, rather than a unified approach. Labelling theorists interpret deviance not as a set of characteristics of individuals or groups, but as a *process* of interaction between deviants and non-deviants. In their view, we have to see why some people become tagged with a deviant label in order to understand the nature of deviance itself. Those who represent the forces of law and order, or are able to impose definitions of conventional morality upon others, provide the main sources of labelling. The labels applied to create categories of deviance thus express the power structure of society. By and large, the rules in terms of which deviance is defined, and the contexts in which they are applied, are framed by the wealthy for the poor, by men for women, by older people for younger people and by ethnic majorities for minority groups. For example, many children engage in activities such as climbing into other people's gardens, breaking windows, stealing fruit or playing truant. In an affluent neighbourhood, these might be regarded by parents, teachers and police alike as relatively innocent aspects of the process of growing up. In poor areas, on the other hand, they might be seen as evidence of tendencies towards juvenile delinquency.

Once a child is labelled as a delinquent, he or she is stigmatized as a criminal and is likely to be considered (and treated as) untrustworthy by teachers and prospective employers. The individual then relapses into further criminal behaviour, widening the gulf with orthodox social conventions. Edwin Lemert (1972) calls the initial act of transgression *primary deviation*. *Secondary deviation* occurs when the individual comes to accept the label that has been given, seeing himself or herself as deviant.

Take, for example, a boy who smashes a shop window while spending a Saturday night out on the town with his friends. The act may perhaps be defined as the accidental result of over-boisterous behaviour, an excusable characteristic of young men. The youth might escape with a reprimand and a small fine. If he is from a 'respectable' background, this is a likely result. The smashing of the window stays at the level of primary deviance if the youth is seen as someone of 'good character' who on this occasion became too rowdy. If, on the other hand, the police and courts have a more punitive reaction, perhaps handing out a suspended sentence and making the boy report to a social worker, the incident could become the first step in a process of secondary deviance. The process of 'learning to be deviant' tends to be accentuated by the very organizations supposedly set up to correct deviant behaviour – borstals, prisons and asylums.

Labelling theory is important because it begins from the assumption that no act is intrinsically criminal. Definitions of criminality are established by the powerful, through the formulation of laws and their interpretation by police, courts and correctional institutions. Critics of labelling theory have sometimes argued that there are in fact a number of acts consistently prohibited across all, or virtually all, cultures, such as murder, rape and robbery (Wellford, 1975). This view is surely incorrect: even within our own culture, killing is not always regarded as murder. In times of war, killing of the enemy is positively approved, and until recently British law did not recognize sexual intercourse forced on a woman by her husband as rape.

We can more convincingly criticize labelling theory on three main grounds. First, in emphasizing the active process of labelling, the processes that *lead* to acts defined as deviant tend to get lost (Fine, 1977). Labelling is clearly not completely arbitrary; differences in socialization, attitudes and opportunities influence how far people engage in behaviour particularly susceptible to being labelled as deviant.

Second, it is still not clear whether or not labelling actually does have the effect of increasing deviant conduct. Delinquent behaviour does tend to increase following conviction, but is this the result of the labelling itself? It is very difficult to judge, since many other factors, such as increased interaction with other delinquents, or learning of new criminal opportunities, may be involved (Farrington, Ohlin and Wilson, 1986, pp. 115–19).

Third, we have to investigate the overall development of modern systems of law, judiciary and police if we are to understand how and why different types of labels come to be applied. As was emphasized above, there has to be a historical dimension to the understanding of deviance. Thus William Nelson investigated changes in criminal law and procedure in Massachusetts from 1760 to 1830. (The system of law and punishment developing at that period did much to structure the later development of the legal system throughout the United States.) From a study of court records, Nelson showed that major changes occurred. Before the American Revolution, in 1776, juries were able to interpret laws as well as decide about particular cases. The property laws of the time discouraged financial speculation and the acquisition of wealth, but after the Revolution, when interest began to shift towards economic expansion, laws were changed to increase the protection of private property. The aggressive acquisition of land and property became 'legal', while crimes against property, including particularly petty theft, became subject to general sanctions (Nelson, 1975).

Rational choice and 'situational' interpretations of crime

None of the theories mentioned so far – which have dominated sociological studies of deviance – finds much place for understanding criminal behaviour as a deliberate and calculated act. Each tends to see criminality as 'reaction' rather than 'action' – as the result of outside influences, rather than as conduct in which individuals actively engage in order to get definite benefits, or because they see a temporary situation of which they can take advantage. Differential association emphasizes interaction with others; anomie theory, the pressure that membership of an achieving society places upon individuals; labelling theory, the effects that external agencies have in categorizing conduct that otherwise might be regarded as innocent. But people who engage in criminal acts, whether regularly or more sporadically, do so in a purposeful way, usually recognizing the risks they are running.

In recent years, there has been an attempt to apply a *rational-choice interpretation* to the analysis of criminal acts (Cornish and Clarke, 1986). This presumes that people do not just get pushed into criminal activities, but actively *choose* to engage in them. They simply think the risk worth taking. People who have a 'criminal mentality' are those who see advantages to be gained from situations in which they break the law, in awareness of the risk of being caught. Research indicates that many criminal actions, particularly in more minor types of crime – like non-violent theft or burglary – are 'situational' decisions. An opportunity presents itself, and seems too good to pass up – as when someone sees that a house is empty, tries the back door and finds that it is easy to get in. There are few 'specialists' in crime; most thieves are 'generalists', supplementing their other sources of income by sporadically taking part in acts of theft or burglary when opportunities to do so crop up (Walsh, 1986).

Floyd Feeney studied a sample of male Californian robbers, some convicted of crimes of robbery with violence (Feeney, 1986). He found that over half said they had not planned in advance the crime or crimes for which they were convicted. Another third reported only minor planning, such as finding a partner, thinking about where to leave a getaway car, or whether to use a weapon. Such planning usually took place the same day as the robbery, often within a few hours of it. Of the 15 per cent who had used a carefully planned approach 9 per cent simply followed a pattern they had established before. Over 60 per cent said that before the robbery they had not even thought of being caught. The belief was perhaps well founded: the sample included one person who had committed over 1,000 robberies by the age of twenty-six, only being convicted once.

The fact that many property crimes are 'situational' emphasizes how similar much criminal activity is to day-to-day decisions of a non-deviant kind. Given that an individual is prepared to consider engaging in criminal activities (a state of mind which some of the other theories might assist in explaining), many criminal acts involve quite ordinary decision-making processes. The decision to take something from a shop when no one is looking is not so different from deciding to buy a particular product which catches the eye – in fact, a person might do both during the same shopping expedition.

Theoretical conclusions

What, then, should we conclude from this survey of the many theories of crime that exist? We must first of all reiterate the point made earlier. Even though 'crime' is only one sub-category of deviant behaviour as a whole, it covers such a variety of forms of activity – from taking a bar of chocolate without paying to mass murder – that it is unlikely that we could produce a single theory which would account for all forms of criminal conduct. Each of the theoretical standpoints we have looked at has a contribution to make to understanding either some aspects or some types of crime. Biological and psychological approaches can serve to identify some of the personality characteristics which – given particular contexts of social learning and experience – predispose certain individuals to contemplate criminal acts. For example, individuals with traits usually termed 'psychopathic' may be more heavily represented among some categories of violent criminal than among the general population. On the other hand, they are probably also over-represented among those recognized as having carried out acts of extreme heroism, or involving themselves in other risk-taking activities.

The general contributions of the sociological theories of crime are twofold. First, these theories correctly emphasize the continuities between criminal and 'respectable' behaviour. The contexts in which particular types of activity are seen as 'criminal', and punishable in law, are widely variable. Second, all agree that there is a strong *contextual* element in the occurrence of criminal activities. Whether someone engages in a criminal act, or comes to be regarded as 'a criminal', is influenced in a fundamental way by social learning, and by the social locations in which individuals find themselves.

In spite of its deficiencies, labelling theory is perhaps the most widely useful approach to understanding aspects of crime and deviant behaviour. When integrated with a historical perspective, labelling theory sensitizes us to the conditions in which some types of activity come to be defined as punishable in law, and the relations of power involved in the forming of such definitions, as well as the circumstances in which particular individuals 'fall foul of the law'. Situational interpretations of crime can be quite easily connected to the labelling approach, because they clarify one feature of criminality about which labelling theory is silent – why many people who are in no obvious way 'abnormal' choose to engage in acts which they know could be followed by legal sanctions.

We now turn to an examination of the levels and character of criminal activities occurring in modern societies, giving particular attention to crime in the United Kingdom.

Crime and criminal statistics

How much crime actually exists, and what are the most common forms of criminal offence? To answer these questions, we can begin by looking at the official crime statistics. Since such statistics are regularly published, there would seem to be no difficulty in assessing crime rates, but this assumption is quite erroneous. Statistics about crime and delinquency are probably the least reliable of all officially published figures on social issues.

The most basic limitation of official crime statistics is that they only include crimes actually recorded by the police. There is a long chain of problematic decisions between a possible crime and its registration by the police. The majority of crimes, especially petty thefts, are never reported to the police at all. People vary in their ability to recognize crimes and their willingness to report them. Of the crimes that do come to the notice of the police, a proportion are not recorded in the statistics; for instance, the police may be sceptical of the validity of some information about purported crimes that comes their way. Surveys estimate that at least half of all serious crimes, including forcible rape, robbery and aggravated assault (assault with the purpose of inflicting severe injury) are not reported to the police.

Table 1   Notifiable offences in England and Wales recorded by the police by offence group, 1963–1983

| Offence group | Number of offences (thousands) | | | | | % increase 1963–83 |
	1963	1968	1973	1978	1983	
Violence against the person	20.1	31.8	61.3	87.1	111.3	454
Sexual offences	20.5	23.4	25.7	22.4	20.4	−0.5
Burglary	219.1	287.1	393.2	565.7	813.4	271
Robbery	2.5	4.8	7.3	13.1	22.1	784
Theft and handling stolen goods	653.4	853.1	998.9	1441.3	1705.9	161
Fraud and forgery	54.4	74.5	110.7	122.2	121.8	124
Criminal damage	6.9	12.2	52.8	306.2	443.3	6325
Other notifiable offences	1.1	2.1	7.8	3.5	8.7	691
Total	978.1	1289.1	1657.7	2561.5	3247.0	232

Source: A. K. Bottomley and K. Pease, *Crime and Punishment: Interpreting the Data* (Milton Keynes: Open University Press, 1986), p. 5.

The Bureau of the Census in the United States has been interviewing people in a random sample of 60,000 households since 1973, to see how many were victims of particular crimes during the preceding six months. This research, which is called the National Crime Survey, has confirmed that much serious crime goes unreported. Reporting is highest for commercial robbery (86 per cent) and lowest for household thefts of under $50 (15 per cent). Until the 1982 and 1984 British Crime Surveys (BCS) there was no official estimate of unrecorded crime in the United Kingdom. The patterns of unreported crime in Britain, as disclosed by the BCS, closely mirror the American findings (Bottomley and Pease, 1986).

To find the true rates of crime we cannot simply add unreported crimes to the official police rate, as practices of local police forces in reporting crime vary. Some report fewer crimes than others, either because of inefficiency or because their arrest record thereby looks better. Studies have shown, for example, that rapid increases in crime shown officially in some large cities in the United States in the 1960s were probably in a large degree the result of changes in reporting practices. Citizens themselves may alter their reporting habits, as attitudes or values change. For instance, rapes are more likely to be reported when women perceive a more sympathetic framework of response developing from police and courts.

Between 1971 and 1980 in the United States the number of officially reported serious crimes rose by 42 per cent. Although this increase gave rise to much public alarm, the real trend was in all probability much less pronounced. Serious crimes, as documented by the National Crime Survey, did not alter greatly over the period, showing only a slight increase, although apparently a consistent one (Rutter and

Giller, 1983, chapter 3). Murder and negligent manslaughter rates rose by 11 per cent between 1977 and 1981. This is likely to represent a real increase, although not necessarily of this exact figure.

Similar findings have come from the United Kingdom. In Britain, the government conducts a regular General Household Survey, sampling households nationally. The survey included a question about burglary in 1972, 1973, 1979 and 1980. Households were asked to mention any burglaries occurring in the twelve months preceding the interview. The 1981 survey concluded that there had been almost no change in the incidence of burglaries between 1972 and 1980, yet over this period the official British crime statistics, based upon crimes reported to the police, showed an increase of 50 per cent (Bottomley and Pease, 1986, pp. 22–3; see also table 1). The apparent rise probably stemmed from increasing public awareness of crime which led to more reporting, plus more effective modes of data collection by the police.

'Victim surveys', like the National Crime Survey, have difficulties of their own. People are more prone to report some crimes to interviewers than to the police, but the reverse may be the case with other criminal activities. A woman may notify the police when assaulted by her husband, but talking to an interviewer several months afterwards might not mention the incident, particularly if the husband is present during the interview. One research study, carried out in San José, California, looked at cases of people who had reported assaults to the police, and who were later interviewed in the National Crime Survey. Only 48 per cent admitted to the assaults in the later interview, the proportion being lowest among those who had reported to the police that the assailant was a relative (Turner, 1981).

Homicide and other violent crime

Homicide

Rates of homicide (murder) are probably the most accurate of crime statistics. Yet even here there are problems. For a death to be classified as a murder it has to be known to have occurred. This usually means a body has to be found; few deaths where a body remains undiscovered are categorized as homicide. Given that a body is located, murder will only be suspected given circumstances which indicate that the death was 'non-natural' – such as severe bruising or lacerations of the skull. Once a case is brought against someone, it may be decided that the accused was guilty of manslaughter (intent to harm, but not kill), rather than murder (figure 5).

Public health statistics, based on coroners' reports, provide a way of measuring the homicide rate that is more or less independent of police reports. These reports are not entirely accurate, since coroners may mistakenly call a homicide an accident, or misinterpret a homicide

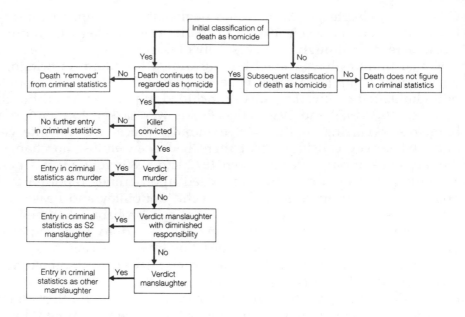

Figure 5   The various ways in which a homicide may be recorded (or not recorded) in criminal statistics
Source: A. K. Bottomley and K. Pease, *Crime and Punishment: Interpreting the Data* (Milton Keynes: Open University Press, 1986), p. 9.

as a suicide. However, such statistics are generally quite close to rates of homicide in police reports, suggesting that these might be in fact fairly accurate.

Violent crime

Nobody disputes one phenomenon disclosed by the crime statistics – the exceptionally high level of violent crime that occurs in the United States as compared to other industrialized countries, including Britain. There are more reported murders each year in Detroit, with a population of just over 1,500,000, than in the whole of the United Kingdom, which has a population of 55,000,000 people. Viewed in comparative context, the United States is a culture in which crimes of violence flourish. Why should this be?

The answer is sometimes given as the widespread availability of handguns and other firearms. This is surely relevant, but cannot on its own be the full answer, as Switzerland has very low rates of violent crime, yet firearms are easily accessible. All males are members of the citizen army and keep weapons in their homes, including rifles, revolvers and sometimes other automatic weapons, plus ammunition. Nor are gun licences difficult to obtain (Clinard, 1978, pp. 114–15). The most likely explanation for the high level of violent crime in the United States is a combination of the availability of firearms, the general influence of the 'frontier tradition' and the existence of sub-cultures of violence in the large cities. Violence on the part of frontiersmen and vigilantes is an honoured part of American history. Some of the first established immigrant areas in the cities developed their own informal modes of neighbourhood social control, backed by violence or threat of violence. Young people in black and Hispanic communities have similarly developed sub-cultures of manliness and honour associated with rituals of violence.

Violence in American society – or in Britain – has absolutely nothing to do with the biological characteristics which separate blacks from whites. Studies demonstrate that homicide rates in African communities are generally extremely low compared to rates for American blacks. Research by Marvin Wolfgang in Philadelphia showed blacks to have an annual rate of 24.6 homicides per 100,000 population between 1948 and 1952. African groups studied at the same period by Paul Bohannan had annual rates of homicide of less than 12 per 1,000,000 population – among the lowest in the world (Wolfgang, 1958; Bohannan, 1960).

It is important to note the relatively mundane character of crimes of violence. Most assaults and homicides bear little resemblance to the murderous, rampaging acts of gunmen given most prominence in the media. Murders generally happen in the context of family and other interpersonal relationships. They are far more often carried out by people under the influence of alcohol than by those under the influence of narcotics – which is hardly surprising, given the prevalence of alcohol consumption (Cook, 1982).

A substantial proportion of homicides are 'victim precipitated' – the victim initiates the fatal outburst by making the first menacing gesture or striking the first blow. Many examples appear in Wolfgang's research in the United States, which initially drew attention to the phenomenon. For example: 'A victim became incensed when his eventual slayer asked for money which the victim owed him. The victim grabbed a hatchet and started in the direction of his creditor, who pulled out a knife and stabbed him' (Wolfgang, 1958, p. 253; see also Campbell and Gibbs, 1986).

A particular form of violent crime, rape, is discussed on pp. 181–6.

Prisons and punishment

For a long time, as was mentioned earlier, prison sentencing has been associated with the aim of correcting criminal behaviour – with the rehabilitation of criminals to become law-abiding citizens. Imprisonment is a mode of punishing wrong-doers, and of protecting citizens from them. But the underlying principle of the prison system is that of 'improving' the individual to play a fit and proper part in society. Do prisons have this effect on those interned in them for specific periods of time? The evidence strongly suggests that they do not.

Prisoners are no longer generally physically maltreated, as was once common practice – although physical beatings are by no means unknown, even in women's prisons (as will be shown below). However, prisoners suffer many other types of deprivation. Not only are they deprived of their freedom, but of a proper income, the company of their families and previous friends, heterosexual relationships, their own clothing and other personal items. They frequently live in over-crowded conditions, and have to accept strict disciplinary procedures and the regimentation of their daily lives.

Living in these conditions tends to drive a wedge between prison inmates and the outside society, rather than adjusting their behaviour to the norms of that society. Prisoners have to come to terms with an environment quite distinct from 'the outside', and the habits and attitudes they learn in prison are quite often exactly the opposite of those they are supposed to acquire. For instance, they may develop a grudge against the ordinary citizenry, learn to accept violence as normal, acquire contacts with seasoned criminals which they maintain when freed, and acquire criminal skills about which they previously knew little. It is therefore not surprising that rates of *recidivism* – repeat offending by those who have been in borstal or prison before – are disturbingly high. Over 60 per cent of all men set free after serving prison sentences are rearrested within four years of their original crimes. The actual rate of reoffending is presumably higher than this, as no doubt some of those returning to criminal activities are not caught.

Although prisons do not seem to succeed in rehabilitating prisoners, however, it is possible that they deter people from carrying out crimes. While those who are actually imprisoned are not deterred, the unpleasant qualities of prison life might well deter others. There is an almost intractable problem here for prison reformers. Making prisons thoroughly unpleasant places to be in probably helps deter potential offenders; but it makes the rehabilitating goals of prisons extremely difficult to achieve. The less harsh prison conditions are, the more imprisonment loses its deterrent effect.

At any one time, many more people who have been convicted of crimes are on probation or parole than in prison. Probation is widely used as a mode of dealing with relatively minor crimes. A person who is put on probation has to hold down a job and commit no further offences within a specified period. At the end of that period the case is closed. Parole is a reduction in the length of a sentence, given to reward 'good behaviour' while an individual is in prison. When a prisoner comes before a parole board, after serving a certain period of the sentence, the board may grant the parole, refuse parole but set a future date for another hearing, or decide that the prisoner must serve the full sentence. Most parole boards recognize the limited rehabilitative effects of prisons, and in practice parole decisions are taken mainly on the basis of an assessment of the seriousness of the crime in relation to the severity of the sentence.

The death penalty

Ever since prison sentencing became the main form of criminal punishment, the death penalty has been increasingly controversial. Given that prisons are supposed to rehabilitate, executing people for crimes has seemed to most reformers illogical as well as barbaric. For clearly to put someone to death is to recognize that altering their behaviour is impossible.

As was mentioned before, the United States is almost the only Western country in which the death penalty is still applied. The death penalty was in fact abolished by the Supreme Court in 1972, but reinstated in 1976. Executions were resumed in some states in 1977, although they remain relatively few in number. The number of people sentenced to death each year is growing, but so far appeals and other factors have limited the proportion of those actually executed.

In various other countries there is public pressure to bring back the death penalty, at least for certain types of crime (like terrorism, or the murdering of a policeman). In Britain, opinion polls consistently show that a majority of the population would like the death penalty reinstated. Many members of the public apparently believe that the threat of execution deters potential murderers, but although the arguments continue, there is little or no evidence to support the idea. Countries which have abolished the death penalty do not have notably higher homicide rates than before. Although the United States retains the death penalty, American rates of homicide are easily the highest in the industrialized world.

Of course, the strength of public feeling on this issue may reflect attitudes about punishment, rather than the idea that the death penalty is a deterrent. People may feel that someone who takes another person's life should be punished in kind. The alternative view is that it is morally wrong for a society to put its citizens to death, whatever their crime. This second view, together with the lack of a deterrent effect, is what has swayed most legislators.

Gender and crime

As in other areas of sociology, criminological studies have traditionally ignored half the population (Morris, 1987). Many textbooks in criminology still include virtually nothing about women, save for sections on rape and prostitution, and most theories of deviance similarly disregard women almost completely. An example is Merton's account of social structure and anomie. The 'pressure to succeed' is supposed to reach virtually everyone in modern societies. Logically, therefore, one could argue that women should figure more prominently in the various categories of deviance identified by Merton than men, including crime, as there are fewer opportunities open for women 'to get on' than for men. Yet rates of criminality of women are – or seem to be – exceptionally low. Even if women are for some reason less prone to participate in deviant activities than men, this is hardly any reason to omit them from consideration.

Male and female crime rates

The statistics on gender* and crime are startling. For example, there is an enormous imbalance in the ratio of men and women in prison, not only in Britain but in all the industrialized countries. Women only make up some 3 per cent of the British prison population. There are also contrasts between the types of crime men and women commit, at least as indicated in the official statistics. The offences of women rarely involve violence, and are almost all small-scale. Petty thefts, like shop-lifting, and public order offences such as public drunkenness and prostitution, are typical female crimes (Gillen, 1978; Flowers, 1987).

Of course, it may be that the real gender difference in crime rates is less than the official statistics show. Police and other officials might perhaps regard female offenders as less dangerous than men, for example, letting pass activities for which males would be arrested. Victimization surveys provide a means of checking upon such a possibility. In one study in the United States, the National Crime Survey materials of 1976 were compared with FBI statistics to see whether there was any divergence in terms of proportions of women involved in criminal activities (Hindelang, 1978). Little variation was found in respect of serious crimes committed by women, the FBI statistics actually showing somewhat *higher* proportions than the survey reports. It has been argued by some observers that the proportion of women involved in 'male' crimes, such as armed robbery, is likely to increase, but there is no clear-cut evidence of such a trend (Dobash et al., 1986).

'Lost letters' experiments have provided one source of information about gender, opportunity and crime (Farrington and Kidd, 1980). In these experiments, letters enclosing money were dropped in public places. Various conditions were altered in differing versions – the amount of money involved, whether it was in cash or another form (like a money order) and the apparent loser (an old lady or an

*In comparing the behaviour of men and women, sociologists often prefer to use the term 'gender' rather than 'sex'. 'Sex' refers to the biological/anatomical differences between women and men; 'gender' to the psychological/social/cultural differences between them – differences between masculinity and femininity (see chapter 6: 'Gender and Sexuality').

affluent man). The characteristics of the individuals who picked up the letters were observed and the researchers could tell from a particular code number whether a letter was posted or kept.

Stealing the money was most common when the apparent victim was an affluent man and cash was involved, but females were as likely to steal as males – except where larger sums of money were concerned. About half of the men observed stole in this situation, compared to less than a quarter of the women. It seems possible that pocketing a small amount of cash is not seen as 'stealing', while taking a large amount is – and that men are more prepared to profit in this way.

The only crime for which the female rate of conviction approximates to that of men is shop-lifting. Some have argued that this indicates that women will engage in criminal activities where they find themselves in a 'public' context – out shopping – rather than a domestic one. In other words, where the opportunity to commit crime is more or less equal between men and women, they are equally likely to commit offences. There have been few investigations comparing female and male rates of shop-lifting, but a relatively recent study found that men are proportionately twice as likely to shop-lift as women (Buckle and Farrington, 1984).

The girls in the gang

There has been little work on female members of youth gangs, or on female gangs where these exist. Numerous accounts of male street-corner groups and male gangs have been written, but in these studies women appear only fleetingly. Anne Campbell, however, has studied girls in New York street gangs (Campbell, 1986a). She selected three gangs for intensive study: one was ethnically mixed, one Puerto Rican, the other black. The members' ages ranged from fifteen to thirty. Campbell spent six months living with each gang, focusing especially upon the gang leaders.

Connie was the leader of the Sandman Ladies, a female group associated with the Sandman Bikers, a gang headed by her husband. She was thirty at the time of the research (1979), and led a mixed Hispanic and black gang in Harlem, New York. The major source of income of the Sandman Bikers was drug-dealing. The group was involved in a long-standing feud with the Chosen Ones, a gang from uptown Manhattan. Those who joined the Sandman Ladies had to prove their fighting capabilities; entry was decided by Connie, who made an initial judgement about whether a girl could 'hang around' for a trial period, and whether she later got her 'patches' (insignia). Connie always carried a flick-knife, and also possessed a gun. She said that when she fought, it was to kill. Fighting involving physical brawls was just as constant a preoccupation of the female as of the male group.

Weeza and the Sex Girls were a Hispanic gang, having a male and female section. Weeza could not read or write, and was unsure of her true age – which was probably twenty-six. At the gang's height, there were more than fifty female members. The women cultivated a reputation for physical toughness; fighting and beatings were commonplace. The male members of the gang admired the women for this, while still encouraging traditional roles in other respects, such as caring for children, cooking and sewing.

The third group studied were the Five Percent Nation, which was a black religious organization. They believe that 10 per cent of the population exploits 85 per cent of the remainder, the other 5 per cent are enlightened believers in Islam, who have the duty of educating blacks. The police regarded the Five Percent Nation as a street gang. The individual on whom Campbell concentrated her attention, Sun-Africa, had rejected what she called her 'government name'. As with the other groups, she and other female members frequently engaged in fighting. Group members had been arrested for robbery, possession of dangerous weapons, burglary and car-theft.

In another study Campbell interviewed working-class schoolgirls about fighting, finding that this is an activity in which they engage more often than is commonly believed (Campbell, 1986b). Almost all those she contacted admitted to having been involved in a fight; a quarter had been in more than six fights. The majority rejected the statement 'I think fighting is only for boys.'

Prison violence among women

The autobiographical accounts collected by Pat Carlen of women prisoners in British prisons contain numerous episodes of violence, which is portrayed as a constant feature of female prison life (Carlen et al., 1985). Josie O'Dwyer, an inmate of Holloway Prison in London, described how the 'heavy mob' of female guards specialized in violent retribution towards prisoners they saw as ill-behaved. Beatings by the 'heavy mob' and by other prisoners were common:

> One particular officer always steamed in and started poking you in the chest because she wanted you to hit her – that's what she got off on, the struggling and the fighting. They carry you by the 'necklace', the key chains, and you can have three chains round your neck at any one time. You get purple bruises round your neck, a necklace of purple . . . you begin to black out and you think, "This is it, I'm going to die now" . . . I could have died. But I didn't and I was lucky. I was a survivor. (Carlen et al., 1985, p. 149)

Evaluation

The studies by Campbell and Carlen show that we must be cautious in supposing that violence is exclusively characteristic of male criminality. Women are much less likely than men to participate in violent crime, but are not always inhibited from taking part in violent episodes. Why, then, are female rates of criminality so much lower than those of men? The reasons are almost certainly the same as those which explain gender differences in other spheres (see chapter 6: 'Gender and Sexuality'). There are, of course, certain specifically 'female crimes' – most notably, prostitution – for which women are convicted while their male clients are not. 'Male crimes' remain 'male' because of differences in socialization and the fact that men's activities and involvements are still more non-domestic than those of most women. The gender difference in crime used often to be explained by supposedly innate biological or psychological differences – in terms of differential strength, passivity or preoccupation with reproduction (Smart, 1977). Nowadays 'womanly' qualities are seen as largely socially generated, in common with the traits of 'masculinity' (see chapter 6: 'Gender and Sexuality'). Many women are socialized to value different qualities in social life from those of males (caring for others and the fostering of personal relationships). Even though a high proportion of women are now in the labour-force, most spend much more of their lives in domestic settings than men do. In the domestic sphere the opportunities and motivation for most forms of criminal activity are less than in the public settings in which men more often move.

At the moment, it is difficult to say with any certainty whether female rates, and patterns, of crime will increasingly resemble those of men as gender divisions become more blurred than once they were. Ever since the late nineteenth century criminologists have predicted that gender equalization would reduce or eliminate the differences in criminality between men and women, but as yet these differences remain pronounced. Whether the variations in female and male crime rates will one day disappear we still cannot say with any certainty.

Crimes of the affluent and powerful

Although they make up the bulk of the prison population, engaging in criminal activities is by no means confined to the poorer sections of society. Many wealthy and powerful people carry out crimes, whose consequences can be much more far-reaching than the often petty crimes of the poor. In the following sections we shall consider some of these forms of crime.

White-collar crime

The term 'white-collar crime' was first introduced by Edwin Sutherland (Sutherland, 1949), and refers to crime carried out by those in the more affluent sectors of society. The term covers many types of criminal activity, including tax-frauds, illegal sales practices, securities and land frauds, embezzlement, the manufacture or sale of dangerous products and illegal environmental pollution, as well as straightforward theft. The distribution of white-collar crimes is even harder to measure than that of other types of crime; most such forms of crime do not appear in the official statistics at all. We can distinguish between **white-collar crime** and **crimes of the powerful**. White-collar crime mainly involves the use of a middle-class or professional position to engage in illegal activities. Crimes of the powerful are those in which the authority conferred by a position is used in criminal ways – as when an official accepts a bribe to favour a particular policy.

Efforts made to detect white-collar crime are usually fairly limited, and it is only on rare occasions that those who are caught go to gaol. A vivid example of differences in judicial attitudes to white-collar and 'orthodox' crime is provided in a case noted in the United States. A partner in a New York firm of brokers was found guilty of illegal trading in Swiss banks involving a sum of $20,000,000. He received a suspended prison sentence plus a fine of $30,000. On the day that this case was tried, the same judge handed down a judgement on an unemployed black shipping clerk who stole a television set worth $100. He was given a year's gaol sentence (Napes, 1970).

Although it is regarded by the authorities in a much more tolerant light than crimes of the less privileged, the cost of white-collar crime is enormous. Far more research has been carried out on white-collar crime in the United States than in Britain. In America, it has been calculated that the amount of money involved in white-collar crime (defined as tax-fraud, securities fraud, frauds involving drugs and medical services, home improvement frauds and car repair frauds) is forty times as great as that in ordinary crimes against property (robberies, burglaries, larceny, forgeries and car thefts) (President's Commission on Organized Crime, 1985). Some forms of white-collar crime, moreover, affect much larger numbers of people than lower-class criminality. An embezzler might rob thousands – or today, via computer fraud, millions – of people, and tainted foods or drugs sold illegally can affect the health of many, and might lead to fatalities.

Violent aspects of white-collar crime are less visible than in cases of homicide or assault, but are just as real – and may on occasion be much more serious in their consequences. For example, flouting regulations concerning the preparation of new drugs, safety in the workplace, or pollution, may cause physical harm or death to large numbers of people (Hopkins, 1980; Geis and Stottland, 1980). Deaths from hazards at work far outnumber murders, although precise statistics about job accidents are difficult to obtain (Box, 1983). Of course, we cannot assume that all, or even the majority, of these deaths and injuries are the result of employer negligence about safety factors for which they are legally liable.

Nevertheless, there is some basis for supposing that many are due to the neglect of legally binding safety regulations by employers or managers.

It has been estimated that about 40 per cent of job injuries in the USA each year are the direct result of illegal working conditions, while a further 24 per cent derive from legal but unsafe conditions. No more than a third are due to unsafe acts on the parts of workers themselves (Hagen, 1988). There are many documented examples of employers knowingly introducing or maintaining hazardous practices even where these are contrary to the law. Some argue that deaths resulting from these circumstances should be called *corporate homicides*, because they effectively involve the illegal (and avoidable) taking of life on the part of business corporations.

Governmental crime

Can government authorities ever be said to engage in crime? If 'crime' is defined more broadly than it was above, to refer to moral wrongdoing which has harmful consequences, the answer is resoundingly clear. States have perpetrated many of the most dreadful crimes in history, including the wiping out of whole peoples, indiscriminate mass bombings, the Nazi holocaust and Stalin's concentration camps. However, even if we define crime in terms of the breaking of codified laws, governments not infrequently act in criminal ways. That is to say, they ignore or transgress the very laws their authority is supposed to defend. In British colonial history, this was the case, for example, when legal guarantees offered to African peoples promising protection of their land and way of life were repeatedly flouted.

The police, the government agency established to control crime, are sometimes themselves involved in criminal activities. This involvement does not just consist of isolated acts, but is a widespread feature of police work. Criminal activities of police officers include intimidating, beating up or killing suspects, accepting bribes, helping organize criminal networks, fabricating or withholding evidence, and keeping some or all of the proceeds when money, drugs or other stolen goods are recovered (Binder and Scharf, 1982).

Organized crime

Organized crime refers to forms of activity that have many of the characteristics of orthodox business, but in which the activities engaged in are illegal. Organized crime in America is a massive business, rivalling any of the major orthodox sectors of economic enterprise, such as the car industry. National and local criminal organizations provide illegal goods and services to mass consumers, and some **criminal**

networks also extend internationally. Organized crime embraces illegal gambling, prostitution, large-scale theft and protection rackets, among other activities. In Britain and the other European countries, organized crime is less prominent – and has also been studied far less.

Precise information about the nature of organized crime is obviously difficult to obtain. In romantic portrayals of gangsters, organized crime in the United States is portrayed as being controlled by a secret society of national dimensions, 'the Mafia'. The Mafia as such – like the cowboy – is in some degree a creation of American folklore. There is almost certainly no group of mysterious mobsters of Sicilian origin who sit at the top of a coherent nationwide organization. Yet it does seem that established criminal organizations exist in nearly all the major American cities, some of which have connections with one another (Bequai, 1980).

The most detailed study yet attempted into organized crime in the United States was carried out by Francis Ianni and Elizabeth Reuss-Ianni (1973). They dealt mainly with an Italian-American crime 'family' in New York City. The Iannis assert that there has never been a single unified Mafia organization in Sicily, let alone in the United States. An organization has not been exported to America, but social values involving the primacy of kin attachments, and a stress on personal honour as more important than law, have been. The Lupullos, the group studied, maintained contacts nationally and internationally, but operated largely independently of any other criminal organizations.

Organized crime in the United States is much more firmly established, pervasive and tenacious than in other industrialized societies. In France, for example, organized crime is quite prominent, but is largely limited in its influence to two major cities, Paris and Marseilles. In southern Italy, the region of the stereotypical gangster, criminal networks are very powerful, but they are linked to traditional patterns of family organization and community control within largely poor, rural areas. Organized crime has probably become so significant in American society because of an early association with – in part being modelled upon – the activities of the industrial 'robber barons' of the late nineteenth century. Many of the early industrialists made fortunes by exploiting immigrant labour, largely ignoring legal regulations on working conditions and often using a mixture of corruption and violence to build their industrial empires. Organized crime flourished in the deprived ethnic ghettos (where people were ignorant of their legal and political rights), using similar methods to curtail competition and build networks of corruption.

Illicit gambling, on horse races, lotteries and sporting events, represents the greatest source of income generated by organized crime. It has been estimated that in 1983 the total amount of money taken in illegal gambling per year was about $30 billion in the United States (President's Commission on Organized Crime, 1984 and 1985). Many Western countries, unlike the United States, have legal off-course betting; in the United Kingdom there are licensed public betting shops. While these do not escape all criminal influence, gambling is not controlled by illegal organizations to anything like the same extent as in the United States.

Although we have little systematic information on organized crime in the United Kingdom, it is known that extensive criminal networks exist in areas of London and other large cities. Some of these have international connections. London in particular is a centre for international criminal operations based in the United States and elsewhere. Discussing the investigation into a bullion robbery at Heathrow Airport in 1987, a Scotland Yard official revealed that the trail of the criminals 'led to the Isle of Man, to the Channel Islands, to the British Virgin Islands, to offshore islands of America, into Florida and Miami. It led us into other areas of organised crime, drug running, conspiracy between our criminals and Italians, French, Spanish and Americans. There were some pretty close connections' (Shawcross and Fletcher, 1987, p. 33).

Despite numerous campaigns by the government and police, the narcotics trade is one of the most rapidly expanding international criminal industries, having an annual growth rate of more than 10 per cent in the 1970s and early 1980s – and an extremely high level of profit. Heroin networks stretch across the Far East, particularly South Asia, and are located also in North Africa, the Middle East and Latin America. The major supply area for the cocaine market is Bolivia, with more than one billion dollars a year being fed into the Bolivian economy as a result of the trading. Supply lines also pass through Paris and Amsterdam, from where drugs are commonly supplied to Britain.

Victimless crime

So-called **victimless crimes** are activities in which individuals more or less freely engage without directly harming others, but which are defined as illegal (taking narcotics, various forms of gambling, or prostitution) (Schur, 1965; Geis, 1972). The term 'victimless crime' is not entirely accurate, because those, for example, who become drug addicts or gamblers, in a sense fall victim to a system of organized crime. However, since whatever harm befalls such individuals is mainly of their own doing, many argue that it is not the role of the government to intervene in such activities – and that these habits should be 'decriminalized'.

Some authors propose that no activities in which people indulge of their own free will should be illegal (so long as they do not impinge upon others' freedom or cause them harm). Opponents claim that government must have a role as moral guardian of the population subject to its administration, and that therefore it is justified to define at least some of these types of activity as criminal. Curiously, this argument is most often advocated by conservatives, who in other respects emphasize freedom of the individual from interference by the state. Of course, the issue is very complicated. Is someone doing harm to others by hurting themselves, e.g. a drug addict hurting her or his family? How far should such arguments be taken?

The concept of mental illness

The second major area of deviant behaviour with which the state is centrally connected, and which also involves the use of carceral organizations, is mental illness. The idea that the insane are mentally 'ill', as has been mentioned, dates from only around two centuries ago. Before that time, people we would now regard as mentally disordered were considered 'possessed', 'unmanageable' or 'melancholic' rather than sick.

Psychosis and neurosis

As insanity came to be seen more and more as a sickness, attempts began to be made to understand its physical origins in the body. The majority of psychiatrists today hold that at least some forms of mental illness have physical causes. They also work with standardized manuals of diagnostic criteria for identifying different types of mental disorder. Psychiatrists divide mental disorder into two main categories, the **psychotic** and the **neurotic**. Psychosis is considered the most serious type, involving a disturbed sense of reality. **Schizophrenia** is the most commonly recognized form of psychosis, and diagnosed schizophrenics make up a substantial proportion of the inmates of mental hospitals. Symptoms characterizing schizophrenia include talking in seemingly illogical or disconnected ways, hearing or seeing hallucinations, having illusions of grandeur or persecution, and being unresponsive to surrounding circumstances or events.

For the most part, neurotic disorders do not inhibit individuals from carrying on their ordinary lives. The main feature of behaviour classified in this way is a pervasive worry about matters that other people would see as fairly trivial. A person might experience extreme anxiety, for instance, when meeting strangers for the first time, or at the thought of travelling in a bus, car or plane. Symptoms of neurosis also sometimes involve *compulsive* activities, which an individual may feel driven to perform. For instance, someone might make and remake a bed thirty or forty times each morning before being satisfied enough to go on to another domestic chore (Prins, 1980).

Physical treatments

Over the past century, many different physical treatments for mental illness have been tried. Claims repeatedly have been made that a physiological basis of the major mental disorders (particularly schizophrenia) has been discovered. Yet both the physical treatment of mental illness, and the thesis that it has an identifiable biological basis, have proved problematic. Physical methods employed to treat schizophrenia include insulin shock therapy, later replaced by electro-convulsive therapy (ECT); and pre-frontal lobotomy (the surgical severing of neural connections between certain parts of the brain). In shock treatments, the patient suffers a short but intense convulsion, followed by memory loss which lasts for weeks or months. At the end of this in theory there is a return to normality. This procedure is still used – more commonly for depression than for schizophrenia today – although many have seen it as little more than a barbaric form of punishment.

Lobotomy was introduced by a Portuguese neurologist, Antonio Egas Moniz, in 1935, and for a period was used extensively in many countries. Wide-ranging claims were made for its effectiveness, but it became apparent that many patients showed a conspicuous deterioration in their intellectual capabilities and developed an apathetic personality. By the 1950s, the technique was largely discarded – although partly because of the discovery of new tranquillizing drugs. These are now very widely used for schizophrenia and other disorders. There is no doubt that the drugs 'work' to some degree – even if no one knows with any clarity why they do so – in the sense that they subdue certain of the symptoms that make it difficult for patients to live effectively in wider society. How effective they are even in this limited respect, however, remains controversial (Scull, 1984).

The diagnosis of mental illness

It would be surprising if drugs had a clear-cut effect on mental illness, because the diagnostic categories employed in psychiatry are quite unreliable. One of the most telling indications of this is to be found in D. L. Rosenhan's study of mental hospital admissions (Rosenhan, 1973). In this research, eight sane people presented themselves to the admissions units of different mental hospitals located on East and West coasts of the United States. They had falsified their employment records, disguising the fact that all had received professional psychological training; they did not change their personal biographies in any other way. They claimed to hear voices.

All were diagnosed as schizophrenic and admitted. Once in the hospitals, they at once went back to their normal behaviour. None were detected by hospital staff as fakes, although the inmates themselves correctly saw them as impostors. All the collaborators in the study regularly and openly took notes on their experiences, but the writing was simply seen by the staff as one aspect of their pathological behaviour. The length of hospitalization of these people ranged from seven to fifty-two days, and each was eventually discharged with a diagnosis of schizophrenia 'in remission'. As Rosenhan points out, the phrase 'in remission' did not mean that the normality of the pseudo-patients had been discerned, because at no time were questions raised about the legitimacy of their hospitalization.

Criticisms have been made of this study, and it is not clear that its results were quite as dramatic as has sometimes been claimed. The nursing reports on the collaborators indicated that they 'exhibited no abnormal indications' (Rosenhan, 1973, p. 3). Length of hospitalization perhaps indicates very little, since it was at that time difficult to be discharged from mental hospitals in the USA at short notice.

The characteristics used by psychiatrists in diagnosing schizophrenia clearly do not exist. A minority of people, for example, persistently hear voices when no one is present, experience hallucinations or display behaviour seemingly quite disjointed and illogical. On the other hand, Rosenhan's experiment demonstrates the vague character of psychiatric diagnosis and the influence of labelling (described earlier in this chapter). If the pseudo-patients had not been collaborators in a research investigation, but had for some other reason found themselves in mental hospitals, there is little doubt that they would have been stuck with the diagnostic label of 'schizophrenic in remission'.

The nature of madness: residual rule-breaking

Sociologists have quite often been sceptical of psychiatrists' tendency to look for a physical basis of mental disorders, and have drawn on labelling theory to interpret the nature of mental illness. Thomas Scheff has suggested that mental disorder, especially schizophrenia, can be understood in terms of **residual rule-breaking** (Scheff, 1966). *Residual norms* are 'deeply buried rules' structuring everyday life. They concern the conventions studied by Goffman and ethnomethodology (as described in chapter 4) – for example, looking at the person who is talking to you, grasping the meaning of what other people say and do, and controlling body posture and gestures. Violating these norms, Scheff suggests, is essentially what schizophrenia is.

Many or all of us are residual rule-breakers in some circumstances. A person who is deeply upset about the death of a loved one, for example, might behave quite 'unnaturally' in interaction with others. In such circumstances, behaviour of this kind is tolerated and even expected. Were an individual to start to act in this way without any apparent reason, however, the reaction of others would be quite different, and it is possible the person would be regarded as mentally ill. Once such a label has been applied, the person's subsequent experiences are likely to reinforce secondary deviance, i.e. to lead them to behave in the expected way (Smith, 1978).

Scheff's theory does not explain *why* some individuals become 'residual rule-breakers'. There may possibly be genetic factors involved; sociological studies and theories of mental illness do not refute the possibility, or even probability, that there is a biological input to some of the main types of mental disorder. (For a critique of sociological discussions of mental illness, see Roth and Kroll, 1986.)

Politics, social pressure and psychiatry

Even if it were true that the major recognized forms of mental illness have a biological foundation, it would not necessarily follow that it is desirable to keep mental patients separated from the wider community, particularly where people were placed in mental hospitals against their will. There is considerable evidence that Soviet dissidents, with no distinguishable signs of mental disorder save for their opposition to the Soviet system, have been declared mentally ill and lodged in mental hospitals. This process allows for the removal of critics of the system from public view without the need of a trial. Active political opposition is equated with lunacy, while a 'cure' is represented by retraction of whatever accusations were made against the state. The practice has been widely condemned by psychiatrists outside the Soviet Union, and is by any token an extreme case of the use of psychiatry as a means of controlling deviance.

Yet it is not as entirely distinct from psychiatric procedures in the West as might be imagined. Thomas Szasz has declared that the whole concept of mental illness is a myth, justifying persecution in the name of mental health (Szasz, 1971). Involuntary detainment in a mental hospital is essentially a form of imprisonment for deviants who have not committed any crimes in law. According to Szasz, what are seen as mental illnesses today should be more properly regarded as 'problems in living' which some individuals experience in an acute way. People currently called 'mentally ill' should be incarcerated (in prisons) only if they transgress laws, like any 'sane' member of the population. Everyone should otherwise be free to express whatever views or feelings they might have, and to live as they wish. Those who feel they need help should be able to seek psychotherapy on a contractual basis, like any other service.

Decarceration

Over the past twenty-five years, in most Western countries, there have been major changes affecting inmates of carceral organizations (Cohen, 1985). The mentally ill and the physically and mentally handicapped have been released in large numbers, with the object of replacing confinement by community care. These reforms have been prompted largely by humanitarian motives, combined to some extent with a desire to cut costs, since the expense to the state of maintaining custodial institutions is very considerable.

Decarceration has most clearly and radically affected mental health. Many liberal reformers were concerned about the effects of prolonged periods of hospitalization upon mental patients, since people kept away from the outside world came to be 'institutionalized' – only able to function within the very organizations that were supposed to care for or rehabilitate them. In addition to pressure from reformers to 'do away with the asylum walls', two other factors in the 1950s and 1960s affected the treatment of the mentally ill. One, first introduced in Britain, was the development of methods of psychiatric therapy that emphasized the need of individuals to relate to groups and communities. The second, and more important, was the marketing of new drugs which apparently provided a breakthrough in the treatment and management of mental illness, as well as forms of mental retardation and the mental disorders of old age. Between 1955 and 1974, the mental hospital population in Britain was reduced by some 30 per cent, although many of those released were old people. In California the numbers of the elderly in state and county hospitals dropped by nearly 95 per cent in only two years, between 1975 and 1977.

What have been the consequences of 'decarceration' – the return of large numbers of people into the outside community – for the mentally ill? Many mental patients in fact seem worse off than they were before. Those discharged from asylums have often found themselves living in circumstances in which others are unwilling or unable to care for them (Wallace, 1987). In many areas there is a serious lack of funds for communal care systems. Government agencies saving on the upkeep of mental hospitals are usually not prepared to devote large-scale expenditure to the creation of community services, and it is not clear to what extent people with serious and persisting mental disabilities can be treated in community medical health centres. Many of those released from mental hospitals, lacking adequate means of support, have drifted to decaying inner-city areas. There they live in poverty and isolation, as trapped in their lodging rooms or dosshouses as they ever were in the asylum, but without security.

Michael Dear and Jennifer Wolch refer to the environments in which many ex-mental patients live as 'landscapes of despair' (Dear and Wolch, 1987), but it would surely be a retrograde step to suggest that such people should be returned to the asylums. Dear and Wolch call for the creation of a 'landscape of caring' that will begin to realize the promise of community care. This would require the provision of adequate shelter and services, backing these up with employment opportunities offered to those released from custodial care. In such a context, we could begin to speak of genuine progress in the community treatment and understanding of people suffering from mental anguish and disability.

Deviance and social order

It would be a serious mistake to regard deviance wholly in a negative light. Any society which recognizes that human beings have diverse values and concerns must find space for individuals or groups whose activities do not conform to the norms followed by the majority. People who develop new ideas, in politics, science, art, or other fields are often regarded with suspicion or hostility by those who follow orthodox ways. The political ideals developed in the American Revolution, for example – freedom of the individual and equality of opportunity – were fiercely resisted by many people at the time, yet they have now become accepted across the world. To deviate from the dominant norms of a society takes courage and resolution, but is often crucial in securing processes of change which later are seen to be in the general interest.

Is 'harmful deviance' the price a society has to pay where considerable leeway is allowed for people to engage in nonconformist pursuits? For example, are high rates of criminal violence a cost which is exacted in a society in exchange for the individual liberties its citizens enjoy? Some have certainly suggested as much, arguing that crimes of violence are inevitable in a society in which rigid definitions of conformity do not apply. But this view does not hold much water when examined closely. In some societies in which a wide range of individual freedoms are recognized, and deviant activities tolerated (such as Holland), rates of violent crime are low. Conversely, countries in which the scope of individual freedom is restricted (like South Africa) may show high levels of violence.

A society that is tolerant towards deviant behaviour need not suffer social disruption. This can probably only be achieved, however, where individual liberties are joined to social justice – in a social order where inequalities are not glaringly large, and in which the population as a whole has a chance to lead a full and satisfying life. If freedom is not balanced with equality, and if many people find their lives largely devoid of self-fulfilment, deviant behaviour is often likely to be channelled towards socially destructive ends.

Summary

1 Deviant behaviour refers to actions which transgress commonly held *norms*. What is regarded as deviant can shift from time to time and place to place; 'normal' behaviour in one cultural setting may be labelled 'deviant' in another.

2 *Sanctions*, formal or informal, are applied by society to reinforce social norms. *Laws* are norms defined and enforced by governments, *crimes* are acts which are not permitted by those laws.

3 Biological and psychological theories have been developed claiming to show that crime and other forms of deviance are genetically determined; but these have been largely discredited. Sociologists argue that conformity and deviance are differently defined in different social contexts. Divergencies of wealth and power in society strongly

influence opportunities open to different groups of individuals and what kinds of activities are regarded as criminal. Criminal activities are learned in much the same way as are law-abiding ones, and in general are directed towards the same needs and values.

4 Labelling theory (which assumes that labelling someone as deviant will reinforce their deviant behaviour) is important because it starts from the assumption that no act is intrinsically criminal (or normal). However, this theory needs to be supplemented with the enquiry: what caused the behaviour (which has come to be labelled deviant) in the first place?

5 The extent of crime in any society is difficult to assess, as not all crimes are reported. But some societies seem to experience much higher levels of crime than others — as is indicated by the high rates of homicide in the USA compared to other Western countries.

6 As 'crime' has varied between different periods and cultures, so have forms of punishment. Prisons have developed partly to protect society and partly with the intention of 'reforming' the criminal. In this they seem to be mostly ineffective. The death penalty has been abolished in most countries.

7 Rates of criminality are much lower for women than for men, probably because of general socialization differences between men and women, plus the greater involvement of men in non-domestic spheres.

8 *White-collar crime* and *crimes of the powerful* refer to crimes carried out by those in the more affluent sectors of society. *Organized crime* refers to institutionalized forms of criminal activity, in which many of the characteristics of orthodox organizations appear, but the activities engaged in are systematically illegal.

9 Sociological studies of mental illness have raised questions about the precision of the diagnostic categories used by psychiatrists, and have indicated that some people 'learn' to become mentally ill by the very process supposed to treat them. Labelling probably plays an important part in this.

10 *Decarceration* is the process whereby inmates of custodial institutions are returned to the community. The unintended consequences of decarceration have often been unfortunate; many former inmates of mental hospitals struggle to survive in unfamiliar, unsupported circumstances 'on the outside'.

Basic concepts

deviance	crime
conformity	mental illness

Important terms

deviant sub-culture	crimes of the powerful
sanction	organized crime
law	criminal network
psychopath	victimless crime
differential association	psychotic states
anomie	neurotic states
gang	schizophrenia
labelling theory	residual rule-breaking
white-collar crime	decarceration

Further reading

A. K. Bottomley and K. Pease, *Crime and Punishment: Interpereting the Data* (Milton Keynes: Open University Press, 1986) — a very useful analysis of problems in documenting the level of occurrence of crime.

S. Box, *Power, Crime and Mystification* (London: Tavistock, 1983) — contains interesting discussions of corporate and police crime, and the relationship between gender and crime.

David Downes and Paul Rock, *Understanding Deviance* (Oxford: Oxford University Press, 1982) — an excellent textbook about crime and deviance.

Ian Taylor, Paul Walton and Jock Young, *The New Criminology* (London: Routledge and Kegan Paul, 1973) — not so new any more, but still a valuable discussion of criminology.

6

Gender and Sexuality

Two newly born infants lie in the nursery of a hospital maternity ward. One, a male baby, is wrapped in a blue blanket; the other, a female, is in a pink blanket. Each baby is only several hours old, and is being seen by its grandparents for the first time. The conversation between one pair of grandparents runs along these lines:

Grandma A: There he is – our first grandchild, and a boy!
Grandpa A: Hey, isn't he a hefty little fellow? Look at that fist he's making. He's going to be a regular little fighter, that guy is. *(Grandpa A smiles and throws out a boxing jab to his grandson)* At-a-boy!
Grandma A: I think he looks like you. He has your strong chin. Oh, look, he's starting to cry.
Grandpa A: Yeah – just listen to that set of lungs. He's going to be some boy.
Grandma A: Poor thing – he's still crying.
Grandpa A: It's okay. It's good for him. He's exercising and it will develop his lungs.
Grandma A: Let's go and congratulate the parents. I know they're thrilled about little Fred. They wanted a boy first.
Grandpa A: Yeah, and they were sure it would be a boy too, what with all that kicking and thumping going on even before he got here.

When they depart to congratulate the parents, the grandparents of the other child arrive. The dialogue between them goes like this:

Grandma B: There she is . . . the only one with a pink bow taped to her head. Isn't she darling.
Grandpa B: Yeah - isn't she little. Look at how tiny her fingers are. Oh, look – she's trying to make a fist.
Grandma B: Isn't she sweet . . . you know, I think she looks a little like me.
Grandpa B: Yeah, she sorta does. She has your chin.
Grandma B: Oh, look she's starting to cry.
Grandpa B: Maybe we better call the nurse to pick her up or change her or something.
Grandma B: Yes, let's. Poor little girl. *(To the baby)* There, there, we'll try to help you.
Grandpa B: Let's find the nurse. I don't like to see her cry . . .
Grandma B: Hmm. I wonder when they will have their next one. I know Fred would like a son, but little Fredericka is well and healthy. After all, that's what really matters.
Grandpa B: They're young yet. They have time for more kids. I'm thankful too that she's healthy.
Grandma B: I don't think they were surprised when it was a girl anyway . . . she was carrying so low.

(Walum, 1977, p. 36)

The contrast between the two sets of conversations sounds so exaggerated that it is tempting to think they were made up. In fact, they are transcripts of actual dialogue recorded in a maternity ward. The very first

question usually asked of a parent – in Western culture at least – is, 'is it a boy or girl?' The experience of people who have lived for part of their lives as men, before undergoing surgery in order to become women, show how fundamentally our images of others are structured around sexual identity (Morris, 1977). Family, friends and colleagues find it enormously difficult to call a 'her' someone they have known as a 'him'. The alterations in behaviour and attitudes this implies are immense.

In this chapter, we study the nature of sex differences, analysing the complex character of what it means to be a 'man' or a 'woman'. We shall first look at the historical differences between the sexes, then at the aspects of socialization which influence **femininity** and **masculinity**. Then we shall discuss the social and economic position of women in modern societies, before moving on to an analysis of sexuality.

Sex, gender and biology

The word 'sex', as used in ordinary language, is ambiguous, referring both to a category of person and to acts in which people engage – that is, when we use the word in phrases like 'having sex'. For the sake of clarity, we must separate these two senses. We can distinguish 'sex' meaning *biological or anatomical differences* between women and men from **sexual activity**. We need also to make a further important distinction, between **sex** and **gender**. While sex refers to physical differences of the body, gender concerns the *psychological, social and cultural* differences between males and females. The distinction between sex and gender is fundamental, since many differences between males and females are not biological in origin.

The origins of sex differences

A first place to start in any discussion of sex is with human genetics. Our sex, and much of our biological makeup, is a result of genes contributed by our father's sperm cell and our mother's egg cell at conception, that is, at the formation of a new cell. All of this genetic material is contained in twenty-three pairs of chromosomes which reside in that new cell. The sperm and egg each contribute genetic information to one member of each pair.

We are concerned with the twenty-third pair of chromosomes, the sex chromosomes. This pair is notated XX for female or XY for male. It is the logic of genetics that an egg (female cell) can contribute only an X to the twenty-third chromosome pair, since it has the XX pair. But since the sperm (male cell) contains the XY pair, it can contribute either an X, resulting in an XX pair (female child) or a Y, resulting in an XY pair (male child).

After conception, the new cell divides and forms new identical cells (with identical chromosomes), which then divide, and before long, the human embryo takes shape. Early on though, the embryo contains the biological apparatus, the gonads, to develop either male testes or female ovaries. The chromosome difference acts like a switch, early in the development of the embryo, moving the physical development of the organism along one or other of two tracks (Lewontin, 1982, pp. 138–9).

Mechanisms of further sexual development are triggered in both sexes later in life, when physical maturity is reached. This is known as puberty. The average age of puberty has been declining in the industrial societies: a hundred years ago, the average age of first menstruation for girls was fourteen and a half; today it is twelve. Boys reach puberty somewhat later than girls. Physical differences in strength reach a maximum at puberty; adult men on average possess ten per cent more muscle than women, and a higher proportion of the muscle fibre associated with physical endurance. How far this is 'in-built' is not easy to assess, however, because it is affected by training and exercise. The biological differences that seem to predispose men more towards active, physically demanding work, as compared to women, are actually slight. Mechanical efficiency (how much force the body can produce per minute for a given unit of fuel consumption) is the same for men and women.

Are behaviour differences biologically based?

How far are differences in the behaviour of women and men the result of sex rather than gender? In other words, how far are they due to biological differences? Opinions are radically opposed on this issue. Many authors hold that there are inbuilt differences of behaviour between women and men which appear, in some guise or another, in all cultures. Some writers believe that the findings of sociobiology point strongly in this direction. They are likely to draw attention to the fact, for example, that in almost all cultures men rather than women take part in hunting and warfare. Surely, they argue, this demonstrates that men have biologically based tendencies towards aggression which women lack? Others are unimpressed by this argument. The level of aggressiveness of males, they say, varies widely between different cultures; women are expected to be more 'passive' or 'gentle' in some cultures than in others (Elshtain, 1987). Moreover, they add, because a trait is more or less universal, it does not follow that it is biological in origin. There may be cultural factors of a very general kind which produce such traits. For instance, in most cultures most women spend a significant part of their lives bearing and nursing children, and could not readily take part in hunting or war at such times. According to this standpoint, differences in the behaviour of men and women develop mainly through the social learning of female and male identities.

The evidence from animals

What does the evidence on this issue show? One possible source of relevant information concerns differences in hormonal make-up between the sexes. Some have claimed that the male sex hormone, testosterone, is associated with the male propensity to violence (Rutter and Giller, 1983). Research has indicated, for instance, that if male monkeys are castrated at birth they become less aggressive; and that female monkeys given testosterone will be more aggressive than normal females. However, it has also been found that providing monkeys with opportunities to dominate actually increases the testosterone level. In other words, aggressive behaviour may affect the production of the hormone, rather than the hormone causing increased aggression.

Another possible source of evidence derives from direct observations of animal behaviour. Writers who connect male aggression to biological influences often lay much emphasis upon male aggressiveness among non-human primates. If we look at the behaviour of the primates, they say, male animals are invariably more aggressive than females. Yet there are in fact large differences between types of primate in this respect. Among gibbons, for instance, there are few noticeable differences in aggression between the sexes, whereas these are marked in baboons. Moreover, many female primates are highly aggressive in some contexts – such as where their young are threatened.

The evidence from humans

Studies of congenital abnormalities found in a few human individuals provide some of the most illuminating evidence we possess about gender differences. One is called **testicular feminization syndrome**, the other

androgenital syndrome. In the first of these conditions, individuals are born with the normal chromosome make-up, testes and distribution of hormones. Were such people to be given the sex examination administered to women Olympic athletes, they would be designated as 'male'. But because their genital tissue does not react to testosterone during the development of the embryo, they appear externally to have female genitals. These children are almost always raised as girls, since their condition is not diagnosed until they fail to menstruate at the time of puberty. Androgenital syndrome is the reverse situation. Individuals with normal female chromosomal characteristics secrete extra androgen hormones before birth, and develop male external genitals. Some of these infants have genitalia of both sexes, which can be altered by surgery to be female in form. But many such children are brought up as males, their abnormality only being noted at a later stage in their development.

On balance, research into each of these types of abnormality points towards the importance of socialization, as opposed to biological influences, in the development of differences between the behaviour of boys and girls. Infants designated as 'female' at birth, even if chromosomally 'male', tend to develop female gender identity, behaviour and attitudes. Babies treated as male since birth, on the other hand, acquire male gender characteristics (Money and Ehrhardt, 1972). A well-known case of identical twins is particularly relevant here. Identical twins derive from a single egg and have *exactly the same* genetic make-up. One of a pair of identical male twins was seriously injured while being circumcised and a decision was taken to reconstruct the genitalia as female. The individual was thereafter raised as a girl. Observations of the behaviour of the twins at six years old demonstrated typical male and female traits as found in Western culture. The little girl enjoyed playing with other girls, helped with the housework and wanted to 'get married' when she grew up. The boy preferred the company of other boys, his favourite toys were cars and trucks, and he wanted to become a fireman or policeman when he grew up.

This case has sometimes been treated as a conclusive demonstration of the overriding influence of social learning upon gender differences. However, the girl, by then a teenager, was later interviewed during a television programme. The interview revealed her to have considerable unease about her gender identity, feeling perhaps she was 'really' a boy after all. (She had by then learned of her unusual background and, of course, the knowledge she acquired about her background may very well have been responsible for this altered perception of herself (Ryan, 1985, pp. 182–3).)

This study does not refute the possibility that there are biological influences upon observed behaviour differences of men and women. If these do exist, though, their physiological origins have not yet been identified. Most observers would probably agree with the conclusions drawn by Richard Lewontin, one of the world's leading geneticists:

The primary self-identification of a person as a man or a woman, with the multitude of attitudes, ideas, and desires that accompany that identification, depends on what label was attached to him or her as a child. In the normal course of events, these labels correspond to a consistent biological difference in chromosomes, hormones and morphology. Thus biological differences became a signal for, rather than a cause of, differentiation in social roles. (Lewontin, 1982, p. 142)

Gender socialization

Reactions of parents and adults

Many studies have been carried out of how gender differences develop. Most forms of gender discrimination are more subtle than the responses of the grandparents noted earlier, but they are still powerful and pervasive.

Studies of mother–infant interaction show differences in treatment of boys and girls even when parents believe their reactions to both are the same. Adults asked to assess the personality of a baby give different answers according to whether or not they believe the child to be a girl or a boy. In one experiment, five young mothers were observed in interaction with a six-month-old called Beth. They tended to smile at her often and offer her dolls to play with. She was seen as 'sweet', having a 'soft cry'. The reaction of a second group of mothers to a child the same age, named Adam, was noticeably different. The baby was likely to be offered a train or other 'male toys' to play with. Beth and Adam were actually the same child, dressed in different clothes (Will, Self and Datan, 1976).

It is not only parents and grandparents whose perceptions of infants differ in this way. One study analysed the words used about new-born babies by the medical personnel attending births. New-born male infants were most often described as 'sturdy', 'handsome', or 'tough'; female infants were more often talked of as 'dainty', 'sweet' or 'charming'. There were no overall size or weight differences between the infants in question (Hansen, 1980).

Gender learning

Early aspects of gender learning by infants are almost certainly unconscious. They precede the stage at which children can accurately label themselves as either 'a boy' or 'a girl'. A range of pre-verbal clues are involved in the initial development of gender awareness. Male and female adults usually handle infants differently. The cosmetics women use contain different scents from those the baby might learn to associate with males. Systematic differences in dress, hair-style, etc., provide visual clues for the infant in the learning process. By age two, children have a partial understanding of what gender is. They know whether they are 'boys' or 'girls', and can usually categorize others accurately. Not until five or six, however, does a child know that a person's gender does not change, that everyone has gender, or that differences between girls and boys are anatomically based.

The toys, picture books and television programmes with which young children come into contact all tend to emphasize differences between male and female attributes. Toy stores and mail order catalogues usually categorize their products by gender. Even some toys which seem 'neutral' in terms of gender are not so in practice. For example, toy kittens or rabbits are recommended for girls, while lions and tigers are seen as more appropriate for boys.

Vanda Lucia Zammuner studied the toy preferences of children in two different national contexts – Italy and Holland (Zammuner, 1987). Children's views of, and attitudes towards, a variety of toys were analysed; stereotypically 'masculine' and 'feminine' toys, as well as toys presumed not to be sex-typed, were included. The children were mostly aged between seven and ten. Both the children and their parents were asked to assess which toys were 'boys' toys' and which were suitable for girls. There was close agreement between the adults and children. On average, the Italian children chose sex-differentiated toys to play with more often than the Dutch children – a finding which conformed to expectations, since Italian culture tends to have a more 'traditional' view of gender divisions than Dutch society. As in other studies, girls from both societies chose 'gender neutral' or 'boys' toys' to play with far more than boys wanted to play with 'girls' toys'.

Books and stories

Lenore Weitzman and her colleagues carried out an analysis of gender roles in some of the most widely used pre-school children's books (Weitzman et al., 1972), finding several clear differences in gender roles. Males played a much larger part in the stories and pictures than females, outnumbering females by a ratio of 11 to 1. Including animals with gender identities, the ratio was 95 to 1. The activities of males and females also differed. The males engaged in adventurous pursuits and outdoor activities demanding independence and strength. Where girls did appear, they were shown as passive and confined mostly to indoor activities. Girls cooked and cleaned for the males, or awaited their return.

Much the same was true of the adult men and women represented in the story-books. Women who were not wives and mothers were imaginary creatures like witches or fairy godmothers. There was not a single woman in all the books analysed who had an occupation outside the home. By contrast, the men were depicted in a large range of roles, as fighters, policeman, judges, kings, and so forth.

Picture-books and story-books written from a non-sexist perspective have still made little impact in the overall market for children's literature. Fairy tales, for example, embody very traditional attitudes towards gender, and towards the sorts of aims and ambitions girls and boys are expected to have. 'Some day my prince will come' – in versions of fairy tales several centuries ago, this usually implied that a girl from a poor family might dream of wealth and fortune. Today, its meaning has become more closely tied to the ideals of romantic love. Feminists have tried to rewrite some of the most celebrated fairy tales, reversing their usual emphases:

> I really didn't notice that he had a funny nose. And he certainly looked better all dressed up in fancy clothes.
> He's not nearly as attractive as he seemed the other night. So I think I'll just pretend that this glass slipper feels too tight. (Viorst, 1987, p. 73)

As in this version of Cinderella, however, these 'rewrites' are mainly in books directed to adult audiences, and have hardly affected the tales told in innumerable children's books.

Television

Although there are some notable exceptions, analyses of television programmes designed for children conform to the findings about children's books. Studies of the most frequently watched cartoons show that virtually all the leading figures are male, and that males dominate the active pursuits depicted. Similar images are found in the commercials that appear at regular intervals through the programmes.

School and peer-group influences

By the time they start school, children have a clear consciousness of gender differences. Schools are not usually supposed to be differentiated by gender. In practice, of course, an array of factors affect girls and boys differently. In many Western countries, there are still differences in the curricula girls and boys follow – home economics or 'domestic science' being studied by the former, for example, woodwork or metalwork by the latter. Boys and girls are often encouraged to concentrate on different sports. The attitudes of teachers may subtly or more openly vary towards their female as compared to their male pupils, reinforcing the expectation that the boys are expected to be the 'performers', or tolerating greater rowdiness among the boys than the girls (see chapter 13: 'Education, Communication and Media'). Peer-group socialization tends to play a major part in reinforcing and further shaping gender identity throughout a child's school career. Children's friendship circles, in and out of school, are normally either all-boy or all-girl groups.

The difficulty of non-sexist child-rearing

June Statham studied the experiences of a group of parents in the UK committed to non-sexist child-rearing (Statham, 1986). Thirty adults in eighteen families were involved in the research, having children aged from six months to twelve years. The parents were of middle-class background, mostly involved in academic work as teachers or professors. Statham found that most of the parents did not simply try to modify traditional sex roles – by seeking to make girls more like boys – but wanted to foster new combinations of the 'feminine' and 'masculine'. They wished boys to be more sensitive to others' feelings and capable of expressing warmth, while girls were encouraged to have an active orientation towards opportunities for learning and self-advancement.

All the parents found existing patterns of gender learning difficult to combat, as their children were exposed to these when with friends and at school. The parents were reasonably successful at persuading the children to play with non-gender-typed toys, but even this proved more difficult than many of them had expected. One mother commented to the researcher:

> If you walk into a toyshop, it's full of war toys for boys and domestic toys for girls, and it sums up society the way it is. This is the way children are being socialised: it's all right for boys to be taught to kill and hurt, and I think it's terrible, it makes me feel sick. I try not to go into toy shops, I feel so angry.

Practically all the children in fact possessed, and played with, gender-typed toys, given to them by relatives.

There are now story-books available with strong, independent girls as the main characters, but few show boys in non-traditional roles. A mother of a five-year-old boy told of her son's reaction when she reversed the sexes of the characters in a story she read to him:

> In fact he was a bit upset when I went through a book which has a boy and a girl in very traditional roles, and changed all the he's to she's and the she's to he's. When I first started doing that, he was inclined to say 'you don't like boys, you only like girls'. I had to explain that that wasn't true at all, it's just that there's not enough written about girls. (Statham, 1986, pp. 43, 67)

Clearly, gender socialization is very deeply ingrained, and challenges to it can be upsetting.

Gender identity and sexuality: three theories

Freud's theory of gender development

Perhaps the most influential – and controversial – theory of the emergence of gender identity is that of Sigmund Freud. According to him, the learning of gender differences in infants and young children is centred on possession or absence of the penis. 'I have a penis' is equivalent to 'I am a boy', while 'I am a girl' is equivalent to 'I lack a penis'. Freud is careful to say that it is not just the anatomical distinctions that matter here; possession or absence of the penis is symbolic of masculinity and femininity.

In the Oedipal phase (see chapter 3: 'Socialization and the Life-Cycle'), a boy feels threatened by the discipline and autonomy which his father demands of him, fantasizing that the father wishes to remove his penis, that is, castrate him. Partly consciously, but mostly on an unconscious level, the boy recognizes the father as a rival for the affections of his mother. In repressing erotic feelings towards the mother, and accepting the father as a superior being, the boy identifies with the father and becomes aware of his male identity. The boy gives up his love for his mother out of an unconscious fear of castration by his father. Girls, on the other hand, supposedly suffer from 'penis envy' because they do not possess the visible organ that distinguishes boys. The mother becomes devalued in the little girl's eyes, because she is also seen to lack a penis and be unable to provide one. When the girl identifies with the mother, she takes over the submissive attitude involved in recognition of being 'second best'.

Once the Oedipal phase is over, the child has learned to repress its erotic feelings. The period from about five years old to puberty, according to Freud, is one of latency – sexual activities tend to be suspended, until the biological changes involved in puberty reactivate erotic desires in a direct way. The latency period, covering the early and middle years of school, is the time at which same-sex peer groups are most important in the child's life.

Assessment

Major objections have been raised against Freud's views, particularly by some feminists, but also by many other authors (Mitchell, 1973; Coward, 1984). First, he seems to identify gender identity too closely with genital awareness; many other, more subtle, factors are surely involved. Second, the theory seems to depend upon the notion that the penis is 'naturally' superior to the vagina, which is thought of as just a lack of the male organ. Yet why shouldn't the female genitals be thought of as superior to those of the male? Third, Freud treats the father as the primary disciplining agent, whereas in many cultures the mother plays the more significant part in the imposition of discipline. Fourth, Freud believes that gender learning is concentrated in the Oedipal phase, at about age four or five. Most later authors, including some strongly influenced by Freud, have emphasized the importance of much earlier learning, beginning in infancy.

Chodorow's theory of gender development

While many writers have made use of Freud's approach in studying gender development, they have usually modified it in major respects. An influential example is the work of Nancy Chodorow (1978, 1988).

Chodorow agrees with later psychoanalytic writers, rather than with Freud himself, that learning to feel male or female is a very early experience, deriving from the infant's attachment to its parents. In addition, she places much more emphasis than Freud does on the importance of the mother, rather than the father. Children tend to become emotionally involved with the mother, since the mother is easily the most dominant influence in their early lives. This attachment has at some point to be broken in order to achieve a separate sense of self – the child is required to become less closely dependent upon the mother.

Chodorow argues that the breaking process – described by Freud as the Oedipal transition – occurs in a different way for boys and girls. Unlike boys, girls remain closer to the mother – able, for example, to go on hugging and kissing her, and imitating what she does. The little girl stays attached to her mother for longer than the boy does. Because there is no sharp break from the mother, the girl, and later the adult woman, has a sense of self which is more continuous with others. Her identity is more likely to be merged with and/or dependent on another's: first her mother, later a man. In Chodorow's view, this tends to produce – and to reproduce across the generations – characteristics of sensitivity and emotional compassion in women.

Boys gain a sense of self via a more radical rejection of their original closeness to the mother, forging their understanding of masculinity from what is *not* feminine. They have to learn not to be 'cissies' or 'mother's boys'. As a result, boys are relatively unskilled in relating closely to others; they develop more analytical ways of looking at the world. They take a more active view of their lives, emphasizing 'achievement'; but they have repressed their ability to understand their own feelings and those of others.

To some extent Chodorow here reverses the Freudian emphasis. Masculinity rather than femininity is defined by a 'loss', the forfeiting of continuing close attachment to the mother. Male identity is formed through separation; thus men unconsciously later in life feel their identity is endangered if they become involved in close emotional relationships with others. Women, on the other hand, feel the opposite; absence of a close relation to another person threatens their self-esteem. These patterns are passed on from generation to generation, because of the primary role women play in the early socialization of children. Women express and define themselves mainly in terms of relationships. Men have repressed these needs, and take a more manipulative attitude towards the world.

Evaluation

Chodorow's work has met with various criticisms. Janet Sayers, for example, has suggested that Chodorow does not explain the struggle of women – particularly in current times – to become autonomous, independent beings (Sayers, 1986). Women (and men), she points out, are more mixed or contradictory in their psychological make-up than Chodorow's theory suggests. Femininity, Sayers argues, may conceal feelings of aggressiveness or assertiveness, which are revealed only obliquely or in certain contexts (Brennan, 1988). In spite of their limitations, Chodorow's ideas are important. They help us to understand the origins of what psychologists have called **male inexpressiveness** – the difficulty men have in revealing their feelings to others (Balswick, 1983). They explain a great deal about the nature of femininity, and are directly relevant to understanding the universal nature of male dominance over women – a phenomenon which we shall document later in this chapter.

Gender, self and morality

Carol Gilligan has developed an analysis of gender differences based on the images adult women and men have of themselves and their attainments (Gilligan, 1982). Women, she agrees with Chodorow, define themselves in terms of personal relationships, and judge their achievements by reference to the ability to care for others. Women's place in the lives of men is traditionally that of caretaker and helpmate. But the qualities developed in these tasks are frequently devalued by men, who see their own emphasis on *individual* achievement as the only form of 'success'. Concern with relationships on the part of women appears as a weakness rather than the strength which it often is.

Gilligan carried out a number of intensive interviews with about two hundred American females and males of varying ages and social backgrounds. She asked all of the interviewees a range of questions concerning their moral outlook and conception of self. Consistent differences emerged between the views of the women and those of the men. For instance, the interviewees were asked: 'What does it mean to say something is morally right or wrong?' Whereas the men tended to respond to this question by mentioning abstract ideals of duty, justice and individual freedom, the women persistently raised the theme of helping others. Thus a female college student answered the question in the following way:

> 'It [morality] has to do with responsibilities and obligations and values, mainly values . . . In my life situation I relate morality with interpersonal relationships that have to do with respect for the other person and myself.' The interviewer then asked: 'Why respect other people?', receiving the answer, 'Because they have a consciousness or feelings that can be hurt, an awareness that can be hurt.' (Gilligan, 1982, p. 65)

The women were more tentative in their moral judgements than the men, seeing possible difficulties between following a strict moral code and avoiding harming others. Gilligan suggests that this outlook reflects the traditional situation of women, anchored in caring relationships rather than in the 'outward-looking' attitudes of men. Women have in the past deferred to the judgements of men, while being aware that they have qualities which most males lack. Their views of themselves are based upon successfully fulfilling the needs of others, rather than pride in individual achievement.

Patriarchy and production

The dominance of men

Although there are considerable variations in the respective roles of women and men in different cultures, there is no known instance of a society in which females are more powerful than men. Women are everywhere primarily concerned with child-rearing and the maintenance of the home, while political and military activities tend to be resoundingly male. Nowhere in the world do men have primary responsibility for the rearing of children. Conversely, there are few if any cultures in which women are charged with the main responsibility for the herding of large animals, the hunting of large game, deep-sea fishing or plough agriculture (Brown, 1977). In industrial societies, the division of labour between the sexes has become less clear-cut than in non-industrial ones; but men still outnumber women in all spheres of power and influence.

Male dominance is usually referred to as **patriarchy**. Why should patriarchy be – in one form or another – universal? Many answers have been suggested, but the most likely explanation is relatively simple. Women give birth to, and nurse, children. The helplessness of the human infant demands that initial care is intensive and prolonged – hence the centrality of 'mothering' to women's experience, as emphasized by Chodorow. The initial physical necessity for mothers to give birth and nurse their children leads easily into the continuing caring and nurturing role which women adopt in all cultures. Because of their role as mothers and carers, women are primarily absorbed in domestic activities. Women become what the French novelist and social critic Simone de Beauvoir called the 'second sex', because they are excluded from the more 'public' activities in which males are free to engage (de Beauvoir, 1972). Men are not dominant over women as a result of superior physical strength, or any special intellectual powers, but because, before the development of birth control, women were at the mercy of their biological constitution. Frequent pregnancy, and continuous caring for infants, made them dependent on males for material provision (Firestone, 1971; see also, however, Mitchell, 1973).

Women and the workplace: the historical view

For the vast majority of the population in pre-industrial societies (and many people in Third World societies today), productive activities and the activities of the household were not separate. Production was either carried on in the home, or nearby. All members of the family in mediaeval Europe participated in work on the land or in handicrafts. In the towns, workshops were normally in the home, and family members contributed to various aspects of the production process. In the weaving trade, for instance, children did carding and combing, older daughters and mothers spun, and the fathers wove. Wives and children similarly directly worked with men in tailoring, shoemaking and baking. Women often had considerable influence within the household as a result of their importance in economic processes, even if they were excluded from the male realms of politics and warfare. Wives of craftsmen often kept business accounts, as did those of farmers, and widows quite commonly owned and managed businesses.

Much of this was changed by the separation of the workplace from the home brought about by the development of modern industry. The movement of production into mechanized factories was probably the largest single factor. Work was done at the machine's pace by individuals hired specifically for the tasks in question, so employers began to contract workers as individuals rather than families. The old way of treating families as one unit took a long time to fade out, however; in the early part of the nineteenth century, in Britain and many other European countries, employers still often hired family units. If the father was hired to work in the factory, for example, the wife and children would be taken on as domestic servants or farm-hands.

As the practice declined, however, an increasing division became established between home and workplace. Women came to be associated with 'domestic' values, although the idea that 'a woman's place is in the home' had different implications for women at varying levels in society. Affluent women enjoyed the services of maids, nurses and domestic servants. The burdens were harshest for poorer women, having to cope with the household chores as well as engaging in industrial work to supplement their husbands' income.

Rates of employment of women outside the home, for all classes, were quite low until well into the twentieth century. Even as late as 1910, in Britain, more than a third of gainfully employed women were maids or house servants. The female labour force consisted mainly of young single women, whose wages, when they worked in factories or offices, were often sent by their employers direct to their parents. When they married, they withdrew from the labour force.

Since then, women's participation in the paid labour-force has risen more or less continuously. One major influence was the labour shortage experienced during the First World War. During the war years, women carried out many jobs previously regarded as the exclusive province of men. On returning from the war, males again took over most of those jobs, but the pre-established pattern had been broken. Today around 50 per cent of women aged between sixteen and sixty in most European countries, including the UK, hold paid jobs outside the home. The most significant rise has been among married women. In the United Kingdom more than 40 per cent of married women with children aged under three are now in gainful employment (Mallier and Rosser, 1987). The proportion of women in the paid labour-force, nevertheless, is still well below that of men. Over 80 per cent of the male population between twenty-five and sixty is in paid employment, and the proportion of men in paid employment has not altered much over the past century. Expanding levels of employment for women are not a result of them ousting men from jobs, but have come about through a general increase in the number of jobs available.

Inequalities at work

Low-status jobs

Women workers today are overwhelmingly concentrated in poorly paid, routine occupations. Changes in the organization of employment as well as sex-role stereotyping have contributed to this. Alterations in the prestige and the work tasks of 'clerks' provide a good example. In 1850, in the UK, 99 per cent of clerks were men. To be a clerk was often to have a responsible position, involving knowledge of accountancy skills and sometimes carried managerial responsibilities. Even the lowliest clerk had a certain status in the outside world. The twentieth century has seen a general mechanization of office work (starting with the introduction of the typewriter in the late nineteenth century), accompanied by a marked downgrading of the skills and status of 'clerk' – together with another related occupation, that of 'secretary' – into a low-status, low-paid occupation. Women filled these occupations as the pay and prestige of such jobs declined. In 1986, nearly 90 per cent of clerical workers, and 98 per cent of all secretaries in the UK were women.

Women have recently made some inroads into occupations defined as 'men's jobs', but so far only to a limited degree. Making up 46 per cent of the paid labour-force in Britain in 1984, women occupied only 17 per cent of higher managerial positions. Women own no more than 5 per cent of all businesses, these producing under 1 per cent of all business receipts. When Margaret Thatcher became Britain's first woman Prime Minister in 1979, it was hailed as a great step forward for women in general. In fact, in 1980 UK legislative bodies comprised 1,762 men and only 87 women, and at present there is little evidence of change in this imbalance.

The problems of success

Women who *are* successful economically have to fit in with a world to which they feel they do not fully belong. Margaret Hennig and

Table 2   Females as a percentage of total civilians in employment

	1950	1960	1970	1980
Australia	*	28.2[b]	28.8	34.1
Belgium	28.7	30.7	32.7	35.9
Canada	21.8	26.8	33.6	39.7
Denmark	*	31.6	39.4	43.6[d]
France	*	*	35.2	38.0
West Germany	35.6	37.8	36.6	38.3
Ireland	26.0[a]	*	26.7	28.5
Italy	*	30.1	28.3	32.1
Japan	*	40.7	39.3	38.7
Norway	27.8	29.0	30.8	41.1
Portugal	23.0	18.7	*	38.8
Spain	16.1	*	25.0	29.0
Sweden	*	36.1[c]	39.4	45.0
UK	32.6	34.4	36.3	40.1
USA	29.4	33.3	37.2	42.4

* Data not available
[a] 1951
[b] 1964
[c] 1962
[d] 1979

Source: A. T. Mallier and M. J. Rosser, *Women and the Economy: A Comparative Study of Britain and the USA* (London: Macmillan, 1987), p. 167.

Anne Jardin have compared the experiences of women executives to someone going to a foreign country for an extended stay. It is essential to take good guides and maps, and to observe the rules of the local inhabitants. A good deal of 'culture shock' is involved, and even the foreigner who stays on permanently is never totally accepted. In the longer run, however, Hennig and Jardin anticipate that women may exert a modifying effect on the masculine value system, bringing family responsibilities and work imperatives into line with one another (Hennig and Jardin, 1977).

One of the major factors affecting women's careers is the male perception that, for female employees, work comes second to having children. A recent British study investigated the views of managers interviewing female applicants for positions as technical staff in the health services. The researchers found that the interviewers always asked the women about whether or not they had, or intended to have, children. They virtually never followed this practice with male applicants. When asked why not, two themes ran through their answers: (a) women with children may require extra time off for school holidays or if a child falls sick and (b) responsibility for child-care is seen as a mother's problem rather than a parental one.

Some managers saw their questions on this issue as indicating an attitude of 'caring' towards women employees, but most saw such questioning as part of their task to assess how far a female applicant would prove a reliable colleague. Thus one manager remarked: 'It's a bit of a personal question, I appreciate that, but I think it's something that has to be considered. It's something that can't happen to a man really, but I suppose in a sense it's unfair – it's not equal opportunity because the man could never find himself having a family as such' (Homans, 1987, p. 92). Yet while men cannot biologically 'have a family' in the sense of bearing children, they can, of course, be involved in and responsible for child-care. Such a possibility was not taken into account by any of the managers studied. The same attitudes were held about the promotion of women: they were seen as likely to interrupt their careers to care for young children, no matter how senior a position they might have reached. A top male manager commented:

> 'Males tend to dominate the higher levels because simply the women drop out to have babies and that sort of thing . . . I don't think that is necessarily selective promotion but just the facts of life that women tend to go off and get married and have their families and therefore they have a fragmented career. They come back and have a gap in experience or training and when you come down to it and you are selecting candidates, it is not the sex of the candidate but what they can contribute to their job. You've got the candidate who is perhaps a woman who has seen three years out of a job for family reasons and a man who has been on the job. It is fairly evident, given that the rest is equal between the candidates, that he is likely to get the job.' (Homans, 1987, p. 95)

The few women who were in senior management posts were all without children, and several of those who planned to have children in the future said they intended leaving their posts, perhaps retraining for other positions subsequently.

How should we interpret these findings? Are women's job opportunities hampered mainly by male prejudices? Some managers expressed the view that women with children should not seek paid work, but occupy themselves with child-care and the home. Most, however, accepted the principle that women should have the same career opportunities as men. The bias in their attitudes was less to do with the workplace itself than with the domestic responsibilities of parenting. So long as most of the population take it for granted that parenting cannot be shared on an equal basis, the problems facing women employees will persist. It will remain a 'fact of life', as one of the managers put it, that women are severely disadvantaged, compared to men, in their career opportunities.

Low pay and the female poverty trap

As might be expected, the average pay of employed women is well below that of men, although the difference has narrowed somewhat over the past twenty years. Women are over-represented in the more poorly paid job sectors, but even within the same occupational categories as men, women on average have lower salaries. For instance, female clerical workers in Britain are paid 60 per cent of the earnings of their male counterparts; women sales employees earn 57 per cent of male earnings in the same occupation.

A substantial proportion of women in the UK live in poverty. This is particularly true of women who are heads of households. The percentage of women among the poor has risen steadily over the past two decades, despite the fact that the percentage of people living in poverty went down in the 1960s and was stable in the 1970s (rising again in the 1980s). Poverty tends to be especially acute for women with very small children, who need constant care. There is a vicious circle here: a woman who can obtain a reasonably well-paid job may be financially crippled by having to pay for child-care, yet if she starts working part-time, her earnings drop, whatever career prospects she may have had disappear, and she also loses other economic benefits – such as pension rights – which full-time workers receive (Rodgers, 1986).

How far are things different in other countries? As a basis for comparison, we shall consider Sweden and the Soviet Union. Each of these countries has introduced a greater range of measures concerned with improving the economic status of women than has been the case in the UK.

The case of Sweden

Sweden leads the Western world in terms of legislation designed to promote the equality of the sexes (Scriven, 1984). A high proportion of women in Sweden are in paid employment – in 1986, 80 per cent of those aged between sixteen and sixty-four did some form of paid work (Allmän/månad statistik, 1987). State benefits, providing for 90 per cent of normal earnings, are available to anyone having a child to cover the period from one month before birth until six months afterwards. These six months can be divided between parents in terms of who takes time off from work to care for the child. A further 180 days' benefit are available, which may be taken by either mother or father at a subsequent period. Many child-care centres exist to provide after-school and holiday-time facilities for children up to the age of twelve.

These measures seem to have been partially successful in terms of providing opportunities for women to achieve positions of influence. For example, women hold a quarter of the seats in the Swedish Parliament, one of the highest percentages internationally. Yet few women are found at the top levels of business firms, and in most occupations women are not much more significantly represented than in other Western societies. In 1985, 45 per cent of Swedish women worked in part-time occupations, which have poorer career opportunities, social benefits and pension rights than full-time jobs (only 5 per cent of men aged between sixteen and sixty-four are in part-time work in Sweden). Many women do not wish to leave their children at the day centres for the long periods necessary for them to take full-time employment, and women continue to be primarily responsible for the home and for child-care. Paradoxically, because of the existence of the day centres, men may think they have less need to participate in child-care than they would do otherwise (Wistrand, 1981).

Women in the Soviet Union and Eastern Europe

The Soviet Union has been said to be 'the first country in the world to declare the equality of men and women and to commit itself to policies to ensure this equality' (Attwood and McAndrew, 1984, p. 269). After the Russian Revolution of 1917, the new Soviet government publicly declared that it would establish equal occupational opportunities for women, coupled with state provision of child-care facilities.

A women's section of the Central Committee of the Bolshevik Party, known as *Zhenotdel*, was set up in September 1919. It was supposed to bring women into a central role in political as well as economic life. *Zhenotdel* has been compared to modern women's centres – putting on exhibitions, meetings and consciousness-raising sessions and organizing campaigns. However, it was regarded with suspicion by the male-dominated Communist Party committees. In some parts of the Soviet Union the women's sections were abolished almost immediately after they were first set up. In other regions of the country they were very active, but met with wide resistance from most of the male-dominated Party organizations. Eventually all were dissolved, becoming incorporated within the orthodox committees of the Party – and instructed to concentrate on increasing productivity rather than upon women's issues as such.

The Communist Party continued none the less to encourage extensive female involvement in the paid labour-force, and there is today a markedly higher proportion of women in paid employment in the Soviet Union, and in other East European societies, than in most Western countries. Compared to the West, rates of participation in paid work are especially high for mothers with small children. In the UK, some 32 per cent of women with children under six years of age are in the labour-force. In Czechoslovakia, by comparison, the figure is over 80 per cent (Heitlinger, 1979). Women are spread far more equally across the range of available jobs than in the West. In Britain, a quarter of all employed women are to be found in five occupations – secretary, shorthand-typist, domestic worker, elementary-school teacher and waitress. Soviet women perform 'physical' work thought in most countries to be the province of men; for example, they work in mining, steel production and the engineering industry, composing about half the blue-collar industrial labour-force. They are also well represented in most professional jobs. Over 75 per cent of doctors and dentists in the Soviet Union, and more than 50 per cent of medical administrators, are women. (By comparison, only about 7 per cent of doctors and dentists in the UK are female.)

But gender equality in the East European countries is much less developed than might appear from such figures. As in the West, occupations in which there is a high percentage of women have lower average wages than comparable occupations in which men dominate. For example, doctors receive lower average wages in the Soviet Union than engineers, a profession in which women are outnumbered by men. Average earnings for women in the USSR are about 75 per cent of those of men. Women are poorly represented in higher positions in the national government.

Equally important, in spite of their high rates of labour-force participation, women in the Soviet Union and Eastern Europe retain primary responsibility for care of the home – and the amount of effort involved in domestic work in the Soviet Union is much larger than in most Western countries. Shopping is time-consuming, as it is often necessary to wait in long queues to purchase even basic items of food; housing space is limited; domestic technology is less advanced. Washing machines and refrigerators are expensive relative to wages, while dishwashers and clothes driers are virtually non-existent. Soviet men mostly have disparaging attitudes towards housework, and although a much higher proportion of women in the Soviet Union work full-time outside the home than in the UK, the average contribution of husbands to housework and child-care is smaller.

Housework

Housework in its current form came into existence with the separation of the home and workplace (Oakley, 1974). The home became a place of consumption rather than production of goods. Domestic work became 'invisible' as 'real work' was defined more and more as that which receives a direct wage. The period of the development of a separate 'home' also saw other changes. Before the inventions and facilities provided by industrialization influenced the domestic sphere, work in the household was hard and exacting. The weekly wash, for example, was a heavy and demanding task. The Maytag Washing Machine Co. carried out research reconstructing what washing involved in the nineteenth century, concluding that 'the old washday was as exhausting as swimming five miles of energetic breast stroke, arm movements and general dampness supplying an almost exact parallel' (quoted in Hardyment, 1987, p. 6).

The introduction of hot and cold running water into homes eliminated many time-consuming tasks; previously water itself had to be carried to the home and heated there whenever hot water was required. The piping of electricity and gas made coal and wood stoves obsolete, and chores such as the regular chopping of wood, carrying of coal and constant cleaning of the stove were thereby largely eliminated. Labour-saving equipment such as vacuum cleaners and washing machines reduced hard work, and declining family size meant fewer children to care for. Yet, surprisingly, the average amount of time spent on domestic work by women did not decline very markedly. The amount of time British women not in paid employment spend on housework has remained quite constant over the past half-century. Household appliances eliminated some of the heavier chores, but new tasks were created in their place. Time spent on child-care, stocking up the home with purchases and meal preparation all increased.

The women's movement has had some effect upon men's attitudes towards work inside and outside the home, but even 'liberated' men still retain conventional masculine standards. Mirra Komarovsky studied sixty-two male final-year students at Columbia University, in New York City, to investigate changing views of masculinity. Many of these individuals were sympathetic to feminist objectives, although they retained the idea of men as strong-willed and assertive. They expressed desire for intellectual companionship, but were cautious about becoming involved with intelligent, self-confident women. Although they did not have a high opinion of women who became full-time house-wives, most still believed that a husband's career should come first. Judgements recognized to be valid in the abstract were disclaimed for the individual. One man commented, for example, 'It is only fair to let a woman do her own thing, if she wants a career. Personally, though, I would want my wife at home' (Komarovsky, 1976).

The trend towards an increasing number of women entering the labour-force has had a discernible impact on housework activities (Vanek, 1974). Married women employed outside the home do less domestic work than others, although they almost always shoulder the main responsibility for care of the home. The pattern of their activities is of course rather different. They do more housework in the early evenings and for longer hours at weekends than do those who are full-time housewives.

Unpaid domestic work is of enormous significance to the economy. It has been estimated that housework accounts for between 25 and 40 per cent of the wealth created in the industrialized countries. Domestic work props up the rest of the economy by providing free services on which many of the working population depend.

Feminist movements

Feminist authors have been largely responsible for pointing out, and analysing, the importance of housework. For many years, sociologists were guilty of defining 'work' as 'paid work outside the home'. Feminists have shown how misleading such a view was, and have prompted studies of women's activities and attitudes in many areas of social life where they were previously largely ignored. Although this particular influence has been a recent one, **feminism** – the struggle to defend and expand the rights of women – in fact has a lengthy history, going back to the late eighteenth century.

One of the earliest works to advance feminist ideas was Mary Wollstonecraft's book *A Vindication of the Rights of Women*, first published in 1792. 'Women', she declared, 'have acquired all the follies and vices of civilisation, and miss the useful fruit' (Wollstonecraft, 1985, p. 67). Sixteen years before, in the United States, Abigail Adams had made a plea for improving the situation of women when writing to her husband John Adams, who was to become the second President, 'I desire you would Remember the Ladies, and be more favourable and generous to them than your ancestors . . . Remember all Men would be tyrants if they could' (Rossi and Calderwood, 1973).

Early feminism in France

The first groups actively organized to promote women's rights date from the period immediately after the French Revolution in 1789 (Evans, 1977). In the 1790s, inspired by the ideals of freedom and equality for which the revolution had been fought, several women's clubs were formed in Paris and major provincial cities. The clubs provided meeting-places for women, but also developed political programmes petitioning for equal rights in education, employment and government. Marie Gouze, a leader of one of the clubs, drew up a statement entitled 'Declaration of the Rights of Women', based upon the 'Declaration of the Rights of Man and Citizen', the main constitutional document of the revolution. Rights of free and equal citizenship, she argued, could not be limited to men; how can true equality be achieved when half the population are excluded from the privileges which men share?

The response from the male revolutionary leaders was less than sympathetic – Marie Gouze was executed in 1793. The women's clubs were subsequently dissolved by government decree. Feminist groups and women's movements have been formed and reformed repeatedly in Western countries since that date, almost always encountering hostility, and sometimes provoking violence, from the established authorities. Marie Gouze was by no means the only feminist to give her life to the cause of achieving equal rights for her sex.

The struggle in the United States

In the nineteenth century, feminism became more advanced in the United States than elsewhere, and most leaders of women's movements in other countries looked to the struggles of American women as a model. In the period from 1830 to 1850, American feminists were closely involved with groups devoted to the abolition of slavery. Anti-slavery petitions usually carried a high proportion of female signatures. Yet, having no formal political rights, women were excluded from the political lobbying through which the reformers pursued their objective. No women were allowed to participate in a world anti-slavery convention held in London in 1840, and this very fact led the women's groups to turn more directly to considering gender inequalities as such. In 1848, just as their French counterparts had done a half a century before, women's leaders in the US met to approve a 'Declaration of Sentiments' modelled on the American Declaration of Independence. 'We hold these truths to be self-evident', it opened, 'that all men *and women* are created equal.' The declaration set out a long list of the injustices to which women were subject (Banner and Hartman, 1974). However, few real gains in improving the social or political position of women were made during this period. When slavery ended, Congress ruled that only freed *male* slaves should be given the vote.

Black women played a part in the early development of the women's movement in the United States, although they often had to contend with hostility from their white sisters. Sojourner Truth was a black woman who spoke out against both slavery and the exclusion of women from the vote, linking the two issues closely. When she forcefully and passionately addressed an anti-slavery rally in Indiana in the 1850s, a white man yelled at her: 'I don't believe you really are a woman.' She publicly bared her breasts to demonstrate her femininity. In 1852, when she lectured at a women's rights convention in Akron, Ohio, white women in the audience heckled to prevent her speaking. She overcame this kind of resistance to play a prominent part in the women's struggles of the period (Hooks, 1986). But other black women who tried to participate alongside white feminists became disillusioned with the prejudice they encountered, and black feminists thenceforth were very few in number.

European developments

One of the most important events in the early development of feminist movements in Europe was the presentation of a petition, signed by 1,500 women, to the British Parliament in 1866. It demanded that the electoral reforms then being discussed include full voting rights for women. The petition was ignored; in response, its organizers set up the National Society for Women's Suffrage the following year. The members of the society became known as the **suffragists**, and throughout the remainder of the nineteenth century petitioned Parliament to extend voting rights to women. By the early twentieth century, the world influence of British feminism rivalled that of the feminists in the United States. In the early 1900s, frequent marches and street demonstrations were organized in both countries. An open-air meeting held in London in June 1908 attracted a crowd of half a million people. During this period, women's movements mushroomed in all the major European countries, together with Australia and New Zealand.

Emmeline Pankhurst, a leading figure among the suffragists, went on several speaking tours of the United States, recounting the British struggles to large audiences. Two Americans who had become involved in the campaigns in Britain, Alice Paine and Harriet Stanton Blatch, organized a series of massive marches and parades through New York and other major Eastern cities from 1910 onwards.

For several decades after 1920, feminist movements in the UK and elsewhere fell into decline. Part of the reason was the very achievement of the right to vote, attained in most Western countries by that date (1928 in Britain). Radical women tended to be absorbed into other movements, such as those engaged in combating Fascism. While many pursued feminist aims in these contexts, as a distinct movement combating male-dominated institutions feminism became less prominent. Yet the achievement of equal political rights did little to extend equality to other spheres.

The Achievement of Women's Right to Vote on an Equal Basis with Men

1893 New Zealand	1945 France, Hungary, Italy,
1902 Australia	Japan, Vietnam,
1906 Finland	Yugoslavia, Bolivia
1913 Norway	1946 Albania, Rumania,
1915 Denmark, Iceland	Panama
1917 USSR	1947 Argentina, Venezuela
1918 Canada	1948 Israel, Korea
1919 Austria, Germany,	1949 China, Chile
the Netherlands, Poland,	1950 El Salvador, Ghana, India
Sweden, Luxembourg,	1951 Nepal
Czechoslovakia	1952 Greece
1920 USA	1953 Mexico
1922 Ireland	1954 Columbia
1928 Great Britain	1955 Nicaragua
1929 Ecuador	1956 Egypt, Pakistan, Senegal
1930 South Africa	1957 Lebanon
1931 Spain, Sri Lanka, Portugal	1959 Morocco
1932 Thailand	1962 Algeria
1934 Brazil, Cuba	1963 Iran, Kenya, Libya
1936 Costa Rica	1964 Sudan, Zambia
1937 Philippines	1965 Afghanistan, Guatemala
1941 Indonesia	1977 Nigeria
1942 Dominican Republic,	1979 Peru, Zimbabwe
Uruguay	(Tuttle, 1986, pp. 370–1)

The resurgence of feminism

In the late 1960s women's movements again came to the fore (Chafe, 1972, 1977). Over the quarter century since then, feminism has become a major influence throughout the world, including many Third World societies. The resurgence of feminism began in the United States, influenced by the civil rights movement and by the student activism of the period. Many women were active in these causes, but found themselves often kept by male activists to a traditionally subordinate role. Civil rights leaders were resistant to women's rights being included in the manifestos of equality for which they fought. Consequently, women began to establish their own independent organizations.

Women's movements recently have addressed a much wider range of issues than their earlier counterparts. They have pressed for economic equality, the availability of abortion and alterations in laws concerning divorce – among other concerns. In addition to significant practical achievements, feminists today have made an intellectual impact far beyond anything previously achieved. Throughout the social sciences, and in many other fields, feminist authors have forced a rethinking of pre-established notions and theories. Much of the research carried out in recent years into historical and cultural factors affecting the position of women, and into gender relations more generally, has been prompted by the influence of modern feminism.

Domestic violence, sexual harassment and rape

We shall now turn to consider some basic problems which very many women face, directly or indirectly. They are all to do with ways in which males use their superior social or physical power against women: domestic violence, sexual harassment and rape. While each of these has occasionally been practised by women against men, in the vast majority of cases men are the aggressors and women the victims.

Domestic violence

The home is often idealized as a haven of security and happiness, but **domestic violence** is part of the experience of many women. This is not a new social ill. Violence towards women was a common aspect of marriage in mediaeval times and in the early days of industrialization. Until the late nineteenth century, there were no laws in the UK prohibiting a man from physically abusing his wife, short of serious injury or murder. Women now have more legal protection, yet such violence remains widespread. Violence against women in the home is sometimes thought to be mostly minor, but evidence from refuges for battered women suggests otherwise. One study noted: 'Some women are appallingly injured; they suffer broken bones, knife wounds and severe bruising; some hit over the head with furniture, some are thrown down-stairs and one had a nail hammered into her foot' (Pahl, 1978, p. 32).

In spite of an improving legal position, recourse to the law for women subjected to domestic violence is difficult. The attitude of the police, who normally have a policy of non-intervention in 'domestic disputes', is very often unhelpful. When called out in such circumstances, they tend to restrict their intervention to calming down the dispute, rather than pressing charges. Women in relationships involving violence often find it difficult to leave the household for a variety of economic and social reasons, including their responsibility for children. Local government housing departments are sometimes wary of women who come to them with complaints of physical abuse, suspecting these to be exaggerated for the purposes of securing alternative housing rapidly.

Sexual harassment

In the work setting, the rights of women are more easily enforceable, and levels of actual violence against women are low. **Sexual harassment**, nevertheless, is extremely common. Sexual harassment in the workplace may be defined as the use of occupational authority or power to try to enforce sexual demands. This may take blatant forms, as when it is suggested to a female employee that she consent to a sexual encounter or be dismissed. Most kinds of sexual harassment are somewhat more subtle. They involve hints, for example, that the granting of sexual favours would bring other rewards; or that if such favours are not offered some kind of punishment, such as a blocked promotion, will ensue.

Choice about where, and with whom, we have sexual relationships is a basic part of exercising control over our lives, and sexual harassment denies this choice. Although the men involved may see the milder forms of sexual harassment as harmless, women often experience them as humiliating. Women are expected to be tolerant of unwanted sexual talk, gestures or physical approaches, and to 'play along'. To do so demands not only tolerance but great skill. A cocktail waitress, whose tips are a major part of her income, and who consequently has to please customers, observes that a woman in her job 'must learn to be sexually inviting at the same time as she is unavailable. This of course means that men will take out their lust through lewd and insinuating words, subtle propositions, gestures. She must manage to turn him off gently without insulting him, without appearing insulted. Indeed she must appear charmed by it, find a way to say no which also flatters him' (quoted in MacKinnon, 1979, p. 78).

It is obviously not easy to draw a line between harassment and what might be regarded as a legitimate approach from a man to a woman. On the basis of self-reporting, however, it has been estimated that seven out of ten women in the UK are affected by sexual harassment in a prolonged way during the course of their working lives. Sexual harassment may be a single occurrence or a consistent pattern of behaviour. Where the second of these is involved, women frequently experience difficulty in maintaining their usual work rate, may take sick leave or quit their jobs altogether (MacKinnon, 1979).

Rape

The extent of **rape** is very difficult to assess with any accuracy. Only a small proportion of rapes actually come to the attention of the police and are recorded in the statistics. The real figure might be as much as five times as high as the official statistics show – although estimates vary widely. A study of 1,236 women in London revealed that one in six had been raped, one in five of the remainder had fought off an attempted rape, and half of the assaults had taken place either in the woman's own house or in that of her assailant (Hall, 1985). The majority of women who are raped either wish to put the incident out of their minds, or are unwilling to participate in what can be a humiliating process of medical examination, police interrogation and courtroom cross-examination. The legal process often takes a long time; it might be as much as eighteen months after the incident before a court verdict is reached.

The trial itself can be intimidating. Courtroom procedure is public and the victim must come face-to-face with the accused. Men are not usually convicted on the basis of the testimony of the victim alone, so confirming evidence has to be obtained from others. Proof of penetration, the identity of the rapist and the fact that the act occurred without the woman's consent all have to be forthcoming. Corroborative evidence of the identity of an assailant is likely to be hard to obtain if the crime occurred in a dark street or alleyway. A woman who walks alone at night is liable to be seen as encouraging the attentions of men. Wherever the rape occurs, the woman may be interrogated about the history of her previous sexual relationships, although a man's sexual history is not deemed relevant in the same way. In fact, prior convictions for rape or assault on the part of an accused cannot be mentioned in rape cases.

According to Sir Matthew Hale, a judge delivering a ruling in 1736, a husband 'cannot be guilty of rape committed by himself upon his lawful wife, for by their mutual matrimonial consent and contract the wife hath given up herself in this kind unto her husband which she cannot retract' (quoted in Hall, James and Kertesz, 1984, p. 20). This formulation remains the law in England and Wales. Unless a non-molestation injunction, personal protection order, or legal separation, has been obtained, even separated women have no legal defence against rape by their husbands. Rape within marriage is illegal only in a minority of Western countries, including Denmark, Sweden, Norway and Canada

– although most countries in East Europe, including the USSR, have passed legislation abolishing the husband's immunity from prosecution. In the United States, the first case of prosecution for rape in marriage was won against James K. Chretien in 1979. Before the Chretien case, rape within marriage was illegal in five states. Since then, many others have brought in legislation or introduced test cases establishing the crime.

Conventional attitudes as to what is and what is not rape can be very strong. Researchers studying forcible sex within established relationships reported the following case. A man who was drunk started to attempt anal intercourse with his girlfriend. She refused and screamed, at which point he became violent, held her down so that she could not move and forced her to submit. Yet when asked by the researchers whether she had ever been forced to have sex against her will, she said 'No' (Finkelhor and Yllo, 1982).

Research has shown many common beliefs about rape to be false. It is not true, for example, that rape cannot happen if the victim resists; that only young, 'attractive' women are likely to be raped; that some women enjoy the experience of being raped; or that most rapists are in some way psychologically disturbed (Hall, 1985). Most rapes are not spontaneous, but at least partly planned in advance (Amir, 1971; Clark and Lewis, 1977). Rape is clearly related to the association of masculinity with power, dominance and toughness. It is not for the most part the result of overwhelming sexual desire, but of the ties between sexuality and feelings of power and superiority. There seems to be little connection between lust and rape. A substantial proportion of rapists in fact are only able to become sexually aroused once they have terrorized and degraded the victim. The sexual act itself is less significant than the debasement of the woman (Estrich, 1987).

Over the last few years, women's groups have pressed for change in both legal and public thinking about rape. They have stressed that rape should not be seen as a sexual offence, but as a type of violent crime. It is not just a physical attack but an assault upon an individual's integrity and dignity. As one writer put it, rape is 'an act of aggression in which the victim is denied her self-determination. It is an act of violence which, if not actually followed by beatings or murder, nevertheless carries with it the threat of death' (Griffin, 1978, p. 342). The campaign has had some real results in changing legislation, and rape is today generally recognized in law to be a specific type of criminal violence.

Rape and female anxiety: Brownmiller's thesis

There is a sense in which all women are victims of rape. Women who have never been raped often experience similar anxieties to those who have. They may be afraid to go out alone at night, even on crowded streets, and may be almost equally fearful of being on their own in a house or flat. Emphasizing the close connection between rape and orthodox male sexuality, Susan Brownmiller has argued that rape is part of a system of male intimidation that keeps all women in fear. Those who are not raped are affected by the anxieties thus provoked, and by the need to be much more cautious in everyday aspects of life than men have to be (Brownmiller, 1975).

Brownmiller's view may sound extreme, but a moment's thought shows how careful a woman has to be if she wishes to minimize the chance of being raped. The following is a list of 'dos' and 'don'ts' for women trying to reduce the risk of rape, published by a women's organization in the United States. This list supplies compelling support for the view that rape is a crime that affects the behaviour of all women (Katz and Mazur, 1979, p. 307).

1 Make your home as safe as possible; locks, windows, and doors should be in good working condition. If you move to a new apartment or home, change the locks. The Crime Prevention Unit of the local police can give advice on making the residence burglar-proof – and thus rape-proof.

2 If you live alone:
  a leave lights on to give the impression of more than one occupant;
  b pretend that there is a male in the house when you answer the door (call out loudly, 'I'll get the door, Bob!');
  c do not list your first name on the doorbell or in the telephone book; instead, use initials.

3 In general, be aloof to strangers and never open the door to a stranger. Always ask for identification from a delivery or service man (their I.D. card can be slipped beneath the door). If children live in the house, be sure that they do not open the door to a stranger.

4 If you live in an apartment house, do not enter or remain alone in a deserted basement, garage, or laundry room.

5 If you receive an obscene telephone call, say nothing but hang up immediately and report the call to the police.

6 Avoid being alone on the streets or on a university campus late at night. However, if necessary, carry in your hand a 'practical' weapon, such as a lighted cigarette, a hat pin, a plastic lemon, an umbrella, a pen, a kitchen fork, a key chain, a hair brush or comb (to slash his face), or a police whistle (not tied around the neck, but on a key chain).

7 Do not hitchhike. (Everyone agrees that this is primary!) If absolutely necessary, go in groups and only in heavy traffic.

8 If you drive a car:
  a be sure your gas tank is never below one-quarter full;
  b always lock your car when you leave it;
  c check back seat and floor before getting into a car;

     d if you have car trouble, do not accept help from a man or group of men; instead, lift the hood, and wait inside the locked car for the police to come.

9 Be wary of picking up strange men in bars, particularly if you have been drinking heavily or using drugs.

10 Do not ride the elevators alone with a man. Either get off immediately or stand by the control panel.

11 On a date, communicate your limits of sexual activity early so that no misunderstandings occur later.

12 Baby-sitters should check on the family's reputation before taking the job. Parents should be very careful in the selection of a baby-sitter.

13 If you are attacked, do *not* cry 'rape', cry 'fire!'

'Normal' sexual behaviour

Cross-cultural differences

Many people suppose that human sexual behaviour is mainly governed by biological influences, since sexual intercourse is obviously a necessity for the reproduction of the species. In fact, unlike most of the animals, our sexual responses are not genetically given, but are almost all learned – and human sexual behaviour includes many other kinds of activities besides heterosexual intercourse (intercourse between a man and a woman). Homosexual behaviour, for example, is common in many cultures. We shall discuss homosexuality in the following section, concentrating for the time being on **heterosexuality**.

Accepted types of heterosexual behaviour vary widely between different cultures, which is one way in which we know that most sexual responses are learned rather than innate. The most extensive survey of sexual practices across different cultures was carried out several decades ago by Clellan Ford and Frank Beach (1951). They surveyed anthropological evidence from more than two hundred societies. Striking variations were found in what is regarded as 'natural' sexual behaviour, and in norms of sexual attractiveness (see also chapter 2: 'Culture and Society'.) For example, in some cultures extended foreplay, perhaps lasting some hours, is thought desirable and even necessary prior to intercourse. In others, foreplay is virtually non-existent. Kissing is an accepted sexual practice in some societies, but either not indulged in, or thought disgusting, among many peoples.

The position adopted by partners in the sexual act is also widely variable. Some cultures accept that a diversity of positions may be adopted in love-making, while in others only one is regarded as 'normal'. Variation was rare in Western culture until recently, the usual position being for the female to lie underneath the male, with the couple face to face. In many other societies this position is hardly ever used, the most common one being where the man enters the woman from the rear, both partners taking a squatting position. In some cultures, it is believed that overly frequent intercourse leads to physical debilitation or illness. Advice on the desirability of spacing out love-making among the Seniang of the South Pacific is given by the elders of the village – who also believe that a person with white hair may legitimately copulate every night!

In most cultures, norms of sexual attractiveness (held by both females and males) focus more on physical looks for women than for men – a situation which seems to be gradually changing in the West as women increasingly become active in spheres outside the domestic environment. The traits seen as most important in female beauty, however, are quite divergent across cultures. In some cultures, for example, a slim, small body build is admired, while in others a much more generous shape is regarded as most attractive. Sometimes the breasts are not seen as a source of sexual stimulus, whereas in other societies great erotic significance is attached to them. Some societies place great store upon the shape of the face, while others emphasize the shape and colour of the eyes, or the size and form of the nose and lips.

Sexuality in Western culture

Western attitudes towards sexual behaviour were for nearly two thousand years moulded primarily by Christianity. Although different Christian sects and denominations have held widely divergent views about the proper place of sexuality in life, the dominant view of the Christian church was that all sexual behaviour is suspect, and to be kept to the minimum needed to secure the production of children. At some periods, and in some places, this view produced an extreme prudishness in society at large. But at other times, many people ignored or reacted against the church's teachings, commonly engaging in various practices (such as adultery) forbidden by religious authorities. As was mentioned in chapter 1 ('Sociology: Problems and Perspectives'), the idea that sexual fulfilment can and should be sought through marriage was rare.

In the nineteenth century, religious presumptions about sexuality became partly replaced by medical ones. Most of the early writings by doctors about sexual behaviour, however, were as stern as the views of the Church. Some argued that any type of sexual activity unconnected with reproduction brings serious physical harm to those indulging in it. Masturbation was said to bring on blindness, insanity, heart disease and many other ailments, while oral sex was claimed to cause cancer (Feldman and MacCulloch, 1980). In Victorian times, sexual hypocrisy abounded. Virtuous women were believed to be indifferent to sexuality, accepting the attentions of their husbands only as a duty. Yet in the expanding towns and cities prostitution was rife, and often more or less openly tolerated, 'loose' women being seen as in an entirely different category from their respectable sisters.

Many men who were on the face of things sober, well-behaved citizens, devoted to their wives, regularly visited prostitutes or kept mistresses. Such behaviour by men was treated leniently, whereas 'respectable' women who took lovers were regarded as scandalous, and shunned in 'polite society' if their behaviour came to light. The differing attitudes towards the sexual activities of men and women formed a *double standard* which has long existed, and whose residues still linger on today.

In current times traditional attitudes of this type exist alongside much more liberal attitudes towards sexuality which developed particularly strongly in the 1960s. Many people, particularly those influenced by Christian teachings, believe that pre-marital sexual experience is wrong, and generally frown upon all forms of sexual behaviour except heterosexual activity within the confines of marriage – although it is now much more widely accepted that sexual pleasure is a desirable and important feature of the marital relationship. Others, by contrast, condone or actively approve of pre-marital sexual activity, and hold tolerant attitudes towards a wide range of sexual practices. Sexual attitudes have undoubtedly become more permissive over the past thirty or so years in most Western countries. In the cinema and theatre scenes are shown which previously would have been completely unacceptable, while pornographic material is readily available to most adults who wish to obtain it.

Sexual behaviour

We can speak much more confidently about public values in relation to sexuality in the past than we can about private practices, for by their nature such practices mostly go undocumented. When Alfred Kinsey began his researches in the United States, in the 1940s and 1950s, it was the first time a major investigation of actual sexual behaviour had been undertaken. Kinsey and his co-researchers faced condemnation from many religious organizations, and his work was denounced as immoral in the newspapers and in Congress. But he persisted, and eventually obtained sexual life-histories of 18,000 people, a reasonably representative sample of the white American population (Kinsey et al., 1948, 1953).

Kinsey's results were surprising to most, and shocking to many, because they revealed a great difference between the public expectations of sexual behaviour prevailing at that time and actual sexual conduct. He found that almost 70 per cent of men had visited a prostitute, and 84 per cent had pre-marital sexual experience. Yet, following the double standard, 40 per cent expected their wives to be virgins at the time of marriage. More than 90 per cent of males had engaged in masturbation, and nearly 60 per cent in some form of oral sexual activity. Among women, about 50 per cent had pre-marital sexual experience, although mostly with their prospective husbands. Some 60 per cent had masturbated, and the same percentage had engaged in oral–genital contacts.

Kinsey's findings demonstrated the gap that can exist between publicly accepted attitudes and real behaviour. But the discrepancy was probably particularly great at that particular period, just after the Second World War. A phase of sexual liberalization had begun rather earlier, in the 1920s, when many younger people felt freed from the strict moral codes that had governed earlier generations. Sexual behaviour probably changed a good deal, but issues concerning sexuality were not openly discussed in the way that has become familiar now. People participating in sexual activities that were still strongly disapproved of on a public level, concealed them, not realizing the full extent to which others were engaging in similar practices. The more permissive era of the 1960s brought openly declared attitudes more into line with the realities of sexual behaviour.

Other factors were also involved in the sexual liberalism of the 1960s. The social movements which challenged the existing order of things – like those associated with the 'New Left', or more generally with counter-cultural or 'hippy' life-styles – also broke with existing sexual norms. Many such groups preached sexual freedom, and the invention of the contraceptive pill for women allowed sexual pleasure to be clearly separated from reproduction. Women's groups also started pressing for greater independence from male sexual values, the rejection of the double standard and the need for women to achieve greater sexual satisfaction in their relationships.

No survey of comparable scope to that carried out by the Kinsey researchers has since been attempted in any country. Because of the fragmentary nature of subsequent research, we cannot be entirely sure how far sexual behaviour today differs from that of the immediate post-war period. But some trends seem fairly clear. There has been a progressive increase in the level of pre-marital sexual experience, particularly among women, in the United States and most European countries. It seems that most Western societies will sooner or later reach the point attained by Sweden in the early 1970s, when about 95 per cent of both women and men in that country had experienced sexual intercourse prior to marriage. Women generally have much higher aspirations towards sexual fulfilment than two decades ago, demanding sexual competence in their lovers and husbands. Extra-marital sexual activity has increased for both sexes, but particularly for women.

Two opposed influences now seem to be at work. Many previously hidden sexual practices have been made public. 'Swinging', spouse-swapping, transvestism (dressing in the clothes of the opposite sex, mainly on the part of males), sadomasochism (inflicting pain to bring sexual pleasure) and other sexual activities and inclinations are now openly discussed. Yet at the same time there is a strong current of 'sexual puritanism', linked to some degree with Rightist thinking in politics. Those involved are highly critical of sexual permissiveness, and preach a return to more rigid standards of behaviour. The spread of AIDS is a further important factor creating pressure towards the sustaining of monogamous relationships – whether inside or outside marriage.

Homosexuality

Homosexuality exists in all cultures. Yet the idea of a 'homosexual person' – someone clearly marked off in terms of their sexual tastes from the majority of the population – is only a relatively recent one. Before the eighteenth century the notion seems barely to have existed. The act of sodomy was denounced by church authorities and by the law; in England and several other countries it was punishable by death. However, sodomy was not defined specifically as a homosexual offence. It applied to relations between men and women, men and animals, as well as men amongst themselves. The term 'homosexuality' was coined in the 1860s, and from then onwards homosexuals were increasingly regarded as being a separate type of people having a particular sexual aberration (Weeks, 1986). Use of the term 'lesbian' dates from a slightly later time.

The death penalty for 'unnatural acts' was abolished in the United States following Independence, and in Europe in the late eighteenth and early nineteenth centuries (Hyde, 1970; Katz, 1976; Greenberg and Bystryn, 1984). Until relatively few decades ago, however, homosexuality remained a criminal activity in Britain in common with virtually all Western countries.

Homosexuality in non-Western cultures

There are many non-Western cultures in which homosexual relations are tolerated or even encouraged, although normally only among certain groups within the population. The Batak people of northern Sumatra, for example, permit male homosexual relationships before marriage. At puberty, a boy leaves his parents' house and sleeps in a dwelling with a dozen to fifteen males of his age or older. Sexual partnerships are formed between couples in the group and the younger boys are initiated into homosexual practices. This situation continues until young men marry. Once married most, but not all, men abandon homosexual activities (Money and Ehrdhardt, 1972).

Among the people of East Bay, a village in Melanesia in the Pacific, homosexuality is similarly tolerated – although again only in males. Prior to marriage, while living in the men's house, young men engage in mutual masturbation and anal intercourse. Homosexual relationships also exist, however, between older men and younger boys, often involving boys too young to be living in the men's house. Each type of homosexual relationship is completely acceptable and discussed openly. Many married men are bisexual, having relations with a younger boy while maintaining an active sexual life with their spouses. Homosexuality without an interest in heterosexual relationships seems to be unknown in this culture – a very common finding (Davenport, 1965; see also Shepherd, 1987).

Homosexuality in Western culture

The extent of homosexuality

Kenneth Plummer has distinguished four types of homosexuality within modern Western culture. *Casual homosexuality* is a passing homosexual encounter that does not substantially structure the overall sexual life of the individual. Schoolboy crushes, or mutual masturbation, are examples. Homosexuality as a *situated activity* refers to circumstances in which homosexual activities are regularly carried on, but where these do not become an individual's over-riding preference. In many carceral settings, such as prisons or military camps, homosexual behaviour of this kind is common. It is regarded as substitute for heterosexual behaviour rather than as preferable to it.

Personalized homosexuality refers to cases of individuals who have a preference for homosexual activities, but who are isolated from groups in which this is easily accepted. Homosexuality here is a furtive activity, hidden away from friends and colleagues. Homosexuality as a *way of life* refers to individuals who have 'come out', and have made associations with others of similar sexual tastes a key part of their lives. Such people usually belong to 'gay' sub-cultures, in which homosexual activities are integrated into a distinct life-style (Plummer, 1975).

The proportion of the population (both male and female) who have had homosexual experiences, or experienced strong inclinations towards homosexuality, is much larger than those who follow an openly gay life-style. The probable extent of homosexuality in Western cultures first became known with the publication of Alfred Kinsey's research. According to his findings, no more than half of all American men are 'completely heterosexual', judged by their sexual activities and inclinations after puberty. Eight per cent of Kinsey's sample had been involved in exclusively homosexual relationships for periods of three years or more. A further 10 per cent had mixed homosexual and heterosexual activities in more or less equal quantities. Kinsey's most striking finding was that 37 per cent of men had had at least one homosexual experience to the level of orgasm. An additional 13 per cent had felt homosexual desires but had not acted upon them.

Rates of homosexuality among women indicated by the Kinsey researchers were lower. About 2 per cent of females were exclusively homosexual. Homosexual experiences were reported by 13 per cent, while a further 15 per cent admitted they had had homosexual desires without acting on them. Kinsey and his colleagues were startled by the level of homosexuality their studies revealed, so the results were rechecked using various different methods, but the conclusions remained the same (Kinsey et al., 1948, 1953). Research since done on a lesser scale in the UK tends to support Kinsey's figures.

Attitudes towards homosexuality

Attitudes of intolerance towards homosexuality have been so pronounced in the past that it is only over recent years that some of the myths surrounding the subject have been dispelled. Homosexuality is not a sickness and is not distinctively associated with any forms of psychiatric disturbance. Homosexual males are not limited to any particular sector of occupations, like hairdressing, interior decorating or the arts, although some popular stereotypes suggest this is so. There is little direct connection between homosexuality and transvestism; the majority of transvestites are heterosexual men (Fisher, 1972; Spada, 1979).

Some kinds of male gay behaviour and attitudes might be seen as attempts to alter the usual connections of masculinity and power – one reason, perhaps, why homosexuals are so often thought to be threatening by the 'straight' community. Gay men tend to reject the image of the effeminate popularly associated with them – deviating from this in two ways. One is through cultivating outrageous effeminacy – a 'camp' masculinity that parodies the stereotype. The other is by developing a 'macho' image. This also is not conventionally masculine. Men dressed as motor-cyclists or cowboys are again parodying masculinity, through exaggerating it (Bertelson, 1986, chapter 7).

Gay sub-cultures

It is difficult to analyse changes in homosexual activities because there was almost no research before the period at which distinct gay sub-communities developed. Gay sub-cultures in large cities today tend to have exclusively homosexual meeting-places, such as clubs and gay bars. Although transient relationships are common, the majority of homosexuals who have 'come out' have long-lasting relationships. Outside the women's movement, lesbian communities tend to be less highly organized than male sub-cultures, and have a lower proportion of casual relationships.

The 1970s and 1980s witnessed a marked change in the public perception of homosexuals, particularly through the high media profile of such performers as David Bowie and Quentin Crisp, and the 'gender bender' movement popularized by the singer Boy George. Nevertheless, it would be wrong to overstate the general tolerance towards gays in

Britain. In 1985, 59 per cent of a national sample interviewed said that gay relationships were always wrong, while 13 per cent said that they were 'not wrong at all'. The 'softening' of public attitudes to gays has not been as radical as is sometimes suggested (Jowell et al., 1986).

Lesbianism

Except within the women's movement, lesbian groups are less highly organized than male gay sub-cultures, and have a lower proportion of casual relationships. Male homosexuality tends to receive more attention than **lesbianism**, and lesbian activist groups are often treated as if their interests were identical with those of male organizations. While there is sometimes close co-operation between male gays and lesbians, there are also differences, particularly where lesbians are actively involved in feminism. The specific character of lesbian women's lives and experiences is now being studied in more detail (Cruikshank, 1982).

Lesbian couples often have children, some through a relationship with a man, others through artificial insemination, but it has been difficult for lesbians to gain custody. In Britain and the United States courts decide whether a mother's lesbianism makes her an 'unfit' parent before allocating custody. Several cases were fought through the American courts in the late 1970s and early 1980s, establishing that lesbianism is not relevant to deciding whether or not a woman should be given custody of her child; but this has in practice only been accepted in a few states in the USA (Rights of Women Lesbian Custody Group, 1986).

AIDS

Recently, male homosexuality has been associated with the social impact of the disease **AIDS** (Acquired Immune Deficiency Syndrome). Media discussion of the illness only dates from late 1981, although within gay circles it was known earlier. AIDS came into public consciousness just at a time when it appeared that many of the pre-established prejudices against homosexuality were collapsing. The illness seemed to those repelled by homosexuality, especially some religious groups, to provide concrete evidence of their accusations. The idea that AIDS is a plague sent by God to punish perversion even found expression in some respectable medical quarters. An editorial in a medical journal asked: 'Might we be witnessing, in fact, in the form of a modern communicable disorder, a fulfilment of St. Paul's pronouncement: "The due penalty of their error"?' (quoted in Altman, 1986, p. 17).

The rapid spread of AIDS was undoubtedly due in some degree to the increased opportunities for homosexual encounters provided by gay sub-cultures in North America and elsewhere. In fact, initially AIDS seemed to be limited almost exclusively to large American cities with significant gay populations. Headlines in the press set the early tone: 'Gay plague baffling medical detectives' claimed the *Philadelphia Daily News* of 9 August 1982. 'Being gay is a health hazard' announced the *Saturday Evening Post* of October 1982, while the *Toronto Star* carried the banner 'Gay plague has arrived in Canada.' The magazine *Us* reported: 'Male homosexuals aren't so gay any more.' At the time it was already known that probably a third of those with AIDS in the United States were not homosexual, but in the initial publicity this was virtually ignored. When Rock Hudson, the film star, died of AIDS in 1985, what shocked much of the world's press was not the nature of his illness, but the fact that this symbol of male virility was homosexual.

Rather than looking for the source of the disease in a particular virus, medical researchers first tried to discover its origins in specific aspects of gay practices. The discovery that AIDS can be transmitted through heterosexual contact then forced a reappraisal. Most of the initial evidence for this came from central Africa, where AIDS was widespread but had no particular relation to male homosexuality. The 'gay plague' soon became redefined by the press as a 'heterosexual nightmare'.

The impact of AIDS is likely to influence many forms of sexual behaviour. In the homosexual community, marked changes are already noticeable, with the level of casual sexual encounters being radically reduced. Some of the most widely condemned homosexual practices, paradoxically, turn out to be the safest. For example, sadomasochistic activities involving the infliction of discomfort or pain on a partner are often entirely safe, because no direct genital contact is involved. The dilemma facing male gay communities is how to foster procedures of 'safe sex', while warding off the renewed attacks to which the gay community is subject.

AIDS and the heterosexual population

In medical terms, AIDS is a moving target, new and elusive. Medical knowledge about the illness dates very fast. AIDS is a condition which causes the body's immune system to collapse; it does not cause death itself, but the sufferer becomes prey to a range of illnesses, including cancers, which are fatal. Much of the evidence so far seems to link AIDS to a virus, or more probably to several related viruses.

AIDS is believed to be transmitted either by direct blood-to-blood contact (as where drug users share needles), or through sexually emitted fluids (semen or vaginal secretion). Homosexual men still account for over 70 per cent of all AIDS cases in the United States, and a higher proportion in most European countries (Vass, 1986).

There is some evidence that fear of AIDS is causing heterosexuals to become less promiscuous. A recent study of London prostitutes found that 70 per cent had changed their behaviour since they had heard of AIDS, and now required all clients to wear condoms for penetrative sex. However, a worrying 10 per cent of the group studied said they would continue to work as prostitutes even if they knew they were infected with the virus (Barton, 1985).

In most countries today controversies are developing about whether there should be compulsory screening for AIDS, and whether or not some discrimination against AIDS sufferers should be legalized. Civil rights groups argue that the introduction of any type of compulsory screening would mark a deterioration in individual freedom, while opponents claim that the price is worth paying if the spread of an awful disease can be halted. Some countries have introduced legal penalties for individuals who knowingly infect others – this carries a sentence of eight years in Norway, for example. In the USA the case of an AIDS patient who spat in the faces of two police officers is awaiting trial; the individual was charged with intent to murder. Under the Texas Communicable Disease and Prevention Act 1982, the city of San Antonio, Texas, has introduced penalties of up to ten years' imprisonment for AIDS sufferers who have sexual intercourse with healthy people. No legislation of this sort has as yet been seriously contemplated in Britain.

Prostitution

Prostitution can be defined as the granting of sexual favours for monetary gain. There is no clear-cut distinction between the paid mistress, whose main reason for granting sexual access to her patron is the money he provides, and prostitution as such, though the main difference is that the prostitute sells sexual access to numerous buyers. The word 'prostitute' began to come into common usage in the late eighteenth century. In the ancient world, most purveyors of sexuality for economic reward were courtesans, concubines (kept mistresses) or slaves. Courtesans and concubines often had a high position in traditional societies.

A key aspect of modern prostitution is that women and their clients are generally unknown to one another. Although men may become 'regular customers', the relationship is not initially established on the basis of personal acquaintance. This was not true of most forms of the dispensing of sexual favours for material gain in early times. Prostitution is directly connected to the break-up of small-scale communities, the development of large impersonal urban areas and the commercializing of social relations. In small-scale traditional communities, sexual relations were controlled by their very visibility. In newly developed urban areas, more anonymous social connections were easily established.

Prostitution today

Prostitutes in the UK today mainly come from poorer social backgrounds, as they did in the past, but they have been joined by considerable numbers of middle-class women. The increasing divorce rate has tempted some newly impoverished women into prostitution. In addition, some women unable to find jobs after graduation work in massage parlours, or in call-girl networks, while looking for other employment opportunities (Rosen, 1982, pp. 173–4).

Paul J. Goldstein has classified types of prostitution in terms of *occupational commitment* and *occupational context*. *Commitment* refers to the frequency with which a woman is involved in prostitution. Many women are only involved temporarily, selling sex a few times before abandoning prostitution for a long time or forever. 'Occasional prostitutes' are those who quite often accept money for sex, but irregularly, to supplement income from other sources. Others are continually involved in prostitution, deriving their main source of income from it. *Occupational context* means the type of work environment and interaction process in which a woman is involved. A 'street-walker' solicits business on the street. A 'call-girl' solicits clients over the phone, men either coming to her home or being visited by her. A 'house prostitute' is a woman who works in a private club or brothel. A 'massage-parlour prostitute' provides sexual services in an establishment supposedly offering only legitimate massage and health facilities.

Many women also engage in barter (payment in goods or other services rather than money) for sexual services. Most of the call-girls Goldstein studied regularly engaged in sexual bartering – sex in exchange for television sets, repairs of cars and electrical goods, clothes, legal and dental services (Goldstein, 1979).

A United Nations Resolution passed in 1951 condemns those who organize prostitution or profit from the activities of prostitutes, but does not ban prostitution as such. A total of fifty-three member states, including the UK, have formally accepted the resolution, although their legislation about prostitution varies widely. In some countries, prostitution itself is illegal. Others, like Britain, prohibit only certain types, such as street soliciting, or child prostitution. Some national or local governments license officially recognized brothels or sex-parlours – such as the 'Eros Centres' in West Germany or the sex houses in Amsterdam. Only a few countries license male prostitutes.

Legislation against prostitution is virtually everywhere confined to one side of the transaction between prostitutes and clients. Those who purchase sexual services are not arrested or prosecuted, and in court procedures their identities may be kept hidden. There are far fewer studies of clients than of those selling sexuality and it is rare for anyone to suggest – as is often stated or implied about prostitutes – that they are psychologically disturbed. The imbalance in research surely expresses an uncritical acceptance of orthodox stereotypes of sexuality, according to which it is 'normal' for men actively to seek a variety of sexual outlets, while those who cater for these needs are condemned.

Child prostitution

Prostitution frequently involves children. David Campagna has analysed the extent of child prostitution in the United States, basing his study on a large-scale research project which collected information from 596 police departments and 125 social service agencies throughout the country (Campagna, 1985). According to his figures, the annual revenue from child prostitution may amount to as much as two billion dollars, but despite these massive sums child prostitution for the most part does not seem to be controlled by networks of organized crime. A study of child prostitutes in the United States, Britain and West Germany indicated that the majority are involved in 'small-scale' operations in which, for example, children who have run away from home and have no income turn to prostitution to gain a livelihood. Most clients do not seem specifically attracted to children, looking rather for youthfulness in those whose sexual services they buy.

The fact that many runaway children turn to prostitution is in part an unintended consequence of laws which protect children against under-age employment, but by no means all child prostitutes have run away from home. Three broad categories of child prostitute can be distinguished (Janus and Heid Bracey, 1980):

1 *Runaways*, who either leave home and are not traced by their parents, or who persistently leave each time they are found and brought back.
2 *Walkaways*, who are basically living at home, but spend periods away, for example staying out periodically for several nights.
3 *Throwaways*, whose parents are indifferent to what they do, or actively reject them.

All categories involve males as well as females.

Child prostitution is part of the 'sex tourism' industry in several areas of the world – in, for instance, Thailand and the Philippines. Package tours, oriented towards prostitution, draw men to these areas from Europe, the United States and Japan. Members of Asian women's groups have organized public protests against these tours, which none the less continue. Sex tourism in the Far East has its origins in the provision of prostitutes for American troops during the Korean and Vietnam wars. 'Rest and recreation' centres were built in Thailand, the Philippines, Vietnam, Korea and Taiwan. Some still remain, particularly in the Philippines, catering to regular shipments of tourists as well as to the military stationed in the region.

Why does prostitution exist? Certainly it is an enduring phenomenon, which resists the attempts of governments to eliminate it. It is also almost always a matter of women selling sexual favours to men, rather than the reverse – although there are some instances, as in Hamburg, West Germany, where 'houses of pleasure' exist to provide male sexual services for women. Of course, boys or men also prostitute themselves with other men.

Thinking about the origins of heterosexual prostitution actually serves to focus the main issues with which this chapter has been concerned. It involves behaviour which is gender-divided (paying for sexual favours) and it is marked for the most part by distinct inequalities (for example, prostitutes are regarded with disapproval and may be subject to legal penalties, while their clients, more often than not, escape each of these social reactions). No single factor can explain prostitution. It might seem that men simply have stronger, or more persistent, sexual needs than women, and therefore require the outlets that prostitution provides. But this explanation is implausible. Most women seem capable of developing their sexuality in a more intense fashion than men of comparable age (Hyde, 1986). If prostitution existed simply to serve sexual needs, there would surely be many male prostitutes catering for women.

The most persuasive general conclusion to be drawn is that prostitution expresses, and to some extent helps perpetuate, the tendency of men to treat women as objects who can be 'used' for sexual purposes. Prostitution is an aspect of patriarchal relations, representing in a particular context the inequalities of power between men and women. Of course, many other elements are also involved. Prostitution offers a means of obtaining sexual satisfaction for people who, because of their physical shortcomings, or the existence of restrictive moral codes, cannot find other sexual partners. Prostitutes cater for men who are away from home, desire sexual encounters without commitment, or have unusual sexual tastes that other women will not accept. But these factors are relevant to the extent of the occurrence of prostitution rather than to its overall nature.

Conclusion: sociology and gender relations

Few areas of sociology have developed as significantly over recent years, or have emerged as so central to the discipline as a whole, as the study of gender relations. In some large part, this reflects changes in social life itself. Pre-established differences between male and female identities, outlooks and typical modes of behaviour are coming to be seen in a new light today. These changes affect numerous other social institutions, as well as sexual behaviour and family life. We shall trace their influence further in many of the chapters which follow.

Summary

1 The term 'sex' is ambiguous. As commonly used, it denotes physical and cultural differences between males and females (as in 'the male sex', 'the

female sex') as well as the sexual act. It is necessary also to distinguish between *sex*, in the physiological or biological sense, and *gender*, which is a cultural construct (a set of learned behaviour patterns).

2 Some people argue that differences in behaviour between the sexes are genetically determined, but there is no conclusive evidence for this.

3 *Gender socialization* begins as soon as an infant is born. Even parents who believe they treat children equally tend to react differently to boys and girls. These differences are reinforced by many other cultural influences.

4 Gender identity and modes of expressing sexuality develop together. It has been argued that masculinity depends upon denial of intimate emotional attachment to the mother, thus producing 'male inexpressiveness'.

5 *Patriarchy* refers to male dominance over women. All known societies are patriarchal, although the degree and character of inequalities between the sexes varies considerably across and between cultures.

6 In all the industrialized countries, women are under-represented in positions of power and influence. The average wage of women is well below that of men; many more women than men in paid employment are in part-time jobs. Women have a disproportionate share of responsibility for domestic work and child-care. Unpaid domestic work is enormously significant to the economy.

7 *Feminist* ideas can be traced back to the eighteenth century. The first significant feminist movements developed in the mid-nineteenth century, concentrating their attention particularly upon attaining the vote for women. Although falling into decline after the 1920s, in the 1960s feminism again burst into prominence, and has had an impact in many spheres of social life and intellectual activity.

8 *Sexual harassment* directly affects a high proportion of women in paid employment. *Domestic violence* and *rape* are also much more common than the official statistics reveal. There is a sense in which all women are victims of rape, since they have to take special precautions for their protection and live with the fear of rape.

9 Sexual practices vary widely between and within cultures. In the West, repressive attitudes to sexuality gave way to a more permissive outlook in the 1960s, the effects of which are still obvious today.

10 *Homosexuality* seems to exist in all cultures, yet the concept of 'a homosexual' is a relatively recent idea. Only in the last hundred years has homosexual activity been considered something that a certain type of person does – a category of abnormality and deviance constructed in opposition to the category of the 'normal heterosexual'.

11 Sexual behaviour is currently being strongly affected by the spread of Acquired Immune Deficiency Syndrome (*AIDS*). AIDS was originally

associated in the public mind only with homosexuality, but is also spread through heterosexual activity. AIDS threatens to become a major epidemic, and will only be contained if people adopt 'safe' sexual practices and avoid casual sexual contacts.

12 *Prostitution* is the granting of sexual favours for payment. Various different types of prostitution exist in modern societies, including male and child prostitution. Licensed prostitution is accepted by national or regional governments in some countries, but in most states prostitutes operate outside the law.

Basic concepts

gender   feminism
patriarchy

Important terms

femininity	domestic violence
masculinity	sexual harassment
sexual activity	rape
sex	heterosexuality
testicular feminization syndrome	homosexuality
androgenital syndrome	lesbianism
male inexpressiveness	AIDS
housework (domestic labour)	prostitution
suffragists	

Further reading

Nancy Chodorow, *The Reproduction of Mothering* (Berkeley: University of California Press, 1978) — a now classic study of gender using psychoanalytic theory to explain gender socialization.

Marilyn J. Davidson and Cary L. Cooper (eds), *Working Women. An International Survey* (New York: Wiley, 1984) — highlights the situations of women in diverse national work-forces and shows how the areas of inequality are often the same.

Hester Eisenstein, *Contemporary Feminist Thought* (London: Unwin, 1984) — a concise dictionary of the main trends in contemporary feminist theory and thinking. Traces how the initial emphasis that the women's movement placed on equality has been supplemented by a concern with the importance of the differences between men and women.

Eleanor Maccoby and Carol Jacklin, *The Psychology of Sex Differences* (Stanford: Stanford University Press, 1975) — a study of the different weights of biological and social influences in shaping the psychology of sex differences, which shows there is little evidence in favour, for example, of female hormones determining maternal behaviour.

Elizabeth M. Meehan, *Women's Rights at Work: Campaigns and Policy in Britain and The United States* (London: Macmillan, 1985) — Meehan's book is a detailed historical study of equal-pay legislation in the United States and Britain.

PART III

Structures of Power

Power is an ever-present phenomenon in social life. In all human groups, some individuals have more authority or influence than others, while groups themselves vary in terms of the level of their power. Power and inequality tend to be closely linked. The powerful are able to accumulate valued resources, such as property or wealth; and possession of such resources is in turn a means of generating power.

In this part, we discuss some of the main systems of power and inequality in society. The first chapter looks at stratification and class structure – the major ways in which inequalities are systematically distributed within societies. This is followed by a discussion of race and ethnicity, examining the tensions and hostilities often found between people who are physically or culturally different from one another.

We then move on to connect power and inequality with varying types of group and organization. Attention is given in particular to the study of the large organizations – like government agencies, industrial firms, hospitals or colleges – which dominate so much of modern social life. The final two chapters analyse two types of organization whose impact is particularly far-reaching – the state and the military. Governments are 'specialists' in power; they are the source of directives which influence many aspects of our daily activities. On the other hand, they are also the focus of resistance and rebellion. From their earliest origins, states have been associated with the development of military power. Military rivalries and wars have shaped human social development in far-reaching ways in the past, and continue to do so in the twentieth century. We look at the change in nature of the military in the modern world, the impact of military power upon social structures, and the possible implications of the world-wide build-up of armaments currently taking place.

PART III

Six Cities of Power

7

Stratification and Class Structure

Why are some groups in a society more wealthy or powerful than others? How unequal are modern societies? How much chance has someone from a lowly background of reaching the top of the economic ladder? Why does poverty persist in affluent countries today? These are some of the questions we shall pose and try to answer in this chapter. The study of social inequalities is one of the most important areas of sociology, because the material resources to which people have access determine a great deal about their lives.

Systems of social stratification

Inequalities exist in all types of human society. Even in the simplest cultures, where variations in wealth or property are virtually non-existent, there are inequalities between individuals, men and women, the young and old. A person may have a higher status than others, for instance, because of particular prowess at hunting, or because he or she is believed to have special access to the ancestral spirits. To describe inequalities, sociologists speak of the existence of **social stratification.** Stratification can be defined as *structured inequalities between different groupings of people.* It is useful to think of stratification as rather like the geological layering of rock in the earth's surface. Societies can be seen as consisting of 'strata' in a hierarchy, with the more favoured at the top and the less privileged nearer the bottom.

Four basic systems of stratification can be distinguished: *slavery, caste, estates* and *class.* These are sometimes found in conjunction with one another: slavery, for instance, existed alongside classes in ancient Greece and Rome, and in the Southern United States before the Civil War.

Slavery

Slavery is an extreme form of inequality, in which some individuals are literally owned by others as their property. The legal conditions of slave ownership have varied considerably between different societies. Sometimes slaves were deprived of almost all rights in law – as was the case in the southern United States – while in other instances their position was more akin to that of servant.

In the United States, South America and the West Indies in the eighteenth and nineteenth centuries, slaves were used almost exclusively as plantation workers and as domestic menials. In classical Athens, by contrast, they were found in many settings, sometimes in positions of great responsibility. Slaves were excluded from political positions and the military, but were found in most other types of occupation. Some were literate and worked as government administrators; many were trained in craft skills. In Rome, where the ruling groups held a low opinion of trade and commerce, slaves sometimes became very wealthy through their business activities, and some rich slaves even owned slaves themselves. At the bottom of the scale, however, those working on plantations or in mines in the ancient world were often treated harshly (Finley, 1968, 1980).

Slavery has frequently provoked resistance and struggle from those subjected to it. History is littered with slave rebellions, in some of which slaves managed collectively to free themselves from their masters. Systems of forced slave labour – such as on plantations – have tended to be unstable; high productivity can only be achieved through constant supervision and the use of brutal methods of punishment. Slave-labour systems break down partly because of the struggles they provoke, and partly because economic or other incentives motivate people more effectively than direct compulsion. Slavery is simply not very efficient. The slave trade carried on by the Western powers up to the nineteenth century was the last – but also the most extensive – system of trading in slaves to be carried on. Since freedom was granted to slaves in North and South America, something over a century ago, slavery as a formal institution has been gradually eradicated, and today has almost completely disappeared from the world.

Caste

Caste is associated above all with the cultures of the Indian sub-continent. The term 'caste' itself is not an Indian one, coming from the Portuguese *casta*, meaning 'race' or 'pure stock' (Littlejohn, 1972, p. 68). Indians themselves have no single term for describing the caste system as a whole, but a variety of words referring to different aspects of it, the two main ones being *varna* and *jati*. The *varna* consist of four categories, each ranked differently in terms of social honour. Below these four groupings are the 'untouchables', those in the lowest position of all. The *jati* are locally defined groups within which the caste ranks are organized.

The caste system is extremely elaborate, and varies in its structure from area to area – so much so that it does not really constitute one 'system' at all, but a loosely connected diversity of varying beliefs and practices. But certain principles are widely shared. Those in the highest *varna*, the Brahmins, represent the most elevated condition of purity, the untouchables the lowest. The Brahmins must avoid certain types of contact with the untouchables, and only the untouchables are allowed physical contact with animals or substances regarded as unclean. The caste system is closely bound up with the Hindu belief in rebirth; individuals who fail to abide by the rituals and duties of their caste, it is believed, will be reborn in an inferior position in their next incarnation. The Indian caste system has never been completely static. Although individuals are debarred from moving between castes, whole groups can change, and frequently have changed, their position within the caste hierarchy.

The concept of caste is sometimes used outside the Indian context where two or more ethnic groups are largely segregated from one another, and where notions of racial purity prevail. In such circumstances, there are strong taboos (or sometimes legal prohibitions) preventing intermarriage between the groups concerned. When slavery was abolished in the southern states of the USA, the degree of separation between blacks and whites remained so strong that some have used the term caste to refer to the stratification system (Cox, 1948; Dumont, 1970). The concept of caste has also been applied to

South Africa, where strict segregation is maintained between black and white, and intermarriage or sexual contact between them was until recently forbidden by law (see chapter 8: 'Ethnicity and Race').

Estates

Estates were part of European feudalism, but also existed in many other traditional civilizations. The feudal estates consisted of strata with differing obligations and rights, some of these differences being established by law. In Europe, the highest estate was composed of the aristocracy and gentry. The clergy formed another estate, having lower status but possessing various distinctive privileges. Those in what came to be called the 'third estate' were the commoners – serfs, free peasants, merchants and artisans. In contrast to castes, a certain degree of intermarriage and individual mobility was tolerated between estates. Commoners might be knighted, for example, to repay special services given to the monarch; merchants could sometimes purchase titles. A remnant of the system persists in Britain, where hereditary titles are still recognized, and business leaders, civil servants and others may be knighted or receive peerages in recognition of their services.

Estates have tended to develop in the past wherever there was a traditional aristocracy based on noble birth. In feudal systems, such as in mediaeval Europe, estates were closely bound to the local manorial community: they formed a local, rather than a national, system of stratification. In more centralized traditional empires, such as China or Japan, they were organized on a more national basis. Sometimes the differences between the estates were justified by religious beliefs, although rarely in as strict a way as in the Hindu caste system.

Class

Class systems differ in many respects from slavery, castes or estates. Four differences should be mentioned in particular:

1 Unlike the other types of strata, classes are not established by legal or religious provisions; membership is not based upon inherited position as specified either legally or by custom. Class systems are typically more fluid than the other types of stratification and the boundaries between classes are never clear-cut. There are no formal restrictions on intermarriage between people from different classes.

2 An individual's class is at least in some part *achieved*, not simply 'given' at birth as is common in other types of stratification system. Social mobility – movement upwards and downwards in the class structure – is much more common than in the other types. (In the caste system, individual mobility from one caste to another is impossible.)

3 Classes depend on *economic* differences between groupings of individuals – inequalities in possession and control of material resources. In

the other types of stratification system, non-economic factors (such as the influence of religion in the Indian caste system) are generally most important.

4 In the other types of stratification system, inequalities are expressed primarily in personal relationships of duty or obligation – between serf and lord, slave and master, or lower- and higher-caste individuals. Class systems, by contrast, operate mainly through large-scale connections of an impersonal kind. For instance, one major basis of class differences is to be found in inequalities of pay and working conditions; these affect all the people in specific occupational categories, as a result of economic circumstances pertaining in the economy as a whole.

We can define a class as a large-scale grouping of people who share common economic resources, which strongly influence the types of life-style they are able to lead. Ownership of wealth, together with occupation, are the chief bases of class differences. The major classes that exist in Western societies are an **upper class** (the wealthy, employers and industrialists, plus top executives – those who own or directly control productive resources); a **middle class** (which includes most white-collar workers and professionals); and a **working class** (those in blue-collar or manual jobs). In some of the industrialized countries, such as France or Japan, a fourth class – **peasants** (people engaged in traditional types of agricultural production) – has also until recently been important. In Third World countries, peasants are usually still by far the largest class.

We will now turn to a discussion of the major theories of stratification that have been developed in sociology, concentrating especially upon their relevance to modern societies.

Theories of stratification in modern societies

The most influential theoretical approaches are those developed by Karl Marx (1818–83) and Max Weber (1864–1920); most subsequent theories of stratification have been heavily indebted to their ideas. We shall also analyse two later theories, those put forward by Erik Olin Wright and Frank Parkin. The ideas of Marx and Weber have made a deep impact on the development of sociology, and have influenced many other areas of the discipline too. Aspects of their writings will be discussed in various subsequent chapters. (For an overall survey of their work, see chapter 22: 'The Development of Sociological Theory'.)

Karl Marx's theory

Marx was born in Germany, but spent much of his life in Britain. Although his ideas have always been controversial, they have been influential world-wide. Many authors (including Max Weber) who reject Marx's political views have drawn widely upon his writings.

Most of Marx's works were concerned with stratification and, above all, with social class, yet surprisingly he failed to provide a systematic analysis of the concept of class. The manuscript Marx was working on at the time of his death (subsequently published as part of his major work, *Capital*) breaks off just at the point where he posed the question 'What constitutes a class?'. Marx's concept of class thus has to be reconstructed from the body of his writings as a whole. Since the various passages in which he discusses class are not always fully consistent, there have been many disputes between scholars about 'what Marx really meant'. The main outlines of his views, however, are fairly clear.

The nature of class

For Marx a class is a group of people who stand in a common relationship to the **means of production** – the means by which they gain a livelihood. Before the rise of modern industry, the means of production consisted primarily of land and the instruments used to tend crops or pastoral animals. In pre-industrial societies, therefore, the two main classes were those who owned the land (aristocrats, gentry or slave-holders) and those actively engaged in producing from it (serfs, slaves and free peasantry). In modern industrial societies, factories, offices, machinery and the wealth or capital needed to buy them become more important. The two main classes are those who own these new means of production – industrialists or **capitalists** – and those who earn their living by selling their labour to them – the working class or, in the now somewhat archaic term Marx sometimes favours, the 'proletariat'.

The relationship between classes, according to Marx, is an exploitative one. In feudal societies, exploitation often took the form of the direct transfer of produce from the peasantry to the aristocracy. Serfs were compelled to give a certain proportion of their production to their aristocratic masters, or had to work for a number of days each month in the lord's fields to produce crops consumed by the lord and his retinue. In modern capitalist societies, the source of exploitation is less obvious, and Marx devotes much attention to trying to clarify its nature. In the course of the working day, Marx reasons, workers produce more than is actually needed by employers to repay the cost of hiring them. This **surplus value** is the source of profit, which capitalists are able to put to their own use. A group of workers in a clothing factory, say, might be able to produce a hundred suits a day. Selling half the suits provides enough income for the manufacturer to pay the workers' wages. Income from the sale of the remainder of the garments is taken as profit.

Marx was struck by the inequalities the capitalist system creates. Although in earlier times aristocrats lived a life of luxury, completely different from that of the peasantry, agrarian societies were relatively poor. Even if there had been no aristocracy, standards of living would inevitably have been meagre. With the development of modern industry, however, wealth is produced on a scale far beyond anything seen before, but workers have little access to the wealth their labour creates. They remain relatively poor, while the wealth accumulated by the propertied grows. Moreover, with the development of modern factories and the mechanization of production, work frequently becomes dull and oppressive in the extreme. The labour which is the source of our wealth is often both physically wearing and mentally tedious – as in the case of a factory hand whose job consists of routine tasks carried on day in, day out, in an unchanging environment.

The complexity of class systems

Although in Marx's theory there are two main classes in society, those who own the means of production and those who do not, he recognizes that actual class systems are much more complex than this model suggests. In addition to the two basic classes, there exist what Marx sometimes calls **transitional classes.** These are class groups left over from an earlier type of production system, which persist for long after that system has disappeared. In some modern Western societies (like France, Italy or Spain, for much of the current century), for example, substantial numbers of people remain peasants, working in much the same way as they did in the feudal system. Marx also draws attention to splits which occur within classes. Some examples can be given as follows.

1 Among the upper classes there are often conflicts between financial capitalists (like bankers) and industrial manufacturers.
2 There are divisions of interest between people with small businesses and those who own or manage large corporations. Both belong to the capitalist class, but policies which favour large businesses are not always in the interests of small ones.
3 Within the working class, the long-term unemployed have worse conditions of life than the majority of workers. These groups often consist largely of ethnic minorities.

Marx's concept of class directs us towards objectively structured economic inequalities in society. Class does not refer to the beliefs people hold about their position, but to objective conditions which allow some to have greater access to material rewards than others.

The theory of Max Weber

Like Marx, Max Weber was also German. Although illness prevented him from following an orthodox academic career, he had a private income, and was able to devote much of his life to scholarly study. He is regarded as one of the main founders of sociology, but his writings ranged much more widely than this, spanning many fields of history, legal theory, economics and comparative religion.

Weber's approach to stratification is built on the analysis developed by Marx, but modifies and elaborates it. There are two main differences between the two theories.

First, although Weber accepts Marx's view that class is founded on objectively given economic conditions, he sees a greater variety of economic factors as important in class formation than are recognized by Marx. According to Weber, class divisions derive not only from control or lack of control of the means of production, but from economic differences which have nothing directly to do with property. Such resources include especially the skills and credentials or qualifications which affect the types of job people are able to obtain. Those in managerial or professional occupations earn more, and have more favourable conditions of work, for example, than people in blue-collar jobs. The qualifications they possess, such as degrees, diplomas, and the skills they have acquired, make them more 'marketable' than others without such qualifications. At a lower level, among blue-collar workers, skilled craftsmen are able to secure higher wages than the semi- or unskilled.

Secondly, Weber distinguishes two other basic aspects of stratification besides class. One he calls *status* and the other *party*. He in fact adapted the notion of status groups from the example of mediaeval estates, the word he used in German (*Stand*) meaning both.

Status

Status refers to differences between social groups in the social honour or prestige they are accorded by others. Status distinctions often vary independently of class divisions, and social honour may be either positive or negative. Positively privileged status groups include any groupings of people who have high **prestige** in a given social order. For instance, doctors and lawyers have high prestige in British society. **Pariah groups** are negatively privileged status groups, subject to discrimination that prevents them taking advantage of opportunities open to most others. The Jews were a pariah group in mediaeval Europe, banned from participating in certain occupations, and from holding official positions.

Possession of wealth normally tends to confer high status, but there are many exceptions. The term 'genteel poverty' refers to one example. In Britain, individuals from aristocratic families continue to enjoy considerable social esteem even when their fortunes have been lost. Conversely, 'new money' is often looked on with some scorn by the well-established wealthy.

Whereas class is objectively given, status depends upon people's subjective evaluations of social differences. Classes derive from the economic factors associated with property and earnings; status is governed by the varying *styles of life* groups follow.

Party

In modern societies, Weber points out, party formation is an important aspect of power, and can influence stratification independently of class and status. 'Party' defines a group of individuals who work together because they have common backgrounds, aims or interests. Marx tended to explain both status differences and party organization in terms of class. Neither, in fact, Weber argues, can be reduced to class divisions, even though each is influenced by them; both can in turn influence the economic circumstances of individuals and groups, therefore affecting class. Parties may appeal to concerns cutting across class differences; for example, parties may be based on religious affiliation or nationalist ideals. A Marxist might attempt to explain the conflicts between Catholics and Protestants in Northern Ireland in class terms, since there are more Catholics than Protestants in working-class jobs. A follower of Weber would argue that such an explanation is ineffective, because many Protestants are also working-class in background. The parties to which people are affiliated express religious as well as class differences.

Weber's writings on stratification are important because they show that other dimensions of stratification besides class strongly influence people's lives. Most sociologists hold that Weber's scheme offers a more flexible and sophisticated basis for analysing stratification than that provided by Marx.

Recent theories of class

The ideas developed by Marx and Weber are still used extensively in sociology today, although rarely without modification. Those who have worked in the Marxian tradition have further developed the ideas Marx himself set out; others have tried to elaborate Weber's concepts. Since the two standpoints are similar in many ways, and complementary in others, some common ways of thinking have emerged. We can give some indication of these by looking briefly at two more recent theoretical perspectives.

Erik Olin Wright's theory of class

The American sociologist Erik Olin Wright has developed a theoretical position which owes much to Marx, but also incorporates ideas from Weber (Wright, 1978, 1985). According to Wright, there are three dimensions of control over economic resources in modern capitalist production, and these allow us to identify the major classes which exist.

1 Control over investments or money capital.
2 Control over the physical means of production (land or factories and offices).
3 Control over labour-power.

Those who belong to the capitalist class have control over each of these dimensions within the production system. Members of the working class have control of none of them. In between these two main classes, however, there are groups whose position is more ambiguous. These people are in what Wright calls **contradictory class locations**, because they are able to influence some aspects of production, but are denied control over others. White-collar and professional employees, for example, have to contract their labour-power to employers in order to obtain a living, in the same way as manual workers do. Yet at the same time they have a greater degree of control over the work setting than most people in blue-collar jobs. Wright terms the class position of such workers 'contradictory', because workers in such class locations are neither capitalists nor manual workers, yet share certain common features with each.

Frank Parkin: a Weberian approach

Frank Parkin, a British author, has proposed an approach drawing more heavily on Weber than on Marx (Parkin, 1971, 1979). Parkin agrees with Marx, as Weber did, that ownership of property – the means of production – is the basic foundation of class structure. Property, however, according to Parkin, is only one form of **social closure** which can be monopolized by a minority and used as a basis of power over others. We can define social closure as any process by which groups try to maintain exclusive control over resources, limiting access to them. Besides property or wealth, most of the characteristics Weber associated with status differences, such as ethnic origin, language or religion, may be used to create social closure.

Two types of process are involved in social closure. *Exclusion* refers to strategies which groups adopt to separate outsiders from themselves, preventing them having access to valued resources. Thus white unions in the USA have in the past excluded blacks from membership, as a means of maintaining their own privileges. *Usurpation* refers to the attempts of the less privileged to acquire resources previously monopolized by others – as where blacks struggle to achieve rights of union membership.

Both strategies may be used simultaneously in some circumstances. Trade unions, for instance, might engage in usurpatory activities against employers (going on strike to obtain a greater share of the resources of a firm) but at the same time may exclude ethnic minorities from membership. Parkin calls this *dual closure*. Here there is clearly a point of similarity between Parkin and Wright. Dual closure concerns much the same processes as those discussed by Wright under the heading of contradictory class locations. Both notions indicate that those in the middle of the stratification system in some part cast their eyes towards the top, yet are also concerned to distinguish themselves from others lower down.

Classes in Western societies today

Some authors have argued that class has become relatively unimportant in modern Western societies. It is generally agreed that a century and a half ago, in the early period of the development of industrial capitalism, there were major class differences. Even those who are most critical of Marx's thought acknowledge that there were yawning gaps between the labouring poor and the wealthy industrialists who employed them. Since then, it has been claimed, material inequalities have been greatly lessened in the industrialized countries. Taxes directed against the rich, combined with welfare benefits for those who cannot easily earn a living for themselves, have flattened out the top and bottom of the scale of inequality. Moreover, with the spread of public education, those who have the necessary talent can find their way to the top levels of the social and economic system.

This picture unfortunately is far from being accurate. The influence of class may be less than Marx supposed, but there are few spheres of social life left untouched by class differences. Even physical differences are correlated with class membership. Working-class people have on average lower birth-weight and higher rates of infant mortality, are smaller at maturity, less healthy, and die at a younger age, than those in higher class categories. Major types of mental disorder and physical illness including heart disease, cancer, diabetes, pneumonia and bronchitis are all more common at lower levels of the class structure than towards the top (Zola and Kosa, 1975; Luft, 1978; Waitzkin, 1986).

Differences of wealth and income

Marx believed that the maturing of industrial capitalism would bring about an increasing gap between the wealth of the minority and the poverty of the mass of the population. According to him, the wages of the working class could never rise far above subsistence level, while wealth would pile up in the hands of those owning capital. At the lowest levels of society, particularly among those frequently or permanently unemployed, there would be an 'accumulation of misery, agony of labour, slavery, ignorance, brutality, moral degradation . . .' (Marx, 1970, p. 645). Marx was right, as we shall see, about the persistence of poverty within the industrialized countries, and in anticipating that large-scale inequalities of wealth and income would continue. He was wrong in supposing that the income of most of the population would remain extremely low, as well as in claiming

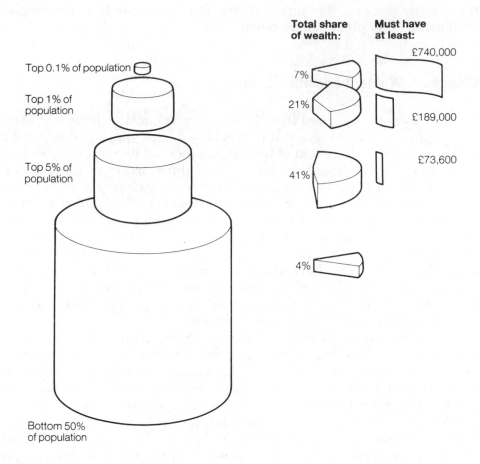

Figure 6   Personal wealth of different sections of the population in Britain, 1987
Source: New Society, 24 April 1987, p. 44.

that a minority would become more and more wealthy relative to the majority. Most people in Western countries today are much better off materially than were comparable groups in Marx's day. To examine how far, and why, this is the case, we have to look at changes in the distribution of wealth and income over the past century or so.

   Wealth refers to all the assets individuals own (stocks and shares, savings and property such as homes or land; items which can be sold). **Income** refers to wages and salaries coming from paid occupations, plus 'unearned' money deriving from investments (usually interest or dividends). While most people get what money they have from their work, the wealthy derive the bulk of their income from investments.

Wealth

Reliable information about the distribution of wealth is difficult to obtain. Some countries keep more accurate statistics than others, but there is always a considerable amount of guesswork involved. The affluent do not usually publicize the full range of their assets; it has often been remarked that we know far more about the poor than we do about the wealthy. What is certain is that wealth is concentrated in the hands of very few. In Britain the top 1 per cent owns some 21 per cent of all personal wealth (owned by individuals rather than organizations). Just over a third of the nation's wealth is at the disposal of 80 per cent of the population. Ownership of stocks and bonds is more unequal than holdings of wealth as a whole. The top 1 per cent in the UK owns some 75 per cent of privately held corporate shares; the top 5 per cent owns over 90 per cent of the total. Some 20 per cent of the population own shares, according to a survey carried out for the Office of Population Censuses and Surveys in 1987. This compares with 14 per cent two years before, suggesting that many people bought shares for the first time during the Conservative government's privatization programme. The increase is even more dramatic when looked at over a longer period, for in 1979 only 5 per cent of the population held shares. Most of these holdings are small (worth less than £1,000 at 1987 prices), and institutional share ownership – shares held by companies in other firms – is growing faster than individual share ownership.

Income

One of the most significant changes in Western countries over the past century has been the rising real income of the majority of the working population (real income is actual income not including rises resulting from inflation, so as to provide a fixed standard of comparison from year to year). Blue-collar workers in Western societies now earn between three and four times as much in real income as their counterparts at the turn of the century. Gains for white-collar, managerial and professional workers have been slightly higher. In terms of earnings per head of the population, and the range of goods and services which can be purchased, the majority of the population today are vastly more affluent than any peoples have been before in human history. One of the most important reasons for the growth in earnings is the increasing *productivity* – output per worker – that has been secured through technological development in industry. The value of the goods and services produced per worker has risen more or less continually, in many industries at least, since the 1900s.

Nevertheless, just as in the case of wealth, income distribution is very unequal. The top 5 per cent of earners in the UK receive 16 per cent of total income; the highest 20 per cent obtain 42 per cent of the total. The bottom fifth of earners receive only 5 per cent of overall income (statistics from 1985). In most Western countries, including Britain, wealth and income have become rather more equally distributed than was the case

How much do people earn per week?

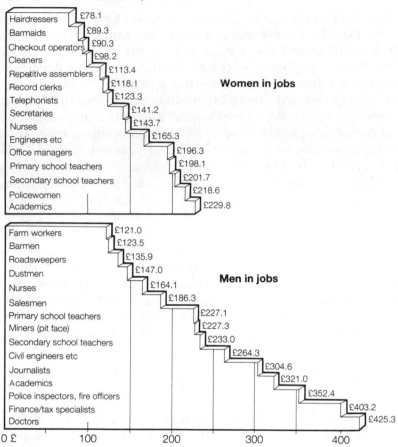

Women in jobs

Hairdressers	£78.1
Barmaids	£89.3
Checkout operators	£90.3
Cleaners	£98.2
Repetitive assemblers	£113.4
Record clerks	£118.1
Telephonists	£123.3
Secretaries	£141.2
Nurses	£143.7
Engineers etc	£165.3
Office managers	£196.3
Primary school teachers	£198.1
Secondary school teachers	£201.7
Policewomen	£218.6
Academics	£229.8

Men in jobs

Farm workers	£121.0
Barmen	£123.5
Roadsweepers	£135.9
Dustmen	£147.0
Nurses	£164.1
Salesmen	£186.3
Primary school teachers	£227.1
Miners (pit face)	£227.3
Secondary school teachers	£233.0
Civil engineers etc	£264.3
Journalists	£304.6
Academics	£321.0
Police inspectors, fire officers	£352.4
Finance/tax specialists	£403.2
Doctors	£425.3

0 £   100   200   300   400

The low paid
Percentage of employed people earning less per week than

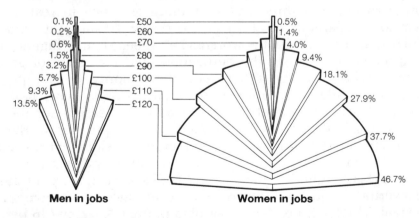

Men in jobs		Women in jobs
0.1%	£50	0.5%
0.2%	£60	1.4%
0.6%	£70	4.0%
1.5%	£80	9.4%
3.2%	£90	18.1%
5.7%	£100	27.9%
9.3%	£110	37.7%
13.5%	£120	46.7%

Men in jobs   **Women in jobs**

Figure 7 Levels of pay for different kinds of work in Britain, 1986. Even when men and women are in the same occupations, they can be receiving very different pay. As the second chart shows, women typically earn much less than men – 46 per cent of women, but only 13.5 per cent of men, earn less than £120 per week
Source: New Society, 24 April 1987, p. 44.

half a century or more ago. This trend has been less pronounced in the United States than elsewhere, and over the past twenty-five years there seems to have been little change in wealth or income inequality in that country. Since the fortunes possessed by the richest Americans are so very large, the disparity between the wealthy and the poor in the USA is considerably greater than in most countries in the industrialized world.

Ownership of wealth, especially ownership of capital, all four theorists discussed above agree, is a basic dimension of the class system. Let us look now at the main class divisions in the United Kingdom.

The upper class

The upper class in British society consists of relatively small numbers of individuals and families who own considerable amounts of property – thinking of them as the top 1 per cent of wealth-holders provides an approximate statistical guide. There tend to be fairly clear status divisions within the upper class between 'old' and 'new' money. Families whose property has been inherited through several generations often look down on those whose wealth is self-made. While they may mix in some contexts, those who have risen from humbler origins often find themselves excluded from most of the circles in which the longer-established wealthy move.

Property, as both Marx and Weber emphasize, confers power, and members of the upper class are disproportionately represented at the higher levels of power. Their influence stems in part from direct control of industrial and financial capital, and in part from their access to leading positions in the political, educational and cultural spheres. Stanworth and Giddens found that in the UK between 1850 and 1970 the proportion of large-company chairmen with upper-class backgrounds remained stable at around 66 per cent (Stanworth and Giddens, 1974).

The British public is under no illusion about the importance of inheritance: 45 per cent of those questioned in a 1986 Gallup poll believed that inheritance and having the 'right' parents were the main ways to get (or stay) rich. By contrast, a similar poll in the USA revealed that 43 per cent, the largest proportion of those interviewed, said 'hard work' was the way to get rich.

The middle class

The phrase *the middle class* covers people working in many differ-ent occupations. According to some observers, the majority of the population of Britain today falls into this class, because the proportion of white-collar jobs has risen markedly relative to blue-collar ones (see chapter 15: 'Work and Economic Life').

There are three fairly distinct sectors within the middle class. The *old middle class* consists of the owners of small businesses, the proprietors of local shops and small farmers. The numbers in this category have declined steadily over the past century, but still compose a significant proportion of the overall working population. Small businesses are much more unstable than larger ones, and most fail within two years of being set up. Only some 20 per cent of those established in any one year in the UK are still in business five years later. Small firms and shops are often unable to compete effectively with the large companies, supermarkets and restaurant chains. If the old middle class has not shrunk as much as some (including Marx) once thought would be the case, it is because there is a large reservoir of people wanting to try their hand at starting a business of their own. Most of those who go out of business are thus replaced by others. Small-business men and women tend to have a fairly distinct social and political outlook. In some countries, such as France, many have been persistent supporters of political parties of the extreme Right.

The *upper middle class* is made up mainly of those holding managerial or professional positions. This category includes large numbers of individuals and families, and generalizing about their attitudes and outlook is risky. Most have experienced some form of higher education, and the proportion holding liberal views on social and political issues, especially among professional groups, is fairly high.

The *lower middle class* is an even more heterogeneous category, including people working as office staff, sales representatives, teachers, nurses and others. For the most part, in spite of the merging of some of their conditions of work, the majority of members of the lower middle class tend to have different social and political attitudes to most blue-collar workers.

The diverse character of the middle class as a whole is captured to some degree by concepts such as those offered by Wright and Parkin. Middle-class people find themselves in 'contradictory' situations of 'dual closure' in the sense that they are caught between conflicting pressures and influences. Many lower-middle-class people, for example, identify with the same values as those in more remunerative positions, but may find themselves living on incomes below those of the better-paid manual workers.

The working class

The working class consists of those working in blue-collar, manual occupations. As with the middle class, there tend to be marked divisions within the working class as a whole. One important source of such divisions is skill-level. The *upper working class*, consisting of skilled workers, has frequently been seen as an 'aristocracy of labour', its members having superior incomes, conditions of work and job security to those in other blue-collar occupations (Mackenzie, 1973). Although some skills have been undermined by technological developments, and the position of the workers in the occupations concerned weakened – as among printers – on the whole the economic circumstances of skilled workers have become even more favourable in recent years. In many trades, their earnings have remained relatively high, and their jobs stable, much less affected by increasing levels of unemployment than those in less skilled blue-collar jobs.

The *lower working class* is made up of those in unskilled or semi-skilled jobs, which need little training. Most of these jobs carry lower incomes than, and inferior job security to, skilled occupations.

Working-class occupations differ in terms of whether they are full-time or part-time, and how much job security workers have. A distinction between *central* and *peripheral* areas of the economy helps to illuminate this. Central sectors are those in which workers are in full-time jobs, obtaining relatively high earnings and enjoying long-term job security. Peripheral sectors are those where jobs are insecure, having low earnings, with a high proportion of part-time workers. Skilled workers, and a proportion of semi- and unskilled employees (mostly male whites) predominate in the central sectors – which are also more often unionized. Others find themselves in the peripheral sector, where the level of unionization is low (Form, 1985).

A major line of demarcation within the working class is between the ethnic majority and underprivileged minorities – who compose an **underclass**. Members of the underclass have markedly inferior conditions of work and living standards to the majority of the population. Many are among the long-term unemployed, or drift in and out of jobs. In Britain, blacks and Asians are disproportionately represented in the underclass. In some European countries, migrant workers who found jobs in times of greater prosperity twenty years ago now make up a large part of this sector of the working class. This is true, for instance, of Algerians in France and Turkish migrants in West Germany.

Studying class consciousness: different approaches

Innumerable surveys have been carried out investigating **class consciousness** – how people think about class and class divisions. Various strategies have been used in such studies.

The reputational method

In the reputational method respondents are asked in which classes they would place other people. One of the most well-known studies of this type was carried out by W. Lloyd Warner and Paul Lunt in Newburyport, a small town in Massachusetts in the United States (Warner and Lunt, 1947; Warner et al., 1949). Lengthy interviews were

Table 3 Self-rated social class in Britain, 1986

Social class (%)	Self	Parents
Upper middle	1	2
Middle	24	17
Upper working	21	12
Working	48	59
Poor	3	8
Don't know/no response	3	2
Sample size (= 100%) (numbers)	3,066	3,066

Source: Social Trends (London: HMSO, 1987), p. 16.

conducted with many residents in order to build up a picture of their views of the class divisions within the community. Terms like 'the folks with the money', 'poor folk but decent' and 'nobodies' were consistently referred to by respondents. Six social classes were identified on the basis of their responses: an upper, middle and lower class, each having sub-divisions.

This approach has quite often been used since the original studies of Warner and his associates, but it can only be effectively applied in small communities. Moreover, it merges two phenomena which should be kept conceptually separate – *class*, and *class consciousness*. Class differences exist regardless of whether or not people are conscious of them.

The subjective method

The subjective method simply involves asking people what class they believe themselves to belong to. An early study of this type was carried out in the United States by Richard Centers, who obtained responses from a national random sample (Centers, 1949). He undertook his research in the wake of a poll organized by the magazine *Fortune*, which claimed that 80 per cent of Americans identified themselves as middle class. Centers observed that the poll had only offered respondents three choices 'upper class', 'middle class' and 'lower class'. He found that if a fourth choice, 'working class', were added about half of those in his sample put themselves in this category. People were prepared to see themselves as 'working class', but were unhappy about placing themselves in the 'lower class'. Since responses vary according to the questions asked in this way, it is difficult to assess the value of results of such studies.

However, Mary and Robert Jackman (1983) have recently tried to build upon Centers' approach to class. They used data from a national survey of attitudes towards and awareness of class in the United States, conducted by the Survey Research Center of the University of Michigan. People were asked to say which of the following classes they considered they belonged to: the poor, the working class, the middle class, the upper middle class, or the upper class. All but 3 per cent of the respondents identified themselves with one of the five class categories. About 8 per cent saw themselves as 'poor', 37 per cent as 'working class', 43 per cent as 'middle class', 8 per cent as 'upper middle class'; and 1 per cent as 'upper class'. There was a high level of agreement over which occupations were associated with these classes. For instance, business executives, doctors and lawyers were almost invariably placed in the 'upper middle' or 'upper class' categories. There were no significant differences between blacks and whites in these assessments. (For a survey of self-rated class in Britain, see table 3.)

Images of the class structure

A third approach to studying class consciousness involves investigating images of the class structure. Research of this sort tends to be more informative than either of the other two approaches, because it looks more directly at *how* people think about the nature and sources of social inequality. For example, there are types of attitude and outlook which do not necessarily even employ the word 'class' itself, but none the less express important aspects of class consciousness. Thus upper-class or upper-middle-class people may sometimes deny that classes exist at all. We may see this sociologically, however, as *itself* an expression of class consciousness. People in such class positions tend to interpret the social world as a hierarchy of positions in which opportunities for advancement are fairly equal for everyone. Their image of stratification corresponds to the contexts of their own experience, but is generalized to the whole society.

Those at lower levels of the class structure, on the other hand, tend more often to see stratification in terms of an opposition between 'us' and 'them'. 'They' are people in authority – officials, bosses or managers. 'We' are those subject to that authority – in similar conditions of work or in a situation of relative powerlessness.

A classic discussion of class imagery was developed by David Lockwood in the 1960s (Lockwood, 1966). He argued that people's images of the class structure are strongly influenced by the local circumstances in which they live. Their communities, towns or neighbourhoods, together with their experiences in the work environment, most directly affect how they see the class system. Lockwood's discussion concentrates on the working class, distinguishing three main types of working-class images of society.

Proletarian traditionalism is the characteristic outlook of groups living in industrial communities which are relatively isolated and where many people work in similar settings, in close co-operation with one another. An example would be the mining towns and villages of South Wales. In

such communities, feelings of shared work experience and class identification are readily generated. Workers holding this type of class imagery see the social world in terms of a division between 'us' and 'them'.
They usually also are inclined to be committed members of trade unions.

Deferential traditionalism is characteristic of working-class groups
living in more diverse community and work environments, such as
farm employees in rural areas. Such workers see the class structure
in more co-operative and harmonious terms. Their view of the social
world is one in which 'everyone knows their place', and where
inequalities express justified differences of talent and responsibility.
These workers are deferential towards their 'superiors', and aware of
the class hierarchy, but accept it as legitimate and necessary. Most
workers with these attitudes are indifferent or hostile to trade unions.

Privatized workers have broken with both of the other types of
outlook. They live away from the older working-class communities and
neighbourhoods (in new suburban housing estates, for example), and
hold 'individualist' attitudes. They see work mainly as a way of achieving
a satisfactory life-style for themselves and their families, and feel few
of the old class loyalties. A study which Goldthorpe, Lockwood and
their colleagues carried out among Luton car-workers showed many
such workers to have this type of outlook (Goldthorpe et al., 1968–9).

Lockwood's typology has stimulated much subsequent research,
although some of this has been critical of the categories he distinguished (Bulmer, 1975). Most studies have found that the three types
of class imagery are not as clear-cut as Lockwood suggested. Workers
whose views approximate to 'proletarian traditionalism', moreover,
are by no means always more militant than others. People having
a 'privatized' outlook are prepared to engage in industrial action,
given a certain level of grievance, and may also at this point shift
to the idiom of 'us' versus 'them'.

The older 'solidary working-class communities' have been to some
considerable degree broken up by various processes of change over
the past several decades. Industries like coal-mining, or iron and steel
production, have for some while been in decline. Many workers have
moved elsewhere in the country, this process also commonly being
associated with the development of more 'privatized' attitudes towards
work. Yet 'us' and 'them' imagery has certainly not disappeared: it
is an outlook that persists in many working-class neighbourhoods.
In areas with substantial minority groups, 'us' and 'them' attitudes
may fuse class and ethnic consciousness.

Gender and stratification

Studies of stratification were for many years 'gender blind' – they
were written as though women did not exist, or as though, for

purposes of analysing divisions of power, wealth and prestige, women were unimportant and uninteresting. Yet gender itself is one of the most profound examples of stratification. There are no societies in which men do not, in some aspects of social life, have more wealth, status and influence than women.

Class divisions and gender

One of the main problems posed by the study of gender and stratification in modern societies sounds simple, but turns out to be difficult to resolve. This is the question of how far we can understand gender inequalities in modern times mainly in terms of class divisions. Inequalities of gender are more deep-rooted historically than class systems; men have superior standing to women even in hunting and gathering societies, where there are no classes. Yet class divisions are so marked in modern societies that there is no doubt that they 'overlap' substantially with gender inequalities. The material position of most women tends to reflect that of their fathers or husbands; hence it can be argued that we have to explain gender inequalities mainly in class terms.

Frank Parkin has expressed this point of view very well:

> Female status certainly carries with it many disadvantages compared with that of males in various areas of social life including employment opportunities, property ownership, income, and so on. However, these inequalities associated with sex differences are not usefully thought of as components of stratification. This is because for the great majority of women the allocation of social and economic rewards is determined primarily by the position of their families and, in particular, that of the male head. Although women today share certain status attributes in common, simply by virtue of their sex, their claims over resources are not primarily determined by their own occupation but, more commonly, by that of their fathers or husbands. And if the wives and daughters of unskilled labourers have something in common with the wives and daughters of wealthy landowners, there can be no doubt that the *differences* in their overall situation are far more striking and significant. Only if the disabilities attaching to female status were felt to be so great as to override differences of a class kind would it be realistic to regard sex as an important dimension of stratification. (Parkin, 1971, pp. 14–15)

Women, it can be argued, tend to be confined to a 'private' domain – the domestic world of the family, children and the household. Men, on the other hand, live in more of a 'public' domain, from which variations in wealth and power primarily derive. Their world is that of paid work, industry and politics (Elshtain, 1981).

The view that class inequalities largely govern gender stratification was often an unstated assumption until recently, but the issue has now become the subject of some debate. John Goldthorpe has defended what he calls the 'conventional position' in class analysis – that the paid work of women is relatively insignificant compared to that of men, and that therefore women can be regarded as being in the same class as their husbands (Goldthorpe, 1983). This is not, Goldthorpe emphasizes, a view based on an ideology of sexism. On the contrary, it recognizes the subordinate position in which most women find themselves in the labour-force. Women have part-time jobs more often than men, and tend to have more intermittent experience of paid employment because of withdrawing for lengthy periods to bear and care for children. Since the majority of women are in a position of economic dependence on their husbands, it follows that their class position is most often governed by the husbands' class situation.

Goldthorpe's argument can be criticized in several ways. First, in a substantial proportion of households the income of women is essential to maintaining the family's economic position and mode of life. In these circumstances women's paid employment in some part determines the class position of households. Second, a wife's employment may strongly influence that of her husband, not simply the other way around. Although women rarely earn more than their husbands, the working situation of a wife might still be the 'lead' factor in influencing the class of her husband. This could be the case, for instance, if the husband is an unskilled or semi-skilled blue-collar worker and the wife, say, the manageress of a shop. The wife's occupation may set the standard of the position of the family as a whole.

Third, many 'cross-class' households exist, in which the work of the husband is in a higher class category than that of the wife, or (less commonly) the other way around. Since few studies have been carried out looking at the consequences of this, we cannot be confident that it is always appropriate to take the occupation of the male as the determining influence. There may be some purposes for which it is more realistic to treat men and women, even within the same households, as being in different class positions. Fourth, the proportion of families in which women are the sole breadwinners is increasing. Unless the woman has an income derived from alimony which puts her on the same economic level as her ex-husband, she is by definition the determining influence upon her own class position (Stanworth, 1984; Walby, 1986).

Recent research has supported the conclusion that the economic position of a woman cannot simply be 'read off' from that of her husband. A study carried out in Sweden showed cross-class families to be common (Leiuffsrud and Woodward, 1987). In most such cases, the husband had the superior occupation, although in a minority of instances the reverse was the case. The research showed that individuals in such families tended to 'import' aspects of their differing class position into the family. Decisions, for instance, about who stays home to care for a sick child were related to the interaction of class and gender in the family. Where the wife's job was superior to that of the husband, he would usually have this responsibility.

The study of women in stratification research

Women have only rarely been directly included in research into occupations and work situations (Stromberg and Harkness, 1977; Barker and Allen, 1976). Even where women do appear in research studies, less attention is paid to their activities and attitudes than to those of males. Roslyn Feldberg and Evelyn Glenn have distinguished two conceptual models used in the study of class and gender differences. One, the *job model*, has been applied mainly to men; the other, the *gender model*, has been used primarily in relation to women (Feldberg and Glenn, 1984). The job model assumes that basic social relationships are determined by work; that families are headed by males; and that employment and financial earnings are the main influence over an individual's life activities. The gender model accepts that the family is male-headed, but sees the family as determining basic social relationships, rather than work, and treats domestic roles as the main focus of a person's life.

Looking at some well-known studies of occupations, Feldberg and Glenn show that the use of these models actively distorts the conclusions reached. One piece of research they examine, for example, is Robert Blauner's work *Alienation and Freedom* (1964). Blauner's research included a comparison of men and women working within the textile industry. The jobs studied were mostly routine and uninteresting. Those of the women were more demanding than the men's, because the women's work was more closely paced by machines requiring a consistently fast rhythm of work. Even though the women had worse working conditions than the men, they did not express greater dissatisfaction with their jobs. Blauner comments that this is because work did not have a central importance in their lives, their most important roles being those of wife and mother. In other words, he invokes the gender model. He provides no evidence to support this interpretation, however, although detailed information was gathered about why men hold the attitudes they do. The reader of Blauner's book is not told what proportion of the women were mothers and housewives, or what their domestic responsibilities were. Women were presumed to be little affected by the nature of the paid work they did, while considerable research effort was expended to document the ways in which the men related to their jobs. Feldberg and Glenn conclude that:

> When several alternative explanations could plausibly be invoked, the one that is most consistent with job or gender models is favoured without adequate discussion . . . the search for alternative interpretations is short-circuited. The models offer a ready-made explanation and the researcher follows the path of least resistance. These distortions are serious enough. An even more serious consequence of the models is that they bias the entire direction of research. As is the case

of basic paradigms in science, the job–gender paradigm determines *what* is studied. (Feldberg and Glenn, 1984, pp. 32–3)

Problems in studying gender and stratification

At present, no adequate framework exists within which problems of gender and stratification can effectively be analysed. Theoretical and conceptual innovations are needed as well as a reorientation of empirical research. The two models identified by Feldberg and Glenn express long-established shortcomings in analyses of class and the domestic sphere. Those interested in stratification have concentrated on men, with their households presumed to be 'pulled along' with them. Where the situation and outlook of women has been studied at all in sociology, it has been almost always in the domestic setting. Not nearly enough is known of the connections between the two environments.

Researchers are, however, starting to explore this issue. Kathleen Gerson has investigated how women make the choices they do about work, careers and motherhood (Gerson, 1985; see also Rowbotham, 1973; Ehrenreich, 1983; Anyon, 1987). Over the past quarter of a century or so, the image of domesticity associated with women's involvement in the private sphere has started to alter. The 'non-domestic woman' has emerged to challenge the pre-eminent position of the 'homemaker'. The traditional household of housewife and breadwinning husband has declined to become a minority of all households in Britain today.

Gerson distinguishes four paths which different women follow in their lives. Some still follow a *traditional* path. They settle down to full-time mothering, and only work outside the home for short periods, if at all. For them, motherhood is a career, with which they are reasonably satisfied. Others have found themselves caught between the traditional outlook and an awareness of the rewards a good job outside the home can offer. They experience *rising work aspirations* and *ambivalence toward motherhood*. These women may have married while in their late teens or early twenties, but either became disillusioned with their married state, or found themselves divorced and on the job market a few years later. A third group follows a *non-traditional* path. Women in this category are clear from early on that they want a career in paid work, and try to ensure that their domestic circumstances permit this. In earlier times, most might have succumbed to pressures to forsake career ambitions in favour of the family and motherhood. But today there are sufficient supports to allow for a more resolute outlook, even though having a successful career and a family remains far harder for women than for men. A fourth pattern is represented by women who experience *falling work aspirations*, and come to see *the home as a haven*. They may enter the world of work with high hopes, but for one reason or another find their ambitions thwarted, and turn to the home as a retreat from the disappointments of work. A complexity of different attitudes, feelings and life experiences influence in which direction a woman chooses to try to channel her activities.

Social mobility

In studying stratification, we have to consider not only the differences between economic positions or occupations, but what happens to the individuals who occupy them. The term **social mobility** refers to the movement of individuals and groups between different socio-economic positions. **Vertical mobility** means movement up or down the socio-economic scale. Those who gain in property, income or status are said to be *upwardly mobile*, while those who move in the opposite direction are *downwardly mobile*. In modern societies there is also a great deal of **lateral mobility**, which refers to geographical movement between neighbourhoods, towns or regions. Vertical and lateral mobility are often combined. For instance, an individual working in a company in one city might be promoted to a higher position in a branch of the firm located in another town, or even in a different country.

There are two ways of studying social mobility. First, we can look at individuals' own careers – how far they move up or down the social scale in the course of their working lives. This is usually called **intragenerational mobility**. Alternatively, we can analyse how far children enter the same type of occupation as their parents or grandparents. Mobility across the generations is called **intergenerational mobility**.

Comparative mobility studies

The amount of vertical mobility in a society is a major index of the degree of its 'openness', indicating how far talented individuals born into lower strata can move up the socio-economic ladder. How 'open' are the industrialized countries in terms of social mobility? Is there more equality of opportunity in Britain than elsewhere? Studies of social mobility have been carried on for a period of more than fifty years, frequently involving international comparisons. One of the earliest works in the field was that of Pitrim Sorokin, published in 1927 (Sorokin, 1927). Sorokin covered a vast array of different societies, including traditional Rome and China, and also carried out one of the first detailed studies of mobility in the United States. He concluded that opportunities for rapid ascent in the USA were much more confined than American folklore suggested. The techniques Sorokin used to gather his data, however, were relatively primitive.

Research carried out by Peter Blau and Otis Dudley Duncan, forty years later, was far more sophisticated and comprehensive (Blau and

Duncan, 1967). Their investigation remains the most detailed study of social mobility yet carried out in any single country. (Wide-ranging though it may have been, like most other studies of mobility it bears out the points made in the previous section – all those studied were men.) Blau and Duncan collected information on a national sample of 20,000 males. They concluded that there is much vertical mobility in the United States, but nearly all of this is between occupational positions quite close to one another. 'Long-range' mobility is rare. Although downward movement does occur, both within the careers of individuals and intergenerationally, it is much less common than upward mobility. The reason for this is that white-collar and professional jobs have grown much more rapidly than blue-collar ones, a shift that has created openings for sons of blue-collar workers to move into white-collar positions.

Perhaps the most celebrated international study of social mobility was that carried out by Seymour Martin Lipset and Reinhard Bendix (Lipset and Bendix, 1959). They analysed data from nine industrialized societies – Britain, France, West Germany, Sweden, Switzerland, Japan, Denmark, Italy and the United States, concentrating on mobility of men from blue-collar to white-collar work. Contrary to their expectations, they discovered no evidence that the United States was more open than the European societies. Total vertical mobility across the blue-collar/white-collar line was 30 per cent in the United States, with the other societies varying between 27 and 31 per cent. Lipset and Bendix concluded that all the industrialized countries were experiencing similar changes in respect of the expansion of white-collar jobs. This led to an 'upward surge of mobility' of comparable dimensions in all of them. Others have questioned their findings, arguing that significant differences between countries are found if more attention is given to downward mobility, and if long-range mobility is also brought into consideration. There is more long-range mobility in Eastern European societies, for instance, than in Western ones. But on the whole the similarities in patterns of mobility are more striking than the differences (Miller, 1960, 1971; Tyree, Semyonov and Hodge, 1979; Heath, 1981, chapter 7; Grusky and Hauser, 1984).

Robert Erikson and John Goldthorpe have carried out a substantial study of cross-national similarities and variations in mobility, including in their work both Western and Eastern European societies (Erikson and Goldthorpe, 1986). They studied nine countries, including England and Wales, France, Sweden, Hungary and Poland. The results showed a general similarity in mobility rates and patterns, but they also found some significant variations. Sweden, for example, was found to be considerably more 'open' than the other Western countries. Poland also showed high rates of mobility, substantially greater than those of Hungary.

There is one respect in which the United States does seem to differ from other Western countries in terms of social mobility. A higher proportion of people from blue-collar backgrounds reach professional jobs than in other countries. The chief reason for this is that professional organizations have grown more in the USA over the past thirty or forty years than in any other Western country – thus creating more chances of mobility for people from modest backgrounds.

Downward mobility

Although downward mobility is less common than upward mobility, it is still a widespread phenomenon. Over 20 per cent of men in the UK are downwardly mobile intergenerationally, although most of this movement is short-range. Downward intragenerational mobility is also common. Mobility of this type is quite often associated with psychological problems and anxieties, where individuals become unable to sustain the life-styles to which they have become accustomed. Redundancy is another of the main sources of downward mobility. Middle-aged men who lose their jobs, for example, either find it hard to gain new employment at all, or can only obtain work at a lower level of income than before.

Many of the downwardly mobile, in terms of intragenerational mobility at any rate, are women. It is still common for women to abandon promising careers on the birth of a child. After spending some years bringing up a family, such women return to the paid work-force at a later date, often at a lower level than that at which they left – for instance, in poorly paid part-time work. This situation is changing, although not as fast as many might wish.

One finding emerges fairly clearly from the literature: levels of mobility are low compared to ideals of equality of opportunity. In Britain, as elsewhere, most people remain close to the same level as the family from which they came. While many do experience vertical mobility, this is most often the result of changes in the occupational structure, not because there is a high level of equality of opportunity.

Opportunities for mobility

Many people in modern societies believe it is possible for anyone to reach the top if they work hard and persistently enough, yet the figures indicate that very few succeed. Why should it be so difficult? In one respect, the answer is very simple. Even in a 'perfectly fluid' society, in which everyone had an exactly equal chance of reaching the highest positions, only a small minority would do so. The socio-economic order at the top is shaped like a pyramid, with only relatively few positions of power, status or wealth. No more than two or three thousand people, out of a total population of fifty-five million in Britain, could become directors of one of the 200 largest corporations.

In addition, however, those who hold positions of wealth and power have many openings available to them to perpetuate their advantages, and to pass them on to their offspring. They can make sure their children have the best available education, and this will often lead them into good jobs. In spite of wealth taxes and death duties, the rich have normally found means of passing on much of their property to their descendants. Most of those who make it to the top have a head start – they come from professional or affluent backgrounds. Studies of people who have become wealthy show that hardly anyone begins with nothing. The large majority of people who have 'made money' did so on the basis of inheriting or being given at least a modest amount initially – which they then used to make more (Jaher, 1980; Rubinstein, 1980).

William Rubinstein has carried out a study of the backgrounds of British millionaires in the 1980s ('The Rich in Britain', *New Society*, 22 August 1986). He based his work on people who died in 1984 and 1985 leaving at least one million pounds. (It is almost impossible to discover reliable facts about living millionaires.) Rubinstein found that those whose fathers were wealthy businessmen or landowners still make up 42 per cent of the ranks of the millionaires. People likely to have received material encouragement from their families (those with parents who were higher professionals) account for an additional 29 per cent. Forty-three per cent of millionaires inherited over £100,000 each, and a further 32 per cent inherited between £10,000 and £100,000. In Britain the surest way to become rich is still to be born rich.

Social mobility in Britain

Social mobility has been fairly extensively studied in Britain over the post-war period – although again virtually all the research has concentrated on men. An early study was directed by David Glass (1954). Glass's work analysed intergenerational mobility for a longish period up to the 1950s. His findings correspond to those noted above in respect of international data (around 30 per cent mobility, from blue- to white-collar jobs). Glass's research was in fact widely drawn on by those making international comparisons. While a good deal of mobility occurred, most of this was short-range. Upward mobility was much more common than downward mobility, and was mostly concentrated at the middle levels of the class structure. People right at the bottom tended to stay there; almost 50 per cent of sons of workers in professional and managerial jobs were themselves in similar occupations.

The largest study carried out since then was produced by John Goldthorpe and his colleagues at Oxford, and was based on a survey carried out in 1972 (Goldthorpe et al., 1980). They sought to investigate how far patterns of social mobility had altered since the time of Glass's study, and concluded that the overall level of mobility of men was in fact higher than in the previous period, with rather more long-range movement being noted. The main reason for this, however, was not that the occupational system has become more egalitarian. Rather, the origin of the changes was the accelerating growth in the number of higher white-collar jobs relative to blue-collar ones. The researchers found that two-thirds of the sons of unskilled or semi-skilled manual workers were themselves in manual occupations. About 30 per cent of professionals and managers were of working-class origins, while some 4 per cent of men in blue-collar work were from professional or managerial backgrounds.

Although the data are incomplete, research by Anthony Heath indicates that the mobility chances of women are severely limited by the lack of opportunities for female employees in professional and managerial occupations (Heath, 1981). Over half of the daughters of professionals or managers are in routine office jobs, no more than 8 per cent obtaining positions of a comparable level to those of their fathers. Only 1.5 per cent of women from blue-collar homes are to be found in such occupations (although 48 per cent are in routine office work).

The original Oxford mobility study was updated on the basis of new material collected about ten years later (Goldthorpe and Payne, 1986). The major findings of the earlier work were corroborated, but some further developments were found. The chances of boys from blue-collar backgrounds getting professional or managerial jobs, for example, had increased. Once again, this was traced to changes in the occupational structure, producing a reduction of blue-collar occupations relative to higher white-collar jobs. Downward mobility was even less frequent than in the preceding research. However, a much higher proportion than before of men from working-class backgrounds were unemployed, reflecting the spread of mass unemployment from the early 1970s onwards.

Problems in studying social mobility

The study of social mobility presents various problems (Hopper, 1981). For example, it is not clear whether mobility from blue-collar to white-collar work is always correctly defined as 'upward'. Skilled blue-collar workers may be in a superior economic position to many people in more routine white-collar jobs. The nature of jobs alters over time, and it is not always obvious that what are regarded as the 'same' occupations are in fact still such. Clerical occupations, for instance, have changed greatly over the past several decades, through the mechanization of office work. Another difficulty is that, in studies of intergenerational mobility, it is difficult to decide at what point of the respective careers to make comparisons. A parent may still be at mid-career when a child begins his or her work life; parents and their offspring may simultaneously be mobile, perhaps in the same direction or (less often) in different directions. Should we compare them at the beginning or the end of their careers?

All these difficulties can be dealt with to some extent. Care can be taken to alter occupational categories when it is clear that the nature of jobs has shifted radically over the period covered by a particular study. For example, we might decide to group higher blue-collar and routine white-collar jobs together, examining mobility into and out of these jobs as a whole. The problem about where in individuals' careers to make comparisons in studying intergenerational mobility can be resolved – where the data permit – by comparing parents and children both at the beginning and at the end of their respective careers. But these strategies are not entirely satisfactory. What may appear to be precise figures offered in mobility studies have to be approached with caution. We can only draw general conclusions from mobility research, particularly where international comparisons are involved.

Your own mobility chances

What implications might be drawn from mobility studies about the career opportunities with which you are faced, as someone searching for a good job in the 1990s? Like previous generations, you are likely to enjoy upward mobility if you do not already come from a privileged background. It seems probable that the proportion of managerial and professional jobs will continue to expand relative to lower-level positions (for more information about changes in the occupational structure, see chapter 15: 'Work and Economic Life'). Those who have done well in the educational system are most likely to fill these 'empty places'.

Yet there are not nearly enough higher status positions open for all who wish to enter them, and some of you are bound to find that your careers do not match up to what you had hoped for. Although a higher proportion of jobs are being created at managerial and professional levels than existed before, the overall number of jobs available in the economy is declining, as compared to people actively seeking work. One reason for this is the growing number of women competing with men for a finite number of jobs. Another (whose consequences are difficult to sort out fully as yet) is the increasing use of information technology in production processes. Because computerized machinery can now handle tasks – even of a highly complicated kind – which once only human beings could do, it is possible, and perhaps even likely, that many jobs will be eliminated in future years.

If you are a woman, although your chances of entering a good career are improving, you face two major obstacles to your progress. Male managers and employers still discriminate against women applicants. They do so at least partly because of their belief that 'women are not really interested in careers', and that they are likely to leave the work-force when they begin a family. The second of these factors does indeed still very substantially affect the chances of women. This is less because they are uninterested in a career than because they are often effectively forced to choose between a career and having children. Men are rarely willing to share full responsibility for domestic work and child-care. Although many more women than before are following Gerson's 'non-traditional path' – determinedly organizing their domestic lives in order to pursue a career – there are still major barriers in their way.

Poverty and inequality

Right at the bottom of the class system, large numbers of people in the United Kingdom exist in conditions of poverty. Many do not have a proper diet, and live in insanitary conditions, having a lower life expectancy than the majority of the population. Yet more affluent people often pay no attention to the existence of poverty.

This is not a new phenomenon. In 1889, Charles Booth published a work which showed that a third of Londoners were living in dire poverty (Booth, 1889). The result was a public outcry. How could it happen that, in a country which at the time was probably the wealthiest on earth, at the centre of a massive empire, poverty should be so widespread? Booth's work was taken up by his namesake, General William Booth of the Salvation Army. His *In Darkest England and the Way Out* (1970, originally published in 1890) opened with figures derived from Charles Booth's calculations, showing there to be 387,000 'very poor' people in London, 220,000 'near starving' and 300,000 'starving'. Almost a quarter of a million copies of William Booth's book were sold within a year, so effectively did he capture the public imagination. Poverty, he proposed, could be drastically reduced by the means of practical programmes of reform and welfare.

Seventy years later, similar events took place in the United States. In his book *The Other America*, Michael Harrington shocked the American public with the fact that many millions of people in the country were too poor to maintain the minimum standards of life (Harrington, 1963). Harrington's book also became a best-seller. In a subsequent State of the Union message, President Lyndon B. Johnson declared an 'unconditional war on poverty', whose object would be 'to eliminate the paradox of poverty in the midst of plenty'. The United States had long since supplanted Britain as the world's richest nation, a country vastly more wealthy than Britain had been at the time of the two Booths. Yet large numbers of the population continued to live in circumstances which denied them the bare essentials of food, health and housing. The 'war on poverty' was designed finally to achieve the objectives that William Booth had planned some three generations earlier.

The war on poverty

After the announcement of the 'war on poverty', there was a large-scale increase in spending on social welfare in the United States. Spending went up by 400 per cent from 77.2 billion dollars in 1965 to 286.5 billion ten years later. This increase did have discernible effects in reducing the level of poverty, although these fell far short of what had optimistically been anticipated when the new programmes were first set up. In 1972, as measured by official statistics, the numbers of the poor fell to their lowest mark in the post-war period. Those living below the officially defined poverty line fell from just under 40 million to about 23 million. Since then, however, the numbers of the poor have again climbed, accelerating steeply since the early years of the Reagan administration.

The level of success achieved with the different programmes that were initiated was limited. The 'Job Corps' was designed to help create the skills needed successfully to enter job markets for those who would otherwise be unemployed. For the most part, however, the openings were simply not there, and in the early seventies a new period of recession set in, reducing job opportunities still further. 'Head Start' and 'Community Action' made some real gains, although both became unpopular among some sections of the white working class.

Welfare payments and social security benefits only partly reach the population to which they are supposedly targeted. Well under two-thirds of the poor below retirement age today in the USA are in receipt of any public assistance, with no more than just over a third receiving cash payments. Even at the peak of the war on poverty, social welfare in the United States was much more fragmented than was the case in most other Western countries. Moreover, welfare spending often benefits the moderately well-off rather than the poorest sections of society. Only about 30 per cent of benefits available through social security pensions, veterans' pensions, or unemployment insurance, were obtained by families in the lowest fifth of the income scale.

What is poverty?

How should *poverty* be defined? A distinction is usually made between *subsistence* or **absolute poverty** and **relative poverty**. Charles Booth was one of the first to try to establish a consistent standard of subsistence poverty, which refers to lack of basic requirements to sustain a physically healthy existence – sufficient food and shelter to make possible the physically efficient functioning of the body. Booth assumed that these requirements would be more or less the same for people of equivalent age and physique living in any country. This is essentially the concept still used most frequently in the analysis of poverty world-wide.

Subsistence definitions of poverty have various inadequacies, especially when formulated as a specific income level. Unless it is set quite high, even allowing for adjustments, a single criterion of poverty tends to mean that some individuals are assessed as above the poverty line when in fact their income does not meet even their basic subsistence needs (Holman, 1978). Some parts of the country, for example, are much more expensive to live in than others. Moreover, the subsistence calculation of poverty does not take into account the impact of generally rising living standards. It is more realistic to adjust ideas about levels of poverty to the changing norms and expectations in a society as economic growth occurs. The majority of the world's population live in dwellings that do not contain a bath or shower; but it would be hard not to see piped water as a necessity in an industrialized society. Problems with formulations of relative poverty are also complex, however. Income criteria are again generally used, but these conceal variabilities in the actual needs people have.

Poverty today

In contrast to the United States, where there is an officially set 'poverty line', in Britain interpretations of poverty as such are not provided by the government, so the level of income at which Supplementary Benefit (SB) allowances are obtainable is often in practice treated as a measure. Using this criterion, according to the statistics of the Department of Health and Social Security, nine million people, about 17 per cent of the total population, were living in poverty in 1986. The last major survey of poverty in the UK was published by Peter Townsend in 1979. Townsend sought to analyse poverty in terms of lack of resources to maintain 'the living conditions and amenities which are customary, or at least widely encouraged or approved' in society (Townsend, 1979, p. 31). Using this definition he calculated that more than half of the British population are likely to experience poverty at some stage in their lives, especially when they become elderly. He has been criticized for using too broad a notion of 'poverty', yet his finding that relative poverty is much more common in Britain than was believed at the time has been widely accepted. The proportion of the population living in poverty as measured by the SB line has increased, rather than declined since then.

Who are the poor? People in the following categories are particularly likely to be in poverty: those in part-time or insecure jobs; the unemployed; older people; the sick and disabled; and the members of large families and/or single-parent families. Although average wage levels have risen consistently this century, well over half a million people in work are so poorly paid that they receive wages below the SB line. About half of all old-age pensioners are living below the SB poverty line. Many people who may have been reasonably paid during their working lives experience a sharp reduction in income on retirement. Single-parent families, nearly all headed by women, make up an increasing proportion of the poor. The high unemployment of the 1970s and 1980s seems unlikely to decline in the near future, and prolonged unemployment for principal breadwinners and their offspring is pushing more and more families – especially female-headed families – into poverty.

As a rule, the media tend to reinforce popular prejudices about the poor. A survey conducted in the last six months of 1976 revealed that no fewer than 30.8 per cent of all media stories about welfare and social security focused on social security abuse – rather than upon the needy themselves (Golding and Middleton, 1972, pp. 195–7). The *Daily Mail* complained of 'Scroungers by the Sea' (13 July 1977) and the *Daily Telegraph* (29 July 1976) ran a story headed: 'How to be a failure and get paid for doing nothing'. In fact, the researchers discovered that in 1975 930,000 eligible claimants, two-thirds of them pensioners, failed to claim £240 million of supplementary benefits to which they were legally entitled.

Why are the poor still poor?

Some general influences on the level of poverty have been well established. Well-developed and systematically administered welfare programmes, in conjunction with government policies which actively assist in keeping down unemployment, reduce poverty levels. Some societies do exist – such as Sweden – in which subsistence poverty has been almost completely eliminated. A social price probably has to be paid for this, not just in terms of high levels of taxation, but in the development of bureaucratic government agencies which may appropriate a great deal of power. Yet the more the distribution of wealth and income in a country is left open to mechanisms of the market – as has been increasingly the case in the UK over the past decade – the greater the material inequalities found. The theory underlying the policies of Mrs Thatcher's government was that cutting tax rates for individuals and corporations would generate high levels of economic growth, the fruits of which would 'trickle down' to the poor. The evidence of the past few years does not support this thesis. Such an economic policy may or may not generate acceleration of economic development, but the result tends to expand the differentials between the poor and the wealthy, actually swelling the numbers of those living in subsistence poverty.

Surveys have shown that the majority of Britons regard the poor as responsible for their own poverty and are suspicious of those who live 'for free' on 'government handouts'. Many believe that people on welfare could find work if they were determined to do so. Unfortunately, these views are completely out of line with the realities of poverty. About a quarter of those officially living in poverty are in work anyway, but earn too little to bring them over the poverty threshold. Of the remainder, the majority are children under fourteen, those aged 65 and over, and the ill or disabled. In spite of popular views about the high level of welfare cheating, fewer than 1 per cent of welfare applications involve fraudulent claims – much lower than in the case of income tax returns, where it is estimated that more than 10 per cent of tax is lost through misreporting or evasion.

Lack of public awareness of the extent of poverty probably partly rests on the low 'visibility' of the poor. Most of those in the more privileged sections of society rarely visit the areas, urban or rural, in which poverty is concentrated. Some issues connected with poverty, such as high rates of crime, regularly command public attention, but the widespread existence of poverty tends otherwise to be overlooked. Poverty has periodically been 'rediscovered' from the time of Charles Booth onwards, and for a while the plight of the poor stirs the conscience of the more favoured – but public concern then rapidly fades away.

Summary

1   *Social stratification* refers to the division of society into layers or strata. When we talk of social stratification, we draw attention to the unequal positions occupied by individuals in society. Stratification by gender and age is found in all societies. In the larger traditional societies, and industrialized countries today, there is stratification in terms of wealth, property and access to material goods and cultural products.

2   Four major types of stratification system can be distinguished: *slavery, caste, estates* and *class*. Whereas the first three depend on legal or religiously sanctioned inequalities, class divisions are not 'officially' recognized, but stem from economic factors affecting the material circumstances of people's lives.

3   Classes derive from inequalities in possession and control of material resources. An individual's class position is at least in some part achieved; it is not simply 'given' from birth. *Social mobility*, both upwards and downwards in the class structure, is a fairly common feature.

4   Most people in modern societies are more affluent today than was the case several generations ago, yet the distribution of wealth and income remains highly unequal. The wealthy use various means to transmit their property from one generation to the next.

5   The most prominent and influential theories of stratification are those developed by Marx and Weber. Marx places the primary emphasis on *class*, which he sees as an objectively given characteristic of the economic structure of society. He sees a fundamental split between the owners of capital and the workers who do not own capital. Weber accepts a similar view, but distinguishes two other aspects of stratification, *status* and *party*. Status refers to the esteem or 'social honour' given to individuals or groups, party to the active mobilizing of groups to secure definite ends.

6   Class is of major importance in modern Western societies, although there are many complexities in the class systems within such societies. Most people in the West accept that the population falls into *upper, middle* and *working* classes, and *class consciousness* is strong.

7   Analyses of stratification have traditionally been written from a male-oriented point of view. This is partly because of the assumption that gender inequalities simply reflect class differences; this assumption is highly questionable. Gender influences stratification in modern societies to some degree independently of class.

8   In the study of social mobility, a distinction is made between *intra-generational* and *intergenerational* mobility. The first of these refers to movement up or down the social scale within an individual's working life. The second concerns movement across the generations, as when a daughter or son from a blue-collar background becomes a professional. Social mobility is mostly of limited range. Most people remain close to the level of the family from which they came, though the expansion of white-collar jobs in the last few decades has provided the opportunity for considerable short-range upward mobility.

9   Poverty remains widespread within the affluent nations. There are two methods of assessing poverty; one involves the notion of 'subsistence poverty', which is a lack of the basic resources needed to maintain health and effective bodily functioning. The other, 'relative poverty', involves assessing the gaps between the living conditions of some groups and those enjoyed by the majority of a population.

Basic concepts

social stratification	status
class	social mobility

Important terms

slavery	contradictory class locations
caste	social closure
estate	wealth
upper class	income
middle class	underclass
working class	class consciousness
peasants	vertical mobility
means of production	lateral mobility
capitalists	intragenerational mobility
surplus value	intergenerational mobility
transitional classes	absolute poverty
prestige	relative poverty
pariah groups	

Further reading

Anthony Heath, *Social Mobility* (London: Fontana, 1981) — a useful overall survey.

Frank Parkin, *Marxism and Class Theory: A Bourgeois Critique* (London: Tavistock, 1979) — a critical account of Marxist theories of class.

Peter Townsend, *Poverty in the United Kingdom* (Harmondsworth: Penguin, 1979) — the most comprehensive recent survey of poverty in the United Kingdom.
Erik Olin Wright, *Classes* (London: Verso, 1985) — a sophisticated discussion of classes and class relationships.

8

Ethnicity and Race

In Japan, there is a group of people who are physically indistinguishable from other Japanese, have lived in the country for hundreds of years and share the same religion, yet are regarded with hostility or disdain by the majority of the Japanese population. The origins of this situation can be traced back to feudal times, when wars between local rulers led to many people being dispossessed from their land. They became outcasts and vagrants, and were called 'Eta' and later on 'Burakumin'. Both names are still used, 'Eta' being the more offensive (Dore and Aoyagi, 1965).

The outcasts were forced to take menial jobs which other people despised. In local religious beliefs, many of these occupations were regarded as unclean, a view which was subsequently extended to the people who worked in them. Consequently, they were systematically discriminated against by the majority. They lived in special settlements, were forbidden to change occupations and compelled to marry only among themselves. With the modernization of Japan, which began in the second half of the nineteenth century, the Eta were made formally equal to everyone else. A decree of the Japanese Emperor stated that they had become full citizens, and were allowed to follow any occupation they desired. The term 'Eta' disappeared from official pronouncements in much the same way as 'nigger' has done in the United States. It continued to be used as an epithet, however, and the actual practices of discrimination changed little. The Burakumin remained concentrated in distinct and poor neighbourhoods, confined to low-paid and generally scorned jobs. The majority of the Japanese population saw marriage into this group as bringing disgrace on a family.

Today the Burakumin still form an oppressed minority within a country that has risen to become the third-ranking economic power in the world. Many Burakumin live in the same areas of overcrowded slums as their ancestors did. Even people from other depressed neighbourhoods nearby look down upon them. Rates of intermarriage with the rest of the population continue to be low and families will often exhaustively check the background of a prospective wife or husband to ensure that there is no Buraku connection. Various organizations seeking to advance the position of the Burakumin within Japanese society have sprung up, but prejudice and discrimination remain strong. The Burakumin are still widely thought to be 'mentally inferior, incapable of high moral behaviour, aggressive, impulsive and lacking any notion of sanitation or manners' (Neary, 1986).

Ethnic groups, minorities and race in plural societies

The case of the Burakumin demonstrates how ingrained and enduring prejudices towards a minority group can be, even when there are no physical differences from the rest of the population. Long-standing persecution of minorities, unfortunately, has been all too common in human history. The Jews have been subject to discrimination and persecution in the Christian West for nearly two thousand years, the most horrific instance of brutal destructiveness against a minority group being the killing of millions of Jews in German concentration camps during the Second World War. Nazi ideology claimed Jews to be a race inferior to the 'Aryan' people of Germany and Northern Europe (Weinstein, 1980). The term 'Aryan' originally referred to a group of languages spoken by people of differing physical stock, and it was appropriated by the Nazis and their so-called 'race scientists' to refer to characteristics that have little or no basis in reality.

The Jews in Germany, like the Burakumin in Japan, were a group with distinct *ethnic* characteristics. **Ethnicity** refers to cultural practices and outlooks that distinguish a given community of people. Members of ethnic groups see themselves as culturally distinct from other groupings in a society, and are seen by those others to be so. Many different characteristics may serve to distinguish ethnic groups from one another, but the most usual are language, history or ancestry (real or imagined), religion, and styles of dress or adornment. Ethnic differences are *wholly learned*, a point which seems self-evident until we remember how often some such groups have been regarded as 'born to rule' or, alternatively, have been seen as 'unintelligent', innately lazy, and so forth.

Most modern societies include numerous different ethnic groups. In Britain, Irish, Asian, West Indian, Italian and Greek immigrants, among others, form ethnically distinct communities within the wider society. The United States and Soviet Union are considerably more differentiated ethnically than Britain, the USA incorporating immigrant communities deriving from all corners of the world. Although Russian is the official language of the USSR, Russia is only one part of the Soviet Union; other regions have their own languages and customs. There are more than a hundred different ethnic groups in the USSR, twenty-three of which have populations of a million or more. The Russians made up 52 per cent of the total population in 1979, when the last census was taken.

Many societies in the world today, in the industrialized and non-industrialized world alike, are **plural societies.** Plural societies are those in which there are several large ethnic groupings, involved in the same political and economic order but otherwise largely distinct from one another. The anthropologist J. S. Furnivall first developed the notion when studying Burma and Java in the Far East:

> In Burma, as in Java, probably the first thing that strikes the visitor is the medley of peoples – European, Chinese, Indian and native. It is in the strictest sense a medley, for they mix but do not combine . . . there is a plural society, with different sections of the community living side by side, but separately within the same political unit. (Furnivall, 1956, p. 304)

Most post-colonial countries are plural societies, because of the political unification imposed on a variety of pre-existing cultures. Virtually all modern societies are pluralistic to some extent, with the United States and Soviet Union being more pluralistic than most European countries (Stone, 1985).

Ethnic distinctions are rarely 'neutral'. They are commonly associated with marked inequalities of wealth and power, as well as with antagonism between groups. Why are ethnic differences so often associated with tension and conflict? What accounts for ethnic prejudice and discrimination? Why do ethnic antagonisms often (though by no means always) centre upon 'racial' differences? Are societies marked by a high degree of pluralism bound to remain unequal? These are the questions we shall try to answer in this chapter. We shall first analyse the nature of ethnic minorities, and discuss the concept of 'race'. Subsequent sections will analyse ethnic divisions and differing systems of race relations.

Minorities

The notion of *ethnic minorities* or **minority groups** is widely used in sociology, and involves more than mere numbers. There are many minorities in a statistical sense, such as people having red hair or weighing more than fifteen stone, but these are not minorities in sociological terms. As understood in sociology, a minority group has the following features.

1 Its members are disadvantaged, as a result of **discrimination** against them by others. Discrimination exists when rights and opportunities open to one set of people are denied to another group. For instance, a landlord may refuse to rent a room to someone because she or he is of West Indian background.
2 Members of the minority have some sense of group solidarity, of 'belonging together'. Experience of being the subject of prejudice and discrimination usually heightens feelings of common loyalty and interests. Members of minority groups often tend to see themselves as 'a people apart' from the majority.
3 Minority groups are usually to some degree physically and socially isolated from the larger community. They tend to be concentrated in certain neighbourhoods, cities or regions of a country. There is little intermarriage between those in the majority and members of the minority group. People in the minority group might actively promote endogamy (marriage within the group) in order to keep alive their cultural distinctiveness.

Some have suggested that, since the notion is sociological rather than numerical, a minority group might in certain circumstances consist of the majority of the population. In South Africa, for example, a relatively small proportion of whites dominates much larger numbers of blacks. However, to use the term 'minority' in such circumstances seems more than a little contradictory. The fact that blacks *are* in such a majority in South Africa makes a major difference to the overall make-up of the society. Similarly, we sometimes hear the phrase 'women and other minorities' in discussions of inequalities in the Western world, although women form over half the population. It seems least likely to confuse us if we use the term 'minority group' only where the people discriminated against do not make up the bulk of the populace.

Minority groups are always to some degree ethnically distinct from the majority, but how far this is so varies. The Burakumin are a minority group in Japan, although the level of ethnic difference between them and the majority population is low. They look and act like other Japanese. Many minorities, however, are both ethnically and physically distinct from the rest of the population of the societies in which they live. This is the case with West Indians and Asians in Britain, for example, and with American Indians, blacks, Chinese and certain other groups in the United States. Physical differences, in skin colour or other characteristics, are commonly called *racial*. Since the notion of **race** has been the subject of much pseudo-scientific thinking, which has influenced public consciousness, it needs to be looked at in some detail.

Race and biology

Many people today believe – mistakenly – that humans can be readily separated into biologically different races. The strength of this belief is perhaps not surprising, because numerous attempts have been made by scholars to categorize the peoples of the world by race. Some authors have distinguished four or five major races, while others have recognized as many as three dozen. But too many exceptions have been found to these classifications to make any of them workable. A commonly used type, for example, that of 'negroid', is supposed to involve dark skin, tightly curled black hair and certain other physical characteristics. Yet the original inhabitants of Australia, the Aborigines, have dark skin but wavy, and sometimes blonde, hair. Many other examples can be found which cut across any clear classifications. Developments in genetics have demolished the theory that there could have been several different lines of racial development from our anthropoid ancestors.

The contrasting appearance of a person with a very dark skin, tightly curled hair and thick lips and one with pale skin, straight or wavy hair and thin lips might suggest basic constitutional differences. The physical divergencies are in fact almost completely confined to such aspects of appearance. A scientist examining a blood sample could not tell whether it came from a black or a white person. Differences in physical types between human beings derive from population inbreeding, which varies according to the degree of contact between different social or cultural units. In other words, human population groups are not distinct, but form a continuum. The genetic diversity *within* populations that share certain visible physical traits is as great as those between groups. These facts lead many biologists, anthropologists and sociologists to believe that the concept of race should be dropped altogether.

There are clear physical differences between human beings and some of these differences are inherited, but the question of why some physical differences, and not others, become matters for social discrimination and prejudice has nothing to do with biology. Racial differences, therefore, should be understood as *physical variations singled out by the members of a community or society as ethnically significant.* Differences in skin colour, for example, are often treated as significant in this way, whereas differences in colour of hair are not (Rex, 1986). **Racism** means falsely attributing inherited characteristics of personality or behaviour to individuals of a particular physical appearance. A *racist* is someone who believes that a biological explanation can be given for characteristics of superiority or inferiority supposedly possessed by people of a given physical stock.

Ethnic antagonism, prejudice and discrimination

Although the concept of 'race' is modern, prejudice and ethnic antagonism have been widespread in human history. In attempting to explain this, we need to look to psychology as well as sociology. But first we must clearly distinguish between **prejudice** and discrimination. Prejudice refers to *opinions* or *attitudes* held by members of one group about another, whereas discrimination refers to *actual behaviour* towards them. Prejudice involves holding preconceived views about an individual or group, often based upon hearsay rather than direct evidence, views which are resistant to change even in the face of new information. People may have favourable prejudices towards groups with which they identify and negative prejudices against others. Someone who is prejudiced against a particular grouping will refuse to give them 'a fair hearing'.

Discrimination refers to activities which serve to disqualify the members of one grouping from opportunities open to others – as when someone of Indian background is refused a job made available to a 'white'. Although prejudice is very often the basis of discrimination, the two may exist separately. People may have prejudiced attitudes which they do not act on. Equally important, discrimination does not necessarily derive directly from prejudice. For example, white house-buyers might steer away from purchasing properties in certain predominantly black neighbourhoods of a city, not because of attitudes of hostility they might feel towards blacks, but because of worries about declining property values in such areas. Prejudiced attitudes here influence discrimination, but in an indirect fashion.

Stereotypes and scapegoats

Prejudice operates mainly through the use of **stereotypical thinking**. All thought involves categories by means of which we classify our experience. Sometimes, however, these categories are both ill-informed and rigid. A person may have a view of blacks or Jews, for example, which is based upon a few firmly held ideas in terms of which information about, or encounters with, them are interpreted.

Stereotypical thinking may be harmless if it is 'neutral' in terms of emotional content and distant from the interests of the individual concerned. The British may have stereotypical views of what the Americans are like, for example, but this might be of little consequence for most people of either nationality. Where stereotypes are associated with anxiety or fear, the situation is likely to be quite different. Stereotypes in such circumstances are commonly infused with attitudes of hostility or hatred towards the group in question. A white person may believe, for example, that all blacks are lazy and stupid, using this belief to justify attitudes of contempt towards them.

One of the traditional stereotypes of the black male in America, for example, was that of the 'Sambo' character. The Southern novelist and poet Robert Penn Warren summed up his traits:

> He was the supine, grateful, humble, irresponsible, unmanly, banjo-picking, servile, grinning, slack-jawed, docile, dependent, slow-witted, humorous, child-loving, childlike, watermelon-stealing, spiritual-singing, blamelessly fornicating, happy-go-lucky, hedonistic, faithful black servitor who sometimes might step out of character long enough to utter folk wisdom or bury the family silver to save it from the Yankees! (Warren, 1965, p. 52)

This stereotype was balanced by that of the black man as 'brute' – a threat to the virtue of white women. Stereotypes of black women varied between seeing them as 'sexual savages', wanton and wild in their behaviour, and as deferential, matronly 'Old Black Mammies' (Staples, 1973).

Stereotyping is often closely linked to the psychological mechanism of **displacement**. In displacement, feelings of hostility or anger become directed against objects that are not the real origin of those anxieties. People vent their antagonism against scapegoats, blamed for whatever is the source of their troubles. **Scapegoating** is common in circumstances in which deprived ethnic groupings come into competition with one another for economic rewards. Those involved in racial attacks directed against blacks, for example, are often in a similar economic position to them. They blame the blacks for sufferings whose real causes lie elsewhere.

Scapegoating frequently involves **projection**, the unconscious attributing to others of one's own desires or characteristics. In circumstances in which people experience considerable frustration, or must carefully control their own desires, they may be unable to recognize their own inner feelings, projecting them on to others. The bizarre ideas held by whites in the old American South about the lustful nature of black men probably originated in their own frustrations, sexual access to white women being limited by the formal nature of courtship.

The authoritarian personality

It is possible that some types of people, as a result of early socialization, are particularly prone to stereotypical thinking and projection on the basis of repressed anxieties. A famous piece of research directed by Theodor Adorno, carried out in the USA in the 1940s, diagnosed a character type the researchers termed the **authoritarian personality** (Adorno et al., 1950). They developed measurement scales, each for a particular area of social attitudes, for assessing levels of prejudice. People were asked to agree or disagree with a series of statements expressing rigid, particularly anti-Semitic, views. Those who were diagnosed as prejudiced on one scale also tended to be so on the others. Prejudice against Jews went along with the expression of negative attitudes towards other minorities. People with authoritarian personalities, the investigators concluded, tend to be rigidly conformist, submissive to those seen as their superiors and dismissive towards inferiors. Such people are also highly intolerant in their religious and sexual attitudes.

Adorno and his colleagues suggest that the characteristics of an authoritarian personality derive from a pattern of upbringing in which parents are unable to express direct love for their children, and are aloof and disciplinarian. The adult brought up this way suffers from anxieties that can be controlled only by adopting a rigid outlook. Such people are unable to cope with ambiguous situations and ignore inconsistencies, thinking in a strongly stereotypical way. This finding was based on the answers given to some contradictory statements. For example, the following items were included:

> Jews tend to remain a foreign element in American society, trying to preserve their old social standards and resist the American way of life.

> Jews go too far in hiding their Jewishness, especially such extremes as changing their names, straightening their noses, and imitating Christian manners and customs.

The majority of people who agreed with the first item also agreed with the second. In much the same way, those who agreed with statements that Jews are too oriented towards the acquisition of money, and control big business, also agreed with the view that Jews are subversive and critical of business enterprise.

The research, and conclusions drawn from it, have been subjected to a barrage of criticism. Some have doubted the value of the measurement scales used; others have argued that authoritarianism is not a characteristic of personality, but reflects the values and norms of particular sub-cultures within the wider society. The investigation may be more valuable as a contribution to understanding authoritarian patterns of thought in general, rather than distinguishing a particular personality type. Yet there are clear similarities between these findings and those of other research on prejudice. For example, a classic study by Eugene Hartley investigated attitudes towards thirty-five ethnic minorities, also finding that those prejudiced against one ethnic group were likely to express negative feelings against others. Jews and blacks were disliked just as much as Wallonians, Pireneans and Danireans (Hartley, 1946). The three latter groups in fact are non-existent! The terms were coined by Hartley in order to see how far people would be prejudiced against groups of whom they could not even have heard.

Ethnicity and childhood

A great deal of research has been carried out into the development of attitudes towards ethnicity among young children. 'I don't like coloured people'; 'He's lazy because he's coloured'; views such as this are common enough in British or American society. However, in this case the first observation was made by a five-year-old white, the second by a four-year-old black (Porter, 1971, p. 1). Children as young as three may be aware of differences between white and black people, these already being associated with variations in attitudes. Kenneth and Mamie Clark studied young American children playing with black and white dolls. They found that both black and white children tended to prefer white dolls. Such a preference has been documented in many other studies, including, for example, Oriental children in Hawaii (Clark and Clark, 1963). Many young black children tend to misidentify themselves as white, whereas white children of the same age are able to classify themselves more accurately.

Until recently children's books in the United Kingdom often contained open stereotypes of blacks. While these are now relatively uncommon, less obvious forms of ethnic misrepresentation still occur. Children's stories are starting to feature more black characters, but for the most part pre-school books are still dominated by whites. Images linking white to purity and black to evil remain prominent in children's stories. The colours have an 'emotional value' which seems to be learned in quite close conjunction with developing awareness of ethnicity. A study carried out of white pre-school children in the United States concluded that they 'are learning the evaluative meanings of black as bad, and white as good, during their pre-school years, the period in which awareness of race is also developing' (Renninger and Williams, 1966).

The attitudes of majority groups

Attitudes learned in early childhood probably continue as important underlying orientations in later life. Blacks often acquire an early sense of their own inferiority that may prove very difficult to dispel later. Whites may have feelings of unease towards blacks, or 'coloured' people, even if in most areas of their behaviour they practise no discrimination and consider themselves without prejudice. Even the most committed liberal may find it difficult to escape these feelings completely, given the influence of early learning (Wellman, 1987).

Robert K. Merton has identified four possible types of members of majority groups in terms of their attitudes and behaviour towards minorities (Merton, 1949):

Type 1

All-weather liberals, who are unprejudiced towards minorities and avoid discrimination, even when it may be personally costly. An example might be a white Southern minister taking part in civil rights demonstrations in the 1960s in the United States even though he might stand to lose his job or be physically attacked.

Type 2
Fair-weather liberals, who consider themselves unprejudiced but will 'bend with the wind' if costs are involved. An example is someone who would tacitly support a protest against a black family moving into his or her street because it would have the effect of reducing house values.

Type 3
Timid bigots are those who hold prejudices against minorities, but because of legal pressure or financial interests act in an egalitarian way. Such would be the case, for instance, with the owner of a shop who feels antipathy towards Asians, but acts in a friendly way towards Asian customers because to do otherwise would be to lose revenue.

Type 4
The active bigot, who both holds strong prejudices against other ethnic groups and practises discrimination against them.

Sociological interpretations

Some of the psychological mechanisms mentioned above – such as stereotypical thinking, displacement or projection – are universal in nature. They are found among members of all societies and are relevant to explaining why ethnic antagonism is such a common element in cultures of many different types. However, they explain little about the social processes involved in concrete forms of discrimination. To study such processes, we must bring into play concepts and materials of a more sociological character. We can separate sociological inter-pretations of ethnic hostilities and conflicts into two types: those which apply generally, like the psychological mechanisms just discussed, and those which relate mainly to ethnic antagonism in the modern world.

General factors

Sociological concepts relevant to ethnic conflicts on a general level are those of *ethnocentrism, group closure* and *resource allocation*. Ethnocentrism – a suspicion of outsiders, combined with a tendency to evaluate the cultures of others in terms of one's own culture – is a concept we have encountered previously (chapter 2: 'Culture and Society'). Virtually all cultures have been ethnocentric to a greater or lesser degree, and it is easy to see how ethnocentrism combines with stereotypical thought. 'Outsiders' are thought of as aliens, barbarians or as morally and mentally inferior. This is how most civilizations have viewed the members of smaller cultures, for example, and it has helped to fuel innumerable ethnic clashes throughout history.

Ethnocentrism and group closure frequently go together. 'Closure' means the process whereby groups maintain boundaries separating themselves from others – we have already discussed it in analysing the boundaries between classes in the previous chapter (chapter 7: 'Stratification and Class Structure'). The anthropologist Frederick Barth (1969) has tried to show how ethnic group boundaries are organized, and how they contribute to conflicts. These boundaries are developed and sustained, he argues, by means of 'exclusion devices', which sharpen the divisions between one ethnic group and another. Such devices include, for instance, the limiting or prohibiting of intermarriage between the groups, restrictions on social contact or economic relationships like trading, and the physical separating of groups from one another (as in the case of ethnic ghettos).

Sometimes groups of equal power may mutually enforce principles of closure: their members keep separate from each other, but neither group dominates the other. More commonly, however, the members of one group are in a position of power over another ethnic group or groups. In these circumstances, ethnic group closure coincides with the *allocation of resources*: in other words, with inequalities in the distribution of wealth and material goods. There are many contexts in which this may happen: for example, through the military conquest of one group by another, or the emergence of an ethnic group as economically dominant over others. Ethnic closure provides a means of defending the privileged position of the dominant group.

An historical perspective

These various concepts, both psychological and sociological, help us to understand factors underlying many forms of ethnic conflicts. But to analyse fully ethnic relations in present times, we must take a more historical perspective. It is quite impossible to comprehend ethnic divisions in the modern era without giving prime place to the impact of the expansion of the West over the past several centuries – especially the impact of Western colonization upon the rest of the world. We have sketched out this history in chapter 2 ('Culture and Society'), and the account given there provides the necessary background for the remainder of this chapter.

From the fifteenth century onwards, the Europeans began to venture into previously uncharted seas and unexplored land masses, pursuing the aims of exploration and trade, but also conquering and subduing native peoples in many areas. Settling in these areas, they poured out in their millions from Europe. By way of the slave trade, they also brought about a large-scale movement of population from Africa to the Americas. The following are the major shifts in population which have occurred over the past 350 years or so (Berry and Tischler, 1978):

Europe to North America   From the seventeenth century to the present, some 45 million people emigrated from Europe to what is now the United States and Canada. Many went back to Europe again, but

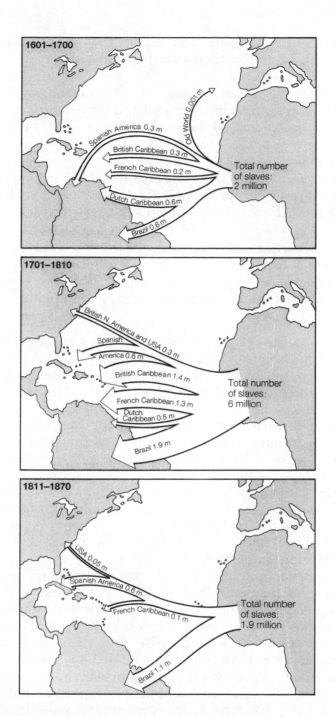

Figure 8 The Atlantic slave trade, 1601–1870. By far the largest single destination was Brazil, with 3.6 million people being taken there over less than 300 years
Source: Ben Crow and Mary Thorpe, *Survival and Change in the Third World* (Cambridge: Polity Press, 1988), p. 15.

most settled permanently and about 150 million people in North America today can trace their ancestry to this migration.

Europe to Central and South America   About 20 million people from Europe, mostly coming from Spain, Portugal and Italy, migrated to Central and South America. Some 50 million people in these areas today are of European ancestry.

Europe to Africa and Australasia   Approximately 17 million people in these continents are of European ancestry. In Africa, the majority are in the state of South Africa, colonized mainly by the British and the Dutch.

Africa to the Americas   Starting in the sixteenth century, about 15 million blacks were transported to the American continent. Under a million came in the sixteenth century; some 2 million in the seventeenth century; in the eighteenth century, about 6 million; and roughly 2 million in the nineteenth century.

These population flows were the main basis of the ethnic composition of the United States, Canada, the countries of Central and South America, South Africa, Australia and New Zealand. In all these countries, the indigenous populations were subjected and came under European rule – they became relatively small ethnic minorities in North America and Australasia. Since the Europeans were from ethnically diverse backgrounds, they implanted numerous ethnic differentiations in their new homelands. At the height of the colonial era, in the nineteenth and early twentieth centuries, Europeans also ruled over native populations in many other regions: for example, throughout most of Africa, parts of the Middle East, and in India, Burma and Malaya.

For most of the period of European expansion, ethnocentric attitudes were rife among the colonists, who believed themselves to be on a civilizing mission to the rest of the world. Even the more liberal European colonists thought themselves superior to the indigenous peoples they encountered. The fact that many of those peoples thought precisely the opposite is not so relevant, since the Europeans possessed the power to make their outlook count. The early period of colonialism coincided with the rise of racism, and ever since then racial divisions and conflicts have tended to have a prime place in ethnic conflicts as a whole. In particular, racist views separating 'whites' from 'blacks' became central to European attitudes.

Why did this happen? There were several reasons. One is that an opposition between white and black as cultural symbols was deeply rooted in European culture. White had long been associated with purity, black with evil. (There is nothing 'natural' about this symbolism; in some other cultures it is reversed.) The symbol 'blackness' held the following meanings *before* the West came into extensive contact with black peoples: 'Deeply stained with dirt; soiled, foul . . . Having dark or deadly purposes, malignant; pertaining to or involving death, deadly; baneful, disastrous, sinister . . . indicating disgrace, censure, liability to punishment' (Kovel, 1970, p. 62).

These symbolic meanings tended to influence reactions to blacks when they were first encountered on African shores. They helped reinforce a sense of radical difference between peoples which, combined with the heathenism of Africans, led many Europeans to regard blacks with a mixture of disdain and fear. As a seventeenth-century observer expressed it, blacks 'in colour as in condition are little other than Devils incarnate' (Jordan, 1968, p. 24). Although the more extreme expressions of such attitudes have disappeared today, it is difficult not to believe that elements of this black/white cultural symbolism remain widespread.

A second important factor influencing modern racism was simply the coinage and diffusion of the concept of 'race' itself. Racist attitudes have existed in many cultures and at early periods of history. In China in 300 AD, for example, we find recorded descriptions of barbarian peoples 'who greatly resemble monkeys from whom they are descended' (Gossett, 1963, p. 4). But the notion of 'race', as referring to a cluster of inherited characteristics, comes from European thought of the eighteenth and nineteenth centuries. Count Joseph Arthur de Gobineau (1816–82) is sometimes called 'the father of modern racism' because he proposed ideas that became influential in many circles. According to de Gobineau, three races exist: the white, black and yellow. The white race possesses intelligence, morality and willpower superior to those of the others, and these inherited qualities underlie the spread of Western influence across the world. Blacks are the least capable of the three races, marked by an animal nature, a lack of morality and emotional instability.

The ideas of de Gobineau and others who proposed similar views were propounded as supposedly scientific theories. They later came to influence Adolf Hitler, who, as mentioned earlier, used them as part of the ideology of the Nazi party. The notion of 'the superiority of the white race', although completely without value factually, remains a key element of white racism today. It is an explicit part, for example, of the ideology of the Ku-Klux-Klan in the United States.

A third reason for the rise of modern racism lies in the exploitative relations which the Europeans established with non-white peoples. The slave-trade could not have existed were it not widely held by Europeans that blacks belonged to an inferior, perhaps even sub-human, race. Racism helped justify colonial rule over non-white peoples, and the denial to them of the rights of political participation which were being won by whites in their European homelands. Using the concept mentioned previously, we can say that racism played an important part in the group closure whereby Europeans were the rulers, and non-whites the ruled.

The racist attitudes of European colonial settlers were almost every-where more extreme in relation to blacks than other non-whites. The early English settlers in North America, for instance, in general saw blacks as markedly inferior to the Indians. Early views of the Indians were cultural rather than racial: seeing them as 'savages' or 'uncivilized', rather than as an inferior race. Later, many colonists did come to see the Indians as a distinct race lacking the qualities of the whites. But this view was never as clear-cut as in the case of attitudes towards blacks. Thomas Jefferson advocated the 'Americanization' of the Indians, meaning by this the teaching of Christian values. Compare this with his attitude towards blacks. Blacks, he wrote, 'in memory are equal to whites; in reason much inferior', adding that 'in imagination they are dull, tasteless and anomalous' (Gossett, 1963, pp. 42–4).

The relations between whites and non-whites varied according to different patterns of colonial settlement, and were also influenced by cultural differences between the Europeans themselves. To demonstrate these points, we now turn to look at race relations in Brazil, the USA and South Africa before analysing racial and ethnic divisions in the UK at greater length.

Ethnic relations in historical perspective: some examples

Comparing ethnic relations in other societies with those in Britain illustrates the ways in which prejudice and discrimination vary with different patterns of historical development. Brazil is sometimes quoted as an example of a society free from ethnic prejudice between black and white, although as we shall see this is not wholly accurate. South Africa, by contrast, is a country in which prejudice and discrimination have developed in an extreme form, and segregation of black and white is institutionalized.

Ethnic relations in Brazil

A little under four million Africans were transported to Brazil before the end of the slave trade in the middle of the nineteenth century. Under a million were taken to the United States, and blacks coming from different African cultures were usually dispersed there, but in Brazil those shipped from the same areas were normally kept together. Hence they were able to retain more of their original culture than was possible for those in the United States. Slaves in Brazil were allowed to marry even if their masters disapproved, as long as they continued serving them as before, and once married, a couple could not be sold as individual slaves. Sexual contact between white men and slave women was frequent, and the children of such unions were often freed, sometimes being fully accepted as part of the white family. Slavery was finally abolished in 1888, but well before then whites had become used to the existence of free blacks.

After the ending of slavery, many black Brazilians moved into the towns and cities. There most of them lived (and live today) in considerable poverty, yet they were not debarred from membership of labour unions, and a proportion have risen to positions of wealth and power. There is a much-quoted Brazilian saying that 'A rich black man is a white and a poor white man is a black.' The phrase neatly catches both the relatively relaxed views of racial differences, as well as the fact that 'whiteness' is still clearly identified with superiority. Whites continue to dominate the higher positions in all sectors of the society.

Brazilians had long interpreted their own system of race relations in a charitable light, comparing it positively to the more segregated patterns of the USA, but in the 1960s and 1970s, as moves to secure greater civil rights for American blacks gathered strength, such comparisons became less favourable to Brazil. In the early 1960s, the Brazilian Congress passed a law forbidding discrimination in public places after a touring American black, Katherine Dunham, complained of being refused accommodation in a São Paulo hotel. The law was largely a symbolic gesture, however, with no effort being made by the government to investigate the extent of possible discrimination.

Most observers agree that such discrimination has been fairly rare in Brazil, but there have been few government programmes designed to improve the social and economic opportunities of non-whites. The Brazilian belief in 'whitening' stands in some contrast to the continued concentration of blacks in the poorest sections of the society. Brazil has none the less avoided the recurrent lynchings and riots which have punctuated the history of the United States, and has escaped most of the more extreme forms of anti-black prejudice (Skidmore, 1974).

The social development of South Africa

In South Africa, the first European settlers were Dutch. Finding the local population resistant to working in European enterprises, they began importing large numbers of slaves from elsewhere in Africa and from the Dutch East Indies. The British later established a dominant position in South Africa, putting an end to slavery in the 1830s. Divisions between whites and indigenous Africans were not at first as absolute as they later became. When slavery was abolished, new taxes were introduced for blacks which effectively forced many of them to contract themselves to European employers, and young African men had to look for employment away from home in order to pay the tax. A system of 'migrant labour' developed which set the pattern for the subsequent evolution of the South African economy. Many Africans went to work in gold or diamond mines, living in special camps well away from the neighbourhoods where Europeans lived.

Gradually a segregated system grew up which was later formalized in law (Western, 1981; D. Smith, 1982; Lapping, 1986).

Under the **apartheid** (meaning separate development) system, introduced after the Second World War, the population of South Africa is classified into four 'registration groups' – the 4.5 million white descendants of European immigrants; the 2.5 million so-called 'coloured people', whose descent is traced from members of more than one 'race'; the 1 million people of Asian descent; and the 23 million black Africans.

It is not just enormous disparities of wealth and opportunity which distinguish South Africa from other industrialized countries, because these exist elsewhere. It is the sharp and all-pervasive contrasts, enshrined in law, which divide white and non-white.

> Exclusive boutiques and luxuriant shopping malls, hushed tree-lined streets, enclosed and well-manicured gardens, and so forth, shape the environment of the affluent white residential areas . . . In contrast, it is difficult to imagine the monotony and abject sparseness of the black townships and ghettos. Pockets of relative affluence do exist, but these are the exception rather than the rule. It is the persistent repetition of identical images – cheerless dusty streets, bare-footed and shabbily dressed children, endless queues of tired travellers, ribbons of exhausted workers trudging home, the sullen stares and probing glances – that creates an unforgettable collage of deprivation. In the townships, daily life is an endless grind, a seemingly ceaseless struggle for existence and survival. (Murray, 1987)

Pierre van den Berghe has distinguished three main levels of segregation in South African society (van den Berghe, 1970).

1 **Microsegregation** – the segregation of public places (such as used also to be the case in the American South). Washrooms, waiting rooms, railway carriages and other public areas have separate facilities for whites and non-whites.
2 **Mezzosegregation** – the segregation of whites and non-whites in terms of the neighbourhoods in which they live in urban areas. Blacks are compelled to live in specially designated zones.
3 **Macrosegregation** – the segregation of whole peoples in distinct territories set up as *native reserves*.

The existence of separate facilities in public places has a strong symbolic value in reinforcing apartheid. However, it provides little or no direct support to the political and economic power which the white minority maintains over the black population. Microsegregation has in fact been relaxed considerably in recent years, as successive South African governments have responded to international pressures to reduce discriminatory practices. The other types of segregation are more significant for the maintenance of white control (Saul and Gelb, 1986).

It has long been impossible for the South African economy to carry on without the labour-power of millions of non-whites, living in or near the cities (Lipton, 1986). At one time there used to be some ethnically mixed neighbourhoods in the major urban areas, but more and more of the blacks have been placed in 'model townships', situated a number of miles away from the white areas. Millions of people have in addition been herded into so-called *homelands* well away from the cities. These regions have been organized into partially autonomous states subject to the overall control of the white central government.

The homelands are supposed to be separate territories where the black majority can exercise the political rights denied them in white South Africa. Under the provisions of the 1970 Homelands Citizenship Act, those in a homeland were automatically deprived of their South African citizenship on the day it became 'independent'. So-called *frontier commuters* live with their families in the homelands and travel daily across the 'national borders' into white South Africa. It has been estimated that 80 per cent of the inhabitants of the homelands live below the officially designated poverty line (Giliomee and Schlemmer, 1985).

Black civil rights in the USA

The abolition of slavery and early developments

Slavery was ended in North America as a result of the Civil War between the northern and southern states. The Emancipation Proclamation was in fact signed in 1863, a year before the war ended. The end of slavery, however, did not signal a dramatic advance in the fortunes of blacks, most of whom remained in circumstances of dire poverty. A series of 'Jim Crow' laws passed in the South between 1890 and 1912 banned blacks from 'white' railway carriages, public toilets and cafés. Such segregation was officially recognized by a Supreme Court decision in 1896, which declared 'separate but equal' facilities constitutional. The activities of the Ku-Klux-Klan, a violent secret society, were directed to ensuring that segregation was maintained.

Struggles by minority groups to achieve equal rights and opportunities have, from the Revolution onwards, been important in American history. Most minorities have been successful in achieving access to political influence and economic rewards, and in pressing claims to equal status with the majority, but blacks were largely excluded from such processes of self-advancement until the early 1940s. The National Association for the Advancement of Coloured People (NAACP) and the National Urban League were founded in 1909 and 1910 respectively. Both fought for black civil rights, but their struggle only began to have some real effect during and after the Second World War.

Before the United States entered the war, the leaders of the NAACP and the Urban League met with President Franklin D. Roosevelt, petitioning for the desegregation of the armed forces. Not only was this refused, but Roosevelt made a public statement to the effect that the civil rights leaders had agreed at the meeting to the continuation of segregation. Angry at this apparent deception, a black union leader who had attended the meeting, A. Philip Randolph, called for a march of a hundred thousand blacks as a protest in Washington. A few days before the march was due to take place, Roosevelt signed an order forbidding discrimination in employment on the grounds of ethnic differences, and pledging action on the issue of segregation in the armed forces (Finch, 1981; Zangrando, 1980).

Two years later, the newly established Congress of Racial Equality (CORE) began challenging segregation in restaurants, swimming-pools and other public areas in Chicago. Although not a great deal was gained, and fierce reaction provoked from whites, this marked the beginning of militant action on behalf of black civil rights – which fifteen years later became a mass movement (Meier and Rudick, 1973).

Shortly after the Second World War, the NAACP instituted a campaign against segregated public education, which came to a head when the organization sued five school boards, challenging the concept of separate and equal schooling which then held sway. In 1954, the Supreme Court unanimously decided that 'separate educational facilities are inherently unequal'. This decision became the platform for struggles for civil rights for the next two decades. When the Supreme Court decision was first reached, several state and local governments made efforts to limit its effects. Public-school integration proceeding under federal orders was violently resisted, leading to the revitalizing of the white racist organization, the Ku-Klux-Klan, 'White Citizens' Councils' and local vigilante groups. Even as late as 1960, well under 1 per cent of Southern black students attended desegregated schools (Issel, 1985; Sitkoff, 1981).

The very strength of the resistance from recalcitrant whites served to persuade black leaders that mass militancy was necessary to give civil rights any real substance. In 1956 a black woman called Rosa Parks was arrested in Montgomery, Alabama, for declining to give up her seat on a bus to a white man. As a result almost everyone among the black population of the town, led by a Baptist minister, Dr Martin Luther King Jnr, boycotted the transportation system for 381 days. Eventually the city was forced to abolish segregation in that transport system.

Further boycotts and sit-ins followed, with the object of desegregating other public facilities. The marches and demonstrations began to achieve a mass following from blacks and white sympathizers. King planned campaigns of active but non-violent resistance to discrimination, but responses to the movement were far from non-violent. Governor Faubus of Arkansas called out state troopers to stop black students entering the Central High School in Little Rock. In Birmingham, Alabama, Sheriff 'Bull' Connor ordered the police to disperse protesters with fire hoses, clubs and police dogs.

After the episode in Birmingham several hundred demonstrations took place in many American cities over a period of some ten weeks, more than 15,000 protesters being arrested. In 1963, a quarter of a million civil rights supporters staged a march in Washington, hearing King announce 'We will not be satisfied until justice rolls down like the waters and righteousness like a mighty stream.' In 1964, a Civil Rights Act was passed by Congress, comprehensively banning discrimination in public facilities, education, employment and any agency receiving government funds. Further bills in following years were aimed at ensuring that blacks became fully registered voters, and outlawed discrimination in housing.

The civil rights movement

The civil rights movement provided a sense of cultural freedom and affirmation for black activists, going well beyond the formal objects for which they were fighting. The Student Nonviolent Coordinating Committee (SNCC) had its 'Freedom Singers', who translated their aspirations into music and song. Vincent Howard has described the energy and sense of a fresh beginning felt by many blacks at the time:

> There was an indescribable hope, idealism, courage and determination in those early months of organising, marching, singing and going to jail . . . They were believers. When they sang in jail, in mass-meetings, in front of policemen and state troopers, 'We shall overcome', they meant it . . . overcoming meant 'freedom' and 'rights' and 'dignity' and 'justice' and black and white together and many other things that people in a movement feel more than they define. (Harding, 1980)

Attempts to implement the new civil rights legislation again met with ferocious resistance from opponents. Civil rights marchers were insulted and beaten up, and some lost their lives. One response was the development of more aggressive black militant groups under the title of 'Black Power' (Carmichael and Hamilton, 1968). Moderates dissociated themselves from this development, continuing to press for reforms in line with established laws. Major riots broke out in black ghetto areas in cities across America between 1965 and 1968.

In spite of the barriers which hampered the full realization of its provisions, the Civil Rights Act proved to be fundamentally important. Its principles applied not just to blacks, but to anyone subject to discrimination including other ethnic groups and women. It served as the starting-point for a range of movements concerned with developing the rights of oppressed groups.

During the struggles of the 1960s, the goals of the black civil rights movement were somewhat altered. The ambition of most civil rights leaders had always been the full integration of blacks into wider American culture. The rise of militant black power groups helped shift these ideals towards a stress upon the dignity of being black and the intrinsic value of black culture. Blacks now began to demand an independent position in the community, looking towards the development of a genuinely plural society rather than assimilation within the white social order. This change in outlook was also prompted by the feeling that equality before the law is of little use if discrimination persists in practice.

The black power groups advocating violence to achieve their ends, like the Black Panthers, were either crushed by the authorities, or broke up into disputing factions. Many black activists turned to the ballot box as a means of generating political power for blacks. In 1975 a group of black musicians recorded the song 'Chocolate City', and this became one of the most popular singles on black-oriented radio stations. Singer George Clinton expressed the hope that black people could achieve real local influence through electoral politics: 'You don't need the bullet when you've got the ballot!' 'Chocolate City' was Washington, in which 'vanilla' suburbs surrounded the black inner core; but it was also all the cities in which blacks could mobilize their political strength. One part of the rap stated:

> There's a lot of Chocolate Cities around
> We got Newark
> We got Gary
> Somebody told me we got LA
> And we' working on Atlanta

> (Gilroy, 1987)

Affirmative action

Although there was such pronounced early resistance to desegregating schools in the South, in the longer term desegregation in the North posed even greater problems. Schools in the North were not segregated in law, but there was (and is) pronounced segregation of black and white because of different patterns of neighbourhood residence. Since blacks and whites live in largely separate neighbourhoods, their children attend different schools. The 'busing' of children between school districts (taking children to schools outside their area in order to place white children in predominantly black schools, and the other way around) to achieve greater integration began as a result of a Supreme Court decision which came into force in 1971. Busing is an example of **affirmative action**, a term which covers all programmes that take positive steps to redress the balance where minority groups are disfavoured. Other examples of affirmative action tried out in the 1970s and 1980s include allocating a certain proportion of college places to minority groups, in the knowledge that their grades might not match up to those of others; and ensuring that at least a certain percentage of those hired for jobs in public agencies come from disadvantaged groups.

Most forms of affirmative action have proved highly controversial. The debates over busing came to a head in Boston in 1976, when whites stormed buses carrying black students to previously white schools. Busing has for the most part progressed peacefully, but almost certainly has had the unintended consequence of adding to the movement of whites away from central areas of cities. The Supreme Court lent partial support to the principle of affirmative action in the case of *Bakke* v. *The University of California* (1977). Bakke was a white student who applied to the medical school of the University of California at Davis. Since his grades and test scores were higher than those of a number of applicants from minority groups, who were accepted while he was rejected, he claimed he had suffered 'reverse discrimination'. The Supreme Court ruled that he should be admitted to the university but decided that universities have the right to use ethnic background as a relevant criterion in deciding student entry. Fixed quotas, on the other hand, were declared illegal.

The history of immigration in the United Kingdom

Early arrivals

The considerable number of Irish, Welsh and Scottish names scattered among the English people today is a reminder of the traditional flow of people from the 'Celtic fringes' to the urban centres of England. In the early nineteenth century, long before the advent of major immigration from distant colonies, it was clear that developing English cities attracted migrants from the less prosperous areas of the British Isles. In 1867 *The Times* lamented the fact that 'there is hardly such a thing as a pure Englishman in this island.' The monarchy, which is today depicted as the most distinctively 'English' of English institutions, has included many 'foreign' elements. England has had French, Scots, Dutch and German monarchs; and the present royal family has so many non-English forebears that it could best be described as 'European'!

There has been a thriving Irish community in London since the seventeenth century. Although at first they worked mainly in unskilled manual jobs, Irish immigrants were able in time to move into more skilled and better-paid positions. Alone among countries in Western Europe, the population of Ireland actually fell in the nineteenth century. London, Manchester, Liverpool and Glasgow received tens of thousands of Irish immigrants, while many more left for the USA. Between 1830 and 1847, 300,000 Irish landed in Liverpool alone. By 1851, half a million Irish people had settled in England and Wales. Why did so many come? Persistent famines in Ireland forced people to seek a new life elsewhere, and the proximity of Ireland to England made it relatively easy for the Irish to travel to English cities and keep up some communication with their native country.

The Irish in mid-nineteenth-century England were the largest immigrant group in a society which, outside London, had largely been sheltered from foreign 'incursions'. The capital itself, however, contained many 'exotic' groups. A Jewish community was established in the seventeenth century, and increased substantially over the following hundred years, as harsh repression drove Jews in other countries to the relative safety of England. By 1800 it was calculated that there were some 6,000 Jews in provincial towns and between 15,000 and 20,000 in London. Criticized when poor, the Jews were also condemned when rich. When Charles Dickens created Fagin in *Oliver Twist*, he employed an immediately recognizable and common caricature.

During the industrial revolution, Dutch immigrants in Britain helped to establish a network of banking and financial agencies known as 'Dutch finance' – which was to prove vital in the economic transformation of the country. Enterprising, well-educated Dutchmen brought to England social and economic qualities which were of abiding and revolutionary importance. Non-British people thus made a significant contribution to the creation of a new socio-economic climate in England.

The influx of Chinese immigrants during the period of English industrial expansion was for employers a welcome source of cheap labour for English factories. Yet on several occasions in the late nineteenth century union leaders spoke out against Chinese immigration because of the threat posed to the wage levels of local workers.

Black settlement in Britain was given an impetus in the late nineteenth century by the expansion of shipping to West Africa and the Caribbean. A few African and West Indian students were admitted to British universities at this period, but the largest black immigrant group consisted of black sailors who had settled in British cities. These were the founders of the first modern black communities in Britain (notably in Cardiff). The need for more fighting men to bolster the British forces during the First World War led to the recruitment of over 15,000 men from the British Caribbean islands to form a black West Indian regiment, and a number of West Indian troops settled in Britain when hostilities ended, preferring to sample whatever Britain had to offer rather than return to the economically depressed West Indies (see Fryer, 1984).

Immigration after 1930

The Nazi persecutions of the early 1930s sent a generation of European Jews fleeing westwards to safety. One survey estimated that 60,000 Jews settled in the UK between 1933 and 1939, but the real figure may well have been even higher. Between 1933 and 1939 some 80,000 refugees arrived from Central Europe, and a further 70,000 came during the

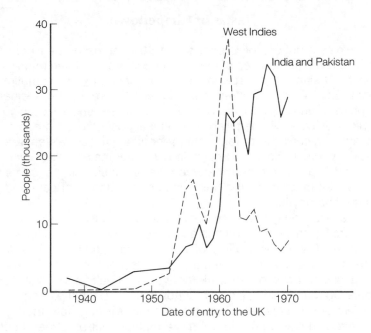

Figure 9 Immigration into the United Kingdom from the West Indies, India and Pakistan, 1940–1970. The graph shows the numbers of people in Great Britain in 1971 with one or both parents born in the West Indies or Pakistan or India, by date of entry into the United Kingdom
Sources: G.B. Lomas, *Census 1971: The Coloured Population of Great Britain* (London: Runnymede Trust, 1974); The Runnymede Trust and The Radical Statistics Race Group, *Britain's Black Population* (London: Heinemann Educational, 1987), p. 27.

war itself. By May 1945, Europe faced an unprecedented refugee problem: millions of people had become refugees. Several hundred thousand of these settled in Britain.

In the post-Second-World-War period, Britain experienced immigration on an unprecedented scale – most of the new residents coming from the Commonwealth countries in response to job opportunities here (Walvin, 1984; Fryer, 1984). There was something of a class division in the way in which the British reacted to this new influx of immigrants. Those in governing circles were influenced by the notion of Britain's great imperial heritage, and therefore felt that West Indians, Indians, Pakistanis and Africans were all British subjects and entitled to settle in Britain. There was also a marked shortage of labour in post-war Britain; employers were for a while keen to attract immigrant labour. Many working people, however, living in the poorer areas (to which the new immigrants gravitated), were more aware of disruptions to their own everyday lives. Their attitudes to the newcomers were often hostile. Nearly a third of all Commonwealth immigrants came to live in certain parts of London; there were further concentrations of immigrants in the West Midlands, in Bradford, and in other impoverished urban areas.

Rastas of Chapeltown

Chapeltown is a suburb of Leeds, about 10 minutes by bus from the city centre. The few square miles of terrace houses are inhabited mainly by Afro-Caribbeans, Asians, Irish, and a few impoverished (and sometimes also idealistic) English. As in other such inner-city areas, the residents are geographically and socially marooned. The streets show little sign of any economic activity. A Sikh family runs the local post office; a group of Rastas own a small record store (an entrepreneurial success often referred to enviously by other blacks). Social life for the mainly black and mainly unemployed population moves between the 'arcades' (single rooms flanked by rows of slot machines), the much raided Bamboo Leaf café and a large urban pub, The Hayfield.

Nigel is a less than typical member of this community. He is young, just 22, black, wears Rasta locks – and has a job. He sits under a large poster of Bob Marley in the Chapeltown office of Ruth Bundley and Co, Solicitors, and describes the long career of unemployment 'schemes' which preceded his present position. 'I was out of work for two and a half years. Wake up in the afternoon. Go round and see if any friends was up. Be in their house. Talk for a while. Go out. Mainly wheeling and dealing. Making dole money last by doing something else with it to get more money. Out on street. Looking for things to buy and sell. That's all.'

And then after a YTS scheme in joinery ('they got rid of me') and a community industries scheme in painting and decorating and yet more unemployment, he finally landed in Ruth's practice as a trainee legal assistant.

He says, 'I wanted to get into Ruth's because other solicitors' firms as soon as they looked at me, they went "No. Not with that hair." Ruth said she wouldn't take me on if I cut my hair. I enjoy work now. Sometimes I get here before everyone else. They gave me a key. I'm determined to go the whole way. I'll take my solicitor's exams. Probably be the first Rastafarian solicitor.'

Most of Nigel's black friends in Chapeltown are far less lucky. (The unemployment figure for under 25s here is nearly 70 per cent.) Like him they may have alternated between 'schemes' and unemployment since leaving school, but many have ended up precisely where they started, as unemployed – 'dolers', in the abusive term they use to describe their plight. And for most that means out on the street. Away from domestic overcrowding but also up with your friends and near the action.

Huey, a 24-year-old Rasta with locks, has tried to break the habit. 'I wake up and I say to myself, "What can I do positively?" But then I do what I do every day. I go down to what we know as the front line. Get down there and think, "I don't want to be down here. I don't want to just be in the street. In a café. I want to do something positive." What else is there to do? Then I go back home again.'

Young unemployed blacks in Chapeltown, as in Brixton, Notting Hill and St Paul's, know that the easiest way to supplement their dole money is to sell a little cannabis. Huey had already done some time in jail for dealing in what he insists on calling 'that herbal plant'. But it was difficult to find any moral concern about the practice either in him or among his friends. 'What's wrong with selling a little to your friends or a few white students from the university?' was more or less the standard response to questions on the subject.

'Crime' is already talked about among such people as an available option. Malcolm liked 'blues' parties because they kept him out of trouble. 'If a friend comes round and says come to the blues and another says how about some burglary, you gotta go to the blues 'cos it won't be there next night.' All in all he didn't think he would go into crime: 'It's a tough life, man. Knowing the police will be on your back all the time. You do crime and buy a car. What's that – you got a car. Next thing you know you locked up. You lose the car.'

Nigel's experience of prison during visits to convicted friends made him even more sceptical of crime as a way out. 'It's too depressing. I wouldn't like nobody to go in there. A lot of my friends have stopped that now. Just want to sit at home, get their little dole money, buy a draw, talk, and that's all. No crime.'

This acceptance of unemployment as almost a way of life is often a cause of division between young blacks and their parents. Nigel captured the incomprehension of the older generation at the street life of their children. '"Oh," they say, "You're all too bad. All you want to do is lie around – go to the blues – stand on the corner."' This is not a culture which parents recognize, which they ever experienced for themselves as youths. 'Perhaps when they came out to England in the 50s and 60s they found it hard but they could still leave a job one day and find another the next. Now there are no jobs.'

(Adapted from L. Taylor, 'Britain now', in *Illustrated London News*, October 1987, pp. 54–5)

Successive governments saw the full integration of the new immigrants into British society as a goal that was both desirable and possible. Roy Jenkins, Labour Home Secretary during the 1960s, offered a definition of integration 'not as a flattening process of assimilation but as equal opportunity, accompanied by cultural diversity, in an atmosphere of mutual tolerance'. In 1966, under the Race Relations Act introduced by the Labour government, a Race Relations Board was established. It provided for intervention in cases of proven discrimination on racial grounds. In 1968, a more substantial Bill against discrimination was introduced, but this was coupled with new legislation to control entry, which thenceforth sharply reduced the number of new immigrants. In the same year, while Parliament was discussing race relations, Enoch Powell (then Conservative front-bench spokesman for defence) delivered a speech in Birmingham in which he envisaged an extraordinary growth of the non-white population: 'like the Romans, I seem to see "the River Tiber flowing with much blood".' A Gallup poll showed that 75 per cent of the population were broadly sympathetic to Powell's views.

The end of the 1970s and the early 1980s witnessed increasing unemployment in Britain concentrated particularly among the ethnic minorities. There were waves of unrest, with racial clashes in Brixton, Handsworth and Tottenham in London, Toxteth in Liverpool and St Paul's in Bristol. Successive governments have been criticized for failing to accept that

Britain is now, irreversibly, a multi-racial nation. The Asian-based communities are different in character from those of West Indian origin, but both are now well established. Some 6 per cent of the population is now officially classified as non-white; approximately half of these were born in the UK.

In a 1985 survey, nine out of ten British whites said that they believed there is prejudice against Asians and blacks. The association between age and the perception of Britain as a racially prejudiced society is fairly strong: the younger a person is, the more likely she or he is to see Britain as prejudiced. The survey also revealed that over a third of whites openly admit to being racially prejudiced themselves (a far higher proportion than in similar surveys in the United States). Men are more likely than women to admit to prejudice, as are older people and those in working-class jobs or the unemployed. Conservative Party supporters, however, are more likely to describe themselves as prejudiced than those supporting the other main parties. Although the whites surveyed were sceptical of the claim that the level of racial prejudice had increased over the past five years (it had), they were generally quite ready to believe that racial prejudice in Britain is likely to grow rather than diminish (see Jowell et al., 1986).

Reactions against racism

There have been several recent examples of attempts at anti-racist intervention in Britain. One important source of counter-attacks on racism was found in the activities of Labour local authorities, especially the Greater London Council (GLC) in the aftermath of riots in 1981. Other groups involved included Rock Against Racism and the Anti-Nazi League in the late 1970s.

The centrepiece of the GLC's strategy was the declaration of London as an 'anti-racist zone'. The year 1984 was designated as an anti-racist year in which the struggle against racism would be a primary focus of the council's work. These commitments relied to some extent on raising public awareness through billboards and press advertisements. One GLC poster pictured people using newspapers to obscure their view of things in front of them, with the caption 'If you're not part of the solution, you're part of the problem.' Another poster asked 'Where would Mrs. Thatcher have got to if she had been black?' The GLC's attempts to develop popular anti-racism lacked the active participation of large numbers of black people, and this fact caused considerable controversy. None the less, the GLC's policy was the most active of any political authority in the country. (The GLC was abolished by Parliament in 1986.)

Rock against Racism (RAR) was formed in August 1976. The organization based itself on youth culture in Britain, seeking to communicate anti-racist themes through popular music. Pop concerts were regularly staged, with performers making a conscious display of their opposition to racial discrimination. New white pop groups began to take an interest in black culture in general and Rastafari in particular, and several influential groups composed of both black and white musicians, such as UB40, emerged.

An organization which sought to attract anti-racist support from politicians, academics, entertainers and others was founded in 1977 as the Anti-Nazi League (ANL). The League's sponsors sought to 'organize on the widest possible scale' and appealed to 'all those who oppose the growth of the Nazis in Britain [to unite] irrespective of other political differences'. The concerns of the League were to combat extremist right-wing views, rather than being solely focused on racism. The ANL's work was a single-issue campaign, more modest in scope than RAR's programme. The ANL sought to isolate and eliminate the Fascist parties at elections, and was brought into being in response to a growth in support of Fascist parties such as the National Front, which was highly visible in the late 1970s and early 1980s. However, in the late 1970s the ANL and RAR co-operated by organizing a series of large demonstrations, 'carnivals', in different parts of the country. These carnivals attracted considerable publicity, and the London carnival of May 1978 drew over 80,000 people (Gilroy, 1987). In the 1980s, the most significant initiatives involving such groups as RAR originated within youth culture. Several leading pop singers have played a part also in such international groups as Artists Against Apartheid.

Commendable as these endeavours may have been, their impact has been relatively slight. This should not be regarded as surprising, as the sources of prejudice and discrimination are deep-rooted; moreover, as has been stressed earlier, racism is in some large degree 'built into' broader social inequalities in British society, and is unlikely to be significantly reduced if these are not also lessened.

Ethnic relations on the Continent

Large-scale migrations took place in Europe during the first two decades after the second World War, the Mediterranean countries providing the nations in the North and West with cheap labour. Migrants moving from areas like Turkey, North Africa, Greece and Southern Spain and Italy were for a period actively encouraged by host countries facing acute shortages of labour. Switzerland, West Germany, Belgium and Sweden all have considerable populations of migrant workers. At the same time, countries that used to be colonial powers experienced an influx of immigrants from their former colonies: this applied primarily to France (Algerians) and the Netherlands (Indonesians) as well as the UK.

Labour migration into and within Western Europe slowed down appreciably over a decade ago, as the boom turned into recession.

Although the transition from migration to settlement is everywhere well advanced, most members of the developing ethnic minorities still suffer serious legal disabilities. In some countries, legal frameworks originally designed to manage temporary labour migration have simply been maintained, despite the fact that they are ill-suited to the current situation. In other nations (such as France and Germany), new restrictive policies have been introduced to control minority populations – for example, limiting the rights of established immigrants to bring in close relatives.

Many West European countries have witnessed campaigns for returning migrants to their countries of origin, threats of deportation in the event of unemployment or committing an offence, and other related policies. Such proposals must seem a particularly disturbing threat to minority youth, often born in their host country, who would face the prospect of being forced to 'return' to countries with which they have no real links.

Not only do racism and ethnic discrimination still persist in Western Europe, but there are signs that it is, if anything, on the increase. The World Council of Churches has presented evidence that there is an 'escalation of racism' throughout Western Europe (World Council of Churches, 1980). In France, opinion polls report that between 60 and 70 per cent of those interviewed think that there are 'too many' North Africans in France, and up to half the respondents feel there are 'too many' Spaniards and Portuguese. In Switzerland, movements against 'foreign swamping' (*Überfremdung*) have led to pressure for the deportation of foreign citizens. Even countries like Sweden and the Netherlands, known for their tolerance, are experiencing growing tensions, and have tightened up their immigration rules.

Racism is thus a daily reality to members of the new ethnic minorities throughout Western Europe today. The West German government estimates that far-right and neo-Nazi organizations have about 20,000 members. Such groups have cultivated strong links with similar ones in other countries, the National Front and Column 88 in the UK, FANE in France and NAR in Italy. These are not movements made up of ageing reactionaries, but rather a *new* generation of men and women holding right-wing beliefs. Of the neo-Nazis – people actively reviving ideas originally proclaimed by Hitler and the National Socialists in the 1930s – convicted of criminal offences in West Germany in 1982, 45 per cent were aged fourteen and 20 per cent were between twenty-one and thirty (Castles, 1984, p. 203).

Likely future developments in ethnic relations

The USA is the most ethnically diverse nation in the West, having been constructed as an 'immigrant society'. The models of possible future ethnic development worked out there have distinct relevance to potential paths of change in Europe. Three types of model have been suggested as characterizing the development of ethnic relations in the United States (Gordon, 1978). One is **assimilation,** meaning that immigrants abandon their original customs and practices, moulding their behaviour to the values and norms of the majority. Generations of immigrants faced pressures towards being 'assimilated' in this way, and many of their children became more or less completely 'American' as a result.

A second model is that of the **melting pot**. Rather than the traditions of the immigrants being dissolved in favour of those dominant among the pre-existing population, all become blended to form new, evolving cultural patterns. Many have believed this to be the most desirable outcome of ethnic diversity. To a limited degree, this model is an accurate expression of aspects of American cultural development. Although the 'Anglo' culture has remained the pre-eminent one, its character in some part reflects the impact of the many different groups that now compose the American population.

The third model is that of **cultural pluralism**. In this view, the most appropriate course is to foster the development of a genuinely plural society, in which the equal validity of numerous different sub-cultures is recognized. The USA has long been pluralistic but ethnic differences have for the most part been associated with inequalities rather than equal but independent membership of the national community.

Turning to Western Europe, we can see similar tensions and similar options. Most official governmental policies, in Britain and elsewhere, are directed towards the first path, that of assimilation. As in the United States, this is likely to prove most problematic where ethnic minorities are physically quite distinct from the majority of the population – as is the case with West Indians, Africans and Asians in Britain. The persistence of racism (often institutionalized) in Europe makes the notion of the melting pot of fairly limited relevance. With many states maintaining or sometimes increasing the strictness of their laws restricting immigration, the social or political climate for ideals of the 'merging' of identities is not encouraging.

The leaders of most ethnic minorities themselves have increasingly emphasized the path of pluralism (Jowell et al., 1986; Castles, 1984). To achieve 'distinct but equal' status will demand major struggles, and as yet this is a very distant option. Ethnic minorities are still perceived by many people as a threat: a threat to one's job, one's safety and the 'national culture'. The scapegoating of ethnic minorities is a persistent tendency (Jowell et al., 1986). With the young in Western Europe quite often still holding similar prejudices to those of older generations, ethnic minorities in most countries face a future of continued discrimination, in a social climate characterized by tension and anxiety.

For the foreseeable future, as in the past, the most likely path is a mixture of the three types, with a stronger emphasis on pluralism than used to be the case. It would be a mistake, however, to see ethnic pluralism as resulting only from differing cultural values and norms 'bought in' from the outside into a society. Cultural diversity has also been *created* by the experience of ethnic groups as they adapt to the wider social environments in which they find themselves.

Summary

1   Sections of a population form ethnic groups by virtue of sharing common cultural characteristics which separate them from others within that population. Ethnic differences are wholly learned, although they are sometimes thought of as 'natural'.

2   A *minority group* is one whose members are discriminated against by the majority population in a society. Members of minority groups often have a strong sense of group solidarity, deriving in part from the collective experience of exclusion.

3   *Race* refers to physical characteristics, such as skin colour, treated by members of a community or society as ethnically significant – as signalling distinct cultural characteristics. Many popular beliefs about race are mythical. There are no clear-cut characteristics by means of which human beings can be allocated to different races.

4   *Racism* means falsely ascribing inherited characteristics of personality or behaviour to individuals of a particular physical appearance. A racist is someone who believes that a biological explanation can be given for characteristics of inferiority supposedly possessed by people of one physical stock or another.

5   *Displacement* and *scapegoating* are psychological mechanisms associated with *prejudice* and *discrimination*. In displacement, feelings of hostility become directed against objects that are not the real origin of these anxieties. People project their anxieties and insecurities on to scapegoats. Prejudice involves holding preconceived views about an individual or group; discrimination refers to actual behaviour which deprives members of a group from opportunities open to others.

6   Ethnic attitudes are assimilated by children at a very young age. They learn, for example, to think of whites as superior and blacks as inferior.

7   Group closure and privileged access to resources are an important part of many situations of ethnic antagonism. However, some of the fundamental aspects of modern ethnic conflicts, especially racist attitudes held by whites against blacks, have to be understood in terms of the history of the expansion of the West and of colonialism.

8   Historical examples illustrate various ways in which societies have dealt with ethnic minorities, ranging from slavery and apartheid to relative acceptance, and the ways those minorities have reacted.

9   *Affirmative action* refers to programmes which take positive steps to reduce the disadvantages suffered by minority groups. Some types of

affirmative action, which have been most widely introduced in the United States, such as the busing of school children, have led to major conflicts.

10 Three models of possible future developments in ethnic relations can be distinguished – the first stressing *assimilation,* the second the *melting pot,* and the third *cultural pluralism.* In recent years there has been an emphasis on the third of these avenues, whereby different ethnic identities are accepted as equally valid within the context of the overall national culture.

Basic concepts

ethnicity	racism
discrimination	prejudice

Important terms

plural society	apartheid
minority group (or ethnic minority)	microsegregation
race	mezzosegregation
stereotypical thinking	macrosegregation
displacement	affirmative action
scapegoating	assimilation
projection	melting pot
authoritarian personality	cultural pluralism

Further reading

Richard Alba (ed.), *Ethnicity and Race in the U.S.A.: Toward the 21st Century* (London: Routledge and Kegan Paul, 1985) — an interesting collection of essays about future developments in ethnic relations.

Cara Bagley Marret and Cheryl Leggon, *Research in Race and Ethnic Relations* (Westfield: JAI Press, 1984) — a useful survey of the current state of research into ethnicity, prejudice and discrimination.

D. Peukert, *Inside Nazi Germany: Conformity, Opposition and Racism in Everyday Life* (London: Batsford, 1987) — Peukert draws upon a wide variety of sources to construct this fascinating account of what Hannah Arendt called the 'banality of racism'.

John Rex and David Mason (eds), *Theories of Race and Ethnic Relations* (Cambridge: Cambridge University Press, 1986) — Rex and Mason analyse the main theoretical interpretations of race and ethnicity, developing a particular perspective of their own.

9

Groups and Organizations

The French philosopher and dramatist Jean-Paul Sartre once wrote that 'hell is other people.' There are indeed many situations, intimate and more impersonal, where our relations with others can be oppressive. One way to make people uncomfortable, and even despairing, is to place them in relationships with others that are too close and continuous – as is often the case, for example, in prisons. Yet a far more severe punishment is to deprive someone of human contact altogether. Being held in solitary confinement, even if allowed a reasonable degree of comfort in other respects, is something most human beings find almost unendurable. Living and interacting with others in groups, associations and organizations is a pervasive aspect of the lives of virtually all human beings.

Most of us belong to numerous groups – including, for example, the families into which we are born, but also a variety of much larger organizations, such as schools, colleges or business firms. Groups and organizations dominate much of our lives, and the systems of authority they involve consistently influence and constrain our behaviour. In this chapter we shall discuss some of the main characteristics of groups, putting particular emphasis on the authority systems of large-scale organizations.

Forms of association

The concept of *social group* should be distinguished from two other related notions, *aggregates* and *social categories*. A **social group** is simply a number of people who interact with each other on a regular basis. Such regularity of interaction tends to weld participants together as a distinct unit with an overall social identity. Members of a group expect certain forms of behaviour from one another that are not demanded of non-members. Groups differ in size, ranging from intimate associations, like a family, up to large collectivities, such as a sports club. **Aggregates** are simply collections of people who are in the same place at the same time, but share no definite connections with one another. Passengers waiting at an airport or a cinema audience, or students waiting in lines to register for courses, are examples of aggregates. To use Erving Goffman's phrase, aggregates are gatherings of people in unfocused interaction with one another (see chapter 4: 'Social Interaction and Everyday Life'). Of course, within aggregates various kinds of group relationship are usually found.

A **social category** is a statistical grouping – people classified together on the basis of a particular characteristic they share, such as having the same level of income or being in the same occupation. People in the same social category neither interact with each other nor gather together in one place; they do not necessarily attach any particular importance to the common characteristic they share. Social categories are nevertheless quite often referred to in sociological research. For instance, if we are interested in race relations in Britain, we might need to analyse the difference in average earnings between blacks and whites as a whole – two statistical categories.

Primary and secondary groups

The groups to which we belong are not all of equal importance to us. Some groups tend to influence many aspects of our lives and bring us into personal and familiar association with others. The American sociologist Charles Horton Cooley (1864–1929) used the term **primary group** to refer to a small association of people connected by ties of an emotionally involving nature. The family is an example, as are friendship groups. Cooley tended to idealize primary groups, but this emphasis should be questioned. Life in families, for example, is not by any means always intrinsically satisfying and enjoyable;

families are often the source of great tension and hostility (see chapter 12: 'Kinship, Marriage and the Family').

A **secondary group** is a number of people who meet regularly, but whose relationships are mainly impersonal. Individuals in secondary groups do not have intimate ties with each other, and normally come together for specific practical purposes. A committee or club is a good example of a secondary group. Of course, in actual social situations, the distinction between primary and secondary groups is not clear-cut. People who regularly attend committee meetings together, for example, might become very friendly and spend time with one another informally.

Formal organizations

In traditional societies, most people live in small-group settings. In a society like traditional China, it was rare for members of a village community ever to meet a government official. Government edicts barely affected their lives. Compare this to our situation today. What we do is constantly conditioned by the decisions of officials; we even speak of such officials now as *the* authorities – as if the authority of others in different settings could be ignored. Every major event – birth, marriage or death – has to be registered. Government organizations provide, or at least are partly responsible for, some of the most basic resources affecting our activities, such as education, sanitation, road systems, public utilities, control of the environment, the national monetary system – the list is almost endlesss.

Many of us are born in large hospitals, and are tagged so that we can be identified among several dozen other new-born babies. Virtually all of us attend schools, and some go on to colleges. We may spend much of our adult lives working within a business firm, financial company, bank, or government agency. Throughout our lives we also depend upon **organizations** in order to communicate with others by means of letters or the telephone, to provide light and heat for our homes, and information or entertainment should we wish to read a newspaper, listen to the radio or watch television.

An organization is a large association of people run on impersonal lines, set up to achieve specific objectives. Most social systems in the traditional world developed over lengthy periods as a result of custom and habit. Organizations, on the other hand, are mostly *designed* – established with definite aims in view, and housed in buildings or physical settings specifically constructed to help realize those aims. The edifices in which hospitals, colleges or business firms carry on their activities are mostly 'custom-built'.

It is easy to see why organizations are so important to us today. In the pre-industrial world, families, close relatives and neighbours provided for most needs – food, the instruction of children, work and leisure-time activities. In modern societies, we are all much more interdependent than was ever the case before. Many of our requirements are catered for by others we never meet, and who indeed may live many thousands of miles away. A tremendous amount of co-ordination of activities and resources – which organizations provide – is needed in such circumstances.

Bureaucracy

All modern organizations are in a large degree bureaucratic in nature. The word **bureaucracy** was invented by a Monsieur de Gournay in 1745. He added to the word 'bureau', meaning both an office and a writing table, a term derived from the Greek verb 'to rule'. 'Bureaucracy' is thus the rule of officials. It was first used only to apply to government officials, but gradually became extended to refer to large organizations in general. The concept was from the beginning used in a disparaging way, by its inventor and by others. De Gournay spoke of the developing power of officials as 'an illness called bureaumania' (Albrow, 1970). The French novelist Balzac spoke of bureaucracy as 'the giant power wielded by pygmies'. This sort of view has persisted into current times. Bureaucracy is frequently associated with 'red tape', inefficiency and wastefulness.

The satirist C. Northcote Parkinson produced a celebrated discussion of bureaucracy, based on the idea that officials informally expand the scope of what they do to take care of any free time they have (Parkinson, 1957). 'Parkinson's Law' states that work expands to fill the time available for its completion. Bureaucracies tend to grow, not because the officials have taken on new duties which they did not have before, but because they have to be constantly seen to be busy. They create tasks where none really exist – and then have to supervise their subordinates, who in turn must spend a great deal of time writing reports and memoranda for them. And so the process continues – most of the form-filling, memo-writing and file-keeping actually being quite unnecessary to carry out the tasks the bureaucracy was set up to do.

Many other writers, however, have seen bureaucracy in a different light – as a model of carefulness, precision and effective administration. Bureaucracy, they argue, is in fact the most efficient form of organization human beings have devised, because all tasks are regulated by strict rules of procedure. The most influential account of bureaucracy, given by Max Weber, steers a way between these two extremes. According to Weber, the expansion of bureaucracy is inevitable in modern societies. The development of bureaucratic authority is the only way of coping with the administrative requirements of large-scale social systems. However, Weber also believes bureaucracy to have a number of major failings, which have important implications for the nature of modern social life.

Weber's view of bureaucracy

A limited number of bureaucratic organizations, Weber points out, existed in the larger traditional societies. For example, there was a bureaucratic officialdom in Imperial China, responsible for the overall affairs of government. The other main type of bureaucracy in the traditional world was the military. But it is only in modern times that bureaucracies have developed fully and are found in most areas of social life. In order to look at the origins and nature of the expansion of bureaucratic organizations, Weber constructs an **ideal type** of bureaucracy. ('Ideal' here does not refer to what is most desirable, but to a 'pure form' of bureaucratic organization. An ideal type is an abstract description constructed by accentuating certain features of real cases so as to pinpoint their most essential characteristics.) Weber lists several characteristics of the ideal type of bureaucracy (Weber, 1978, pp. 956–63).

1 There is a clear-cut *hierarchy of authority*, such that tasks in the organization are distributed as 'official duties'. A bureaucracy looks like a pyramid, with the positions of highest authority at the top. There is a 'chain of command', stretching from top to bottom, making co-ordinated decision-making possible. Each higher office controls and supervises the one below it in the hierarchy.
2 *Written rules* govern the conduct of *officials* at all levels of the organization. This does not mean that bureaucratic duties are just a matter of routine. The higher the office, the more the rules involved tend to encompass a wide variety of cases and demand flexibility in their interpretation.
3 **Officials** *are full-time and salaried*. Each job in the hierarchy has a definite and fixed salary attached to it. The individual is expected to make a career within the organization. Promotion is possible on the basis of capability, seniority, or a mixture of the two.
4 *There is a separation between the tasks of the official within the organization and life outside.* The 'home life' of the official is distinct from her or his activities in the workplace, and is also physically separated from it.
5 *No member or members of the organization own the material resources with which they operate.* The development of bureaucracy, according to Weber, separates workers from control of their means of production. In traditional communities, farmers and craft workers usually had close control over their processes of production, and owned the tools they used. In bureaucracies, officials do not own the offices in which they work, the desks at which they sit or the office machinery they utilize.

The effectiveness of bureaucracy

Modern bureaucracy, Weber argues, is a highly effective mode of organizing large numbers of people. There are several reasons for this:

1 Bureaucratic procedures might in some ways limit initiative, but they also ensure that decisions are taken according to general criteria rather than individual whim or caprice.
2 Training officials to be experts in the area to which their duties apply cuts out the 'talented amateur', but ensures a general level of overall competence.
3 Making official positions salaried and full-time reduces, although it does not eliminate, possibilities of corruption. Traditional systems of authority were actually based in large part on what we would today regard as corrupt practices. Office-holders used their position, for instance, to tax those they governed, taking most of the money for their own use.
4 The fact that performance is judged by examinations or other public means reduces – although it does not entirely put a stop to – the obtaining of positions through personal favour or kinship connections.

Weber believes that the more an organization approaches the ideal type of bureaucracy, the more effective it will be in pursuing the objectives for which it was established. He often likens bureaucracies to sophisticated machines. Yet he recognizes that bureaucracy can cause 'red tape' problems, and accepts that many bureaucratic jobs are dull, offering little opportunity for the exercise of creative capabilities. Bureaucratic routine, and the authority of officialdom over our lives, are prices we pay for the technical effectiveness of bureaucratic organizations.

Formal and informal relations within bureaucracies

Weber's analysis of bureaucracy gives prime place to **formal relations** within organizations. The more bureaucratized an organization is, in Weber's terms, the more tasks are fixed and detailed. He has little to say about the informal connections, and small-group relations, that exist in all organizations. In bureaucracies, informal ways of doing things are often the chief means by which a measure of flexibility is achieved.

In a classical study, Blau studied **informal relations** in a government agency (Blau, 1963). The tasks of the officials in the agency involved investigating possible income-tax violations. Agents who came across problems which they were unsure how to deal with were supposed to discuss them with their immediate supervisor. The rules of procedure stated that they should not consult colleagues working at the same level as themselves. Most officials were wary of approaching their supervisors, however, because they felt this might suggest a lack of competence on their part, and reduce their promotion chances. Hence, they usually consulted each other, violating the official rules. This not only helped to provide concrete advice; it also reduced the anxieties involved in working alone. A cohesive set of loyalties, of a *primary group* kind, developed among those working at the same level. The problems these workers faced, Blau concludes, were probably coped with much more effectively as a result. The group was able to evolve informal procedures allowing for more initiative and responsibility than was provided for by the formal rules of the organization.

Informal networks tend to develop at all levels of organizations. At the very top, personal ties and connections may be more important in the real structure of power than the formal situations in which decisions are supposed to be taken. For example, meetings of boards of directors and shareholders supposedly determine the policies of business corporations. In practice, a few members of the board often really run the corporation, taking their decisions informally and expecting the board to approve them. Informal networks of this sort can also stretch across different corporations. Business leaders from different firms frequently consult one another in an informal way, and belong to the same clubs and leisure-time associations.

Deciding how far informal procedures generally help or hinder the effectiveness of organizations is not a simple matter. Systems that resemble Weber's ideal type tend to give rise to a forest of unofficial ways of doing things. This is partly because the flexibility that is lacking can be achieved by unofficial tinkering with formal rules. For those in dull jobs, informal ways of doing things often also help to create a more satisfying work environment. Informal connections between officials in higher positions may be effective in ways which aid the organization as a whole. On the other hand, those involved may be more concerned to advance or protect their own interests than to further those of the organization as such.

Bureaucracy and oligarchy

It follows from Weber's model of bureaucracy that power tends to be concentrated at the top. A large organization is a pyramid, with the majority being in relatively powerless positions near the bottom. A student and colleague of Weber's, Robert Michels, made use of this observation to set out what he termed the *iron law of oligarchy* (Michels, 1967). **Oligarchy** means rule by the few. According to Michels, the larger and more bureaucratized an organization becomes, the greater the degree to which power is concentrated in the hands of a small number of people in high positions. Michels based his thesis upon the development of the Social Democratic Party in Germany, which was explicitly committed to ideals of mass participation in political decision-making. The party was developing into a major force in German politics at that period (the first decade of this century). Its very success brought about increasing internal bureaucracy, as the party grew in size.

Real power, Michels tried to show, was increasingly coming to be monopolized by those running the party bureaucracy at the top – a few high party officials. Ironically, the Social Democratic Party had become dominated by a small clique in just the same way as were the conservative parties it opposed. Every large-scale organization, according to Michels, shows the same tendencies. Rule by the few is simply an inevitable aspect of the bureaucratic nature of large organizations. If Michels's argument is valid, the consequences are serious for anyone who values democratic participation. Michels himself progressively abandoned the socialist ideals he once supported.

In common with Weber, Michels identified a genuine source of tension in modern societies between trends towards *bureaucracy* on the one hand and the development of **democracy** on the other. Mass democracy can only exist if there are regular voting procedures and well-developed party organizations, but these bring about the advance of bureaucracy, because there have to be full-time officials to supervise or run the parties. Democracy is supposed to involve mass participation in the political system; yet the very furtherance of democratic parties leads to the development of large, bureaucratized party machines, dominated by cliques of leaders. (For further discussion of mass democracy, see chapter 10: 'Politics, Government and the State'.)

Was Michels right? It surely is correct to say that large-scale organizations involve the centralizing of power, yet there is good reason to suppose that the 'iron law of oligarchy' is not quite as hard and fast as Michels claimed. The connections between oligarchy and bureaucratic centralization are more ambiguous than he supposed.

We should recognize first of all that unequal power is not just a function of size. In modest-sized groups there can be very marked differences of power. In a small business, for instance, where the activities of employees are directly visible to the directors, much tighter control might be exerted than in offices in larger organizations. As organizations expand in size, power relationships often in fact become looser. Those at the middle and lower levels may have little influence over general policies forged at the top. But on the other hand, because of the specialization of expertise involved in bureaucracy, people at the top lose control of many administrative decisions, which come to be handled by those lower down (Crozier, 1964). Individuals in subordinate positions always have some form of control over their superiors. For example, a civil service official is often able to present the background of a case to a superior in such a way that only one decision appears plausible.

Power is also quite often openly delegated from superiors to subordinates within organizations. Ray Pahl and Jack Winkler studied business directors in corporations of differing sizes (Pahl and Winkler, 1974). They found that open transfer of power downwards was *more* common in the larger than in the smaller firms. In the larger companies, directors were so busy co-ordinating different departments, coping with crises and analysing budget and output or sales figures, that they had little time for original thinking. They handed over consideration of policy issues to others below, whose task was to consider the issues and develop proposals. Many directors frankly admitted that for the most part they simply accepted the conclusions given to them.

Non-oligarchical organizations

Since Michels wrote, there have been many attempts to set up organizations so as to counter tendencies towards the centralization of power. Two examples are the Israeli **kibbutzim** and the system of workers' self-management in Yugoslavian industry. The kibbutzim were set up specifically to create an egalitarian system of production, in which there would be few differences of income or power. (For further information about them, see chapter 12: 'Kinship, Marriage and the Family'.) The Yugoslavian enterprises have a formal system of industrial democracy, with workers voting to elect directors of firms.

Tannenbaum and his colleagues carried out a comparative study of firms in five countries, including the kibbutzim and industrial plants in Yugoslavia (Tannenbaum et al., 1974; see also Rosner and Tannenbaum, 1987). Business organizations were also studied in Austria, Italy and the United States. Small and large firms were included in the research, which was explicitly addressed to Michels's views on organization and oligarchy.

The results showed substantial differences between organizations in the various societies. Size of organizations did not prove to be the main link between centralization and hierarchy. Both within and across different countries some small firms were more hierarchical than larger ones. In the kibbutzim and the Yugoslavian enterprises, whether small or large, there was less hierarchy than in the industrial plants in the other countries. The kibbutzim, for example, showed few graduations of authority, and no large differences in income between those at the various levels; individuals rotated between different tasks frequently (see also Bartolle et al., 1980). The researchers also found, however, variations in the degree to which informal participation alleviated hierarchy. In Yugoslavia, participation in decision-making is formally part of the organizational structure. Informal practices tended to produce *more*, rather than less, hierarchy in such a setting. In the case of American firms, on the other hand, the reverse was more often true. In Yugoslavia, informal connections were used to get round procedures of industrial democracy, while in the United States they served to alleviate hierarchical inequalities.

Japanese corporations

Let us now look at organizations in a very different cultural setting – that of Japan, the only country from a wholly non-Western context to have become fully industrialized. Its economic progress is remarkable for several reasons. At the mid-point of the nineteenth century, just before industrialization got fully under way, Japan was still essentially a feudal society – far more traditional and rural than most Western countries at that period – yet it experienced very rapid industrial development in the late 1800s and the early twentieth century. After its defeat by the United States in the Second World War, the Japanese economy was shattered. Yet – aided in fact by financial resources provided by the American victors – Japan has since shot to near the top of the league table of economic powers. In terms of volume of wealth produced, Japan is today the third largest economy in the world. The rates of economic growth of the two biggest economic systems, the United States and the Soviet Union, are currently well behind that of Japan. If present trends are maintained, Japan will be the wealthiest country in the world shortly after the year 2000 (Pascale and Athos, 1982).

Japan's economic success is frequently said to stem mainly from the distinctive characteristics of large Japanese corporations – which differ substantially from most business firms in the West (Vogel, 1979). Japanese companies also diverge from the characteristics that Weber associated with bureaucracy.

(1) The big Japanese corporations do not form a pyramid of authority as Weber portrayed it, with each level being responsible only to the one above. In Japanese firms, workers low down in the organization are consulted about policies being considered by management, and even the very top executives regularly meet them. The Japanese refer to this system as 'bottom-up' decision-making.

(2) In Japanese organizations, employees specialize much less than their counterparts in the West. Take as an example the case of Sugao, as described by William Ouchi (1981). Sugao is a university graduate who has just joined the Mitsubeni Bank in Tokyo. He will enter the firm in a management training position, spending the first year learning in a general way how the various departments of the bank operate. He will then work in a local branch for a while, directly with the tellers, before being brought back to the bank's headquarters to learn commercial banking. Then he will move out to yet another branch dealing with loans, learning about that side of the business. From there he is likely to come back again to headquarters, working in the personnel department. Ten years will have elapsed by this time, and Sugao will have reached the position of section chief. But the process of job rotation will not stop there. He will move on to a further branch of the bank, perhaps dealing with the financing of small businesses, and then return to yet a different job at the headquarters. By the time Sugao reaches the peak of his career, some thirty years after having begun as a trainee, he will have mastered all the important tasks in which the bank is involved. His likely career contrasts dramatically with that stretching ahead of a typical

American bank management trainee of the same age. The American trainee will almost certainly specialize in one area of banking early on, and stay in that specialism for the remainder of his or her working life.

(3) The large corporations in Japan are committed to the life-time employment of those they hire – the employee is guaranteed a job. Pay and responsibility are geared to seniority – how many years a manager has been with the firm – rather than to a competitive struggle for promotion. At all levels of the corporation people are involved in small teams or work-groups. The groups, rather than individual members, are evaluated in terms of their performance. Unlike their Western counterparts, the organization charts of Japanese companies – maps of the authority system – show only groups, not individual positions.

(4) In Weber's depiction of bureaucracy, there is a clear division between the work of the individual within the organization, and her or his activities outside. This is in fact true of most Western corporations, in which the relation between firm and employee is largely an economic one. Japanese corporations, by contrast, provide for many aspects of their employees' needs, expecting in return a high level of loyalty to the firm. Japanese employees, from workers on the shop-floor right through to top executives, often wear company uniforms. They may assemble to sing the company song each morning, and regularly take part in leisure activities organized by the corporation at weekends. (A few Western corporations, for example IBM or Apple, now also have company songs.) Workers receive many material benefits from the company over and above their salaries. The electrical firm Hitachi, for example, studied by Ronald Dore, provides housing for all unmarried workers and nearly half of its married male employees (Dore, 1973). Company loans are provided for the education of children, and to help with the cost of weddings and funerals.

The implications of the Japanese system for organization theory

Many observers have argued that firms in the USA and Europe should copy the Japanese corporations if the Western economies are to match Japan's rate of development. This is an important issue, not only on an economic level, but for our understanding of the nature of organizations and bureaucracy in general. For the Japanese companies are definitely in some ways more 'democratic' than Western corporations – there is far more effort to secure consultation at all levels, and to encourage a developed sense of corporate loyalty. In their authority system, emphasis on work teams, promotion by seniority rather than competition, and overall provision for employees' needs, the Japanese firms diverge quite substantially from Weber's model of bureaucracy. If they are efficient *because* of these deviations from bureaucratic hierarchy, considerable doubt would be thrown on conclusions usually drawn from the study of organizations in a Western context. For, in spite of the criticisms to which it has been subject, Weber's interpretation of bureaucracy is still taken by most observers to be correct in its broad outlines. That is to say, it is generally agreed that Weber's 'ideal type' of bureaucratic organization does promote productive efficiency.

How far are there factors other than their 'non-bureaucratic' nature which might explain the effectiveness of Japanese corporations? It is actually not difficult to point to other potential influences. Consultation at all levels is perhaps only possible because of the marked attitudes of deference that subordinates in Japan show towards their superiors, which means that the final decisions of supervisors and managers are accepted even where subordinates disagree with them. In Japan, it is common to see junior managers carrying the briefcases of their seniors as a matter of course. Life-time employment is only guaranteed in large firms (and not in all of these). The Japanese economy also contains a high proportion of small firms, in which pay and employment conditions are often very poor.

Japan's superior economic performance may come in part from the sheer intensity of work and the long hours involved. Satoshi Kamata, a freelance journalist, worked for a period at Toyota, the Japanese car-manufacturer, and described his experiences there in vivid detail in a book published not long afterwards (Kamata, 1982). The company housing in which he lived was regulated like an army camp. Health standards in the living-quarters and in the workplace were bad, and the working conditions oppressive. Kamata wrote:

> Workers are urged on to production, day and night. So tightly are their lives bound to the conveyor belts in the plants that they cannot even take days off when they want to. The thoroughgoing enforcement of rationalisation has eliminated all relief workers. Not only team leaders, the lowest management people, but also unit leaders have been required to work on conveyor lines. Even foremen, normally part of higher management, may sometimes put on working gloves and lend a hand. Then these men have to take home their paper work such as the writing of daily reports and the calculation of day-to-day work units. Through it all the conveyor belts are kept running, with the absolute minimum number of men necessary . . . Workers are forced to work on Sundays and holidays. The reinforcement work and Sunday-holiday work are a lubricant without which the conveyors could not run . . . Whenever I come to this city and talk with the workers, I feel as though I have strayed into some foreign land. But this is a nightmare that I have lived, and the anger will not go away. (Kamata, 1982, pp. 203, 206, 211)

One test of how far Japanese managerial methods depend on an especially compliant, deferential and hard-working labour-force is provided by the experience of Japanese-run firms recently set up in Western countries. The number of studies carried out so far is small, and the evidence patchy. But it does seem that Japanese

management practices can be detached from the cultural environment of Japan and operate effectively. It appears that they can be
applied with some success among a more individualistic labour-force
used to reasonable working conditions.

Studies of Japanese-run plants in Britain and the United States
indicate that 'bottom-up' decision-making does work outside the Japanese cultural context. Workers seem to respond positively to the
greater level of involvement these plants provide, as compared to the
Western-style firms in which they were previously employed (White
and Trevor, 1983). It seems reasonable to conclude, therefore, that the
'Japanese model' does carry some lessons relevant to assessing the
Weberian conception of bureaucracy. Organizations which closely
resemble Weber's 'ideal type' are probably much less effective than
they appear on paper, because they do not permit lower-level employees
to develop a sense of autonomy over, and involvement in, their work
tasks and the way work is organized.

Drawing on the example of Japanese corporations, William Ouchi
(1979, 1981) has argued that bureaucratic hierarchy as emphasized by
Weber has clear limits to its effectiveness. Overtly bureaucratized
organizations lead to 'internal failures' of functioning because of their
rigid, inflexible and uninvolving nature. What Ouchi terms *clan forms* of
authority contrast with bureaucratic systems – and in many settings of
modern societies are more efficient than bureaucratic types. 'Clans' are
groups that have close ties and personal connections with one another.
The work-groups in Japanese firms are one example, but clan-type
systems also often develop informally within Western organizations.

Influences on organizations in the modern world

Professionals

All modern organizations depend on knowledge, expertise and the
transmitting of information. **Professionals** specialize in the development
of technical knowledge. Because a long period in higher education is
necessary, and because professionals belong to national and even international bodies defining the nature of their tasks, professional expertise
cannot easily be reduced to bureaucratic duties. When professionals are
employed within large organizations, they do not fit neatly within the
hierarchy of authority. They usually have more autonomy in their work
than others in middle and lower levels of organizations. Professors and
lecturers, for example, are employed by universities and colleges, and
paid to teach students in them, but in their writing and research they are
oriented to the international scholarly communities in their disciplines.
They usually have a large amount of control over the syllabus that is
taught, deciding how courses should connect with one another and

what combinations of courses provide sufficient qualification for a degree. To a large extent, they stand outside the bureaucratic hierarchy. The administrative officials tend to control the financial and material resources necessary for setting up a teaching programme and their jobs are more clearly defined as bureaucratic duties. Much the same is true of the divisions between doctors and administrators in a hospital.

How much control professionals within organizations enjoy over their work tasks varies according to several factors – the size and level of bureaucratization of the organization, the nature of the profession in question, and the strength of the professional association to which the individual worker belongs (Freidson, 1986). As contrasting examples, we might take nursing and law. Nurses are usually recognized to be professionals, but the amount of control most have over their conditions of work is relatively limited. Hospitals are strongly bureaucratized organizations, in which nurses are subordinate to nursing supervisors as well as to other medical staff. Nursing associations set out guidelines for the employment of nurses, but do not have much power over how far these are followed within the National Health Service.

Even when working in large organizations rather than specialized practices, lawyers normally have more control over their work tasks than nurses do. The professional associations in law are very strong, and are able to define the codes of conduct which lawyers follow. Lawyers accept some administrative constraints, but their work can only be fully assessed or supervised by others who are themselves also members of the legal profession. Suppose a lawyer working in a given company has to prepare a legal case defending the firm against a suit which a disgruntled customer has brought against it. The company can instruct the lawyer to take charge of the case, but would not ordinarily insist that she or he argues the case in court in a particular way. This is almost always assumed to be within the sphere of the lawyer's professional autonomy, and not subject to interference on the part of the employer.

Part of the power of professionals in organizations derives from their role as *gatekeepers* for the wider publics to which these organizations cater. A gatekeeper is someone who controls access (in this case, to qualifications). For example, professional surveyors or engineers control the licences needed before building construction can be undertaken; professors and lecturers determine who shall get degrees and diplomas, and their grades; case-workers assess who is eligible for various types of welfare benefit. How much autonomy professionals have in these matters is influenced by the factors noted in the previous paragraph.

A general increase is taking place in the proportion of people working in professional occupations in modern societies. As organizations come increasingly to rely upon specialized knowledge and skills, hierarchical systems of the bureaucratic type are liable to come under strain. A growing tendency exists for professionals to work outside large organizations, founding smaller firms of their own and hiring out their services as they are needed. Organizations involving a high proportion of professional workers tend to have a more flexible administrative character than do traditional types of organization.

Information technology

The development of **information technology** – computers and electronic communication devices – is another factor currently influencing organizational structures. Automatic data-processing systems have been widely introduced in a range of settings. Anyone who draws money out of a bank, or buys an airline ticket, depends on a computer-based communications system. Since data can be processed instantaneously in any part of the world linked to such a system, there is no need for physical proximity between those involved (Winch, 1983; Sommerville, 1983; Gill, 1985; Davies, 1986).

A fully fledged 'electronic office', in which the bulk of the work is carried out by machines rather than humans, is still a long way off, and there are many problems in the way of its realization. Nevertheless, there is a strong trend towards the transfer of many office activities to electronic machinery. Word-processors, computer networks, teleprinter links and other electronic systems have already altered the nature of much office work. In some leading American banks, the trust department, where stock transfers are made, has been completely automated. Banks have also automated many aspects of the processing of bank accounts. A study carried out in a branch of Citycorp, New York, showed that, before the introduction of automation, fourteen people needed three days to process a single letter of credit. After the introduction of electronic equipment, one person using a mini-computer, which stores records electronically, could carry out the same job in a matter of minutes (Matteis, 1979). The bank in question reduced its clerical staff from 10,000 to 6,000 during the 1970s.

In 1982, Rank Xerox found the sales of some of its products falling, and was faced with the need to reduce costs. The traditional route to be taken in such circumstances was to lay off staff. Instead of following such a policy, Rank Xerox set up the people involved as independent consultants, and established a computerized support network called Xanadu to provide basic office services to each of them working from home. The company then bought back a substantial proportion of their working time for a number of years, leaving them free to use the other time to work for different clients. The idea was that the new system would provide the corporation with access to the skills possessed by their erstwhile employees, but at a cheaper rate and in a more flexible way than if they were full-time members of the company. The former employees, in their turn, would have the opportunity to build up their own businesses. So far, at least, the scheme seems to have worked well for both parties (Handy, 1984).

It might appear from such experiences that large organizations will become leaner, as the more routine tasks disappear, reinforcing the tendency towards smaller, more flexible types of enterprise. Yet we should be cautious about reaching such conclusions. Some trends along these lines are observable, but their impact is as yet fairly limited. In principle, organizations could become much more decentralized than they are at present. A good deal of office work, for instance, could be carried out at home through computer terminals linked through the telecommunications system. Several large firms in Britain and the United States and elsewhere have set up computer networks connecting employees who work from home. However, these schemes have not yet become nearly as widespread as many anticipated. Computer terminals are not an attractive substitute for face-to-face interaction with colleagues and friends at work; and management cannot easily monitor the activities of such invisible employees.

The physical settings of organizations

As mentioned earlier, many modern organizations function in specially designed physical settings. The buildings in which organizations are housed have specific features relevant to their activities, but also share important architectural characteristics with those of other organizations. The architecture of a hospital, for instance, differs in some respects from that of a business firm or a school. In the hospital, there are separate wards, consulting rooms, operating rooms, and offices, which give the overall building a definite layout, while a school has classrooms, laboratories and a sports hall. Yet there is a general resemblance between hospital buildings and those of schools. Both are likely to have a large number of hallways with doors leading off, and to have standard decoration and furnishings throughout. Apart from the differing dress of the people moving through the corridors, the buildings in which modern organizations are usually housed have a definite 'sameness' to them. They often look quite similar from the outside as well as within their interiors. It would not be at all unusual to ask, on passing a building, 'Is that a school?', and get the response, 'No, it's a hospital.' Although major internal modifications are required, it can happen that a school takes over buildings which once housed a hospital.

For many years, sociologists discussed organizations as though they floated in some kind of ethereal void. It is still common to find large tomes written on organizations which make no mention at all of the fact that they operate in definite physical settings. Yet, as Michel Foucault and others have shown, the architecture of organizations is very directly involved with their social make-up and system of authority (Foucault, 1971, 1979; Gregory and Urry, 1985). By analysing the physical characteristics of organizations we can shed new light on the problems Weber analysed. The 'offices' which Weber discussed abstractly are also *architectural settings* – rooms, separated by corridors – within organizations. The buildings of large firms are sometimes actually constructed physically as a hierarchy, in which the more elevated one's position in the hierarchy of authority, the nearer the top of a skyscraper one's office is – the phrase 'the top floor' is sometimes used to mean 'those who hold ultimate power' in the organization.

In many other ways the geography of an organization will affect its functioning, especially in cases where systems rely heavily on informal relationships. Physical proximity enables the formation of 'primary groups', while physical distance can enhance the polarization of groups – a 'them' and 'us' attitude between departments, for example.

Surveillance and discipline in organizations

Surveillance

The arrangement of rooms, hallways and open spaces in an organization's buildings can provide basic clues to how its system of authority operates. (Of course, many organizations exist in buildings *not* purposefully designed for them, and this can affect the activities of the staff in significant ways.) In some kinds of organization, open settings are provided, in which groups of people work collectively. Because of the dull, repetitive nature of certain kinds of industrial work – like assembly-line production – regular supervision is needed to ensure that the pace of labour is sustained. The same is often true of routine work carried out by typists, who sit together in the typing pool, where their activities are visible to their superiors. Foucault lays great emphasis on how *visibility*, or lack of it, in the architectural settings of modern organizations influences and expresses patterns of authority. How far what subordinates do is visible to those of higher grades affects whether they can easily be subject to what Foucault calls **surveillance.**

Surveillance refers to the supervision of activities in organizations. In modern organizations everyone, even in relatively high positions of authority, is subject to surveillance; but the more lowly a person is, the more his or her behaviour tends to be closely scrutinized. Surveillance takes two forms. One is that just noted – the direct supervision of the work of subordinates by superiors.

Consider the example of a school classroom. Pupils sit at tables or desks, usually arranged in rows, all in view of the teacher. The teacher often sits or stands on a raised platform, allowing a clear sight of the pupils' activities. Children are supposed to look alert more or less continually, or otherwise to be absorbed in their work. Of course, how far this actually happens in practice depends on the abilities of the teacher and the inclinations of the children to conform to what is expected of them.

The second type of surveillance is more subtle, but equally important. It consists in keeping files, records and case-histories of employees. Weber saw the importance of written records (nowadays often computerized) in modern organizations, but did not fully bring out how they can be used to regulate behaviour. Employee records usually provide complete work-histories, registering personal details and often giving character assessments. Such records are used to monitor employees' behaviour and assess recommendations for promotion. In many business firms, individuals at each grade in the organization prepare annual reports on the performance of those in the grades just below them. School records and college grade transcripts are other examples of case-history records, used to monitor individuals' performance as they move through the organization. References are kept on file for academic staff too.

Of course, individuals in lower grades do not simply passively accept the surveillance to which they are subject. They find all sorts of ways to create 'free space' and 'free time' for themselves, out of sight of supervisors. People may get to look at their records even when they are not supposed to do so, and discover means of encouraging or pressurizing their superiors to write good reports about them. The creation of 'back regions', away from supervisory control, is one main method used to combat over-strict supervision (see chapter 4: 'Social Interaction and Everyday Life'). Middle-level supervisors often connive in this, because they both want to keep the trust of the workers and have to be seen to be 'doing a good job' when they themselves are inspected by superiors. Thus an early sociological study of a shipyard reported:

> It was amusing to watch the sudden transformation whenever word got round that the foreman was on the hull or in the shop or that a front-office superintendent was coming by. Quartermen and leadermen would rush to their groups of workers and stir them to obvious activity. 'Don't let him catch you sitting down,' was the universal admonition, and where no work existed a pipe was busily bent and threaded, or a bolt which was already in place was subjected to further and unnecessary tightening. This was the formal tribute invariably attending a visitation by the boss, and its conventions were as familiar to both sides as those surrounding a five-star general's inspection. (Archibald, 1947, p. 159)

Discipline

Surveillance is important in modern organizations because of their strong connection with *discipline* – the co-ordinated regulation of people's behaviour. Organizations cannot operate effectively if what goes on in them is haphazard. In business firms, for example, as Weber pointed out, people are expected to work regular daily hours. We have come to take this more or less for granted, but in the

"Franklin can't discuss that—he's under constant electronic surveillance."

Drawing by Mulligan; © 1976 The New Yorker Magazine, Inc.

early days of industrialization it was a long time before people could be persuaded to work for the same number of hours each day, every week. Rural work in traditional communities was irregular and seasonal, and people were used to working only as long as they needed to in order to meet their needs. The setting up of factories and separate workplaces, which made constant supervision possible, was a means of achieving the necessary labour discipline (Thompson, 1967).

Discipline is promoted both by the physical settings of organizations and by the precise scheduling provided by detailed timetables. Timetables regularize activities across time and space – in Foucault's words, they 'efficiently distribute bodies' around the organization. Timetables are the condition of organizational discipline, because they slot the activities of large numbers of people together. If a university did not have a lecture timetable which was fairly strictly observed, for example, it would soon collapse into complete chaos. A timetable makes possible the intensive use of time and space: each can be packed with many people and many activities.

Carceral organizations

In common with Erving Goffman, Foucault has given much attention to studying organizations in which individuals are physically separated for long periods from the outside world. In such organizations, people are *incarcerated* – kept hidden away – from the external social environment. According to Goffman, prisons, asylums and other carceral systems differ radically from other organizations, because of their 'totally closed' nature (Goffman, 1961). Foucault agrees with this, but also tries to show that the study of **carceral organizations** can illuminate how other organizations are run. Surveillance and discipline were pioneered in carceral settings before being widely used in other types of organizations. Prisons, asylums and barracks illustrate in clear detail the nature of surveillance and discipline, precisely because they seek to maximize control over their inmates' behaviour. Hence Foucault clearly intends the answer to be in the negative when he asks, 'Is it surprising that prisons resemble factories, schools, barracks, hospitals, which all resemble prisons?' (Foucault, 1979, p. 228).

The development of carceral organizations

Carceral organizations were rare in mediaeval times. Gaols and dungeons sometimes existed, but they were few and far between, and were not places in which convicted criminals served fixed sentences. People were kept in them either as a means of stifling political opposition, to be tortured in order to extract information, or to await trial. The mentally ill either lived within the community, or were forced to roam the countryside. There were no asylums or mental hospitals.

Carceral institutions can be traced back to the early 1700s, although prisons and asylums only became common more than a century afterwards (Ignatieff, 1978). Both grew out of the earlier foundations of what were called 'general hospitals'. As the word was used then, 'hospital' did not mean primarily a place where the sick were cared for. Rather, it signified a place of confinement, mostly filled with vagrants, the feeble-minded and the mentally ill. The 'hospitals' were supposed to help reform their inmates, and to this end they were often places where forced labour, for very low wages, was carried on.

Mental asylums began to be built in the late eighteenth century in Europe and somewhat afterwards in the United States. Prisons in the form we recognize now were first set up at about the same period. It took some while, however, for these to become more or less completely disentangled from the older hospitals. The prison reformer John Howard wrote of his visit in 1781 to a Berlin hospital that it was full of 'idlers', 'rogues and libertines', 'infirm and criminals' and 'destitute old women and children', all mixed together.

According to Foucault, the 'Panopticon' – designed by Jeremy Bentham in the mid-nineteenth century – expressed in purest form the differences between the old hospitals and the new prisons. The Panopticon was the name Bentham gave to an ideal prison he designed, which he tried on various occasions to sell to the British government. The design was never fully implemented, but some of its main principles were taken up in prisons built in the nineteenth century in the United States, Britain and several countries of continental Europe. The Panopticon was circular in shape, with the cells built around the outside edge. In the centre was an inspection tower. Two windows were placed in every cell, one facing the inspection tower and the other facing the outside. The aim of the design was to make prisoners visible to guards at all times. The windows in the tower itself were to be covered by venetian blinds, so that while the prison staff could keep the prisoners under constant observation, they themselves would be invisible.

Among other influences, the plan of the Panopticon helped spread the principle of separate cells for individuals or small numbers of prisoners. In the old houses of internment, people had been kept together in very large rooms, in which they both worked and slept. The architectural design of prisons influenced the design of other types of organization in a very direct way, some of the early factories, for example, being planned by architects who had earlier designed prisons.

Carceral organizations, of course, remain in a minority among modern organizations. People either only spend part of the day or week on the site in most institutions, as in schools or at work, or they are only inmates for short periods, as in hospitals. Yet there are evident similarities between carceral and non-carceral organizations, and Foucault is right to point out that studies of each can aid our understanding of the other.

Non-bureaucratic organizations: self-help groups

Sociologists often suppose that the only social associations of any importance in modern societies are primary groups and bureaucratic organizations, but this is far from true. There have long been a variety of voluntary associations, charities and self-help organizations besides. In the early period of industrialism, for example, many workers' groups were established, such as working men's clubs or workers' education associations. In this discussion we will concentrate on self-help organizations, which often contrast most markedly with bureaucratic systems.

The number and variety of self-help groups as a whole has risen substantially over the past century. Housing associations, Alcoholics Anonymous, drug rehabilitation groups and hundreds of other self-help associations have come into existence (Robinson, 1979; Hatch and

Collection Particulière/photograph D.R.

Kickbusch, 1983). A few have a continuous history going back a hundred years or more, while others come and go with some rapidity.

The right to form self-help groups has by no means always been accepted in law. In many countries the early workers' associations met with hostile reactions from the authorities, and were sometimes prohibited. The right to form groups according to freely chosen interests and objectives was one that had to be fought for in most societies.

Self-help groups are made up of people who are in a similar situation, and who come together to assist one another in pursuing shared interests or coping with common problems. Such groups tend to be non-hierarchical and lack the fixed positions associated with bureaucracies. They often have a fluctuating membership: individuals may come for one or a few meetings, then leave the group. Such groups are normally dependent on money collected by members, or on donations, rather than having fixed forms of income. If paid staff exist, they usually have low salaries compared to their counterparts in orthodox organizations. Usually some kind of moral ideal binds the members of the group to each other.

Features of self-help groups

The two main characteristics of self-help groups can be designated as *sharing* and *project work*. Sharing means the pooling of information and similar experiences, either in face-to-face meetings or via other contacts. In TOUCH, for example, a self-help group for parents of mentally handicapped children, people contact one another through correspondence magazines. Parents participate in exchanges of letters; magazines circulate around the group continuously, so that every member receives up to a dozen letters every few weeks, although they only write one each themselves.

Self-help groups ordinarily seek to influence both their members and the attitudes of others outside. One of the aims of TOUCH is to educate the general population about the problems of the mentally handicapped. *Project work* usually consists of co-operative activities organized to achieve these and other goals. For example, much of the programme of Alcoholics Anonymous is made up of projects designed to help fellow alcoholics. When a person recounts his or her past experiences and current problems, the information is used to develop discussion and policies in the group as a whole.

Self-help groups have frequently been set up in opposition to estab- lished bureaucratic organizations. For example, some medical self-help groups have been started to permit patients to care for themselves directly, on the basis of the belief that orthodox medical settings fail to give them sufficient responsibility for their own well-being. Self-help groups clearly are in some ways a counter to bureaucracy: they provide spheres outside bureaucratic organizations where individuals can meet in circumstances of co-operation and equality. Yet they are always likely to exist alongside formal organizations, rather than replacing them. Self-help groups that become permanent, and grow in size, usually tend to become like other formal organizations. They develop specialized authority positions, have to ensure a regular income, and generally take on more of the trappings of bureaucracy.

Concluding comment

It does seem that there are important shifts towards more flexible types of organization in modern societies. We are not (as Weber and many others have feared) all about to become tiny cogs in a vast administrative machine that runs our lives. Bureaucratic systems are more flexible internally than Weber believed, and their dominance is constantly challenged by less hierarchical types of group and association. Yet it is wishful thinking to suppose, as some have, that large impersonal organizations will progressively disappear, being replaced by more decentralized and flexible agencies (Toffler, 1981). Rather, there is likely to be a continuing 'push and pull' between tendencies towards large size, impersonality and hierarchy in organizations and opposing influences.

Summary

1 A *group* is a number of people who interact with each other on a regular basis. This regularity encourages familiarity, solidarity and shared habits. *Aggregates* are collections of people, such as a bus queue, without a common sense of identity. A *social category* is a statistical grouping – people classified together on the basis of a particular characteristic they share.

2 All modern organizations are in some degree bureaucratic in nature. *Bureaucracy* involves a clear-cut hierarchy of authority; written rules governing the conduct of *officials* (who work full-time for a salary); and a separation between the tasks of the official within the organization and life outside it. Members of the organization do not own the material resources with which they work. Max Weber argued that modern bureaucracy is a highly effective means of organizing large numbers of people, ensuring that decisions are taken according to common criteria.

3 Informal networks tend to develop at all levels both within and between organizations. The study of these informal ties is as important as the more formal characteristics concentrated on by Weber.

4 The work of Weber and Michels identifies a tension between bureaucracy and democracy. On the one hand, long-term processes of centralization of decision-making are associated with the development of modern societies. On the other hand, one of the main features of the past

two centuries has been growing pressure towards democracy. The trends conflict, with neither one in a position of dominance.

5   Japanese corporations differ significantly from most Western companies in terms of their characteristics as organizations. There is more consultation of lower-level workers by managerial executives, pay and responsibility are linked to seniority, and groups, rather than individuals, are evaluated for their performance. Some Western firms have adopted aspects of Japanese management systems in recent years, although it is by no means proven that these help explain why Japan's economic performance has outstripped that of most Western countries.

6   All modern organizations depend upon the specialization of knowledge and the transmitting of information. *Professionalization*, together with the increasing use of *information technology*, may be leading to a general increase in the flexibility of organizations. The impact of these changes – thus far, at any rate – has often been exaggerated.

7   The physical settings of organizations strongly influence their social features. The architecture of modern organizations is closely connected to surveillance as a means of securing obedience to those in authority. *Surveillance* refers to the supervision of people's activities, as well as to the keeping of files and records about them.

8   *Carceral organizations* are those in which individuals spend virtually the whole of their time, separated from the outside world. The main types of carceral organization are prisons and mental hospitals. Carceral organizations maximize discipline and supervision, but these are to some degree characteristic of all bureaucratic organizations.

9   *Self-help groups* (and voluntary associations of various types) contrast with bureaucratic organizations, tending to be non-hierarchical and participatory. Large numbers of such groups are found in most modern industrial societies. They exist alongside, and sometimes in a relationship of tension with, larger, more bureaucratic systems. Some grow to become bureaucratic.

Basic concepts

social groups	formal relations
organization	informal relations

Important terms

aggregate	oligarchy
social category	democracy
primary group	kibbutzim
secondary group	professionals
bureaucracy	information technology
ideal type	surveillance
officials	carceral organization

Further reading

Amitai Etzioni and Edwin Lehman, *A Sociological Reader on Complex Organizations*, 3rd edition (New York: Holt, Rinehart and Winston, 1980) — a well-organized collection of readings on organizations.

M. Meyer et al., *The Limits to Bureaucratic Growth* (New York: Walter de Gruyter, 1985) — attempts to assess and predict future organizational trends.

Charles Perrow, *Complex Organizations* (New York: Random House, 1986) — the latest edition of this classic study of the development of organizational theory.

D. Pugh et al., *Writers on Organizations*, 3rd edition (Harmondsworth: Penguin, 1983) — contains succinct thumb-nail sketches of most writers on organizations.

Anselm Strauss, *Negotiations: Varieties, Contexts, Processes and Social Order* (San Francisco: Jossey-Bass, 1978) — begins with interesting readings of Goffman and Blau and raises both empirical and theoretical questions.

10

Politics, Government and the State

As we saw in the previous chapter, the state and government impinge on many aspects of our lives today; yet, for the greater part of human history, states did not exist at all. In hunting and gathering communities, and in small agrarian cultures, there were not separate political authorities. Such **stateless societies** did not relapse into chaos: they had informal mechanisms of government through which decisions affecting the community were channelled and disputes managed. Decisions were generally made within family groups; should several groups of kin living within one band fundamentally disagree, they split off into separate units, subsequently perhaps recombining with others.

Other small cultures had an element of political centralization, without becoming fully fledged states. In these societies, there was a male chief to whom the rest of the population owed allegiance. Chiefs were normally themselves either warriors or priests, or both, and sometimes had the right to call upon armed retainers to back up whatever decisions they made. The chief usually ruled with the assistance of a council or court. In **state societies** (traditional civilizations), these chiefly rulers became kings or emperors, had elaborate courts and households and controlled armed forces used to ensure obedience and extend the scope of their dominion. They had full-time officials who dealt with regular issues of administration, together with specialized courts within which trials were organized and criminals punished.

All states, traditional and modern, share some general characteristics. A **state** exists where there is a **political apparatus** (governmental institutions, such as a court, parliament or congress, plus civil-service officials), ruling over a given *territory*, whose authority is backed by a *legal system* and by the capacity to use **force** to implement its policies. Looking at each aspect of this definition in turn will provide a clear understanding of the nature of states. In the rest of the chapter, we shall concentrate upon analysing modern states, comparing the different types of political system which exist in the modern world.

Characteristics of states

The political apparatus

Anthropologists and archaeologists accept that by far the greater number of societies in history have been stateless. The concept of *state* simply has no application to these societies. They are more divided on the question of whether **government** and **politics** can be said to exist in them. Since there are no specialized political institutions, or agencies of political administration, it can be argued that government and politics are absent, but the issue is largely a definitional one. All societies have forms of government if that word is defined broadly enough – for example, to refer to any systematic means of reaching decisions affecting most people in a community. This is too vague a definition, however, to be of much use. It is better to opt for a narrower understanding of both government and politics.

Government will be used here to refer to the regular enactment of policies and decisions on the part of the officials within a political apparatus. These officials include kings or emperors, their courts, elected representatives and members of the civil service. We can speak of government as a process, or of *the* government, referring to the apparatus responsible for the administrative process. *Politics* concerns the means whereby power is used to affect the scope and content of the governmental activities. The sphere of the *political* may therefore range well beyond that of state institutions themselves. For there may be many ways in which those who are not part of the governmental apparatus seek to influence it. In modern societies, for instance, social movements operating outside accepted political channels may try to exert pressure on a government, or even overthrow it.

Territory

Hunting and gathering societies had no fixed territories, but moved around over large areas of land. Small agrarian communities were more fixed in one spot, but usually they had no clear conception of boundaries separating them from other groups. Once definite political authorities were established, however, specific territories, corresponding to the area over which they claimed to rule, came to be distinguished. In contrast to preceding types of society, states have consistently been expansionist. Where rulers have seen an opportunity to acquire more territory – and thus expand the scope of their dominion – they have normally taken advantage of it.

Law and the use of force

A legal system exists where there are individuals who specialize in the administration of justice. In smaller societies, conflicts are resolved by a meeting of the whole community, or by the actions of kinship units. There is no group in such societies which holds prime responsibility for using force to back up communal decisions. Sometimes a family or kinship group will take matters into its own hands, initiating a *blood feud*. With the development of states, however, a specialized judicial system emerges – codified laws and law courts – backed by the ability to use force in cases where decisions are not complied with. In traditional states there was usually no clear distinction between the army and specialized police forces; the military were used to back up juridical decision-making.

Modern states

Definitions

All modern states are **nation-states**. Nation-states incorporate each of the characteristics mentioned in the definition of the state given previously. They involve an apparatus of government laying claim to specific territories, possessing formalized codes of law, and backed by the control of military force. Some of their main characteristics, however, contrast rather sharply with those of traditional states.

1 The territories ruled by traditional states were always poorly defined, the level of control wielded by the central government being quite weak. The notion of **sovereignty** – that a government has authority over an area with clear-cut borders, within which it is the supreme power – had little relevance to traditional states. All nation-states, by contrast, are sovereign states.

2 In traditional states, most of the population ruled by the king or emperor had little awareness of, or interest in, those who governed them. Normally only the dominant classes, or more affluent groups felt a sense of belonging to an overall community of those ruled by that figure. In nation-states, by contrast, most of those living within the borders of the political system are **citizens,** having common rights and duties, and knowing themselves to be part of a *nation*. While there are some people who are political refugees and 'stateless', almost everyone in the world today is identified as a member of a definite national political order.

3 Nation-states are associated with the rise of **nationalism** (A. D. Smith, 1979; Breuilly, 1982; Gellner, 1983). Nationalism can be defined as a set of symbols and beliefs providing the sense of being part of a single political community. Thus, individuals feel a sense of pride and belonging in being 'British', 'American' or 'French'. Probably people have always felt some kind of identity with social groups of one form or another – for example, their family, clan or religious community. Nationalism, however, only made its appearance with the development of the modern state. It is the main expression of feelings of identity with a distinct sovereign community.

Nationalistic loyalties do not necessarily always fit the borders demarcating the territories of states in the world today. Virtually all nation-states were built from communities of diverse backgrounds. *Local nationalisms* have frequently arisen in opposition to those fostered by the development of states. Thus, in Britain, for instance, Scottish and Welsh nationalism offer a challenge to the feeling of 'Britishness' (Nairn, 1977). Yet while the relation between the nation-state and nationalism is a complicated one, the two have come into being as part of the same set of processes.

In the light of these considerations, we can now offer a comprehensive definition of the concept of nation-state. A nation-state refers to a *political apparatus*, recognized to have sovereign rights within the borders of *a demarcated territorial area*, able to back its claims to sovereignty by *control of military power*, many of whose citizens have positive feelings of *commitment to its national identity*.

Citizenship rights

Most nation-states became centralized and effective political systems through the activities of monarchs who successfully concentrated more and more power in their own hands. The sovereign state was not at first one in which citizenship carried with it rights of political participation. These were achieved largely through struggles which limited the power of monarchs, or actively overthrew them – sometimes by a process of revolution, as in the cases of France or the United States.

T. H. Marshall has distinguished three types of rights associated with the growth of citizenship (Marshall, 1973). **Civil rights** refer to the rights of the individual in law. These include prerogatives many of us take for granted today, but which took a long while to achieve (and which are by no means fully recognized in all countries). Civil rights involve the freedom of individuals to live where they choose; freedom of speech and religion; the right to own property; and the right to equal justice before the law. These rights were not fully established in most European countries until the early nineteenth century. Even where they were generally achieved, some groups were omitted. Although the constitution granted such rights to Americans well before most European states had them, blacks were excluded. Even after the Civil War, when blacks were formally given these rights, they were not able to exercise them.

The second type of citizenship rights are **political rights**, especially the right to participate in elections and to stand for public office. Again, these were not won easily or quickly. Except in the United States, the achievement of full voting rights even for all men is relatively recent, and had to be struggled for in the face of governments reluctant to admit the principle of the universal franchise. In most European countries, the vote was at first limited to male citizens owning a certain amount of property – effectively limiting voting rights to an affluent minority. Not only women, but the majority of the male population was excluded. Universal franchise for men was mostly obtained by the early years of the present century. Women had to wait longer; in most Western countries the vote for women was achieved partly as a result of the struggles of women's movements, and partly as a consequence of the mobilization of women into the formal economy during the First World War (see chapter 6: 'Gender and Sexuality').

While legal and political rights were being won in Europe, colonization was proceeding in many other parts of the world. Almost without exception, colonized peoples were excluded from full citizenship of the parent states of the colonial regimes (and normally also within the colonial states themselves). Those who were not enslaved were regarded by white administrators as too primitive to be allowed to participate in government. The possibility of their being treated as equals to the white settler communities was barely even thought of. The majority of the population only acquired legal and political rights with the disappearance of colonialism in the twentieth century.

The third type of citizenship rights Marshall identifies are **social rights.** These concern the prerogative of every individual to enjoy a certain minimum standard of economic welfare and security. They include such rights as sickness benefits, social security in case of unemployment, and the setting of minimum levels of wages. Social rights, in other words, concern *welfare provisions*. Although in some countries, such as nineteenth-century Germany, various kinds of welfare benefits were introduced before legal and political rights were fully established, in most societies social rights have been the last to develop. This is because the achievement of civil, and particularly political, rights has usually been the basis upon which social rights have been fought for. Social rights have been established largely as a result of the political strength which poorer groups or classes have been able to develop through obtaining the vote.

The broadening of social rights is the basis of what has come to be called the **welfare state**, which has been firmly established in Western societies only since the Second World War. A welfare state exists where government organizations provide material benefits for those who are unable to support themselves adequately through paid employment – the unemployed, the sick, the disabled and the elderly. The foundations of the welfare state in Britain were set up in the 1930s, largely as a result of the policies of the Labour government elected immediately after the war (Ashford, 1987). All Western countries today have extensive welfare provisions. State-provided welfare benefits are even more extensive in East European societies, including the Soviet Union. On the other hand, in many of the poorer countries of the world these benefits are virtually non-existent.

Democracy

One of the most important aspects of the development of the modern state is its association with **democracy.** The word has its roots in the Greek term *demokratia*, the parts of which are *demos* (people) and *kratos* (rule), and its basic meaning is therefore a political system in which the people, not monarchs or aristocracies, rule. This sounds simple and straightforward, but it is not. As David Held has pointed out, questions can be raised about each part of the phrase: *rule*, *rule by* and *the people* (Held, 1987). If we start with *the people*:

1 Who are to be considered 'the people'?
2 What kind of participation is envisaged for them?
3 What conditions are assumed to be conducive to participation?

As regards *rule*:

1 How broadly or narrowly should the scope of rule be? Should it be confined, for example, to the sphere of government, or can there be democracy in other spheres – such as industrial democracy?

2 Can rule cover the day-to-day administrative decisions which governments must take, or should it refer only to major policy decisions?

In the case of *rule by*:

1 Must the rule of 'the people' be obeyed? What is the place of
obligation and dissent?
2 Are there circumstances in which some of 'the people' should act
outside the law, if they believe existing laws to be unjust?
3 Under what circumstances, if any, should democratic governments
use coercion against those who happen to disagree with their
policies?

Answers to these questions have taken contrasting forms, both at
varying periods and in different societies. For example, 'the people'
has been variously understood as owners of property, white men,
educated men, men and adults. In some societies, the officially
accepted version of democracy is limited to the political sphere,
whereas in others it is held to extend to other areas of social life.

Types of democracy

Some of the main differences between types of democracy are those
separating *representative multi-party democracy*, *representative one-party
democracy* and *participatory democracy*. (This third type is also sometimes
called *direct democracy*.)

Representative democracy means that decisions affecting a community are taken, not by its members as a whole, but by people they have
elected for this purpose. Versions of representative democracy exist
in many organizations: for instance, a sports club run by a council
elected from among the club's members. In the area of national
government, representative democracy takes the form of elections
to congresses, parliaments or similar national bodies. Representative
democracy also exists at other levels where collective decisions are
taken, such as in provinces or states within an overall national
community: cities, counties, boroughs and other regions.

Representative multi-party systems

Representative multi-party democracy is found at any or all of these
levels when voters have at least two parties to choose from in the
political process. Nations which practise multi-party representational
democracy, in which the mass of the adult population has the right
to vote at various levels, are usually called **liberal democracies.** The
United States, the Western European countries, Japan, Australia and
New Zealand all fall into this category. Some Third World countries,
such as India, also have liberal democratic systems.

Representative one-party systems

When people living in the West use the term *democracy* without qualification, they are usually referring to liberal democratic systems. Yet the Soviet Union, East European societies, and many Third World countries in which there is effectively only one party (such as China), also regard themselves as democracies. In these countries, while voters do not have a choice between different parties, there are elections in which representatives are appointed at the various local and national levels. Moreover, democracy is held to extend to the sphere of industrial organization as well as to the arena of government.

The principle usually underlying **representative one-party democracy** is that the single party expresses the overall will of the community. According to Marxist thinkers, the parties in liberal democracies represent divisive class interests. In socialist societies, which have supposedly eliminated antagonistic classes, there is presumed to be a need only for one party. Voters choose, therefore, not between parties, but between different *candidates*, proposing divergent policies. Most one-party democracies are organized through **democratic centralism,** which is a pyramid structure in which each level elects representatives to a council, which, in turn, elects representatives to the body above it, and so forth. In the USSR there is a pyramid of councils, or 'Soviets', descending from the Supreme Soviet to those at local village and neighbourhood levels. At each stage there are executive committees, all members of which are elected. A separate, but somewhat similar, system operates at the various levels of the Communist Party, and there are also complex connections between the party and levels of union representation in industry, supposed to render the economic sphere democratic.

Participatory democracy

In **participatory democracy** (or *direct democracy*), decisions are taken communally by those affected by them. This was the 'original' type of democracy found in ancient Greece. Those who were *citizens*, a small minority of the society, regularly assembled together to consider policies and take major decisions. Participatory democracy is of limited importance in modern societies, where the mass of the population have political rights, and it would be impossible for everyone actively to participate in the taking of all the decisions that affect them. Yet some aspects of participatory democracy do have relevance to modern societies, and there are many organizations within such societies in which it is practised. The holding of referenda, for example, in which a decision is based upon the expressed views of the majority on a particular issue, is one form of participatory democracy.

Referenda are regularly used at national level in some European countries. They are also employed quite frequently on a state level in the USA to decide controversial issues, and other elements of participatory democracy, such as meetings of the community, are found at local level in some townships in New England, for example (Mansbridge, 1983).

The universal appeal of democracy and the decline of monarchies

While some modern states (such as Britain or Belgium) still have monarchs, these are now few and far between. Where traditional rulers of this sort are still found, their real power is usually limited or virtually non-existent. In a tiny number of countries, such as Saudi Arabia and Jordan, monarchs continue to hold some degree of control over government, but in most cases where monarchies still exist, they are symbols of national identity rather than having any direct power in political life. The Queen of England, the King of Sweden, or even the Emperor of Japan, are all **constitutional monarchs** – the amount of real power they have is severely restricted by the constitution, which vests authority in the elected representatives of the people. The vast majority of modern states are republican; in almost every state, including constitutional monarchies, there is a professed adherence to democracy.

Even in countries subject to military rule, elections may be held and a certain façade of democratic politics adhered to. Most military rulers profess allegiance to democratic principles and claim that their rule is a means of achieving stability until there can be a return to some form of representative democracy (see chapter 11: 'War and the Military').

Why has the appeal of democracy become a near-universal feature of modern states? The answer is no doubt partly to be found in the intrinsic attractiveness of democratic ideals, which promise an escape from subjection to arbitrary power. But a fundamental factor is the integrated character of nation-states compared to traditional civilizations. Modern states are internally unified systems; those who rule in such states cannot do so unless they secure the active compliance of the majority of the population. Democratic ideals represent a way of expressing, as well as securing, that compliance.

Democratic elitism and pluralist theories

Professed democratic ideals, of course, do not necessarily correspond to reality. The fact that appeals to democracy are so consistently made by ruling authorities today shows little about the actual composition of different forms of governmental regime. Theorists of democracy disagree, in fact, about the potentialities and limitations of forms of democratic involvement in modern societies.

Democratic elitism

One of the most influential views of the nature and limits of modern democracy was set out by Max Weber and, in rather modified form, by the economist Joseph Schumpeter (Schumpeter, 1976). The ideas they developed are sometimes referred to as the theory of **democratic elitism.**

Max Weber's view

Weber started from the assumption that participatory democracy is impossible as a means of regular government in large-scale societies. This is not only for the indisputable reason that millions of people cannot regularly meet to take political decisions, but because the running of a complex society demands *expertise*. Participatory democracy can only work, Weber believes, in small organizations in which the tasks to be carried out are fairly simple and straightforward. Where more complicated decisions have to be taken, or policies worked out, even in modest-sized groups – like a small business firm – specialized knowledge and skills are necessary. Experts have to carry out their jobs on a continuous basis; positions which require expertise cannot be subject to the regular election of people who may only have a vague knowledge of the necessary skills and information. While higher officials, responsible for overall policy decisions, are elected, there must be a large substratum of full-time bureaucratic officials who play a large part in running a country (Weber, 1978, vol. 2, pp. 967–80).

In Weber's view, the development of mass citizenship, which is so closely involved with the idea of general democratic participation, greatly expands the need for bureaucratic officialdom. For example, provision for welfare, health and education demands large-scale administrative systems of a permanent kind. As Weber expresses this, 'It is obvious that technically the large modern state is absolutely dependent upon a bureaucratic basis. The larger the state, and the more it is a great power, the more unconditionally this is the case . . .' (Weber, 1978, vol. 2, p. 971).

Representative multi-party democracy, according to Weber, helps defend society both against arbitrary decision-making on the part of political leaders and against power being completely appropriated by bureaucrats. Yet in both respects the democratic institutions have been less effective than many advocates of democracy have hoped. 'Rule by the people' is possible in only a very limited sense. Parties must become organized in a systematic way to hope to achieve power – they must become bureaucratized. *Party machines* develop, which threaten the autonomy of parliaments or congresses as places in which policies are discussed and formulated. If a party with a majority is simply able to dictate what is decided, and if that party is itself mainly run by permanent officials, the level of democracy that has been achieved is slim indeed.

In order for democratic systems to have some degree of effectiveness, Weber argues, two conditions have to be met. First, there must be parties which represent different interests and have different outlooks. If the policies of competing parties are more or less the same, voters are denied any effective choice. Weber rejects the idea that one-party systems can be democratic in any meaningful way. Second, there must be political leaders who have the imagination and verve necessary to escape the dull weight of bureaucracy. Weber places great emphasis on the importance of *leadership* in democracy – which is why his preferred system is referred to as 'democratic elitism'. He argues that rule by elites is inevitable, and that the best we can hope for is that those elites effectively represent our interests and that they do so in wise and innovative ways. Parliaments and congresses provide a breeding-ground for capable political leaders, able to counter the influence of bureaucracy and to command mass support. Weber values multi-party democracy more for the quality of leadership it generates than for the mass participation in politics it makes possible.

Joseph Schumpeter's ideas

Schumpeter fully agreed with Weber about the limits of mass political participation. For Schumpeter, as for Weber, democracy is more important as a method of generating effective and responsible government than as a means of providing significant power for the majority. Democracy cannot offer more than the possibility of replacing a given political leader or party by others. Democracy, Schumpeter states, is the rule of the *politician*, not the *people*. Politicians are 'dealers in votes' much as brokers are dealers in shares on the stock exchange. To achieve voting support, however, politicians must be at least minimally responsive to the demands and interests of the electorate. Only if there is some degree of competition to secure votes can arbitrary rule effectively be avoided. Like Weber, Schumpeter believes that the mechanisms of political democracy should be kept largely separate from economic life. A competitive market provides for a measure of consumer choice, just as a competitive system of parties provides at least a small measure of political choice.

Pluralist theories

The ideas of Weber and Schumpeter strongly influenced the pluralist theorists of modern democracy. **Pluralist theories** were developed particularly on the basis of studies of American politics, but their conclusions – if valid – have wide application. Pluralists accept that individual citizens can have little or no direct influence on political decision-making. But they argue that tendencies towards the centralization of power in the hands of government officials are limited by the presence of multiple **interest groups**. Competing interest groups or factions are vital to democracy because they divide up power, reducing the exclusive influence of any one group or class.

According to pluralists, government policies in a democracy are influenced by continual processes of bargaining between numerous groups representing different interests – business organizations, trade unions, ethnic groups, environmental organizations, religious groups and so forth. A democratic political order is one in which there is a balance between competing interests, all having some impact on policy but none dominating the actual mechanisms of government. Elections are also influenced by this situation, for to achieve a base of support broad enough to lay claim to government, parties must be responsive to numerous diverse interest groups. The United States, it is argued, is the most pluralistic of industrialized societies and, therefore, the most democratic. Competition between diverse interest groups occurs not only at the national level but within the states and in the politics of local communities.

Criticisms and evaluation of the theories

Democratic elitism and pluralist theories have met with considerable criticism (Held, 1987). Let us start with those of the democratic elitist approach. First, the mass of the electorate, critics argue, is portrayed as passive and unenlightened, without evidence being given to show that this is so. Second, the only choice seen by Weber and Schumpeter is between creatively led elite rule and unresponsive bureaucratic rule. Yet there are wider variations between types of bureaucracy, some being more open and responsive to public interests and needs than others, and the requirements of expertise can often be fulfilled by professionals, rather than bureaucratic officials. Third, there might be possibilities for introducing co-operative enterprises and 'open' forms of association, which reduce bureaucratic tendencies – in both the political and the economic spheres.

The interest groups referred to by pluralists, critics point out, are not equivalent in their power. Business interest groups in particular usually have far greater sway over government policies than others. It is misleading, in any case, to see the influence of business as expressed through specific interest groups. Business enterprise supplies an overall *framework* in the context of which political processes occur and decisions are taken (Lindblom, 1977; Mintz and Schwartz, 1985). In the light of these and other objections, at least one of the early advocates of pluralist theories has revised his views: Robert A. Dahl has recently stressed the need to introduce programmes of economic democracy which would counterbalance the undue influence of large corporate interests (Dahl, 1985b).

These criticisms all have some validity; but it is impossible to deny the force of some of the arguments developed in democratic elitism and pluralism. Participatory democracy may function well in settings where relatively few people are involved, but it could not work as a regular system of government in a large-scale society. There can be occasional referenda, but voting on each and every issue after prolonged discussion of all the elements involved would be impossible if thousands, let alone millions, of people were involved (Bobbio, 1987). In modern societies, groups have many different interests and these cannot find recognition unless they can organize to make their views known. Competition between such groups can in principle serve to produce something of a 'balance': the strongest do not simply impose their views on others, while minorities can get their interests represented.

Moreover, Weber and Schumpeter were right to raise the question of expertise. The mass of the electorate cannot master the intricacies of the decisions which governments constantly have to take, but civil service officials and elected members of representative bodies have the time to acquire specialist knowledge of issues. While experts need to be constrained by the views of those affected by policies they formulate, they can make decisions on an informed basis. Where their activities are overseen by elected representatives, these decisions can be made responsive to broad social interests and pressures.

We cannot analyse such issues solely on an abstract level, of course; we have to look at the operation of actual political systems. This is the task to which we now turn, beginning with the nature of political parties and going on to look at women's role (or lack of it) in politics. We then consider who actually holds power in various systems, and consider the nature of concentrated political power in the shape of 'totalitarianism'.

Political parties and voting in Western countries

A **political party** may be defined as an organization oriented towards achieving legitimate control of government through an electoral process. In some situations, there may be political organizations which seek to achieve power but are denied the opportunity to do so through orthodox means. Such organizations are best regarded as political sects or movements until they achieve recognition. In late nineteenth-century Germany, for example, the Social Democrats were outlawed by Bismarck. They were then an organized political movement, operating outside orthodox channels, but they later achieved recognition as a party, and have held power for several periods in this century.

There are many types of party system within the overall category of *multi-party states*. Whether a two-party system, or one involving more parties, flourishes depends in large part on the nature of electoral procedures in a given country. Two parties tend to dominate the political system where elections are based on the principle of winner-take-all. The candidate who gains the most votes wins the election, no matter what proportion of the overall vote he or she gains (Duverger, 1954). Where elections are based on different principles, such as proportional representation (where seats in a representative assembly are allocated in terms of proportions of the vote attained), two-party systems are less common.

In Western European countries there are many types of party organization, not all of which are found in British politics. Some parties are based upon religious denomination (like the Parti Social Chrétien in Belgium or the Katholieke Volkspartij); some are ethnic parties, representing specific nationalist or linguistic groups (such as the Scottish National Party in Britain or the Svenska Folkpartiet in Finland); others are rural parties, representing agrarian interests (for example, the Centerpartiet in Sweden or the Schweizerische Volkspartei in Switzerland); yet others are environmental parties, concerned with ecological objectives (such as the Greens in West Germany). There are also numerous parties representing different shades of political opinion (Kesselman et al., 1987).

Socialist or labour parties have formed governments at some point since the Second World War in most West European societies. There are officially recognized Communist parties in virtually all such countries, some of which are large (those in Italy, France and Spain). There are many conservative parties (like the Parti Républicain in France or the Conservative and Unionist Party in Britain), and 'centrist' parties which occupy the 'middle ground' between *Left* and *Right* (such as the Social and Liberal Democrats in Britain). (The term 'Left' is used to refer to radical or progressive political groups who lean towards socialism; 'Right' refers to more conservative groups.)

Party systems

In some countries, the leader of the majority party, or of one of the parties in a coalition, automatically becomes prime minister, the highest public official in the land. In other cases (like the United States) a president is elected separately from party elections to the main representative bodies. Hardly any of the electoral systems in Western countries are exactly the same as one another, and most are more complicated than that of the United Kingdom. West Germany can serve as an example. In that country, members are elected to the *Bundestag* (parliament) by a system which combines winner-take-all and proportional election rules. Half the members of the Bundestag are elected in constituencies in which the candidate getting the most votes wins. The other 50 per cent are elected according to the proportions of the vote they poll in particular regional areas. This is the system which has enabled the Green Party to win parliamentary seats. A 5 per cent limit has been set to prevent undue proliferation of small parties – at least this proportion of the vote must be achieved before a party obtains parliamentary representation. A similar system is also used in local elections.

Two-party systems, like that of Britain, tend to lead to a concentration upon the 'middle ground', where most votes are to be found, excluding more radical views. The parties in these countries usually cultivate a moderate image, and sometimes come to resemble one another so closely that the choice they offer is slight. A plurality of interests may supposedly be represented by each party, but they quite often become blended into a bland programme with few distinctive policies. Multi-party systems allow divergent interests and points of views to be expressed more directly, and provide scope for the representation of radical alternatives. On the other hand, no one party is likely to achieve an overall majority, leading to coalitions which can suffer from an inability to make decisions because of major conflicts, or a rapid succession of elections and new governments, none able to stay in power for long and thus very limited in their effects.

Voting and class

In most Western states, the largest parties are those associated with general political interests – socialist, communist, liberal or conservative parties. There is usually a fairly clear connection between voting patterns and class differences. Liberal and leftist parties tend to gain most of their votes from those in lower-class occupations, while conservative or rightist parties are more strongly supported by affluent groups.

The party system in the United States is quite distinct from that of virtually all other Western societies, since there is no large leftist party. Class-based voting is less pronounced there than in other Western democracies. While the Democratic Party has tended to appeal more to lower-class groups, and the Republicans have drawn support from the more affluent sectors of the population, the connections are not clear-cut. Each party has a conservative wing; it is relatively common for conservative and liberal members of one party to vote with those holding parallel opinions in the other party on particular issues.

Internal party organization in the American parties is much weaker than in most large European ones. The European parties usually have ways of ensuring that their members follow the 'party line' on contentious issues, and try to maintain strong party solidarity.

Parties and voting in Britain

In Britain until the nineteenth century parties were regarded only as temporary devices, needed to mobilize support in relation to specific events or crises. As parties developed into more stable organizations, they became associated with the idea that support for their leadership could bring specific rewards. Party membership and loyalty came to be linked to various forms of patronage, in which the faithful would be rewarded by receiving specific positions in a new administration. For most of the twentieth century, two major parties (Labour and Conservative) have dominated the national political scene, and *adversarial politics* has developed through the raising of support for two alternative governmental teams, each consisting of members of a single party. In the post-war years the two parties have come increasingly under pressure – both external and internal. Externally, we can note three manifestations of this pressure:

1 *Loss of voting support.* In 1951, historically a peak for the two-party system, the Labour and Conservative parties jointly polled 96.8 per cent of the votes cast in the general election. By 1974, in the October general election this percentage had fallen to 75 per cent. The February 1974 election was the first in forty-five years not to produce a single-party majority in the House of Commons. The Liberal-SDP Alliance used these facts in the early 1980s to back its demand for electoral reform.
2 *Loss of members.* Both major parties have suffered a decline in their membership since 1953. Reliable membership figures are not issued by either party, but it is generally agreed that their current levels are relatively low.
3 *Loss of resources.* In real terms, the parties' income has diminished in similar proportion to the membership decline, although contributions from members are not the major source of either party's income. The effect of this decline in resources has been to increase the financial dependence of the Conservatives on private business firms and of Labour on the trade unions.

For several reasons, British electoral politics have changed significantly over the past twenty years or so. One factor is structural: the proportion of the economically active population involved in traditional blue-collar occupations – in manufacture especially – has dropped considerably. There is little doubt that this has eroded some traditional sources of Labour support. A second factor is the split that occurred in the Labour Party at the beginning of the 1980s, which led to the founding of the Social Democratic Party (SDP). Although in 1988 support for the 'centre' parties has dropped away considerably, a significant 'additional force' in British politics seems to have emerged. A third influence has been that of the Conservative Prime Minister, Mrs Thatcher, elected for three successive terms of office. The vigorous programme of change initiated by Mrs Thatcher and her cabinets expresses a significant move from earlier Tory philosophy. 'Thatcherism' gives prime emphasis to restricting the role of the state in economic life, and makes faith in market forces the basis of both individual liberties and economic growth.

Before 1970, the two major parties enjoyed stable voting support (Heath et al., 1986), most of the electorate having strong Tory or Labour loyalties. This was recognized in party campaigns, which concentrated more on rallying the faithful than on trying to convert those holding alternative views. The two elections held in 1974 showed these traditional loyalties to have become markedly weaker. In surveys of political affiliation, the numbers of those describing themselves as 'very' or 'fairly' strong supporters of a particular party declined from about 80 per cent to 60 per cent between 1970 and 1986 (Crewe, 1987). At each election, this percentage has dropped progressively, and the

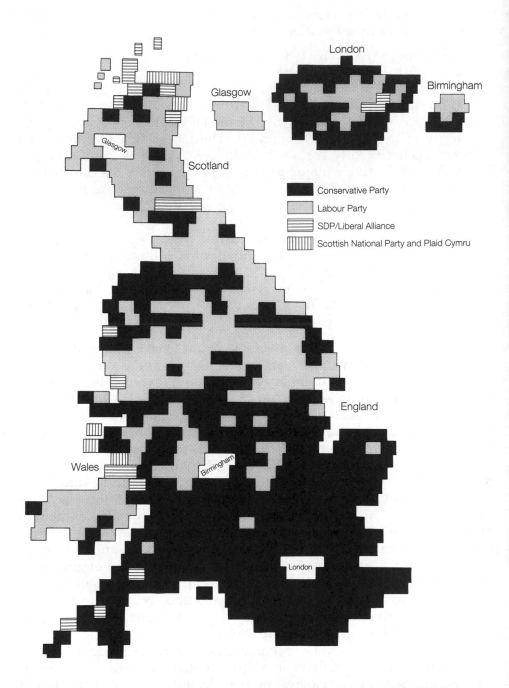

Figure 10 Regional variations in the strength of the main parties at the British General Election of 11 June 1987. Each constituency has been drawn with the same space, to give a more accurate visual representation of the strength of the various parties. Northern Ireland has been omitted
Source: Sunday Telegraph, 14 June 1987.

proportion of voters who say they made up their minds during the final campaign has increased markedly. It seems likely, therefore, that the campaigns have become more important to the election results than they used to be. Television has probably been a significant influence here, as a means of 'selling' the images of parties and politicians.

Television perhaps acts as a balance to the politically partisan nature of the British press in current times. As a result of changes in newspaper ownership and circulation, papers backing the Tories dominate the market. In the 1960s, papers supporting Labour had 43 per cent of the total circulation of dailies. Today only the *Daily Mirror* is unequivocally pro-Labour, holding 22 per cent of total circulation. It has been suggested that one effect of the increasing prominence of television in election campaigning is to focus undue attention on the party leaders. Some have claimed that British elections are becoming like American presidential campaigns. This does not in fact seem to be true: although more of the electorate preferred Callaghan to Thatcher as a potential prime minister in 1979, the Tories won the election.

In the 1987 general election, the Conservatives lost seventeen seats, but held on to all but 0.3 per cent of their 1983 vote. Labour gained twenty seats, adding 3.2 per cent to the percentage of the vote the party received in 1983, which had been at its lowest in the post-war period. The Alliance (SDP and Liberals) slipped by 2.9 per cent emerging with twenty-two MPs rather than twenty-three; all but five of their existing MPs were defeated at the polls, the remainder representing new gains. The results of the election showed the country to be radically divided regionally. Labour holds no seats in the South-East, outside London, and the Conservatives have very few Scottish seats (see figure 10).

'Thatcherism'

One of the most distinctive features of British politics in the 1980s has been the influence of the political ideas associated with Mrs Thatcher which came to be known as 'Thatcherism'. What were the sources of Thatcherism? What was its appeal to such an apparently wide section of the British electorate? It is easy to suppose that the policies associated with Mrs Thatcher's governments (which came to power in 1979) were more unified and consistent than is in fact the case. Thatcherism has certain guiding threads, but is in most respects a fairly loose collection of programmes and initiatives. Some were adopted for pragmatic reasons, while others evolved, or were largely abandoned, with the progress of time (Riddell, 1985; Kavanagh, 1987).

Mrs Thatcher did not become Conservative Party leader, or Prime Minister, because of any early groundswell of support for the policies later to be called Thatcherism. She was not initially thought of as the most likely person to succeed Edward Heath as Tory leader, but she

was prepared to challenge Heath at a time, in the late 1970s, when –
the party having suffered two election defeats – many MPs wanted a
change in the leadership. Her victory was not seen by most at the time
as marking a decisive ideological shift in Tory philosophy, although
she was closely involved in the rethinking of the party's outlook
begun by Keith Joseph. Once she became leader, ideas suggested
by Joseph, together with views based on those of the economist
Milton Friedman, were welded together to initiate new policies.

The Conservative Manifesto of 1979 in fact for the most part contained
the doctrines associated with Mr Heath, although it promised a
reversal of Britain's economic decline and spoke of radically expanding
individual freedoms by reducing the power of the state. The Tory
victory in the 1979 general election was interpreted by most political
commentators as a reaction to the inability of Labour to control the
unions, rather than as a triumph for a new political philosophy. During
her first term of office Mrs Thatcher's policies were most concentrated
on 'monetarism'. Controlling the money supply was believed to be
the key to reducing inflation and promoting the sound management
of the economy. The targets set for monetary control, however,
proved impossible to achieve, and monetarism was in effect largely
abandoned subsequently. An initial commitment to reduce public
expenditure has also been revised, since expenditure has steadily risen
over the period since Mrs Thatcher first came to power.

Since the 1983 election, the momentum of Thatcherism in economic
matters has been maintained by the privatizing of public companies.
The sale of shares in British Telecom, British Gas, British Airways and
British Petroleum (BP) drew a wide response. The sale of council
houses has also proved popular among the electorate. Far-reaching
changes are planned in education and in the system of domestic
rates for local authority spending, although it is not clear that these
enjoy equivalent popular support.

'The lady's not for turning!', Mrs Thatcher declared in one of her
more celebrated public pronouncements. Perhaps the strongest element
of continuity in Thatcherism has been the personality and moral style of
Mrs Thatcher herself. Her crusading outlook has not won the affection
of many of the electorate, but it has brought respect for her qualities
as a national leader. Mrs Thatcher's refusal to back down in the face
of the Argentinian occupation of the Falkland Islands seemed to many
to give concrete expression to these qualities, and her dominant role
within the government was also reinforced by her progressive dismissal
of Cabinet members who were out of sympathy with her views.

The level of support for Thatcherism has also altered over time.
Initially, her victory was more the result of a vote *against* Mr Callaghan's
government. In the early 1980s, there were major expressions of popular
dissent from Mrs Thatcher's policies, including marches and demonstrations against unemployment. Support for the Conservatives had

declined substantially, but was revived by the positive public response to the government's show of strength and determination in the Falklands War – a major factor in the 1983 Tory election victory. The government could have been brought down by the miners' strike in 1984, but when the miners were defeated the government became even more popular.

There is no doubting the widespread support that the general outlook fostered by Mrs Thatcher's successive administrations has commanded. This support has extended to at least some parts of the population previously more inclined towards Labour. Stuart Hall has argued that Mrs Thatcher created a form of *authoritarian populism* that appealed to popular sentiments in several ways (Hall and Jacques, 1983). Many welcomed her attacks upon state collectivism, together with her endorsement of self-help and individual initiative. This is the populist element in her appeal. There was also considerable sympathy with her attempts to discipline the unions, her 'harsh economic medicine', and her strong endorsement of a 'law and order' state. These were the authoritarian overtones to the populist sentiments.

Party politics: breaking the mould in the late twentieth century?

In spite of the long period of her rule, Mrs Thatcher has never enjoyed the support of more than a minority of the population. In fact, in Britain and in many other Western countries, there seems to be growing scepticism and disenchantment with traditional party politics, coupled with increased instability in party support. This coincides with a period (from the early 1970s to the present day) in which the gradual extension of social rights, as diagnosed by Marshall, seems to have gone into reverse. Rightist parties, such as those led by Mrs Thatcher in Britain, or Helmut Kohl in West Germany, together with the Reagan administration, have attempted to cut back on welfare expenditure (Krieger, 1986). Even in states led by socialist governments, like France under President Mitterrand (1981–6), commitment to government provision of public resources was restricted (Ross, Hoffman and Malzacher, 1987). One reason has been decline in government revenues stemming from the world recession which began in the early 1970s. Yet there also seems to have been an increase in scepticism about the effectiveness of the welfare state, felt not only by governments, but also by many citizens. These views seem closely related to changing patterns of party support.

The theories of state overload and legitimation crisis

Two contrasting theories have been developed which are relevant to this changing political situation. One is the theory of **state overload**

(Brittan, 1975; Nordhaus, 1975). According to this view, as governments have taken on more and more tasks, including public ownership of industries, utilities and transport, as well as welfare provision, they have acquired more than they can fund and manage. Political parties have tried to woo voter support since the Second World War by promising more and more benefits and services, but once elected they have been unable to deliver, because the level of state expenditure has risen to exceed the revenue from taxation on which governments depend. Large government agencies develop their own momentum, and become increasingly unwieldy and unresponsive to the needs they are supposed to serve (Etzioni-Halévy, 1983).

Consequently, it is argued, voters become sceptical about claims made by governments and political parties. Leftist parties, and the Democrats in the United States, lose some of their traditional support from working-class groups, who feel that state expenditure has got out of hand in relation to the benefits they actually experience. The rise of 'New Right' politics is explained as an attempt to cope with this situation by trimming back the state and encouraging private enterprise.

The rival theory is that of **legitimation crisis**, as developed by the German social thinker, Jürgen Habermas, and others (Habermas, 1976; Offe, 1984, 1985). The starting-point of this theory is the observation that modern governments as a whole find it difficult to generate the resources they need to carry out their appointed tasks. State intervention in economic life and provision of welfare resources is necessary to keep the economy stable, but where a society depends extensively on goods and services generated by private capitalist production, economic life tends to be fluctuating and uncertain. Governments have to provide many services which private companies are unwilling to fund because they are insufficiently profitable. While the state must take on more and more tasks, there is resistance to providing the revenue necessary to do this, since taxes must be raised from private individuals and businesses. Governments cannot cope adequately with these contradictory demands. The pressures have become more acute than before in recent years, because the range of services provided by governments has constantly expanded. The capabilities of parties – particularly those advocating a large role for the state – to live up to their promises has diminished. This has led to a partial withdrawal of public support, and general disillusionment with the abilities of politicians – a 'legitimation crisis'. New forms of Rightist politics have arisen from resistance to high levels of taxation by those in higher income groups.

Assessment of the theories

The two theories have common elements. Each holds that government authority and established patterns of party support are undermined in the face of growing demands. Both suggest that governments find it difficult to control the aspects of social and economic life they promise to influence in their programmes. The suggestions for practical remedies which flow from the two theories, however, are quite different. Overload theory suggests that attempts to roll back levels of state spending can be fruitful. The alternative theory implies that such attempts will rebound, probably causing worsening social conflicts because there will be inadequate funding to cope with needs such as those of health, welfare provision, or deteriorating inner cities.

Overload theory is probably the less illuminating of the two. There seems to be a 'push and pull' in the provision of resources between governments and private bodies which Habermas successfully analyses. Those who feel they pay most towards providing services – the more affluent – are likely to believe they gain least from them. Thus in many countries there are persistent debates about how far health services should be funded from taxation, and provided by the state, and how far they should be directly paid for by those who consume them. Many current social conflicts centre on such issues.

The political participation of women

Voting patterns and political attitudes

Voting has a special meaning for women against the background of their struggle to obtain universal suffrage, which virtually everywhere took a long time to gain. The members of the early women's movements saw the vote both as the symbol of political freedom and the means of achieving greater economic and social equality. In Britain and the United States, where the attempts of women to gain voting rights were more active, and provoked more violence, than elsewhere, women's leaders underwent considerable hardship to reach this end. Even today women do not have the same voting rights as men in all countries, although Saudi Arabia is the only state where women cannot vote at the national level (Randall, 1982). Has the hard-fought struggle to acquire voting rights produced the results that were hoped for?

The short answer is 'no'. In most Western countries, when they first achieved voting rights, women voted in far smaller numbers than males. In the first national election for which they were eligible in Britain, in 1929, only about one-third of women voted, as compared to two-thirds of men. The proportions were roughly the same in the USA, and a similar pattern is found in other states in the early period after the instituting of universal voting rights (Baxter and Lansing, 1983; Flanz, 1983). Women still do not vote in the same proportions as men in many nations, although in some cases the discrepancy has almost completely disappeared. Voter turnout of women in the last three American presidential elections has only been between 3 and 6 per cent less than that of men. In Britain, in Parliamentary elections since 1970 (including the election of that year), the differential has not been more than 4 per cent. Gender differences in voting have completely disappeared in Sweden, West Germany and Canada, while in Italy, Finland and Japan women vote at slightly higher rates than men.

These figures indicate that the real obstacle to equality between the sexes was not the vote, but the more deeply buried social divisions between men and women, which restricted women to the household and domestic tasks. Changes in these social divisions have brought about alterations in the political participation of women, rather than the other way around. As the differences in power and status between men and women begin to narrow, women's level of voting climbs.

How far do the political attitudes of women differ from those of men? Many suffragists, early supporters of women's right to vote, believed that the entry of women into politics would radically transform political life, bringing a new sense of altruism and morality. Those who were against the extending of the vote to women similarly argued that the political participation of women would have momentous consequences – but of a disastrous kind. A prominent male opponent of female franchise in Britain warned that 'a revolution of such boundless significance cannot be attempted without the greatest peril to England' (quoted in Currell, 1974, p. 2). Women's involvement in politics, it was widely held, would trivialize political life and at the same time undermine the stability of the family.

Neither of these extreme consequences has come to pass. The obtaining of the vote by women has not greatly altered the nature of politics. Women's voting patterns, like those of men, are shaped by party preferences, policy options and the choice of available candidates, though there are some differences between female and male voting that are fairly consistently found. Women voters on the whole tend to be more conservative than men, as judged by level of voting for Rightist parties. This is true, for example, in France, West Germany and Italy. The relationship is more ambiguous in Britain and the United States. In Britain young women vote in higher numbers for the Labour Party than young men, but older women disproportionately vote Conservative. The two tendencies more or less balance one another. In the United States a conservative orientation cannot be easily associated with either of the two main parties, since the contrast between the Republicans and Democrats is not a straightforward opposition between political Right and Left. In recent elections, women have voted Democrat in slightly higher proportions than men, with younger women being particularly inclined to favour the Democrats.

The influence of women on politics cannot be assessed solely in terms of voting. Feminist groups have made an impact on political life independently of the franchise, particularly in recent decades. The National Organization of Women (NOW) and other women's groups in the USA, since the early 1960s, have pressed for a range of issues directly affecting women to be placed on the political agenda. Such issues include equal rights at work, the availability of abortion, changes in family and divorce law, and lesbian rights. In most European countries, comparable national women's organizations have often been lacking, but the 'second wave' of feminism characteristic of the 1960s and since has brought the same issues to the centre of the political stage. Many of these matters – like the question of how far abortion should be freely available – have proved highly controversial among women as well as men.

Women's groups played a significant role in Britain in the passing of the 1967 Abortion Act and legislation against sex discrimination at work, and women's organizations have pressed for other changes which have been recognized in law, such as protection for the victims of domestic violence secured under the Domestic Violence and Matrimonial Procedures Act of 1976. Whatever happens in the future, it seems clear that many problems and concerns that particularly affect women, and which previously may have seemed to be 'outside politics', are now central to political debates.

Women in political organizations

Women have never been complete strangers to political power. In past times, individual women have on occasion wielded vast influence as heads of state – from Cleopatra onwards. Where they have not been formally installed as rulers, women have sometimes held great power informally, as the wives or mistresses of monarchs, presidents and prime ministers. One of the most famous of such examples is that of Madame de Pompadour, the mistress of Louis XIV of France, who was able effectively to take most of the important decisions of state. In the twentieth century, women have relatively often been heads of government – examples include Golda Meir in Israel, Indira Gandhi in India, and Margaret Thatcher in the United Kingdom.

Yet in general, as in so many other areas of social life, women are poorly represented among political elites. In Britain, after the 1983 election, there were 19 female Members of Parliament making up 3 per cent of the membership of the House of Commons. In the preceding Parliament there had been 27 women MPs, representing 4.5 per cent of the total. After the 1980 national elections in the United States, there were 19 women members in the House of Representatives, making up just over 4 per cent of the total membership (Randall, 1982, chapter 3). This proportion has remained more or less stable since the early 1970s. In 1981 there were only two women in the American Senate, representing 2 per cent of those sitting in the upper chamber. There were no women at all in the preceding session, and in its entire history there have only been a total of 13 women members. Women have fared somewhat better in the legislatures of some other countries. In West Germany in 1981, women made up 8.5 per cent of the parliament, the Bundestag. Women formed 28 per cent of legislators in Sweden, 26 per cent in Finland, and 24 per cent in Norway.

The representation of women in local government is generally greater than in national assemblies. Women composed some 16 per cent of local councillors in the United Kingdom in 1981. In most other European countries, women are more strongly represented in local than in national assemblies, with the exception of the Scandinavian countries, where the local and national percentages are more similar. In 1983, 9.8 per cent of the members of state assemblies in the USA were women. The overall pattern of women's representation in government parallels that of most other spheres of society. While at the middle levels of power there may be a fairly substantial proportion of women – although nothing approaching equal numbers with men – the higher we go up the system, the fewer women are to be found.

Exactly the same pattern is found within political party organizations. In Britain, 11 per cent of Labour Party Annual Conference delegates in 1980 were women, with the comparable figure for the Conservative Party being 38 per cent. Women make up about a third of delegates to the Democratic and Republican Party Conventions in the United States. At the top of the party hierarchies, however, the proportion of women shrinks dramatically. In the American Carter administration, there were 2 women in a Cabinet of 11 people. The Cabinet formed by President Reagan after the 1980 election contained no women at all. The Scandinavian countries are virtually the only ones in which women have figured reasonably prominently. The Cabinets in Sweden, Finland and Norway have long included women, although still in a clear minority. In 1980, for example, 5 out of 20 Cabinet members in Sweden were women.

What is surprising about the figures on women's involvement at the higher levels of political organizations is not this lack of representation itself, but the slowness with which things seem to be changing. In the business sector, men still monopolize the top positions, but women are now making more inroads into the strongholds of male privilege than ever before. As yet at least, this does not seem to be happening in the political sphere – in spite of the fact that nearly all political parties today are nominally committed to securing equal opportunities for women and men. The factors that present difficulties for women's advancement in the economy also exist in the realm of politics. To rise within a political organization normally requires a great expenditure of effort and time, which women who have major domestic burdens can rarely generate. But there may be an additional influence. A high level of power is concentrated in the political arena; perhaps men are especially reluctant to abandon their dominance in such a sphere.

Non-institutionalized political action

Political life is by no means carried on only within the orthodox framework of political parties, voting and representation on government bodies. It often happens that groups find that their objectives or ideals cannot be achieved within, or are actively blocked by, this framework. The most dramatic and far-reaching example of non-orthodox political action is revolution – the overthrow of an existing political order by means of a mass movement, using violence. Since revolutions are discussed extensively in chapter 19 ('Revolutions and Social Movements'), we shall not analyse them here. But an idea must be given of the scope and nature of non-institutionalized political activity.

The most common type of such activity is represented by protest movements, normally but not always springing up among the poorer and more underprivileged groups in society. In Western countries today, it is legally permissible to form political associations of more or less any sort, and some kinds of extra-parlimentary action are also permitted – such as the staging of street demonstrations or marches. These rights mostly had to be won from the political authorities. During the nineteenth century, for example, 'Combination Acts' were introduced in several European countries banning the assembling of large numbers of people in public places for political purposes. These attempts at government regulation were mostly abandoned when it became clear that they could not be realistically enforced. People turned out *en masse* to demonstrate against them – such laws tended to stimulate the very activities they were supposed to prevent.

It is characteristic of protest movements, however, that they operate near the margins of what is defined as legally permissible by governments at any particular time or place. A police licence, for example, normally has to be obtained before a mass demonstration is staged. Where such a licence is denied, the organizers may decide to go ahead anyway, bringing them into confrontation with the authorities. Protesters who feel strongly about a cause may quite often be prepared to transgress the law in order to make their actions more effective. People

Table 4 Attitudes to protest actions on the part of a national British sample (men and women) in 1977

	Have done (%)	Might do (%)	Would never do (%)
Signing a petition	63	28	9
Attending lawful demonstrations	9	33	58
Joining in boycotts	6	31	63
Joining unofficial strikes	8	16	76
Occupying buildings or factories	2	10	87
Damaging things like breaking windows, removing road signs, etc.	2	1	97
Using personal violence like fighting with other demonstrators or the police	1	3	96

Source: Mark Abrams, David Gerrard and Noel Timms, *Values and Social Change in Britain* (London: Macmillan, 1986), p. 165.

involved in peace movements over the past few years, for instance, have blockaded army camps in an endeavour to stop weapons being moved in and out, climbed over the wire to stage sit-ins, and entered missile silos.

Government leaders have three main options when confronted by extra-parliamentary action. First of all, they may simply ignore it. Groups which can muster little support are likely simply to draw little response from government circles. In such circumstances, a particularly determined group or movement may turn to the use of violence, since this inevitably calls forth a reaction, even if only a punitive one. Small political sects, for example, which have few followers among the population at large, might turn to terrorism as a means of furthering their cause.

A second response on the part of government authorities might be to clamp down immediately on those involved, or believed to be involved, in the activities in question. Repressive measures have very frequently been used by political authorities to quell what are seen as 'disturbances to public order'. Sometimes such responses have been savage: armed troops have been used against unarmed marchers, for example, occasionally with extensive loss of life.

The third possible reaction is to blunt the edge of protest by agreeing to at least some of the demands. The three responses might very well follow on from one another. In the first stage of the development of a protest movement, the authorities may pay little attention to it, or believe that it will fade away of its own accord. If the movement gathers strength, especially if it is directly hostile to government policies, the response might be to control its impact by the use of force. If this fails, or produces a public outcry, the political authorities might at that point give way on some issues, and perhaps incorporate them within their own political programme.

Extra-parliamentary political action quite often produces major revisions in official policies (Piven and Cloward, 1977). Such was the case, for example, with the civil rights movement in the United States in the late 1950s and 1960s – described in more detail in chapter 8 ('Ethnicity and Race'). Involving a mixture of poor Southern blacks, middle-class black leaders, and white liberals recruited mostly from the North, the civil rights movement brought about far-reaching political changes. Reactions to the movement by the government broadly followed the sequence mentioned above. At first, neither central nor local government agencies were particularly interested, treating the marches and disturbances as phenomena that would evaporate of their own accord. When it became clear that this was not to be the case, some local authorities began to harass the movement's leaders and tried to prevent marches and demonstrations by a show of force. Later on, however – the Federal Government having taken the lead – they were compelled to introduce legislative changes promoting greater equality between black and white, such as the desegregation of schooling.

Who rules?

Pluralist theory, as described earlier in the chapter, was based on an interpretation of the political system of modern societies which emphasizes the competitive nature of group interests. Such competition supposedly prevents power falling too much into the hands of any one group or class. Like the advocates of the theory of democratic elitism, the pluralists agree that 'the people' do not, and cannot, rule. But they see the United States, and other Western societies, as essentially democratic. The view suggested by C. Wright Mills in his celebrated work, *The Power Elite*, was quite different (Mills, 1956). He felt that, in earlier periods of its history, American society did in fact show considerable flexibility and diversity at all levels, but that this has since changed.

Mills argues that during the course of the twentieth century a process of institutional centralization occurred in the political order, the economy and the sphere of the military. The political system was once largely organized through the separate states, loosely co-ordinated by the federal government. Political power today, according to Mills, has come to be tightly co-ordinated at the top. Similarly, the economy was once made up of many small units, but has now become dominated by a cluster of very large corporations. Finally, whereas once the armed forces were restricted in size, and supplemented by militia, they have now grown to form a giant establishment in a key position among the country's institutions.

Not only has each of these spheres become more centralized; according to Mills, they have become increasingly interconnected with one another to form a unified system of power. People in the highest positions in all three institutional areas come from similar social backgrounds, have parallel interests and often know one another on a personal basis. They have come to be a single **power elite** which runs the country – and given the international position of the United States, also influences much of what happens in the rest of the world.

The power elite, in Mills's portrayal, is composed mainly of (male) wealthy white Anglo-Saxon professionals (WASPs), many of whom have been to the same prestigious universities, belong to the same clubs and sit on government committees with one another. They have closely connected concerns. Business and political leaders work together, and both have close relationships with the military through weapons contracting and the supply of goods for the armed forces. There is a great deal of movement back and forth between top positions in the three spheres. Politicians have business interests; business leaders often stand for public office; higher military personnel come to sit on the boards of the large companies.

In opposition to pluralist interpretations, Mills argues that there are three distinct levels of power in the United States. The power elite occupies the highest level, formally and informally taking the most important policy decisions affecting both the domestic arena and foreign policy. The interest groups on which the pluralists concentrate their attention operate at the middle levels of power, together with more local agencies. Their influence over major decisions is limited. At the bottom is the large mass of the population, having virtually no influence on decisions at all, since these are taken within the closed settings in which the members of the power elite come together. The elite spans the top of both party organizations, each party being run by individuals with similar overall interests and outlooks. Thus the choices open to voters in Presidential and congressional elections are so small as to be of little consequence.

Since Mills published his study, there have been numerous other research investigations analysing the social background and interconnections of leading figures in the various spheres of American society (Dye, 1986). All studies agree that the social backgrounds of those in leading positions are highly unrepresentative of the population as a whole. Individuals in top positions in each of the three spheres discussed by Mills are men drawn quite disproportionately from WASP families with high incomes, having attended a limited range of select private schools and top universities. G. William Domhoff studied the members of the American upper class, defined as those persons listed in the select publication *The Social Register* (Domhoff, 1967, 1970, 1979). Although *The Social Register* is only published for twelve cities, with the South and South West more or less completely excluded, it provides something of a guide to the distribution of the rich and powerful in the United States. Domhoff found that, thus defined, the upper class were heavily over-represented in the high-level positions, not only in the three areas analysed by Mills but in many others as well. These include the boards of trustees of universities and colleges, the mass media, charitable foundations and the diplomatic service. Domhoff has documented connections through marriage, membership of the same clubs and committees, and the holding of top positions simultaneously in several spheres.

Like Mills, he concludes that a power elite exists, within which the most important decisions affecting the country are taken, its members being largely drawn from the upper class. He differs from Mills in arguing that the military form a fairly closed system, having a major influence upon political and economic decisions only in times of crisis or war.

The 'inner circle' in the USA

Michael Useem has more recently studied the leadership of large corporations in the United States, drawing a contrast with patterns of business leadership in Britain (Useem, 1984). He argues that similar trends can be found in both societies in respect of the interrelation of business and political decision-making. According to him, leaders in some of the largest corporations have come to take more and more of a directly political role in national affairs. The large majority of business executives are not part of what Useem calls the *inner circle* – a small network of business leaders in regular connection with each other and with political leaders. The few who are, however – mostly drawn from the top levels of large corporations – exercise an influence on government on behalf of the whole business community.

During the 1970s and early 1980s, according to Useem, a marked intensification of corporate political activities occurred. These now operate through the direct support of candidates, lobbying at the highest levels, membership of government decision-making bodies and through personal contacts in informal contexts. The increased political mobilization of big business, Useem argues, is a response to economic difficulties resulting from the recent world recession. Corporate leaders in the USA and United Kingdom have also become more influential through the political climate fostered by the Reagan administration and Thatcher government, both of which are firmly pro-business.

Elites in Britain

Closely connected as the different areas of leadership may be in the United States, in Britain and in most other European countries they are even more tightly knit. Only a tiny minority of the population in Britain attends fee-paying schools, or goes to the two leading universities, Oxford and Cambridge. These people are heavily over-represented in top positions in many spheres – although less so in industry than in most others, the prestige of business in Britain generally having been much lower than in the United States. Between 60 and 80 per cent of those in top positions in the armed forces, the Church, judiciary, civil service, and Conservative members of parliament, were educated at fee-paying schools and/or Oxford or Cambridge (Stanworth and Giddens, 1974).

The practice of issuing regular 'honours lists', which developed at the end of the nineteenth century, maintains a tie between distinguished people of the present and the hereditary aristocracy. The Prime Minister puts forward a list, which is scrutinized by a parliamentary committee and endorsed by the monarch. In the civil service and the military there are formal channels of nomination, and receipt of honours or titles closely follows promotion to high positions. In other areas, nomination more commonly depends on networks of informal connections which link the powerful and the prestigious with one another.

The highest rank in the peerage is that of duke, followed in descending order by marquess, earl, viscount and baron. Dukes are easily the most exclusive of these groups, and include a number of descendants of families of ancient lineage. Only five of the twenty-six non-royal dukes possess titles dating from the nineteenth century, and the dukes include some of wealthiest private land-owners in the country. The large majority of peers are barons; virtually all of these have titles created in the nineteenth and twentieth centuries. The honours system is more than a minor ritual of recognition of 'services rendered to the country'.

It expresses a cohesiveness among the wealthy and powerful, and provides public indication of acceptance for newcomers who might otherwise be inclined to separate themselves from established circles.

Three other substantial influences serve to consolidate an elite group. One is intermarriage. Marriage of children to 'eligible' mates has always been to some degree a matter of deliberate policy on the part of parents, but it is today largely dependent upon the sharing of life-styles and pursuits. The country-house life and social contexts like 'coming out' parties create a common outlook, set of values and language (Sampson, 1982). A second factor is shared educational background, with the public schools and Oxbridge being prominently represented. The third is the maintenance of friendships, stretching across different elite spheres. The 'old-boy network' is sustained by membership of exclusive clubs and associations, and by a social round of dinners and parties – as well as by ties developed in more formal contexts of business or government.

Of course, there are many schisms and conflicts both between and within the major elite spheres. In the economic area, divergencies of interest and outlook between leading industrial figures and city banking

Table 5   Educational background of Conservative MPs in Britain, 1945–1974

Education	Number of MPs at each election									
	1945	*1950*	*1951*	*1955*	*1959*	*1964*	*1966*	*1970*	*1974a*	*1974b*
Eton	55	77	75	75	70	66	56	62	54	47
All public	169	240	216	264	274	232	199	243	222	206
Oxford	62	94	99	106	104	66	80	93	89	76
Cambridge	46	62	68	74	79	88	64	75	76	76
All universities	131	187	199	217	219	190	169	208	198	186
Total no. of Conservative MPs	213	297	320	343	365	301	253	330	297	277

The two entries for 1974 relate to the two elections of that year (February and October).
Source: John Scott, *The Upper Classes: Property and Privilege in Britain* (London: Macmillan, 1982), p. 163.

Table 6   Educational background of top army officers in Britain, 1897–1971

Education	Number of officers					
	1897	*1913*	*1926*	*1939*	*1959*	*1971*
Major boarding school	17	29	31	33	21	24
Other public school	6	5	6	4	8	5
Private	17	12	5	6	0	0
Other	23	12	6	2	7	3
Total	63	58	48	45	36	32

The figures relate to the ranks of lieutenant-general and above.
Source: John Scott, *The Upper Classes: Property and Privilege in Britain* (London: Macmillan, 1982), p. 168.

or financial groups are long established (Ingham, 1984). There tend to be chronic tensions between 'insiders' and people who are 'self-made', and church leaders may sometimes speak out against the policies of governments. In so far as the Labour Party represents the interests of the less well off, the political arena cannot remain the monopoly of the privileged. Even if their influence has been sharply reduced since the period of Mrs Thatcher's leadership, trade-union leaders have often mingled with the 'high and mighty'; yet they are plainly distinct in their backgrounds and careers from other powerful figures.

Assessment

How should we assess Mills's thesis in the light of subsequent discussion and empirical research? It seems reasonable to conclude that in Britain and the United States, as in other Western countries, there is a distinguishable upper class, holding a disproportionate share of the wealth of the country; its members have much higher chances of achieving top positions in a variety of areas than others from less privileged backgrounds. There is a strong meshing of business and governmental interests, often facilitated by direct personal contacts. Many major decisions are taken in contexts outside the public arena – in boardrooms, meetings of the Prime Minister and a few cabinet colleagues, and in the more informal settings in which some of these individuals come into regular contact with each other.

On the other hand, it is dubious whether, either in Britain or elsewhere, there exist groups as co-ordinated and cohesive as Mills's power elite. There are major divisions of opinion and interest between powerful groups, who may collaborate in some circumstances, but are more diverse and fragmented than in Mills's portrayal. The truth lies somewhere between the picture painted by the pluralists and the analysis offered by Mills.

Elites in the Soviet Union

One way of obtaining a perspective on structures of political power in the West is to look at leadership positions in the East European countries. Although information about these is much less easy to obtain, a good deal of research into the nature of Soviet leadership has been carried out.

The Soviet Union differs from Britain or the United States in so far as there are no large privately owned corporations, and the political system is dominated by a single party, the Communist Party of the Soviet Union (CPSU). In spite of the pre-eminent position of the party, the official view is that there are no favoured elites in the Soviet Union, let alone a distinct upper class. The party regards itself as the 'tried and tested militant vanguard of the Soviet people', the 'leading and guiding force of Soviet society' (quoted in Hill and Frank, 1983,

p. 1). As the representative of the industrial workers, the party claims to express the collective interests of the majority of the population.

Membership of the CPSU is in principle open to any citizen of the Soviet Union. In practice, entry tends to be controlled by members of local party organizations, through which individuals are co-opted. Applications for membership may be rejected by the local party branches. Party members are expected regularly to attend meetings and take part in discussions; membership is more than just a process of formal registration. Formally, party membership is not a prerequisite for entry into the majority of high positions in the country, but it greatly facilitates chances of reaching the top in most spheres. Full-time party officials make up only a small proportion of the overall membership, but include within their ranks some of the most powerful individuals in the Soviet Union.

About seventeen million people belong to the CPSU today. In 1977, 42 per cent of the membership was composed of manual workers, 14 per cent were agricultural workers, and the remainder were in white-collar and professional jobs (Hill and Frank, 1983, p. 36). The Politburo, Central Secretariat and Central Committee stand at the apex of the party organization. The Central Committee is in fact a large body with over 400 members; top leadership is concentrated in the Politburo and Central Secretariat. The former consists of about twenty men (only one woman has ever been a member), the latter about a dozen, with some people being members of both. The post of Secretary-General of the CPSU has come to be acknowledged as that of the country's main political leader, the equivalent of the American presidency.

Recruitment, prestige and privilege

In terms of social background, recruitment to top party positions is much more open than in the case of political leadership in Western countries. Thus all the members of the Politburo in 1957 came from working-class or peasant backgrounds. Of the members of the Central Committee in 1961, more than 85 per cent had such origins. Much the same was true of those in leading positions in industry, the military, education and the arts (Matthews, 1972, pp. 72–107). This situation has since altered, with a trend towards a higher proportion of the leadership being drawn from white-collar homes; yet the party elite continues to include a far higher proportion of people drawn from the lower classes than is typical in the West. Among members of the Politburo and secretaries of the Central Committee in 1985, only one came from a background of some privilege – the son of a senior official in a government ministry (Walker, 1986, p. 188).

In spite of the egalitarian ideology of the Soviet Union, top leadership in the CPSU carries privileges denied to most of the rest of the popula-tion. Party officials have access to international travel outside the Soviet bloc, and to special shops containing superior goods; they can jump food queues, obtain the best accommodation and may possess second homes in the countryside. Yet because there is no private ownership of industrial enterprise, opportunities for the accumulation of large fortunes are lacking. There is no propertied upper class in the Soviet Union which, by means of its wealth, can transmit material advantages across the generations. Although those in leading positions in the party have sometimes been regarded as a 'new class', it is more appropriate to see them as a distinctively privileged elite (Djilas, 1967; Gouldner, 1979).

There are persistent divisions of interest and viewpoint both within the top party officialdom and between party officials and leaders in other organizations. For example, there have often been tensions between managers of large industrial enterprises, who wish for greater autonomy, and party officials concerned with formulating economic policy. Although there are no formal pressure groups of the Western type in the Soviet Union, there are many different factions which can and do influence top policy-making, at least on certain issues (Skilling and Griffith, 1971; Barghoorn and Remington, 1986, chapter 8). Some observers have suggested that, in part precisely because of the extreme centralization of decision-making in the Soviet Union, interest groups can often make their opinions count very effectively. How far this is so depends in part upon the personality and position of the Soviet leader. In Stalin's time, such groups had little influence; under Brezhnev and Gorbachev, these non-party factions gained in power.

The Soviet Union is far from being a monolithic or unidimensional society. In terms of ethnic, regional and religious differences, it is at least as diverse as the United States. There is widespread political participation through the vehicle of the Communist Party, combined with a relative openness of recruitment to top positions. At the same time, political, economic and military power are tightly co-ordinated. In the Soviet political system there is almost no open, legal opposition, and central control over public information is more intensive than in any Western country. Although Mills coined the term 'power elite' to apply to the United States, it surely has its clearest reference to the Soviet Union.

Totalitarianism

The Soviet Union – and sometimes the East European societies as a whole, together with other Communist systems such as that of China – have often been labelled **totalitarian.** The term has also been used to characterize Fascist regimes, such as those of Germany and Italy during the Second World War. The word was in fact coined by a philosopher whose ideas became important in Italian **Fascism**, Giovanni Gentile, and was used in an approving way by the Italian dictator, Mussolini, to describe his own regime. Thereafter, the term acquired a pejorative sense (Schapiro, 1972). The notion has been commonly applied not only to Communist countries but to traditional states, and even to fictional societies like Plato's republic.

Carl Friedrich's definition of totalitarianism has probably been most influential. According to Friedrich (1954), totalitarianism involves four elements:

1 *A totalist ideology* – a set of political doctrines of an inclusive kind, to which everyone is expected to adhere (for example, the commitment to the 'fatherland' stressed by the Nazis).
2 *A single party* committed to this ideology and usually led by one individual, a dictator.
3 *A secret police*, seeking out and punishing those said to be enemies of the regime.
4 *Monopoly control* of economic organizations, the mass media and the military.

Is totalitarianism, thus defined, a useful way of referring to the Communist societies? Most scholars today are agreed that it is not (Hill and Frank, 1983; Holmes, 1986; Walker, 1986). The Soviet Union and the East European societies are more internally diverse than such a definition presumes, and their governments command at least a considerable measure of popular support. They are not ruled over by dictators, but by party bureaucrats.

Totalitarianism should rather be seen as a form of political regime of a more transitional sort, in which a dictator rises to power, promoting totalist ideologies with the use of mass terror. The periods of rule by Stalin in the Soviet Union, Hitler in Germany, or Pol Pot in Cambodia may be regarded as examples of totalitarian government. In these circumstances, Friedrich's four characteristics can be clearly identified. Each involved an extreme concentration of power in the hands of an individual, supported by an ideology to which no exceptions were permitted. All were, in addition, marked by great savagery and killing directly instigated by the state authorities. As Barghoorn writes:

> Totalitarianism describes not so much a type of political system as a historical situation in which a dictator integrates and mobilises a society beset by a crisis that threatens disintegration, barring emergency measures. If we identify totalitarianism with practices and perspectives implicit perhaps in Leninism but fully developed only by Stalin, then the Russia of today still has not fully recovered from the trauma of totalitarian rule. However, its dynamism and rigour have in large measure been supplanted by business-as-usual routines and rituals. (Barghoorn, 1986, p. 13)

Differences between East and West

What conclusions can we draw about the similarities and differences between the political systems of the West and the Soviet Union? In both cases there is a considerable concentration of power at the top. By any reckoning, this concentration is more pronounced in the Soviet Union than in the Western nations as a result of the dominance of the Communist Party. On the other hand, the USSR is a more pluralistic system than many Western observers allow. There are interest groups in the Soviet Union, although their scope for independent action is less than in Western countries; and there are divisions of interest between different sections of the elite.

Elite recruitment is notably more open in the Soviet Union than in the West, and there is a sense in which the level of political participation is higher, because of mass involvement in party activities. Yet since there are no competing parties, there is no way in which the public can directly influence the selection of political leaders. Leaders are chosen as a result of deliberations of top party officials. Whatever the limitations of Western liberal democracy, it allows the citizens at least some influences over who rules them, and how long they stay in power.

Summary

1 A *state* exists where there is a political apparatus, ruling over a given territory, whose authority is backed by a legal system and by the ability to use force to implement its policies.

2 *Government* refers to the regular enactment of policies, decisions and matters of state on the part of the officials within a political apparatus. *Politics* concerns the means whereby power is used to affect the scope and content of governmental activities. The sphere of the *political* may range well beyond that of state institutions themselves.

3 Modern states are *nation-states*, usually having some form of congressional or parliamentary system. The notion of *sovereignty* (the authority of a government over a clearly defined territorial order) suggests both the acknowledged legitimacy of the nation-state and the recognition of the state's borders by others. Each community acquires a distinct character through its association with *nationalism*.

4 Citizenship is associated with certain rights: civil, political and social. Where these have been established in some form a nation can be said to be democratic.

5 There are several major types of democratic system. *Representative multi-party democracy* involves the right to vote of the mass of the adult population, with a choice of party. *Representative one-party democracy* entails the right to vote of the mass of the adult population, with no choice of party. *Participatory democracy* allows decisions to be discussed and taken communally by those to whom they relate.

6 According to Weber and Schumpeter, the level of democratic participation which can be achieved in a modern, large-scale society is

limited. The rule of elites is inevitable, but multi-party systems provide the possibility of choosing *who* exercises power. The pluralist theorists add the claim that the competition of interest groups limits the degree to which ruling elites are able to concentrate power in few hands.

7   A *political party* is an organization oriented towards achieving legitimate control of government through an electoral process. In most Western states, the largest parties are those associated with general political interests – socialism, communism, liberalism or conservatism. There is usually some connection between voting patterns and class differences. In many Western countries there has recently been a decline in allegiance to traditional parties and a growing disenchantment with the party system in general.

8   Women achieved the right to vote much later than men in all countries, and continue to be poorly represented among political elites. They have been influential in certain areas, such as in achieving legal protection for victims of domestic violence.

9   Political activity is not confined to political parties. *Protest movements* and *pressure groups* can be very influential.

10   In Western societies there is a distinguishable upper class, holding a disproportionate share of the country's wealth, whose members have higher chances of achieving and retaining top positions in a variety of areas than have others from less privileged backgrounds.

11   The Soviet Union, and other East European societies, are more 'open' than Western countries in terms of the social backgrounds of top leaders. Yet Communist Party elites have many distinctive privileges compared to the rest of the population. They are also more powerful than Western elites in terms of their control over economic and political life.

12   *Totalitarianism* involves a totalist ideology, a single party led by a dictator, a secret police and monopoly control of major institutions. It is not a term that usefully describes Soviet-type societies, referring rather to the exceptional circumstances in which a dictator wields immense power.

Basic concepts

the state	politics
government	nation-state

Important terms

stateless society	liberal democracy
state society	representative one-party democracy
political apparatus	democratic centralism
force	participatory democracy
sovereignty	constitutional monarch

citizen	democratic elitism
nationalism	pluralist theories of democracy
civil rights	interest groups
political rights	political party
social rights	state overload
welfare state	legitimation crisis
democracy	power elite
representative multi-party	totalitarianism
democracy	Fascism

Further reading

Klaus von Beyme, *Political Parties in Western Democracies* (London: Gower, 1985) — a comparative study of political parties, with particular emphasis on their development and ideological changes.

Ronald J. Hill, *Governing Soviet Society* (Brighton: Wheatsheaf, 1987) — a recent study which analyses the political system of the USSR.

Alan James, *Sovereign Statehood* (London: Allen and Unwin, 1986) — an examination of the meanings, uses and contexts of the concept of sovereignty.

Adam Przeworski, *Capitalism and Social Democracy* (Cambridge: Cambridge University Press, 1985) — argues that the struggle for economic improvement and the ideal of socialist transformation are distinct historical phenomena.

Alan Ware (ed.), *Political Parties: Electoral Change and Structural Response* (Cambridge: Polity Press, 1987) — looks at how parties and voters interact; the relations between party elites and party membership; the financial arrangements of party organization and elections.

11

War and the Military

On 1 July 1916 the British and French armies launched an attack against German forces occupying an area close to the River Somme, in North-eastern France. The First World War had been in progress for some two years, and each side had prepared a complex array of trenches and fortifications. Neither army had made much progress in pushing back the other. The Allied plan at the Battle of the Somme was to launch an all-out offensive which would drive the Germans back decisively from the lines they occupied. The British army bore the brunt of the responsibility for the attack. After a massive artillery bombardment of the German encampments, thousands of men swept out of their trenches across 'no-man's land' towards the Germans.

Although many German soldiers died in the artillery bombardment, most of their defensive fortifications remained intact. As the attackers advanced, they were met by a pitiless stream of rifle and machine-gun fire. The larger German guns behind the lines also sent over a hail of explosive shells, jagged pieces of which sprayed across the battlefield wherever they landed. Small groups of British forces did manage to penetrate the German front line, and a few even pressed beyond, but behind them the enemy fire continued to dominate no-man's land, and only meagre numbers of other troops got through to reinforce them. By the end of the first day's fighting, the British had advanced only on one small sector of the front – and no more than a mile from their own trenches. As a result, 57,000 British troops, and 8,000 German troops, died.

The offensive was resumed on 3 July, and the attacks continued for over four months thereafter. Some got further through the German lines than before, but only with appalling casualties. By mid-November, when the campaign ended, the German front remained largely intact. Well over half a million Allied soldiers, and an equivalent number of Germans, were killed at the Battle of the Somme. No other military encounter in human history had involved so many soldiers on a single battlefield; and none had generated casualties even remotely approaching those suffered by both sides (Wilson, 1986).

Since the First World War, developments in the destructive strength of weaponry have continued apace. In the Second World War, and subsequent military engagements all over the world, horrific levels of casualties have been suffered by armed forces and civilians alike. The acceleration in the scale and intensity of war is as distinctive an aspect of modern societies as any other institutional changes since the emergence of industrialism. How and why has modern war developed to such a pitch? What impact have war and the military had on modern social development? How should we analyse war and military power in sociological terms? These are the problems we shall tackle in this chapter.

Warfare in the past

Ancient societies

In hunting and gathering societies, and smaller agrarian cultures, there were few if any specialized warriors. If skirmishes with rival groups occurred, some or all of the adult men who were not too old to fight would be called on. It is misleading to speak of 'war' among such peoples, as long battles were rarely, if ever, fought. Since everyone was routinely engaged in the day-to-day production of food, which usually could not be extensively stored, there were no bands of men free to engage in chronic fighting. Conflicts between small societies are fundamentally different from those involving large-scale ones. Such societies have no armies, little technology of war (for example, no metal shields, swords or pikes) and very little wish for the conquest or subjugation of other cultures (Otterbein, 1985).

The fighting of wars, which were often protracted and very bloody, is one of the most obvious features of the first development of states. The larger traditional states were empires, usually built by the military conquest and subordination of less powerful groups. The development of methods of working metal to produce armour and weapons was pioneered within these civilizations. In traditional states there were **standing armies**, that is to say, bodies of men who were full-time professional soldiers. In societies whose wealth and strength depended on the use of ships, there were also specialized warrior navies. Standing armies and navies were usually fairly small, often primarily providing protection for the sovereign or emperor's court and household. Larger armies were raised by conscripting peasants and by forming alliances with other military leaders.

The early civilizations mostly used armour and weaponry made from bronze, but the waging of war was not always co-ordinated with technological development, as has come to be the case now. Arms and armour took skilled craftsmen a long time to make, and once constructed, equipment was used for many years, and there were always very few armourers compared to the numbers of soldiers. When iron began to be smelted, somewhere around 1400 BC, metal weapons became much cheaper. A far higher proportion of the male population could acquire weaponry and, less frequently, armour, without themselves being full-time soldiers.

Before the sixteenth and seventeenth centuries, the Chinese and the Mongols were the most powerful civilizations in military terms. In military equipment, as in the arts and literary culture, the Chinese were far more developed than the societies of the West. Evidence relating to two Chinese government arsenals in the late eleventh century shows that they were producing 32,000 suits of armour every year, indicating a very extensive scale of military development (Needham, 1975, pp. 19–22). The Chinese pioneered the use of gunpowder and invented the first guns. Their ships also ranged far and wide. An edict of the Chinese Emperor in 1371, prohibiting foreign trade, put a stop to these voyages and the Chinese then withdrew to within their own territories. If the Emperor had not made this prohibition, the subsequent history of the world might have been completely different. Only slightly later the Europeans began to make the voyages of discovery which were to provide the basis for the expansion of Western power.

Warfare in Europe and its colonies

The economic development of Europe, coupled with changes in military organization and technology, have propelled Western states into a commanding global position; wars and battles have played a primary role in shaping the map of the world. Within Europe itself, military strength was a major factor influencing which states survived and which did not. In 1500 there were some 500 or more states in Europe; by 1900 the number had shrunk to 25 (Tilly, 1975). Wars have also served to forge national borders in Europe in the present century – for example, the division between West Germany and East Germany after the Second World War.

The success of European invasions into other parts of the world depended substantially on their superior military organization and weaponry. Cultures like those of the Indians of the Americas were only intermittently able to hold up the advance of white colonists into their territories, and it was warfare between the Europeans themselves which largely determined the distribution of social and political units in North and South America. While the Spanish and Portuguese divided up South and Central America between them, the shape of North American society was resolved by military encounters between the British and French, and the British and the American colonists. The victory of the British over the French settled the boundaries and ethnic character of Canada, with a French Canadian culture surviving only in the area around Quebec. The triumph of the American colonial settlers over their British government in the War of Independence made possible the survival and enlargement of the United States.

The industrialization of war

From the early eighteenth century onwards, the armed forces of the leading states became vastly larger than ever before – in some part a reflection, of course, of the fact that populations expanded. Very large standing armies came into being, swelled by systems of regular conscription. Just as important, the nature of army organization changed in basic ways (McNeill, 1983). Soldiers became subject to regular discipline and training; armies were bureaucratized like other organizations. The officer corps was increasingly professionalized. War also became directly fused with industry, the new industrial techniques making possible an immense acceleration in the destructive power of weaponry.

These processes are often referred to as the **industrialization of war**. By 1860, the Woolwich Arsenal in London, the main supplier of the British military, was able to produce a quarter of a million bullets a day and nearly as many completed cartridges (Ropp, 1959). While governments sponsored their own arsenals devoted to military production, industrialists also started producing weapons sold both nationally and internationally. The **arms trade** in its modern sense came into being during the second part of the nineteenth century. Large corporations, devoted either wholly or partly to the manufacture

Table 7 Nineteenth- and twentieth-century wars in which 100,000 or more people died

Nineteenth century			
Location	*Date*	*Identification of conflict*	*Deaths*
North America			
United States	1861–5	Civil war, Confederacy vs Union govt	650,000
Latin America			
Brazil	1864–70	Peru vs Brazil and Argentina	1,000,000
Colombia	1899–1903	Liberals vs Conservative govt	150,000
Cuba	1868–78	Cuba vs Spain	200,000
	1898	US vs Spain over Cuba and Philippines	200,000
Europe			
Germany	1870–1	France vs Germany/Prussia	250,000
Greece	1821–8	Greek revolt against Turkey	120,000
Turkey	1828–9	Russia vs Turkey	130,000
	1877–8	Russia vs Turkey	285,000
Russia	1853–6	Turkey vs Russia; UK, Fr., It., invading	267,000
Far East			
China	1860–4	Taiping rebellion; UK intervening	2,000,000
	1860–72	Muslim rebellions vs China	150,000
Indonesia	1873–8	Achinese vs Netherlands	200,000
Philippines	1899–1902	Philippine revolt against US	215,000
Total			5,817,000

Twentieth century			
Location	*Date*	*Identification of conflict*	*Deaths*
Latin America			
Bolivia	1932–5	Paraguay vs Bolivia	200,000
Colombia	1949–62	'La Violencia': civil war, Libs. vs Conserv. govt	300,000
Mexico	1910–20	Liberals and Radicals vs govt	250,000
Europe			
Greece	1945–9	Civil war; UK intervening	160,000
Poland	1919–20	USSR vs Poland	100,000
Spain	1936–9	Civil war; Italy, Portugal and Germany intervening	1,200,000
Turkey	1915	Armenians deported	1,000,000
Russia	1904–5	Japan vs Russia	130,000
	1918–20	Civil war; Allied intervention	1,300,000
Europe and other			
	1914–18	First World War	38,351,000
	1939–45	Second World War	19,617,000
Middle East			
Iraq	1961–70	Civil war, Kurds vs govt; massacre of Christians	105,000
	1982–8	Iran attack following Iraq invasion	600,000
Lebanon	1975–6	Civil war, Muslims vs Christians; Syria intervening	100,000
Yemen, AR	1962–9	Coup; civil war; Egypt intervening	101,000
South Asia			
Afghanistan	1978–86	Civil war, Muslims vs govt; USSR intervening	500,000

Table 7 continued

Location	Date	Identification of conflict	Deaths
Bangladesh	1971	Bengalis vs Pakistan; India invading; famine and massacres	1,500,000
India	1946–8	Muslims vs Hindus; UK intervening; massacres	800,000
Far East			
Cambodia	1970–5	Civil war, Khymer Rouge vs govt; NV, US intervening	156,000
	1975–8	Pol Pot govt vs people; famine and massacres	2,000,000
China	1928	Muslim rebellion vs govt	200,000
	1930–5	Civil war, Communists vs govt	500,000
	1937–41	Japan vs China	1,800,000
	1946–50	Civil war, Communists vs Kuomintang govt	1,000,000
	1950–1	Govt executes landlords	1,000,000
	1956–9	Tibetan revolt	100,000
Indonesia	1965–6	Abortive coup; massacres	500,000
	1975–80	Annexation of East Timor; famine and massacres	100,000
Korea	1950–3	Korean war; UN intervening	2,889,000
Vietnam	1945–54	War of independence from France	600,000
	1960–5	Civil war, Vietcong vs govt; US intervening	300,000
	1965–75	Peak of Indo-China War; US bombing	2,058,000
Africa			
Algeria	1954–62	Civil war, Muslims vs govt; France intervening	320,000
Burundi	1972	Hutu vs govt; massacres	100,000
Ethiopia	1974–86	Eritrean revolt and famine	545,000
Mozambique	1981–6	Famine worsened by civil war	100,000
Nigeria	1967–70	Civil war, Biafrans vs govt; famine and massacres	2,000,000
Rwanda	1956–65	Tutsis vs govt; massacres	108,000
Sudan	1963–72	Christians vs Arab govt; massacres	300,000
Tanzania	1905–7	Revolt against Germany; massacres	150,000
Uganda	1971–8	Civil war, Idi Amin coup; massacres	300,000
	1981–5	Army vs people; massacres	102,100
Zaire	1960–5	Katanga secession; UN, Belgium intervening	100,000
Total			83,642,000

Source: Ruth Leger Sivard, *World Military and Social Expenditures* (Washington DC: World Priorities, 1983), p. 26.

of armaments and placing considerable stress on technical innovation, have played a leading part in military development and war ever since.

Total war

The industrialization of war brought about a transition from **limited** to **total war** – epitomized by the Battle of the Somme. Before the twentieth century, even when large battles were fought, they involved very small parts of the population – soldiers directly involved with fighting (normally a small percentage of the adult males of a society), or people living in the areas fought over. The two world wars were not limited in this sense, because high proportions of the male population were involved in battle, and the waging of war came to depend upon the mobilization of the whole economies of the nations involved. The First World War, or 'Great War', was in many ways a watershed in military development. It fully justified its name; in terms of the numbers of countries involved, from Europe to Russia, Japan and the United States, there were no previous historical parallels. The numbers of combatants and non-combatants killed were much higher than in any previous episodes of armed conflict.

Never before had war been fought so unremittingly, with the soldiers so consistently under fire. Some features of the First World War remained largely confined to it, such as its immobile trench battles, but in many other respects it set the pattern for other twentieth-century wars. As the social historian Maurice Pearton observes, 'war had changed from being the concern of the army as an elite to being the business of society as a whole, and from the limited and rational application of force to unrestricted violence' (Pearton, 1984, p. 33).

During the Great War processes of scientific discovery were applied in a concerted way to develop new forms of weaponry. A good example was the development of the tank (first introduced in the Battle of the Somme). Tanks were originally the equivalents of armed and plated ships brought ashore and made manoeuvrable on land. They were commonly known as 'land cruisers' – or, more popularly, as 'motor-monsters', 'touring forts', or 'giant toads'. While the part they played in the First World War was limited, they have subsequently become basic to war on land. After the Great War, the research and development programmes of which tanks and other military machinery were part became a continuous process.

Three technological developments that now dominate military power were pioneered during the Second World War: the creation of nuclear weapons, the invention of rocket-propelled missiles and the use of radar tracking to organize offensive and defensive strategies. In the post-Second-World-War period, all three have come to be used together: missiles can be furnished with nuclear warheads and guided by electronic tracking equipment. Some of the most important technological innovations influencing civilian life over the past half-century had their origins in the Second World War or in weapons-related developments shortly afterwards. These include advances in jet travel, telecommunications and information technology (Milward, 1984).

In terms of numbers of lives lost, the twentieth century is easily the most war-ridden in human history. During the century so far, more than a hundred million human beings have been killed in war, an average of 3,500 a day. The majority of these people were killed in the two world wars, but wars have been carried on more or less continuously, somewhere across the face of the globe, throughout the century.

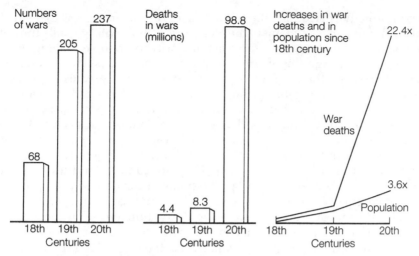

Figure 11   Three centuries of war: numbers of wars and war-deaths 1700–1986. The figures are for wars with estimated annual death tolls of 1,000 or more
Source: Ruth Leger Sivard, *World Military and Social Expenditures* (Washington DC: World Priorities, 1983), p. 26.

War and aggression

Why do wars happen? It might seem as though the tendency of human beings to engage in warfare rests on innate inclinations towards aggression. Perhaps we are just inherently aggressive, and this finds an outlet in the destructiveness of war? Such a view does not in fact stand up to examination. War has little to do with the expression of aggressive impulses, although the battlefield may provide some people with the chance to express murderous feelings they would otherwise keep concealed. Aggression is a feature of many aspects of human activity, but it leads very few of us to murder anyone. The vast majority of those who have killed others have done so in war-time; some of us no doubt know, or have met, such people. But we do not usually fear them, because we recognize that their actions in war are quite different from the personal aggression that individuals can feel in ordinary life.

All armies involve drill training and the learning of discipline. Training develops physical fitness and the group solidarity important for success in battle, but it also helps alter people's usual attitudes towards indiscriminately shedding blood. Gwynne Dyer, who has made a systematic study of war and aggressiveness, comments as follows:

> The business of armies, at the end, is killing, and so a crucial part of training people to be soldiers is teaching them to ignore the limits

they normally place on the actual use of violence, so that in the right circumstances against the 'enemy', they will go all the way and actually kill him. For the vast majority of people, killing has to be taught – though there are exceptions. There is such a thing as a 'natural soldier': the kind of man who derives his greatest satisfaction from male companionship, from excitement, and from the conquering of physical and psychological obstacles. He doesn't necessarily want to kill people as such, but he will have no objections if it occurs within a moral framework which gives him a justification – like war – and if it is the price of gaining admission to the kind of environment he craves. . . . But armies are not full of such men. They are so rare that they form only a modest fraction even of small professional armies, mostly congregating in the commando-type paid forces. In large conscript armies they virtually disappear beneath the weight of numbers of more ordinary men. And it is those ordinary men, who do not like combat at all, that the armies must persuade to kill. (Dyer, 1985, pp. 117–18)

A US army colonel, Colonel S. L. A. Marshall, carried out a large number of interviews with men in some four hundred infantry companies during the Second World War, to investigate their reactions to battle. The results greatly surprised him. He found that on average only 15 per cent of troops fired their guns at all in battle, even when their positions were directly under attack and their lives in danger. The findings were as startling to the infantrymen as to their officers, because each had believed himself to be alone in defecting from his duty. They fired their weapons when others were present, especially officers, but not when more isolated. Their unwillingness to fire had nothing to do with fear, but reflected a disinclination to kill when there was 'no need' (Marshall, 1947).

The fighting of war, then, does not derive directly from human aggression. The origins of war, and the frequency with which wars have been fought, must be traced to other factors. The most important influence is the rise of state-based societies – from traditional states to the nation-states of today. As was mentioned earlier in the chapter, among hunting and gathering peoples war did not exist in any recognizable sense. The armed conflicts they staged were exciting and dangerous rituals, more like sport than war, in which bloodshed was minimized rather than deliberately sought. With the development of larger societies, having centralized forms of government, things changed. Armies were established and military discipline introduced. From that time onwards, hundreds or thousands of men operating in tight formations met on the fields of battle.

War, simply, is an ever-present possibility in a world in which states possess the means of wielding military violence. Although the events precipitating an outbreak of war are very varied, warfare is what happens when states clash and their disagreements cannot be handled successfully through negotiation, treaty or diplomacy. A government may go to war because of desire to acquire some or all of the territory of another, because of a struggle over resources (such as control of a major sea-route), or as a result of ideological or religious clashes. There is no single 'cause' of war. It is the ultimate test of power in the international arena. The most famous theorist of war, the nineteenth-century German thinker Karl von Clausewitz, put the point precisely when he declared in a celebrated statement, 'War is not merely a political act, but also a real political instrument, a continuation of political commerce, a carrying out of the same by other means' (von Clausewitz, 1908, p. 85).

Patterns of military organization

The word *discipline* originally meant a process of learning. It is sometimes still used in this way, as when we speak of sociology or other academic subjects as 'disciplines'. During the seventeenth century, however, it came to refer to military training and the controlled behaviour it produces. First of all in the Dutch armies, and then rapidly spreading throughout Europe, standardized forms of military organization were developed. Maurice, Prince of Orange (1567–1625), set up the first military academy in Europe; his doctrines later became standard practice throughout the continent. The modern sense of *uniform* as well as that of *discipline* can be traced to his teachings.

Uniform was originally only an adjective, but became a noun as the wearing of standard clothes came to be the norm in armies. Previously troops had often dressed more or less as they pleased. During the seventeenth century, the wearing of uniforms became firmly established among all ranks. Maurice also developed regularized marching, keeping men in step. He set up chains of command extending from generals to the enlisted men, and armies provided a model for the development of bureaucracy in the civil service and other organizations (de Feld, 1977). From this period onwards, large standing armies, in which professional careers could be made, became a major feature of modern societies.

Until the early nineteenth century, officers were usually either aristocrats or mercenaries. For the first of these groups war was still something of a hobby, while for the second it was an activity pursued for profit; mercenary officers would be at the call of whatever commander cared to pay them. Prussian military reforms in the early nineteenth century initiated moves towards the professionalizing of the officer corps. Policies of open recruitment, written examinations and systematic criteria of promotion were established, although originally in a somewhat haphazard way. By 1900 all the major European countries, as well as the United States and Russia, had set up training schools using bureaucratic modes of recruitment and advancement. The regular soldiery came to consist of men recruited for particular periods of time in regular service. They were augmented in times of war or potential war by conscripts; governments started to introduce large-scale conscription as the scale of war increased. The practice had its origins in France; in 1813 Napoleon was able to call up an army of one million, three hundred thousand men (Challener, 1965; Finer, 1975).

Universal conscription, involving a period of national service undertaken by all young males, was a significant development. It was an explicit recognition that everyone should be involved in wars waged for national objectives. The need for conscription in the early twentieth century was one influence which helped promote universal voting rights for males. Except in the United States, in most Western countries these rights were only established in the current century.

Modern armies are bureaucracies, staffed at officer level by full-time officials. The terms *officer* and *official* have a common origin, referring to the office or position which individuals occupy in a hierarchy. In armies some bureaucratic elements tend to be especially prominent. For example, divisions of rank are often the same throughout all branches of the military organization, no matter how large it is or how far-flung its personnel. In other respects the armed forces are quite distinctive, compared to most modern organizations. Entry into the military is not voluntary, where conscription or *national service* exists. Anyone who attempts to leave before their period of service is ended, whether they are national service conscripts or soldiers on longer contracts, is subject to military trial and imprisonment. The army is a *carceral organization* in which most members spend their waking and sleeping hours. Even those military personnel who do not live in barracks tend to reside in housing set aside for them, physically separate from the civilian population. (See chapter 9: 'Groups and Organizations'.)

Characteristics of the modern military

According to Samuel Huntington, the modern military has four basic characteristics.

1 Expertise in the **management of violence**. Military technology has become highly complex and possesses immense destructive capabilities. The military specializes in the control and use of this weaponry. In pre-modern armies, the contrast between weapons used in the military and that available to the civilian population was not large. Swords, bows and shields were owned by many who were not themselves professional soldiers, although they might be sometimes pressed into the service of a monarch or lord. Today, the armaments possessed by the military are vastly more powerful than those available to civilian populations – especially, of course, where nuclear weapons are involved.

2 **Clientship**. With the exception of guerrilla and revolutionary movements, the armed forces in modern times are responsible to their

major 'client', the government of the state of which they are part. In some pre-industrial cultures, a military leader could quite often 'opt out' of a political organization or alliance to which he and his armies were connected. He could move off elsewhere, subjugate the indigenous population and set up a new administrative regime. This is no longer possible in the modern world, in which the military depend on finance provided by the state through taxation and on arms manufactured in industrial production.

3 **Corporateness**. The armed forces, especially on the officer levels, tend to have a strong sense of corporate identity, separating them from civilians. The military often have their own schools, associations, publications and customs. Those who reach high ranks in the armed forces have to start at the lowest officer grades and progress within the organization. Unlike, say, in business firms, there are no opportunities for moving into higher management or obtaining directorships from a background in other firms or other careers. Since members of the armed forces tend to live and work separately from the rest of society, their contacts and informal friendships tend to be all within the military sphere.

4 The ideology of the **military mind**. Pre-modern warfare tended to emphasize warrior values, in which battle was glorified for its own sake. These values have become redundant, or at least greatly reduced in their influence, in the military today. The modern 'military mind' emphasizes attitudes of co-operation, the subordination of individual motives to group demands, and the primacy of order and discipline.

Paradoxical though it might appear, military leaders in the developed world are usually not keen to engage in war and may oppose politicians more belligerent than themselves. The outlook of the military is based on a desire to maintain its organizational strength and level of technological advancement. As Huntington puts it,

> the military man rarely favours war. He will always argue that the danger of war requires increased armaments; he will seldom argue that increased armaments make war practical or desirable. He always favours preparedness, but he never feels prepared. Accordingly, the professional military man contributes a cautious, conservative, restraining voice to the formulation of state policy. This has been his typical role in most modern states including fascist Germany, Communist Russia and democratic America. (Huntington, 1981, p. 69)

The military in Britain

The development of the British military over the past several centuries has been affected by two major factors: the geographical situation of the country as an island, relatively immune from the large troop-movements which have governed continental warfare; and its position as the centre of an empire which at its height was the largest the world had ever seen. British military strength was long based as much on its naval power as on land-based forces; and a good proportion of its fighting strength, from the eighteenth century onwards, was on duty abroad.

Before the Second World War

The seventeenth-century English Parliament resisted the formation of a standing army, and refused to vote the taxes necessary to support one. In the English Civil War, both sides had to raise armies more or less from scratch. The first true standing army in England was that developed by Cromwell. It was both well paid and well disciplined, but after the Restoration, Cromwell's army was largely disbanded. English armies, of course, played a key role in the 'internal colonial expansion' which created modern Britain through the uniting of Scotland, Wales, England and Ireland into a 'United Kingdom'. The activities of Cromwell in Ireland, together with the importation of Protestant settlers into the country, created divisions there which continue actively to smoulder today – British troops still being involved in regular action in the North.

Britain's overseas involvements necessitated the maintenance of a strong navy, which rarely met with the hostility felt (by all classes) to the presence of a large standing army. Distrust of standing armies was reinforced by the fact that, from the defeat of Napoleon up to the outbreak of the First World War a century later, Britain was not seriously menaced by the threat of external military invasion. However, British armed forces were more or less continuously involved in wars or skirmishes in the colonial domains during this period. Thus some of the most distinctive traditions developed in the British military derived from practices established in the acquisition or control of territories abroad. The size of Britain's army in the nineteenth and twentieth centuries lagged well behind the level of growth in the population as a whole. The home army was in large degree a recruiting and training force for units abroad (Ropp, 1959, chapter 5). Parliament continued to see a standing army as a necessary evil, leaving it mainly in the hands of the country gentry (the recruitment source for the officer corps) and rural workers (the source of the rank and file). Until the 1870s, officers still bought their commissions, and normally spent two-thirds of their army careers in colonial service.

The result was that although Britain had a leading place in industrial development, its military leaders resisted the introduction of mechanization. The British were among the last to adopt new methods of industrialized war. (Aron, 1954). No trained reserve, of the sort adopted by continental countries well before the end of the nineteenth century, existed in Britain. The 'Blue Water' doctrine developed by British military strategists held that, if the strength of the navy was maintained, British armies would never again have to fight on mainland Europe. By the turn of the century, only Britain and the United States among major powers had not adopted a system of mass conscription or national service.

British participation in the First World War forced a re-examination of most of these attitudes. The British army and navy became equipped with modern weaponry, generated by a massive war effort involving the creation of a 'war economy' during 1914–18. Yet at the very same time, British military power began to be decisively outstripped by that of others. The British navy, the supreme force at sea for well over a century, was overtaken by that of the United States. The rebuilding of German military strength in the 1930s, the general development of the United States' military power, plus the growing might of the Soviet Union and of Japan, left Britain trailing.

The post-Second-World-War period

Since 1945, the end of the Second World War, the status of Britain as a second-rank military power has become more and more evident, especially given the 'superpower' dominance of the United States and the Soviet Union. Britain is no longer at the centre of a global empire, but a medium-sized power among numerous others. British armed forces have been involved in several conflicts in colonial domains (now all decolonized) since 1945 – such as in Malaya, Kenya and Cyprus. They have also taken part in several sporadic military engagements, such as those at Suez in the 1950s and more recently in the Falklands. Yet the post-war period is basically one of the progressive contraction of British military power, in conjunction with the process of decolonization.

British post-war policy has moved away from compulsory military service (still in force in many other countries), placing reliance on a relatively small military establishment, coupled with the possession of nuclear weapons. A White Paper of 1957 set out what it referred to as 'the biggest change in military policy ever made in normal times'. The armed forces were cut by half at the same time as national service was abolished; plans were instituted to equip all three services with nuclear weapons.

Britain had in fact been the first country to try to build an atomic bomb. The work was transferred to the USA during the war, on the grounds that it would be less vulnerable to attack there and because of the greater resources the Americans could muster for the project. As early as 1945, a committee chaired by Sir Henry Tizard concluded that possession of atomic weapons would need to be the basis of future British defence policy (Rumble, 1985, chapter 4). A programme to make atomic weapons in Britain was initiated in 1947; work was begun on the manufacture of hydrogen bombs in 1952. Although a rocket-based delivery system – the 'Blue Streak' – was promised in the mid-1950s, it never became effective. Bombers remained the only operational means of delivering nuclear weapons until the Polaris system (currently scheduled to be replaced by another American system, Trident, in the 1990s) was purchased from the United States, and brought into service in 1967–9.

One of the most significant influences affecting Britain's military involvements over the past several decades has been a series of agreements permitting the USA to deploy nuclear forces in the country. This policy was initiated in 1958, when the then Prime Minister, Harold Macmillan, agreed to the stationing of sixty American Thor missiles in Britain. An American Polaris base was set up at Holy Loch some two years later. Today, a multiplicity of American military establishments exists in Britain. According to Duncan Campbell, there are more than a hundred American military bases in the country (Campbell, 1982).

The presence of nuclear weapons in Britain has from the first provoked widespread public protest, although opinion polls consistently show that a majority of the population supports the 'British nuclear deterrent'. The Campaign for Nuclear Disarmament (CND) has been, since the 1950s, the main organization actively campaigning against nuclear weapons. Its public presence, and the support it is able to command for mass demonstrations and marches, has waxed and waned over the years. The development of Cruise and Pershing II missiles served to promote a resurgence of support for CND in Britain in the late 1970s, as well as for other peace movements in Europe. From about 3,200 in 1978, membership of CND rose to more than 100,000 in 1984, with some 140,000 further people belonging to affiliated organizations.

Women and war

War has always been pre-eminently a male activity. Men have everywhere staffed the fighting forces of armies, and have been the commanders and generals; warrior values, emphasizing adventure, daring and 'esprit de corps' (the sense of involvement with people other than the family in the pursuit of shared ends) have always been mainly associated with men rather than women. The enthusiasm of men for war, and the absence of women from the ranks of the warriors, has led some to speculate that genetic factors must be responsible. In other words, men are biologically disposed to engage in aggressive behaviour – fighting against others – while women are not. Authors who have held such a view include writers influenced by sociobiology (see chapter 2: 'Culture and Society'), as well as some feminists. An early feminist writer, Elizabeth Cady Stanton, expressed this idea forcefully when she wrote in 1868:

> The male element is a destructive force, stern, selfish, aggrandising, loving war, conquest, acquisition, breeding in the material and moral world alike discord, disorder, disease and death. See what a record of

blood and cruelty the pages of history reveal! . . . The male element has held high carnival thus far, it has fairly run riot from the beginning, overpowering the feminine element everywhere, crushing out the diviner qualities in human nature. (Stanton, Anthony and Gage, 1889, p. 145)

Perhaps we might hope, Stanton went on to add, that in the future the female values of gentleness, caring and sympathy will be brought more to the fore in society, balancing the aggressive impulses of men. The female values are held by one half of humankind, but because of the dominance of men in public activities, they have never had much influence.

How valid is the view that men are constitutionally predisposed towards war, whereas women are not? On the whole, the evidence is against this thesis. As was discussed earlier, the fighting of wars cannot be directly connected with aggressive impulses. Warfare (in the sense of violent and bloody battles, in which many are killed) barely existed before the emergence of traditional states, and states fight wars for reasons not directly connected with aggressiveness as such.

Moreover, women have sometimes been combatants in times of war, and as non-combatants have frequently supported war aims. Although the vast majority of commanders have been men, there are historical cases of women military leaders who have actively led soldiers on the battlefield. Two of the best-known examples are Boadicea, the Saxon warrior monarch, and Joan of Arc, who led French forces against the English in the fifteenth century. Female monarchs (like Queen Elizabeth I of England) have assumed overall control over their country's fighting forces, and have not hesitated to proclaim militaristic values (Elshtain, 1987).

Women's regiments have been formed in most modern armies, although the majority of these do not participate in actual combat. In some armies, women recruits are not instructed in the handling of weapons or in techniques of fighting, but in most they are. Israeli women soldiers have formed part of fighting units, and during the Second World War Soviet women were regularly engaged in combat. Some 8 per cent of militarily active Soviet personnel in 1943, the time of peak strength of the Soviet armed forces during the war, were women. They served as machine-gunners and snipers, and in the artillery and tank corps (Cottam, 1980). A Soviet bomber-pilot, Nadya Popova, wrote of her wartime experiences in a way which closely parallels countless male observations of war: 'They were destroying us and we were destroying them . . . I killed many men, but I stayed alive . . . War requires the ability to kill, among other skills. But I don't think you should equate killing with cruelty. I think the risks we took and the sacrifices we made for each other made us kinder rather than cruel' (quoted in Saywell, 1985, p. 38).

Women today form a larger percentage of the armed forces in most Western countries than ever before. The United States has the highest proportion of women military personnel (10 per cent). These soldiers are not posted to areas away from possible combat zones, but are evenly distributed across the various 'hot spots' of the world (like parts of West Germany, which border on Eastern Europe). Among the more militant, there is strong pressure to lift the regulations which prevent them being in combat units. The majority of women in the American armed forces, surveys show, are strongly in favour of such a move. It is worth noting, too, that many modern terrorist groups include active female members, whose roles do not differ from those of the men.

Non-combatant women have not infrequently protested against the barbarism of war, but just as commonly have supported and praised military values. Women have cared for the wounded and dying, 'kept the home fires burning', have staged celebrations when soldiers went off to war and when they returned. During the two world wars, women contributed to the war effort of most countries in a crucial way by entering the paid labour-force in large numbers. In the world wars, particularly the first, women played a major role in pacifist organizations; but the majority of organizations in which women were prominently involved were dedicated to victory. Emmeline Pankhurst, one of the leaders of the women's movement in Britain in the early 1900s, declared her support for the Allied war aims near the beginning of the First World War. The magazine she ran, the *Suffragette*, was in fact reoriented to war propaganda, and renamed *Britannia* in 1915 (Wiltsher, 1985). In the United States, the National American Woman Suffrage Association proclaimed women's loyalty to the war effort, and promised its dedication to the virtues of patriotism and duty.

If most women have normally supported war-making activities, there have been many men by contrast who have rejected war and military values. Some of the most notable male religious leaders in history, such as Buddha or Jesus, have condemned military violence (their followers, of course, have by no means always conformed to their teachings). Mahatma Gandhi, the Indian political activist who led the opposition to British colonial rule in India, was a celebrated twentieth-century advocate of non-violence. Although many men who held **pacifist** views before the two world wars found themselves drawn into the conflict, a minority refused to take part in any military activities. They did so in the face of great pressure from government authorities, and hostility from much of the rest of the population. During the Second World War, it was possible for men to register as conscientious objectors (people who refuse to participate in war activities for religious or moral reasons). One conscientious objector in the USA described a typical experience when travelling across the country by train to reach a work camp in which he had been placed. A group of marine recruits were on the same train, and when the men got off the train, women who were waiting to hand out food and magazines initially thought they were all soldiers: 'We'd spill out of the cars onto the railroad tracks, and the ladies didn't know who the hell was which, so we ended up with a lot of these goodies. When word got round that there was some yellowbellies (conscientious objectors) on this train, the ladies would actually go around and yank us by the arm and say, "Are you one of those damn yellowbellies? I want my cookies back" ' (Terkel, 1984, p. 165).

Modern feminist authors have quite frequently expressed views on gender and war similar to those which Stanton proposed well over a century ago. In her work, *The Second Stage*, for example, Betty Friedan argues that women soldiers have a more compassionate outlook than their male counterparts, and that this could help diminish likely brutalities in any future armed conflicts (Friedan, 1981). But such a view does not really seem convincing. As Elshtain has said, after surveying the attitudes of women soldiers: 'Women soldiers do not speak that way. They are soldiers. Period' (Elshtain, 1987, p. 243).

If warfare – or at least active participation in combat – has been an overwhelmingly male preserve in the past, then, this probably has little to do with any biologically given differences which make one sex more gentle than the other. Men have monopolized war as they have the other institutions in which power is concentrated. Participation in war involves long periods of military training and discipline, and demands that the soldier be able to go wherever military duties require. Wars have been mostly fought by young men, at the ages which roughly equate to the main childbearing years for women. Women's confinement to the domestic sphere has separated them decisively, in most previous periods of history, from the role of warrior.

Women's campaigns against war

Although these differences are probably not genetically given – and are far from universal – women have often held differing attitudes towards war from those of most men. Ancient Greek dramas contain episodes in which women try to dissuade husbands and sons from going off to fight, or protest about the futility of warfare. From the early origins of modern feminism, in the late eighteenth century, sections of the women's movement have consistently maintained a pacifist stance. As in the case of men, women's pacifist groups have normally represented the views of only a minority of their sex; but such groups have had a significant part to play in the struggles which women's associations have carried on against a male-dominated society.

Women's pacifist organizations were particularly active during the First World War. Before the war, women had played a substantial part in the international peace movements which gained momentum in the early years of the twentieth century. While many women later followed Emmeline Pankhurst and other feminist leaders in changing their views to support the war effort, others vigorously defended an anti-war stance. In the United States, which didn't enter the war until 1917, women opposing the war were not subjected to harassment by government authorities, as happened in Europe. In August 1914, 15,000 women participated in a peace parade in New York, rejecting offers of co-operation from males holding similar views (Steinson, 1980). A Women's Peace Party (WPP), formed in the same year, drew widespread support (although a counter-organization, the Woman's Section of the Navy League, argued for a build-up of American military strength). Without female participation, there would have been very little agitation in favour of peace in the USA during the First World War.

Two European feminist pacifists, Rosika Schwimmer and Emmeline Pethik-Lawrence, organized an international women's peace conference at The Hague, in Holland, in 1915, in conjunction with the WPP. Delegates came from several countries, in spite of the efforts of some of their governments to dissuade or prevent them from attending. The conference was the first international meeting to press for peace, or to outline what the principles of a peace settlement might be between the warring nations. The women had to face a great deal of ridicule and adverse publicity. The London *Evening Standard* carried a typical comment. 'Women peace fanatics', it proclaimed, 'are becoming a nuisance and a bore' (quoted in Wiltsher, 1985, p. 99), yet the long-term influence of the conference was considerable. President Wilson of the United States was the only leading Western leader to display public sympathy for the women's objectives, and his 'Fourteen Points', which he offered as the basis of the peace settlement in 1919, reflected several of the ideas put forward by the women.

Feminist pacifist organizations played a lesser role (like their male counterparts) during the Second World War – there was general agreement that Nazism was such a menace that military violence was necessary to stop it. But in the post-war period, particularly since nuclear weapons have become widespread, women's groups have again become prominent in peace movements. Female pacifist groups have developed in most Western countries – such as Women's Action for Nuclear Disarmament in the USA or Women for Peace in West Germany and the Netherlands. Counterparts exist in some Eastern European countries, but have been greatly harassed by the authorities.

Perhaps the most notable example of women's involvement in peace issues was the camp set up at Greenham Common, in Britain. Greenham Common is the site of a military base at which nuclear missiles were located. Women established a 'peace camp' near the perimeter of the base in 1981 which continued for several years. Men were not allowed to join. The camp members concentrated on publicizing their resistance to the existence of nuclear weapons, but also often blockaded the road out of the base to try to prevent nuclear convoys from entering or leaving. As one participant remarked: 'The peace camps are more than just a brave gesture of defiance. It's an experiment in non-violent resistance, the taking of responsibility by ordinary people, not just for what's being done in our name, but for how we behave towards each other . . . In the past, men have left home to go to war. Now women are leaving home for peace' (Cook and Kirk, 1983, pp. 29–30).

The military, politics and society

Military rule and influence

In many countries throughout the world the leaders of the armed forces are, or have been at some recent period, the rulers. Military take-overs in the present century have happened in most South American countries, and in many Third World states in Africa, the Middle East and Asia. In one guise or another, military rule is 'normal' in some parts of the world, and over the past fifty years has become more rather than less common. Two types of society have been relatively immune from military rule: the industrialized, liberal democratic societies of the West and the East European societies, including the Soviet Union. Why should this be so? Why aren't all societies ruled by the military, given that they are far more tightly organized than any civilian groups, and have a monopoly over the most powerful weapons?

There are several reasons. First, the higher the level of a society's industrialization, the more complicated its administrative system needs to be. Depending as they do on their own internal codes of discipline and duty, the armed forces are not equipped to undertake the task of administering a complex social order. Specialist civilian administrators are necessary to govern such systems, as can be seen from the experiences of the Allied military governments of occupation in Germany and Italy following the Second World War. Although faced with defeated and compliant populations, rather than rebellious ones, the occupying powers found it necessary to reinforce their military personnel with large numbers of specialized civilian officials.

Second, the military lacks the **legitimacy** – the morally accepted right – to rule. Government by force can only be transitory. To sustain continuing political power, a group must be widely recognized as having the right to govern. In societies with established traditions of civilian rule, this is very difficult for the military to achieve. Whether in multi-party systems, as in the West, or single-party systems as in Eastern Europe, there are well-developed party organizations geared to mechanisms of government.

Third, in societies without histories of military government, there is normally a clear separation between the military and the police force, developed over a period of time. During the development of modern Western police forces, in the early to middle nineteenth century, the military were often called in to quell civil disturbances. The more civil order is maintained by the police, however, the more well-defined is the role of the armed forces as concerned with *external* threat. The police may be armed, and have their own paramilitary anti-riot squads, but the fire-power available to the police is vastly less than that of the armed forces, and the police could not stage a *coup d'état* (seizure of government) as the military could (Finer, 1962). Where civil order is maintained by a clearly defined police force, with the armed forces concerned only with 'defence', the chances of a military takeover of government are minimized.

It does not follow from these observations that military governments could never come into being in the industrialized countries, or that there is a clear line of division between the developed world and the Third World in terms of military rules. Some First and Second World countries have experienced periods of rule by the armed forces – including Spain, Portugal, Greece and Poland.

Even in societies in which they do not rule, the military are an important influence on political life. This is virtually guaranteed by the fact that the modern armed forces depend on tax revenue, channelled through the government. The sway that the military seek to achieve over political decisions varies considerably within modern societies. Military leaders can use various means to try to affect, or control, political and economic policies. At one end of the spectrum, they might confine themselves to employing 'usual' channels in influencing politicians and business leaders. That is to say, they form a lobby or pressure group like any other, not straying outside conventional processes of political bargaining. At the other end of the spectrum, they may blackmail or intimidate civilian authorities by the threat or actual use of violence. Thus in Japan, in the 1930s, the army was implicated in the murders of prominent politicians and trade union leaders, carrying on a campaign of threats against others. The French armed forces in Algeria blackmailed the government by refusing to co-operate with any of its policies unless General de Gaulle was brought to power.

The military–industrial complex

In those states in which the direct role of the military in politics is fairly confined, a close meshing of military and industrial interests may still develop. Some observers believe this has come to be the case increasingly in industrialized societies which have large military establishments. President Eisenhower used the term **military–industrial complex** to describe the close integration of military and economic development in the context of modern war. He originally coined the phrase in an attempt to promote the systematic application of science and technology to military production. Later, however, he came to see the development of such connections as threatening, fearing that the military–industrial complex had achieved such power that major decisions affecting social and economic life were taken out of the political domain. Many subsequent observers have argued that, as a result of the Cold War (the hostility between the USA and USSR which led to a build-up of arms on both sides in the 1950s and 1960s), the military–industrial complex has become especially prominent in the United States and the Soviet Union.

How valid is this view? Unfortunately, the idea of the military–industrial complex has often been used in a vague way, and the extent of its power over decision-making hinted at rather than directly specified. If such a system is said to *dominate* a modern economy, however, two conditions are implied: (1) that large areas of economic activity are dependent on military production for their prosperity; (2) that in consequence of this, those in government positions find themselves compelled to acquiesce to the industrial demands of military leaders and armaments manufacturers.

In some Western countries defence contractors are giant corporations. About three-quarters of firms having the biggest military contracts with the government in the United States are among the largest 500 American corporations (Kennedy, 1983, p. 156). There are many documented ties between military leaders and the top executives within these corporations. In the Soviet Union, as has been mentioned, arms-related industries outstrip all others in terms of their level of technological advancement. Industries concerned with military needs account for a higher proportion of Soviet economic activity as a whole than in most Western countries. Yet it does not follow that in either economy the main productive organizations are primarily dependent upon military-related activities for their prosperity. Few of the largest American corporations are engaged in military production. Those whose scale of business does depend on military contracts tend to move in and out of this production area according to shifts in the political and economic climate (Lieberson, 1972).

During the Vietnam War, the largest twenty-five military contractors in the United States derived some 40 per cent of their business from defence production. Fifteen years after the end of the war, this had slumped to under 10 per cent (Gansler, 1980). The level of involvement in military production, in other words, tends to respond to political needs and pressures, rather than the other way around. Much the same is true in the Soviet Union. It is the Communist Party leaders who retain the final say in questions of military expenditure.

We can conclude that there is not a military–industrial complex manipulating civilian policies in either of these societies. None the less, production of military-related goods and services is a major part of the economy of both, and expenditure on these is a matter of prime political concern. Hence, military leaders and manufacturers, sometimes acting as combined pressure groups, are often able to wield considerable direct and indirect influence over political policies. Much the same can be said for the other industrialized countries, although there are some (such as Canada) where the influence of the military is particularly weak.

Armed force in the Third World

Why should there be so many *coups d'état*, and military governments, in developing countries? To reach an answer, we have to understand the distinctive nature of these societies. Many have only a low degree of administrative unity. They are the legacy of colonial regimes, or are 'new nations' established in areas in which there was previously little or no centralized government. Colonial regimes did not encourage ideals of democratic participation, and when they ended there was often little basis for feelings of national unity. In countries in which there are multiple ethnic, tribal and regional loyalties, and where most of the population may have little knowledge of or interest in mechanisms of central government, party systems are highly unstable. Specific interest groups are much more important, and in these circumstances, as an internally coherent group with its own interests, the military frequently steps directly into the political arena. In many such countries the distinction between the military and the police is ambiguous, the two often being connected through military intelligence units used to maintain compliance among the civilian population (Janowitz, 1977). A separate system of internal policing, similar to those of the industrialized countries, has not been effectively developed.

In most Third World countries in which the armed forces are a major presence, **military rule** is relatively indirect. The military leaders place puppet politicians in power, whose activities they control. Should the politicians deviate from approved policies, a *coup d'état* will be staged. The military leaders temporarily assume power before handing over to another puppet regime.

Types of military rule

Where the armed forces try to maintain direct governmental power, they are always compelled to develop some basis of legitimacy among at least substantial sections of the population. Amos Perlmutter distinguishes three main types of military rule (Perlmutter, 1977). In the **autocratic** type, there is a simple military tyranny, the military rule of one individual. In this situation, a military leader uses control of the armed forces to achieve and maintain power. The leader normally, however, attempts to secure a large measure of popular support and may assume a presidential post. Little or no attempt is made to hold even nominal elections, but the ruler's position only becomes relatively secure if some measure of real popular support is generated by the policies followed. An example would be the rule of Idi Amin in Uganda some years ago. This type of military government is unstable, because too much diffuse power is vested in one individual, and support among the general population is either largely lacking or volatile. A revolt against such a ruler may succeed if a section of the armed forces support it.

A second type is **oligarchic military rule**. In this system, a *cabal* or *junta* (council) of military leaders governs the country. The chief executive in the oligarchy might either be a military figure or a civilian whose support comes exclusively from the armed forces. In order to promote its stability, this type of ruling group usually seeks to create a façade of electoral support – in fact, however, controlling the results of whatever voting processes are followed. Numerous recent governments in South American countries fall into this category including, for instance, the military regime in power in Argentina until 1985.

The third type is **authoritarian praetorianism**. Here there is a fusion between military and civilian government. The country is ruled by a coalition of military and civilian leaders. Elections take place, but the range of choice is limited to a party or parties approved of by the ruling group. A case in point is the government which was in power in Pakistan in 1987, led by General Zia.

On the whole, military governments are as unstable as the civilian ones they irregularly replace. There are not many societies with a consistent history of stable military government; rather, the picture is usually one of periods of direct military rule followed by phases of civilian power. Most military governments are conservative in orientation, often being linked to the interests of major landowners and industrialists. On the other hand, there are some examples of military governments espousing socialist or radical causes. An example is the government of Colonel Gadhafi in Libya.

Terrorism and guerrilla movements

As compared to traditional social orders, modern societies are highly *pacified* – internally peaceful. Of course, much criminal, domestic and other types of violence exists. Yet except where strong revolutionary movements arise, no agencies internal to the society are capable of challenging the armed forces. This was very rarely the case in traditional societies, where the power of the ruling authority was often threatened by local warlords, pirates, brigands and others.

Terrorism

We can only understand what has come to be called **terrorism** against the background of the internal pacification of states. Terrorism can be defined as the threat or use of violence, for political ends, on the part of individuals or groups who otherwise have no formal political power. Understood in this way, terrorism acquires a particular significance within modern states, precisely because governments claim a monopoly over the right to use violence – as a threat against other nations, or in actual wars – for political motives. Terrorism thus draws upon the same symbols of legitimacy as the governments to which it is opposed. Terrorists tend to assert that their actions are 'legal', and often call themselves soldiers, adopting military terms for their organizations – such as the Irish Republican Army (IRA), the Red Brigades in Italy and so forth. They talk of 'political rights' and announce 'trials', 'sentences' and 'executions' (Wardlaw, 1983; Wilkinson, 1986).

If the majority of the population do not accept the claim that the activities of terrorist groups are legitimate military ones, they are likely to see the group as engaging in wanton violence. One of the characters in Sean O'Casey's play *The Shadow of a Gunman* describes this attitude when talking of armed resistance to the British presence in Ireland:

> It's the civilians that suffer; when there's an ambush they don't know where to run. Shot in the back to save Ireland. I'm a Nationalist myself, right enough . . . I believe in the freedom of Ireland, an' that England has no right to be here, but I draw the line when I hear about the gunmen dyin' for the people, when it's the people that are dyin' for the gunmen! (O'Casey, quoted in Wilkinson, 1974, p. 87)

The word *terrorism* has its origins in the French Revolution of 1789. Thousands of people – originally aristocrats, but later many other more ordinary citizens – were hunted down by the political authorities and put to the guillotine. Terror, in the sense of the use of violence to intimidate, has been used by governments on a large scale since that time. The practices of the Nazis in Germany, or of the Russian secret police under Stalin, are particularly horrific examples.

States have been responsible for far more outrages against human dignity and life over the past two centuries than have insurrectionary groups. For purposes of clarity, however, it is perhaps best to reserve the term 'terrorist' for those who specifically set out to *challenge* the authority of states. Even this cannot be an entirely clear-cut definition, however. Terrorists might receive support from, or be part of, larger organizations, which at some point themselves can become governing authorities. Some people who later became leading figures in the Israeli government participated in terrorist activities when endeavouring to set up a new state in what was then Palestine in the 1940s. Conversely, the Palestine Liberation Organization (PLO) today is seen by many Palestinians as their legitimate government – although it has supported acts which other states regard as terroristic.

Guerrilla movements

Terrorism in the twentieth century has been closely connected with **guerrilla movements**, and the two really have to be considered together. The only real difference between the two is that *guerrillas* are usually thought of as operating against specifically military targets, and *terrorists* against civilian ones – but this distinction is blurred in practice. Guerrillas are irregular fighters, lacking the organized military power and personnel commanded by regular armed forces. They use sporadic acts of violence as means of drawing attention to their cause, because they cannot hope to win in open battle. There are many examples of guerrilla movements and wars in the twentieth century, involving groups of a variety of different political persuasions. Sometimes such movements have remained weak, or have been wiped out by superior military force; on other occasions they have been successful enough to bring about wholesale political change.

The resistance movements which harassed the Germans during the Nazi occupation of the Second World War, in France, Holland, Belgium, Scandinavia, the occupied parts of Russia and elsewhere, were guerrilla organizations. So too were the movements led by Mao Tse-tung in China, or by Fidel Castro in Cuba, before their successful take-overs of governmental power. Guerrilla movements include the Algerian insurrectionists who forced the French to put an end to their colonial government of that country in the 1960s; the Mau Mau revolts in Kenya of roughly the same period; the Tupamaros in Uruguay and Monteneros in Argentina in the 1960s and 1970s; the groups who operated in South Vietnam fighting the Americans during the period of the Vietnam war; and the Islamic groups opposed to the Russian presence in Afghanistan in the 1980s.

Guerrilla organizations have mostly sprung up in circumstances in which there is either acute political oppression, or a very unequal distribution of wealth. Yet there are many differences between the situations in which guerrilla activity has existed and, as Walter Laqueur says, guerrilla movements 'are an awkward topic for generalisation' (Laqueur, 1976, p. 389).

Laqueur provides a description of some of the main characteristics of twentieth-century guerrilla war which can be summarized as follows.

1 Guerrilla movements develop in relatively inaccessible areas, in which the regular military cannot easily use their superior numbers and fire-power. Guerrillas normally operate out of inhospitable mountain areas, forests, jungles or swamps. They usually change their bases periodically, seeking to escape offering a clear target for enemy attack.
2 Guerrilla wars often occur in areas where numerous wars and battles have occurred before. This is obviously in some part because such regions tend to be fiercely contested in terms of political

Table 8 Major incidents of terrorism April 1985 – April 1986, in Europe and the Mediterranean, excluding Northern Ireland and the Spanish Basque Province

Date	Location	Target	Casualties	Group allegedly responsible
12 April 1985	Madrid	Restaurant	18 dead; 82 injured	Islamic Holy War
13 April 1985	Paris	3 bombs at offices and at an Israeli bank	None	Action Directe and Commando Sana Mheidleh(?)
14 June 1985	Beirut	TWA Boeing hijacked	1 dead	Palestinian group possibly linked to Hezbollah
19 June 1985	Frankfurt	Airport	3 dead; 42 injured	Arab unit from Abu Nidal(?)
1 July 1985	Madrid	TWA and British Airways offices	1 dead; 27 injured	Group of the Oppressed
8 August 1985	US Rhine base	Car bomb	2 dead	Action Directe and Red Army Faction
3 September 1985	Athens	Hotel bombs	18 injured	Possibly Black September
16 September 1985	Rome	Café de Paris	38 injured	Revolutionary Socialist Muslims
25 September 1985	Rome	British Airways office	1 dead; 14 injured	Palestinian claim from Revolutionary Socialist Muslims
7 October 1985	Mediterranean	Achille Lauro cruise ship hijacked	1 dead	Palestinian group
23 November 1985	Athens	Egyptian aircraft hijacked	58 dead	Groups from Egypt and Abu Nidal
24 November 1985	Frankfurt	US Army PX shop	35 injured	Not known
7 December 1985	Paris	Bombs in shops	39 injured	Palestine Liberation Organization
27 December 1985	Rome and Vienna	Airports	20 dead; 110 injured	Revolutionary Council of El Fatah
3 February 1986	Paris	Champs-Elysées bomb	8 injured	Committee for Middle Eastern Political Prisoners[a]

Table 8 continued

Date	Location	Target	Casualties	Group allegedly responsible
4 February 1986	Paris	Book shop bomb; Bomb on Eiffel Tower (defused)	4 injured None	Not known Not known
5 February 1986	Paris	Bomb in Les Halles	9 injured	Not known
20 March 1986	Paris	Bomb in Champs-Elysées; defused bomb in metro	2 dead; 28 injured	Committee for Solidarity with Middle Eastern Prisoners[a]
2 April 1986	Athens	Bomb exploded on TWA airliner on Rome flight	4 dead	Not known
5 April 1986	West Berlin	Discotheque bomb	2 dead; 230 injured	Anti-American Front for Arab Liberation(?)

In the incidents shown in this table 113 people lost their lives, and nearly 700 were injured.
[a] The name of this group appears to have changed during the early part of 1986; it now seems to be known as the 'Solidarity Committee for Arab Political Prisoners' and is referred to as such in table 9.
Source: Social Studies Review, March 1987, p. 3.

Table 9   Some of the principal terrorist groups active during the last decade

Name	Aim/type of group	Target	Area of operation
Abu Nidal	Palestinian state	Israel and Israeli support	Western Europe
Action Directe	Revolutionary anti-capitalism	Military, business, US and defence	France
Al Jihad al-Islam	Palestinian state	Israel and USA connections	Western Europe Middle East
Autonomia	Anti-capitalist	Business and military	Italy
Avanguardia Nazionale	Fascist group	Random attacks	Italy
Bakounine-Gdansk-Paris	Revolutionary anti-capitalism	Businesses	France
Black September	Palestinian state	Israel and Israeli support	Western Europe
Cellules Communistes Combattantes (CCC)	Revolutionary anti-capitalism	Military and business	Belgium (links with France)
El Fatah	Palestinian state	Israeli and Israeli support	Western Europe Middle East
Euzkadi ta Askata-suna (ETA)	Basque nationalism	Spanish police and administration	Spain (sometimes France)
Factions Armées Révolutionnaires Libanaises (FARL)	Palestinian state	Israel and Israeli support	France Middle East

Table 9 continued

Name	Aim/type of group	Target	Area of operation
Front de Libération de la Bretagne – Armée Républicaine Bretonne (FLB–ARB)	Breton nationalism	French state	France
Front de la Libération Nationale Corse (FLNC)	Corsican nationalism	French state and property, especially businesses	France
Francia	Anti-Corsican nationalism	Nationalists	Corsica
Groupes d'Actions Révolutionnaires Internationales (GARI)	Revolutionary socialism	Capitalist concerns	France
Anti-fascist Resistance Groups (GRAPO)	Anti-fascism	Random attacks	Spain
Irish National Liberation Army (INLA)	Irish nationalism	Security forces and random attacks	United Kingdom
Irish Republican Army (IRA)	Irish nationalism	Security forces	United Kingdom
Noyaux Armées pour l'Autonomie Populaire	Revolutionary socialism	Random attacks	France
Provisional Irish Republican Army (PIRA)	Irish nationalism	Security forces and random attacks	United Kingdom
Palestine Liberation Organisation (PLO)	Palestinian state	Israel and Israeli support	Western Europe Middle East
Portere Operaio	Revolutionary socialism	Businesses	Italy
Red Army Faction (RAF)	Revolutionary socialism	Military and business	West Germany (suspected of Italian link)
Red Brigades	Revolutionary socialism	Military and business	Italy
Solidarity Committee for Arab Political Prisoners	Release of Arab prisoners; Palestinian state	Currently French government personnel and installations	France
Ulster Freedom Fighters (UFF)	Northern Irish unity with UK	IRA/PIRA; Irish nationalists	United Kingdom

Many other groups, particularly nationalists and regionalists, operate in Europe; these include Armenians, Jugoslavs, South Tyroleans and Jurassians.
Source: Social Studies Review, March 1987, p. 5.

affiliations and loyalties. The factors which give rise to military rule also facilitate the emergence of guerrilla movements, opposed to the military leaders.

3 Guerrilla warfare is most commonly found in less-developed countries, where traditional social structures have been broken down by the impact of political or economic ties with the industrialized world. Peasants whose livelihood has suffered, or who wish to escape the influence of large landowners, form a source of recruitment to guerrilla movements.

4 There have been three main types of guerrilla war in this century. One consists of hostilities waged against foreign invaders; a second is warfare conducted by separatist movements in conflict with the central government (such as the IRA); the third consists of guerrilla activities conducted against governments thought to be corrupt or exploitative (as in the case of the Tupamaros or Monteneros in South America).

5 Guerrilla war has developed in conjunction with the modernization of warfare generally. Guerrilla movements cannot deploy the range of sophisticated weaponry available to orthodox armies. On the other hand, particularly given appropriate terrain, they can and do develop means of countering or frustrating it. Thus the Vietcong guerrillas in Vietnam had very little weaponry, compared to that of the Americans, but were still able to use tactics that in the end defeated the sophisticated military technology deployed against them – such as the elaborate system of underground tunnels into which they disappeared after carrying out raids.

6 Most guerrilla movements do not operate autonomously; they are funded or supported by states outside the particular region in which they operate. Funding and support received from one or other of the two major military alliances (centred on the United States and Soviet Union) means that guerrilla struggles today are frequently extensions of the global competition between the major powers. Thus both the United States and Soviet Union have provided resources for guerrilla movements in several parts of Africa, Latin America and South East Asia. (Laqueur, 1976, chapter 9)

Urban guerrillas

Over the past twenty years, tactics originally used mainly by guerrilla movements have been widely adopted by groups operating within urban settings, especially in Europe and Japan. The hijacking of aeroplanes, kidnapping, murder of prominent individuals, and bombings have become familiar events in many countries. Those involved hold political views ranging from extreme Left to extreme Right, and include a variety of separatist and nationalist groups. In the late 1960s and early 1970s, bombings, kidnappings and assassinations were carried out by the Rengo Sekigun in Japan, the Red Army Faction in West Germany and the Red Brigades in Italy. In the United States the Weathermen and Black Panthers advocated strategies of urban violence. In the mid-1980s, a further wave of urban guerrilla activity occurred, in Milan, Paris, Berlin and other European cities. Most of the groups involved have proved to be fairly transient, either meeting with widespread condemnation and so failing to recruit members or obtain money, or being broken up by the authorities. Others have more sustained sources of funding, and represent causes having some measure of popular support, particularly where they are connected with separatist movements. Such groups include the Irish Republican Army (IRA) and ETA, the Basque separatist organization (Lodge, 1981).

Most of even the more permanently organized groups remain small. Violence is used to dramatize particular causes, to create anxieties that might reflect badly on the competence of the government, and to achieve a following among those impressed by the fact that such movements do not merely 'talk' but 'mean business'. As such groups are increasingly persecuted by state, and forced to operate more and more secretively, so their links with the wider community weaken and their use of violence sometimes becomes more ruthless than before (Mommsen, 1982).

In the popular press terrorists are often represented as driven by bloodlust and as having incomprehensible motives for their actions (Schmid, 1982; Crenshaw, 1983). This sort of characterization is usually far from the truth. Most groups prepared to use violence to further their ends have a coherent philosophy about why they act as they do. Controversial though their ideas may be, these groups are not normally composed of people who claim to value violence for its own sake. Political authorities and the general public often have ambivalent, or even hypocritical, attitudes towards terrorism. They may feel outrage at the brutality of activities carried out within their own borders by groups using violent means, but at the same time support and encourage guerrilla movements using identical tactics in other regions of the world. What is the difference between a 'freedom fighter' and a 'terrorist'? Terrorists and guerrillas appropriate to themselves a power that states seek to maintain as their monopoly – the right to use violent means to pursue political objectives.

Global military expenditure and weapons

Global military expenditure has been climbing since the late nineteenth century, and continues to mount today (Oberg, 1980). Since the Second World War, military budgets have become much larger than previously in peacetime, and the military equipment available in many parts of the world has become increasingly sophisticated.

In 1977, world military expenditure passed one billion dollars a day, representing a rate of spending of 50 million dollars each hour. Since then, overall spending has almost doubled again, amounting to a total of 663 billion dollars in 1985 (SIPRI, 1986). By far the greatest proportion of this is spent by First World countries, their share amounting to 480 billion dollars in that year. World military expenditure is greater than the overall gross product of the whole of the African continent, South Africa included. It is more than that of all of Asia, if Japan is left out. The gross national product of Japan, which is the third largest economy in the world, is only about twice the size of the wealth dispensed for military ends globally. As one author puts it, 'it is as if half a "Japan" existed within the world economy, but was unrecognised diplomatically' (Kennedy, 1983, p. 45).

The ratio of military spending to total government expenditure within particular countries varies. Among Western countries, the lowest rate of spending as a percentage of gross domestic product (overall home production per year) is recorded by Luxemburg, with 0.9 per cent (1983). West Germany allocates 3.3 per cent of its overall home production for military purposes, Britain 5.4 per cent and the United States 6.6 per cent (SIPRI, 1986). The Soviet Union does not provide figures which allow accurate comparison with these countries, but its rate of military expenditure is certainly higher than that of the United States.

The nuclear stock-pile

Although there are non-proliferation treaties, supposed to limit the spread of nuclear weapons, the world's stock-pile of nuclear armaments continues to increase. About 50,000 nuclear warheads are currently controlled by those countries with a nuclear capability – the vast majority of these held by the United States and the Soviet Union. Over the past ten years, both the United States and the USSR have increased their numbers of new warheads by some 400 per cent, although the total will be cut back somewhat by the treaty signed by the USA and the USSR early in 1988. The nuclear arsenals of other countries are much smaller, but even the possession of a few nuclear weapons yields immense destructive capacity. Countries that have nuclear weapons include Britain, France, India, Pakistan, China – and probably Israel and South Africa.

Chemical weapons

Technological developments on various fronts are adding new military capabilities. In spite of international agreements to ban it, research on chemical and biological weapons has gone ahead in various countries. According to the Geneva Protocol of 1925, chemical and biological weapons may not be used in warfare. This followed widespread repugnance at the fate of soldiers exposed to mustard gas attacks during the First World War. Several of the signatories to the agreement, including the United States and the Soviet Union, accepted the terms of the treaty, but reserved the right to use such weapons in retaliation when they were employed by other states. They therefore hold stocks of chemical and biological weapons, and have not stopped research and development connected with them.

The USA has a programme to develop binary nerve-gas weapons, which are chemicals kept separately and only mixed to become lethal once they have been fired. The Reagan administration made strong efforts in 1982–4 to persuade Congress to provide funds to move from research to the full-scale production of binary nerve-gas weapons. This was not approved, but discussions have been carried on within NATO to keep the matter open. The toxic chemicals would be fired against an enemy by the use of missiles or multiple rocket-launchers (Turner, 1985, pp. 51–8).

The Soviet Union accused the United States of using chemical and biological weapons in Vietnam in the early 1970s. The United States, in its turn, announced that North Vietnamese forces were using toxic substances supplied from Soviet sources. These substances came to be known as Yellow Rain, since there were claimed to be eye-witness accounts of the yellow poison falling from the sky. It has proved difficult to assess the validity of these claims and counter-claims. However, it is undisputed that chemical weapons have been used in the recent war between Iran and Iraq. United Nations investigators, visiting Iranian victims in hospital, were able to establish that mustard gas had been used against them. Since this seems to have been produced in Iraq itself, it raises the possibility that many countries may have been covertly developing chemical or biological weapons.

Little can be done to prevent states using modern industrial techniques to produce chemical and biological weapons. There are bound to be connections between scientific development, industry and the potential to produce certain types of arms. There are also major links between nuclear power and the capacity to manufacture nuclear weapons. If dependence on nuclear power as a source of energy becomes widespread throughout the world (and some Western countries are encouraging this), it will offer more and more states the potential to develop their own nuclear weapons. In 1981, the Israeli Air Force bombed Iraq's nuclear reactor just outside Baghdad. The Israelis alleged that what was claimed to be a power station was in fact producing nuclear weapons. Israel was universally condemned by other states for its action, but it is generally agreed that the Iraqi technology programme was being put to military purposes (Durie and Edwards, 1982). In 1986 there were nuclear reactors in twenty-six countries which are not as yet known to possess nuclear weapons.

The arms trade

The pattern of world military organization is strongly influenced by the arms trade. Governments, as well as industrial firms, sell arms, and the arms trade, like so much in the military sphere today, is dominated by the United States and the Soviet Union. Each of the superpowers transfers arms within its global system of alliance, often coupling this to the military training of the armies of allied states. Since the Second World War, the United States has provided some 80,000 million dollars, in the form of loans or grants, to assist military projects in countries covered by the various alliances it has developed. It has also made available many experts to train personnel in those countries. Soviet military assistance has been lent to its allies in similar ways, but less extensively. The Soviets have concentrated attention on Eastern Europe and a few strategically important clients, particularly in the Middle East, although they have provided very large stocks of weapons for these.

Arms exports are controlled by the governments of the leading producing countries: arms trading requires export licences. Consequently, with the exception of the small illegal traffic in arms, it is quite easy to identify the flow of arms from one country to another. The United States is by a large margin the leading exporter, with the USSR lagging some way behind. About two-thirds of the arms trade involves weapons passing between the industrialized and Third World countries, and a high proportion of this consists of major weapons systems, rather than just small arms and support equipment (Kaldor, 1982). In the first twenty years after the Second World War, much of the weaponry exported to developing countries was old fashioned, and being phased out of use by the USA and its Western allies. Today, however, even the most sophisticated weapons systems, with the exception of those involving nuclear capability, are sold to those with the money to buy. Thus, some Third World countries possess equipment almost as advanced as that of the American or Soviet military. Several leading Western industrial powers besides the United States are also major arms exporters, including especially France and Britain.

Since the early 1980s, the overall volume of the world arms trade has declined slightly. Many Third World countries, suffering from the global economic recession and growing foreign debts, can no longer afford major arms purchases. On the other hand, an increasing number of developing countries now have their own arms industries. Not only are they less reliant upon Western or Soviet sources, they are actively starting to compete with them in offering their own military goods for sale on world markets.

The arms trade has important effects on the economies of many countries, in the First, Second and Third worlds. The leading Western exporting countries, and the Soviet Union, gain financially from the world trade in weapons. Governments and businesses which produce military hardware put a great deal of investment into research and development, pioneering new weapons technologies. The costs of such investment can be significantly lessened by selling the weapons to customers outside their own countries (although this can

Table 10   Comparison of Soviet and American military technologies (1985)

United States' lead		
Increasing	*No change*	*Decreasing*
Computers and software	Electronic signal processing	Ground and aerospace propulsion
	Electro-optical sensors	High-strength materials
	Guidance and navigation	Radar sensing devices
	Life sciences and biotechnology	Submarine detection
	Microelectronics	
	Production and manufacturing	
	Robotics and machine intelligence	
	Stealth designs	
	Telecommunications	

US–Soviet parity
Aerodynamics and fluid dynamics
Conventional warhead design
Lasers
Nuclear warhead design
Optics
Power sources and energy storage

Soviet lead
No areas found

Source: Rip Bulkeley and Graham Spinardi, *Space Weapons: Deterrence or Delusion* (Cambridge: Polity Press, 1987), p. 154.

potentially rebound in times of war, when a country could find itself attacked by weapons it originally produced).

Third World countries which purchase armaments from the industrialized nations, on the other hand, quite often do so at the price of placing great strain on their economies – which are mostly much weaker than those of the industrialized world. For them, the arms trade has unfortunate consequences. Where the military are particularly powerful, or actually governing, they are able to push for the constant importing of new equipment. This in turn further strengthens their position, while draining away economic resources that might be desperately needed for other projects – such as buying agricultural machinery, power plants or manufacturing technology.

The arms race

The arms trade helps foster a global **arms race** – competition between states to match, or surpass, others in their level of military strength. To understand the origins of such competition, we have to understand why states in general are usually concerned to build up their military strength.

First, a country which is militarily strong can hope to *deter* others from using force against it. Second, military strength can be used to acquire new territories or pursue national interests through victory in active conflict or war. According to von Clausewitz, war is a means of achieving national ends where peaceful or diplomatic measures fail (von Clausewitz, 1908). Third, in times of peace, military power can be used as a means of *coercion*, because the threat of its use might be sufficient to achieve a desired objective. Fourth, military power provides a basis for *defence* if one country is attacked by another. 'Defence' has come to be used as a synonym for military needs, because no government wants to advertise itself as a likely aggressor against others.

These considerations have underlain competition in military development between different countries since the early phase of the industrialization of war in the late eighteenth century. From that time onwards, it has been recognized that warfare depends upon technological sophistication and the constant upgrading of weaponry.

The main focus of the arms race today is between the two dominant producers of weapons in the world: the United States and the Soviet Union. The arms race between the two superpowers is characterized by what has been called **action-reaction** – the government of each country looks to innovations going on in the other in order to adjust its own programme of weapons development. The military in each society also presses its claims on the basis of what it believes military leaders on the other side are planning. Research must go on continuously to make all this possible. Quite often political or military leaders set out objectives for scientists to try to meet. This was the case, for example, with the construction of the first atomic bombs towards the end of the Second World War. One of the largest scientific teams ever assembled was brought together specifically to create an atomic weapon. On the other hand, since scientific work on weapons development has become permanent, weapons are sometimes invented which the armed forces then usually find a reason for needing. Thus when it was discovered that several warheads could be put on one inter-continental missile, having multiple targets, the armed forces enthusiastically adopted the new technology. Their reasoning as to why it was necessary changed as the technology altered further (Sheehan, 1983).

The deterrence debate

The arms race has been decisively influenced by the advent of nuclear weapons, particularly since the development of long-range missiles. There is no effective defence against nuclear missiles. Deterrence used to be only one among other reasons why states kept themselves armed, but in the case of massively destructive nuclear weapons, it is the *only* possible reason. As the effect of using them would be catastrophic to all, nuclear weapons are supposedly kept only to deter the other side from using them.

The American view

Deterrence is essentially a psychological concept, since what is important is that each side believes both that the other would retaliate if attacked and that the outcome would be so devastating that no military aggression can be risked. The deterrent strategy of the United States has for several years been based upon two concepts. Mutual assured destruction (MAD) describes the situation in which each side possesses such large nuclear arsenals that neither could immobilize the other by suddenly mounting an attack. It is not rational for either country to precipitate a nuclear war, because each knows that its population and resources would be largely wiped out. This outlook has been criticized from a number of standpoints. Activists in peace movements argue that in fact the doctrine produces a paradoxical situation of extreme danger. For MAD to work, each side must believe that the other would be willing to unleash its missiles, if it itself were attacked, and simultaneously believe that the other has no intention of using its nuclear weapons. Each must be frightened into holding back from using its weaponry, and must believe the other to be so deterred; yet each must accept that the other *would* use that weaponry if called upon to do so. Jonathan Schell remarks:

> We cannot both threaten ourselves with something and hope to avoid that same thing by making the threat – both intend to do something and intend not to do it. The head-on contradiction between these aims has set up a cross current of tension within the policies of each super-power. Safety may be emphasised at one moment, and at the next moment it is the 'terror' that comes to the fore. And since the deterrence doctrine pairs the safety and the terror, and makes the former depend on the latter, the world is never quite sure from day to day which one is in the ascendent – if, indeed, the distinction can be maintained in the first place. (Schell, 1982, pp. 201–2)

Others, closer to government circles, have argued (against the MAD doctrine) that if the Soviet Union struck first, the results might be so devastating to the West that few, if any, retaliatory weapons would get through. In a surprise attack, the USSR might eliminate the American nuclear weapons before they could be despatched. They reason that what is important is not the overall size of the nuclear force, but its *residual capability* – what is left after an initial attack. The Soviet Union could only effectively be deterred if it were clear that, even after a surprise attack by its forces, wholesale damage could be inflicted upon it. This argument was accepted by the United States government in the early 1960s, and so the notion of the *triad*, or *three-fold* system of deterrence, was developed. If nuclear weapons are kept not only in land-based missiles, but also in fleets of aircraft some of which are constantly airborne, and thirdly in missile-carrying submarines, no surprise attack can destroy retaliatory capability.

The Soviet view

One consequence of this alteration in doctrine was an acceleration in the arms race. Each element of the triad had to be capable of destroying large areas of the Soviet Union on its own, should both the others be wiped out. This, in turn, of course, led to an intensification of weapons development in the Soviet Union. There is evidence that the USSR tends to respond to real or perceived American military build-up very rapidly, partly because of differences in strategy. Soviet strategic thinking has been built around the experience of the Soviet Union in the Second World War, when so many millions of lives were lost. The geographical position of the United States makes it more or less immune from large-scale invasion, whereas the Soviet Union was invaded by the Nazis even though it was militarily strong. Deterrence did not seem to work for the Soviet Union at that time.

According to Soviet thinking the military strategy of the country must be based on the knowledge that the Soviet Union would *win* a war. It is assumed that the Western powers, especially the United States, are hostile, and would attack if they could do so with some chance of achieving a favourable result. Soviet strategic planning is based on making it clear that any such ventures would lead to military defeat. There is no exact equivalent to the word 'deterrence' in Russian; the official Soviet view is that MAD is an ideology that actually fuels the arms race. Successive Soviet leaders have refused to subscribe to the idea that each country must be able to survive a 'first strike' in order to achieve a credible defence posture. For this reason, the Soviet nuclear forces are not nearly as dispersed as those of the United States, and are in fact quite vulnerable to a first strike on the part of the United States.

'Star wars'

It was to some degree the realization of the Soviet attitude that led to a retreat from the MAD theory in the United States during the 1970s. MAD assumes some rough level of parity between the superpowers' nuclear capabilities, but the very furtherance of the doctrine led to a Russian arms build-up beyond that consistent with the feeling of safety the balance was supposed to generate. In any case, it is difficult to believe that the balance of weaponry presumed by MAD can ever be achieved. It is based on offensive weapons; therefore, the very armaments that give one side a sense of security inherently

"It's hard to believe that everything doesn't have a military solution."

Drawing by Dana Fradon; © 1983 The New Yorker Magazine, Inc.

threaten the other, which is then motivated to increase the destructive potential of its own weapons . . . and so on. The impulse to try to halt this runaway process alternates with succumbing to it.

Strategic Arms Limitations Talks (SALT) have been held by the superpowers on several occasions, leading to two sets of agreements, one signed in 1972 and the other in 1979. These have not, however, prevented a resurgence of military spending by the superpowers in the late 1970s and the 1980s. Such spending has also been prompted by President Reagan's 'Star Wars' programme – officially known as the Strategic Defence Initiative (SDI). This programme aims to develop a system of defence against missiles using space weapons and lasers. It seems probable that the Soviet Union is also working on similar lines, although not investing so much money as the United States. Certainly both the USA and the Soviet Union are known to have been developing space weapons for at least twenty years (Bulkeley and Spinardi, 1986).

Given the irrationalities of MAD, MAS (mutually assured security) would obviously be vastly preferable if it worked (if defensive weapons could be effectively deployed by both sides). Even the establishing of such a policy tends to undermine whatever credibility MAD might have had, because it presumes that effective defence against nuclear attack is after all feasible. Critics argue that SDI can never work, because to do so it must be virtually perfect. A system could be 99.9 per cent effective, and yet with current missile deployments still allow eight warheads through, capable of killing sixty million people in the United States. Since the level of expenditure required for MAS is so huge, the result could be a further surge in the arms race. Moreover, the Soviets might well decide that their best counter-strategy is to build up their offensive weapons so as to overwhelm even the sophisticated SDI shield. Supporters, on the other hand, claim that SDI will in fact increase stability by turning the emphasis from destructive to protective systems. SDI, according to them, offers far greater possibilities of world peace in the relatively near future than the current reliance upon offensive weapons.

The USA and the Soviet Union reached agreement in 1988 to scrap medium-range nuclear missiles stationed in Europe. This initiative was originally proposed by Western leaders, but made a realistic option by a concrete agenda put forward by Mr Gorbachev, the Soviet premier. If the agreement is successfully put into practice, it will mark the first effective reversal in the arms race.

A world without war?

The threat of nuclear annihilation is now ever-present. In the event of a full-scale nuclear exchange, the global effects would be so horrendous that probably only small numbers of people in more remote regions would survive. No one can be sure just how complete the destruction would be; it is possible that, because of atmospheric and ecological effects, after a short period the human race – along with most other life on the planet – would disappear altogether. The result might be 'a republic of insects and grass' – with all the higher animals eliminated (Schell, 1982, chapter 1).

Precisely because the implications are so cataclysmic – depending on circumstances that are supposed to be unthinkable – most of us manage to carry on our day-to-day lives without constantly worrying about the threat of nuclear oblivion. We are the first generation in the history of the human race to live with the fact that the end of our individual lives might coincide with the termination of humanity itself. If this only rarely impinges upon the thinking of many people, it is no doubt partly because of resigned acceptance of a possibility that most of us have little chance of preventing. Yet psychological studies of the effects of living in a nuclear age indicate that there may be buried fears and anxieties that relatively few are able openly to acknowledge. Particularly among children, the atmosphere of fear that is essential to nuclear deterrence seems to have powerful psychological consequences (Lifton et al., 1982).

The development of weapons capable of destroying humanity is the outcome of the industrialization of war, a process initiated some 200 years ago. Unless there should be some fundamental political turn-around, with all states agreeing to outlaw nuclear weapons, everyone must live for the indefinite future in the shadow of a possible nuclear holocaust. Even if all nuclear weapons were completely scrapped (which looks unlikely), the knowledge that produced them cannot be destroyed. Moreover, it seems improbable that the continuing application of science and technology to weapons development will diminish. Nuclear weapons are not necessarily the most horrific or destructive armaments that human beings are capable of inventing and constructing.

Yet, in spite of all this, and notwithstanding the fact that wars have been so prevalent this century, it is possible to envisage a world without war. Some of the chief ambitions which led to war in the past, particularly the acquisition of new territories, have become less and less relevant in the contemporary world. Modern societies are today much more interdependent on a global level than ever was the case before, and for the most part their boundaries have been fixed (Rosecrance, 1986). Nuclear war is so cataclysmic in its consequences that it cannot be used to achieve any realistic political or economic objectives. The industrialization of war has thus brought about a situation in which armed conflict using the highest technology it has generated has no rational purpose.

Recognition of this situation might perhaps lend weight to the view that non-violent means of resolving global social conflicts must be found. But it would be naive to be too optimistic. A nuclear war might be triggered by accident, by technical malfunctioning or by the activities of irresponsible political leaders. Also, the absence of full-scale nuclear war does not necessarily prevent the occurrence of wars in which smaller nuclear weapons are used, or wars using conventional weapons. Yet it is not wholly unrealistic in the long-term future to envisage a world free from war.

Summary

1　The fighting of wars is one of the most obvious features of the first development of states, and wars and battles have played a primary role in shaping the map of the world as it exists today. The development of the modern military was closely intertwined with the emergence of industrialization in the eighteenth century. Large corporations, devoted either wholly or partly to the manufacture of armaments and stressing technical innovation, have ever since played a leading part in military development and war.

2   Wars are not the result of innate aggressive instincts. People have to be *trained* to kill. Wars are usually fought to acquire territory or resources or because of ideological or religious clashes.

3   Modern armies are bureaucracies, staffed on the officer level by full-time officials. Armies are highly organized, specialized and hierarchical. Although the sheer complexity of most modern states works against the possibility of military dominance, the army still often has a significant voice in the policy-making process.

4   War has always been pre-eminently a male activity, although women have tended to support wars, and today some armed forces include women in combat roles. Women have also played a prominent part in campaigning for peace. There is unlikely to be any innate reason why women are less involved in wars than are men.

5   Some countries are directly ruled by the military, although most military governments are unstable. While most have been concentrated in the Third World, several industrialized countries have experienced periods of military rule.

6   An important characteristic of modern societies is the degree to which the military and police are able successfully to acquire more or less exclusive control over the use of force. Terrorist groups and guerrilla movements draw upon the same symbols of legitimacy as established armies and governments.

7   As guerrilla groups become more persecuted by the state, and forced to operate more and more secretly, their use of violence sometimes becomes more ruthless than before. Although governments oppose the activities of terrorists within their own borders, they none the less often encourage guerrilla movements using identical tactics in other regions of the world.

8   The pattern of world military organization is strongly influenced by the arms trade, which is carried on by governments as well as by industrial firms. The competitive development of conventional weapons and nuclear arms by the USA and the USSR has been called the *arms race*.

9   We are the first generation in the history of the human race to live with the threat of extinction. The industrialization of war has led to this situation. Yet states are now so interdependent, and the consequences of nuclear war are known to be so cataclysmic, that the hope that a world without war can be achieved lives on.

Basic concepts

the industrialization of war   military rule

Important terms

standing army	legitimacy
arms trade	military–industrial complex
limited war	autocratic military rule
total war	oligarchic military rule
universal conscription	authoritarian praetorianism
management of violence	terrorism
clientship	guerrilla movement
corporateness	arms race
military mind	action-reaction
pacifism	deterrence

Further reading

Mary Kaldor et al. (eds), *The World Military Order: The Impact of Military Technology on the Third World* (New York: Praeger, 1979) — essays dealing with the transfer of military technology to the Third World and questioning the claim that these are justified by defence requirements.

Werner Kaltefleiter et al. (eds), *Peace Movements in Europe and the United States* (New York: St Martin's Press, 1985) — a comparative analysis seeking common features among eight national peace movements.

R. D. McKinlay et al., *Global Problems and World Order* (London: Frances Pinter, 1986) — a comparative approach to world order examining competing concepts of global problems in the fields of international economy and security.

Michael Mandelbaum, *The Nuclear Revolution: International Politics before and after Hiroshima* (New York: Cambridge University Press, 1981) — studies how nuclear weapons have affected international politics.

Greville Rumble, *The Politics of Nuclear Defence: A Comprehensive Introduction* (Cambridge: Polity Press, 1985) — a detailed introduction to the debate on nuclear weapons.

Martin Shaw (ed.), *War, State and Society* (New York: St Martin's Press, 1984) — a collection of papers studying the relationship of war and capitalism, with special reference to academic sociology and Marxism.

PART IV

Social Institutions

Social institutions are the 'cement' of social life. They provide the basic living arrangements that human beings work out in their interaction with one another and by means of which continuity is achieved across the generations.

This part begins with a look at the institutions of kinship, marriage and the family. Although the social obligations associated with kinship vary widely between different types of society, the family is everywhere the context within which the young are provided with care and protection. Marriage is in turn more or less universally connected to the family, since it is a means of establishing new kin connections, and forming a household in which children are brought up. In traditional cultures, much of the direct learning or formal instruction a child receives occurs within the family context. In modern societies, however, children spend many years of their lives in special places of instruction outside the family – that is, in schools and colleges. The second chapter in this part looks at the ways in which formal education is organized, concentrating particularly on how the educational system relates to wider processes of learning and communication.

The two remaining chapters deal with religion and the economic order. Although religious beliefs and practices are found in all cultures, the changes affecting religion in modern societies have been particularly acute. We analyse the nature of these changes, considering the ways in which traditional types of religion still maintain their influence. Finally, we study work and economic life. Economic institutions affect many aspects of social activity, and although the nature of work varies widely both within and between different societies, it is one of the most pervasively important of all human pursuits.

12

Kinship, Marriage and the Family

The study of the family and marriage is one of the most important areas of sociology. Virtually everyone, in all societies, is brought up in a family context; and in every society the vast majority of adults are, or have been, married. Marriage is a very pervasive **social institution**. Yet as with other aspects of social life there is great variation in the family and marriage patterns across different cultures. What counts as a *family*, its connections with other kin, whom one is permitted to marry, how spouses are selected, the connections between marriage and sexuality – all these differ widely. In this chapter we shall study some of these variations, showing how they help illuminate distinctive aspects of family life and patterns of marriage and divorce in the modern West. The Western family has changed markedly over the centuries, and we shall compare family life and marriage relationships in the modern period with those of earlier times. Fundamental shifts in the nature of the family and marriage are occurring in the current era also, and in the concluding sections of the chapter these will be analysed in some detail.

We need first of all to define the basic concepts of **family**, **kinship** and **marriage**. A *family* is a group of persons directly linked by kin connections, the adult members of which assume responsibility for caring for children. *Kinship* ties are connections between individuals, established either through marriage, or through the lines of descent that connect blood relatives (mothers, fathers, other offspring, grandparents, etc.). *Marriage* can be defined as a socially acknowledged and approved sexual union between two adult individuals. When two people marry, they become kin to one another; the marriage bond also, however, connects together a wider range of kinspeople. Parents, brothers, sisters and other blood relatives become relatives of the partner through marriage.

Kinship

In most Western societies, kinship connections are for all practical purposes confined to a limited number of close relatives. Most people, for example, have only a vague awareness of relatives more distant than first or second cousins. In many other cultures, however, especially small-scale ones, kinship relations are of overriding importance in most spheres of life. In some small societies, all individuals are, or believe themselves to be, related to the others (Beattie, 1964). Western kinship terminology cannot always easily be translated into the kinship connections recognized in other cultures. For example, we have the single term 'uncle' for relatives both on the mother's and on the father's side. Some cultures, by contrast, possess separate terms for the mother's brother and father's brother, and these are regarded as very different types of kin relationship.

Clan groups

In most traditional societies there are large kinship groupings which go well beyond immediate family relationships. One important grouping of this sort is the **clan**. A clan is a group from which all members believe themselves to be descended, either through men or through women, tracing their origin to a common ancestor several generations back. They see themselves, and are seen by others, as a collectivity with a distinct identity. The clans in Scotland were groups of such a kind; and there are many African and Pacific societies where such corporate groups remain significant.

Normally members of the same clan share similar religious beliefs, have economic obligations to one another, and live in the same locality. Clan groups may be fairly small, but sometimes number hundreds or even thousands of individuals. Clan membership often affects almost every part of an individual's life. In such groups, kinspeople who for us would be only very distant relatives may be thought of, and treated, in the same ways as those who are close. A man might call his father's father's father's brother's son's son (a third cousin in Western kinship terminology) his brother and recognize the same obligations towards him as he does towards his biological brothers.

Sometimes kinship categories recognized in clan groups completely cut across those we would take to be 'natural'. For example, a father's sister may be called 'father', with the addition of the qualification 'female'; a mother's brother might be called 'mother', with the added qualification 'male'. In these groups, it is not unusual to hear a man refer to another man, who may be much younger than himself, as his 'mother'. Strange as this sounds to us, it is entirely logical within a society organized in terms of clans. The individual is aware of who his real mother is. When he uses the word, he identifies the person referred to as coming from the same descent group as his mother, and therefore having strong ties to himself.

An example of a clan group is the *tsu* of traditional China. A *tsu* sometimes numbered thousands of people. Each had a council of elders which discussed issues of interest to the whole group. Members of the *tsu* had common religious obligations, and the *tsu* also carried out economic and educational tasks for its members. It provided a credit system for money loans to members and also served as a court of law for judicial disputes. The *tsu* was also the basis of Chinese criminal organizations, which once flourished in the large cities such as Shanghai, and remain active today in Hong Kong.

Family relationships

Family relationships are always recognized within wider kinship groups. In virtually all societies we can identify what sociologists and anthropologists have come to call the **nuclear family**, which consists of two adults living together in a household with their own or adopted children. In most traditional societies, even when there are no clans, the nuclear family is embedded in larger kinship networks of some type. Where kin other than a married couple and children live either in the same household, or in close and continuous contact with one another, we speak of the **extended family**. An extended family can be defined as a group of three or more generations living either within the same dwelling or very close to each other. It may include grandparents, brothers and their wives, sisters and their husbands, aunts, uncles, nieces or nephews.

Whether nuclear or extended, so far as the experience of each individual is concerned, families can be divided into families of **orientation** and families of **procreation**. The first is the family into which a person is born; the second is the family into which an individual enters as an adult and within which a new generation of children is brought up. A further important distinction concerns place of residence. In Britain when a couple marry they are usually expected to set up a separate household. This can be in the same area as the bride's parents or the groom's parents, but may very well be elsewhere. In many societies, however, everyone who marries is expected to live close to, or within the same dwelling as, the parents of the bride or groom. Where the couple moves to live near or with the bride's parents, the arrangement is called **matrilocal**. A **patrilocal** pattern is one where the couple goes to live near to or with the parents of the groom.

Monogamy and polygamy

In Western societies, marriage, and therefore the family, is associated with **monogamy**. It is illegal for a man or woman to be married to more than one individual at any one time. Monogamy is not the most common type of marriage style in the world as a whole. In a comparison involving 565 societies, George Murdock found that polygamy was permitted in over 80 per cent of them (Murdock, 1949). **Polygamy** describes any type of marriage which allows a husband or wife to have more than one spouse. There are two types of polygamy: **polygyny**, in which a man may be married to more than one woman at the same time; and **polyandry** (which is much less common), in which a woman may have two or more husbands simultaneously.

Polyandry

Murdock found that only four societies out of the 565 he analysed practised polyandry – under 1 per cent. Polyandry creates a situation absent in polygyny – the biological father of a child is usually not known. Among the Todas of southern India, a polyandrous culture, husbands seem uninterested in establishing biological paternity. Who is deemed the father of a child is established by means of a ceremony in which one of the husbands presents the pregnant wife with a toy bow and arrow. If other husbands subsequently wish to become fathers, the ritual is re-enacted during further pregnancies. Polyandry seems to exist only in societies living in extreme poverty, in which female infanticide is practised.

Polygyny

Most men in polygynous societies in fact only have one wife. The right to have several wives is often limited to individuals of high status; where there are no such restrictions, the sex ratio and economic factors keep polygyny in check. There are no societies, obviously, in which women so far outnumber men that the majority of males could have more than one wife.

In polygynous families, co-wives sometimes live in the same dwelling as one another, but often have different households. Where separate households exist, each including the children of one wife, there are effectively two or more family units. The husband usually has one home as his primary dwelling, but may spend a certain number of nights per week or month with each wife in rotation. Co-wives are frequently co-operative and friendly; but their situation is obviously one that can lead to rivalry and tension, since they may see themselves as competitors for the husband's favours. Among the Ruanda of East Africa, the word for 'co-wife' is the same as that for 'jealousy' (Macquet, 1961). The discord provoked by polygyny is sometimes eased by a system of hierarchical grading among wives. The senior wife or wives have more authority over family decisions than juniors.

Western missionaries have always been extremely hostile to polygyny, and from the days of colonialism onwards sought to eradicate it. Polygyny still exists in many parts of the world, but where Western influence is strong, attitudes have often become mixed. The anthropologist John Beattie quotes a case of a young school-teacher he got to know while working in Bunyoro in Western Uganda. This man had one wife, whom he had married in the Christian church, and with whom he cohabited when he lived at the school. He had another wife and two children in his home village. This wife he had married in the traditional way of his people. He hid the existence of the second wife from his superiors at the school, and asked Beattie to keep the matter completely secret (Beattie, 1964, p. 255).

The family and marriage in European history

Before industrialization, most families were also units of production, working the land or engaged in crafts. Even people who did not establish their own families of procreation tended to live and work in the family settings of others. Selection of marriage partners was not usually determined by love or affection, but by social and economic interests involved in the continuation of the family enterprise and care of dependents. Landlords often directly influenced the choice of their tenants' marriage partners, because they were concerned to ensure the effective working of their estates (Mitterauer and Sider, 1982). In most parts of central Europe, a person wishing to be married had to obtain the landlord's permission. The landless poor, who had little hope of obtaining a cottage or farm, were sometimes prohibited from marrying altogether.

Sexual relationships before and outside marriage were common in many areas of mediaeval Europe, among both poor and wealthier people. In some regions, it was permissible for a man to test the child-bearing capacity of his future wife by trying to impregnate her before marriage. If she became pregnant, the marriage would go ahead, but if no such result was forthcoming she would stay unmarried. Rates of illegitimacy in many parts of Europe (particularly Central Europe) were extraordinarily high by modern standards. Little shame was attached to illegitimacy, and children of extra-marital unions were frequently taken into the family and raised alongside legitimate offspring. As was mentioned in chapter 1 ('Sociology: Problems and Perspectives'), sexual passion within marriage seems to have been rare among most groups in the population. Within the aristocracy and gentry, erotic liaisons were recognized, but were almost always extra-marital.

Many sociologists used to suppose that the predominant form of family in mediaeval Europe was of the extended type, but more recent research indicates that the nuclear family was the usual form – at least, in Western parts of the continent. Households were larger than in the present day, but the difference is accounted for by domestic servants rather than kin. In England throughout the seventeenth, eighteenth and nineteenth centuries, the average household size was 4.75 people (Anderson, 1981). The current average is 3.04. Extended family groups were, apparently, more important in Eastern Europe and Russia.

In the modern family, children grow up in the household and continue to live there while at school. The obtaining of a job is a mark of adult status, and tends to be soon thereafter accompanied by marriage and the establishing of a separate household. This was not the typical sequence in mediaeval Europe. Children usually began helping their parents on the farm or at their craft from about the age of seven or eight. Those who did not help with domestic production frequently left the parental household at an early age to do domestic work in the houses of others, or to follow apprenticeships. Children who went away to work in other households might rarely or never see their parents again.

In mediaeval Europe, a quarter or more of all infants did not survive beyond the first year of life (in contrast to well under 1 per cent today). Other factors also made family groups more impermanent than they are now – in spite of the high rates of divorce in current times. Illness was a major killer, and wives frequently died in childbirth. Rates of mortality (numbers of deaths per thousand of population in any one year) were much higher than those of today, and the deaths of children, or of one or both spouses, frequently dislocated or shattered family relationships. Remarriages, with their attendant step-relationships, were common.

The development of family life

The historian Lawrence Stone has charted some of the changes leading from mediaeval to modern forms of family life (Stone, 1977). He distinguishes three main phases in the development of the family over a period of three hundred years from the 1500s to the 1800s. The dominant family form in the early part of this period, and for hundreds of years before, was what Stone calls the **open lineage family**. This was a type of nuclear family, living in a fairly small household, but deeply embedded in community relationships, including those with other kin. The family was not clearly separated from the community. According to Stone (although other historians have challenged this), at that time the family was not a major focus of emotional attachment or dependence for its members. People did not get, or look for, the emotional intimacies we associate with family life today. Sex within marriage was not regarded as a source of pleasure, but as necessary in order to propagate children.

Individual freedom of choice, in contracting marriage and in other aspects of family life, was subordinated to the interests of others, such as parents, other kin or the community. Outside aristocratic circles, erotic or romantic love was regarded by moralists and theologians as a sickness. As Stone puts it, the family during this period 'was open to support, advice, investigation and interference from the outside, from neighbours and from kin, and internal privacy was non-existent. The family, therefore, was an open-ended, low-keyed, unemotional, authoritarian institution. . . . It was also very short-lived, being frequently dissolved by the death of the husband or wife or the death or very early departure from the home of the children. . .' (Stone, 1977, p. 6).

The open lineage family was succeeded by what Stone calls the **restricted patriarchal family**, lasting from the early sixteenth century to the start of the eighteenth century. This form was largely confined to the upper reaches of society, and was a transitional type. It was nevertheless very important, because from it spread attitudes that have since become more or less universal. The nuclear family became a more separate entity, distinct from ties to other kin and to the local community. This phase of family development was associated with a growing stress on the importance of marital and parental love, although there was also a growth in the authoritarian power of fathers.

According to Stone, the restricted patriarchal family was progressively replaced by the **closed domesticated nuclear family**, a group tied by close emotional bonds, having a high degree of domestic privacy, and preoccupied with the rearing of children. This is the type of family organization that persists into the twentieth century. The closed domestic nuclear family was marked by the rise of **affective individualism**, the formation of marriage ties on the basis of personal selection, guided by norms of affection or romantic love. Sexual aspects of love began to be glorified inside marriage instead of only in extra-marital relationships.

Originating among more affluent groups, this family type gradually became more or less universal in Western countries with the spread of industrialization. The choice of a mate became based on the desire for a relationship offering affection or love. Western marriage and the family took on the overall shape they still have today.

Origins of the changes

In mediaeval times, as we have seen, the household and the local community were the chief focus of the production of goods and services. The family produced most of the resources needed for the day-to-day lives of its members, sometimes buying and selling a few goods in the village or town market. The family group was usually an integrated production unit, with all family members – wife, husband and children – working co-operatively in the production process. Although women had the main responsibility for child-rearing, they also had an important economic role in the household, production being something of an economic partnership (a situation which remains the case in rural areas in many Third World countries).

From about the seventeenth century in Europe, and rather later in the United States, smaller farming families began to be displaced from their landholdings as large-scale commercial farming started to develop. This process of displacement was subsequently greatly accelerated as industrialization got under way, and the production of goods and services was carried on in workshops, factories and offices. People (especially men and, initially, children) left the household to 'go out to work'. The family was no longer a production unit, the 'workplace' having become separate from the 'home'.

These changes broke up the 'open lineage family' among all classes. Some of the changes, however, first affected higher-status groups. The early commercial farmers, traders and industrialists freed themselves from the ties of tradition and community involvement characteristic of previous periods. They pioneered the 'restricted patriarchal family', the characteristics of which later spread to lower-class groups, eventually creating a situation in which the 'closed domesticated nuclear family' became more or less universal.

The roles of men, women and children in the family were all affected by the changes. From the early years of industrialization, many women have gone out to work as well as caring for children inside the home. But among more affluent groups it became widely believed that 'a woman's place is in the home', while the male should be the 'breadwinner'.

Many married women became 'housewives', unpaid workers in the household, whose role was to care for the husband and children. The situation of children also changed as laws were passed restricting their employment, while other statutes enforced their attendance at school.

Changes in the nature of love and its relation to sexuality were intertwined with these other developments. Ideals of romantic love arose at the same time as marriage lost its economic basis. In the patriarchal family, new ideals of family love became prominent, but these still emphasized duty rather than romantic attachment. With the separation of the home from the workplace, moreover, 'personal' relationships in the family became clearly distinguished from relationships in the sphere of work. Affective individualism began to emerge, forming the main basis of marriage and altering the relationships of women and men. By the turn of the twentieth century, it was generally held that the family is a private world of fulfilment – or should be – in which emotional and sexual intimacy between wife and husband is given primary emphasis (Cancian, 1987).

Changes in family patterns world-wide

There remains a diversity of family forms in different societies across the world. In some areas, such as remote regions in Asia, Africa or the Pacific, traditional family systems involving extended families, clans and polygamy have altered little. In most Third World countries, however, widespread changes are occurring. The origins of these changes are complex, but several factors can be picked out as especially important. They include above all, as in the West at an earlier period, the impact of modern industry and urban life. In general, these changes are creating a world-wide movement towards the predominance of the nuclear family, breaking down extended family systems and other types of kinship group. This was first documented by William J. Goode in his book *World Revolution in Family Patterns* (1963). Goode probably over-simplified some of the changes, but his claim that a general shift is occurring towards the increased prominence of the nuclear family has been borne out by subsequent research.

Directions of change

The following points summarize the most important changes occurring world-wide.

1 Clans and other corporate kin groups are declining in their influence. The post-war history of China offers an example. When the Communist government came to power in 1949, it set out to try to dissolve the influence of the *tsu* over family life and economic affairs. *Tsu* land-holdings were broken up and redistributed among

the peasants. Communes largely replaced the traditional *tsu* organization. Since then, other changes in social and economic life have further undermined its influence.

2 There is a general trend towards the free choice of spouse. Although there is by no means a complete correlation, extended family systems tend to be associated with arranged marriages. Obligations to the family group are of overriding importance in the establishing of marriage ties. Partly because of the influence of Western ideas, emphasizing individualism and romantic love, and partly because of the other factors weakening extended family systems, marriage by arrangement is coming under strain. Members of the younger generation – particularly those living and working in urban areas – often claim the right to choose their own marriage partners.

3 The rights of women are becoming more strongly recognized, in respect both of choice in marriage and decision-making within the family. Higher levels of employment for women outside the home, coupled with the liberalizing of divorce, are bound up with these changes. In some societies, husbands traditionally had almost complete discretion in divorcing their wives – needing, for example, only to tell the wife in front of witnesses that she was no longer wanted. Women's organizations are now widely pressing for equal rights of divorce – although there are many societies where little progress has been made in this respect.

4 Most marriages in traditional cultures used to be 'kin marriages'. People were expected, or obliged, to marry a partner chosen from a specific range of people, defined by means of kinship relations. For example, where strong clan groups existed, individuals were usually not allowed to marry anyone who was a member of the same clan, however distant might be the kin connection. This practice is called **exogamy**. **Endogamy** is the reverse, where individuals are obliged to marry others *within* a kin group. In both instances, kin membership is the organizing factor for the formation of marriage relationships. This is generally becoming less and less the case.

5 Higher levels of sexual freedom are developing in societies which were very restrictive. Sometimes this process has not proceeded very far, and there have been changes in the opposite direction, as happened following the Islamic Revolution in Iran in the late 1970s. (The Iranian authorities have sought to revive laws and customs limiting sexual freedom.) None the less, such examples are exceptional. In fact, many traditional societies were more liberal sexually than has ever been the case in the West, up to and including the present day.

6 There is a general trend towards the extension of children's rights. In many countries children are still subject to extreme deprivation, or sexually exploited and abused. Most governments have established legal frameworks protecting children's rights, although there is a long way to go before these are universal.

It would be a mistake to exaggerate these trends, or to suppose that the nuclear family has everywhere become the dominant form. In most societies in the world today, extended families are the norm and traditional family practices continue. Moreover, family systems are diverse, and begin from all kinds of starting-points in this process of change. There are differences in the speed at which change is occurring, and there are many reversals and counter-trends. In a study in the Philippines, for example, a higher proportion of extended families was found in urban areas than in surrounding rural regions. These were not just a development from traditional extended family households, but represented something new. Leaving the rural areas and coming to the cities, cousins, nephews and nieces went to live with their relatives to try to take advantage of the employment opportunities available there. Parallel examples have also been noted elsewhere in Third World countries (Stinner, 1979). Similar processes have been observed in some industrialized nations. In certain regions of Poland, for instance, a rejuvenation of the extended family has been documented. Many industrial workers in Poland have farms which they tend part-time. Grandparents move in with their children's family and help to run the household and bring up the children, while the younger generation is engaged in outside employment (Turowski, 1977).

Family and marriage in the United Kingdom

Overall characteristics

There are many differences in family organization within British society as a whole – some of these will be identified a little later. But there are also a number of general characteristics which apply to the majority of the population:

1 The British family is *monogamous*, monogamy being established in law. Given the high rate of divorce that now exists in the United Kingdom, however, some observers have suggested that the British marriage pattern should be called **serial monogamy**. That is to say, individuals are permitted to have a number of spouses in sequence, although no one may have more than one wife or husband at any time. It is misleading though, to muddle legal monogamy with sexual practice. It is obvious that a high proportion of Britons engage in sexual relations with individuals other than their spouses.
2 British marriage is based upon the idea of romantic love. *Affective individualism* has become the major influence. Couples are expected to develop mutual affection, based on personal attraction and compatibility, as a basis for contracting marriage relationships. Romantic love as part of marriage has become 'naturalized' in contemporary

Britain; it seems to be a normal part of human existence, rather than a distinctive feature of modern culture. Of course, the reality is divergent from the ideology. The emphasis on personal satisfaction in marriage has raised expectations which sometimes cannot be met, and this is one factor involved in increasing rates of divorce.

3 The British family is patrilineal and neo-local. **Patrilineal inheritance** involves children taking the surname of the father, and property usually passes down the male line. (Many societies in the world are **matrilineal** – surnames, and often property, pass down the female line.) A **neo-local residence** pattern involves married couples moving into a dwelling away from both of their families of orientation. Neo-localism, however, is not an absolutely fixed trait of the British family. Many families, particularly in lower-class neighbourhoods, are matrilocal – the newly-weds settle in an area close to where the bride's parents live.

4 The British family is nuclear, consisting of one or two parents living in a household with their children. However, nuclear family units are by no means completely isolated from other kin ties.

Trends of development

New forms of variation in family patterns

The Second World War disrupted marriages and family life. Divorces in 1947 were ten times the pre-war figure, although the rate subsequently dropped, rising sharply again in the early 1960s. The passing of the Legal Aid Act two years later opened the possibility of divorce to many who had previously been deterred by the expense. There was, however, no serious change in the popularity of marriage; three-quarters of those divorced remarried. A brief 'baby boom' occurred in the immediate post-war period, with the birth-rate (numbers of live births per thousand adults in any one year) reaching a peak of 20.5 in 1947. Thereafter, the birth-rate levelled off again, and has since remained quite stable.

According to Rapoport, 'families in Britain today are in a transition from coping in a society in which there was a single overriding norm of what family life should be like to a society in which a plurality of norms are recognized as legitimate and, indeed, desirable' (Rapoport and Rapoport, 1982, p. 476). Substantiating this argument, Rapoport identifies five types of diversity: *organizational, cultural, class, life-course* and *cohort*.

Families today *organize* their respective individual domestic duties and their links with the wider social environment in a variety of ways. The contrasts between 'orthodox' families – the woman as 'housewife', the husband as 'breadwinner' – with dual-career or one-parent families, illustrate this diversity. *Culturally*, there is greater diversity of family beliefs and values than used to be the case. The presence of ethnic minorities (such as West Indian, Asian, Greek or Italian communities), and the influence of movements such as feminism, have produced considerable cultural variety in family forms. Persistent *class* divisions, between the poor, the skilled working class, and the various groupings within the middle and upper classes, sustain major variations in family structure. Variations in family experience during the *life course* are fairly obvious. For instance, one individual might come from a family in which both parents had stayed together, and herself or himself become married and then divorced. Another person might be brought up in a single-parent family, be multiply married and have children by each marriage.

The term *cohort* refers to generations within families. Connections between parents and grandparents, for example, have probably become weaker than they were. On the other hand, more people now live into old age, and three 'ongoing' families might exist in close relation to one another: married grandchildren, their parents, and the grandparents.

South Asian families

Among the variety of British family types, there is one pattern distinctively different from most others – that associated with South Asian groups. The South Asian population of the UK numbers more than one million people. Migration began in the 1950s from three main areas of the Indian sub-continent: Punjab, Gujarat and Bengal. In Britain, these migrants formed communities based on religion, area of origin, caste and, most importantly, kinship. Many migrants found their ideas of honour and family loyalty almost entirely absent among the indigenous British population. They tried to maintain family unity, but housing proved a problem. Large old houses were available in run-down areas; moving up-market usually meant moving into smaller houses and breaking up the extended family.

South Asian children born in the UK are exposed to two very different cultures. At home parents expect or demand conformity to the norms of co-operation, respect and family loyalty. At school they are expected to pursue academic success in a competitive and individualistic social environment. Most of these children choose to organize their domestic and personal lives in terms of the ethnic sub-culture, as they value the close relationships associated with traditional family life. Yet exposure to British culture has brought changes. Young people of both sexes are demanding greater consultation in the arrangement of their marriages (see Ballard, 1982).

Influences on the family and marriage today

One of the most important factors influencing family life today is the large numbers of married women now working in paid employment (see chapter 6: 'Gender and Sexuality'). As was mentioned before, a proportion of married women have been employed outside the home since the early period of industrialization. Since the Second World War, however, the numbers of women in paid work have increased dramatically. This increase has helped to produce changes in family patterns as well as reflecting alterations in those patterns themselves.

Although they are mostly in inferior occupations to their partners, married women in paid work have more economic independence than those who are full-time housewives. Many women still see their wages or salaries as 'topping up' the income earned by their husbands, regarded by both as the chief source of their revenue. Yet increasing numbers of women regard success in a career as a major aspiration of their lives, rather than accepting that their sole place is as homemaker.

How far have these developments altered the respective roles of women and men within the home? Are men assuming larger respon- sibilities for domestic chores, and for child-care, than used to be the case? The evidence suggests that there have been some changes over the past three or four decades, but they have been relatively limited. Heidi Hartmann collected together the results of a range of researches carried out in the United States in the 1960s and 1970s (Hartmann, 1981). She found that, on average, women who were full-time housewives spent 60 hours a week on domestic tasks. Men spent an average of only 11. In families with young children, women gave 70 hours a week to domestic tasks, including child-care. While men spent an average of 5 hours a week on child-care, they reduced the amount of time they gave to other domestic duties accordingly.

Fewer systematic studies have been carried out in Britain than in the USA, but research that has been done indicates a similar picture. Elston studied couples in which both wife and husband were doctors (Elston, 1980). The results showed that the male doctors carried out far fewer domestic tasks than their wives. For instance, only 1 per cent of the male doctors regularly went shopping, cooked, or cleaned the house; over 80 per cent of the women doctors engaged in the first two activities, and over 50 per cent in the third. Only in a minority of cases were both partners largely relieved of domestic duties by employing domestic cleaners and child-minders. Even women in high-status and well-paid careers, then, still tend overwhelmingly to be regarded as primarily housewives and mothers in their homes.

Studies of decision-making in marriage show that men usually retain power over the economic resources of families. Men mostly decide how the overall financial management of families is organized – something which sets the framework for many other aspects of family life. A study of white-collar and professional males and their wives divided decisions into those which couples thought 'very important' and those considered 'important'. Many of the 'very important' decisions – concerning, for example, financial matters – were taken by husbands alone. 'Important' decisions – about children's education, for instance – were often taken jointly. But virtually no decisions in either category were taken by wives alone. Women usually only took sole responsibility for decisions both partners saw as trivial – such as choice of decoration (Edgell, 1980).

Women are frequently powerful within families, but they may exercise their influence in an indirect way. Whereas men can legitimately be assertive in a family context, women often disguise whatever power they may possess, because it is seen as illegitimate. A woman may have a 'nag' her husband, or risk appearing 'bossy', or use stratagems to 'get round him' to get her own way. While men may use similar devices on occasion, they are generally able to assert their influence more directly. If these inequalities are changing, it is only quite slowly.

Divorce and separation in the West

The growth in divorce

The past thirty years have seen major increases in rates of divorce, together with a decline in disapproval of it. For many centuries in the West marriage was regarded as virtually indissoluble. Divorces were granted only in very limited cases, such as non-consummation of marriage. Some countries, such as Spain, still do not recognize divorce, and in a referendum in Ireland in 1986, the majority voted against permitting couples to divorce. Yet these are now isolated examples. Most countries have moved rapidly towards making divorce more easily available. The so-called *adversary system* used to be characteristic of virtually all industrialized countries. Under it, for a divorce to be granted, one spouse had to bring charges (for example, cruelty, desertion or adultery) against the other. The first 'no fault' divorce laws were introduced in some countries in the mid-1960s. Since then, many Western states have followed suit, although the details vary. In the UK, the Divorce Reform Act, which made it easier for couples to obtain a divorce, and contained 'no fault' provisions, was passed in 1969, and came into effect in 1971.

Between 1960 and 1970, the divorce rate in Britain grew by a steady 9 per cent each year, doubling within that decade. By 1972, it had doubled again, partly as a result of the 1969 Act, which made it easier for many in long-'dead' marriages to become divorced. Since 1980, the divorce rate has stabilized to some degree, but remains at a very high level compared to any previous period (Burgoyne, Ormrod and Richards, 1987).

Divorce makes an increasing impact upon the lives of children. It has been estimated that nearly 40 per cent of children born in the UK in 1970 will at some stage before adulthood be members of a one-parent

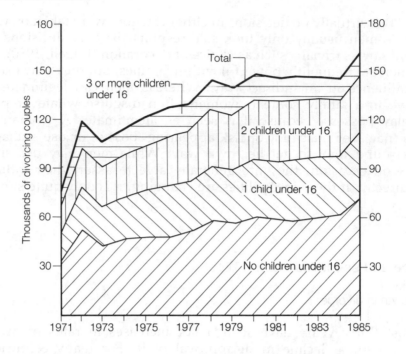

Figure 12   The rising total of divorces in England and Wales, 1971–1985, by number and age of children
Source: Social Trends (London: HMSO, 1987), p. 51.

family. Since 75 per cent of women and 83 per cent of men who are divorced remarry within three years, they will none the less grow up in a family environment. Only just over 2 per cent of children under fourteen in the UK today are not living with either parent.

Divorce rates are obviously not a direct index of marital unhappiness. For one thing, rates of divorce do not include people who are separated but have not been legally divorced. Moreover, people who are unhappily married may choose to stay together – because they believe in the sanctity of marriage, or worry about the financial or emotional consequences of a break-up, or wish to remain with one another to give their children a 'family' home.

Why is divorce becoming more common? Several factors are involved, to do with wider social changes. Except for a very small proportion of wealthy people, marriage today no longer has much connection with the desire to perpetuate property and status from generation to generation. As women become more economically independent, marriage is less of a necessary economic partnership than it used to be. Greater overall prosperity means that it is easier to establish a separate household, in case of marital disaffection,

"Darling, let's get divorced."

Drawing by Koren; © 1975 The New Yorker Magazine, Inc.

than used to be the case. The fact that little stigma now attaches to divorce is in some part the result of these developments, but also adds momentum to them. A further important factor is the growing tendency to evaluate marriage in terms of the levels of personal satisfaction it offers. Rising rates of divorce do not seem to indicate a deep dissatisfaction with marriage as such, but an increased determination to make it a rewarding and satisfying relationship.

The experience of divorce

It is extremely difficult to draw up a balance sheet of the social advantages and costs of high levels of divorce. More tolerant attitudes mean that couples can terminate an unrewarding relationship without incurring social ostracism. On the other hand, marriage break-up is almost always emotionally stressful and may create financial hardship for one or both parties.

Uncoupling

Diane Vaughan has analysed relationships between partners during the course of separation or divorce (Vaughan, 1986). She carried out a series of interviews with 103 recently separated or divorced people (mainly from middle-class backgrounds) to chart the transition from living together to living apart. The notion of *uncoupling* refers to the change out of long-term intimate relationships and into living alone. She found that in many cases before the physical parting there had been a *social separation* – at least one of the partners developed a new life-pattern, becoming interested in new pursuits, and making new friends, in contexts in which the other was not present. This usually meant keeping secrets from the other – especially, of course, when a relationship with a lover was involved.

According to Vaughan's research, uncoupling is often unintentional at first. One individual – whom she called the *initiator* – becomes less satisfied with the relationship than the other, and creates a 'territory' independent of the activities in which the couple engages together. For some time before this, the initiator may have been trying unsuccessfully to change the partner, to get him or her to behave in more acceptable ways, foster shared interests and so forth. At some point, the initiator feels that the attempt has failed and that the relationship is fundamentally flawed. From then onwards, he or she becomes preoccupied with the ways in which the relationship or the partner is defective. Vaughan suggested that this is the opposite of the process of 'falling in love' at the beginning of a relationship, when an individual focuses on the attractive features of the other, ignoring those which might be less acceptable.

Initiators seriously considering a break normally discuss their relationship extensively with others, 'comparing notes'. In so doing, they weigh the costs and benefits of separation. Can I survive on my own? How will friends and parents react? Will the children suffer? Will I be financially solvent? Having thought about these and other problems, some decide to try again to make the relationship work. For those who proceed with a separation, these discussions and enquiries help make the break less intimidating, building confidence that they are doing the right thing. Most initiators become convinced that a responsibility for their own self-development takes priority over commitment to the other.

Of course, uncoupling is not always wholly led by one individual. The other partner may also have decided that the relationship cannot be saved. In some situations, an abrupt reversal of roles occurs. The person who previously wanted to save the relationship becomes determined to end it, while the erstwhile initiator wishes to carry on.

Transitions in divorce

Should a couple decide to divorce, a number of major transitions of life-style and outlook have to be made. Paul Bohannan distinguishes six overlapping *stations of divorce* that a couple who part have to face (Bohannan, 1970). All may create difficulties and tensions, affecting the two people themselves, their children, relatives and friends:

1 *The emotional divorce*, expressing the deteriorating marriage itself – increasing tension between partners, leading usually to separation.
2 *The legal divorce*, involving the grounds upon which the marriage is ended.
3 *The economic divorce*, concerned with the division of wealth and property.
4 *The co-parental divorce*, covering issues of child custody and visiting rights.
5 *The community divorce*, concerning the alterations in friendships and other social relations that a divorced person undergoes.
6 *The psychic divorce*, whereby the individual has finally to sever ties of emotional dependence, and face the demands of living alone.

A series of interviews which Robert Weiss carried out with divorced men and women in the United States showed a definite 'trajectory' of adjustment (Weiss, 1976). Women suffer from divorce far more than men on an economic level, but the process of psychological and social adjustment seems similar for both sexes. In the majority of instances Weiss studied, the respect and liking a couple may have felt for one another disappears some while before they separate. Hostility and mistrust take their place. At the same time, a sense of being bound emotionally to the other person persists. Thus, even though a couple may row bitterly just before parting, they tend to experience profound feelings of what Weiss calls *separation distress*. The sudden absence of the spouse creates feelings of anxiety or panic. A minority of individuals have an opposite experience – a feeling of euphoria in response to being free and able to deal with their lives on their own. Feelings of depression and euphoria can also alternate with one another. After a time, distress and euphoria both give way to sensations of loneliness. People feel separated from the secure family worlds in which others, for all their problems, seem to live. Friendship relations in fact do almost always alter. Although friends may attempt to maintain contact with both ex-partners, gradually they tend to see much more of one than the other.

Divorce and children

The effects of parents divorcing on children are difficult to gauge. How much conflict there is between the parents before separation; the age of the children at the time; whether or not they have brothers or sisters; the availability of grandparents and other relatives; their relationships with their individual parents; how far they continue to see both parents frequently – all these and other influences can affect the process of adjustment. Since children whose parents are unhappily married but stay together may be affected by the resulting tension, assessing the consequences of divorce for children is doubly difficult.

Research indicates that children do often suffer marked emotional anxiety after the separation of their parents. Judith Wallerstein and Joan Kelly studied the children of sixty recently separated couples in Marin County, California (Wallerstein and Kelly, 1980). They contacted the children at the time of the divorce in court, a year and a half afterwards, and five years later. According to the authors, almost all the 131 children involved experienced intense emotional disturbance at the time of the divorce. The children of pre-school age were confused and frightened, tending to blame themselves for the separation. Older children were better able to understand their parents' motives for divorce, but frequently worried deeply about its effects upon their future and often expressed sharp feelings of anger. At the end of the five-year period, however, the researchers found that two-thirds of the children were coping at least reasonably well with their home lives and their commitments outside. A third remained actively dissatisfied with their lives, subject to depression and feelings of loneliness, even in some cases where the parent with whom they were living had remarried.

We cannot say, of course, how the children might have fared if their parents had stayed together. The people studied all came from an affluent white area, and might or might not be representative of the wider population. Moreover, the families were self-selected, in the sense that they had approached counsellors seeking help. Those who actively seek counselling might be less (or more!) able to cope with separation than those who do not. One finding that does seem to emerge from this and other research is that children fare better when they have a continuing relationship with both parents after separation than when they see only one parent regularly.

Remarriage and step-parenting

Remarriage

Remarriage can involve various circumstances. Some remarried couples are in their early twenties, neither bringing a child to the new relationship. People who remarry in their late twenties, thirties or early forties each might take one or more children from the former marriage or marriages to live in the same dwelling as their new partner. Those who remarry at later ages might have adult children who never live in the new homes the parents establish. There may also be children within the new marriage itself. Either one of the new couple may previously have been single, divorced or widowed, adding up to eight possible combinations. Generalizations about remarriage therefore have to be made with considerable caution, although some general points are worth making.

In 1900, about nine-tenths of all marriages in the United Kingdom were first marriages. Most remarriages involved at least one widowed person. With the rise in the divorce rate, the level of remarriage also began to climb, and an increasing proportion of remarriages began to involve divorced people. In the' 1960s, the remarriage rate increased rapidly, tailing off during the 1970s and early 1980s.

Today, twenty-eight out of every hundred marriages involves at least one previously married person. Up to the age of thirty-five, the majority of remarriages involve divorced people. After that age, the proportion of remarriages involving widows or widowers rises, and by fifty-five the proportion of such remarriages is larger than those following divorce.

Odd though it might seem, the best way to maximize the chances of marriage, for both sexes, is to have been married before! People who have been married and divorced are more likely to marry again than single people in similar age-groups are to marry for the first time. At all age levels, divorced men are more likely to remarry than divorced women: three in every four divorced women, but five in every six divorced men, remarry. In statistical terms, at least, remarriages are less successful than first marriages. Rates of divorce of people from second marriages are higher than those from first marriages.

This does not show that second marriages are doomed to fail. People who have been divorced may have higher expectations of marriage than those who have not. Hence they may be more ready to dissolve new marriages than those only married once. The second marriages which endure might be more satisfying, on average, than first marriages (Glenn and Weaver, 1956).

Step-families

A **step-family** may be defined as a family in which at least one of the adults is a step-parent (Vischer and Vischer, 1979). Using such a definition, the number of step-families is much greater than shown in available official statistics, since these usually refer only to families with whom step-children live. Many who remarry become step-parents of children who visit regularly, but don't live permanently in the same household.

The existence of step-families brings into being kin ties which resemble those of some traditional societies. Children may now have two 'mothers' and two 'fathers' – their natural parents and their step-parents. Some step-families regard all the children and close relatives from previous marriages as 'part of the family'. If we consider that at least some of the grandparents may be closely involved, the result is a situation of some complexity.

An added feature is the practice of adoption. Brenda Maddox has estimated that more than one-third of all adoptions in the United States are of step-children. The proportion in Britain is lower, but the rate is climbing (Maddox, 1975). Adoption is a method by which the non-biological parent makes up in some way for the lack of genetic connection, by making a public declaration of affiliation to the child. Adoptive parents have legal rights and obligations towards their children. Other step-parents lack these, and in most cases their relationship with their step-children endures only as long as the marriage lasts. According to the law in most countries, if the biological parent in a step-family dies or is divorced from the step-parent, the step-parent has no legal rights of custody over the children. Even if a child has lived with a step-parent for many years, if the natural parent dies the step-parent has little recourse in law if the other natural parent wishes to have custody.

Certain difficulties tend to arise in step-families. In the first place, there is usually a biological parent living elsewhere whose influence over the child or children is likely to remain powerful. Secondly, co-operative relations between divorced individuals are often strained when one or both remarries. Take the case of a woman with two children who marries a man who also has two, and all live together. If the 'outside' parents insist that children visit them at the same times as before, the major tensions involved in welding such a newly established family together will be exacerbated. For example, it may prove impossible ever to have the new family together at weekends.

Thirdly, step-families merge children from different backgrounds, who may have varying expectations of appropriate behaviour within the family. Since most step-children 'belong' to two households, the likelihood of clashes in habits and outlook are considerable. Finally, there are few established norms which define the relationship between step-parent and step-child. Should a child call a new step-parent by name, or is 'Dad' or 'Mum' more appropriate? Should the step-parent discipline the children as a natural parent would? How should a step-parent treat the new spouse of his or her previous partner when collecting the children?

This letter and response appeared in Dear Abbie, a 'problem column' syndicated in many American newspapers.

> *Dear Abbie*
>
> A year ago I married Ted. His wife (Maxine) died and left him with two children, ages six and eight. This is my first marriage. I say that after Maxine died, Ted is no longer related to Maxine's relatives. Ted says Maxine's parents will always be his in-laws. Well, I have parents, too, so where does that leave them? A person can only have one set of in-laws at a time, and *my* parents should be regarded as grandparents, too, and they aren't. The titles of 'grandma' and 'grandpa' go to Maxine's parents. My parents are called 'papa Pete' and 'mama Mary'. Do you think this is fair? . . . and what can I do about it? [*signed* In-law trouble]
>
> *Dear In-law trouble*
>
> Even though technically Ted is no longer the son-in-law of Maxine's parents, I advise you not to be so technical. There is a strong bond between Ted's former in-laws and their grandchildren, so if you're wise

you won't tamper with these bonds because they were established before
you came into the picture. Grandparents are grandparents for ever.
(Quoted in Vischer and Vischer, 1979, p. 132)

Step-families are developing types of kinship connection which are new
to modern Western societies, although the problem experienced by 'In-
law trouble' would have been common in mediaeval Europe and other
traditional societies. The difficulties created by remarriage *after divorce*
are really new. Members of these families are developing their own
ways of adjusting to the relatively uncharted circumstances in which
they find themselves. (It is an interesting example of the ways in which
we are all usually governed or at least influenced by cultural norms;
where norms are absent, insecurity, confusion and misunderstanding
are frequent problems, and will persist until norms become established.)
Perhaps the most appropriate conclusion to be drawn is that while marriages are broken up by divorce, families on the whole are not. Especially
where children are involved, many ties persist despite the reconstructed
family connections brought into being through remarriage.

The dark side of the family

Since family or kin relations form part of everyone's existence, family
life encompasses virtually the whole range of emotional experience.
Family relationships – between wife and husband, parents and children,
brothers and sisters, or between distant relatives – can be warm and
fulfilling. But they can equally well be full of the most pronounced
tensions driving people to despair, or filling them with a deep sense of
anxiety and guilt. The 'dark side' of family life is extensive, and belies
the rosy images of harmony with which we are relentlessly bombarded
in TV commercials and elsewhere in the popular media. There are many
aspects to the unattractive side of the family, including the conflicts
and hostilities that lead to separation and divorce, just discussed, and
the association of family relationships with the onset of mental illness.
Among the most devastating in their consequences, however, are the
incestuous abuse of children and domestic violence.

Sexual abuse

The sexual abuse of children is a widespread phenomenon and much
of it happens in the context of the family. *Sexual abuse* can most easily
be defined as the carrying out of sexual acts by adults with children
below the age of consent (sixteen years old in Britain). *Incest* refers to
sexual relations between close kin. Not all incest is sexual abuse. For
example, sexual intercourse between brother and sister is incestual,

but does not fit the definition of abuse. In sexual abuse, an adult is essentially exploiting an infant or child for sexual purposes (Ennew, 1986). The most common form of incest is one that is also sexual abuse – incestuous relations between fathers and young daughters.

Incest, and child sexual abuse more generally, are phenomena which have been 'discovered' only over the past ten to twenty years. Of course it has long been known that such sexual acts occasionally occur, but it was assumed by most social observers that the strong taboos which exist against this behaviour meant that it was not widespread. Such is not the case. Child sexual abuse is proving to be disturbingly commonplace. It is probably found more often among lower-class families, but exists at all levels of the social hierarchy. Statistics reported to the nation-wide data collection system in the United States charted an increase of 600 per cent in reported cases of child sexual abuse between the years 1976 and 1982 (Finkelhor, 1984).

It is almost certain that this increase results from more direct attention being paid to the problem by welfare agencies and the police. It is equally certain that such statistics represent no more than the tip of the iceberg. In some surveys carried out in Britain and the US in the 1980s, more than a third of women were found to have been victims of sexual abuse in childhood, meaning that they had experienced unwanted sexual touching. The figure for males is about 10 per cent (Russell, 1984).

Why have incest and child sexual abuse come into public view so suddenly? Part of the answer seems to be that the taboos against such activity led welfare workers and social researchers in the past to be wary of asking questions about it to parents or children. The women's movement played an important role in initially drawing public attention to sexual abuse through their inclusion of it as one element in wider campaigns against sexual harassment and exploitation. Once researchers began to probe into suspected cases of child sexual abuse, many more came to light. The 'discovery' of child sexual abuse, beginning in the United states, has been an international phenomenon (CIBA Foundation, 1984).

We do not know exactly what proportion of child sexual abuse is incestuous, but it is likely that most cases occur in a family context. Both the nature of the incestuous relation, and the sexual acts committed, vary quite widely. Most studies indicate that 70–80 per cent of incest cases are father–daughter or stepfather–daughter relationships. However, uncle–niece, brother–sister, father–son, mother–daughter and even grandparent–grandchild relationships also occur. Some incestual contacts are transitory and involve simply a fondling of the child's sexual organs by the adult, or the child being encouraged to touch the adult's genitals. Others are much more extensive and may be repeated over several years. The children involved are usually over two years old, but there are many reported instances of sexual acts with infants. In one case, for example, a baby died from suffocation induced by fellatio (oral sex) (Goodwin, 1982).

Sometimes multiple incestuous relationships exist within the same family group. One study, for instance, reported a case in which the father had had sexual intercourse with his daughter, aged fourteen, and had also committed buggery with his thirteen-year-old son who, in turn, had had sexual intercourse with his sister, as had another brother. The mother knew of these activities, but was too frightened of her husband to report any of them to the authorities. The full extent of the abuse only came to light when the father was arrested for physically beating his daughter (CIBA Foundation, 1984, p. 128).

Force or the threat of violence is involved in many cases of incest. Children are in some instances more or less willing participants, but this seems quite rare. Children are sexual beings, of course, and quite often engage in mild sexual play or exploration with one another. But the large majority of children subject to sexual contact from adult family members find the experience repugnant, shameful or disturbing. There is now considerable material to indicate that child sexual abuse might have long-term consequences for its sufferers. Studies of prostitutes, juvenile offenders, adolescent runaways and drug-users show that a high proportion have a history of child sexual abuse. Of course, correlation is not causation (see chapter 21: 'Working with Sociology: Methods of Research'). Demonstrating that people in these categories have been sexually abused as children does not show that such abuse was a causal influence over their later behaviour. Probably a range of factors is involved, such as family conflicts, parental neglect, physical abuse and so on.

Explanations

To explain why incest and, more broadly, child sexual abuse occur, we have to account for two things. First, why adults should be attracted to sexual activities involving children and, second, why men should make up the vast majority of abusers. Each of these raises complex issues, given the variable nature of the acts and the relationships concerned. We can say with some certainty that only a minority of the perpetrators of child sexual abuse are mentally ill. In other words, we cannot explain adult attraction to sexual involvement with children in terms of mental disorder.

Most child abusers do not seem to have a *preference* for sexual relationships with children as opposed to other adults. Rather, it is a matter of availability coupled with power. Children within the family are dependent beings and highly vulnerable to parental demands or pressures. Adults involved in incest with their children often seem to be timid, awkward and inadequate in their dealings with other adults. Many appear not just to be satisfying sexual impulses, but searching for affection they cannot obtain elsewhere. We can make a connection here with the fact that the large majority of abusers are men. In an earlier chapter (chapter 6: 'Gender and Sexuality') we discussed 'male inexpressiveness' – the difficulty many men have in expressing feelings, a phenomenon which probably has deep psychological origins. Men come to associate the expression of feeling directly with sexuality, whereas women focus more on whole relationships. Males also associate sexuality with the assertion of power and with submissiveness in their partners. There is less of a difference, therefore, for men between adult sexuality and sexual attraction to children than for women.

As one of the leading students of child abuse, David Finkelhor, has argued, such an interpretation provides clear implications about some of the social and psychological changes which would help reduce the sexual exploitation of children:

> First, men might benefit from the opportunity to practise affection and dependency in relationships that did not involve sex, such as male-to-male friendships and nurturant interaction with children. Second, the accomplishment of heterosexual sex might be de-emphasized as the ultimate criterion of male adequacy. Third, men might learn to enjoy sexual relationships based on equality. Men who are comfortable relating to women at the same level of maturity and competence will be less likely to exploit children sexually. As men's relations with women change, so will their relations with children. (Finkelhor, 1984, p. 13)

Violence within the family

Violence within family settings is also primarily a male domain. We may define domestic violence as physical abuse directed by one member of the family against another or others. Studies show that the prime targets of physical abuse are again children, especially small children under the age of six. Violence by husbands against wives is the second most common type, a phenomenon we have also referred to in chapter 6. Women, however, can also be the perpetrators of physical violence in the household, violence directed against young children and husbands.

The home is in fact the most dangerous place in modern society. In statistical terms, a person of any age or of either sex is far more likely to be subject to physical attack in the home than on the street at night. One in four murders in the UK is committed by one family member against another.

It is occasionally claimed that women are almost as violent as men in the home towards both spouses and children. Some surveys indicate that wives hit husbands nearly as often as the reverse (Straus, Gelles and Steinmetz, 1980). However, violence by females is more restrained and episodic than that of men, and much less likely to cause enduring physical harm. 'Wife-battering' – the regular physical brutalizing of wives by husbands – has no real equivalent the other way around.

Men who physically abuse children are also much more likely to do so in a consistent way, causing longstanding injuries, than are women.

Why is domestic violence so commonplace? Several sets of factors are involved. One is the combination of emotional intensity and personal intimacy characteristic of family life. Family ties are normally charged with strong emotions, often mixing love and hate. Quarrels which break out in the domestic setting can unleash antagonisms that would not be felt in the same way in other social contexts. What seems only a minor incident can precipitate full-scale hostilities between spouses, or between parents and children. A man tolerant towards eccentricities in the behaviour of other women may become furious if his wife talks too much at a dinner party, or reveals intimacies he wishes to keep secret.

A second influence is the fact that a good deal of violence within the family is actually tolerated, and even approved of. Although socially sanctioned family violence is relatively confined in nature, it can easily spill over into more severe forms of assault. There are few children in Britain who have not at some time been slapped or hit, even in a minor way, by one of their parents. Such actions quite often meet with general approval on the part of others, and they are probably not even thought of as 'violence'. If a stranger slapped a child in a shop because he disapproved of something she said or did, it would be a different matter. Yet there is no difference in the assault involved.

Although it is less clear-cut, there is also social approval of violence between spouses. Murray Straus has argued that parenthood provides a 'licence for hitting' and 'the marriage licence is a hitting licence' (Straus, 1978, p. 455). The cultural acceptability of this form of domestic violence is expressed in the old ditty:

> A woman, a horse and a hickory tree
> The more you beat 'em the better they be.

In the workplace and other public settings, it is a general rule that no one can hit anyone else, no matter how objectionable or irritating they may be. This is not the case within the family. Many research studies have shown that a substantial proportion of couples believe that in some circumstances it is legitimate for a spouse to strike the other. About one in four Americans of both sexes takes the view that there can be a good reason for a husband to strike a wife. A somewhat lower proportion believe that the reverse also holds (Greenblat, 1983).

However, violence within the family does also reflect broader patterns of violent behaviour. Many husbands who physically abuse their wives and children have records of violence in other contexts. A study by Jeffrey Fagan and his co-researchers (1983) of a national sample of battered wives showed that more than half their husbands were violent with others as well as their partners. More than 80 per cent of these men had in fact been arrested at least once for episodes of violence of a non-domestic kind.

Alternatives to marriage and the family

Communes

The family has long had its critics. In the nineteenth century, numerous thinkers proposed that family life should be replaced by more communal forms of living. Some of these ideas were acted on, one of the best-known examples being the Oneida Community, of New England in the USA, set up in the middle of the nineteenth century. It was based on the religious beliefs of John Humphrey Noyes. Every man in the community was married to every woman, and all were supposed to be parents to the community's children. After various initial difficulties, the group expanded to include about three hundred people and endured for about thirty years before breaking up. Many other communes have been founded since then, in Britain as well as many other Western countries. A large variety of communal groups were established in the 1960s, often involving free sexual relations within the group and collective responsibility for the raising of children. A small number of these are still in existence.

The most important current example of communal domestic life is that of the **kibbutzim** in Israel. A kibbutz is a community of families and individuals which co-operates in the raising of children. Most of the kibbutzim were originally collective farming enterprises, but today many have also moved into industrial production. There are more than 240 kibbutzim in Israel, having nearly 100,000 members in all. Some are small, with no more than 50 members, while others include as many as 2,000 people. Each kibbutz operates as though it were a single household, child-care being treated as the responsibility of the whole community rather than the family. In some, children live in special 'children's houses' rather than with their parents, although they usually spend weekends with their families.

The kibbutzim were originally established with a radical intent. Communal ownership of property, together with the group rearing of children, were to allow kibbutzim members to escape the individualistic, competitive nature of life in modern societies. These ideals have by no means been abandoned, yet over the years the majority of kibbutzim have opted for more conventional living arrangements than those favoured in the early stages. It is more common for children to sleep in their parents' quarters, for instance, than used to be the case.

Cohabitation

Cohabitation – where a couple lives together in a sexual relationship without being married – has become increasingly widespread in most Western societies. In Sweden, East Germany, and some other countries, it has become the norm for couples to live together before marriage. Since it is only relatively recently that a high proportion of people have been cohabiting in this way, it is difficult as yet to say how far it signals primarily a postponement of marriage, and how far a permanent situation. In a Swedish survey of unmarried people living together to whom children were born in 1971, the majority were shown still to be living together in 1975, by the time the offspring had reached the age of four. Only 43 per cent of these couples had married (Agell, 1980).

In Britain until very recently cohabitation was generally regarded as somewhat scandalous. During the 1970s, however, the number of unmarried men and women sharing a household went up by nearly 300 per cent. Cohabitation has become widespread among college and university students. Virtually no research has been carried out into cohabitation in the UK, but surveys in the United States indicate that about one in four students there lives with a partner with whom they are involved in a sexual relationship at some point during the course of their college careers (Macklin, 1978). In a national survey of cohabitation in the USA, a sample of 2,510 unmarried men aged twenty to thirty were contacted. While only 5 per cent were living with a woman at the date of the interview, 18 per cent had cohabited for at least six months at previous times in their lives (Clayton and Voss, 1977).

Cohabitation in Britain today seems to be for the most part an experimental stage before marriage. Young people come to live together usually by drifting into it, rather than through calculated planning. A couple who are already having a sexual relationship spend more and more time together, eventually giving up one or other of their individual homes. Young people living together almost always anticipate getting married at some date, but not necessarily to their current partners. Only a minority of such couples pool their finances. Living with a member of the opposite sex remains a rather furtive activity for many people in their late teens. Most young women still attempt to conceal the true nature of their living arrangements from parents – although men are less troubled by this.

It does not seem likely that trends towards extensive cohabitation in Britain will proceed in the near future as far as they have in Sweden. Living together is not yet established as a significant alternative to marriage. In some countries, including Britain, the law now recognizes that people living together have rights similar to those of married couples. Should the relationship be broken up, individuals can sue for a property settlement and for maintenance. The most internationally publicized case in recent years concerned the relationship between the actor Lee Marvin and his companion Michelle Triola Marvin. When their relationship ended, Michelle Marvin claimed financial support, some of which was ultimately granted by a California court.

Gay-parent families

Many homosexual men and women live in stable relationships as couples, and some gay couples have been formally 'married' even

Table 11   Percentages of people living alone in private households in Great Britain

Age groups	1973	1984	1985
Males and females			
16–24	1.5	3.4	3.6
25–44	2.4	5.4	5.3
45–64	8.1	10.4	10.6
65–74	25.7	28.0	28.9
75 or over	40.0	46.6	47.0
All aged 16 or over	9.1	12.3	12.3
Males			
65–74	13.1	15.8	16.5
75 or over	24.2	29.4	26.2
Females			
65–74	35.8	37.4	38.8
75 or over	48.0	56.3	58.1

Source: Social Trends (London: HMSO, 1987), p. 44.

if these ceremonies have no standing in law. Relaxation of previously intolerant attitudes towards homosexuality has been accompanied by a growing tendency for courts to allocate custody of children to mothers living in gay relationships. Techniques of artificial insemination mean that gay women may start a family without any heterosexual contacts. While virtually every gay family with children in Britain involves two women, for a period in the late 1960s and early 1970s social welfare agencies in several cities in the USA placed homeless gay teenage boys in the custody of gay male couples. The practice was discontinued, largely because of adverse public reaction.

Staying single

Several factors have combined to increase the numbers of people living alone in modern Western societies (see table 11). One is a trend towards later marriages – people now marry on average about three years later than was the case in 1960 – another is the rising rate of divorce. Yet another is the growing numbers of old people in the population whose partners have died. Being single means different things at different periods of the life-cycle. A larger proportion of people in their twenties are unmarried than used to be the case. By their mid-thirties, however, only a small minority of men and women have never been married. The majority of single people aged thirty to fifty are divorced and 'in between' marriages. Most single people over fifty are widowed.

Peter Stein interviewed sixty single individuals in the age range twenty-five to forty-five (Stein, 1980). Most felt ambivalent about being single. They recognized that being single often helped their career opportunities because they could concentrate whole-heartedly upon work, made available a wider variety of sexual experiences, and promoted overall freedom and autonomy. On the other hand, they acknowledged the difficulty of being single in a world where most people their age were married, and suffered from isolation or loneliness. On the whole, most found the pressures to marry greater than the incentives to stay single.

The decline of the family?

In 1859, a contributor to the *Boston Quarterly Review* wrote that 'The family, in its old sense, is disappearing from our land, and not only our free institutions are threatened but the very existence of our society is endangered' (quoted in Lantz, Schultz and O'Hara, 1977). This sort of judgement has echoed down the years in most Western countries, anxiously and regularly expressed. The Conservative Party made the family a political issue in Britain during the 1980s. Margaret Thatcher told the 1986 Conservative Women's Conference: 'Our policy starts with the family, its freedom and its well-being.' Critics of the family, on the other hand, have looked forward with approval to the decline, and even the disappearance, of family institutions.

Since it has so often been said – with little real justification – that the family is disappearing, we should be sceptical of sweeping judgements. Yet it would be difficult to deny that major shifts in the nature of both marriage and the family are taking place today, which both express and contribute to broader social changes. It seems almost certain that a continuing variety of social and sexual relationships will flourish. It seems equally clear that the family is not on the verge of crumbling or falling into decay.

Summary

1   *Kinship, family* and *marriage* are closely related terms of key significance for sociology and anthropology. *Kinship* comprises either genetic ties or ties initiated by marriage. A *family* is a group of kin having responsibility for the upbringing of children. *Marriage* is a bond between two people living together in a socially approved sexual relationship.

2   A *nuclear family* is a household in which a married couple (or single parent) live together with their own or adopted children. Where kin other than a married couple and children live in the same household, or are involved in close and continuous relationships, we speak of the existence of an *extended family*.

3   In Western societies, marriage, and therefore the family, are associated with *monogamy* (a culturally approved sexual relationship between one

woman and one man). Many other cultures tolerate or encourage *polygamy*, in which an individual may be married to two or more spouses at the same time. *Polygyny*, in which a man may marry more than one wife, is far more common than *polyandry*, in which a woman may have more than one husband.

4   In Western Europe and the USA, nuclear family patterns were strongly implanted well before the development of industrialization, although they were profoundly influenced by it. Elsewhere there is a diversity of family forms. Changes in family patterns are generated by such factors as the development of centralized government, the expansion of towns and cities, and employment within organizations outside family influence. These changes are tending to produce a worldwide movement towards nuclear family systems, eroding extended family forms and other types of kinship group.

5   There have been major changes in patterns of family life in the West during the post-war period. A high percentage of women are in the paid labour-force, divorce rates are rising, and substantial proportions of the population are either in single-parent households or are living within step-families. *Cohabitation* (where a couple lives together in a sexual relationship outside of marriage) has become increasingly common in many industrial countries.

6   Family life is by no means always a picture of harmony and happiness. The 'dark side' of the family is found in the patterns of sexual abuse and domestic violence which often occur within it. Most sexual abuse of children is carried out by males, and seems to connect with other types of violent behaviour in which some men are involved.

7   Marriage has ceased to be (if it ever was) the condition of regular sexual experience, for either sex; it is no longer the basis of economic activity. It seems certain that varying forms of social and sexual relationships will flourish still further, yet marriage and the family remain firmly established institutions.

Basic concepts

social institution	kinship
family	marriage

Important terms

clan	restricted patriarchal family
nuclear family	closed domesticated nuclear family
extended family	affective individualism
family of orientation	exogamy
family of procreation	endogamy

matrilocal family	serial monogamy
patrilocal family	patrilineal inheritance
monogamy	matrilineal inheritance
polygamy	neo-local residence
polygyny	step-families
polyandry	kibbutzim
open lineage family	cohabitation

Further reading

Tamara K. Haraven, *Family Time and Industrial Time* (Cambridge: Cambridge University Press, 1982) — an interesting account of the changes brought about in family life by the development of factory production.

Christopher Harris, *The Family and Industrial Society* (London: Allen and Unwin, 1983) — a useful general survey of the sociology of marriage and the family.

Peter Laslett, *The World We Have Lost* (London: Methuen, 1979) — a classic study of how family patterns, and other related institutions, have been transformed over the past several centuries.

Martin Richards, Jackie Burgoyne and Roger Ormrod, *Divorce Matters* (Harmondsworth: Penguin, 1987) — a recent discussion of trends in divorce.

Lawrence Stone, 'Family history in the 1980s', *Journal of Interdisciplinary History*, XII (1981) — an article which examines how and why we study the history of the family.

13

Education, Communication and Media

Imagine you are in the shoes – or the wooden clogs – of Jean-Paul Didion, a peasant boy growing up in a French farming community about two centuries ago. Jean-Paul is fourteen years old in 1750. He cannot read or write, but this is not uncommon; only a few of the adults in his village have the ability to decipher more than the odd word or two of written texts. There are some schools in nearby districts, run by monks and nuns, but these are completely removed from Jean-Paul's experience. He has never known anyone who attended school, save for the local priest. For the past eight or nine years, Jean-Paul has been spending most of his days helping with domestic tasks and working in the fields. The older he gets, the longer each day he is expected to share in the hard physical work involved in intensive tilling of his father's plot of land.

Jean-Paul is likely never to leave the area in which he was born, and may spend almost his whole life within the village and surrounding fields, only occasionally travelling to other local villages and towns. He may have to wait until he is in his late fifties before inheriting his father's plot, then sharing control of it with his younger brothers. Jean-Paul is aware that he is 'French', that his country is ruled by a particular monarch, and that there is a wider world beyond even France itself. But he only has a vague awareness even of 'France' as a distinct political entity. There is no such thing as 'news' or any regular means by which information about events elsewhere reaches him. What he knows of the wider world comes from stories and tales he has heard from adults, including a few visiting travellers. Like others in his community, he only learns about major events – like the death of the king – days, weeks, or sometimes months, after they have occurred.

Although in modern terms Jean-Paul is uneducated, he is far from being ignorant. He has a sensitive and developed understanding of the family and children, having had to care for those younger than himself since he was very young. He is already highly knowledgeable about the land, methods of crop production and modes of preserving and storing food. His mastery of local customs and traditions is profound, and he can turn his hand to many tasks other than agricultural cultivation, such as weaving or basket-making.

Jean-Paul is an invention, but the description above represents the typical experience of a boy growing up in early modern Europe. Compare our situation today. In the industrialized countries, virtually everyone can read and write. We are all aware of being members of a particular society, have at least some knowledge of its geographical position in the world, and of its past history. Our lives are influenced at all ages beyond infancy by information we pick up through books, newspapers, magazines and television. We have all undergone a process of formal schooling. The printed word, electronic communication, combined with the formal teaching provided by schools and colleges, have become fundamental to our way of life.

In this chapter, we shall study how present-day education has developed, and analyse its social influence, moving on to discuss the nature of modern systems of communication.

The early development of literacy and schooling

The term 'school' has its origins in a Greek word meaning leisure or recreation. In pre-industrial societies, schooling was available only to the few who had the time and money available to pursue it. Religious leaders or priests were often the only fully literate groups, using their knowledge to read and interpret sacred texts. For the vast majority of people, growing up meant learning by example the same social habits and work skills as their elders. As we have seen, children normally began assisting in domestic, farm and craft work at a very young age. Reading was not necessary or even useful in their daily lives.

Another reason why so few were able to read was that all texts had to be laboriously copied by hand, and so were scarce and expensive. Printing, an invention which came to Europe from China, altered that situation. The first printing press in the West was invented by Johann Gutenberg in 1454. Printing made texts and documents widely available. These included books and pamphlets, but also many kinds of routine materials essential to the running of an ever complex society. Codes of law, for instance, were written down and widely diffused. Records, reports and the collection of routine data increasingly became part of government, economic enterprises and organizations in general. The increasing use of written materials in many different spheres of life led to higher levels of **literacy** (the ability to read and write at a basic level) than had ever previously been the case. **Education** in its modern form, involving the instruction of pupils within specially constructed school premises, gradually began to emerge. Yet until a century and a half ago, and even beyond, the children of the wealthy were frequently educated by private tutors. Most of the population continued to have no schooling whatsoever until the first few decades of the nineteenth century, when in the European countries and the United States systems of primary schools began to be constructed.

The process of industrialization, and the expansion of cities, served to increase demands for specialized schooling. People now work in many different occupations, and work skills can no longer be passed on directly from parents to children. The acquisition of knowledge becomes increasingly based upon abstract learning (of subjects like maths, science, history, literature and so forth), rather than upon the practical transmission of specific skills. In a modern society people have to be furnished with basic skills, such as reading, writing and calculating and a general knowledge of their physical, social and economic environment; and it is also important that they know how to learn, so that they are able to master new, sometimes very technical, forms of information.

The development of schooling in the United Kingdom

Between 1880 (when compulsory education was first established in Britain) and the Second World War, successive governments increased expenditure on education. The school leaving age rose from ten to fourteen, and more and more schools were built, but education was not really considered to be a major area for government intervention (Chapman, 1986). Most schools were run by private or church authorities under the supervision of local government boards. The Second World War changed this attitude. Recruits to the armed forces were given ability tests; the results startled the authorities by showing widespread ignorance. Concerned about prospects for post-war recovery, the government began to rethink the existing educational system.

Up to 1944, the vast majority of British children attended a single free school, the *elementary* school, until the age of fourteen. *Secondary* schools existed alongside the elementary system, but parents had to pay. This system divided children along clear lines of social class – children from poorer backgrounds were almost all confined to elementary schooling. Less than 2 per cent of the population attended university. The Education Act of 1944 initiated several major changes, including free secondary education for all; the raising of the school leaving age to fifteen; and a commitment to equality of opportunity in education.

As a result of the Act, the majority of local education authorities adopted academic selection as a means of providing secondary education tailored to children's needs. Academic selection at age eleven – the age of transition from primary to secondary school – was supposed to sort out the more able from duller children, regardless of social background. Results in the 'eleven-plus' examination determined whether pupils went on to *grammar schools* (for the more 'academic' children), or to *secondary modern schools* (for those presumed to be more suited to vocational learning). The option of staying on at school until seventeen was available for those who wanted to continue their education.

By the 1960s – partly as a result of sociological research – it had become clear that the results of the eleven-plus had not come up to expectations. The Crowther Report of 1959 showed that only 12 per cent of pupils continued in school until the age of seventeen, and early leaving was shown to be more closely related to class background than to academic performance. The Labour government which was returned to power in 1964 was committed to establishing *comprehensive schools*, abolishing the division between grammar and secondary modern, and thus mixing together children of diverse class backgrounds. However, there was confusion over what the comprehensive school should offer: 'grammar schools for all', or a completely new type of education. No one solution was found to the problem, and different schools and regions developed their own approaches. Some local authorities resisted the change, and in a few areas grammar schools still exist.

Since the early 1970s state education has been strongly affected by the jolting transition from a situation in which labour-power was in short supply, to one in which there is too much – a time of rising unemployment and reduced government revenue. Educational expansion, which had characterized the whole of the post-war period, was suddenly replaced by contraction and attempts at the reduction of government expenditure. From the mid-1970s to the mid-1980s, state spending on education dropped from 6.3 per cent of public expenditure as a whole to just over 5 per cent.

The picture would not be complete without mentioning the privately owned and run schools which existed alongside the state system throughout the period. They all depended on fees from parents, and were thus largely restricted to children from affluent backgrounds.

Comparisons of school systems in the industrialized world

In all states in the world today, including Third World countries, education has become a major area of investment (Ramirez and Boli, 1987). There are wide differences, however, in modes of organizing educational institutions and in the proportion of the population receiving different types and levels of education.

Some types of **educational system** are highly centralized. In France, for example, all students follow nationally determined curricula, sitting uniform national examinations. The American system is much more decentralized than those of most other industrialized countries. Local states provide substantial funding to schools, contributing about 40 per cent of the necessary finance, with the federal government being responsible only for some 10 per cent. The rest comes from taxation revenue in local school districts. Schools are administered by local boards, elected by community vote; the boards have a wide range of powers including the hiring of teachers and other school officials, and control of the curriculum.

Community control of schooling has mixed consequences. It has clear benefits in the sense that schools are kept responsive to the needs and interests of the people they serve. On the other hand, the system also leads to very wide differences in school funding, depending upon how wealthy or otherwise a given community is. Class size, available facilities, and the ability to attract well-qualified teachers, all vary enormously from district to district.

In most industrialized countries, private schools and colleges coexist with the publicly funded system. Central or local government agencies sometimes provide subsidies for schools controlled by religious denominations. In Ireland, for instance, all schools are church schools, although they receive extensive public funding. Schools run by religious bodies in Britain, on the other hand, receive little income from public sources and operate largely independently of the public system. In many countries, governments struggled in the past to wrest control of education away from religious authorities. Even in societies where most educational facilities are now publicly organized and financed, religious organizations frequently fight to keep at least some of their traditional rights in education.

Higher education

International comparisons

There are also large differences between societies in the organization of **higher education** (education after school, usually at university or college). In some countries, all universities and colleges are public agencies, receiving their funding directly from government sources. Higher education in France, for instance, is organized nationally, with centralized control being almost as marked as in primary and secondary education. All course structures have to be validated by a national regulatory body responsible to the Minister of Higher Education. Two types of degree can be gained, one awarded by the individual university, the other by the state. National degrees are generally regarded as more prestigious and valuable than those of specific universities, since they are supposed to conform to guaranteed uniform standards. A certain range of occupations in government are only open to the holders of national degrees, which are also favoured by most industrial employers. Virtually all teachers in schools, colleges and universities in France are themselves state employees. Rates of pay and the broad framework of teaching duties are fixed centrally.

The United States is distinctive among developed countries in terms of the high proportion of colleges and universities which are in the private sector. Private organizations make up 54 per cent of organizations of higher education in the United States. These include some of the most prestigious universities, such as Harvard, Princeton and Yale. The distinction between *public* and *private* in American higher education, however, is not as clear-cut as is the case in other countries. Students at private universities are eligible for public grants and loans, and these universities receive public research funding. Public universities often possess substantial endowments, and may be given donations by private firms. They also often obtain research grants from private industrial sources.

The system in Britain

The British system of higher education is considerably more decentralized than that of France, but more unitary than that of the USA. Universities and colleges are government-financed, and teachers at all levels of the educational system have their salaries determined according to national wage-scales. Yet there is considerable diversity in the organization of institutions and curricula.

There were twenty-one universities in Britain in the immediate pre-war period. Most of the universities at this time were very small by today's standards. In 1937, the total number of undergraduates in British universities was only slightly more than the number of full-time university academic staff in 1981 (Carswell, 1985, p. 1). Graduate work was only weakly developed, even in Cambridge or Oxford, the oldest universities. In 1937 75 per cent of all the graduate students in the country were registered at the University of London.

Between 1945 and 1970, the higher education system in Britain grew to be four times as large. The older universities were expanded, and new, 'red-brick' or concrete universities built (such as Sussex, Kent, Stirling and York). A *binary* system was set up with the creation of polytechnics. This second layer of higher education is today relatively large, comprising some 400 colleges offering a wide range of courses. The polytechnics concentrate more on vocational courses than the universities. The Council for National Academic Awards was set up as a validating body to ensure their degrees were of a uniform standard.

Today, British institutions of higher education have what has sometimes been called a 'standard coinage'. This means that a degree from Leicester or Leeds, at least in theory, is the same standard as one from Cambridge, Oxford or, for that matter, from a polytechnic or college of higher education. Yet Oxford and Cambridge are noted for a highly selective intake, about half of which comes from *public schools* (fee-paying schools). An Oxford or Cambridge degree confers greater chances of reaching a high economic position than a qualification from most other universities.

In spite of post-war expansion, the proportion of the British population in universities, and in higher education more generally, is still well below that of other Western countries. In 1986, only 6.6 per cent of eighteen-year-olds entered university; the proportions in most other European countries are well over 10 per cent and, in Italy, closer to 30 per cent.

In the 1980s, the Conservative government demanded a leaner, cheaper, more utilitarian system of higher education – a reversal of a previously widely held view that universities should be places where ideas are freely explored and academic excellence is pursued for its own sake. Between 1981 and 1985, 5,600 academic posts in universities disappeared and 18,000 undergraduate places were lost (Kogan and Kogan, 1988, p. 11). Despite the government's aim to reduce waste and 'academic drift', there is growing opposition to a set of policies which seem to jeopardize the universities' distinctive contribution to national life: the commitment to rational, disinterested solutions to all kinds of problems.

The government's aim to cut down on expenditure on higher education has led to demoralization in some sectors of the university system, and to the feeling that the universities' ability to train and teach the students whose skills will be needed in the years to come is endangered.

Education and inequality

The expansion of education has always been closely linked to ideals of mass democracy. Reformers value education, of course, for its own sake – for the opportunity it provides for individuals to develop their abilities and aptitudes. Yet education has also consistently been seen as a means of equalization. Universal education, it has been argued, will help reduce disparities of wealth and power by providing able young people with skills to enable them to find a valued place in society. How far has this happened? Much sociological research has been devoted to answering this question. Its results are clear: education tends to express and reaffirm existing inequalities far more than it acts to change them.

Coleman's study of inequalities in American education

Studies carried out in a variety of countries demonstrate that social and family background are the major influences over school performance, and are thus reflected in subsequent levels of income. One of the classic investigations was undertaken in the United States in the 1960s. The 1964 Civil Rights Act required the United States Commissioner of Education to report on educational inequalities resulting from differences of ethnic background, religion or national origin. James Coleman, a sociologist, was appointed director of the research programme. The results were published in 1966, after one of the most extensive research investigations ever carried out in sociology.

Information was collected about more than half a million pupils, who were also given a range of tests assessing verbal and non-verbal abilities, reading levels and mathematical skills. Sixty thousand teachers also completed forms providing data about four thousand schools. The results provided a general survey of schooling in the country, and gave rise to some surprising results, which had significant practical impact on policy-making.

The report found that the large majority of children were in schools effectively segregated into black and white. Almost 80 per cent of schools attended by white students contained 10 per cent or less black students. Whites and Asian Americans scored higher in achievement tests than blacks or other ethnic minorities. Coleman had supposed the study would show that mainly black schools would have worse facilities, larger classes and inferior buildings to those that were predominantly white, but the results showed far fewer differences of this type than had been anticipated.

He concluded that the material resources provided in schools made little difference to educational performance; the decisive influence was the children's backgrounds. In Coleman's words, 'Inequalities imposed on children by their home, neighbourhood, and peer environment are carried along to become the inequalities with which they confront adult life at the end of school' (Coleman et al., 1966, p. 325). There was, however, some evidence that students from deprived backgrounds who had close friendships with others who were better off were likely to be more successful at school.

The Coleman report influenced public debates about school integration in Britain as well as the USA, since it suggested that children from minority groups would do better in school if mixed with students from more affluent backgrounds.

Later research

While subsequent research has confirmed some of Coleman's findings, aspects of his work have been challenged. Since his study was confined to a single point in time, it could not analyse changes. A study by Michael Rutter, carried out in London, looked at the educational development of groups of boys over several years. The children studied were first contacted in 1970, when they were about to finish their primary schooling, and information was collected on social background and academic performance. The survey was repeated in 1974, when the boys had been in secondary school for three years. Within the group, a number of schools were selected for intensive study: pupils and teachers were interviewed and classroom activities observed.

The findings indicated that schools do in fact have an influence upon the academic development of children. The factors Rutter found to be important had been left largely unanalysed in Coleman's investigation: they included, for example, the quality of teacher–pupil interaction, an atmosphere of co-operation and caring between teachers and students, and well-organized course preparation. Schools which provided superior learning environments were not always best equipped in terms of material resources or buildings.

Rutter's results do not negate the finding that influences prior to, and outside, school are most decisive in perpetuating social inequalities. Since the factors to which Rutter pointed are often maximized in schools catering to well-motivated students, and which provide good support for their teachers, his results help us to understand just why schooling tends to maintain inequalities. There is a self-repeating cycle in which students from relatively privileged homes attend a particular school, and perpetuate its qualities; good teachers are attracted and motivation is maintained. A school mainly attended by deprived children will have to work far harder to achieve a similar result. Nevertheless Rutter's conclusions do suggest that differences in school organization and atmosphere can counteract outside influences on academic attainment. Improvements in teaching quality, the social climate of the school and patterns of school work can help deprived children improve academic performance. In later research Coleman in fact reached similar conclusions (Coleman, Hoffer and Kilgore, 1981).

Christopher Jencks's *Inequality*, published in 1972, reviewed some of the empirical evidence which had accumulated by then on education and inequality, concentrating mainly from American research (Jencks et al., 1972). Jencks reaffirmed the findings that educational and occupational attainment are governed mainly by family background and non-school factors, and that educational reforms on their own can have only minor effects on existing inequalities. Jencks's work has been criticized on methodological grounds, but his overall conclusions remain persuasive (Oakes, 1985).

Much information now exists on patterns of inequality in education in the United Kingdom. Research reported by A. H. Halsey and his colleagues in 1980 developed various comparisons between educational opportunities open to working-class boys and those available to boys from the 'service class' (people of professional and managerial background). A boy from the service class during the post-war period was ten times as likely as one from the working class to be in school at the age of eighteen, and was eleven times as likely to go to university.

Other studies have looked at the relation between ethnicity and educational achievement. Black pupils in Britain, on average, fare considerably worse in the educational system than whites. The Swann Report of 1985 showed that only 5 per cent of West Indian school-leavers obtained one or more passes at 'A' level in 1981–2, compared to 13 per cent of the white population. Black pupils come disproportionately from poorer backgrounds, which partly explains this difference. Other studies, however, have shown that an imbalance remains even when class background is accounted for (Craft and Craft, 1985).

Theories of schooling

Bernstein: language codes

There are several theoretical perspectives on the nature of modern education and its implications for inequality. One approach emphasizes linguistic skills. Basil Bernstein has argued that children from varying backgrounds develop different *codes*, or forms of speech, during their early lives, which affect their subsequent school experience (Bernstein, 1975). He is not concerned with differences in vocabulary or verbal skills, as these are usually thought of; his interest is in systematic differences in ways of using language, particularly contrasting poorer and wealthier children.

The speech of lower-class children, Bernstein argues, represents a **restricted code** – a way of using language containing many unstated assumptions which speakers expect others to know. A restricted code is a type of speech tied to the cultural setting of a lower-class community or district. Many lower-class people live in a strong familial or neighbourhood culture, in which values and norms are taken for granted, and not expressed in language. Lower-class parents tend to socialize their children directly by the use of rewards or reprimands to correct behaviour. Language in a restricted code is more suitable for communication about practical experience than for discussion of more abstract ideas, processes or relationships. Restricted code speech is thus characteristic of children growing up in lower-class families, and of the peer-groups in which they spend their time. Speech is oriented to the norms of the group, without anyone easily being able to explain *why* they follow the patterns of behaviour they do.

The language development of middle-class children, by contrast, according to Bernstein, involves the acquisition of an **elaborated code** – a style of speaking in which the meanings of words can be *individualized* to suit the demands of particular situations. The ways in which children from middle-class backgrounds learn to use language are less bound to particular contexts; the child is able more easily to generalize and express abstract ideas. Thus, middle-class mothers, when controlling their children, frequently explain the reasons and principles which underlie their reactions to the child's behaviour. While a lower-class mother might tell a child off for wanting to eat too many sweets by simply saying, 'No more sweets for you!', a middle-class mother is more likely to explain that eating too many sweets is bad for one's health and the state of one's teeth.

Children who have acquired elaborated codes of speech, Bernstein proposes, are more able to deal with the demands of formal academic education than those confined to restricted codes. This does not imply that lower-class children have an 'inferior' type of speech, or that their codes of language are 'deprived'. Rather, the way in which they use speech clashes with the academic culture of the school. Those who have mastered elaborated codes fit much more easily within the school environment.

There is some evidence to back up Bernstein's theory, although its validity is still debated. Joan Tough has studied the language of working- and middle-class children, finding systematic differences. She backs up Bernstein's thesis that lower-class children generally have less experience of having their questions answered, or of being offered explanations about the reasoning of others (Tough, 1976). The same conclusion was reached in subsequent research by Barbara Tizard and Martin Hughes (1984). On the other hand, some who have studied the speech of lower-class groups have denied that their use of language can in any sense be termed a 'restricted' code. Lower-class language, they say, is as elaborate, and abstract, as middle-class speech, although its grammatical character is different (Labov, 1978).

If they are right, Bernstein's ideas will help us understand why those from low socio-economic backgrounds tend to be 'under-achievers' at school. The following traits have been associated with restricted code speech, all of which inhibit the lower-class child's educational chances:

1 The child probably receives limited responses to questions asked at home, and therefore is likely to be both less well-informed and less curious about the wider world than those mastering elaborated codes.
2 The child will find it difficult to respond to the unemotional and abstract language used in teaching, as well as to appeals to general principles of school discipline.
3 Much of what the teacher says is likely to be incomprehensible, depending upon different forms of linguistic usage from those to which the child is accustomed. The child may attempt to cope with this by *translating* the teacher's language into that with which she or he is familiar – but then could fail to grasp the very principles the teacher intends to convey.
4 While the child will experience little difficulty with rote or 'drill' learning, she or he will have major difficulties in grasping conceptual distinctions involving generalization and abstraction.

Bowles and Gintis: schools and industrial capitalism

The work of Samuel Bowles and Herbert Gintis is concerned mainly with the institutional background to the development of the modern school system (Bowles and Gintis, 1976). Bowles and Gintis base their ideas on schooling in the United States, but claim they apply also to other Western societies. Quoting studies such as that by Jencks (1972), they begin from the observation that education has not been a powerful influence towards economic equality. Modern education, they suggest, should be understood as a response to the economic needs of industrial capitalism. Schools help to provide the technical and social skills required by industrial enterprise; and they instil respect for authority and discipline into the labour-force. Relations of authority and control in school, which are hierarchical and include an emphasis upon obedience, directly parallel those dominating the workplace. The rewards and punishments held out in school also replicate those in the world of work. Schools help to motivate some individuals towards 'achievement' and 'success', while discouraging others, who find their way into low-paid jobs.

Bowles and Gintis accept that the development of mass education has had many beneficial effects. Illiteracy has been virtually eliminated, and schooling provides access to learning experiences which are intrinsically self-fulfilling. Yet because education has expanded mainly as a response to economic needs, the school system falls far short of what enlightened reformers hoped from it.

According to Bowles and Gintis, modern schools reproduce the feelings of powerlessness which many individuals experience elsewhere. The ideals of personal development central to education can only be achieved if people can control the conditions of their own lives, and develop their talents and abilities of self-expression. Under the current system, schools 'are destined to legitimate inequality, limit personal development to forms compatible with submission to arbitrary authority, and aid in the process whereby youth are resigned to their fate' (p. 266). If there were greater democracy in the workplace, and more equality in society at large, Bowles and Gintis argue, a system of education could be developed providing for greater individual fulfilment.

Illich: the hidden curriculum

One of the most controversial recent writers on educational theory is Ivan Illich. He is noted for his criticisms of modern economic development, which he describes as a process whereby previously self-sufficient peoples are dispossessed of their traditional skills, and made to rely on doctors for their health, teachers for their schooling, television for their entertainment and employers for their subsistence. With Everett Reimer, Illich argues that the very notion of compulsory schooling – now accepted throughout the world – should be questioned (Illich, 1973). Like Bowles and Gintis, Illich stresses the connection between the development of education and economic requirements for discipline and hierarchy. He argues that schools have developed to cope with four basic tasks: the provision of custodial care, the distribution of people among occupational roles, the learning of dominant values and the acquisition of socially approved skills and knowledge. The school has become a *custodial* organization because attendance is obligatory, and children are 'kept off the streets' between early childhood and their entry into work.

Illich stresses the **hidden curriculum** of schools. Much is learnt there which has nothing to do with the formal content of lessons. Schools tend to inculcate what Illich called *passive consumption* – an uncritical acceptance of the existing social order – by the nature of the discipline and regimentation they involve. These lessons are not consciously taught; they are implicit in school procedures and organization. The hidden curriculum teaches children that their role in life is 'to know their place and to sit still in it' (Illich, 1973).

Illich advocates *de-schooling* society. Compulsory schooling is a relatively recent invention, he points out; there is no reason why it should be accepted as somehow inevitable. Since schools do not promote equality or the development of individual creative abilities, why not do away with them in their current form? Illich does not mean by this that all forms of educational organization should be abolished. Education, he argues, should provide everyone who wants to learn with access to available resources – at any time in their lives, not just in their childhood or adolescent years. Such a system should make it possible for knowledge to be widely diffused and shared, not confined to specialists. Learners should not have to submit to a standard curriculum, and they should have personal choice over what they study.

What all this means in practical terms is not wholly clear. In place of schools, however, Illich suggests several types of *educational framework*. Material resources for formal learning would be stored in libraries, rental agencies, laboratories and information storage banks, available to any student. 'Communications networks' would be set up, providing data about the skills possessed by different individuals and whether they would be willing to train others, or engage in mutual learning activities. Students would be provided with vouchers allowing them to use educational services as and when they wished.

Are these proposals wholly Utopian? Many would say so. Yet if, as looks possible, paid work is substantially reduced or restructured in the future, they appear less unrealistic (see chapter 15: 'Work and Economic Life'). Should paid employment become less central to social life, people might instead engage in a wider variety of pursuits. Against this backdrop, some of Illich's ideas make good sense. Education would not just be a form of early training, confined to special institutions, but would become available to whoever wished to take advantage of it.

Education and cultural reproduction

Perhaps the most illuminating way of connecting some of the themes of these three theoretical perspectives together is through the concept of **cultural reproduction** (Bourdieu, 1986, 1988; Bourdieu and Passeron, 1977). Cultural reproduction refers to the ways in which schools, in conjunction with other social institutions, help perpetuate social and economic inequalities across the generations. The concept directs our attention to the means whereby, via the hidden curriculum, schools influence the learning of values, attitudes and habits. Schools reinforce variations in cultural values and outlooks picked up early in life; when children leave school, these have the effect of limiting the opportunities of some, while facilitating those of others.

The modes of language-use identified by Bernstein no doubt connect to such broad cultural differences, which underlie variations in interests and tastes. Children from lower-class backgrounds, particularly those from minority groups, develop ways of talking and acting which clash with those dominant in the school. As Bowles and Gintis emphasize, schools impose rules of discipline upon pupils, the authority of teachers being oriented towards academic learning. Children from lower-class backgrounds experience a much greater cultural clash when they enter school than those from more privileged homes. The former find themselves in effect in a foreign cultural environment. Not only are they less likely to be motivated towards high academic performance; their habitual modes of speech and action do not mesh with those of the teachers, even if each is trying their best to communicate.

Children spend long hours in school. As Illich stresses, they learn much more there than is contained in the lessons they are actually taught. Children get an early taste of what the world of work will be like, learning that they are expected to be punctual and apply themselves diligently to the tasks which those in authority set for them.

Willis: an analysis of cultural reproduction

A brilliant discussion of cultural reproduction is provided in the report of a field-work study carried out by Paul Willis in a school in Birmingham (Willis, 1977). The question he set out to investigate was how cultural reproduction occurs – or, as he puts it, 'how working-class kids get working-class jobs'. It is often thought that, during the process of schooling, children from lower-class or minority backgrounds simply come to see that they 'are not clever enough' to expect to get highly paid or high-status jobs in their future work lives. In other words, the experience of academic failure teaches them to recognize their intellectual limitations; having accepted their 'inferiority', they move into occupations with limited career prospects.

As Willis points out, this interpretation does not conform at all to the reality of people's lives and experiences. The 'street wisdom' of those from poor neighbourhoods may be of little or no relevance to academic success, but involves as subtle, skilful and complex a set of abilities as any of the intellectual skills taught in school. Few if any children leave school thinking 'I'm so stupid that it's fair and proper for me to be stacking boxes in a factory all day.' If children from less privileged backgrounds accept menial jobs, without feeling themselves throughout life to be failures, there must be other factors involved.

Willis concentrated on a particular boys' group in the school, spending a lot of time with them. The members of the gang, who called themselves 'the lads', were white; the school also contained many black and Asian children. Willis found that the lads had an acute and perceptive understanding of the school's authority system – but used this to fight that system rather than working with it. They saw the school as an alien environment, but one which they could manipulate to their own ends. They derived positive pleasure from the constant conflict – which they kept mostly to minor skirmishes – they carried on with teachers. They were adept at seeing the weak points of the teachers' claims to authority, as well as where they were vulnerable as individuals.

In class, for instance, the children were expected to sit still, be quiet and get on with their work. But the lads were all movement, save when the teacher's stare might freeze one of them momentarily; they would gossip surreptitiously, or pass open remarks that were on the verge of direct subordination but could be explained away if challenged.

Willis describes all this beautifully:

'The lads' specialise in a caged resentment which always stops just short of outright confrontation. Settled in class, as near a group as they can manage, there is a continuous scraping of chairs, a bad-tempered 'tut-tutting' at the simplest request, and a continuous fidgeting about which explores every permutation of sitting or lying on a chair. During private study, some openly show disdain by apparently trying to go to sleep with their heads sideways down on the desk, some have their backs to the desk gazing out of the window, or even vacantly at the wall. . . . A continuous hum of talk flows around injunctions not to, like the inevitable tide over barely dried sand and everywhere there are rolled-back eyeballs and exaggerated mutterings of conspiratorial secrets. . . . In the corridors there is a foot-dragging walk, an over-friendly 'hello' or sudden silence as the deputy [senior teacher] passes. Derisive or insane laughter erupts which might or might not be about someone who has just passed. It is as demeaning to stop as it is to carry on. . . . Opposition to the school is principally manifested in the struggle to win symbolic and physical space from the institution and its rules and to defeat its main perceived purpose: to make you 'work'. (Willis, 1977, pp. 12–13, 26)

The lads referred to conformist children – those who accepted the authority of the teachers, and concerned themselves with academic values – as 'the ear-'oles'. The ear-'oles actually *listened* to the teachers, and did as they were told. The ear-'oles would go on to be far more 'successful', in terms of getting well-paid, comfortable jobs on leaving school, than the lads. Yet their awareness of the complexities of the school environment, according to Willis, was in many respects less profound than that of the lads. They accepted them in an unquestioning way.

Most pupils were somewhere between the lads on the one side and the ear-'oles on the other – less openly confrontational than the first group, and less consistently conformist than the second. Styles and modes of opposition, however, were also strongly influenced by ethnic divisions. The teachers were mostly white, and in spite of their distaste for the school, the lads had more in common with them than black children did. These were children from West Indian families, some groups of whom were much more openly, and violently, hostile to the school than the lads. The lads themselves were openly racist, and distinguished themselves sharply from the black gangs.

The lads recognized that work would be much like school, but they actively looked forward to it. They expected to gain no direct satisfaction from the work environment, but were impatient for wages. Far from taking the jobs they did – in tyre-fitting, carpet-laying, plumbing, painting and decorating – from feelings of inferiority, they held an attitude of dismissive superiority towards work, as they had towards school. They enjoyed the adult status which came from working, but were uninterested in 'making a career' for themselves. As Willis points out, work in blue-collar settings often involves quite similar cultural features to those the lads created in their counter-school culture – banter, quick wit, and the skill to subvert the demands of authority figures where necessary. Only later in their lives might they come to see themselves as trapped in arduous, unrewarding labour. When they have families, they might perhaps look back on education retrospectively – and hopelessly – as the only escape. Yet if they try to pass this view on to their own children, they are likely to have no more success than their own parents did.

Intelligence and inequality

The discussion so far neglects the possible importance of inherited differences in ability. Suppose it were the case that differences in educational attainment, and in subsequent occupational position and income, directly reflected differential intelligence? In such circumstances, it might be argued, there is in fact equality of opportunity in the school system, for people find a level equivalent to their innate potential.

What is intelligence?

For many years psychologists have debated whether a single human ability which can be called **intelligence** actually exists, and, if so, how far it rests upon innately determined differences. Intelligence is difficult to define, because it covers many different, often unrelated, qualities. We might suppose, for example, that the 'purest' form of intelligence is the ability to solve abstract mathematical puzzles. However, people who are very good at such puzzles sometimes have low abilities in other areas, such as history or art. Since the concept has proved so resistant to accepted definition, some psychologists have proposed (and many educators have by default accepted) that intelligence can simply be regarded as 'what **IQ** (intelligence quotient) tests measure'. The unsatisfactory nature of this is obvious enough, because the definition of intelligence becomes wholly circular.

IQ and genetic factors: the Jensen controversy

Scores on such tests do in fact correlate highly with academic performance. They therefore also correlate closely with social, economic and ethnic differences, since these are associated with variations in levels of educational attainment. White students score better, on average, than blacks or members of other disadvantaged minorities. On this basis, some have suggested that the IQ differences between blacks and whites are partly the result of hereditary factors. An article published by Arthur Jensen in 1967 caused a furore by attributing differences in IQ between blacks and whites in part to genetic variations (Jensen, 1967, 1979).

Jensen's views have been widely criticized, and most psychologists reject them. Jensen drew largely upon the work of the British psychologist Cyril Burt (Burt, 1977), who was later shown to have fabricated evidence relating IQ to heredity. We do not really know whether IQ tests measure constant abilities, let alone whether such abilities are inherited. Critics of Jensen deny that the IQ difference between blacks and whites – usually amounting to an average of about fifteen IQ points – is genetic in origin. IQ tests relate to a range of linguistic, symbolic and mathematical skills, and arguments such as those advanced by Bernstein and others suggest that these may be strongly influenced by early learning processes. The tests leave out other intellectual aptitudes not usually thought significant in school curricula. These may include, for instance, the abilities that the 'street-wise' person may possess in abundance.

IQ tests are probably always to some degree *culture-bound*. They pose questions – to do with abstract reasoning, for example, more likely to be part of the experience of middle-class white students rather than of blacks or other ethnic minorities. Scores on IQ tests may also be influenced by factors that have nothing to do with the abilities supposedly being measured – such as whether the testing is experienced as stressful. Research has demonstrated that blacks score some 6 points lower on IQ tests when the tester is white than when the tester is black (Kamin, 1977).

Differences in average IQ scores between blacks and whites are almost certainly the result of social and cultural influences, not of differences in genetic inheritance. There may be genetic variations between individuals which influence scores on IQ tests; but these have no overall connection to racial differences. The average degree of difference in IQ between blacks and whites is much smaller than variations found within each grouping.

Disentangling genetics and IQ: identical twins

We do not actually know how far genetic factors influence IQ scores. There is no way of disentangling, for any particular individuals, the relative influence of heredity and environment on their development. The only means whereby an approximate assessment can be attempted is through comparison of identical twins, who by definition have exactly the same genetic characteristics. There have been a few studies of identical twins separated at birth and reared in different environments (including the now partly discredited research work of Cyril Burt), but the number of separated twins traced and studied is small, and it is not even always possible to be sure that the twins were in fact identical (*fraternal* twins are those born from separate eggs and therefore having different innate characteristics; twins may look physically alike even when they are in fact fraternal).

After assessing the evidence provided by several studies of identical twins, L. J. Kamin concluded that nothing could really be learned from them. The material is too unreliable, and the number of cases too few, to supply any authoritative conclusions about the influence of heredity on IQ. In Kamin's words, 'There are no data sufficient for us to reject the hypothesis that differences in the way in which people answer the questions asked by testers are determined by their palpably different life experiences' (Kamin, 1977, p. 176).

Gender and schooling

Perhaps if there are in fact differences in average intelligence between people of varying racial backgrounds, we should create different educational programmes for them? An experiment of this type was tried out in the 1960s. It took place in Farrington Elementary School in Southern California. The school was initiating a Programme for Educational and Occupational Needs (PEON), founded on a study of the aptitudes and interests of several generations of previous graduates of Farrington. Two ethnic groups, white Americans and Mexican Americans, were taking part in the programme. Research had made clear that white students have a definite aptitude for, and interest in, professional and managerial occupations, while Mexican Americans tend more to turn to agricultural labour. The white students hence were taught using more academic methods, while the Mexican American classes put heavy emphasis on physical exercise, in order to increase the strength and agility needed to harvest crops satisfactorily. Since Mexican Americans do not usually aspire to positions of leadership, the games they were taught to play emphasized submissiveness and docility. The teaching staff were enthusiastic about the programme, believing it to be ideally tailored to the needs of the two groups.

Does this sound shocking? Certainly it should do. Does it appear ridiculous? It might well do, because of course the episode as described here is fictional. Even those who believe that there are inherited differences in intelligence between people of varying physical stock would not suggest such policies. Yet the programme was a real one, except that it referred not to ethnic groups but to the sexes.

An article which appeared in 1966 in a widely read journal, the *National Elementary Principal*, outlined a new programme of teaching children, grouped by gender, in Wakefield Elementary School, Fairfax County, Virginia. When the article was written, pupils were being

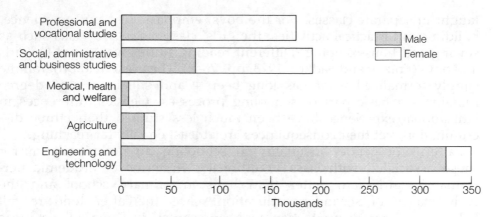

Figure 13 Men and women are disproportionately represented as students on non-advanced college courses, England and Wales, 1984
Source: New Society, 26 September 1986, p. 44.

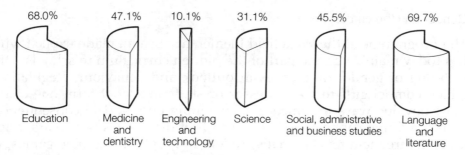

Figure 14 What do women in Great Britain study in university? Women as a proportion of university undergraduates, 1984
Source: New Society, 26 September 1986, p. 44.

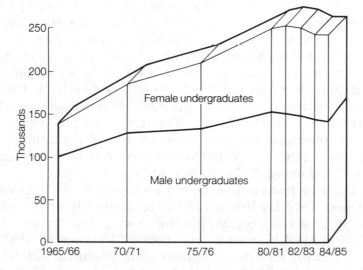

Figure 15 Numbers of men and women attending university in Great Britain, 1965–1984
Source: New Society, 26 September 1986, p. 44.

taught in separate classes. For the boys, emphasis was put on science, building and practical activities; the girls' classes stressed tasks such as sewing and housekeeping. Different reading stories were used for girls and boys (Frazier and Sadker, 1973, pp. 76–8). The Wakefield programme simply formalized what has long been – and still in a large degree remains – a basic part of schooling processes. Gender differences in educational experience have been much less studied than ethnic discrimination, yet their consequences are at least equally far-reaching.

Patterns of gender inequality in schooling do not wholly mirror those associated with class or ethnicity. In terms of academic performance, girls fare better than boys in primary school and the early stages of secondary education. Girls thereafter tend to fall behind, and are disproportionately represented in some subject-areas rather than others. Science, engineering and medicine at college and university level are still dominated by male students.

Gender and the curriculum

The programme at the Wakefield Elementary School made explicit what has today mainly become part of the hidden curriculum in schools – the fostering of gender differences in outlook and behaviour. Regulations which compel girls to wear dresses or skirts in school form one of the most obvious ways in which gender typing occurs. The consequences go beyond mere appearance. As a result of the clothes she wears, a girl lacks the freedom to sit casually, to join in rough and tumble games, or sometimes to run as fast as she is able. School reading texts also help to perpetuate gender images. Although this again is changing, story books in primary schools often portray boys as showing initiative and independence, while girls, if they appear at all, are more passive and watch their brothers. Stories written especially for girls often have an element of adventure in them, but this usually takes the form of intrigues or mysteries in a domestic or school setting. Boys' adventure stories are more wide-ranging, having heroes who travel off to distant places or in other ways are sturdily independent (Statham, 1986).

Studies of teacher reactions to gender differences in the classroom are relatively few and far-between. The research which exists indicates that girls are rewarded for silence, neatness and conformity, whereas somewhat more rebellious behaviour is tolerated in boys (Frazier and Sadker, 1973; Delamont, 1976; Walker and Barton, 1983).

Female children from ethnic minorities are in some respects doubly disadvantaged. Beverley Bryan and her colleagues have described what it was like to be a black female pupil in a school in the area of Britain where Willis studied his white boys' group (Bryan et al., 1987). Unlike the lads, the black girls were initially enthusiastic about school, but altered their attitudes because of the difficulties encountered there. Even when they were quite small, aged seven or eight, teachers would disperse the girls if they stood chatting in the playground. Being seen as 'trouble-makers', they rapidly became so (Bryan et al., 1987).

Women in higher education

Women's organizations in Britain and elsewhere have often attacked sex discrimination in school and higher education. Women are still heavily under-represented among the teaching staff in colleges and universities. A survey of 454 colleges and universities in the USA, published in 1970, showed that no more than 8 per cent of those in top-level administrative positions were women (Oltman, 1970, pp. 14–15). Women hold only 10 per cent of full professorships and 25 per cent of associate professorships. In the United Kingdom in 1981, women held 2 per cent of full professorial posts, 6 per cent of those of reader or senior lecturer and 14 per cent of those of lecturer (Szreter, 1983).

A comparative investigation of women academics in Britain and the United States disclosed that in both countries women on average have higher teaching loads than male colleagues, and are less often involved in postgraduate teaching. Heavy teaching loads are likely to cut into time available for research and publication; and levels of both publication and postgraduate supervision are important criteria for promotion (Blackstone and Fulton, 1975).

Education and literacy in the Third World

We now turn to look at education in non-industrialized countries. Living in the West, we have become used to circumstances in which the vast majority of the population can read and write, and attends school for years. But universal education is far from fully established throughout the world. Over the past quarter-century, the educational systems of most Third World countries have expanded rapidly; yet there are still several societies (such as Senegal, in Africa), where well under half of the children receive no formal schooling whatsoever. Literacy – the ability to read and write with a reasonable level of competence – is the basis of education. Without it, schooling cannot proceed. We take it for granted in the West that the majority of people are literate, but, as has been mentioned, a few hundred years ago the vast majority were illiterate.

In 1986 it was estimated that 30 per cent of the population of Third World countries were illiterate. In India alone over 250 million people are thought by the government to be illiterate. Even if the provision of primary education increases with the level of population growth, illiteracy will not be much reduced for many years, because a high proportion of illiterates are adults. The absolute number of those who cannot read or write is actually rising (Coombs, 1985, chapter 9).

Many countries have instituted literacy programmes, but these have mostly made only a small contribution to a huge problem. Television, radio and the other electronic media can be used, where these are available, to convey education directly to illiterate people, without their having to go through the laborious process of learning to read, but educational programmes are far less popular than commercial entertainment.

During colonial rule, education was regarded by the colonial powers with some suspicion. Until the twentieth century, most believed indigenous populations to be too primitive to benefit from education, although education came to be seen as a way of making local elites responsive to European interests and ways of life. At the same time, it was recognized that educating colonized peoples could serve to foment discontent and rebellion. To some extent this did happen, since the majority of those who led anti-colonial and nationalist movements were from educated elites. Many of these people had attended schools or colleges in Europe itself, and were able to compare directly the democratic institutions of the European countries with the absence of democracy in their colonies.

The educational systems introduced by the colonizers were usually European, not very relevant to the colonial areas themselves. Africans, for instance, had to learn the language of their European masters, and learn about European history and culture. Educated Africans in the British colonies knew about the kings and queens of England, read Shakespeare, Milton and the English poets, but knew next to nothing about their own history or culture. Policies of reform in education since the end of colonialism have not completely altered this situation even today.

Colonial education left another legacy: the educational system in many Third World countries is 'top-heavy'. Higher education is disproportionately developed, relative to primary and secondary schools. The result is an educated elite, some of whom, having attended college or university, cannot find white-collar or professional jobs. Given the low level of industrial development, most of the better-paid positions are in government; and there are not enough of these to go around.

Many Third World countries have tried in recent years to redirect their educational efforts towards the rural poor, recognizing the shortcomings of the colonial inheritance. These have had limited success, because they have been restricted in scope by lack of money. Some countries, such as India, have promoted *self-help education*, by which communities draw upon their own resources in ways which do not demand high expenditure. Those who can read and write, and perhaps possess job skills, are encouraged to take on others as 'apprentices', whom they coach in their spare time. Some of these schemes bear a close similarity to ideas suggested by Illich in his critique of orthodox education – not surprisingly, because

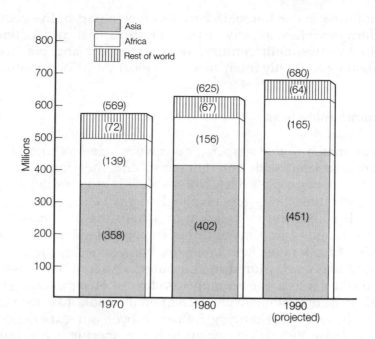

Figure 16 UNESCO estimates of the number of illiterate people in the world,1970 and 1980, and a projection for 1990
Source: Philip H. Coombs, *The World Crisis in Education: The View from the Eighties* (New York: Oxford University Press, Inc., 1985), p. 268.

he developed his ideas in Third World contexts where, apart from basic teaching of literacy, formal school systems often bear little relation to the real needs of the population.

Communication and media

The modern world depends on continuous **communication** or interaction between people widely separated from one another. If we were not so dependent upon *communication across distance*, schooling on a mass basis would be neither necessary nor possible. In traditional cultures – as in the example with which we opened the chapter – most knowledge was what the anthropologist Clifford Geertz has called **local knowledge** (Geertz, 1983). Traditions were passed on through the local community, and although general cultural ideas gradually spread across large areas, processes of cultural diffusion were long-drawn-out, slow and inconsistent. Today, we live in 'the whole world' in a way which would have been quite inconceivable to Jean-Paul Didion, or anyone living before about 1800. We are aware of situations and events thousands of miles away – electronic communication makes such awareness almost instantaneous. Changes in the spread of information, and in information technologies, are as much a part of the development of modern societies as any aspect of industrial production (Kern, 1983). In the twentieth century, rapid transport and electronic communication have greatly intensified the global diffusion of information.

Mass communications

The **mass media** – newspapers, magazines, cinema and television – are often associated with entertainment, and therefore seen as rather marginal to most people's lives. Such a view is quite misleading.

Mass communications are involved in many aspects of our social activities. For instance, monetary transactions are now mainly founded on the exchange of information held in computers. A bank account is not a pile of bank notes kept in a safe, but a series of digits printed on an account sheet and stored in computers. Anyone who uses a credit card is hooked into a very complex system of electronically stored and transmitted information. Even 'recreational' media like newspapers or television have a wide-ranging influence over our experience. This is not just because they affect our attitudes in specific ways, but because they are the *means of access* to the knowledge upon which many social activities depend. Voting in national elections, for example, would be impossible if information about current political events, candidates and parties were not generally available. Even those who are largely uninterested in politics, and have little knowledge of the personalities involved, have some awareness of national and international events. Only a complete hermit could be completely detached from the 'news events' which impinge on all of us – and we might well suspect that a twentieth-century hermit would possess a radio!

The development of newspapers

Newspapers in their modern form derive from pamphlets and information sheets printed and circulated in the 1700s. Newspapers only became 'daily', with many thousands or millions of readers, from the end of the nineteenth century onwards. The newspaper was a fundamentally important development in the history of modern media, because it packaged many different types of information within a limited, and easily reproducible, format. Newspapers contained in a single item information on current affairs, entertainment and advertising. News and advertising developed together, and indeed the distinctions between news, advertising and entertainment are shifting and difficult to define. For example, the announcement that a ship is leaving or arriving may in one context be news, in another an advertisement, or if it concerns particular passengers and is written as part of a gossip column, it becomes entertainment (Smith, 1980a, p. 11).

The cheap daily press was pioneered in the United States. The one-cent daily paper was originally established in New York, then copied in other major Eastern cities. By the early 1900s there were city or regional newspapers covering most of the American states. (In contrast to the smaller countries of Europe, national newspapers did not develop.) During the period of mass immigration, many foreign-language newspapers were published in the United States. For example, in 1892 ninety-seven German-language daily papers were being published in cities in the mid-West and North-East (Tunstall, 1977, p. 27). The invention of cheap newsprint (the paper used) was the key to the mass diffusion of newspapers from the late nineteenth century onwards.

The two prime examples of prestige newspapers at the turn of the century were the *New York Times* and *The Times* of London. Most of the influential papers in other countries took these as their models. Newspapers at the top end of the market became a major political force and have remained so to the present day.

For half a century or more, newspapers were the chief way in which information was conveyed quickly and comprehensively to a mass public. Their influence has waned with the rise of radio, cinema and – much more important – television. As recently as 1960, more than one newspaper per household was sold each day in the UK: an average of 112 newspapers for every 100 households, but the ratio has steadily declined since then. Today less than 90 papers are sold for every 100 households (Smith, 1980a, pp. 34–5). Sales to young adults have fallen particularly (Bogart, 1975).

Newspaper publishing

Newspapers have long been associated with the image of the powerful tycoon, the head of a publishing empire. The picture is not an inaccurate one. In many countries, newspaper ownership is concentrated in the hands of a few large corporations often owned and dominated by particular individuals or families. Many of these firms today also have extensive holdings in television and the entertainments industry. In Britain, huge companies run by *press barons*, the Lords Northcliffe, Beaverbrook and Kemsley, developed, based on the success of their mass-circulation papers in the 1920s and 1930s. France has seen the development of the Hersant information empire; the German Springer and Grüner organizations are vast. In the United States, the number of cities in which there are competing newspaper firms has steadily declined, from more than 500 at the turn of the century to just over 30 in 1984. Only 3 per cent of American cities have competing papers – local newspaper publishing has become a monopoly enterprise.

With the exception of the USA, all Western countries boast a number of national newspapers. There is a choice between nationally available papers, often geared to different political standpoints. Although news-papers in the United States are local, they are by no means all locally owned: more than 70 per cent are controlled by publishing chains. In some of these, as with many mass-circulation papers in Europe, the owners set the editorial policies which editors and journalists must follow. In the Hearst chain of newspapers, several editorials are sent every day to the editors of the eight major papers, some of which *have* to be used, while others *may* be. The editors do not write their own.

Mass-circulation papers are extremely expensive to establish and run. There have been some successful new newspapers (like the *Sun* in Britain, owned by Australian entrepreneur Rupert Murdoch), mostly in the 'low-brow' part of the market, but there have been many more failures. The fact that newspaper ownership is so concen-trated has worried most Western governments (Jenkins, 1986). In many countries, governments have taken action to prevent the take-over of newspapers by large chains, although these have frequently failed. Sometimes states have tried to enforce political balance in the press: in Norway, for example, a scheme was set up in the 1970s to equalize investments between newspapers representing different sides of the political spectrum, and most local communities in that country now have two or more well-produced and comprehensive papers providing different points of view on national and international news.

It is possible that the development of computer-based technologies will lead to greater numbers of newspapers, as they have recently become much cheaper to print and produce than used to be the case. On the other hand, electronic communication might in fact bite further into newspaper circulation. For instance, tele-text systems provide news information constantly updated during the course of the day and available on the TV screen.

The impact of television

The increasing influence of television is probably the single most impor-tant development in media of the past thirty years or so (Barnouw, 1975). If current trends in TV-watching continue, by the age of eighteen the average child born today will have spent more time watching television than in any other activity except sleep. Virtually every household now possesses a TV set. In the UK, the average set is switched on for between five and six hours a day. Much the same is true in the United States and the other West European countries (Goodhardt, Ehrenberg and Collins, 1987). The number of hours individuals watch TV is lower than this, of course, since the set is viewed by different members of the household at different times, but the average adult in Britain watches for three hours.

The advent of television has strongly influenced patterns of day-to-day life, since many people schedule other activities around particular pro-grammes. One study, covering eleven countries, sought to analyse the

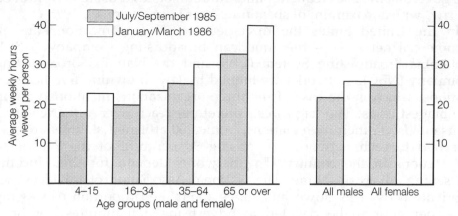

Figure 17 Hours spent watching television in the United Kingdom, July/September 1985 and January/March 1986, by age groups and by sex
Source: Social Trends (London: HMSO, 1987), p. 164.

influence of television-watching on daily life, comparing the activities of owners and non-owners of television sets. The countries covered included the United States, a range of West and East European countries, and Peru in Latin America. Respondents were asked to list all their activities over the course of a twenty-four-hour period. In all countries, those with televisions spent less time on other leisure activities, meeting friends, conversation, household duties and sleeping.

The researchers concluded that television has had a larger impact on daily life than any other technical innovation outside the sphere of paid employment. Those who own automobiles, for instance, spend on average only 6 per cent more time travelling than non-owners, and time spent on housework tends not to alter when domestic appliances like refrigerators, washing machines and dryers are acquired (see chapter 6: 'Gender and Sexuality') (Robinson, in Rubenstein et al., 1972).

Television companies

Like mass newspapers, television today is big business, and in most countries the state has been directly involved with its administration. In Britain the British Broadcasting Corporation, which initiated the first television programmes ever produced, is a public organization (although in 1988 its status is being re-examined by the government). It is funded by licence fees paid by every household that owns a set. For some years the BBC was the only organization permitted to broadcast either radio or television programmes in Britain, but today, alongside the two BBC TV channels, BBC 1 and 2, there exist two commercial TV channels (ITV channels 3 and 4), put together from programmes produced by regional companies whose number is strictly limited by the government. The frequency and duration of advertising is controlled by law, with a maximum of six minutes per hour (Pragnall, 1985).

In the United States the three leading TV organizations are all commercial networks – the American Broadcasting Company (ABC), Columbia Broadcasting System (CBS) and the National Broadcasting Company (NBC). Networks are limited by law to owning five licensed stations, which in the case of the three organizations mentioned are in the biggest cities. The 'big three', therefore, reach over a quarter of all households via their own stations. Some 200 affiliated stations are also attached to each network, comprising 90 per cent of the 700 or so TV stations in the country. The networks depend for their income on selling advertising time. The National Association of Broadcasters, a private body, lays down guidelines about the proportion of viewing time per hour to be devoted to advertising: 9.5 minutes per hour during 'prime time' and 16 at other periods. TV companies use regularly collected statistics (ratings) of how many people watch specific programmes in setting advertising fees. The ratings also, of course, strongly influence whether or not a series continues.

The effect of television on behaviour

Vast amounts of research have been done to try to assess the effects of television programmes. Most research about the influence of television has concerned children – understandably enough, given the sheer volume of their viewing and the possible implications for socialization. The three most commonly researched topics are television's impact on propensities to crime and violence, the effects of news broadcasting, and the role of television in political life. We shall concentrate here on the first of these.

The incidence of violence in television programmes is well documented. The most extensive studies have been carried out by Gerbner and his collaborators, analysing samples of prime-time and weekend daytime television for all the major American networks each year since 1967. The number and frequency of violent acts and episodes is charted for a range of varying types of programme. Violence is defined in the research as the threat or use of physical force, directed against the self or others, in which physical harm or death is involved. Television drama emerges as highly violent in character: on average 80 per cent of such programmes contain violence, with a rate of 7.5 violent episodes per hour. Children's programmes show even higher levels of violence, although killing is less commonly portrayed. Cartoons contain the highest number of violent acts and episodes of any type of television programme (Gerbner et al., 1979, 1980; Gunter, 1985).

In what ways, if at all, does the depiction of violence influence the audience? F. S. Anderson collected the findings of sixty-seven studies conducted over the twenty years from 1956 to 1976 investigating the influence of TV violence on tendencies to aggression among children. About three-quarters of the studies claimed to find some such association. In 20 per cent of cases there were no clear-cut results, while in 3 per cent of the researches the investigators concluded that watching television violence actually decreases aggression (Anderson, 1977; Liebert, Sprafkin and Davidson, 1982, chapter 5).

The studies Anderson surveyed, however, differ widely in the methods used, the strength of the association supposedly revealed, and the definition of 'aggressive behaviour'. In crime dramas featuring violence (and in many children's cartoons) there are underlying themes of justice and retribution. A far higher proportion of miscreants are brought to justice in crime dramas than happens with police investigations in real life, and in cartoons harmful or threatening characters usually tend to get their 'just deserts'. It does not necessarily follow that high levels of the portrayal of violence create directly imitative patterns among those watching, who are perhaps more influenced by the underlying moral themes. In general, research on the 'effects' of television on audiences has tended to treat viewers – children and adults – as passive and undiscriminating in their reactions to what they see.

Robert Hodge and David Tripp emphasize that children's responses to TV involve interpreting or *reading* what they see, not just registering the content of programmes (Hodge and Tripp, 1986). They suggest that most research has not taken account of the complexity of children's mental processes. TV-watching, even of trivial programmes, is not an inherently low-level intellectual activity; children 'read' programmes by relating them to other systems of meaning in their everyday lives. For example, even very young children recognize that media violence is 'not real'. According to Hodge and Tripp it is not the violence as such in television programmes that has effects on behaviour, but rather the general framework of attitudes within which it is both presented and 'read'.

Yet it is difficult to believe that the continuing depiction of violence on television has no impact at all on children's attitudes or behaviour. A US government investigation into the influence of television on violent behaviour among children and young people, initiated by the Surgeon General, included many different studies. It produced an ambiguous and inconclusive final report, which masked differences of opinion among the various researchers concerned (Surgeon General, 1972). The report did, however, fuel efforts to use television in a constructive and positive way in children's development – particularly through public service television (television funded by state grants and the raising of subscriptions, rather than by advertising). Although they only have about 5 per cent of the revenue obtained by commercial broadcasters, public television stations put on numerous educational programmes. *Sesame Street* was an example of a programme specifically designed to entertain yet also foster the intellectual and cultural development of children (Cook et al., 1975).

Television as purveyor of social attitudes

The influence of television as a cultural medium cannot properly be assessed in terms of the content of programmes offered. Television helps to provide the *frames of experience*, the overall cultural outlooks, within which individuals in modern societies interpret and organize information. Television is as important as books, magazines and newspapers in today's expansion of indirect forms of communication. It frames the ways in which individuals interpret and respond to the social world by helping to *order our experience* of it. Assumptions built into the overall character of TV production and distribution may perhaps be more significant than whatever particular programmes are shown.

For instance, television has served in some degree to change the nature of modern elections, because of its importance in providing a platform for presentation of issues and candidates. To take another example: the symbols involved in advertising might have a more profound influence on social behaviour than the stated 'messages' the advertisers wish to get across. Thus, gender divisions are often symbolized in what goes on in the setting or the background of a commercial rather than what it is explicitly selling. In many ads, men appear as mentally and physically alert, while women are shown as gazing into the distance in a dreamy way (Goffman, 1979).

Conclusion

As in the case of schooling, television and the 'culture industry' raise questions about the balance between power, responsibility and freedom. Schools provide for many learning experiences – inside and outside the formal curriculum – which are inherently fulfilling and contribute towards individual development. The teaching of reading and writing is the most obvious example of this: if we did not have access to such skills, our existence would be radically impoverished. On the other hand, the school system helps perpetuate social and economic inequalities.

The modern media of communication are similarly central to our lives, providing many necessary information services as well as offering possibilities for self-enlightenment and entertainment. Yet the media on the whole tend to reflect the outlook of dominant groups in society. This is not mainly because of direct political censorship (as in Eastern Europe), but results from the fact that ownership of television, newspapers, data banks, and so forth, is concentrated in relatively few hands. Who should control the media? How can the less privileged make their voices heard? These are complex and difficult problems, which now have an international dimension, given the domination of world communications by a limited number of countries. This phenomenon is discussed in chapter 16 ('The Globalizing of Social Life').

Summary

1   Education in its modern form, involving the instruction of pupils within specially designated school premises, began to emerge with the spread of printed materials and higher levels of *literacy*. Knowledge could be retained, reproduced and consumed by more people in more places. With industrialization, work became more specialized, and knowledge is increasingly acquired in more abstract rather than practical ways – the skills of reading, writing and calculating.

2   The expansion of education in the twentieth century has been closely tied to perceived needs for a literate and disciplined work-force. Although reformers have seen the use of education for all as a means of reducing inequalities, its impact in this respect is fairly limited. Education tends to express and reaffirm existing inequalities more than it acts to change them.

3   According to Bernstein's theory, children who have acquired *elaborated codes* of speech are more able to deal with the demands of formal academic education than those confined to *restricted codes*. Intelligence tests, such as IQ tests, rely on a standardized conception of 'useful' abilities and skills; they are culture-bound and thus limited in application.

4   The formal school curriculum is only one part of a more general process of *cultural reproduction* influenced by many informal aspects of learning, education and school settings. The 'hidden curriculum' plays a significant role in cultural reproduction.

5   The organization of and teaching within schools have tended to sustain gender inequalities. Rules specifying distinct dress for girls and boys encourage sex-typing, as do texts containing established gender images. There is evidence that teachers treat girls and boys differently, and there is a long history of separating the sexes: certain subjects are thought more suitable for girls than boys and *vice versa*. Women are still under-represented among students and teachers in higher education and this situation is unlikely to improve until the other factors change.

6   Universal primary education is far from being established throughout the world; there are still some Third World countries in which most children receive no formal education whatsoever. The absolute number of people in the world who are illiterate is rising rather than declining at present.

7   Schooling has to be understood as one element in the systems of mass communication that have emerged with industrialization. A tremendous expansion of information communicated between people widely separated from one another has occurred. Modern political systems depend on an informed citizenry: through mechanical printing and the

electronic media of telephone, radio, television and computer-transmitted information, the *global* and the *local* have moved nearer to each other.

8   In spite of many studies of television and violence, it is still not clear how far, and in what ways, the portrayal of violence on TV encourages aggressive behaviour in real life. Most of the research has underestimated how far viewers selectively interpret what they see, and the complex ways in which the 'fictional' and the 'real' interrelate.

9   The influence of TV, and other mass media, upon our lives is profound. The media do not only provide entertainment, but provide and shape much of the information which we utilize in our daily lives. Questions about who owns the media, and how far the media allow for the expression of diverse viewpoints, are of great importance.

Basic concepts

education   communication
cultural reproduction

Important terms

literacy   hidden curriculum
educational system   intelligence
higher education   IQ
restricted code   local knowledge
elaborated code   mass media

Further reading

David Altheide, *Creating Reality: How TV News Distorts Events* (Beverly Hills, California: Sage, 1976) — a discussion, still relatively accurate, of the influence of the medium on the message.

T. P. Barwise, A. S. C. Ehrenberg and G. J. Goodhardt, 'Glued to the Box?', *Journal of Communication*, vol. 6, 1982 — article on the effects of television, particularly on children.

Ray Hiebert and Carol Reuss (eds), *The Impact of Mass Media* (New York: Longman, 1986) — looks at impact of mass communications on gender, society and violence.

Robert Hodge and David Tripp, *Children and Television: A Semiotic Approach* (Cambridge: Polity Press, 1986) — focuses on the 'violence' controversy, and argues that children are active 'readers' of TV.

Ronald Meighan, *A Sociology of Educating* (London: Holt, Rinehart and Winston, 1981) — a review of the standard debates.

Jean S. Phinney and Mary Jane Rotheram (eds), *Children's Ethnic Socialisation* (London: Sage, 1987) — a study of ethnicity and the social factors which impinge on it.

Jason E. Square (ed.), *The Movie Business Book* (London: Columbus Books, 1986) — essays by film-makers explaining how modern films are planned, produced, directed, marketed and exhibited.

14

Religion

How can we live in a world without God? This question has reverberated through Western culture since the eighteenth century, when social observers and theologians perceived that the influence of religion seemed to be sharply declining. For close to two thousand years, Christianity had provided a moral and spiritual framework for Western development – supplying the impulse for numerous wars as well as comfort and guidance for believers.

We tend to forget in modern times that it had a strong material presence too. Until relatively recently, the churches rivalled, and frequently surpassed, monarchs and governments in the political power they wielded and the wealth they managed to accumulate. The priesthood maintained a monopoly over the skills of literacy, scholarship and learning. Even when education became more widespread, the churches continued to have a leading role in its organization. As industrialization took hold, as with so many other areas of social life, the place of religion changed. Churches and religious bodies in Western countries lost much of the secular power they had formerly wielded. Governments took over many of the tasks previously managed by churches, including the provision of education.

On the level of ideas, scientific thought and technology increasingly challenged **religion** and magic as modes of understanding and coping with the world. In mediaeval times, many people believed not only in Christian ideas, but in ghosts, spirits, witches and demons (Camporesi, 1988). The more physical explanations science provided, the less the world was thought to be governed by spiritual beings or ghostly entities. In the middle ages, mystical experiences had been commonplace among the general population. Joan of Arc was not unusual, for example, in claiming to have heard the voices of angels instructing her to save France from the marauding English. Three centuries later, not only was it rare for anyone to claim to experience mystical states; any such experiences were regarded as symptoms of mental disorder.

Towards the end of the nineteenth century, the German philosopher Friedrich Nietzsche announced that 'God is dead!' The teachings of Christianity used to be a point of reference for our sense of purpose and meaning; henceforth we have to live, Nietzsche asserted, without this security, and indeed without any fixed moral reference-points at all. Living in a world without God means creating our own values and getting used to what Nietzsche called 'the loneliness of being' – understanding that our lives are without purpose, and that no superior entities watch over our fate.

Secularization describes the processes whereby religion loses its influence over the various spheres of social life. As we shall see later in this chapter, secularization is a complex phenomenon, and it is not clear, as Nietzsche thought, that the influence of religion has declined to vanishing-point. We shall return to the theme of secularization later, because it is the backdrop to all current sociological discussions of religion. But first of all, we must investigate what religion actually is, describe some of the main types of religious belief and practice, and analyse the leading sociological theories of religion.

Defining religion (and magic)

The variety of religious beliefs and organizations is so immense that scholars have found great difficulty in reaching a generally accepted definition of religion. In the West, most people identify religion with Christianity – a belief in a supreme being, who commands us to behave in a moral fashion on this earth, and promises an after-life to come. Yet we certainly cannot define religion as a whole in these terms. These beliefs, and many other aspects of Christianity, are absent from most of the world's religions.

What religion is not

In order to overcome the pitfalls of culturally biased thinking about religion it is probably best to begin by saying what religion *is not*, considered in general terms (Wilson, 1972). First, religion should not be identified with **monotheism** (belief in one God). Nietzsche's thesis of the 'death of God' was strongly ethnocentric, relating only to Western religious ideas. Most religions involve many deities. Even in some versions of Christianity, there are several figures with sacred qualities: God, Jesus, Mary, the Holy Ghost, Angels, and saints. In certain religions there are no gods at all.

Second, religion should not be identified with *moral prescriptions* controlling the behaviour of believers – like the Commandments Moses was supposed to have received from God. The idea that the gods are very interested in how we behave on this earth is alien to many religions. To the ancient Greeks, for example, the gods were largely indifferent to the activities of humanity.

Third, religion is not necessarily concerned with *explaining how the world came to be as it is*. In Christianity, the myth of Adam and Eve purports to explain the origin of human existence, and many religions have *myths of origin* of this sort; but equally many do not.

Fourth, religion cannot be identified with the *supernatural*, as intrinsically involving belief in a universe 'beyond the realm of the senses'. Confucianism, for example, is concerned with accepting the natural harmony of the world, not with finding truths that 'lie behind' it.

What religion is

Characteristics that all religions *do* seem to share are as follows. Religions involve a set of *symbols*, invoking feelings of *reverence* or *awe*, and are linked to **rituals** or ceremonials (such as church services) practised by a community of *believers*. Each of these elements needs some elaboration. Whether or not the beliefs in a religion involve gods, there are virtually always beings or objects inspiring attitudes of awe or wonder. In some religions, for example, people believe in and revere a 'divine force', rather than personalized gods. In other religions, there are figures who are not gods, but are thought of with reverence – such as Buddha or Confucius.

The rituals associated with religion are very diverse. Ritual acts may include praying, chanting, singing, eating certain kinds of food – or refraining from doing so – fasting on certain days, and so on. Since ritual acts are oriented towards religious symbols they are usually seen as quite distinct from the habits and procedures of ordinary life. Lighting a candle to honour or placate a god differs completely in its significance from doing so to provide illumination. Religious rituals are often carried on by individuals in isolation, but all religions also involve ceremonials practised collectively by believers. Regular ceremonials normally occur in special places – churches, temples or ceremonial grounds.

The existence of collective ceremonial is usually regarded by sociologists as one of the main factors distinguishing religion from magic, although the borderlines are by no means clear-cut. **Magic** is the influencing of events by the use of potions, chantings, or ritual practices. It is generally practised by individuals, not by a community of believers. People often choose to resort to magic in situations of misfortune or danger. Thus Bronislaw Malinowski's classic study of the Trobriand islanders of the Pacific describes a variety of magical rites performed before any hazardous voyage by canoe (Malinowski, 1982). The islanders omit such rites when they are simply going fishing on the safe and placid waters of a local lagoon.

Although magical practices have mostly disappeared from modern societies, in situations of danger magic-like superstitions are still common. Many who work in occupations that either are dangerous or where chance factors can drastically affect performance – such as miners, deep-sea fishermen or sports players – indulge in small superstitious rituals or carry particular items in times of stress. An example might be a tennis-player who insists on wearing a particular ring during big matches. Astrological beliefs, which have been inherited from magical ideas in mediaeval Europe, still command a following, although probably most people do not take them too seriously (Adorno, 1974).

Varieties of religion

In traditional societies, religion usually plays a central part in social life. Religious symbols and rituals are often integrated with the material and artistic culture of the society – music, painting or carving, dance, story-telling and literature. In small cultures, there is no professional priesthood, but there are always certain individuals who specialize in knowledge of religious (and often magical) practices. Although there are various sorts of such specialists, one common type is the **Shaman** (a word originating among North American Indians). A Shaman is an individual believed to be able to direct spirits or non-natural forces through ritual means. Shamans are sometimes essentially magicians rather than religious leaders, however, and are often consulted by individuals dissatisfied with what is offered in the religious rituals of the community.

Totemism and animism

Two forms of religion found frequently in smaller cultures are **totemism** and **animism**. The word 'totem' originated among North American Indian tribes, but has been widely used to refer to species of animals or plants believed to have supernatural powers. Usually each kinship group or clan within a society has its own particular totem, with which various ritual activities are associated. Totemic beliefs might seem alien to those living in industrialized societies, yet in certain relatively minor contexts, symbols similar to those of totemism are familiar – as when a sports team has an animal or plant for its emblem. Mascots are totems.

Animism is a belief in spirits or ghosts, thought to populate the same world as human beings. Such spirits may be seen as either benign or malevolent, and may influence human behaviour in numerous respects. In some cultures, for example, spirits are believed to cause illness or madness, and may also *possess* or take over individuals in such a way as to control their behaviour. Animistic beliefs are not confined to small cultures, but are found to some degree in many religious settings. In mediaeval Europe, those believed to be possessed by evil spirits were frequently persecuted as sorcerers or witches.

Small, seemingly 'simple' societies frequently have complex systems of religious belief. Totemism and animism are more common among these societies than in larger ones, but some small societies have far more complex religions. The Nuer of southern Sudan, for instance, described by E. E. Evans-Pritchard, have an elaborate set of theological ideas centred on a 'high god' or 'sky spirit' (Evans-Pritchard, 1956). Religions which incline towards monotheism, however, are found relatively infrequently among smaller traditional cultures. Most are **polytheistic** – there is a belief in many gods.

Judaism, Christianity and Islam

The three most influential monotheistic religions in world history are *Judaism*, *Christianity* and *Islam*. All originated in the Near East and each has influenced the others.

Judaism

Judaism is the oldest of the three religions, dating from about 1,000 BC. The early Hebrews were nomads, living in and around ancient Egypt. Their **prophets**, or religious leaders, partly drew their ideas from existing religious beliefs in the region, but differed in their commitment to a single, almighty God. Most of their neighbours were polytheistic. The Hebrews believed that God demands obedience to strict moral codes, and insisted on their claim to a monopoly of truth, seeing their beliefs as the only true religion (Zeitlin, 1984, 1988).

Until the creation of Israel, not long after the end of the Second World War, there was no state of which Judaism was the official religion. Jewish communities survived in Europe, North Africa and Asia, although they were frequently persecuted – culminating in the murder of millions of Jews by the Nazis in concentration camps during the war.

Christianity

Many Judaic views were taken over and incorporated as part of Christianity. Jesus was an orthodox Jew and Christianity began as a sect of Judaism; it is not clear that Jesus wished to found a distinctive religion. His disciples came to think of him as the *Messiah* – a Hebrew word meaning 'the anointed', the Greek term for which was 'Christ' – awaited by the Jews. Paul, a Greek-speaking Roman citizen, was a major initiator of the spread of Christianity, preaching extensively in Asia Minor and Greece. Although the Christians were at first savagely persecuted, the Emperor Constantine eventually adopted Christianity as the official religion of the Roman Empire. Christianity spread to become a dominant force in Western culture for the next two thousand years.

Christianity today commands the greatest number of adherents, and is more generally spread across the world, than any other religion. Over a thousand million individuals regard themselves as Christians, but there are many divisions in terms of theology and church organization, the main branches being Roman Catholicism, Protestantism and Eastern Orthodoxy.

Islam

The origins of Islam, today the second largest religion in the world, overlap with those of Christianity. Islam derives from the teachings of the prophet Mohammed in the seventh century AD. The single God of Islam, Allah, is believed to hold sway over all human and natural life. The *Pillars of Islam* are the five essential religious duties of Muslims (as believers in Islam are called). The first is the recitation of the Islamic creed, 'There is no god but Allah, and Mohammed is the apostle of Allah.' The second is the saying of formal prayers five times each day, preceded by ceremonial washing. The worshipper at these prayers must always face towards the holy city of Mecca in Saudi Arabia, no matter how far away that is.

The third pillar is the observance of Ramadan, a month of fasting during which no food or drink may be taken during daylight. The fourth is the giving of alms (money to the poor), set out in Islamic law, which often has been used as a source of taxation by the state. Finally, there is the expectation that every believer will attempt, at least once, to make a pilgrimage to Mecca.

Muslims believe that Allah spoke through earlier prophets – including Moses and Jesus – before Mohammed, whose teachings most directly express his will. Islam has come to be very widespread, having some 600 million adherents throughout the world. The majority are concentrated in North and East Africa, the Middle East and Pakistan. (For a brief discussion of Muslim beliefs, see the section on the Islamic Revolution below.)

The religions of the Far East

Hinduism

There are major contrasts between Judaism, Christianity and Islam and the religions of the Far East. The oldest of all the great religions still prominent in the world today is *Hinduism*, the core beliefs of which date back some 6,000 years. Hinduism is a polytheistic religion. It is so internally diverse that some scholars have suggested it should be regarded as a cluster of related religions rather than a single religious orientation; many local cults and religious practices are linked by a few generally held beliefs.

Most Hindus accept the doctrine of the cycle of *reincarnation* – the belief that all living beings are part of an eternal process of birth, death and rebirth. A second key feature is the caste system, based on the belief that individuals are born into a particular position in a social and ritual hierarchy, according to the nature of their activities in previous incarnations. A different set of duties and rituals exists for each caste, and one's fate in the next life is governed mainly by how well these duties are performed. Hinduism accepts the possibility of numerous different religious standpoints, not drawing a clear line between believers and non-believers. There are as many Hindus as Muslims – about 600 million, but these are virtually all situated on the Indian sub-continent. Hinduism does not seek to convert others into 'true believers', unlike Christianity and Islam.

Buddhism, Confucianism, Taoism

The **ethical religions** of the East encompass *Buddhism, Confucianism* and *Taoism*. These religions have no gods. Rather, they emphasize ethical ideals that relate the believer to the natural cohesion and unity of the universe.

Buddhism derives from the teachings of Siddhartha Gautama, the Buddha (*enlightened one*) who was a Hindu prince in a small kingdom in south Nepal in the sixth century BC. According to the Buddha, human beings can escape the reincarnation cycle by the renunciation of desire. The path of salvation lies in a life of self-discipline and meditation, separated from the tasks of the mundane world. The overall objective of Buddhism is the attainment of *Nirvana*, complete spiritual fulfilment. The Buddha rejected Hindu ritual and the authority of the castes. Like Hinduism, Buddhism tolerates many local variations, including belief in local deities, not insisting upon a single view. Buddhism today is a major influence in several states in the Far East, including Thailand, Burma, Sri Lanka, China, Japan and Korea.

Confucianism was the basis of the culture of the ruling groups in traditional China. 'Confucius' (the latinized form of the name K'ung Fu-Tzu), lived in the sixth century BC, the same period as Buddha. Like Lao-Tsze, the founder of Taoism, Confucius was a teacher, not a religious prophet in the manner of the Near Eastern religious leaders. Confucius is not seen by his followers as a god, but as 'the wisest of wise men'. Confucianism seeks to adjust human life to the inner harmony of nature, emphasizing the veneration of ancestors. *Taoism* shares similar principles, stressing meditation and non-violence as means to the higher life. Although some elements survive in the beliefs and practices of many Chinese, Confucianism and Taoism have lost much of their influence in China as a result of determined opposition from the government.

Theories of religion

Sociological approaches to religion are still strongly influenced by the ideas of the three 'classical' sociological theorists: Marx, Durkheim and Weber. None of the three were themselves religious, and all thought that the significance of religion would decrease in modern times. Each believed that religion is in a fundamental sense an illusion. The advocates of different faiths may be wholly persuaded of the validity of the beliefs they hold and the rituals in which they participate, yet the very diversity of religions, and their obvious connection to different types of society, the three thinkers held, make these claims inherently implausible. An individual born into an Australian society of hunters and gatherers would plainly have different religious beliefs from someone born into the caste system of India or the Catholic Church of mediaeval Europe.

Marx and religion

In spite of his influence on the subject, Karl Marx never studied religion in any detail. His ideas mostly derived from the writings of several early nineteenth-century theological and philosophical authors. One of these was Ludwig Feuerbach, who wrote a famous work called *The Essence of Christianity* (Feuerbach, 1957; originally published 1841). According to Feuerbach, religion consists of ideas and values produced by human beings in the course of their cultural development, but mistakenly projected on to divine forces or gods. Because human beings do not fully understand their own history, they tend to attribute socially created values and norms to the activities of gods. Thus the story of the ten commandments given to Moses by God is a mythical version of the origins of moral precepts which govern the lives of Jewish and Christian believers.

So long as we do not understand the nature of the religious symbols we ourselves have created, Feuerbach argues, we are condemned to be prisoners of forces of history we cannot control. Feuerbach uses the term **alienation** to refer to the establishing of gods or divine forces distinct from human beings. Humanly created values and ideas come to be seen as the product of *alien* or separate beings – religious forces and gods. While the effects of alienation have in the past been negative, the understanding of religion as alienation, according to Feuerbach, promises great hope for the future. Once human beings realize that the values projected on to religion are really their own, those values become capable of realization on this earth, rather than being deferred to an after-life. The powers believed to be possessed by God in Christianity can be appropriated by human beings themselves. Christians believe that while God is all-powerful and all-loving, human beings themselves are imperfect and flawed. However, the potential for love and goodness, and the power to control our own lives, Feuerbach believed, are present in human social institutions and can be brought to fruition once we understand their true nature.

Marx accepts the view that religion represents human self-alienation. It is often believed that Marx was dismissive of religion, but this is far from true. Religion, he writes, is the 'heart of a heartless world' – a haven from the harshness of daily reality. In Marx's view, religion in its traditional form will, and should, disappear; yet this is because the positive values embodied in religion can become guiding ideals for improving of the lot of humanity on this earth, *not* because ideals and values themselves are mistaken. We should not fear the gods we ourselves have created, and we should cease endowing them with values we ourselves can realize.

Marx declared, in a famous phrase, that religion has been the 'opium of the people'. Religion defers happiness and rewards to the after-life, teaching the resigned acceptance of existing conditions in this life. Attention is thus diverted away from inequalities and injustices in this world by the promise of what is to come in the next. Religion has a strong ideological element: religious beliefs and values often provide justifications of inequalities of wealth and power. For example, the teaching that 'the meek shall inherit the earth' suggests attitudes of humility and non-resistance to oppression.

Durkheim and religious ritual

In contrast to Marx, Emile Durkheim spent a good part of his intellectual career studying religion, concentrating particularly on religion in small-scale, traditional societies. Durkheim's work, *The Elementary*

Forms of the Religious Life, first published in 1912, is perhaps the single most influential study in the sociology of religion (Durkheim, 1976). Durkheim does not connect religion primarily with social inequalities or power, but with the overall nature of the institutions of a society. He bases his work upon a study of totemism as practised by Australian aboriginal societies, and he argues that totemism represents religion in its most 'elementary' or simple form – hence the title of his book.

A totem, as has been mentioned, was originally an animal or plant taken as having particular symbolic significance for a group. It is a *sacred* object, regarded with veneration and surrounded by various ritual activities. Durkheim defines religion in terms of a distinction between the **sacred** and the **profane**. Sacred objects and symbols, he holds, are treated as *apart* from the routine aspects of existence – the realm of the profane. Eating the totemic animal or plant, except on special ceremonial occasions, is usually forbidden, and as a sacred object, the totem is believed to have divine properties which separate it completely from other animals that might be hunted, or crops gathered and consumed.

Why is the totem sacred? According to Durkheim, it is because it is the symbol of the group itself; it stands for the values central to the group or community. The reverence which people feel for the totem actually derives from the respect they hold for central social values. In religion, the object of worship is actually society itself.

Durkheim strongly emphasizes the fact that religions are never just a matter of belief. All religion involves regular ceremonial and ritual activities, in which a group of believers meets together. In collective ceremonials, a sense of group solidarity is affirmed and heightened. Ceremonials take individuals away from the concerns of profane social life into an elevated sphere, in which they feel in contact with higher forces. These higher forces, attributed to totems, divine influences or gods, are really the expression of the influence of the collectivity over the individual.

Ceremony and ritual, in Durkheim's view, are essential to binding the members of groups together. This is why they are found not only in regular situations of worship, but in the various life crises at which major social transitions are experienced, for example birth, marriage and death. In virtually all societies, ritual and ceremonial procedures are observed at such gatherings. Durkheim reasons that collective ceremonials reaffirm group solidarity at a time when people are forced to adjust to major changes in their lives. Funeral rituals demonstrate that the values of the group outlive the passing of particular individuals, and so provide a means for bereaved people to adjust to their altered circumstances. Mourning is not the spontaneous expression of grief – or, at least, it is only so for those personally affected by the death. Mourning is a duty imposed by the group.

In small traditional cultures, Durkheim argues, almost all aspects of life are permeated by religion. Religious ceremonials both originate new ideas and categories of thought and reaffirm existing values. Religion is not just a series of sentiments and activities; it actually conditions the *modes of thinking* of individuals in traditional cultures. Even the most basic categories of thought, including how time and space are thought of, were first framed in religious terms. The concept of 'time', for instance, was originally derived from counting the intervals involved in religious ceremonials.

Durkheim's expectations of religious change

With the development of modern societies, Durkheim believes, the influence of religion wanes. Scientific thinking increasingly replaces religious explanation, and ceremonial and ritual activities come to occupy only a small part of individuals' lives. Durkheim agrees with Marx that traditional religion – that is, religion involving divine forces or gods – is on the verge of disappearing. 'The old gods', Durkheim writes, 'are dead.' Yet he says that there is a sense in which religion, in altered form, is likely to continue. Even modern societies depend for their cohesion upon rituals that reaffirm their values; new ceremonial activities can thus be expected to emerge to replace the old. Durkheim is vague about what these might be, but it seems that he has in mind the celebration of humanist and political values such as freedom, equality and social co-operation.

It could be argued that most industrialized states have in fact fostered **civil religions**. In Britain, symbols such as the flag, songs like *Land of Hope and Glory*, and rituals such as coronations, all act to reaffirm the 'British way of life' (Bellah, 1970). These symbols are linked to traditional religious institutions, such as the Church of England. The Soviet Union, by contrast, is openly hostile to traditional religion, on the basis of Marx's ideas; yet Marx, Engels and Lenin have themselves become powerful symbols within a state-sponsored civil religion. The May Day celebrations held annually in Red Square in Moscow, and other rituals, reinforce a commitment to the ideals of the Russian Revolution.

Whether we can really justify speaking of 'religion' in these contexts is debatable; these symbols and practices co-exist with traditional religions. Yet it is difficult to deny that civil symbols and rituals draw upon similar social mechanisms to those found in traditional forms of religion.

Weber and the world religions

Durkheim bases his arguments on a very small range of examples, even though he claims his ideas apply to religion in general. Max Weber, by contrast, embarked on a massive study of religions world-wide. No scholar before or since has undertaken a task of such scope. Most of his attention was concentrated on what he called the *world religions* – those that have attracted large numbers of believers and decisively affected the course of global history. He made detailed studies of Hinduism, Buddhism, Taoism and ancient Judaism (Weber, 1958, 1951, 1952, 1963), and in *The Protestant Ethic and the Spirit of Capitalism* (1976; originally published 1904–5) and elsewhere he wrote extensively about the impact of Christianity on the history of the West. He did not, however, complete his projected study of Islam.

Weber's writings on religion differ from those of Durkheim in concentrating on the connection between religion and social change, something to which Durkheim gave little attention. They contrast with the work of Marx because Weber argues that religion is not necessarily a conservative force; on the contrary, religiously inspired movements have often produced dramatic social transformations. Thus Protestantism – particularly Puritanism – was the source of the capitalistic outlook found in the modern West. The early entrepreneurs were mostly Calvinists. Their drive to succeed, which helped initiate Western economic development, was originally prompted by a desire to serve God. Material success was for them a sign of divine favour.

Weber saw his research on the world religions as a single project. His discussion of the impact of Protestantism on the development of the West is part of a comprehensive attempt to understand the influence of religion on social and economic life in varying cultures. Analysing the Eastern religions, Weber concludes that they provided insuperable barriers to the development of industrial capitalism, such as took place in the West. This is not because the non-Western civilizations are backward; they simply have accepted values different from those which came to predominate in Europe.

In traditional China and India, Weber points out, there was at certain periods a significant development of commerce, manufacture and urbanism, but these did not generate the radical patterns of social change involved in the rise of industrial capitalism in the West. Religion was a major influence in inhibiting such change. For example, Hinduism is what Weber calls an 'other-worldly' religion. That is to say, its highest values stress escape from the toils of the material world to a higher plane of spiritual existence. The religious feelings and motivations produced by Hinduism do not focus upon controlling or shaping the material world. On the contrary, Hinduism sees material reality as a veil hiding the true concerns to which humankind should be oriented. Confucianism also acted to direct effort away from economic development, as this came to be understood in the West, emphasizing harmony with the world rather than promoting active mastery of it. Although China was for a long while the most powerful and culturally most developed civilization in the world, its dominant religious values acted as a brake on a strong commitment to economic development for its own sake.

Weber regards Christianity as a *salvation religion*, involving the belief that human beings can be 'saved' if they adopt the beliefs of the religion and follow its moral tenets. The notions of sin, and of being rescued from sinfulness by God's grace are important here. They generate a tension and an emotional dynamism essentially absent from the Eastern religions. Salvation religions have a 'revolutionary' aspect. While the religions of the East cultivate an attitude of passivity towards the existing order within the believer, Christianity involves a constant struggle against sin, and hence can stimulate revolt against the existing order of things. Religious leaders – like Jesus – arise, who reinterpret existing doctrines in such a way as to challenge the existing power-structure.

Assessment

Marx, Durkheim and Weber each identify some important general characteristics of religion, and in some ways their views complement one another. Marx is right to claim that religion often has ideological implications, serving to justify the interests of ruling groups at the expense of others: there are innumerable instances of this in history. Take as an example the influence of Christianity on the European colonialists' efforts to subject other cultures to their rule. The missionaries who sought to convert 'heathen' peoples to Christian beliefs were no doubt sincere, yet the effect of their teachings was to reinforce the destruction of traditional cultures and the imposition of white domination. Various Christian denominations almost all tolerated, or endorsed, slavery in the United States and other parts of the world up to the nineteenth century. Doctrines were developed claiming slavery to be based on divine law, disobedient slaves being guilty of an offence against God as well as their masters (Stampp, 1956).

Yet Weber is certainly correct to emphasize the unsettling, and often revolutionary, impact of religious ideals on pre-established social orders. Despite the churches' early support for slavery in the United States, many church leaders later played a key role in the fight to abolish it. Religious beliefs have prompted many social movements seeking to overthrow unjust systems of authority, for instance, playing a prominent part in the civil rights movements of the 1960s in the USA. Religion has also influenced social change – often provoking much bloodshed – through the armed clashes and wars fought for religious motives.

These divisive influences of religion, so prominent in history, find little mention in Durkheim's work. Durkheim emphasizes above all the role of religion in promoting social cohesion. Yet it is not difficult to redirect his ideas towards explaining religious division, conflict and change as well as solidarity. After all, much of the strength of feeling which may be generated *against* other religious groups derives from the commitment to religious values generated *within* each community of believers.

Among the most valuable aspects of Durkheim's writings is his stress on ritual and ceremonial. All religions involve regular assemblies of believers, at which ritual prescriptions are observed. As he rightly points out, ritual activities also mark the major transitions of life – birth, entry to adulthood (rituals associated with puberty are found in many cultures), marriage and death (Van Gennep, 1977).

In the rest of this chapter we shall make use of ideas developed by all three authors. First, we'll look at different types of religious organization, and consider the different gender roles in religious practice. Then we'll go on to discuss religious movements which set out to challenge the existing social order – the *millenarian* movements of mediaeval Europe and some non-European cultures in the twentieth century. We shall then go on to discuss one of the most important instances of religious revival in current times: the rise of Islamic fundamentalism, before discussing religion in Western societies today.

Types of religious organization

Weber and Troeltsch: churches and sects

All religions involve communities of believers, but there are many different ways in which such communities are organized. One way of classifying religious organizations was first put forward by Max Weber and his colleague, the religious historian Ernst Troeltsch (Troeltsch, 1981). Weber and Troeltsch distinguished between **churches** and **sects**. A church is a large, well-established religious body – like the Catholic Church or the Church of England. A sect is a smaller, less highly organized grouping of committed believers, usually setting itself up in protest against a church – as Calvinists or Methodists have done. Churches normally have a formal, bureaucratic structure, with a hierarchy of religious officials, and tend to represent the conservative face of religion, since they are integrated within the existing institutional order. Most of their adherents are children of church-members.

Sects are comparatively small; they usually aim at discovering and following 'the true way', and tend to withdraw from the surrounding society into communities of their own. The members of sects regard established churches as corrupt. Most have few or no officials, all members being regarded as equal participants. A small proportion of people are born into sects, but most actively join them in order to further their beliefs.

Becker: denominations and cults

Other authors have further developed the church/sect typology as originally set out by Weber and Troeltsch. An example is the work of Howard Becker who has added two further types: the **denomination** and the **cult** (Becker, 1950). A denomination is a sect which has 'cooled down' and become an institutionalized body rather than an active protest group. Sects which survive over any period of time inevitably become denominations. Thus Calvinism and Methodism were sects during their early formation, when they generated great fervour among their members; but over the years they have become more 'respectable'. Denominations are recognized as more or less legitimate by churches and exist alongside them, quite often co-operating harmoniously with them.

Cults resemble sects, but have different emphases. They are the most loosely knit and transient of all religious organizations, being composed of individuals who reject what they see as the values of the outside society. Their focus is on individual experience, bringing like-minded individuals together. People do not formally *join* a cult, but rather follow particular theories or prescribed ways of behaviour. Members are usually allowed to maintain other religious connections. Like sects, cults quite often form around an inspirational leader. Instances of cults in the West today would include groups of believers in spiritualism, astrology or transcendental meditation.

Evaluation

The four concepts just discussed are useful for analysing aspects of religious organization, but have to be applied with caution, partly because they reflect specifically Christian traditions. As the case of Islam indicates, there is not always a distinct *church* separate from other institutions in non-Christian religions, and other established religions do not have a developed bureaucratic hierarchy. Hinduism, for example, is such an internally heterogeneous religion that it is hard to find within it features of bureaucratic organization. Nor would it make much sense to call the various sub-divisions of Hinduism 'denominations'.

The concepts of sect and cult perhaps have broad application, but here again a degree of caution is necessary. Sect-like groupings have often existed within the major world religions. They show most of the characteristics – commitment, exclusiveness, divergence from orthodoxy – characteristic of Western sects. However, many of these groups, for instance in Hinduism, are more like traditional ethnic communities than they are like Christian sects (Wilson, 1982). Many such groups lack the fervour of 'true believers' commonly found in Christianity, because in the 'ethical religions' of the East there is more tolerance of diverse outlooks. A group may 'go its own way' without necessarily meeting opposition from other more established organizations. The term cult has wide usage, and can be applied, for instance, to some kinds of millenarian movement, yet these are often more similar to sects than to the types of cult Becker had in mind in formulating the concept.

The concepts of church, sect and denomination may be somewhat culture-bound; but they do help us to analyse the tension which all religions tend to generate between revivalism and institutionalization.

Religious organizations which have been in existence for some while tend to become bureaucratic and inflexible. Yet religious symbols have extraordinary emotive power for believers, and resist becoming reduced to the level of the routine. New sects and cults are constantly arising. We can find a use here for Durkheim's distinction between the sacred and the profane. The more religious activities become standardized, a matter for unthinking re-enactment, the more the element of sacredness is lost and religious ritual and belief become like mundane parts of the everyday world. On the other hand, ceremonials can help revitalize a sense of the distinct qualities of religious experience, and lead to inspirational experiences that may diverge from established orthodoxy. Groups might break away from the main community, mobilize protest or separatist movements, or otherwise differ from patterns of established ritual and belief.

Gender and religion

Churches and denominations, the preceding discussion has indicated, are religious organizations with defined systems of authority. In these hierarchies, as in other areas of social life, women are mostly excluded from power. This is very clear in Christianity, but is also characteristic of all the major religions.

Religious images

The Christian religion is a resolutely male affair in its symbolism as well as its hierarchy. While Mary, the mother of Jesus, may sometimes be treated as if she had divine qualities, God is *the Father*, a male figure, and Jesus took the human shape of a man. Woman is portrayed as created from a rib taken from man. There are many female characters in the biblical texts, and some are portrayed as acting charitably or bravely, but the prime parts are reserved for males. There is no female equivalent to Moses, for example, and in the New Testament all the apostles are men.

These facts have not gone unnoticed by those involved in women's movements. In 1895, Elizabeth Cady Stanton published a series of commentaries on the scriptures, entitled *The Woman's Bible* (Stanton, 1985). In her view, the deity had created women and men as beings of equal value, and the Bible should fully reflect this fact. Its masculine character, she believed, reflected not the authentic view of God, but the fact that it was written by men. In 1870, the Church of England had established a committee to do what had been done many times before – revise and up-date the biblical texts. As she pointed out, the committee contained not a single woman. She asserted that there is no reason to suppose that God is male, since it was clear in the scriptures that *all* human beings were fashioned in the image of God. When one of her colleagues opened a women's rights conference with a prayer to 'God, our Mother', there was virulent reaction from church authorities, yet Stanton pressed ahead in organizing a Women's Revising Committee of twenty-three women to advise her in preparing *The Woman's Bible*.

In her introduction she summed up her position:

> The canon and civil law; church and state; priests and legislators; all political parties and religious denominations have alike taught that woman was made after man, of man, and for man, an inferior being, subject to man. The fashions, forms, ceremonies and customs of society, church ordinances and discipline all grow out of this idea. . . . Those who have the divine insight to translate, transpose and transfigure this mournful object of pity into an exalted, dignified personage, worthy of our worship as the mother of the race, are to be congratulated as having a share of the occult mystical power of the eastern Mahatmas. (Stanton, 1985, pp. 7–8; see also Gage, 1980, originally published 1893)

Female deities are quite often found in religions across the world. These are sometimes thought of as 'womanly', gentle and loving; in other instances, goddesses appear as fearful destroyers. Women warrior-gods, for example, are found fairly often, even though in actual social life women are only very occasionally military leaders. No wide-ranging study of the symbolic and material involvement of women in different religions has yet been undertaken. But there seem to be few, if any, religions in which females are the dominant figures, either symbolically or as religious authorities (Bynum et al., 1986).

Take Buddhism as an example. Females appear as important figures in the teachings of some Buddhist orders. In one branch of the religion especially, Mahayana Buddhism, women are represented in a particularly favourable light. But as a prominent scholar writing on the issue has remarked, on the whole Buddhism – like Christianity – is 'an overwhelmingly male-created institution dominated by a patriarchal power structure', in which the feminine is mostly 'associated with the secular, powerless, profane and imperfect' (Paul, 1985, p. xix). Contrasting pictures of women appear in the Buddhist texts, mirroring no doubt the ambiguous attitudes of men towards women in the secular world. On the one hand, females appear as wise, maternal and gentle; on the other, as mysterious, polluting and destructive, threatening evil.

It cannot be surprising that religions have stressed masculine images, if one accepts Feuerbach's view that religion expresses the deeply held values of society.

Women in religious organizations

In Buddhism, women have traditionally been allowed a role as nuns, which has also been the main avenue for the direct expression of female religious conviction within Christianity. The monastic life derives from the practices of very early Christian groups, who lived a life of extreme poverty given over to meditation. These individuals (many of whom were hermits) and groups had few connections with the established church, but by the early Middle Ages, the church had managed to gain control of most of the orders these groups founded. Monasteries became fixed buildings, with their inmates bound to the authority system of the Catholic Church. Some of the most influential male monastic orders, such as the Cistercians and Augustinians, were founded in the twelfth and thirteenth centuries – the same era as the Crusades. The first orders for women were not established until some two centuries later. Their membership remained relatively small, however, until the nineteenth century. Many women at this time became nuns partly because of the careers which were thereby opened up to them in teaching and nursing, since these occupations were controlled by the religious orders. As the professions became separated from the church, the proportion of women in the orders fell.

Although the rituals and observations of different orders vary, all nuns are regarded as 'brides of Christ', renouncing sexuality. Until changes were made in some of the orders in the 1950s and 1960s, elaborate 'marriage' ceremonies were carried out, during the course of which the novitiate would cut her hair, receive her religious name, and be given a wedding ring. A novice is free to leave, or can be dismissed. After several years, however, vows of perpetual membership are taken; thereafter leaving the convent entails excommunication – being rejected by the Catholic Church.

Women's orders today show a considerable diversity in their beliefs and modes of life (Campbell-Jones, 1979). In some convents, sisters dress in full traditional habit, and keep to established routines. Other convents, by contrast, are not only housed in modern buildings, but have dropped many of the old regulations, the nuns wearing ordinary dress. Restrictions on talking to others at certain periods of the day have been relaxed, together with rules about the position of the body, such as walking with the hands folded and hidden under the habit. These changes were made possible by edicts from the Vatican Council in the 1960s.

Those in monastic orders by definition wield little or no authority within the church hierarchy, even though they are subject to it. The existence of women's orders has never given women any direct power in the wider religious organizations, which in the Catholic and Anglican churches remain almost exclusively dominated by men, although they are now under strong pressure from women's organizations. In 1977, the Sacred Congregation for the Doctrine of the Faith, in Rome, declared formally that women were inadmissible to the Catholic priesthood. The reason given was that Jesus did not call a woman to be one of his disciples (Noel, 1980). The year 1987 was officially designated by the Catholic Church as the 'Year of the Madonna' in which women were advised to recall their traditional roles as wives and mothers.

In the Church of England, women are permitted to be deaconesses, but this position is ambiguous. They are officially part of the laity, and until recently were not allowed to conduct basic religious rituals, like pronouncing blessings or solemnizing marriages. On the other hand, at the direction of a minister, a deaconess may administer certain sacraments and conduct baptisms, among other duties. A report was issued by the standing committee of the General Synod, the church of England's governing body, in 1986 to examine the legislation which would be needed were women to be admitted to the priesthood. The group consisted of ten men and two women. Their task was to consider the 'safeguards' necessary to meet the objections of 'those within the Church of England who are unable to accept, for one reason or another, the ordination of women as priests' (quoted in Aldridge, 1987, p. 377). The feelings and aspirations of women themselves received little mention.

The Christian religion was born of what was in a fundamental sense a revolutionary movement, but in their attitudes towards women, some of the major Christian churches are among the most conservative organizations in modern societies. Women priests have long been accepted in some sects and denominations, but the Catholic and Anglican churches persist in formally supporting inequalities of gender. The Anglican Bishop of London, Graham Leonard, was asked on a radio programme in August 1987 if he thought the Christian notion of God would be affected by seeing a woman regularly up at the altar. He replied: 'I think it would. My instinct when faced with her would be to take her in my arms . . .' The possibility of sexual attraction between a woman priest and members of the congregation, he claimed, was a reason why women should not be admitted as full members of the priesthood. In religion as elsewhere, 'it is the male who takes the initiative and the female who receives' (Jenkins, 1987).

Millenarian movements

The cargo cult discussed at the beginning of chapter 2 ('Culture and Society') is an example of a **millenarian movement**. The existence and number of such movements show very clearly that religion frequently inspires activism and social change. A millenarian group is one that anticipates immediate, collective salvation for believers, either because of some cataclysmic change in the present, or through a recovery of a golden age supposed to have existed in the past. (The term 'millenarian' actually derives from the thousand-year reign of Christ, the *millennium* prophesied in the Bible.) Millenarian movements are deeply entwined with the history of Christianity, and they have arisen in two major contexts – among the Western poor in the past, and among colonized peoples in other parts of the world.

The followers of Joachim

One European mediaeval millenarian movement was known as Joachimism, and flourished in the thirteenth century (Cohn, 1970a and b). At this period, Europe's economic prosperity was increasing rapidly, and the dominant Catholic Church was becoming richer. Many abbots converted their monasteries into luxurious castles, bishops built palaces where they lived as magnificently as secular feudal lords, and the popes maintained splendid courts. Joachimism developed in protest against these tendencies in the official church.

In the mid-thirteenth century, a number of Franciscan monks (whose order stressed avoidance of material pleasure and wealth), began to protest against the indulgent habits of church officials. They based their movement on the prophetic writings of the abbot Joachim of Fiore, who had died about fifty years earlier. Joachim's writings were interpreted to foretell that in 1260 the 'Spirituals', as they called themselves, would inaugurate the Third and Last Age of Christendom. This would lead to the millennium, in which all human beings, regardless of their previous religion, would unite in a life of Christian devotion and voluntary poverty. It was prophesied that the existing church would be disbanded and that the clergy would be massacred by the German emperor.

When the year 1260 passed without the occurrence of this cataclysm, the date of the millennium was postponed – and put off again and again. The fervour of the followers of Joachim did not diminish. Condemned by the religious authorities, the Joachimite Spirituals came to see the official church as the Whore of Babylon, the Pope as Anti-Christ and the Beast of the Apocalypse. They expected a saviour to emerge from their own ranks to ascend the papal throne as the 'Angelic Pope', chosen by God to convert the whole world to a life of voluntary poverty. Among the groups within the movement was one led by Fra Dolcino, who, with more than a thousand armed men, waged war against the armies of the Pope in Northern Italy until eventually defeated and massacred. Dolcino was burned to death at the stake as a heretic, but for many years afterwards other groups arose claiming to draw inspiration from him.

The Ghost Dance

A quite different example of a millenarian movement is the Ghost Dance cult that arose among the Plains Indians of North America in the late nineteenth century. Prophets preached that a general catastrophe would occur, heralding the millennium, in which storms, earthquakes, whirlwinds and floods would destroy all the white intruders. The Indians would survive to see again the prairies covered with herds of buffalo and other game. After the catastrophe all ethnic divisions would be dissolved, and any whites who came to the land would live amicably with the Indians. The Ghost Dance ritual spread from community to community in the area, just as cargo cults have spread more recently from village to village in New Guinea (Burridge, 1971). The rituals of the Ghost Dance, which included singing, chanting and the attainment of trance-like states, were based partly on ideas derived from contact with Christianity, and partly on the traditional Sun Dance which the Indians used to perform before the whites' arrival. The Ghost Dance died out after the massacre at Wounded Knee, at which 370 Indian men, women and children were slaughtered by white soldiers.

The nature of millenarian movements

Why do millenarian movements occur? A number of common elements which most or all share can be identified. Virtually all seem to involve the activities of *prophets* ('inspired' leaders or teachers), who draw upon established religious ideas, and proclaim the need to revitalize them. They successfully develop a following if they manage to put into words what others only vaguely feel, and if they tap emotions that stir people to action. Prophecy has always been strongly associated with salvation religions, especially Christianity, and most of those who have led millenarian movements in colonized areas have been familiar with Christian practices and beliefs. Many have in fact been mission teachers, who have turned their adopted religion against those who schooled them in it.

Millenarian movements often arise where there is either radical cultural change, or a sudden increase in poverty (Worsley, 1970). They tend to attract people who have a strong sense of deprivation as a result of such changes, which leads them to abandon their earlier acceptance of the *status quo*. In mediaeval Europe, millenarian movements were frequently the last, desperate resort of those who found themselves suddenly impoverished. Peasants in times of famine, for example, were drawn to follow prophets who offered a vision of a 'world turned upside down', in which the poor would finally inherit the earth. Millenarian movements among colonized peoples tend to develop when a traditional culture is being destroyed by the impact of Western colonizers, as was the case with the Ghost Dance.

Millenarianism has sometimes been interpreted as essentially a rebellion of the poor against the privileged (Lantenari, 1963), or the oppressed against the powerful, and this is obviously a factor in many cases. But it is too simplistic: some millenarian movements, such as that of the Joachimite Spirituals, are forged through influences and sentiments that initially have little to do with material deprivation.

Current developments in religion: the Islamic revolution

One view that Marx, Durkheim and Weber all shared was that traditional religion was becoming more and more marginal to the modern world

– that *secularization* was an inevitable process. Of the three, probably only Weber would have suspected that a traditional religious system like Islam could undergo a major revival, and become the basis of important political developments in the late twentieth century; yet this is exactly what has occurred in the 1980s in Iran. In recent years, Islamic fundamentalism has also had a significant impact on other Middle Eastern countries, including Egypt, Syria and Lebanon. What explains this large-scale renewal of Islam?

The development of the Islamic faith

To understand the phenomenon, we have to look both to aspects of Islam as a traditional religion and to secular changes that have affected modern states within which its influence is pervasive. Islam, like Christianity, is a religion that has continually stimulated activism: the Koran – the Islamic holy scripture – is full of instructions to believers to 'struggle in the way of God'. This struggle is against both unbelievers and those who introduce corruption within the Muslim community. Over the centuries there have been successive generations of Muslim reformers, and Islam has become as internally divided as Christianity. *Kharigism* and *Shi'ism* split from the main body of orthodox Islam early in its history. The Kharigites were the first distinct sect to develop within Islam (Mortimer, 1982). They held strongly egalitarian beliefs, rejecting all forms of material privilege and proclaimed that those guilty of serious sins should no longer be regarded as Muslims. They did not last long as a sect, but they were in some respects forerunners of all subsequent *fundamentalist* Muslim revival movements – that is, movements claiming to return to the 'essentials' of Islam.

The other major sect, the Shi'ites, has remained influential. Shi'ism is today the official religion of Iran and was the source of the ideas behind the Iranian Revolution. The Shi'ites trace their beginnings to Mohammed Ali, a seventh-century religious and political leader who is believed to have shown qualities of personal devotion to God and virtue outstanding among the worldly rulers of the time. Ali's descendants came to be seen as the rightful leadership of Islam, since they were held to belong to the prophet Mohammed's family, unlike the dynasties actually in power. The Shi'ites believed that the rule of Mohammed's rightful heir would eventually be instituted, doing away with the tyrannies and injustices associated with existing regimes. Mohammed's heir would be a leader directly guided by God, governing in accordance with the Koran.

Shi'ism has been the official religion of Iran (earlier known as Persia) since the sixteenth century. There are large Shi'ite populations in other Middle Eastern countries, including Iraq, Turkey and Saudi Arabia – and in India and Pakistan. Islamic leadership in these countries, however, is in the hands of the majority, the Sunnis. The Sunni Muslims follow the 'Beaten Path', a series of traditions deriving from the Koran which tolerate considerable diversity of opinion, in contrast to the more rigidly defined views of the Shi'ites. Sunni doctrines have themselves changed considerably, particularly since the expansion of Western power over the last two or three centuries.

Islam and the West

During the Middle Ages, there was a more or less constant struggle between Christian Europe and the Muslim states, which controlled large sections of what is now Spain, Greece, Yugoslavia, Bulgaria and Romania. Most of the lands conquered by the Muslims were reclaimed by the Europeans, and many of their possessions in North Africa were in fact colonized as Western power grew in the eighteenth and nineteenth centuries. These reverses were catastrophic for Muslim religion and civilization, which Islamic believers held to be the highest and most advanced possible, transcending all others. In the late nineteenth century, the inability of the Muslim world effectively to resist the spread of the West led to reform movements seeking to restore Islam to its original purity and strength. A key idea was that Islam should respond to the Western challenge by affirming the identity of its own beliefs and practices.

This idea has been developed in various ways in the twentieth century, and formed a backdrop to the 'Islamic Revolution' in Iran of 1978/9. The revolution was fuelled initially by internal opposition to the Shah, Mohammed Reza, who had accepted and tried to promote forms of modernization modelled on the West – for example, land-reform, extending the vote to women, and developing secular education. The movement that overthrew the Shah brought together people of diverse interests, by no means all of whom were attached to Islamic fundamentalism, but a dominant figure was the Ayatollah Khomeini, who provided a radical reinterpretation of Shi'ite ideas.

Khomeini established a government organized according to traditional Islamic law, calling that government the 'Representative of Ali'. The Islamic Revolution according to Khomeini makes religion, as specified in the Koran, the direct basis of all political and economic life. Under the revived Islamic law, men and women are kept rigorously segregated, women obliged to cover their bodies and heads in public, practising homosexuals sent to the firing squad and adulterers stoned to death. The strict code is accompanied by a very nationalistic outlook, rejecting especially Western influences. Although the ideas underlying the revolution are supposed to unite the whole of the Islamic world against the West, governments of countries where the Shi'ites are in a minority have not aligned themselves closely with the Islamic Revolution in Iran. Yet Islamic fundamentalism has achieved significant popularity in most of these states, and various forms of Islamic revivalism elsewhere have been stimulated by it.

Islamic revivalism plainly cannot be understood wholly in religious terms; it represents in part a reaction against the impact of the West, and is a movement of national or cultural assertion. It is doubtful whether Islamic revivalism, even in its most fundamentalist forms, should be seen only as a renewal of traditionally held ideas. What has occurred is something more complex. Traditional practices and modes of life have been revived, but are combined with concerns that relate specifically to modern times.

Let us now turn to looking at the recent development of religion in the West, concentrating particularly upon Britain and the United States.

Religion in the United Kingdom

According to the 1851 census of religion, about 40 per cent of adults in England and Wales attended church each Sunday; by 1900 this had dropped to 35 per cent, by 1950 to 20 per cent and today the total is approximately 11 per cent. The main British denominations lost an average 5 per cent of churchgoers during the second half of the 1970s, with the most substantial decline (of 8 per cent) among Roman Catholics. Until then this had been the only church showing any growth – partly because of immigration from Ireland, together with high birth-rates. Today, the only exceptions to the general Christian decline are the small African and West Indian and Pentecostal churches.

The influence of religion over government has also faded during the post-war period. Bishops still have their place in the House of Lords, but their effective authority in public debate is much reduced. Half a century ago, the church had a major say in the abdication crisis; recently, there have been occasions when Prime Minister Margaret Thatcher has been 'too busy' to see the Archbishop of Canterbury. On several occasions in the 1980s the Conservative government criticized religious leaders (such as the Bishop of Durham) for their speeches on 'political' issues.

Religious membership and beliefs

Most of the adult population of Britain in fact regard themselves as belonging to a religious organization. In survey, only about 5 per cent of Britons stated they have no religious affiliation at all (Brothers, 1971, pp. 11–12). Almost 70 per cent of the total population saw themselves as belonging to the Church of England, even though most may not have actually attended church more than a few times in their lives, if at all.

In addition to the Church of England, the Presbyterian Church of Scotland, and the Catholic Church, a variety of other religious groups exist in Britain. These include Jews, Mormons, Muslims, Sikhs and Hindus. Smaller sects include the Plymouth Brethren, the Rastafarians, and the Divine Light Mission. Only a few of the new religious groups which have flourished in the USA have managed to obtain a toe-hold in Britain. An example is the Children of God, subsequently known as the Family of Life. The members of this community give up their orthodox careers and live in 'colonies' (Annett, 1976).

There is a discernible pattern to religion in the UK in terms of age, sex, class and geography. Generally, older people are more religious than those in younger age-groups. Church-going among young people reaches a peak at the age of fifteen, after which average levels of attendance slump until people reach their thirties and forties and enthusiasm returns; church-going thereafter rises with increasing age. Women are more likely to be involved in organized religion than men. In Anglican churches this is only marginally the case, but in Christian Science churches, for example, women outnumber men by four to one.

In general, church attendance and professed religious belief is higher among more affluent than among poorer groups. The Church of England has been called 'the Conservative Party at prayer', and there is still some truth in this. Catholics are more likely to be working-class. This class orientation shows itself in voting patterns: Anglicans tend to vote Conservative and Catholics to vote Labour, as do many Methodists, Methodism having originally been closely connected with the rise of the Labour Party. Religious participation also varies widely according to where people live: 35 per cent of adults in Merseyside and 32 per cent in Lancashire are church members, compared with only 9 per cent in Humberside and 11 per cent in Nottinghamshire. One reason for this is immigration – Liverpool has a large population of Irish Catholics, just as North London has its Jews, and Bradford its Muslims and Sikhs.

In terms of their consequences for day-to-day behaviour, religious differences are much more marked in Northern Ireland than anywhere else in Britain. The clashes between Protestants and Catholics which occur there only involve a minority from either faith, but are often acute and violent. The influence of religion in Northern Ireland is not easy to disentangle from other factors involved in the antagonisms there. The belief in a 'united Ireland', in which Eire and Northern Ireland would become one state, is generally held among Catholics, and rejected by Protestants, in the North. But political considerations and ideas of nationalism play an important role alongside religious beliefs.

Religion in the United States

Diversity

The position of religious organizations in the United States is unusual in several respects. Freedom of religious expression was made an article of the American Constitution long before tolerance of varied religious beliefs and practices was widespread in any other Western society. The early settlers were refugees from religious oppression by political authorities, and ensured the separation of state and church.

The United States also contains a far greater diversity of religious groups than any other industrialized country. In most Western societies the majority of the population are formally affiliated to a single church, such as the Anglican Church in Britain or the Roman Catholic Church in Italy. Some 90 per cent of the American population is Christian, but belongs to a diversity of churches and denominations. Many groups number only hundreds, but more than ninety religious organizations claim memberships of more than 50,000, twenty-two of these reporting memberships of over a million. The largest body by far in the United States is the Catholic Church, which has some fifty million members. However, it makes up only about 27 per cent of total membership of religious organizations. About 60 per cent of the population are Protestant, divided among numerous denominations. The Southern Baptist Convention is largest, with over thirteen million members, followed by the United Methodist Church, the National Baptist Convention, the Lutheran and Episcopal Churches. Among non-Christian groups, the largest are the Jewish congregations, numbering about six million members.

Some 40 per cent of the American population on average attends a church service each week (Wuthnow, 1986). Almost 70 per cent belong to churches, synagogues or other religious organizations, and the majority of these claim to be active within their congregations. When questioned about their personal attitudes, virtually all Americans – some 95 per cent – say they hold religious beliefs of one kind or another. Most express beliefs in God and life after death and accept that the Bible was divinely inspired (Stark and Bainbridge, 1985). A survey carried out in sixty countries showed the United States to have a higher level of stated religious commitment than any other country except India. Over 70 per cent of Americans, for example, say they believe in life after death, compared to 46 per cent in Italy, 41 per cent in Britain or 35 per cent in Scandinavia (Gallup Opinion Index, 1976).

Since the Second World War, the USA has witnessed a far greater proliferation of religious movements than at any previous time in its history, including an unprecedented series of mergers and divisions between denominations. Most have been short-lived, but a few have achieved remarkable followings. An example is the Unification Church, founded by the Korean Sun Myung Moon. The sect was introduced into the United States at the beginning of the 1960s, displaying all the characteristics of a millenarian movement. Moon's followers accepted his prediction that the world would come to an end in 1967, but the fact that the world carried on in much the same way after that year did not spell the end of the sect. As many previous leaders of millenarian movements have done, Moon readjusted his ideas in the light of his failed prediction. His new doctrines in fact gained even more adherents than before, a claimed membership now of 40,000 people. The beliefs of the Unification Church mix Eastern teachings with aspects of fundamentalist Christianity and anti-communism, and new members undergo strict religious training.

Religious fundamentalism

The growth of fundamentalist religious organizations in the United States is one of the most notable features of the past twenty years or so. **Fundamentalism** is a loose label for a variety of viewpoints which emphasize a return to literal interpretations of the biblical texts. Christian fundamentalism is a reaction against liberal theology and against *in-church secularization* – attendance at church by people who do not really take much active interest in religion. The fundamentalist groups are mostly affiliated to the political Right and have not refrained from direct activism in the political sphere.

One expression of this trend is the Moral Majority, founded by the Reverend Jerry Falwell in 1980. It is nominally a political body, but gains its membership and financial resources from its association with fundamentalist organizations. The secular influence of the Moral Majority is considerable: Falwell claims to have recruited 72,000 ministers and four million lay citizens to his cause, raising millions of dollars to intervene in political campaigns. The 'Religious Right' has made extensive use of radio and television in seeking to extend its influence; religious groups now own many radio and TV stations and their leading programmes reach audiences of millions. Unlike some older sects (such as the Plymouth Brethren), the Religious Right has embraced new electronic technology, rather than being hostile to it. Fundamentalism is much more prominent in the United States today than in other industrialized countries. Its progress in Britain, for example, has been relatively slight.

Some have suggested that there are direct parallels between Christian and Islamic fundamentalism, both representing a need for doctrinal certainty in a troubled and insecure world, but this is probably too superficial. Islamic fundamentalism, having its origins in the clash between Western modernity and traditional cultures, is in most respects very different from religious fundamentalism in the United States. On the other hand, each is linked with strong nationalistic sentiments, and in both cases fundamentalist religious leaders support an aggressive posture in international relations. One factor promoting fundamentalism in each instance seems to be a felt need to reaffirm a 'strong nation' by restoring basic religious and cultural values.

The problem of secularization

This chapter opened with the point that, with the development of modern societies, religion underwent a serious decline – which many observers saw as a terminal condition, religion being consigned to the category of obsolete traditional beliefs and customs. Yet, when questioned in surveys, over 80 per cent of Britons today say they believe in a deity of some sort, and in the USA hundreds of sects and cults thrive alongside the established churches. In Iran, and other areas of the Middle East, Africa and India, a dynamic Islamic fundamentalism challenges Westernization. In Northern Ireland, Protestants and Catholics keep alive a set of divided religious loyalties established for centuries, while more aggressively activist members of each denomination engage in open warfare with one another. The Pope tours South America and the United States, his progress followed by millions of Catholics. Can all this be reconciled with the idea that 'God is dead'?

This question can only be answered effectively if we understand that *secularization* has a number of aspects or dimensions. One concerns the *level of membership* of religious organizations – how many people belong to a church or other religious body, and are active in attending services or other ceremonials. With the exception of the USA, the industrialized countries have all experienced considerable secularization as indexed in this way. The pattern of religious decline found in Britain is found in most of Western Europe, including Catholic countries such as France or Italy. More Italians than French attend church regularly, and participate in the major rituals (such as Easter communion), but the overall pattern of declining religious observance is similar in both cases (Acquaviva, 1979).

A second dimension of secularization concerns how far churches and other religious organizations *maintain their social influence, wealth and prestige*. In earlier times, as we saw, religious organizations usually wielded considerable influence over governments and social agencies, and commanded high respect in the community. How far is this still the case? The answer to the question is clear. Even if we only confine ourselves to the present century, religious organizations have progressively lost much of the social and political influence they previously had, and the trend is world-wide, although there are some exceptions (such as Poland). Church leaders can no longer automatically expect to be influential with the powerful. Although some established churches remain very wealthy by any standards, and new religious movements may rapidly build up fortunes, the material circumstances of many long-standing religious organizations are insecure. Churches and temples have to be sold off, or are in a state of disrepair.

The third dimension of secularization concerns beliefs and values. We can call this the dimension of *religiosity*. Levels of church-going, and the degree of social influence of churches, are obviously not necessarily a direct expression of the beliefs or ideals held. Many who have religious beliefs do not regularly attend services or take part in public ceremonials. Regularity of such attendance or participation, on the other hand, does not always imply the holding of strong religious views – people may attend out of habit or because it is expected of them in their community.

As in the other dimensions of secularization, we must have an accurate understanding of the past to see how far religiosity has declined today. In many traditional societies, including mediaeval Europe, commitment to religious belief was less strong, and less important in day-to-day life, than might be supposed. Research into English history, for example, shows that lukewarm commitment to religious beliefs was common among the ordinary people (Thomas, 1978). Religious sceptics seem to have been found in most cultures, particularly in the larger traditional societies (Ginzburg, 1980).

Yet there can be no doubt at all that the hold of religious beliefs today is less than was generally the case in the traditional world – particularly if we include under the term 'religion' the whole range of the supernatural in which people believed. Most of us simply do not any longer experience our environment as permeated by divine or spiritual entities. Some of the major tensions in the world today – like those which afflict Israel and neighbouring Arab states – derive primarily, or in some part, from religious differences. But the majority of conflicts and wars are now mainly secular in nature – concerned with divergent political creeds or material interests.

Concluding assessment

The influence of religion has diminished along each of the three dimensions of secularization. Should we conclude that the nineteenth-century authors were correct after all? Perhaps the death-throes of religion have merely been more long-drawn-out than they anticipated? Such a conclusion would be mistaken. The appeal of religion, in its traditional and novel forms, is likely to be long-lasting. Modern rationalist thought and a religious outlook exist in an uneasy state of tension. A rationalist perspective has conquered many aspects of our existence, and its hold seems unlikely to be weakened in the foreseeable future. Nevertheless there are bound to be reactions against rationalism, leading to periods of religious revival. There are probably few people on the face of the earth who have never been touched by religious sentiments, and science and rationalist thought remain silent on such fundamental questions as the meaning and purpose of life – matters which have always been at the core of religion.

Summary

1   There are no known societies in which there is no form of religion, although religious beliefs and practices vary from culture to culture.

All religions involve a set of *symbols*, involving feelings of *reverence*, linked to *rituals* practised by a community of believers.

2   *Totemism* and *animism* are common types of religion in smaller cultures. In totemism, a species of animal or plant is perceived as possessing supernatural powers. Animism means a belief in spirits or ghosts, populating the same world as human beings, sometimes *possessing* them.

3   The three most influential monotheistic religions (religions in which there is only one God) in world history are *Judaism, Christianity* and *Islam. Polytheism* (belief in several or many gods) is common in other religions. In some religions, like Confucianism, there are no gods or supernatural beings.

4   Sociological approaches to religion have been most influenced by the ideas of the three 'classical' thinkers: Marx, Durkheim and Weber. All held that religion is in a fundamental sense an illusion. They believed that the 'other' world which religion creates is *our* world, distorted through the lens of religious symbolism.

5   Several different types of religious organization can be distinguished. A *church* is a large, established religious body, having a bureaucratic structure. *Sects* are small, and aim at restoring the original purity of doctrines which have become 'corrupted' in the hands of official churches. A *denomination* is a sect which has become institutionalized, having a permanent form. A *cult* is a loosely knit group of people who follow the same leader or pursue similar religious ideals.

6   Religious organizations are generally dominated by men. In most religions, particularly Christianity, the images and symbols are mostly masculine; female imagery stresses gentleness and passivity.

7   A *millenarian* movement is one that anticipates immediate, collective salvation – either because of some fundamental change in the present or a recovery of a long-lost golden age. Virtually all such movements involve the activities of prophets – professional or 'inspired' interpreters of established religious ideas.

8   Secularization refers to the declining influence of religion. Measuring the level of secularization is complicated, because several dimensions of change are involved. Although the influence of religion has definitely declined, religion is certainly not on the verge of disappearing, and continues to show great diversity in the modern world. Religions can act as both conservative and revolutionary forces in society.

Basic concepts

religion	ritual
secularization	magic

Important terms

monotheism	profane
Shaman	civil religion
totemism	church
animism	sect
polytheism	denomination
prophets	cult
ethical religions	millenarianism
alienation	fundamentalism
sacred	

Further reading

I. Bradley, 'Religious Revival', *New Society*, 6 November 1987, pp. 16–18 — Bradley discusses the idea of the 'post-secular society' in the 1980s.

C. W. Bynum, S. Harrell and P. Richman (eds), *Gender and Religion: On the complexity of symbols* (Boston: Beacon Press, 1986) — an examination of religious rituals and texts in several different cultures.

E. Cashmore, *Rastaman: The Rastafarian Movement in England* (London: Allen and Unwin, 1979) — a detailed historical account of the influence of Rastafarianism in the UK.

David Martin, *The Dilemmas of Contemporary Religion* (Oxford: Basil Blackwell, 1978) — this book looks at the tensions between traditional and modern life for religious faith and practice.

15

Work and Economic Life

All human beings depend on systems of production. We could not survive were it not for regular provision of food, drink and shelter. Even in societies where no food is cultivated – the hunting and gathering cultures – there are systematic arrangements for the supply and distribution of necessary material resources. For most people in all societies, productive activity, or **work**, occupies a larger part of their lives than any one other type of activity. In modern societies, we are used to people working in a large variety of occupations, but this has only come about with industrial development. The majority of the population in traditional cultures were engaged in one main pursuit – food-gathering or food production. Various crafts, such as carpentry, stone-masonry or ship-building, were practised in the larger societies; but only a small minority of the population engaged in them full-time.

Work may be defined as the carrying out of tasks, involving the expenditure of mental and physical effort, which have as their objective the production of goods and services that cater to human needs. An **occupation** or *job* is work which is done in exchange for a regular wage or salary. Work is in all cultures the basis of the *economic system*, or **the economy**, which consists of those institutions that provide for the production and distribution of goods and services.

The study of economic institutions is of major importance in sociology, because the economy to a greater or lesser degree influences all other segments of society. Economic activity does not have the degree of controlling influence that Marx attributed to it, but in every society the impact of economic practices is considerable. Hunting and gathering, pastoralism, agriculture, industrialism – these different ways of gaining a livelihood have a fundamental influence on the lives people lead. The distribution of goods, and variations in the economic position of those who produce them, also strongly influence *social inequalities* of all kinds. Wealth and power do not inevitably go together, but in general the richest are among the more powerful groups in a society.

In this chapter, we shall analyse the nature of work in modern industrial societies, and discuss the major changes currently affecting the economic order. We shall investigate the origins of industrial conflict and the ownership structure, and importance, of large business corporations. Then we shall take up some of the most significant work-related issues today – unpaid work, the informal economy, large-scale unemployment, and the possibility that work may be becoming less central to social life than ever before.

The division of labour

One of the most distinctive characteristics of the economic system of modern societies is the development of a highly complex and diverse **division of labour**. In other words, work is divided into an enormous number of different occupations, in which people specialize. In traditional societies, non-agricultural work was based on the mastery of crafts, and such skills were learned through a lengthy period of apprenticeship. The worker normally carried out all aspects of the production process from beginning to end. For example, a metal-worker making a plough would forge the iron, shape it, and assemble the implement itself. With the rise of modern industrial production, many traditional crafts disappeared altogether, while those that remained mostly became part of more large-scale production processes. An electrician working in an industrial setting today, for instance, may inspect and repair only a few parts of a particular type of machine; different people deal with the other jobs and other machines.

The contrast between the division of labour in traditional and modern societies is truly extraordinary. Even in the largest traditional societies, there usually existed no more than twenty or thirty major craft trades, together with a few other specialized pursuits, such as those of merchant, soldier or priest. In a modern industrial system, there are many thousands of distinct occupations. The UK census lists some 20,000 distinct jobs in the British economy. In traditional communities, most of the population (who worked in farming) were economically self-sufficient, producing food, clothes and other necessities of life for themselves. One of the main features of modern societies, by contrast, is an enormous expansion of **economic interdependence**. All of us are dependent on an immense number of other workers for the products and services involved in sustaining our lives. With some minor exceptions, the vast majority of people in modern societies do not produce the food they eat, the dwellings in which they live, or the material goods they consume.

Primary, secondary and tertiary sectors

It is useful to divide work in an industrial economy into three sectors: the *primary*, *secondary* and *tertiary* sectors. The proportion of the labour-force within the three sectors tends to vary at different stages of industrialization. Primary industries are those involving the collection or extraction of natural resources. The **primary sector** of an economy includes agriculture, mining, forestry and fishing, among others. In the first phases of industrial development, most workers are to be found in the primary sector. As the use of machinery and the construction of factories increase, a larger proportion of workers is drawn into the **secondary sector**. Secondary industries are those which convert raw materials into manufactured goods. The **tertiary sector** refers to **service industries** – to occupations that, instead of directly producing goods, offer services to others. Medicine, teaching, managerial and clerical jobs are examples of types of work usually included as service occupations.

Although it is a relatively crude indicator, the distinction between primary, secondary and tertiary sectors allows us to draw contrasts between different types of society. In most Third World countries, some three-quarters of the work-force is engaged in agriculture, with the remainder distributed about equally between manufacture and services. In the industrialized countries, on the other hand, only a tiny proportion of the population is engaged in agricultural production. For example, less than 2 per cent of the British labour-force now works in agriculture – as compared to 22 per cent in 1851. Another trend of major importance within the industrialized societies is the expansion of the service sector. In Britain in 1911, only 19 per cent of the labour-force worked in the tertiary sector. Today, the proportion is just over half.

Industrial division of labour: Taylorism and Fordism

Writing in the late 1700s, Adam Smith, one of the founders of modern economics, identified various advantages which the division of labour provides in terms of increasing productivity. His most famous work,

The Wealth of Nations, opens with a description of the division of labour in a pin-factory. A person working alone could perhaps make twenty pins per day. By breaking down the task into a number of simple operations, however, ten workers carrying out specialized jobs in collaboration with one another could produce 48,000 pins per day. The rate of production per worker, in other words, is increased from 20 to 4,800 pins, each specialist operator producing 240 times as much as if he or she were working in isolation (Smith, 1910, pp. 2–5).

Charles Babbage (who also invented an early form of computer) subsequently extended Smith's analysis (Babbage, 1835). According to the 'Babbage Principle', technological progress in production can be measured by the degree to which the tasks of each worker are simplified and integrated with those of other workers. This process reduces the price employers have to pay for hiring workers, and the time needed to learn each job, as well as weakening the workers' bargaining power and thus keeping wage costs down.

Sixty years later, these ideas reached their most developed expression in the work of Frederick Winslow Taylor, an American management consultant (Braverman, 1974). Taylor's approach to what he called *scientific management* involved the detailed study of industrial processes, in order to break them down into simple operations that could be precisely timed and organized. **Taylorism** had a widespread impact on the organization of industrial production and technology in many countries, although its influence varied. Japan was particularly resistant, and Japanese industrialization followed a substantially different path from that of most Western societies. In Japanese industry, from the beginning the use of work teams and work groups, lacking precise job divisions and offering considerable job flexibility, was a major element.

Taylor was concerned with improving industrial efficiency, but gave little consideration to how products should be sold. Mass production needs mass markets, and the industrialist Henry Ford was among the first to see and exploit this fact. **Fordism** is the name used to designate the system of mass production, tied to the cultivation of mass markets, which he developed (Hounshell, 1984). Ford established his first plant at Highland Park, Michigan, in 1913. It made only one product – the Model T Ford – thereby allowing the introduction of specialized tools and machinery designed for speed, precision and simplicity of operation (Sabel, 1982). One of Ford's most significant innovations was the construction of a moving assembly-line – said to have been inspired by Chicago slaughterhouses, in which animals were 'disassembled' section by section on a moving line. Each worker on Ford's assembly-line had a specific task, such as fitting the left-side door-handles, as the car bodies moved along the line. Before 1929, when production of the Model T ceased, fifteen million cars were made. At that date, 80 per cent of the cars in the world were registered in the United States.

Work on the assembly-line

Having apparently maximized productive efficiency, Ford began to discover problems with assembly-line production. Rates of absenteeism and labour turnover soon became extremely high. According to the head of Ford's personnel department, it cost only 38 dollars to train a new worker in 1913, so simple and routine were the tasks required. Yet because the annual turnover was more than 50,000 workers, the total cost of training amounted to $2,000,000 per year (Meyr, 1981). Ford sought to develop worker discipline by extending his influence outside the factory gates. His 'Five Dollar Day' offered workers wage incentives for changing their personal as well as their work habits. Bonuses, and possibilities of obtaining company loans, depended on employees behaving soberly and respectably, and limiting their alcohol and tobacco consumption. The company even set up its own 'Sociological Department' to investigate and report on workers' private lives.

Fordism – manufacture carried on in large plants, producing for mass markets using assembly-line processes – became central to the automobile industry world-wide and was adopted in other industrial settings. Ford, and its main competitor, General Motors, set up subsidiary companies in Britain, Germany, Japan and other countries. Citroën, in France, introduced assembly-line production as early as 1919, hiring American engineers as advisers. It was followed in France by Renault, by Fiat in Italy and later by Austin-Morris in the UK. Fordism was imported into Japan as well, being adopted first of all by Toyota.

A vivid picture of work on the production line is provided by an employee in a Citroën factory in the 1970s:

> each man has a well-defined area for the operations he has to make, although the boundaries are invisible: as soon as a car enters a man's territory, he takes down his blow torch, grabs his soldering iron, takes his hammer or his file, and gets to work. A few knocks, a few sparks, then the soldering is done and the car's already on its way out of the 3 or 4 yards of this position. And the next car's already coming into the work area. And the worker starts again. Sometimes, if he's been working fast, he has a few seconds respite before a new car arrives: either he takes advantage of it to breathe for a moment, or else he intensifies his effort and 'goes up the line' so that he can gain a little time . . . if, on the other hand, the worker's too slow, he 'slips back', that is he finds himself progressively behind his position, going on with his work when the next labourer has already begun his. Then he has to push on fast, trying to catch up. And the slow gliding of the cars, which seems to me so near to not moving at all, looks as relentless as a rushing torrent which you can't manage to dam up . . . sometimes it's as ghastly as drowning. (Linhart, 1981, pp. 15–16)

The limitations of Fordism and Taylorism

At one time, it looked as though Fordism represented the likely future of large areas of industrial production. This has not happened for several reasons, and the 'high point' of Fordism has already passed (Sabel, 1982). In fact, it only ever became prominent in some industrial sectors – most notably, the car industry itself. The system can only be developed in industries producing standardized products for large markets; to set up mechanized production lines is enormously expensive. Once a Fordist system is established, it is quite rigid – to alter a product, for example, substantial reinvestment is usually needed. Fordist production, too, is relatively easy to copy, if sufficient funding is available to set up the plant, and firms in countries in which labour-power is expensive find it difficult to compete with those in areas where wages are cheaper. This was a factor involved in the first successes of the Japanese car industry (although Japanese wage-levels today are no longer low) and, more recently, that of South Korea.

Taylorist techniques of management do not necessarily involve expensive capital investment. The limitations of Taylorism are much more bound up with the fact that human beings are not like machines, and resent being treated as though they were. Where jobs are sub-divided into monotonous tasks, they offer little scope for the creative involvement of the worker (Salaman, 1986). In such circumstances, it is difficult to motivate workers to do more than the bare minimum necessary to get by, and levels of job dissatisfaction are high (Wood, 1982). In its extreme form, as promoted by Taylor himself, 'scientific management' did not have a wide influence. But some of the features of modern industry to which Taylor drew attention have become very widespread indeed. For to some degree he simply accentuated characteristics of the division of labour towards which the mechanization of production naturally tends.

Work and alienation

Marx was one of the first writers to grasp that the development of modern industry would reduce many people's work to dull, uninteresting tasks. According to Marx, the division of labour *alienates* human beings from their work. In traditional societies, he points out, work was often exhausting – peasant farmers sometimes had to toil from dawn to dusk, caring for their fields. Yet peasants held a real measure of control over their work, which involved many forms of knowledge and skill. Many industrial workers, by contrast, have little control over the nature of the task, only contribute a fraction to the creation of the overall product, and have no influence over how or to whom it is eventually sold. Work thus appears as something *alien*, a task which the worker must carry out in order to obtain an income, but which is intrinsically unsatisfying.

Marx sees a major paradox at the heart of modern societies. On the one hand, the development of industry generates enormous wealth, far greater than was found in any preceding type of society. But large numbers of those whose labour is the very source of this wealth are denied any effective control of the work they do. He describes this phenomenon in graphic terms:

> What constitutes the alienation of labour? First, that work is *external* to the worker, that it is not part of his nature; and that, consequently, he does not fulfil himself in his work but denies himself, has a feeling of misery rather than wellbeing, does not develop freely his mental and physical energies but is physically exhausted and mentally debased. The worker, therefore, feels himself at home only during his leisure time, whereas at work he feels homeless. His work is not voluntary but imposed, *forced labour*. It is not the satisfaction of a need, but only a *means* for satisfying other needs. Its alien character is clearly shown by the fact that as soon as there is no physical or other compulsion it is avoided like the plague. . . . We arrive at the result that man (the worker) feels himself to be freely active only in his animal functions – eating, drinking and procreating, or at most also in his dwelling and personal adornment – while in his human functions he is reduced to an animal. The animal becomes human and the human becomes animal! (Marx, 1963a, pp. 124–5)

For Marx, **alienation** does not refer only to feelings of indifference or hostility to work, but to the overall framework of industrial production within a capitalist setting. Alienation expresses the material lack of control workers have over the settings of their labour. Most recent studies of alienation in sociology, however, have concentrated on workers' feelings and attitudes rather than the objective nature of the work situation. An example is a report produced by the United States Department of Health, Education and Welfare, entitled *Work in America*. Unlike most official reports, this study attracted major public attention, and became a best-seller. The investigation found many work settings involved 'dull, repetitive, seemingly meaningless tasks, offering little challenge or autonomy', thereby 'causing discontent among workers at all occupational levels' (1973).

Blue-collar workers, the report indicated, feel they have little control over their working conditions and are denied the opportunity of influencing decisions about their jobs. Their work schedules tend to be fixed and they are subject to close and continuous supervision. Only 24 per cent of blue-collar workers studied said they would choose the same kind of job if they could have their lives over again. Almost twice as many white-collar workers said they would do so. However, levels of dissatisfaction with work were high among those in white-collar jobs too. Those in lower-level office work found their jobs routine and boring, providing little scope for initiative, and many middle managers expressed similar dissatisfaction. They felt called upon to put into practice policies they had no influence in setting up. Those in higher positions were more likely to be satisfied with their work, considering themselves to have a measure of independence, challenge and variety.

No wide-ranging survey of such a type has been carried out in Britain. The fragmentary research that exists, however, suggests parallel conclusions. Many people enjoy their work in spite of the tasks they are called on to perform, rather than because of them. They value the social contact with others, for example, more than their actual jobs (Littler and Salaman, 1984).

Low-trust systems/high-trust systems

Fordism and Taylorism – systems of production which maximize worker alienation – have been called by some industrial sociologists **low-trust systems** (Fox, 1974). Tasks are set by management and are geared to machines. Those who carry them out are closely supervised and are allowed little autonomy of action. **High-trust** positions are those in which people are permitted to control the pace, and even the content, of their work, within overall guidelines. Such positions are usually concentrated at the higher levels of industrial organizations. Where there are many low-trust positions, the level of worker alienation is high, industrial conflict common, and rates of absenteeism often acute.

From the early 1970s onwards, firms in various industries in Western Europe, United States and Japan have experimented with alternatives to low-trust organizations. These include, among other schemes, the automation of assembly lines, reducing routine work done by humans to a minimum; and the introduction of *group production*, in which the work-group has a recognized role in influencing the nature of the task. Although they have rarely found favour among employers, there have also been some notable attempts to establish systems of industrial democracy (Kelly, 1982). We'll now look at these alternatives.

Automation

Automation has so far affected relatively few industries, but with advances in the design of *industrial robots*, its impact is certain to become greater (P. Marsh, 1982; Large, 1984). A robot is an automatic device which can perform functions ordinarily done by human beings.

The term 'robot' came from the Czech word *robota*, or serf, popularized about fifty years ago by the playwright Karel Capek. The concept of programmable machinery goes back much further: Christopher Spencer, an American, invented the Automat, a programmable lathe that made screws, nuts and gears, in the mid-1800s. Robots were first introduced into industry in significant numbers in 1946, when the first device able to regulate machinery automatically was introduced into some simple areas of production technology in the engineering industry.

Robots of any complexity, however, only date from the recent development of microprocessors – basically from the 1970s onwards.

The first robot controlled by a minicomputer was developed in 1974 by Cincinnati Milason. Robots today can do numerous tasks like welding, spray-painting, lifting and carrying, and are controlled by microprocessors. Some robots can distinguish parts by 'feel' or touch, while others can 'see' by distinguishing a certain range of objects visually.

As Robert Ayres and Steven Miller have pointed out,

> there can be no more dedicated and untiring factory worker than a robot. Robots can repeat tasks such as spot-welding and spray-painting flawlessly on a variety of workpieces, and they can quickly be reprogrammed to perform entirely new tasks . . . In the next few years, we can expect to see many industrial robots installed in medium-batch manufacturing plants. Robots will feed workpieces to clusters of automatic machines in 'workcells', which may be serialised to form a 'closed loop' manufacturing system controlled by microprocessors. (Ayres and Miller, 1985, p. 342)

These systems will form the factories of the future; their precursors have already been built in the USA and Japan.

The main stage on the way to the completely automated factory is the flexible manufacturing system (FMS). This consists of a computer-controlled machining centre that sculpts metal parts at high speed, robots that handle the parts, and guided cars which transport materials to and from the site of production. FMSs can be instantly reprogrammed to make new parts or projects. They are able to manufacture goods cheaply in small volumes; different products can be made on the same line at will. The implications are far-reaching. In the era of Fordism, economies were only realizable with massive production schedules. Flexible manufacturing systems can turn out a small batch of goods as efficiently as a production line designed to turn out a million identical items.

FMSs are at the moment most developed in Japan. In the Japanese plants, skeleton crews work with the machines during the day, while at night the robots and machines work alone. In the factory of Fanuc Inc., near Mount Fuji, automatic machining centres and robots toil through the night, the unmanned delivery carts rolling quietly through the semi-darkness, which is relieved only by the subdued flashing of blue warning lights. At night a single controller supervises the whole operation, watching the machinery on closed-circuit television. If anything goes wrong, the supervisor can close down part of the operation and reroute production around it. A new factory is planned by Yamazaki, which will be operated by remote control from the firm's headquarters twenty miles away. The work done in the factory (making machine tools) will be fully programmed from the headquarters. The plant will have 200 workers, producing as many goods as 2,500 would be able to do in a conventional factory (Ayres and Miller, 1983).

Most of the large motor-car companies have automated part of their production lines, using robots for assembling, welding and spraying. The majority of the robots utilized in industry world-wide, in fact, are to be found in automobile manufacture. In spite of the imminent arrival of automated factories, the usefulness of robots in production so far is relatively limited, because their capacity to recognize different objects and manipulate awkward shapes is still at a fairly rudimentary level. Yet it is virtually certain that automated production will spread rapidly in coming years. The sophistication of robots is fast increasing, while their costs decrease.

Group production

Group production – abandoning the production line and establishing collaborative work-groups – has sometimes been used in conjunction with automation as a basis for the reorganization of work. Underlying the idea is a recognition of the importance of groups and group problem-solving to production problems. An experiment set up by Volkswagen in one of its German engine plants in 1975 is a good example. Car engines are usually built on an assembly-line, with each worker having about one or two minutes to complete a standard task. Volkswagen instead set up four groups each of seven workers; within each group, four worked on assembly, two on testing, and one was in charge of supplying materials. The members of each group were trained so that they could carry out all the team jobs, and were allowed to rotate job assignments as they wanted. The group had to meet a quota of making seven engines per day. Levels of production, however, were not high enough to satisfy the Volkswagen management (although the groups met their quotas), and in 1978 the experiment came to an end.

A comparable innovation is that of so-called *quality circles* (QCs). These are groups of between five and twenty workers, which meet regularly to study and resolve production problems. Workers who belong to quality circles receive extra training in order to be able to contribute technically to discussion of production issues. QCs were initiated in the United States, taken over by a number of Japanese companies and then re-popularized in the West in the late 1970s.

Quality circles represent a break from the assumptions underlying Taylorism, since they recognize that workers have the expertise to contribute to the definition and method of the tasks they carry out. In 1980, the Ford Corporation, under the stimulus of Japanese competition, decided to set up quality circles in all its twenty-five manufacturing and assembly plants in Western Europe, in a bid to improve the quality of its products and their reliability, together with encouraging worker involvement.

Industrial democracy

The idea of **industrial democracy** is much older than notions of group production. Marx pointed out in the nineteenth century that rights of political participation enjoyed by the citizenry stopped short at the gates of the work-place. Political democracy, he suggested, should be complemented by the introduction of democratic rights within industry. These claims have been taken seriously by the national governments of some countries and by the founders of co-operative firms in certain sectors of industry. Workers' self-management is built into Yugoslavian industry, with workers having the right to elect directors and have a say in personnel policies. According to Swedish law, workers must be represented on the boards of directors of companies with more than a hundred employees. Worker-directors also exist in West Germany and Norway.

Good evidence exists to show that organizations where workers have some influence over decision-making have high morale and a good productivity record. In an early analysis of seventeen experiments with systems of industrial democracy, Paul Blumberg concluded that 'there is hardly a study in the entire literature which fails to demonstrate that satisfaction in work is enhanced or that other generally acknowledged beneficial consequences accrue from a genuine increase in workers' decision-making power. Such consistency of findings, I submit, is rare in social research' (Blumberg, 1968, p. 123). Blumberg's findings have been criticized because the cases he discussed were mostly short-lived, lasting only some two or three years. But subsequent research supports his conclusion. A study of plywood co-operatives in the Pacific Northwest of the United States showed that firms with a co-operative system were 30–50 per cent more efficient than orthodox companies of similar size in the same industry (Berman, 1982).

Co-operative organizations, in which workers have a range of powers usually held by management, can be found in several Western European countries. For example, the Mondragon co-operatives, in the Basque country of Northern Spain, have achieved a high degree of economic success in the manufacture of various consumer goods. Yet there is often resistance to the extension of industrial democracy by both management and unions. Managers are loath to accept that workers should have decision-making powers previously kept to themselves, while unions sometimes see industrial democracy as eroding their rights of collective bargaining (Thornley, 1981).

Trade unions and industrial conflict

There have long been conflicts between workers and those in economic and political authority over them. Riots against military conscription and high taxes, and food riots at periods of harvest failure, were common in urban areas of Europe in the eighteenth century. These 'pre-modern' forms of labour conflict continued up to not much more than a century ago in some countries. For example, there were food riots in several large Italian towns in 1868 (Geary, 1982). Such traditional forms of confrontation were not just sporadic, irrational outbursts: the use or threat of violence had the effect of limiting the price of grain and other essential foodstuffs (Thompson, 1971; Booth, 1977).

The development of unions

Industrial conflict between workers and employers in the first half of the nineteenth century was frequently only semi-organized. Where there was confrontation, workers would quite often leave their places of employment and form crowds in the streets; they would make their grievances known through their unruly behaviour or by engaging in acts of violence against the authorities. Workers in some parts of France in the late nineteenth century retained the practice of threatening disliked employers with hanging (Holton, 1978)! Use of the strike, which is now associated with organized bargaining between workers and management, developed slowly and sporadically. The Combination Acts passed in Britain in 1799 and 1800 made the meeting of organized workers' groups illegal, and banned popular demonstrations. The Acts were repealed some twenty years later, when it became apparent that they stimulated more public disturbances than they quelled. *Trade unionism* soon became a mass movement, and union activity was legalized in the last quarter of the nineteenth century, after which membership increased to cover 60 per cent of male manual workers in Britain by 1920. The British trade union movement is co-ordinated by a central body founded in 1868, the Trades Union Congress (TUC), which developed strong links with the Labour Party.

In the early development of modern industry, there was little direct connection between the existence of unions and the tendency to strike. Most early strikes were spontaneous, in the sense that they were not called by any specific organizations of workers. A report of the US Commissioner of Labor in 1907 showed that somewhere near half all the strikes at the time were not initiated by unions (Ross, 1954). Much the same was probably true in Britain. This situation had changed by the end of the First World War, since when the proportion of strikes occurring among non-unionized workers has become small.

The development of the union movement has varied considerably between countries, as has the influence of the unions over the work-force, employers and government. In Britain and the United States unions have been established for longer than in most European societies. The German unions, for example, were largely destroyed by the Nazis in the 1930s, and set up afresh after the Second World War, whereas the main development of the French union movement did not in fact occur until the 1930s, when the freedom to organize unions and negotiate collective labour contracts was formally recognized.

Some 50 per cent of the labour-force in Britain today are union members, compared to under 20 per cent in the United States. Most European countries are below the British figure in terms of membership levels; but Belgium and Denmark have rates of around 65 per cent, while in Sweden membership is as high as 90 per cent. Sweden provides a good example of a country in which the labour movement plays a major and direct part in influencing government policies. In that country, there is continuous consultation at a national level between union representatives, employers and the government.

Why do unions exist?

Although their levels of membership, and the extent of their power, varies widely, union organizations exist in all Western countries. All such countries (unlike the Soviet Union and Eastern Europe) legally recognize the right of workers to strike in pursuit of economic objectives. Why have unions become a basic feature of Western societies? Why does union–management conflict seem to be a more or less ever-present feature of industrial settings?

Some have proposed that unions are effectively a version of mediaeval guilds – associations of people working in the same trade – reassembled in the context of modern industry. Thus Frank Tannenbaum has suggested that unions are associations built on the shared outlook and experience of those working in similar jobs (Tannenbaum, et al. 1974). This interpretation might help us understand why unions often emerged first among craft workers, but does not explain why they have been so consistently associated with wage-bargaining and industrial conflict. A more satisfactory explanation must look to the fact that unions developed to protect the material interests of workers in industrial settings in which they hold very little formal power.

In the early development of modern industry, workers in most countries were without political rights and had little influence over the conditions of work in which they found themselves. Unions developed in the first instance as means of redressing the imbalance of power between workers and employers. Whereas workers had little power as individuals, through collective organization their influence was considerably increased. An employer can do without the labour of any particular worker, but not without that of all or most of the workers in a factory or plant. Unions were originally mainly 'defensive' organizations, providing the means whereby workers could counter the overwhelming power over their lives which employers enjoyed.

Workers now have voting rights in the political sphere, and there are established forms of negotiation with employers, by means of which economic benefits can be pressed for and grievances expressed. Yet union influence, both at the level of the local plant and nationally, still remains primarily *veto power*. In other words, using the resources at their disposal, including the right to strike, unions can normally only *block* policies or initiatives of employers, not help formulate them in the first place. There are various partial exceptions to this, as in instances where unions and employers negotiate periodic contracts covering conditions of work. There is an increasing tendency for these to include 'no-strike' agreements for the duration of the contract. Nationally – especially in the Scandinavian countries – union officials may have a significant role in formulating economic policies.

Yet unions in some countries have faced a constant battering from hostile employers and governments. The rights of industrial negotiation workers hold have had to be won in the face of much bitter opposition, and once achieved have frequently been subjected to further attacks. Employers in some industries have consistently refused to employ union members or allow company union branches to be established. The employers' resistance to the unions has been especially pronounced in the United States – one factor in the low incidence of union membership in the country. For instance, in the 1920s and 1930s, under the slogan of the 'American Plan', the National Association of Manufacturers fought against some of the key bargaining rights claimed by unions. 'Yellow-dog' contracts (under which employees agree not to join a union) were promoted, together with more positive schemes, like profit-sharing, designed to show workers that rewards could be achieved without unions.

Recent developments

Unions themselves, of course, have altered over the years. Some have grown very large and, as permanent organizations, have become bureaucratized. Unions are staffed by full-time officials, who may themselves have little direct experience of the conditions under which their members work. The activities and views of union leaders can thus become quite distant from those of the members they represent. Shop-floor groups sometimes find themselves in conflict with the strategies of their own unions. Most unions have not been successful in recruiting a high level of women workers. Although some have initiated campaigns to increase their female membership, many have in the past actively discouraged women from joining.

In current times, unions in Western countries are facing a threat from three connected sets of changes – the recession in world economic activity, associated with high levels of unemployment, which weakens the unions' bargaining position; the decline of the older manufacturing industries, in which the union presence has traditionally been strong; and the increasing intensity of international competition, particularly from Far Eastern countries, where wages are often lower than in the West. In the United States and several European countries, including Britain, France, Germany and Denmark, Rightist

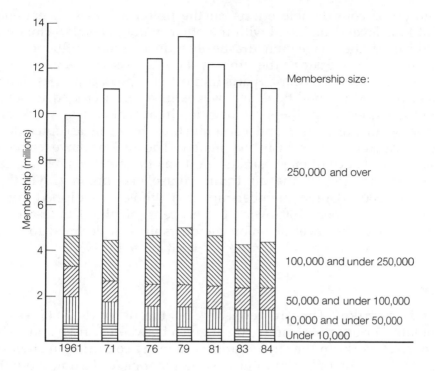

Figure 18 Trade union membership in the United Kingdom, 1961–1984, by size of union
Source: Social Trends (London: HMSO, 1987), p. 178.

governments came to power in the 1970s or 1980s, mostly determined
to limit what they saw as excessive union influence in industry.

Under Mrs Thatcher, the Conservative government in Britain has
followed policies designed to give fuller play to market forces. The
Conservatives believed that the unions were too powerful, and introduced a range of measures designed to reduce the scope of their
activities. The unions, it was argued, drive wages up to levels where
British products become uncompetitive in world markets. Union power
is held to prevent firms from laying off workers when they need
to do so in order to maximize efficiency. Consultations between
government ministers and union leaders became much less frequent
than they had been under preceding (Labour) administrations.

Employment Acts passed in 1980 and 1982 introduced new limitations
on the legal rights of unions. The official definition of a 'trade union
dispute' was tightened up, to exclude such activities as picketing the
suppliers of an employer. The Trade Union Act of 1984 required that
unions hold a ballot of members before undertaking industrial action,
as well as introducing other restrictions on union prerogatives. The civil
servants employed at the government communications centre (GCHQ)
were deprived of their right to belong to a union, a move which was justified by arguing that industrial action at GCHQ could represent a threat
to national security (Manwaring and Sigler, 1985). These measures have

certainly had considerable effects on the union movement, nationally and at local level. Combined with the other, more general, factors mentioned earlier, they have quite drastically reduced union influence.

In the United States, the unions face a crisis of even greater dimensions than their counterparts in most European countries. Union-protected working conditions and wages have been eroded in several major industries over the past decade. In recent years, workers in the road transport, steel and car industries have all accepted lower wages than those previously negotiated. The unions have come out second-best in several major strikes, perhaps the most notable example being the crushing of the air traffic controllers' union (PATCO) in the early 1980s. Union membership as a whole has dipped considerably. From a peak of over 30 per cent of the labour-force in the mid-1950s, the level of union membership has declined to 19 per cent today (Edwards and Podgursky, 1986; Goldfield, 1987).

Strikes

What is a **strike**? The answer is by no means obvious or easy to formulate. For example, can we distinguish between a strike and a short stoppage of work? In the strike statistics of many countries an attempt is made to do so, by only counting as strikes stoppages lasting more than a specific time (like half a day), or where more than a certain number of workers is involved. Are overtime bans, or 'working to rule', examples of strike activity? Is it appropriate to speak of a strike if tenants get together and refuse to pay the rents demanded of them? The term *rent strike* is sometimes applied to such a situation, and indeed stoppages of activity in many contexts are often referred to as strikes – as, for instance, where students refuse to attend lectures to draw attention to a grievance.

On the whole it seems preferable to define 'strike' in a reasonably narrow sense, or else the term loses all precision. We can define a strike as a temporary stoppage of work by a group of employees in order to express a grievance or enforce a demand (Hyman, 1984). All the components of this definition are important in separating strikes from other forms of opposition and conflict. A strike is *temporary*, since workers intend to return to the same job with the same employer; where workers quit altogether, the term is not appropriate. As a *stoppage of work*, a strike is distinguishable from an overtime ban or 'going slow'. A *group* of workers has to be involved, because a strike refers to a collective action, not the response of one individual worker. That those acted against are *employers* serves to separate strikes from protests such as may be conducted by tenants or students. Finally, a strike involves *seeking to make known a grievance or press a demand*; workers who were absent solely to attend a sports event could not be said to be on strike.

Strikes represent only one aspect or type of conflict in which workers and management may become involved. Other closely related expressions of organized conflict are *lock-outs* (where employers rather than workers bring about a stoppage of work), output restrictions, and clashes in contract negotiation. Less organized expressions of conflict may include high labour turnover, absenteeism and interference with production machinery.

Strike statistics

Since there is a fairly large arbitrary element in specifying exactly what a strike is, it is not surprising that different countries have varying practices in the registering of strike statistics. International comparisons of strike levels can be made, but have to be interpreted with caution. What is regarded as a strike in one country, and thus included in the statistics, may not count as such in another. For example, in Britain a stoppage has to involve only ten workers or more before it is reported as a strike, whereas in the United States (since 1982) only stoppages involving 1,000 or more workers are registered in the strike statistics.

Three measures of strike activity are usually published – the number of strikes per year, the proportion of the labour-force involved in strikes for that year, and the number of working days lost through strike activity. The three taken together provide a rough idea of differences in strike levels between countries. In terms of all three criteria, Italy and Canada are among the most strike-prone countries, the least being Germany and the Scandinavian countries. The United States and United Kingdom are in the middle range. There seems to be no particular connection between strike levels, as measured by the official statistics, and levels of economic performance. Countries with low strike rates, in other words, do not necessarily show higher levels of economic growth than those having more strikes. This is hardly surprising; the value of comparative strike statistics is in any case suspect, and industrial conflict or tensions can be expressed in many ways other than strikes. In addition, it does not follow that because industrial relations are harmonious, productivity will inevitably be high (Jackson, 1986).

Recent trends in industrial conflict

In a well-known work published at the beginning of the 1960s, some observers argued that strikes were 'withering away'. According to these authors, prolonged and intense disputes are mainly characteristic of the early phases of industrialization. Once agreed-upon frameworks of industrial bargaining are firmly in place, they argued, strike activity declines (Ross and Hartman, 1960). No sooner was this thesis proclaimed than there was an upsurge of industrial conflict in many Western countries, including Britain. A notable feature of strike activity in the British context during the 1960s and early 1970s was a sharp rise in the number of unofficial strikes. It seems that many workers at this period were as disaffected with their official union organizations as with their employers (Thompson, 1983).

In the 1980s the focus of strike activity shifted back to the official unions. At the same time, the strike rate in Britain has declined substantially, owing in large part to the constrained political and economic climate in which the unions now find themselves. Easily the most important confrontation was the miners' strike in 1984. A national strike of coal-miners was called after a Coal Board announcement in March that twenty pits would be closed and 20,000 jobs lost within twelve months. A further fifty pits were also scheduled to cease production within the following five years, involving a loss of 50,000 more jobs. The strike was protracted and bitter, eventually ending in the defeat of the miners' union. Clashes which occurred between miners and the police raised a number of issues about civil liberties, whose implications have yet to be fully worked out in law.

We now turn to the other side of the coin, moving away from workers to look at their employers – the business corporations (although it should not be forgotten that many people today are employees of government organizations).

Corporations and corporate power

Since 1900, modern economies have been more and more influenced by the rise of large business corporations. The share of total manufacturing assets held by the 200 largest manufacturing firms in Britain has increased by 0.5 per cent each year from 1900 to the present day. These 200 corporations now control over half of all manufacturing assets. The 200 biggest *financial* organizations – banks, building societies and insurance companies – account for more than half of all financial activity. In both business and finance, there are many connections between large firms. For example, financial institutions hold well over 30 per cent of the shares of the largest 200 firms.

Of course, many thousands of smaller firms and enterprises still exist within the British economy. In these companies, the image of the **entrepreneur** – the boss who owns and runs the firm – is by no means obsolete, but the large corporations are a different matter. Ever since Adolf Berle and Gardiner Means published their celebrated study, *The Modern Corporation and Private Property* more than half a century ago, it has been accepted that most of the largest firms are not run by those who own them (Berle and Means, 1967 – originally published 1932). In theory, the large corporations are the property of their shareholders, who have the right to take all important decisions affecting them. Since share-ownership is so dispersed, however, Berle and Means argued, actual control over decisions in large corporations has passed into the hands of the managers who run the firms on a day-to-day basis. *Owner-ship* of the corporations has thus become separated from their *control*.

On the basis of the findings of Berle and Means, and subsequent research, some authors have diagnosed major shifts in the nature and outlook of the large corporations. The managers who now control the giant companies, they claim, do not have the same interests as shareholders. While shareholders want to maximize the returns they get on their investment, managers are more concerned with the growth of the corporation and its image in the outside world. It has been suggested that, as a consequence, the large corporations have become more 'socially responsible' than before, looking as much to their public role as to cultivating their profits.

However, this view is of dubious validity. Many managers in fact own considerable stocks in their own companies as well as in other corporations, and presumably wish to gain a high return on these. The salaries of executives tend to be linked to the financial success of firms, that success usually being measured by the profit they generate. When asked where their priorities lie, managers themselves emphasize profitability. A study of about 190 senior executives and directors of a number of large corporations in the United Kingdom, for example, showed that precedence was given to 'maximizing growth of total profits' and 'maximizing rate of return on capital'. Objectives such as 'provision of service to the community at large' were well down the list (Francis, 1980).

Just how many of the large corporations are manager-controlled is difficult to gauge. An individual (or family) who owns even as little as 15–20 per cent of the total shares may be able effectively to control the company, if the remainder of the share-holding is widely fragmented between different individuals. Moreover, a good deal of the share-holding in large companies is now in the hands of *other* corporations – usually banks, insurance firms and financial organizations. Where these corporations are still dominated by share-owning interests themselves, a whole network of firms may be in the control of shareholders rather than managers. Nevertheless, there is general agreement that the majority of very large corporations are under management control (Scott, 1981).

Whether run by owners or managers, the power of the major corporations is very extensive. Where one, or a handful, of firms dominate in a given industry, they often co-operate in setting prices rather than freely competing with one another; thus the giant oil companies normally follow one another's lead in the price charged for petrol. Where one firm has a commanding position in a given industry, it is said to be in a **monopoly** position. More common is a situation of **oligopoly**, in which a small group of giant corporations predominate. In situations of oligopoly, firms are able more or less to dictate the terms on which they buy in goods and services from smaller firms.

Table 12 The world's twenty-five largest industrial companies (1987)

Rank	Company	Headquarters	Industry	Sales ($)	Net income ($)
1	General Motors	Detroit	Motor vehicles and parts	102,813,700	2,944,700
2	Exxon	New York	Petroleum refining	69,888,000	5,360,000
3	Royal Dutch/Shell Group	The Hague/London	Petroleum refining	64,843,217	3,725,779
4	Ford Motor	Dearborn, Mich.	Motor vehicles and parts	62,715,800	3,285,100
5	International Business Machines (IBM)	Armonk, NY	Computers	51,250,000	4,789,000
6	Mobil	New York	Petroleum refining	44,866,000	1,407,000
7	British Petroleum	London	Petroleum refining	39,855,564	731,954
8	General Electric	Fairfield, Conn.	Electronics	35,211,000	2,492,000
9	American Tel. & Tel.	New York	Electronics	34,087,000	139,000
10	Texaco	White Plains, NY	Petroleum refining	31,613,000	725,000
11	IRI	Rome	Metals	31,561,709	197,118
12	Toyota Motor	Toyota City (Japan)	Motor vehicles and parts	31,553,827	1,717,733
13	Daimler-Benz	Stuttgart	Motor vehicles and parts	30,168,550	831,600
14	E.I. du Pont de Nemours	Wilmington, Del.	Chemicals	27,148,000	1,538,000
15	Matsushita Electric Industrial	Osaka	Electronics	26,459,539	946,571
16	Unilever	Rotterdam/London	Food	25,141,672	973,983
17	Chevron	San Francisco	Petroleum refining	24,351,000	715,000
18	Volkswagen	Wolfsburg (W. Germany)	Motor vehicles and parts	24,317,154	286,133
19	Hitachi	Tokyo	Electronics	22,668,085	679,609
20	ENI	Rome	Petroleum refining	22,549,921	342,275
21	Chrysler	Highland Park, Mich.	Motor vehicles and parts	22,513,500	1,403,600
22	Philips' Gloeilampenfabrieken	Eindhoven (Netherlands)	Electronics	22,471,263	414,418
23	Nestlé	Vevey (Switzerland)	Food	21,153,285	994,566
24	Philip Morris	New York	Tobacco	20,681,000	1,478,000
25	Siemens	Munich	Electronics	20,307,037	629,353

Types of corporate capitalism

Three general stages can be distinguished in the development of today's large business **corporations** – although each overlaps with the others, and all continue to coexist today. The first phase, characteristic of the nineteenth and early twentieth centuries, was dominated by **family capitalism**. Even large firms were mostly run either by individual entrepreneurs or by a handful of members of the same family – and then passed on to their descendants. The famous corporate 'dynasties' – such as the Rockefellers or Fords – belong in this category. These families owned not just a single large corporation, but a diversity of economic interests, and stood at the apex of economic empires.

Most of the big firms founded by entrepreneurial families have since become public companies and passed into managerial control. But important elements of family capitalism remain, even within some of the very largest corporations – like the Ford Motor Company in the USA, where Henry Ford IV has a leading managerial role. Among small firms, such as local shops run by their owners, small plumbing and house-painting businesses and so forth, family capitalism of course continues to be the primary type of enterprise. Some of these firms are also 'dynasties' on a minor scale – a shop may remain in the hands of the same family for two or more generations. However, the small-business sector is highly unstable, and economic failure in it is very common; the proportion of firms which are owned by members of the same family for very long periods of time is minute.

The family corporations were not always concerned overwhelmingly with amassing profit through aggressive business practice. Some owners had a 'paternalistic' outlook towards their employees, providing them with material benefits – including occasionally housing and financial aid – that most firms today would not contemplate. Sometimes, too, the interests of the family would be put ahead of those of the company: a member of the family known not to have much concern for, or perhaps even competence in, business might nevertheless be given a prime position in the firm.

In the large corporate sector, family capitalism was increasingly succeeded by **managerial capitalism**. As managers came to have more and more influence, through the growth of very large firms, the entrepreneurial families were displaced. The result has been described as 'the replacement of family role of the company by the supremacy of the company itself' (Useem, 1984, p.16). The corporation emerged as a more clear-cut *economic* entity, having priority over the concerns of the founding family. The family once controlled the destinies of the firm; but now, where family connections remain, the reverse is usually the case. Preservation of the company's profits by its managerial executives governs the returns accruing to family members. The difference has been documented empirically: studying 200 large industrial corporations,

Michael Allen found that, in cases where profit showed a decline, family-controlled enterprises were unlikely to replace their chief executive, but manager-controlled firms did so rapidly (Allen, 1981).

Managerial capitalism has today partly ceded place to a third form of corporate system, **institutional capitalism**. This term refers to the emergence of a consolidated network of business leadership, concerned not only with decision-making within single firms, but also with the development of corporate power outside. Institutional capitalism is based upon the spread of share-holding by corporations in other firms, and to some degree reverses the process of increasing managerial control. It is marked by the increasing significance of collaboration between corporate leaders from different companies, and share-holding of this type often takes effective control away from managers within the firms. One of the main reasons for the spread of institutional capitalism is a shift in patterns of investment which has occurred over the past thirty years or so. Increasingly, individual members of the population invest in building societies, trusts, insurance and pension funds, and other financial organizations, which in turn invest their savings in industrial corporations (Scott, 1981; Stollman, Ziegler and Scott, 1985).

Most of the large corporations today are *transnationals* – they operate on an international basis, having subsidiary offices and factories in many countries. We shall look at this aspect of corporate enterprise in some detail in a subsequent chapter (see chapter 16: 'The Globalizing of Social Life').

Unemployment, women's work and the informal economy

In studying work and the economy, we cannot just concentrate on people who are in stable, full-time employment. At any one time, only a minority of the adult population are in the paid work-force. The young, older people, a high proportion of women, those who live off unearned incomes, and the unemployed, are all outside. Most of these individuals certainly work as hard or harder than people holding full-time, paid jobs. Children and college students work at their academic studies; retired people work caring for their houses and gardens; and housewives work on the domestic chores and caring for children (they may also have part-time paid work). Only for a tiny minority of the wealthy at the top of the class system, who can live off investments, and the much larger numbers of the unemployed, is the average day not dominated by work activities. For most people, unemployment is not a happy state. Being without work when one wants it, and without the resources to lead a satisfying life, brings psychological as well as material hardship.

Unemployment

Rates of unemployment have fluctuated considerably over the course of this century. In Western countries, unemployment reached a peak in the early 1930s, with some 20 per cent of the labour-force being out of work in Britain. The ideas of the economist John Maynard Keynes strongly influenced public policy in Europe and the United States during the post-war period. Keynes believed that unemployment results from lack of sufficient purchasing power to buy goods; governments can intervene to increase the level of demand in an economy, leading to the creation of new jobs. State management of economic life, many came to believe, meant that high rates of unemployment belonged to the past. Commitment to *full employment* became part of government policy in virtually all Western societies. Until the 1970s, these policies seemed successful and economic growth was more or less continuous.

Over the past fifteen years or so, however, unemployment rates have shot up in many countries, and Keynesianism has been largely abandoned everywhere as a means of trying to control economic activity. For some quarter of a century after the Second World War, the British unemployment rate was less than 2 per cent. Today it has risen to 12 per cent – in spite of a change in the method of accounting which restricted those registered as unemployed to people entitled to unemployment benefit.

Analysing unemployment

Large-scale unemployment is a phenomenon of major importance in the 1980s. Interpreting official unemployment statistics, however, is not straightforward. Unemployment is not easy to define. It means 'being out of work'. But 'work' here means 'paid work', and 'work in a recognized occupation'. People who are properly registered as

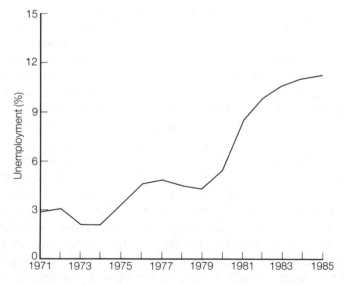

Figure 19 The unemployment rate in the United Kingdom, annual averages 1971–1985
Source: Social Trends (London: HMSO, 1987), p. 80.

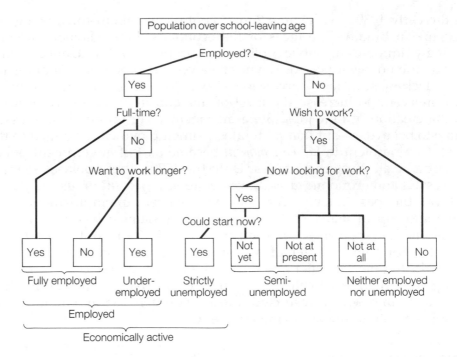

Figure 20   A taxonomy of possible employment, unemployment and non-employment states
Source: Peter Sinclair, *Unemployment: Economic Theory and Evidence* (Oxford: Basil Blackwell, 1987), p. 2.

unemployed may engage in many forms of productive activity, like painting the house or tending the garden. Many people are in part-time paid work, or only in paid jobs sporadically; the retired are not counted as 'unemployed' (Sinclair, 1987). Statistics collected by governments are not strictly comparable, and usually leave out many people who would like to find paid work, but have not been able to do so.

Variations in the distribution of government-defined unemployment within Britain are well documented. Unemployment is higher for men than for women, and for ethnic minorities than whites. Ethnic minorities also have much higher rates of long-term unemployment than the average for the rest of the population. The recent rise in unemployment has especially affected young people, again being more pronounced for ethnic minority groups than for whites. Unemployment rates for those aged between sixteen and nineteen stand at some 20 per cent. To some extent this is artificially high, because it includes numbers of students who work part-time, or in casual employment. However, a substantial proportion of young people are among the long-term unemployed, especially the members of minority groups. Youth unemployment is largely concentrated among relatively small proportions of individuals out of work for extended time-periods. More than half the male teenage unemployment involves those out of work for six months or more.

The experience of unemployment can be very disturbing to those who have become accustomed to having secure jobs. Obviously the most immediate consequence is a loss of income. The effects of this vary between countries, because of contrasts in the level of unemployment benefits. In Britain, for instance, long-term welfare benefits are provided for the unemployed. Unemployment may produce acute financial difficulties, but does not affect access to health care and other welfare benefits, since these are provided by the state. In the United States, Spain, and some other Western countries on the other hand, unemployment benefits last a shorter time and the economic strain on those without work is correspondingly greater.

Being in and out of work

In modern societies, having a job is important for maintaining self-esteem. Even where work conditions are relatively unpleasant, and the tasks involved dull, work tends to be a structuring element in a people's psychological make-up and the cycle of their daily activities. The experience of unemployment can therefore only be properly understood in terms of what holding a job provides. Six main characteristics of paid work are relevant here.

1 *Money*. A wage or salary is the main resource most people depend on to meet their needs. Without such an income, anxieties about coping with day-to-day life tend to multiply.
2 *Activity level*. Employment often provides a basis for the acquisition and exercise of skills and capacities. Even where work is routine, it offers a structured environment in which a person's energies may be absorbed. Without employment, the opportunity to exercise such skills and capacities may be reduced.
3 *Variety*. Employment provides access to contexts that contrast with domestic surroundings. In the working environment, even when the tasks are relatively dull, individuals may enjoy doing something different from home chores. Unemployment reduces this source of contrast with the domestic milieu.
4 *Temporal structure*. For people in regular employment, the day is usually organized around the rhythm of work. While this may sometimes be oppressive, it provides a sense of direction in daily activities. Those who are out of work frequently find boredom a major problem and develop a sense of apathy about time. As one unemployed man remarked, 'Time doesn't matter now as much as it used to. . . . There's so much of it' (Fryer and McKenna, 1987).
5 *Social contacts*. The work environment often provides friendships, and opportunities to participate in shared activities with others. Separated from the work setting, a person's circle of possible friends and acquaintances is likely to dwindle.

6 *Personal identity*. Employment is usually valued for the sense of stable social identity it offers. For men in particular, self-esteem is often bound up with the economic contribution they make to the maintenance of the household.

Against the backdrop of this formidable list, it is not difficult to see why unemployment may undermine individuals' confidence in their social value. Thus an unemployed teacher remarked: 'It's difficult when you strip away all the things that supposedly hold you together in terms of an identity. Your work, your money, whatever is power to you, whatever is responsibility, whatever means freedom and choice. I have to ask myself, "Who am I now? What will I do now?" ' (Holt, 1979).

In some part, recent rises in unemployment in the West are the result of the decline of the older, manufacturing industries. This means that unemployment rates vary substantially between the different regions of a country – a situation hidden by national unemployment rates. In areas where heavy industry has traditionally been concentrated, 20 per cent or more of the work-force may be unemployed. In old-established industrial neighbourhoods or towns, the outcome is a partial disintegration of long-standing social communities. Mining or steel towns, for example, from South Wales and the Ruhr to Detroit and Pittsburgh now quite often lie almost in decay. As the pits and factories close down, property values plummet; while many of the unemployed are moving away, others can no longer afford to do so.

Similar changes can now be seen in Japan, the last fully developed industrial society to be affected by them. Many Japanese workers have in the past enjoyed much greater security of employment than their Western counterparts, the large corporations having pursued a policy of 'life-time employment' – taking on their employees for life (see chapter 9: 'Groups and Organizations'). For such workers, the experience of unemployment is even more disturbing than it is for most employees in the West. A recent description of unemployment in Japan quoted the case of forty-seven-year-old Atsuhiko Tateuchi, fired from his job as a section chief in a middle-sized company. Seeing unemployment as utterly demeaning, he didn't tell his family. Instead, he continued to leave home at 7.30 every morning, dressed in a suit and tie. He spent the day in coffee shops, parks or cinemas. Eventually his wife and children became suspicious, because he came home at 6.30 p.m. rather than midnight!

The same article describes the fate of the citizens of Kamaishi, a steel town in Northern Japan. Most employment in the town depends on a steel-mill run by the Nippon Corporation, the largest steel-producer in the world. It was the first steel-mill in Japan, having opened in 1886, but is now to be shut down completely by 1990, with the loss of 2,300 jobs. Several thousands of people in the town, whose businesses depend on the mill, will also become unemployed. The mayor of

Kamaishi says the town will return to what it was a hundred years ago, 'just a village' (McGill, 1987). But the dislocation in the local economy and in people's lives will be profound.

Why have rates of unemployment risen?

A combination of factors probably explains the sharp increase in unemployment levels in the West in recent years.

1 An important element is the rise of international competition in industries on which Western prosperity used to be founded. In 1947 60 per cent of world steel production was carried out in the United States. Today the figure is only about 15 per cent, while steel production has risen by 300 per cent in Japan and the Third World countries (principally Singapore, Taiwan and Hong Kong – which are now undercutting Japanese prices).
2 There is a world-wide economic recession, which was either caused or triggered by the 'Oil Crisis' of 1973 – a recession which is not yet over.
3 The increasing use of micro-electronics in industry has reduced the need for labour-power.
4 More women than ever before are seeking paid employment, with the result that more people are chasing the limited number of available jobs.

It is not clear whether the current high rates of unemployment will continue – or perhaps become even more pronounced – in the immediate future. Some countries seem to be better placed to combat large-scale unemployment than others. Rates of unemployment have been reduced more successfully in the United States than in Britain, or some of the other major European nations. This is perhaps because the sheer economic strength of the country gives it more power in world markets than smaller, more fragile economies. Alternatively, it may be that the exceptionally large service sector in the USA provides a greater source of new jobs than in countries where more of the population has traditionally been employed in manufacturing.

Women and work

Housework

In much of the sociological literature about work, at least until very recently, unwaged work – labour carried on without direct payment and outside the scope of a particular 'occupation' – was never considered. Marx's discussion of alienated labour concentrates wholly on the worker in the enterprise, and most discussions in industrial sociology since that time have followed suit. Unpaid work, particularly that of women in the domestic sphere, was largely ignored, yet such work is just as necessary to the economy as paid employment. It has been estimated that **housework** is equivalent in value to about a third of the total production per year in a modern economy.

The association of women with domestic work – concentrating on maintaining the home and raising children – had little meaning when the home was a production unit, before industrialization. A proportion of married women, and virtually all unmarried women, were engaged in paid work from the first beginnings of industrialization. But many women also became confined to the domestic sphere ('not working') as paid employment for men in separate work-places became the norm (Oakley, 1976, 1982). This process was accompanied by a decline in the numbers of household servants. J. K. Galbraith has remarked that from the early twentieth century onwards, servants are now only employed by a small minority, but 'the servant-wife is available, domestically, to almost the entire present male population . . .' (Galbraith, 1974, p. 33). It is true that many men are enabled, by their wives' work at home, to do far more in their 'paid' jobs than would be possible were they looking after themselves.

Before urbanization, most women carried out a variety of tasks, in addition to caring for children and chores in the home. For example, women would cultivate gardens in which vegetables consumed in the home were grown, tend sheep, goats, cows and other animals, make their own bread and preserve food for storage. Except in the homes of the wealthy, the tasks associated with housework today – cleaning, tidying, dusting, shopping and so forth – were not the major chores. Rooms in pre-modern houses did not have individual uses, and were sparsely furnished. For the average household, there was little to clean or tidy. Cooking, eating, and working at the spinning wheel or loom all occupied the same space (Tilly and Scott, 1978). Women's tasks were often closely co-ordinated with those of men, the household forming an integrated productive unit.

With the development of workplaces separate from the home, production also became separated from consumption. Men, the 'producers', 'went out to work'; the home, the domain of women, became a place in which goods were consumed in the process of family life. The housewife became a 'consumer', someone 'who does not work', her productive activity concealed from view. Yet housework patently *is* work, as exhausting and demanding as most types of industrial labour. In Oakley's study of housework, women frequently drew attention to its 'unending' character – it is work that can never be finished, is 'never done' (Oakley, 1974). Housewives value the fact that they have a considerable amount of control over what they do, and when they do it. Like industrial workers, however, they dislike most the tasks that are purely routine – such as ironing or dusting.

Women's work outside the home

Between the two world wars, the numbers of women who were solely housewives reached a peak. Although it was common for unmarried women to be in paid employment, the large majority of married women at that time did not 'work'. In both wars women were encouraged to enter employment to take the place of men who joined the armed forces; after the First World War they were displaced, but after the Second the expulsion was not so thorough. The growth in women's employment since then (see chapter 6: 'Gender and Sexuality') has been closely connected with the expansion of service jobs. Women are disproportionately concentrated in the service sector, although not in managerial or professional positions. Women's jobs are concentrated in *secondary labour markets*. The **primary labour market** consists of work in large corporations, unionized industries or government agencies. In these contexts, workers receive relatively high wages, enjoy good job security and promotion possibilities. **Secondary labour markets** include forms of employment which are unstable, where job security and wages are low, there are few opportunities for promotion, and working conditions are frequently poor. Waitressing, retail sales work, cleaning, and many other service jobs mostly carried out by women fall into this category.

Women are also much more heavily concentrated than men in part-time paid work. Women make up 90 per cent of part-time workers in the UK; about 40 per cent of all working women are in part-time paid employment. Many women move to part-time work after the birth of a first child, if they do not leave the work-force altogether. Older women who return to paid work once their children are grown up often take part-time jobs – either from choice or because few full-time positions are available to them.

The informal economy

Sociologists and economists often think in terms of people being either 'employed' or 'unemployed', as though these were exhaustive categories; but this is an over-simplified view of work. Not only housework, but other kinds of non-paid labour (such as repairing one's own car) loom large in many people's lives; many types of work do not conform to orthodox categories of paid employment. Much of the work done in the **informal economy** is not recorded in any direct way in the official employment statistics. The term *informal economy* refers to transactions outside the sphere of regular employment, sometimes involving the exchange of cash for services provided, but also often involving the direct exchange of goods or services (Henry, 1978; Feige, 1981; Gaertner and Wenig, 1985; Pahl, 1987).

Someone who comes round to fix the tap, for example, may be paid in cash, without any receipt being given or details of the job recorded. People exchange 'cheap' – that is to say pilfered or stolen – goods with friends or associates in return for other favours. The informal economy includes not only 'hidden' cash transactions, but many forms of *self-provisioning* which people carry on inside and outside the home. DIY activities, domestic machinery and household tools, for instance, provide goods and services which would otherwise have to be purchased (Gershuny and Miles, 1983).

To illustrate this, Ray Pahl gives the example of fixing a leaking roof. The roof might be mended in several ways:

1 The owner of the home might do the work with the help of other members of the household. The materials needed could be bought from a shop, or could be acquired from a friend or neighbour who had saved them from some other job. In such a case, it might be that no money changes hands at all. The members of the household may choose to fix their own roof because they cannot afford to pay a contractor to do it, or perhaps because they take pride in their ability to maintain the dwelling without outside assistance.

2 The roof might be mended by a friend or neighbour in exchange either for cash or for benefits provided in return. The work relations here are based on informal ties, quite different to those between employer and employee. If the work is done by a relative, payment may not be made for months or even years.

3 A contractor could be hired to do the work. In this case, the transaction might be a 'normal' one in which a full fee is paid for the service and receipted in the accounts of the contractor. Alternatively, the contractor might charge a lower rate, be paid in cash, not recording the transaction in order to avoid declaring income which might be taxed. (Pahl, 1984, pp. 134–6)

The informal sector is particularly significant among poorer groups and in areas of high unemployment. Many goods or services that could not otherwise be paid for are provided in this way. Self-provisioning, of course, is not just a matter of economic necessity; it may bring satisfactions that cannot be derived from the environment in which paid work is done.

The household is usually the main setting in which connections between the informal and formal economies are handled. Members of households often make collective decisions about what constitutes an overall level of income that will meet their needs, and to some degree – where circumstances allow – distribute paid and unpaid labour tasks accordingly. For example, a husband or wife might work overtime in their paid employment to cover various domestic costs (like paying a carpenter to put in new cupboards). Alternatively, opportunities to work overtime might be rejected, the couple undertaking the tasks in the home themselves.

The future of work

What counts as *work*, then, is a complex matter, involving many types of activities in addition to orthodox employment. 'Everyone has the right to work' states the Universal Declaration of Human Rights, signed at the United Nations after the Second World War. At the time, this meant the right to a paid job. If, however, the trend towards large-scale unemployment proves to be long-term, the aim may prove to be unrealizable. Perhaps we should rethink the nature of paid work, and in particular the dominant position it often has in people's lives?

Unemployment tends to be seen by employers and workers alike as a negative phenomenon, but this outlook needs examining. After all, the identification of 'work' with 'paid employment' is peculiarly limiting. If someone expends enormous effort on a hobby, such as cultivating a beautiful garden, for interest rather than for any material reward, why should this not be regarded as work? The word 'unemployment' only came into the language in the late nineteenth century; perhaps it might disappear in the late twentieth, if not having a job ceases to be regarded as the same as being 'out of work'. Why not, some observers suggest, classify all the unemployed as self-employed, giving subsidies to those who need them to follow their chosen pursuits? (Handy, 1984; Jones, 1982; Merritt, 1982).

In all the industrialized countries the average length of the working week is gradually being reduced. Many workers still undertake long stretches of overtime, but some governments are introducing new limits on permissible working hours. In France, for example, overtime is restricted to a maximum of 130 hours a year. In most countries, men retire at the age of sixty-five and women at sixty, but there seems to be a move towards shortening the average working career (Blyton, 1985). More people would probably quit the labour-force at sixty, or earlier, if they could afford to do so.

If the amount of time given to paid employment continues to shrink, and the need to have a job becomes less central, the nature of careers might be substantially reorganized. Job-sharing, or the working of flexible hours, for example, may become increasingly common. Some work analysts have suggested that sabbatical leave, such as exists in universities, should be extended to workers in other spheres, so that everyone would be entitled to take a year off to study or pursue some form of self-improvement. Perhaps more and more individuals will engage in *life planning*, by which they arrange to work in different ways (paid, unpaid, full- or part-time, etc.) at different stages in their lives. Thus some people might choose to enter the labour-force only after a period of formal education followed by one devoted to pursuits like travel. Many people might opt to work part-time throughout their lives, rather than being forced to do so because of lack of full-time opportunities.

Some recent surveys of work indicate that, even under existing conditions, part-time workers register higher levels of job satisfaction than those in full-time employment. This may be because most part-time workers are women, who have lower expectations of their careers than men, or who are particularly relieved to escape from domestic monotony. Yet many individuals seem to find reward precisely in the fact that they are able to balance paid work with other activities and enjoy a more varied life (Humphries, 1983).

Some people might choose to 'peak' their lives, giving full commitment to paid work from their youth to their middle years, then perhaps changing to a second career which would open up new interests. Studies of those choosing deliberately to retire early provide some idea of ways in which they might organize their activities. A study by Ann McGoldrick of men who had retired early showed much diversity in their styles of life. Of the 1,800 people studied, 75 per cent described themselves as 'more at ease' and 'under less stress and strain' than they were in their jobs. (A minority, however, were disappointed with their new lives, including some individuals living in financial hardship or suffering from some form of debility or illness (McGoldrick, 1973).)

The French sociologist and social critic André Gorz has used findings like McGoldrick's to criticize traditional ideas about the development of modern societies, and to provide an alternative mapping of their likely future organization. Gorz bases his views upon a critical assessment of Marx's work. Marx believed that the working class – to which more and more people supposedly belong – would lead a revolution that would bring about a more humane type of society, in which work would be central to the satisfactions life has to offer. Although writing as a Leftist, Gorz rejects this view. Rather than the working class becoming the largest grouping in society (as Marx suggested) and leading a successful revolution, it is actually shrinking. Blue-collar workers have now become a minority – and a declining minority – of the labour-force.

It no longer makes much sense, in Gorz's view, to suppose that workers can take over the enterprises of which they are a part, let alone seize state power. There is no real hope of transforming the nature of paid work, because it is organized according to technical considerations which are unavoidable if an economy is to be efficient. 'The point now', as Gorz puts it, 'is to free oneself *from* work . . .' (Gorz, 1982, p. 67). This is particularly necessary where work is organized along Taylorist lines, or is otherwise oppressive or dull.

Rising unemployment, together with the spread of part-time work, Gorz argues, have already created what he calls a 'non-class of non-workers', alongside those in stable employment. Most people, in fact, are in this 'non-class', because the proportion of the population in stable paid jobs at any one time is relatively small – if we exclude the young, the retired, the ill and housewives, together with people who are in part-time work or unemployed. The spread of micro-technology, Gorz believes, will further reduce the numbers of full-time jobs available. The result is likely to be a swing towards rejecting the 'productivist' outlook of Western society, with its emphasis on wealth, economic growth and material goods. A diversity of life-styles, followed outside the sphere of permanent, paid work, will be pursued by the majority of the population in coming years.

According to Gorz, we are moving towards a 'dual society'. In one sector, production and political administration will be organized to maximize efficiency. The other sector will be a sphere in which individuals occupy themselves with a variety of non-work pursuits offering enjoyment or personal fulfilment.

How valid is this viewpoint? That there *are* major changes going on in the nature and organization of work in the industrialized countries is beyond dispute. It does seem possible that more and more people will become disenchanted with 'productivism' – the stress upon constant economic growth and the accumulation of material possessions. It is surely valuable, as Gorz has suggested, to see unemployment not wholly in a negative light, but as offering opportunities for individuals to pursue their interests and develop their talents. Yet, thus far at least, progress in this direction has been slight; we seem to be far from the situation Gorz envisages. With women pressing for greater job opportunities, there has been a rise, not a fall, in the numbers of people actively interested in securing paid employment. Paid work remains for many the key basis of generating the material resources necessary to sustain a varied life.

Summary

1   *Work* is the carrying out of tasks, involving the expenditure of mental and physical effort, which have as their objective the production of goods and services catering for human needs. An *occupation* is work which is done in exchange for a regular wage. Work is in all cultures the basis of the *economic system*.

2   A distinctive characteristic of the economic system of modern societies is the development of a highly complex and diverse *division of labour*. The economy of the industrialized countries consists of three sectors: the *primary sector* (involving the collection or extraction of natural resources), the *secondary sector* (converting raw materials into commodities), and the *tertiary sector* (providing services).

3   Union organizations, together with recognition of the right to *strike*, are characteristic features of economic life in all Western countries. Unions

emerged as *defensive* organizations, concerned to provide a measure of control for workers over their conditions of labour. Today, union leaders quite often play an important role in formulating national economic policies – although this is less true of Britain at present than formerly.

4   The modern economy is dominated by the large *corporations*. When one firm has a commanding influence in a given industry, it is in a *monopoly* position. When a cluster of firms wield such influence, a situation of oligopoly exists. Through their influence upon government policy, and upon the consumption of goods, the giant corporations have a profound effect on our lives.

5   A *primary labour market* consists of workers in large corporations, in unionized industries or government agencies. A *secondary labour market* consists of unstable forms of employment, where job opportunities are restricted and insecure, and working conditions are poor.

6   Unemployment has been a recurrent problem in the industrialized countries in the twentieth century. As work is a structuring element in a person's psychological make-up, the experience of unemployment is often disorientating. The impact of new technology seems likely further to increase unemployment rates.

7   *Work* should not be understood as a term only covering paid employment. Domestic work and the *informal economy* are major spheres of non-waged work, which make a major contribution to the overall production of wealth. The term *informal economy* refers to transactions involving either the direct exchange of cash for services or the direct exchange of goods for services; apart from sometimes being a matter of economic necessity, *self-provisioning* may provide satisfactions unavailable from paid employment.

8   The nature of women's work has been greatly affected by the separation of the workplace from the home. Many married women become 'housewives' and are regarded as 'not working' – even though the hours of labour they put into domestic tasks may be far more than the working hours of their husbands. Far more women are now in paid employment than was the case some decades ago; but women are disproportionately concentrated in low-paid jobs.

9   Major changes are currently taking place in the nature and organization of work, which seem certain to become even more important in the future. None the less, paid work remains for many people the key way of generating the resources necessary to sustain a varied life.

Basic concepts

work	division of labour
the economy	alienation

Important terms

occupation	strike
economic interdependence	entrepreneur
primary sector	monopoly
secondary sector	oligopoly
tertiary sector	corporations
service industries	family capitalism
Taylorism	managerial capitalism
Fordism	institutional capitalism
low-trust systems	housework
high-trust systems	primary labour market
automation	secondary labour market
group production	the informal economy
industrial democracy	

Further reading

Marie Jahoda, *Employment and Unemployment* (Cambridge: Cambridge University Press, 1982) — a study of the employed and unemployed, giving material on the psychological consequences of unemployment.

S. Lonsdale, *Work and Inequality* (London: Longman, 1985) — a useful survey of some main areas of industrial sociology.

S. R. Parker et al., *The Sociology of Industry* (London: Allen and Unwin, 1983) — an analysis of major problems of industrial organization.

Charles F. Sabel, *Work and Politics* (Cambridge: Cambridge University Press, 1982) — an analysis of the impact of Fordism, which stresses the variations found in the development of industry in different countries.

PART V

Social Change in the Modern World

All the chapters in this book emphasize the sweeping nature of the social changes which have taken place in the modern era. For virtually the whole of human history, the pace of social change was relatively slow; most people followed more or less the same ways of life as their parents. By contrast, we live in a world subject to dramatic and continuous transformation. In the chapters in this part, we look at some of the areas in which change is most marked.

The first chapter analyses a particular direction of change which affects us all, the increasing involvement of different societies within global systems. The globalizing of social life both influences, and is influenced by, changing patterns of urbanization. Urbanism – the factors swelling the numbers of people living in cities all over the world – is the subject of the succeeding chapter. We then discuss one of the most far-reaching changes currently taking place – the tremendous growth in global population. Population growth has been greatly influenced by the spread of Western techniques of hygiene and medicine, and in this chapter we study the social contexts of health and disease. One effect of people living longer has been to change the age-distribution (proportions of the population in different age groups) of modern populations, creating major contrasts between the industrialized and less developed nations.

The concluding two chapters in this part look directly at processes of change. A major characteristic of the modern era is the deliberate attempt to secure social and political change through collective action. We study some of the major forms of revolutionary change from the eighteenth century to the present day, and also analyse some general mechanisms of protest and collective violence. In the final chapter, we consider overall interpretations of the nature of social change. We discuss what social change actually is, and why change has become so profound and constant in current times. We then take a look into the future, considering where present-day patterns of change are likely to lead us as we move into the twenty-first century.

16

The Globalizing of Social Life

Take a close look at the array of products on offer the next time you walk into the local shop or supermarket. The diversity of goods which we in the West have come to take for granted as available, for anyone with the money to buy them, depends on amazingly complex economic connections stretching across the world. The products on display have been made in, or use ingredients or parts from, a hundred different countries. All these have to be regularly transported across the globe, and constant flows of information are necessary to co-ordinate the millions of daily transactions involved.

'Until our day', the anthropologist Peter Worsley has written, 'human society has never existed' (Worsley, 1984, p. 1), meaning that it is only in quite recent times that we can speak of forms of social association which span the earth. The world has become in important respects a *single social system*, as a result of growing ties of interdependence which now affect virtually everyone. The global system is not just an *environment* within which particular societies – like Britain – develop and change. The social, political and economic connections which cross-cut borders between countries decisively condition the fate of those living within each of them. The general term for the increasing interdependence of world society is **globalization**.

It would be a mistake to think of globalization simply as a process of the growth of world unity. The globalizing of social relations should be understood primarily as the reordering of time and distance in our lives. Our lives, in other words, are increasingly influenced by activities and events happening well away from the social contexts in which we carry on our day-to-day activities. Although rapidly developing today, globalization is by no means completely new, dating from the time at which Western influence started to expand across the world some two or three centuries ago. (We have already discussed aspects of this phenomenon in chapter 2, 'Culture and Society'.)

Our main concern in this chapter will be to analyse the *uneven*, or *fragmented*, nature of the processes which have drawn different parts of the globe into interrelation with one another. The globalizing of social relations has not proceeded evenly: from the beginning it has been associated with inequalities between different regions in the world. Especially important are the processes that created the **Third World** societies. Large disparities of wealth and living standards separate the industrialized (First and Second World) countries from those in the Third World – in which most of the planet's population live. We shall begin by looking at how the Third World societies have developed, and their relationship to the industrialized nations today. We shall then discuss some of the most important theories of world development, before moving on to analyse international organizations and the media.

Third World societies

The formation of nations

The large majority of Third World societies are in areas that underwent colonial rule – in Asia, Africa and South America. One or two are still colonies (Hong Kong, for example, is a British colony, although control is due to pass to China in 1997). A few colonized areas gained independence early, like Haiti, which became the first autonomous black republic in January 1804. The Spanish colonies in South America acquired their freedom in 1810, while Brazil broke away from Portuguese rule in 1822. In most early examples of the formation of independent states, European settlers were usually instrumental in the separation from the original colonizing country (Haiti was an exception). This was the case, of course, with the founding of the United States.

Some countries which were never ruled from Europe were none the less strongly influenced by colonial relationships, the most notable example being China. By force of arms China was compelled to enter into trading agreements with European powers, by which the Europeans were allocated the government of certain areas, including a number of major sea-ports. Hong Kong is the last remnant of these.

Most Third World nations have only become independent states since the Second World War – often following bloody anti-colonial struggles. Examples include India, which very shortly after achieving self-rule split into India and Pakistan; a range of other Asian countries (like Burma, Malaysia or Singapore); and many states in Africa (including, for example, Kenya, Nigeria, Zaire, Tanzania and Algeria).

Many Third World countries were not distinct societies before colonization. Their boundaries derive from the imposition of European rule, the colonists usually having forced together many different cultures under a single administration, or split cultures where territorial boundaries between two European powers were established. Although substantial colonial expansion occurred from the sixteenth century onwards, most of the regions that have now become Third World states were only colonized in the nineteenth century. India did not come fully under British rule until the 1860s, around the same period as the consolidation of British administration in Malaya, Singapore and Burma.

Africa was the 'dark continent' to Europeans and was largely unexplored until the mid-nineteenth century. In the 1870s and 1880s, the leading European countries competed with one another to acquire different parts of Africa, and effective systems of colonial government were established there somewhat later. The period of colonial rule was thus in some cases very short, not long enough to integrate a diversity of indigenous groups under an effective administration. This explains why many Third World states today are internally so diverse and fragmented. At the time of Kenyan independence in 1963, for instance, some people could remember personally the period before the establishment of white rule (Goldthorpe, 1984, chapter 3).

The economic consequences of colonialism

The European powers acquired colonies for a number of reasons.

1 Colonial possessions added to the political influence and power of the parent country and provided sites for military bases.
2 Most Westerners also saw colonialism as a civilizing enterprise, helping upgrade native peoples from their 'primitive' conditions. Missionaries wished to bring Christianity to the heathen.
3 There was an important economic motive. From the early years of Western expansion, food, raw materials and other goods were taken from the colonized areas to fuel Western economic development.

Even where colonies were not acquired primarily for economic gain, the colonizing country nevertheless almost always strove to achieve sufficient economic return to cover the costs of its administration of the area.

In some regions, the existing economic activities of the local peoples generated a sufficient basis for trade. However, in the majority of instances, particularly in tropical areas, the Europeans encouraged the development of **cash crops** – crops produced for sale on international markets. The colonizers often set up plantations, farms and mines, in which they were the overseers, drawing their labour-power from the native populations, and in most cases large tracts of land were taken over to become the property of European settlers. A significant economic invention on the part of the colonial countries was the setting up of **concession companies** – companies licensed by the colonizing state to have a monopoly over the production of certain goods or crops within a particular area (Weatherby et al., 1987). A few of these companies, including both state-controlled enterprises and private firms, became very large, having a leading influence over the regions in which they operated. The descendants of some of the concession companies are very prominent in world trade today.

Many, although not all, of the Third World countries are impoverished compared to the industrialized nations. The main reason for this is their lack of an industrial base. Most of their populations are engaged in agriculture, using traditional methods of production. In some cases, they were drained of resources by the colonizing countries, who kept them in a state of subjection. In addition, most of the Third World societies have experienced high rates of population growth over the course of the present century (see chapter 18: 'Population, Health and Ageing'). This has made it very difficult for them to achieve any sustained economic development, because increases in production are taken up by the extra mouths which have to be fed.

In the poorer Third World countries, many people live in conditions that are almost inconceivable to those who live in the West. Agostino Neto, the first President of Angola, in Southern Africa, wrote a poem which graphically describes the life of a poor quarry worker. With deliberate irony, it is entitled 'Western Civilization':

Sheets of tin nailed to posts
driven in the ground
make up the house.

Some rags complete
the intimate landscape.

The sun slanting through cracks
welcomes the owner.

After twelve hours of slave
labour.

breaking rock
shifting rock
breaking rock
shifting rock
fair weather
wet weather
breaking rock
shifting rock

Old age comes early

a mat on dark nights
is enough when he dies
gratefully
of hunger.

(Quoted in Bennett and George, 1987, p. 113)

Poverty

Conditions in the poorer Third World countries have deteriorated during the world recession of the past fifteen years or so. The recession also significantly affected the First World countries: high rates of inflation, coupled with increasing unemployment, were for a period found in most industrialized countries – Japan being an exception. Inflation has since been brought down, and although unemployment has remained high in many Western societies, the difficulties they face are slight compared to those confronting the Third World.

The economic adjustments made by wealthier countries to combat the recession had serious consequences for poor Third World countries. First, the richer countries cut down on imports from the poorer ones, which depressed prices; prices for some cash-crops, such as tea and rubber, are today at their lowest for thirty years. Some countries (like Mexico, Brazil or Nigeria) have by now accumulated debts which they cannot pay back in the foreseeable future; nor can they even afford the high interest rates payable on money already borrowed. Secondly, the level of aid (as opposed to loans) going from richer to poorer countries has actually declined. Given high rates of population growth, the outlook for the poorest Third World countries is bleak indeed (Brandt Commission, 1983).

The newly industrializing countries

The Third World is not a unity. While the majority of Third World countries lag well behind the Western societies and those of Eastern Europe, some have now successfully embarked upon a process of industrialization (Saunders, 1981). These are sometimes referred to as the **newly industrializing countries**, and include Brazil and Mexico in

South America, and Hong Kong, South Korea, Singapore and Taiwan in East Asia. To these we have to add the oil-rich countries of the Middle East, like Kuwait or Saudi Arabia. Some of this group actually have a high level of income per head, as a result of oil revenues. They have no developed industrial base of their own, but are striving to build one.

The rates of economic growth of the most successful NICs, such as Taiwan, are several times those of most of the Western industrial economies (Harris, 1987). No developing economy figured among the top thirty exporters of manufactured products in the world in 1965, but twenty years later, Hong Kong and South Korea were in the top fifteen, with export shares similar to those of Sweden and Switzerland. However, the relative success of these countries has few spin-offs for the rest of the Third World.

Brazil is easily the largest of the NICs – it is in fact the eighth biggest non-communist economy in the world. The country increased its GNP by an average of 6.5 per cent annually from 1932 to the mid-1980s. In the late 1960s and 1970s in particular, growth-rates were spectacular compared to those of most of the industrialized world. Mexico's growth-rate paralleled this, averaging just below 8 per cent for these two decades. On the other hand, as has been mentioned, both countries are very heavily indebted to Western banks, with little chance of being able to repay even in the moderate-term future. Much of the newly created wealth is monopolized by the privileged, rather than filtering down to the urban and rural poor.

The divergence between rich and poor countries

About twenty countries in the world today (the Western countries, Japan, Australia and New Zealand) are markedly wealthier than any others. At the top of the league are the United States, Canada, Sweden and Switzerland, with the highest **gross national products** in the world. (The gross national product (GNP) of a society is the value of all the goods and services produced in that country each year. *GNP per head of population* is the normal measure used for comparing differences in wealth between nations, although it is a very limited indicator. For example, being an average, it conceals variations between rich and poor *within* countries.) There is another group whose GNP per head of population approaches that of the industrialized countries; the oil-rich states in the Middle East. Their position fluctuates as the price of oil changes, however, and their domestic economies have not developed non-oil-based industries to the same extent as those of the West and Japan. The Soviet Union and Eastern Europe (the Second World societies) have lower per capita (per head of population) GNPs than the Japanese and Western economies, although there is a good deal of variation within this block, East Germany being the most prosperous. The poorest countries in the world are mostly in Asia and Africa.

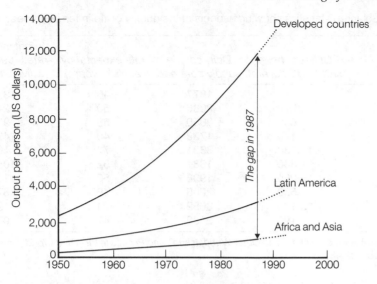

Figure 21 The development gap since 1950, including predicted growth
Source: Andrew Reed, *The Developing World* (London: Bell and Hyman, 1987), p. 16.

If we take the wealthiest forty countries, and the forty poorest (each making up about a quarter of humankind), we find that the second group produces about 5 per cent of the GNP of the first. In other words, the population of the richest forty countries has a 'cake' twenty times larger than that shared between the equivalent number of poorest nations. This gap is currently widening, rather than narrowing. It has been estimated that, at current rates of development, the gap between the wealthiest and poorest countries will have widened by a further 300 per cent by the year 2000 (Kubalkova and Cruickshank, 1981, p. 81).

The position of Third World countries within the world economy is made especially precarious by their dependence on cash-crop production. There are many countries in which just one or two crops form the main basis of the economic system, and some of these crops (like coffee or cocoa) are strongly affected by climatic fluctuations from year to year. Their prices on world markets vary far more than those for manufactured goods. Problems caused by this are often exacerbated by the fact that the national economy is more dependent on foreign trade than is the case for the wealthier nations (Goldthorpe, 1984, pp. 94–6; Stavrianos, 1981).

Connections between the First and Third Worlds

The term 'Third World' (originally coined by the French demographer, Alfred Sauvy) has become a conventional way of referring to the less developed societies, but in some respects it is not very satisfactory. The label makes it sound as though these societies are quite separate from the industrialized countries – a world apart from ours. But this is

Table 13   Selected statistics showing aspects of the quality of life in ten countries

Country	GNP per head (1982: US dollars)	Daily calorie supply per head	Life expectancy at birth (years)	Infant mortality rates (per 1,000 live births)
Bangladesh	140	1877	40	132
Bolivia	570	2086	50	124
Egypt	690	2950	56	97
Ethiopia	140	1729	40	143
France	11,680	3381	74	10
Haiti	300	1881	52	108
India	260	1998	50	118
Indonesia	580	2296	49	87
USA	13,160	3652	74	12
Zaire	190	2133	47	107

Source: Joseph Weatherby et al., *The Other World: Issues and Politics in the Third World* (New York: Macmillan, 1986), p. 43.

not true at all; the Third World societies have long been bound up with the industrialized countries, and the other way around. As has been mentioned, they were shaped by the impact of colonialism and by the trading links forged with the Western states. In turn, the connections which the West established with other parts of the world have strongly affected their own development. For example, the fact that there is a large black population in the United States, and in Brazil, is a result of the 'trade in people' – the slave trade – which the colonizers developed.

In current times, as a result of the accelerating process of globalization, the ties between the First and Third World countries are becoming ever more complex. Many raw materials used in Western manufacture are imported from the Third World. Large numbers of food products (cash crops) come regularly from the Third World to the industrialized nations. Finally, to an increasing degree, goods are now manufactured in Third World countries, where many Western companies have established plants. We shall analyse these developments later in the chapter.

Food production and world hunger

The distribution of the world's food supply reflects the general inequalities between rich and poor countries. The World Health Organization estimates that ten million children under five in Third World nations are close to starvation levels. Many more than ten million children die in infancy or early childhood each year, through illness brought about by their own or their mother's malnutrition. There are also probably about 700 million adults who are seriously under-nourished (Bennett and George, 1987; Lappé and Collins, 1980).

Yet world food supplies have been steadily increasing, and have not, as many feared some years ago, so far been outstripped by population growth. The average world yield of grain over the past few years has been about 1,300 million tonnes, which is sufficient to feed the five billion (thousand million) people alive today.

Virtually all surplus food, however, is produced within the industrialized societies. North America is easily the largest source of exportable food supplies. Before the Second World War, it shared this position with South America, Argentina being especially prominent as a source of grains and livestock. Since then, population growth in South America, combined with lack of agricultural reform and modernization, has eliminated that continent's surplus; today, most South American countries do not produce sufficient food to meet their own needs. In North America and Europe, by contrast, there is a large excess capacity in agricultural production. On both continents, governments regularly pay farmers to keep some of their acreage idle, and store very large amounts of food which cannot find buyers on world markets.

Under Public Law 480, passed in 1954, it was declared that the United States' policy is to use its 'abundant productivity to combat hunger and malnutrition and to encourage economic development in the developing countries', through providing direct food aid, and low-priced food to the needy. Levels of aid supplied under the programme, however, have varied, and never involved more than a slight proportion of the available surplus. Moreover, political considerations have strongly influenced the food's destinations. In the mid-1970s, about half of all American food aid went to just two countries: South Vietnam and Cambodia. During the same period the United States rejected a request from Chile, at that time governed by the socialist administration of Salvador Allende, to buy wheat on credit. The refusal probably contributed to the downfall of Allende's government, something which the United States government had been trying to encourage for some time.

The Soviet Union is not in a position to contribute to world food supplies, since its own agriculture is inefficient compared to that of most Western countries. The USSR is in fact from time to time dependent on grain exports from the United States. In the early 1960s, the Soviet Union managed to buy up a large share of the exportable wheat crop of the United States surreptitiously, purchasing some 28 million tonnes of grain through various Third World agencies. It was thus able to buy at a much lower price than normal, taking advantage of United States government subsidies to which the country was not entitled. Available food exports to the rest of the world were severely reduced, while the Soviet Union got its grain at bargain prices.

Famine

If extreme hunger in Third World countries is largely ignored by the richer states, it is partly because the nature of famine has changed.

Famine is commonly seen as a temporary condition affecting a particular area as a result of specific, and transient, circumstances. Thus, for instance, there was famine in Ireland at certain periods of the nineteenth century when the potato crop failed. Famines of this sort still do occur – as in Uganda in 1985 and 1986 – but severe shortage of food has become general among the poor of the world, rather than being confined to particular times and places.

The most widespread conditions of malnutrition and famine today are found in Africa. Most African countries are net importers of food, but the proportion of their national income which can be devoted to this purpose is shrinking. A spiral of deteriorating conditions has set in, as population increase combines with lack of foreign currency to buy the fertilizers, pesticides and agricultural machinery that could increase levels of food production. Wars, political upheavals and unusual periods of drought have made matters even worse. Countries in which two-thirds or more of the labour-force are engaged in agriculture now have to import nearly 10 per cent of all their food (Cannon, 1987).

Even if the richer countries were more generous in providing food aid than in fact they are, fundamental problems would still remain. The provision of aid does nothing to improve the capacity of poor countries to develop more effective agriculture, and may even have the opposite effect. In some parts of Africa, for example, imports of wheat and rice have changed local diets, and also tastes. In tropical parts of the continent these products are extremely expensive to grow, so money is spent to import them which previously might have been devoted to local agriculture. Such paradoxical consequences have led some people to argue that food aid should actually be confined to emergency situations. Certainly what is really needed is a large-scale transfer of *production* resources (for example, agricultural machinery and the means to run and repair it), which would create more effective methods of indigenous agriculture (Brandt Commission, 1983, pp. 123–33).

Agribusiness

Despite the fact that many among their own populations go hungry, Third World countries are important food suppliers to the West. Western food-producing companies – the **agribusiness** enterprises – are the main influences here. The term *agribusiness* was coined by Ray Goldberg of the Harvard Business School, referring to the fact that food production has become largely *industrialized* – produced using machinery, and organized through systematic processing, transport and storage. Many millions of people – mostly in the industrialized countries – no longer directly provide their own food. The food products they consume include large numbers of crops, minerals and other goods imported from the Third World. These are mainly not 'basic' foods (like grain or meat), but include many that are a frequent part of Western diets (such as coffee, tea and cane sugar).

Many of the large agribusiness firms operating in Third World countries have developed from the concessionary companies established there by colonial governments. For instance, one of the first plantations owned by a foreign company in Africa was that set up by William Hesketh Lever in the nineteenth century. Lever was the prime mover in the development of Lever Brothers, which has since become Unilever, the largest food business in the world. Its activities in Africa originally involved the control of palm-oil supplies used in the company's soap factories in North-west England.

Other examples are the Firestone Rubber Company and the Brooke Bond Tea Company. The former bought a million acres from the government of Liberia in 1926, establishing a huge rubber-plantation. While the resources fed permanently into the Liberian economy were few, the country none the less became so dependent on the company that it was often called the 'Firestone Republic' (Dinham and Hines, 1983, pp. 21–2). Brooke Bond set up the first tea-plantation in Africa in the 1920s, later establishing plantations also in India, Pakistan and Ceylon (now Sri Lanka).

Several sectors of the world's production of exportable crops are controlled today by a small number of large agribusiness companies. Three corporations (Gill and Duffus, Cadbury-Schweppes and Nestlé) handle 60 to 80 per cent of world cocoa sales. Ninety per cent of the tea marketed in Western Europe and North America is controlled by five European and three United States companies. A third of the world trade in margarine and table oil is in the hands of one firm (Unilever). Prices paid for crops are primarily governed by activities on the New York and London stock exchanges, far removed from the circumstances of local producers.

Taxation of agribusiness enterprises provides a source of foreign currency for Third World governments, and the corporations often provide employment at rates of pay higher than those available in competing local industries. Yet the overall effects are usually largely negative for the host countries. While agribusiness enterprises are generally highly efficient, the bulk of their production is devoted to the needs of the industrialized regions of the world. More traditional modes of agricultural production tend to be undermined, as workers are drawn into agribusiness employment. Once this has happened, local populations are at the mercy of foreign corporations should they decide to switch their investment elsewhere. Local elites generally become richer through their connections with the agribusiness enterprises, while divisions between them and the peasantry grow larger.

Theoretical perspectives

What accounts for the huge differences in wealth and power between the industrialized countries and those of the Third World? Three theoretical approaches have been proposed to try to explain why such marked global inequalities have developed over the past several centuries: *imperialism, dependency theory* and *world system theory*.

Imperialism

The theory of **imperialism** was first advanced by the English historian J. A. Hobson, and taken up by the Soviet leader Lenin, who was influenced by Marx. Hobson's work was published in the early 1900s, at the time of the 'scramble for Africa' among Western nations. In Hobson's view, colonialism derived from the attempt to find new markets for investment, as capacity for production expanded beyond what could profitably be sold in the home markets. According to him, the majority of the population are only able to afford to buy a relatively small proportion of the goods that can be produced, so there is a constant striving both for new markets in which to sell, and for ways of cheapening production by finding sources of inexpensive raw materials and labour-power in other parts of the world. What Hobson terms *imperialism* – the drive to conquer and subjugate other peoples, of which colonialism was one expression – results from these pressures towards external expansion (Hobson, 1965).

This process both assisted the Western countries' economic development, and impoverished much of the rest of the world, because resources were drained off from the non-industrialized regions. This set in motion the increasing divergence between the wealth of the West and the poverty of the Third World. Lenin argued that large business corporations play a leading role in these developments, although with support from their national governments. They lead the way in exploiting the non-industrialized areas, establishing trading relations with poorer countries on terms highly favourable to themselves.

Neo-imperialism

Subsequent authors have borrowed from the ideas of Lenin and Hobson to develop theories of **neo-imperialism**. They are more concerned with the present-day world than with the period which Hobson and Lenin analysed. The old colonial empires, like the British empire, have more or less completely disappeared; virtually all the old colonial areas have become self-governing countries; yet, so it is argued, the industrialized states still maintain control through their leading economic position in world trade, and through the influence of large corporations operating on a global basis. The Western countries are able to perpetuate their privileged position by ensuring that they control the terms upon which world trade is carried on (Warren, 1981).

Dependency theory

An approach linked to theories of neo-imperialism is **dependency theory**. This approach was developed initially in a South American context (Cardoso, 1972; Furtado, 1984). According to the dependency theorists, global society has developed in an *uneven* way, such that the main **core** of the industrialized world (United States, Europe and Japan) has a dominant role, with the Third World countries being *dependent* upon it. The origins and nature of dependence vary according to how far a specific country was colonized and by whom. Dependence usually involves the reliance of Third World countries on selling cash crops to the developed world.

For example, Brazil became – and remains today – the major producer of coffee for export. Other cash-crops include sugar, rubber and bananas (hence the name *banana republics*, scornfully applied to the unstable political regimes of South America by those surveying them from the more prosperous North (Munck, 1986)). The strong presence of traditional forms of agriculture, combined with cash-crop production for export, prevented the development of modern manufacturing production. Once the South American countries had fallen too far behind the industrialized countries of Europe and North America, and had become dependent on them for manufactured goods, stagnation set in.

The economist André Gunder Frank has coined the phrase 'the development of under-development' to describe the evolution of the Third World countries. These societies have become impoverished, he holds, as a direct result of their subordinate position in relation to the industrialized countries. The industrialized countries have become rich *at the expense* of the Third World, which they have created through colonialism and neo-imperialism. In Frank's words, 'development and under-development are two sides of the same coin' (Frank, 1969, p. 4). The rich countries form a *metropolitan centre*, around which *satellite* (Third World) countries are grouped, their economies being dependent upon those of the more advanced countries, while they themselves become largely impoverished.

World system theory

World system theory, pioneered by Immanuel Wallerstein, is the most sophisticated of these attempts to interpret world patterns of inequality. According to Wallerstein, from the sixteenth century onwards a world system has developed – a series of economic and political connections stretching across the globe – based on the expansion of a *capitalist world economy* (Wallerstein, 1974, 1979). The capitalist world economy is made up of the *core* countries (which correspond roughly to Frank's *metropolitan centre*), the **semi-periphery**, the **periphery** and the **external arena**. The *core* states are those in which modern economic enterprise first emerged and which subsequently underwent processes of industrialization: Britain, Netherlands and France initially, with other societies located in North-west Europe, such as Germany, later joining them. The core areas contained a range of emerging manufacturing industries and relatively advanced forms of agricultural production, and had centralized forms of government.

Societies situated in the south of Europe, around the Mediterranean (such as Spain), became a *semi-periphery* of the core countries. In other words, they were linked in various kinds of dependent trading relationships with the northern states, but remained economically fairly stagnant. Until two centuries ago, the *periphery* – the 'outer edge' – of the world economy was mainly in the eastern fringes of Europe. From these areas, such as what is now Poland, cash-crops were sold directly to the core countries.

Much of Asia and Africa at this time were part of the *external arena* – that is to say, they remained untouched by the commercial connections established by the core countries. As a result of colonialism, and subsequently through the activities of large corporations, these regions have been drawn into the world economy. The Third World nations currently form the periphery of what is by now a very comprehensive world system, in which the United States and Japan have joined, and now dominate, the core. The Soviet Union and the East European societies (the Second World societies), whose economies are centrally planned, are the only large group of countries today which remain to some degree outside the global economy.

Since the core countries dominate the world system, Wallerstein argues, they are able to organize world trade to favour their interests. Much as the dependency theorists say, the First World countries have established a position in which they are able to exploit the resources of Third World societies for their own ends.

Critical assessment of the theories

How valid are these theories? They all agree that the imbalance in wealth and resources between the First and Third Worlds has its origins in colonialism. In this they are surely correct, and without doubt it is also right to claim that the dependency relationships established during the colonial period have been maintained, and even accentuated, since then. Most Third World countries find themselves enmeshed in economic relations with the core states which hamper their economic development, but from which it is very difficult for them to break free. The result is that the industrialized areas of the world become increasingly prosperous, while many Third World countries stagnate.

But it is false to argue, as Frank does in particular, that the prosperity of the industrialized societies has been achieved *as a result* of their exploitation of the poorer countries. The resources they derived from these countries were of minor importance compared to the processes of industrial growth generated within themselves (Blomstrom and Hettne, 1984).

Wallerstein's theory is especially important, because it is not just concerned with global inequalities, but with analysing the world as an overall social system. The industrialized societies and the Third World countries emerged as different parts of a single set of processes of development. This perspective is vital, even if the details of Wallerstein's account can be criticized (Brenner, 1977; Skocpol, 1977; Stinchcombe, 1982).

A basic weakness of each of these theories is that they concentrate almost exclusively on economic factors in the development of the world system. Economic influences are very important, but so are others. Political considerations, the impact of war, and cultural factors, have all had a major impact on the forging of increasing global interdependence. We shall study these later in the chapter.

The transnational corporations

The theories described above rightly give great weight to the role of large business corporations in shaping twentieth-century world development. Let us now go on to look at these corporations in more detail. They are usually referred to as **transnational** or *multinational* companies. The term 'transnational' is preferable, indicating that these companies operate *across* different national boundaries rather than simply *within* several or many nations. A transnational corporation is a company that has plants or offices in two or more countries.

The largest transnationals are gigantic companies, their wealth outstripping that of many countries. Half of the hundred largest economic units in the world today are nations; the other half are transnational corporations! (Benson and Lloyd, 1983, p. 77). The scope of the operations of these companies is staggering. Combining industrial and service corporations, the sales of the top 200 companies in 1986 were equivalent to one third of the world's total production. The revenues of the largest 200 companies rose ten-fold between the mid-1970s and the mid-1980s. Over the past twenty years, the transnationals' activities have become increasingly global: only three of the world's 315 largest companies in 1950 had manufacturing subsidiaries in more than twenty countries; some fifty do so today. These are still, of course, a small minority; the majority of transnationals have subsidiaries in between two and five countries.

Eighty-nine of the top 200 transnational corporations in the world today are based in the United States, contributing just over half the total sales. The share of American companies has, however, fallen significantly since 1960, a period in which Japanese companies have grown dramatically. Only five were in the top 200 in 1960, as

Table 14   A comparison of the world's top ten transnational corporations with the GNPs of some Third World countries (1983)

Rank	Corporation	Headquarters	Sales (thousand US dollars)	Equivalent to the GNP in
1	Exxon	USA	88,561,134	Indonesia[a]
2	Royal Dutch/Shell Group	England/ Netherlands	80,550,885	Algeria, Peru, and Libya combined[b]
3	General Motors	USA	74,581,600	Thailand, Pakistan, and Uruguay combined[b]
4	Mobil	USA	54,607,000	Venezuela[b]
5	British Petroleum	England	49,194,886	Iraq and Ecuador[b]
6	Ford Motors	USA	44,454,600	Sudan, Chile, and Bangladesh
7	IBM	USA	40,180,000	Syria, Ivory Coast, Zaire, and Singapore combined[b]
8	Texaco	USA	40,068,000	Algeria[b]
9	El du Pont	USA	35,378,000	Colombia
10	Standard Oil (Indiana)	USA	27,635,000	Egypt[b]

[a] 1981 GNP; [b] 1980 GNPs.
Source: Joseph Weatherby et al., *The Other World: Issues and Politics in the Third World* (New York: Macmillan, 1986), p. 29.

compared to twenty-five in 1983. Contrary to common belief (including among some of the theorists mentioned above), most of the investment by transnational companies is within the industrialized world: three-quarters of *all* foreign direct investment is between the industrialized countries. Nevertheless, the involvements of transnationals in Third World countries are very extensive, with Brazil, Mexico `and India showing the highest levels of foreign investment. Since 1970 the most rapid rate of increase in corporate investment by far has been in the Asian newly industrializing countries of Singapore, Hong Kong, South Korea and Malaysia (Dicken, 1986, pp. 62–4).

Types of transnational corporation

The transnationals have assumed an increasingly important place in the world economy over the course of this century. Just as national economies have become increasingly *concentrated* – dominated by a limited number of very large companies – so has the world economy. In the case of the United States and several of the other leading industrialized countries, the firms that dominate nationally also have a very wide-ranging international presence. In many sectors of world production (as in agribusiness) the largest companies are *oligopolies* – production is controlled by three or four corporations, which dominate the market. Over the past two or three decades, international oligopolies have developed in motor-car production, micro-processors, the electronics industry and some other goods marketed world-wide.

A particularly important recent trend is the growth of **conglomerates** – companies straddling many different types of production and service. An example is the US firm, R. J. Reynolds, the producer of Winston cigarettes. Reynolds owns, among other companies, Del Monte (fruit), Heublein (alcohol), Sealand Services (shipping), Kentucky Fried Chicken (food retailing) and Aminoil (oil and petroleum).

H. V. Perlmutter divides transnational corporations into three types. One consists of **ethnocentric** transnationals, in which company policy is set, and as far as possible put into practice, from a headquarters in the country of origin. Companies and plants which the parent corporation owns around the world are cultural extensions of the originating company – its practices are standardized across the globe. A second category is that of **polycentric** companies, where overseas subsidiaries are managed by local firms in each country. The headquarters in the country or countries of origin of the main company establish broad guidelines within which local companies manage their own affairs.

Finally, there are **geocentric** transnationals, which are international in their management structure. Managerial systems are integrated on a global basis and higher managers are very mobile, moving from country to country as needs dictate (Perlmutter, 1972). According to Perlmutter, the large majority of transnationals at the moment are polycentric, but there is a strong movement towards the geocentric type; many companies are becoming more and more truly international in character.

Of all transnationals, the Japanese companies tend to be most strongly ethnocentric in Perlmutter's terms. Their world-wide operations are usually controlled tightly from the parent corporation, sometimes with the close involvement of the Japanese government. The Japanese Ministry of International Trade and Industry (MITI) plays a much more direct part in the overseeing of Japanese-based foreign enterprise than Western governments do. MITI has produced a series of development plans co-ordinating the overseas spread of Japanese firms over the past two decades. One distinctive Japanese type of transnational consists of the giant trading companies or *sogo shosha*. These are colossal conglomerates whose main concern is with the financing and support of trade. They provide financial, organizational and information services to other companies. About half of Japanese exports and imports are routed through the ten largest *sogo shosha*. Some, like Mitsubishi, also have large manufacturing interests of their own.

The growth of the transnationals

What accounts for the growth of the transnational companies? First, they are an expression of the tendency of modern economic enterprise to internationalize. Firms which buy and sell goods at a profit – the very rationale for their existence – would be foolish to confine their operations to one country. The more they seek to expand, the more it makes sense to look for sources of profitable investment wherever they can be found. Second, by expanding overseas, a firm can take advantage of sources of cheap labour-power and, often, the absence of trade unions. Third, having subsidiaries in several countries may permit access to a diversity of natural resources. Fourth, transnational companies with subsidiaries in many markets can sometimes gain tax advantages by spreading their profits between branches. Finally, the transnational corporations are able to *internalize* numerous transactions which otherwise are sources of uncertainty for a company. By integrating plants and services in several countries, they can avoid depending on other companies for raw materials and services they need. The parent firm can set its own prices for goods and services transferred between its various subsidiaries (Buckley and Casson, 1976).

The growth of the transnationals over the past thirty years would not have been possible without advances in transport and communications. Jet travel now allows people to move around the world at a speed that would have seemed inconceivable even half a century ago. The development of extremely large ocean-going vessels (super freighters), together with containers that can be shifted directly from one type of transport to another, makes possible the easy transport of bulk materials.

Telecommunications technologies now permit more or less instantaneous communication from one part of the world to another. Satellites have been used for commercial telecommunications since 1965, when the first satellite could carry 240 telephone conversations at once. Current satellites can carry 12,000 simultaneous conversations! The larger transnationals now have their own satellite-based communications systems. The Mitsubishi corporation, for instance, has a massive network, across which five million words are transmitted to and from its headquarters in Tokyo each day (Naksase, 1981).

International economic integration

The transnational companies have helped create a new **international division of labour** – economic interdependence between societies – which now profoundly affects all countries in the world (Fröbel et al., 1980; Nyilas, 1982). Although it is true that the Third World countries are much more *dependent on* – vulnerable to – movements in some global markets than the industrialized societies are, there is a sense in which *all* economies have become more dependent upon one another. For even the most highly industrialized countries cannot control their own economic development to the degree that they formerly could (Kahn, 1986).

The transnationals have contributed to global economic interdependence by the sheer scale of their activities, but also by the way in which the largest companies have integrated their administrative and production systems world-wide.

An example: the motor-car industry

Car making, together with the goods and services associated with it – the production and refining of oil, the building of petrol stations, hotels and motels, and highway construction – have been at the heart of post-war Western development. The car industry directly employs about one in ten of all manufacturing workers in France and Japan, and one in twenty in Britain and the United States, and the related industries and services employ many millions more.

The industry is controlled by a small number of huge corporations, all of which are transnationals. In the early 1980s, twenty-two firms provided some 90 per cent of global car production (Tolliday and Zeitlin, 1986). The United States used to be the leading producer of cars in the world; in 1980 it was surpassed by Japan. Its share is now only 18 per cent, compared to the 25 per cent produced by Japanese manufacturers. Well over 50 per cent of the cars manufactured by Japanese companies are exported.

Car producers have pioneered the **vertical integration** of their companies and their subsidiaries, welding together a diversity of plants and companies operating in different areas of the world within a single administrative framework. The Ford company has the most extensive range of subsidiaries, organized on a collaborative basis. The production

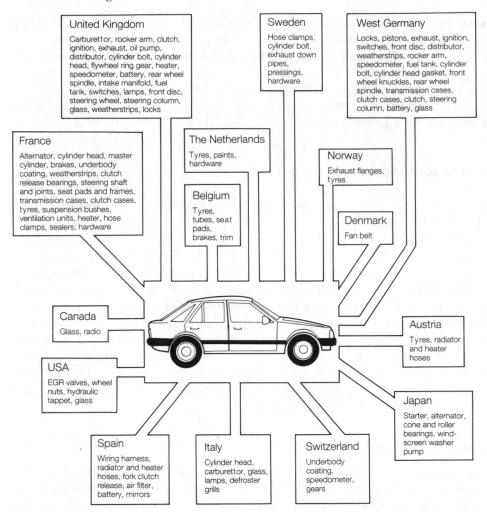

United Kingdom

Carburettor, rocker arm, clutch, ignition, exhaust, oil pump, distributor, cylinder bolt, cylinder head, flywheel ring gear, heater, speedometer, battery, rear wheel spindle, intake manifold, fuel tank, switches, lamps, front disc, steering wheel, steering column, glass, weatherstrips, locks

Sweden

Hose clamps, cylinder bolt, exhaust down pipes, pressings, hardware

West Germany

Locks, pistons, exhaust, ignition, switches, front disc, distributor, weatherstrips, rocker arm, speedometer, fuel tank, cylinder bolt, cylinder head gasket, front wheel knuckles, rear wheel spindle, transmission cases, clutch cases, clutch, steering column, battery, glass

France

Alternator, cylinder head, master cylinder, brakes, underbody coating, weatherstrips, clutch release bearings, steering shaft and joints, seat pads and frames, transmission cases, clutch cases, tyres, suspension bushes, ventilation units, heater, hose clamps, sealers, hardware

The Netherlands

Tyres, paints, hardware

Norway

Exhaust flanges, tyres

Belgium

Tyres, tubes, seat pads, brakes, trim

Denmark

Fan belt

Canada

Glass, radio

Austria

Tyres, radiator and heater hoses

USA

EGR valves, wheel nuts, hydraulic tappet, glass

Japan

Starter, alternator, cone and roller bearings, windscreen washer pump

Spain

Wiring harness, radiator and heater hoses, fork clutch release, air filter, battery, mirrors

Italy

Cylinder head, carburettor, glass, lamps, defroster grills

Switzerland

Underbody coating, speedometer, gears

Figure 22　Global manufacturing: the component network for the European model of the Ford Escort
Source: Peter Dicken, *Global Shift* (New York: Harper and Row, 1986), p. 304.

of the Ford Escort was designed to provide a car produced from parts made and assembled in numerous countries, and suitable for motoring on all continents. In Europe, the car is built of parts manufactured by Ford's subsidiaries in twelve European countries, Canada, the USA and Japan. Final assembly is carried out in Germany, Britain and Spain. It is not yet truly a 'world car', however, because the degree of integration between European and North American production is fairly low. The Escort in the United States and Canada is assembled primarily from parts made on the North American continent.

Like the Western companies, the Japanese car firms have integrated production systems stretching across different countries, centred mainly in the East. However, in the 1970s and 1980s they set up manufacturing plants in the United States and Europe, largely because many countries limit the numbers of Japanese cars that can be imported each year. Honda set up a plant in Ohio in 1982, followed by Nissan in Tennessee; Toyota, Mazda and Mitsubishi have subsequently opened plants in the United States. Toyota and Nissan have also set up assembly plants in Australia and Europe. Cars are now also produced in South Korea by the Hyundai Group, which is a large conglomerate company, that first began to build cars under licence from Ford. It has since developed its own models and has begun to capture a significant portion of the North American import market.

Current developments

Changes taking place in the car industry are part of a global process of the spatial reorganization of industry which is gaining pace. These have profound consequences for the Western countries (Morgan and Sayer, 1988). The overall proportion of manufacturing jobs in the world economy has gone up at a period when rates of unemployment have risen rapidly in many countries in the West. Job creation in manufacture, in other words, is proceeding in non-Western states (especially the newly industralizing countries) – either where the transnationals have set up production, or the local government has successfully promoted economic development, or a combination of the two.

Given the staggering economic success of Japan, the increasing prosperity of other, smaller Asian countries – and the possibility that rapid economic advancement might potentially be achieved by China – is the centre of global power shifting back to where it lay before the rise of Europe? Will Asia and the Pacific become the new 'core' of global social and economic relationships, and the USA and Europe become more marginal? This is a possibility, but there are other factors involved. Not all the major expansion is happening in the Far East. It is possible that some South American countries, notably Brazil, will rise to world prominence. Moreover, what happens over the next few decades will depend not only on economic changes, but also on political and military developments. The military and political strength of the United States and the Soviet Union is likely to set limits on the degree to which a fundamental 'Eastward shift' of world power will occur.

Non-state actors

It is not only in terms of the international division of labour and economic relationships that the world is becoming more interdependent. Since early this century – but again, particularly after the Second World War – the number of non-commercial organizations with an international role has been growing. Together with the transnational corporations, these are often referred to as **non-state actors**, because their activities are not bound to the policies of particular states or governments.

Several major types of non-state actor exist alongside the trans-nationals. First, there are organizations representing the international community of states, including especially the United Nations and its affiliated organizations (like UNESCO, the UN Educational, Scientific and Cultural Organization). Secondly, there are a great many organizations concerned with processes that demand international collabora-tion or communication, such as postal services, telecommunications, navigational regulations for shipping and so forth. Thirdly, there are organizations linking states or other economic enterprises with mutual international interests. The largest of such organizations is the EEC (European Economic Community). We shall look briefly at each of these types in turn.

The United Nations

After the First World War, there was widespread revulsion at the huge loss of life suffered. Political leaders were united in the view that war on such a scale must never be repeated (although, of course, their hopes turned out to be vain). To provide an organization that might stand above international squabbles, the League of Nations was set up shortly after the war. President Woodrow Wilson of the United States was a major figure in its planning and organization, seeing the League as a body that would help secure the future peace of the world and enhance international co-operation. In Wilson's words, 'we [i.e. nations] are all participants, whether we would or not, in the life of the world. The interests of all nations are our own also. We are partners with the rest . . . citizens of the world' (Scott, 1918, p. 270).

Wilson's vision was not realized. Some of the other political leaders involved saw the League more as a means of pursuing their own national interests than as a force transcending them. In addition, it did not include countries all over the world, but was made up mainly of those who had fought in the war. The Soviet Union was expressly excluded. In the end, after much debate, the United States did not join either, since the organization differed so much from that envisaged by Wilson. While the League was only a partially representative organization, and was unable to prevent another world war, it did become the focus of numerous new forms of international agency that still exist today. For example, it established its own health organization, concerned with documenting and checking the spread of infectious diseases throughout the world. This was later renamed the World Health Organization (WHO) when the League of Nations was replaced by the United Nations after the Second World War.

The United Nations has today come to include virtually all states in the world, but this process was not an uncomplicated one. The

American government at first tried to use the organization to advance its own political aims. For this and other reasons, in 1950 the Soviet Union withdrew to start a rival body, the Partisans of Peace. In the Russians' absence the Americans gained UN support for their military intervention in South Korea a short while later, which had been invaded from the Communist North. Alarmed by the prospect of the UN being used to further Western interests, the Russians returned to full participation.

Like the League of Nations before it, the United Nations has little chance of independently protecting or enhancing world peace. The only military forces it possesses are small and drawn from member states. Yet it has had a profound influence upon the world system, for example, because discussions carried on under its auspices led to the establishment of a large number of new Third World nations. In the mid-1950s, there was a mass admission to the UN of Asian and African post-colonial countries.

Even though it is not in any sense a form of 'world government', with a membership of over 150 countries the United Nations expresses the increasing integration of the world system. Of course, it also reflects the material and ideological conflicts which divide the global social order.

Other international organizations

Many organizations of the second type mentioned above (bodies concerned with international collaboration) are linked to the United Nations in one way or another. For instance, the Universal Postal and International Telecommunications Union existed before the foundation of the United Nations, but has since become connected to it. This organization establishes standard measures of payment for letters or packages sent across the world and messages passed through airborne communications systems, such as telephone calls beamed off satellites.

We tend to take much of the organization of the international order for granted, because the activities of such bodies are not very visible, but the standardization of many forms of global relationship is relatively recent. For example, in 1850 there were some 1,200 different postal rates operating in the various parts of Europe, and standardization of European postal charges was not fully accomplished until the turn of the present century. The co-ordination of world-wide postal systems took much longer (Luard, 1977, pp. 11–24). Many similar international organizations now exist, concerned with diverse aspects of the co-ordination of global activity. *The Year Book of International Organizations* listed 1,000 agencies in 1958. By 1972 this had grown to 2,190; the number today is over 4,000.

Trading networks

The EEC (often also called the Common Market) was set up shortly after the Second World War, consisting originally of six European countries. Membership has now expanded to twelve. It began as a first step towards the development of a European Federation, which some of the founders believed would eventually become a strong political union. There is, as part of the EEC, a European Parliament, but so far its powers have been relatively restricted. The EEC is basically an economic network, offering favourable conditions for trading and economic exchange between member countries.

Many similar **trading networks**, although smaller in size, have been formed in other areas of the world; the Soviet Union, for instance, set up the Council for Mutual Economic Assistance (COMECON), to facilitate trading relationships among the Eastern European societies. One of the most important international economic networks was established by the Organization of Petroleum Exporting Countries (OPEC). The control that OPEC established over world oil-supplies allowed its members to quadruple the price of oil in the early 1970s, causing shock-waves throughout most of the world economy. With the decline in demand for oil from the early 1980s onwards, its influence has declined, but various attempts have been made to set up similar organizations among producers of scarce goods. Organizations of this type, of course, are partial rather than world-wide. Yet they still express – and are at the same time a response to – the acceleration of globalizing influences.

The globalizing of media

If today we all live in 'one world', it is in large part a result of the international scope of the communications media. Anyone who switches on the television and watches 'the world news' usually gets just that: a presentation of some of the events which took place that day or shortly before in many different parts of the world. Television programmes and films are sold to large international markets; hundreds of millions of people watch such programmes and series. This process is part of the development of a **world information order** – an international system of the production, distribution and consumption of information. Like other aspects of global society, the new information order has developed unevenly and reflects divisions between the developed societies and Third World countries.

News

Flows of news are dominated by a small number of news agencies, which supply up-to-date information to newspapers, as well as to radio and TV stations, throughout the world. Reuters, a British agency, was one of the first in the field. In 1870, together with HAVAS, a French company, it divided up the globe into exclusive news territories. Reuters dealt with Britain, Holland and their imperial dependencies, which at that time stretched across large segments of Africa and Asia. HAVAS took France, Italy, Spain, Portugal and part of the Middle East. In 1876, Reuters agreed that HAVAS could have exclusive claim to South America, Reuters being given the whole of the Far East, except for what was then Indo-China but including Australasia. Both agencies exchanged news with the most prominent American agency, Associated Press (AP).

AP was thus at that time largely dependent on the two European agencies for material used by newspapers in the United States, but after the First World War, the leading American agencies began to compete with their European rivals in many parts of the world. The two largest agencies, AP and UPI (United Press International) still gain much of their revenue from newspapers, radio and television in the United States, but have become very influential in providing news material used internationally.

Together with Agence France-Presse, which has replaced HAVAS, Reuters, AP and UPI are responsible for most of the international news transmitted throughout the world, partly excluding the Soviet bloc. UPI, today the biggest of the four, has 6,400 clients in 114 countries and its releases are translated into 48 languages (Mattelart, 1979, p. 215). Information assembled by these agencies, once sent by Morse code, or telephone line, is now sent via computer and satellite links. Between them the four agencies send out 34 million words each day, claiming to provide nine-tenths of the total news output of the world's press, radio and television (Smith, 1980b, p. 73).

Another agency of world importance is TASS (the Telegraphic Agency of the Union of Soviet Socialist Republics). TASS provides virtually all the international news that reaches provincial newspapers and broadcasting stations in the Soviet Union. The major national newspapers and television also rely heavily on its services, although a few have their own offices overseas which directly supply them with material. When TASS was first set up, in 1925, it was given sole authority to distribute information about the Soviet government inside the country and abroad. TASS maintains offices in many parts of the world, although it is particularly well established in Eastern Europe (Hopkins, 1970). It is essentially an arm of the Soviet government, explicitly dedicated not only to reporting international news but to portraying the Soviet Union in a favourable light to the rest of the world. Information supplied by TASS is free to foreign clients, leading many Third World countries to make use of the agency.

Partly to counter the dominance of TASS, the Union of Journalists and Writers in the USSR established NOVOSTI in 1961. This agency has no direct links with either the Soviet Government or the Communist Party, although like all organizations in the Soviet Union it is subject to their general supervision. NOVOSTI has grown rapidly, publishing foreign-language magazines and newspapers as well as maintaining a large chain of foreign bureaux. These are linked through communication technologies as sophisticated as those possessed by the leading Western media organizations. Outside the Soviet Union, TASS and NOVOSTI have nothing like the global influence of the Western agencies. Western media use TASS and NOVOSTI as sources of official Soviet pronouncements, or for news events in the Soviet Union that Western agencies for one reason or another are unable to cover. However, the press and TV in Eastern Europe – especially in countries other than the Soviet Union itself – make extensive use of the Western agencies for international reporting.

Cinema, television, advertising and electronic communication

American sources are dominant in the production and distribution of television programmes, films, advertisements, and various forms of electronic communication.

Cinema

In the 1920s, when 'feature films' first saw the light of day, Hollywood made four-fifths of all films screened in the world, and the United States continues to be easily the largest influence in the cinema industry. The governments of many countries provide subsidies to aid their own film industries, but no other country rivals the United States as an exporter of feature films. In Britain, for instance, American films account for 40 per cent of all films shown each year in cinemas (Smith, 1981, p. 41). Most of the other countries which have a film export industry, such as Italy, Japan and West Germany, also import large quantities of American films. In South America the proportion is often over 50 per cent, and a similar ratio applies in many parts of Asia, Africa and the Middle East. In Thailand, as many as 90 per cent of all films shown per year are American.

Television

In television programmes, the British are an important global presence alongside American corporations. If feature films on television are excluded, earnings for British television exports are about the same as those for the USA. However, a far higher proportion of British programmes are sold to a single market – the United States itself – than in the case of American products, so the world-wide influence of American television programmes is in fact more considerable.

Advertising

Nine of the largest ten advertising firms in the world are North American. Half the major agencies in Canada, West Germany, France,

Britain and Australia are American; in many states in Asia, Africa and South America the largest agencies are either American or owned by US companies. The top ten advertising agencies are transnationals, some with a host of subsidiaries in other countries. The large advertising agencies, like McCann Erikson or Saatchi and Saatchi, are regularly employed by the giant transnational corporations to co-ordinate programmes of advertising put out simultaneously in many countries.

Electronic communication

American influence is strong over the electronic channels used to communicate much of the information upon which modern states and large corporations depend. Telecommunication links now essential to banking, world monetary transactions, and some kinds of TV and radio broadcasting, are mostly in American hands. International Business Machines (IBM), based in the United States, is one of the largest of all transnational corporations, and has enormous influence over international information flow, particularly in the supply of computer resources. It has been estimated that nine-tenths of all records held in databases throughout the world are accessible to the American government or other organizations in the United States (Schiller, 1978).

Media imperialism

The paramount position of the industrialized countries, above all the United States, in the production and diffusion of media has led many observers to speak of *media imperialism*. A cultural empire, it is argued, has been established. Third World countries are held to be especially vulnerable, because they lack resources with which to maintain their own cultural independence.

Herbert Schiller has claimed that control of global communications by United States firms has to be seen in relation to various factors. He argues that American TV and radio networks have fallen increasingly under the influence of the federal government and particularly the Defence Department. He points out that RCA, which owns the NCB television and radio networks, is also a leading defence sub-contractor to the Pentagon, the headquarters of the US armed forces. American television exports, coupled with advertising, propagate a commercialized culture which corrodes local forms of cultural expression. Even where governments prohibit commercial broadcasting within their borders, radio and television from surrounding countries can often be directly received (Schiller, 1969). Alan Wells has advanced a similar perspective, concentrating particularly on South America. In most Latin American countries, television has been run largely through North American finance and US-based companies, mostly alongside US advertising agencies (Wells, 1972).

Control of the world's news by the major Western agencies, it has been suggested, inevitably means the predominance of a 'First World' outlook in the information conveyed. Thus it has been claimed, for example, that attention is given to the Third World in news broadcasts mainly in times of disaster, crisis or military confrontation. The daily files of other types of news kept on the industrialized world are not maintained for Third World coverage (Tatarian, 1978).

Schiller and Wells perhaps overstate their case. The quantity of television and film exports coming from the United States, as a proportion of the world's total, has declined since a peak in the late 1960s. After studying the development of radio and television networks in ten Third World countries, Elihu Katz and his colleagues put forward the view that there are *phases of institutionalization* in the introduction of radio and television in the less developed societies. In the first phase, a model of broadcasting is adopted from elsewhere, usually from the United States, Britain or France, and serves as the basis for the fledgling system. During this period, the media are saturated by imported products. In the second phase, local production facilities are developed, and the system becomes more oriented towards the local society. In the third stage, governments tend to intervene to promote conditions in which the onslaught of Western influence can in some degree be resisted (Katz et al., 1978).

Yet it would be impossible to deny the prime role that Western media in general, and English-speaking countries and organizations in particular, play in the global production and diffusion of media. As in other areas of production, Third World societies are especially vulnerable. Some Third World leaders have pressed for controls on information production and flow which would create more equality in communications media. At a conference of nations not affiliated by treaty either to the United States or to the Soviet Union, a 'Non-aligned News Pool' was set up in the early 1970s. The eighty-five countries involved agreed to share information from their national news agencies, in order to encourage more informed or relevant news releases than those coming from Western and Soviet agencies. Its influence so far, however, has been limited. Many of the national agencies involved are hardly known for scrupulous or unbiased reporting of events in their homelands, and it has seemed to critics that some Third World governments try to control their own media internally, ensuring that the 'official' way of seeing things is maintained – while denouncing 'bias' from abroad (McPhail, 1987).

Some observers believe that world inequalities in telecommunications technology are likely to become even more pronounced in the future. In the words of a prominent media researcher, Anthony Smith,

> the threat to independence in the late twentieth century from the new electronics could be greater than was colonialism itself. We are beginning to learn that de-colonisation and the growth of supra-nationalism were not the termination of imperial relationships but merely the extending of

a geo-political web which has been spinning since the Renaissance. The new media have the power to penetrate more deeply into a 'receiving' culture than any previous manifestation of Western technology. The results could be immense havoc, an intensification of the social contradictions within developing societies today. In the West we have come to think of the 2,500 communications satellites which presently circle the earth as distributors of information. For many societies they may become pipettes through which the data which confers sovereignty upon a society is extracted for processing in some remote place. (Smith, 1980b, p. 176)

Conclusion

What will be the result of the processes described in this chapter? Is the whole globe likely at some future point to become a single political system, supervised by some form of world government? Certainly processes of globalization are among the most important social changes occurring at the current time, and sociological analysis that confines itself to the study of single societies is becoming increasingly archaic. Many of the fundamental problems which beset human life today, such as ecological issues or avoiding large-scale military confrontation, are necessarily global in scope.

Yet in spite of growing economic and cultural interdependence, the world global system is riven with inequalities, and divided up into a patchwork of states that have divergent as well as common concerns. There is no real indication of a political consensus which will overcome the conflicting interests of states in the near future. A world government may eventually come into being, but if this does happen it will be as a result of a long-term process of development. One of the most worrying features of world society today is that increasing globalization is not matched either by political integration or by the reduction of international inequalities of wealth and power. In many ways, the world is becoming more united, and some traditional sources of conflict between nations are disappearing (see chapter 11: 'War and the Military'). Yet the divisions between rich and poor societies are quite extreme, and could easily be the source of great international tensions. There is no central global agency which could effectively control these tensions, or enforce a world redistribution of wealth.

Summary

1   World society has become increasingly interdependent – a process known as *globalization*. The development of world social relations

involves large-scale inequalities between the industrialized and Third World societies. The largest disparities of wealth and living standards are those separating the rich industrialized countries from the poorer Third World states.

2   Most Third World societies are in areas of the world which underwent Western colonial rule. Many have only become independent states in the period since the Second World War. Although most Third World societies are impoverished compared to the industrialized nations, a minority (the NICs, or newly industrializing countries) have recently experienced rapid economic development.

3   Millions of people in the world each year die of hunger or diseases associated with malnutrition. Yet, even with rapid population growth, sufficient food is produced to feed everyone in the world. Large amounts of food are destroyed or stored indefinitely by the Western countries, even though people in other parts of the world are starving. The level of regular food aid provided by the rich to the poor countries is low.

4   The distribution of the world's food supplies is strongly influenced by the impact of agribusiness – the industrial production, processing and storage of food. Agribusiness firms operating in Third World countries are geared to export for Western markets rather than stimulating local agriculture.

5   Three types of theoretical thinking have contributed to our under-standing of the developments leading to global inequalities. Theories of *imperialism* and *neo-imperialism* see the forces behind such devel-opments as economic pressures towards the external expansion of industrial enterprise. *Dependency theories* emphasize the ability of the industrialized countries to dominate the terms of their relationships with Third World states. *World system theory* describes a centralized world economy linking *core* countries, the *semi-periphery*, the *periphery*, and the *external arena*.

6   A significant feature of the process of world development is the growth of *transnationals* – companies operating in two or more countries *across* national boundaries. Countries in the world economy have become interdependent largely as a result of the activities of the transnationals.

7   The invention of telecommunications technologies permits more or less instantaneous communication from one part of the world to the other. Advances made in transport have also facilitated a frequent and rapid exchange of goods from country to country. *Non-state actors* – organi-zations concerned with processes demanding international collaboration or communication – have emerged to help cope with these trends.

8   The sense today of inhabiting *one world* is in large part a result of the international scope of media of communication. TV news programmes provide a mosaic of international images. A world information order – an international system of the production, distribution and consumption of informational goods – has come into being. Given the paramount position of the industrial countries in the world information order,

many believe that the Third World countries are subject to a new form of *media imperialism*.

Basic concepts

globalization   world system
imperialism

Important terms

Third World	external arena
cash-crop production	transnational companies
concession companies	conglomerates
newly industrializing countries	ethnocentric transnationals
gross national product (GNP)	polycentric transnationals
agribusiness	geocentric transnationals
neo-imperialism	international division of labour
dependency theory	vertical integration
core	non-state actors
world system theory	trading networks
semi-periphery	world information order
periphery	

Further reading

H. Bull et al. (eds), *Expansion of International Society* (Oxford: Oxford University Press, 1986) — examines the expansion of the international society of European States across the rest of the globe.

Charles F. Doran et al. (eds), *North/South Relations: Studies of Dependency Reversal* (New York: Praeger, 1983) — develops the view that dependency is a two-way process and examines the possibilities of dependency reversal from a global perspective.

Susan George, *How the Other Half Dies: The Real Reasons for World Hunger* (Harmondsworth: Penguin, 1976) — an analysis of the role of agribusiness in Third World starvation.

Ankie M. M. Hoogvelt, *The Third World in Global Development* (London: Macmillan, 1982) — this book discusses the differentiation of Third World development, changes in the world's financial markets and internationalization of production. It looks at a number of theoretical frameworks which could help to explain these phenomena.

Charles P. Kindleberger et al. (eds), *The Multinational Corporation in the 1980s* (Cambridge, Mass.: MIT Press, 1983) — a collection of essays discussing current research on the theory, and selected case studies, of the multinational corporation.

P. Worsley, *The Three Worlds – Culture and World Development* (London: Weidenfeld and Nicolson, 1984) — a study of cultural, political and economic aspects of Third World development.

17

Modern Urbanism

The traditional city

Cities in traditional societies were mostly very small by modern standards. Babylon, for example, one of the largest ancient Near-eastern cities, only extended over an area of 3.2 square miles – and probably at its height had a population of no more than fifteen or twenty thousand people. The world's first cities appeared in about 3500 BC, in the river valleys of the Nile in Egypt, the Tigris-Euphrates in what is now Iraq, and the Indus in what is today Pakistan. Rome under Emperor Augustus was easily the largest ancient city outside China, having some 300,000 inhabitants.

Certain common features have been found in most cities of the ancient world, despite the variety of their civilizations. Cities were usually walled; the walls, primarily for military defence, emphasized the separation of the urban community from the countryside. The central area, often including a large public space, was sometimes enclosed within a second, inner wall. Although it usually contained a market, the centre was quite different from the business districts found at the core of modern cities. The main buildings were nearly always religious and political, such as temples and palaces or courts (Sjoberg, 1960, 1963; Cox, 1964; Wheatley, 1971). The dwellings of the ruling class or elite tended to be concentrated in or near the centre, while the less privileged lived towards the edges of the city, with some living outside the walls but able quickly to get within them if they came under attack.

Different ethnic and religious groups were often allocated to separate neighbourhoods, where their members would both live and work. Sometimes these neighbourhoods were also surrounded by walls. The central square, in which ceremonial gatherings took place, was usually too small to hold more than a minority of the citizens, and communication between the city-dwellers was usually erratic; public pronouncements might be made by officials shouting at the tops of their voices. Although a few traditional cities had large thoroughfares, in most there were few 'streets' in the modern sense; paths were usually strips of land on which no one had yet built. For most people, the home and workshop were part of the same building, sometimes even the same room. The 'journey to work' was more or less unknown.

In a few traditional states sophisticated road systems linked the cities, but these existed mainly for military purposes, and communication for the most part was slow and limited in nature. Travel was largely a specialized affair, merchants and soldiers being the only people who regularly travelled any distance. Cities were the main focus of science, the arts and cosmopolitan culture in traditional states, but their level of influence over the rural areas was always relatively low. No more than a tiny proportion of the population lived in the cities, and the division between cities and countryside was pronounced. By far the majority of people lived in small rural communities, rarely if ever coming into contact with more than the odd state official or merchant from the towns.

In studying modern cities in this chapter, we shall be analysing some of the most basic changes which separate our world from the traditional one. For in all industrialized countries most of the population lives in urban areas. Moreover, modern urban life affects everyone, not only those who live in cities themselves. We shall first study the vast growth in the number of city-dwellers that has occurred over the past century and analyse some of the main theories of urbanism, before going on to compare different patterns of **urbanization,** contrasting Britain, the United States, Eastern Europe, and Third World cities.

Features of modern urbanism

All modern industrial societies are very heavily urbanized. The most populous cities in the industrialized countries include up to twenty million inhabitants, and urban **conurbations** – clusters of cities making large built-up areas – may include much larger numbers. The most extreme form of urban life today is represented by what some have called the **megalopolis**, the 'city of cities'. The term was originally coined in ancient Greece to refer to a city-state that was planned to be the envy of all civilizations, but in current usage it bears little relation to that dream. It was first used in modern times to refer to the north-eastern seaboard of the United States, a conurbation covering some 450 miles from north of Boston to below Washington DC. In this region about forty million people live at a density of over 700 persons per square mile. An urban population almost as large and dense is concentrated in the Great Lakes area of the United States and Canada.

Britain, the first society to undergo industrialization, was also the earliest to move from being a rural to a predominantly urban country. In 1800, well under 20 per cent of the population lived in towns or cities of more than 10,000 inhabitants. By 1900, this proportion had become 74 per cent. The capital city, London, was home to about 1.1 million people in 1800; it increased in size to a population of over 7 million by the start of the twentieth century. London was then by far the largest city ever seen in the world, a vast manufacturing, commercial and financial centre at the heart of a still-expanding British empire.

The urbanization of most other European countries and the United States took place somewhat later – but in some cases, once under way, accelerated even faster. In 1800, the United States was a more rural society than the leading European countries at the same date. Less than 10 per cent of the population lived in communities with populations of more than 2,500 people. Today, well over three-quarters of Americans do so. Between 1800 and 1900, the population of New York leapt from 60,000 people to 4.8 million!

Urbanization in the twentieth century is a global process, into which the Third World is increasingly being drawn. Before 1900 nearly all the growth in cities was in the West: there was some expansion in Third World cities over the following fifty years, but the main period of their growth has been over the last forty years or so. Overall, urban populations are growing much faster than the world's overall population: 39 per cent of the world's population lived in urban localities in 1975; the figure is predicted to be 50 per cent in 2000, and 63 per cent in 2025, according to United Nations estimates. East and South Asia will contain about half of the world's population in 2025, and by that date the urban populations of Africa and South America will each exceed that of Europe.

The development of modern cities: consciousness and culture

Only at the turn of the twentieth century did statisticians and social observers begin to distinguish between the town and the city. Cities with large populations were recognized to be usually more cosmopolitan than smaller centres, with their influence extending beyond the national society of which they were a part.

The expansion of cities came about as a result of population increase, plus the migration of outsiders from farms, villages and small towns. This migration was often international, with people moving from peasant backgrounds directly into cities in the countries to which they came. The immigration of very large numbers of Europeans from poor, farming backgrounds into the United States is the most obvious example.

Cross-national immigration into cities was also widespread between countries in Europe itself. Peasants and villagers migrated to the towns (as they are doing on a massive scale in Third World countries today) because of lack of opportunities in the rural areas, coupled with the apparent advantages and attractions of cities, where the streets were 'paved with gold' (jobs, wealth, a wide range of goods and services). Cities, moreover, became concentrated centres of financial and industrial power, entrepreneurs sometimes creating new urban areas almost from scratch. Chicago grew to a population of well over two million by 1900, in an area which was almost completely uninhabited until the 1830s.

The development of modern cities has had an enormous impact, not only on habits and modes of behaviour, but on patterns of thought and feeling (Lees, 1985). From the beginning of large urban agglomerations, in the eighteenth century, views about the effects of cities on social life have been polarized – and remain so today. Some saw cities as representing 'civilized virtue', the fount of dynamism and cultural creativity (Schorske, 1963). For these authors, cities maximize opportunities for economic and cultural development, and provide the means of living a comfortable and satisfying existence. James Boswell frequently praised the virtues of London, which he compared to a 'museum, a garden, to endless musical combinations' (Byrd, 1978, p. 92). Others branded the city as a smoking inferno thronged with aggressive and mutually distrustful crowds, riddled with crime, violence and corruption.

Interpretations of city life

During the nineteenth and early twentieth centuries, as cities mushroomed in size, these contrasting views found new forms of expression. Critics found easy targets for their attacks, as the living conditions of the poor in the most rapidly developing urban areas were frequently appalling. George Gissing, an English novelist and social analyst, personally experienced extreme poverty in both London and Chicago in the 1870s. His descriptions of the East End of London, the poorest sections of the city, convey a grim picture. Gissing portrayed the area as:

a region of malodorous market streets, of factories, timberyards, grimy warehouses, of alleys swarming with small trades and crafts, of filthy courts and passages leading into pestilential gloom; everywhere toil in its most degrading forms; the thoroughfares thundering with high-laden waggons, the pavements trodden by working folk of the coarsest type, the corners and lurking-holes showing destitution at its ugliest. (Gissing, 1973, pp. 25–6)

At this time, poverty in American cities received less attention than European poverty. Towards the end of the century, however, reformers began increasingly to condemn the squalor of large parts of New York, Boston, Chicago and other major cities. A Danish immigrant, Jacob Riis, who became a reporter for the *New York Tribune*, travelled extensively across the United States, documenting conditions of poverty, and lecturing about needed reforms. Riis's book, *How the Other Half Lives*, which appeared in 1890, reached a wide audience (Riis, 1957; Lane, 1974). Others added their voices to his. As one poet put it, speaking of the Boston poor:

In a great, Christian city, died friendless, of hunger!
Starved to death, where there's many a bright banquet hall!
In a city of hospitals, died in a prison!
Homeless, died in a land that boasts free homes for all!
In a city of millionaires, died without money!

(Quoted in Lees, 1985, pp. 128–9)

The extent of urban poverty, and the vast differences between city neighbourhoods, were among the main factors prompting early sociological analyses of urban life. Unsurprisingly, the first major sociological studies of, and theories about, modern urban conditions originated in Chicago – a city marked by a phenomenal rate of development, and by very pronounced inequalities.

Theories of urbanism

The Chicago School

A number of writers associated with the University of Chicago from the 1920s to the 1940s, especially Robert Park, Ernest Burgess and Louis Wirth, developed ideas which were for many years the chief basis of theory and research in urban sociology. Two concepts developed by the 'Chicago School' are worthy of special attention. One is the so-called **ecological approach** to urban analysis, the other the characterization of **urbanism** as a *way of life*, developed by Wirth (Park, 1952; Wirth, 1938; McKenzie, 1933).

Urban ecology

Ecology is a term taken from a physical science: the study of the adaptation of plant and animal organisms to their environment. In the natural world, organisms tend to be distributed in systematic ways over the terrain, such that a balance or equilibrium between different species is achieved. The Chicago School believed that the siting of major urban settlements, and the distribution of different types of neighbourhoods within them, can be understood in terms of similar principles. Cities do not grow up at random, but in response to advantageous features of the environment. For example, large urban areas in modern societies tend to develop along the shores of rivers, in fertile plains or at the intersection of trading routes or railways.

'Once set up', in Park's words, 'a city is, it seems, a great sorting mechanism which . . . infallibly selects out of the population as a whole the individuals best suited to live in a particular region or a particular milieu' (Park, 1952, p. 79). Cities become ordered into 'natural areas', through processes of competition, invasion and succession – all of which occur in biological ecology. If we look at the ecology of a lake in the natural environment, we find that competition between various species of fish, insects and other organisms operates to reach a fairly stable distribution between them. This balance is disturbed if new species 'invade' – try to make the lake their home. Some of the organisms which used to proliferate in the central area of the lake are driven out to suffer a more precarious existence around its fringes. The invading species are their successors in the central sections.

Patterns of location, movement and relocation in cities, according to the ecological view, have a similar form. Different neighbourhoods develop through the adjustments made by inhabitants as they struggle to gain their livelihoods. A city can be pictured as a map of areas with distinct and contrasting social characteristics. In the initial stages of the growth of modern cities, industries congregate at sites suitable for the raw materials they need, close to supply-lines. Population clusters around these workplaces, which, as the number of the city's inhabitants grows, come to be more and more diversified. The amenities thus developed become correspondingly more attractive, and greater **competition** develops for their acquisition. Land values and property taxes rise, making it difficult for families to carry on living in the central neighbourhood, except in cramped conditions or in decaying housing in which rents are low. The centre becomes dominated by businesses and entertainment, with the more affluent private residents moving out to newly forming suburbs around the perimeter. This process follows transport routes, since these minimize the time taken in travelling to work; the areas between these routes develop more slowly.

Cities can be seen as formed in concentric rings, broken up into segments. In the centre are the **inner-city** areas, a mixture of big business prosperity and decaying private houses. Beyond these are older-established neighbourhoods, housing stably employed lower-class workers. Further out still are the suburbs in which higher income groups tend to live. Processes of **invasion** and **succession** occur within the segments of the concentric rings. Thus as property decays in a central or near-central area, ethnic minority groups might start to move into it. As they do so, more of the pre-existing population start to leave, precipitating a wholesale flight to neighbourhoods elsewhere in the city, or out to the suburbs.

Although for a period the **urban ecology** approach fell into disrepute, it was later revived and elaborated in the writings of a number of authors, particularly Amos Hawley (Hawley, 1950, 1968). Rather than concentrating on competition for scarce resources, as his predecessors did, Hawley emphasizes the *interdependence* of different city areas. *Differentiation* – the specialization of groups and occupational roles – is the main way in which human beings adapt to their environment. Groups on which many others depend will have a dominant role, often reflected in their central geographical position. Business groups, for example, like large banks or insurance companies, provide key services for many in a community, and hence are usually to be found in the central areas of settlements. But the zones which develop in urban areas, Hawley points out, arise from relationships not just of space, but of time. Business dominance, for example, is expressed not only in patterns of land-use, but in the rhythm of activities in daily life – an illustration being the rush hour. The ordering in time of people's daily lives reflects the hierarchy of neighbourhoods in the city.

The ecological approach has been as important for the amount of empirical research it has helped to promote as for its value as a theoretical perspective. Many studies of cities as a whole, and of particular neighbourhoods, have been prompted by ecological thinking – concerned, for example, with the processes of 'invasion' and 'succession' just mentioned. However, various criticisms can justifiably be made. The ecological perspective tends to under-emphasize the importance of conscious design and planning in city organization, regarding urban development as a 'natural' process. The models of spatial organization developed by Park, Burgess and their colleagues were drawn from American experience, and only fit some types of city in the United States, let alone many cities in Europe, Japan, Eastern Europe or the Third World.

Urbanism as a way of life

Wirth's thesis of urbanism as a *way of life* is concerned less with the internal differentiation of cities than with what urbanism *is* as a form of social existence. Wirth observes:

> the degree to which the contemporary world may be said to be 'urban' is not fully or accurately measured by the proportion of the total population living in cities. The influences which cities exert on the social life of man are greater than the ratio of the urban population would indicate; for the city is not only increasingly the dwelling-place

and the workshop of modern man, but it is the initiating and controlling
centre of economic, political and cultural life that has drawn the most
remote communities of the world into its orbit and woven diverse areas,
peoples and activities into a cosmos. (Wirth, 1938, p. 342)

In cities, Wirth points out, large numbers of people live in close
proximity to one another, without knowing most others personally
– a fundamental contrast to small, traditional villages. Most contacts
between city-dwellers are fleeting and partial, and are means to
other ends rather than being satisfying relationships in themselves.
Interactions with sales clerks in shops, cashiers in banks, passengers
or ticket-collectors on trains, are passing encounters, entered into not
for their own sake but as means to other aims.

Since those who live in urban areas tend to be highly mobile,
there are relatively weak bonds between them. People are involved
in many different activities and situations each day – the 'pace of
life' is faster than in rural areas. Competition prevails over co-operation.
Wirth accepts that the density of social life in cities leads to the
formation of neighbourhoods having distinct characteristics, some
of which may preserve the characteristics of small communities.
In immigrant areas, for example, traditional types of connections
between families are found, with most people knowing most others
on a personal basis. The more such areas are absorbed into wider
patterns of city life, however, the less these characteristics survive.

Wirth's ideas have deservedly enjoyed wide currency. There are any
number of examples of the impersonality of cities and the lack of involvement of their residents with one another. One is the infamous case of
the murder of Katherine Genovese on 13 March 1964 in New York City.
Genovese was returning to her apartment late at night in an affluent,
tree-lined section of Queens, an area quite close to Manhattan. She was
attacked on three separate occasions on her journey. The third assault,
which happened in the hallway of her building, proved fatal. The impersonality of city life is shown in the apparent apathy of the onlookers. A
total of thirty-eight respectable citizens witnessed the attacks, but not a
single person either came to Genovese's help or even called the police.
A newspaper editorial declared that 'The city has robbed Katherine
Genovese of friends' (Latane and Darley, 1970). But she certainly had
friends. Where were they when she needed them? Given the far-flung
nature of big-city life, they were no doubt in their homes elsewhere
– in Manhattan, Long Island or Brooklyn – and ignorant of her plight.

The impersonality of many day-to-day contacts in modern cities
is undeniable – and to some degree this is true of social life in general in
modern societies. Wirth's theory is important for its recognition that
urbanism is not just *part* of a society, but expresses and influences the
nature of the wider social system. Aspects of the urban way of life are
characteristic of social life in modern societies as a whole, not just the
activities of those who happen to live in big cities. Yet Wirth's ideas also

have marked limitations. Like the ecological perspective, with which it has much in common, Wirth's theory is based mainly on observations of American cities, yet generalized to urbanism everywhere. Urbanism is not the same at all times and places. As has been mentioned, for example, ancient cities were in many respects quite different from those found in modern societies. Life for most people in the early cities was not much more anonymous or impersonal than for those living in village communities.

Wirth also exaggerates the impersonality of modern cities. Communities involving close friendship or kinship links are more persistent within modern urban communities than he supposed. Everett Hughes, a colleague of Wirth's at the University of Chicago, wrote of his associate: 'Louis used to say all those things about how the city is impersonal – while living with a whole clan of kin and friends on a very personal basis' (quoted in Kasarda and Janowitz, 1974). Groups such as those Herbert Gans calls 'the urban villagers' are common in modern cities (Gans, 1962). His 'urban villagers' are Italian Americans living in an inner-city Boston neighbourhood. Such 'white ethnic' areas are probably becoming less significant in American cities than was once the case, but they are being replaced by inner-city communities involving newer immigrants.

More importantly, neighbourhoods involving close kinship and personal ties seem often to be actively *created* by city life; they are not just remnants of a pre-existing way of life which survive for a period within the city.

Claude Fischer has put forward an interpretation of why large-scale urbanism tends actually to promote diverse sub-cultures, rather than swamp everyone within an anonymous mass. Those who live in cities, he points out, are able to collaborate with others of like background or interests to develop local connections; and they can join distinctive religious, ethnic, political and other sub-cultural groups. A small town or village does not allow the development of such sub-cultural diversity (Fischer, 1975, 1984). Those who form ethnic communities within cities, for instance, might have little or no knowledge of one another in their land of origin. When they arrive, they gravitate to areas in which others from a similar linguistic and cultural background are living, and new sub-community structures are formed. An artist might find few others in a village or small town with whom to associate, but in a large city, on the other hand, he or she might become part of a significant artistic and intellectual sub-culture.

Other studies show that characteristics which Wirth regarded as urban are frequently found in small towns or villages. Peter Mann compared a small rural community in Sussex, in Southern England, with Huddersfield in the North. The village is on fast rail and road routes to London, and many of its inhabitants are commuters. They are more sophisticated and cosmopolitan than most of the inhabitants of the northern city, which is much further from London. There are probably more personal kinship ties between those living in various areas of Huddersfield than is the case among the residents of the Sussex village (Mann, 1965, pp. 105–7). Of course, it could be argued that the village represents a part of urban culture, its older, personal links having been destroyed by an influx of people whose lives are centred on the city. If this is so, it could be that *change* is the depersonalizing agent, rather than the existence of modern cities themselves.

A large city is a 'world of strangers', yet supports and creates personal relationships. This is not paradoxical. We have to separate urban experience into the public sphere of encounters with strangers, and the more private world of family, friends and work colleagues. It may be difficult to 'meet people' when one first moves to a large city. But anyone moving to a small, established rural community may find the friendliness of the inhabitants largely a matter of public politeness – it may take years to become 'accepted'. This is not the case in the city. As Edward Krupat has commented:

> The urban egg . . . has a harder shell to crack. Lacking the occasion and circumstances for making an entrée, many persons who see each other day after day at a bus or railroad station, in a cafeteria or passing in the hallways at work, never become anything more than 'familiar strangers'. Also, some people may remain totally on the outside because they lack social skills or initiative. Yet the overwhelming evidence is that because of the diversity of strangers – each one is a *potential friend* – and the wide range of lifestyles and interests in the city, people do move from the outside in. And once they are on the inside of one group or network, the possibilities for expanding their connections multiply greatly. As a result, the evidence indicates that the positive opportunities in the city often seem to outweigh the constraining forces, allowing people to develop and maintain satisfying relationships. (Krupat, 1985, p. 36)

Wirth's ideas retain some validity, but in the light of subsequent contributions it is clear that they are over-generalized. Modern cities frequently involve impersonal, anonymous social relationships, but they are also sources of diversity – and, sometimes, intimacy.

Urbanism and the created environment

Recent theories of urbanism have stressed that urbanism is not an autonomous process, but has to be analysed in relation to major patterns of political and economic change. The two leading writers in urban analysis today, David Harvey and Manuel Castells, have both been strongly influenced by Marx (Harvey, 1973, 1982, 1985; Castells, 1977, 1983).

Harvey: the restructuring of space

Urbanism, Harvey emphasizes, is one aspect of **the created environment** brought about by the spread of industrial capitalism. In traditional societies, city and countryside were clearly differentiated. In the modern world, industry blurs the division between city and countryside. Agriculture becomes mechanized and run simply according to considerations of price and profit, just like industrial work, and this process lessens the differences in modes of social life between urban and rural people.

In modern urbanism, Harvey points out, space is continually *restructured*. The process is determined by where large firms choose to place their factories, research and development centres and so forth; the controls which governments operate over both land and industrial production; and the activities of private investors, buying and selling houses and land. Business firms, for example, are constantly weighing up the relative advantages of new locations against existing ones. As production becomes cheaper in one area than another, or as the firm moves from one product to another, offices and factories will be closed down in one place and opened up elsewhere. Thus at one period, when there are considerable profits to be made, there may be a spate of office-block building in the centre of large cities. Once the offices have been built, and the central area 'redeveloped', investors look for potential for further speculative building elsewhere. Often what is profitable in one period will not be so in another, when the financial climate changes.

The activities of private home-buyers are strongly influenced by how far, and where, business interests buy up land, as well as by rates of loans and taxes fixed by local and central government. After the Second World War, for instance, there was vast expansion of suburban development in major cities in the United States. This was partly due to ethnic discrimination and the tendency of whites to move away from inner-city areas. However, it was only made possible, Harvey argues, because of government decisions to provide tax concessions to home-buyers and construction firms, and by the setting up of special credit arrangements by financial organizations. These provided the basis for the building and buying of new homes on the peripheries of cities, and at the same time promoted demand for industrial products such as the motor-car. The growth in size and prosperity of towns and cities in the South of England since the 1960s is directly connected to the decline of older industries in the North, and the consequent movement of investment to new industrial opportunities (Massey, 1984).

Castells: urbanism and social movements

Like Harvey, Castells stresses that the spatial form of a society is closely linked to the overall mechanisms of its development. To understand cities, we have to grasp the processes whereby spatial forms are created and transformed. The lay-outs and architectural features of cities and neighbourhoods express struggles and conflicts between

different groups in society. In other words, urban environments represent symbolic and spatial manifestations of broader social forces. For
example, skyscrapers may be built because they are expected to provide
profit, but the giant buildings also 'symbolise the power of money over
the city through technology and self-confidence and are the cathedrals
of the period of rising corporate capitalism' (Castells, 1983, p. 103).

In contrast to the Chicago sociologists, Castells sees the city not
only as a distinct *location* – the urban area – but as an integral
part of processes of **collective consumption**, which in turn are an
inherent aspect of industrial capitalism. Homes, schools, transport
services and leisure amenities are ways in which people 'consume'
the products of modern industry. The taxation system influences
who is able to buy or rent where, and who builds where. Large
corporations, banks and insurance companies, which provide capital
for building projects, have a great deal of power over these processes.
But government agencies also directly affect many aspects of city
life, by building roads and public housing, planning green belts and
so forth (Lowe, 1986). The physical shape of cities is thus a product
of both market forces and the power of government.

But the nature of the created environment is not just the result
of the activities of wealthy and powerful people. Castells stresses
the importance of the struggles of under-privileged groups to alter
their living conditions. Urban problems stimulate a range of social
movements, concerned with improving housing conditions, protesting
against air pollution, defending parks and green belts, and combating
building development that changes the nature of an area. For example,
Castells has studied the gay movement in San Francisco, which
succeeded in restructuring neighbourhoods around its own cultural
values – allowing many gay organizations, clubs and bars to flourish
– and gained a prominent position in local politics.

Cities, Harvey and Castells both emphasize, are almost wholly
artificial environments, constructed by ourselves. Even most rural
areas do not escape the influence of human intervention and modern
technology, for human activity has reshaped and reordered the world of
nature. Food is not produced for local inhabitants, but for national and
international markets, and in mechanized farming, land is rigorously
sub-divided and specialized in its use, ordered into physical patterns
which have little relationship to natural features of the environment.
Those who live on farms and in isolated rural areas are economically,
politically and culturally tied to the larger society, however different
some of their modes of behaviour may be from those of city-dwellers.

Evaluation

The views of Harvey and Castells have been widely debated (Pahl,
1977; Pickvance, 1985; Saunders, 1986), and their work has been important

in redirecting urban analysis. In contrast to the ecologists' approach, it places emphasis, not upon 'natural' spatial processes, but upon how land and the created environment reflect social and economic systems of power. This marks a significant shift of emphasis. Yet the ideas of Harvey and Castells are often stated in a highly abstract way, and have not stimulated such a large variety of research studies as did the work of the Chicago School.

In some ways, the views set out by Harvey and Castells and those of the Chicago School usefully complement each other, and can be combined to give a comprehensive picture of urban processes. The contrasts between city areas described in urban ecology do exist, as does the overall impersonality of city life. But these are more variable than the members of the Chicago School believed, and are primarily governed by the social and economic influences analysed by Harvey and Castells (Micklin and Choldin, 1984). John Logan and Harvey Molotch have suggested an approach that directly connects the perspectives of authors like Harvey and Castells with some features of the ecological standpoint (Logan and Molotch, 1987). They agree with Harvey and Castells that broad features of economic development, stretching nationally and internationally, affect urban life in a quite direct way. But these wide-ranging economic factors, they argue, are focused through local organizations, including neighbourhood businesses, banks and government agencies, together with the activities of individual housebuyers.

Places – land and buildings – are bought and sold, according to Logan and Molotch, just like other goods in modern societies, but the markets which structure city environments are influenced by how different groups of people want to *use* property they buy and sell. Many tensions and conflicts arise as a result of this process – and these are the key factors structuring city neighbourhoods. For instance, an apartment block is seen as a 'home' for its residents, but as a 'source of rent' by its landlord. Businesses are most interested in buying and selling property in an area to find the best production sites, or to make profits in land speculation. Their interests and concerns are quite different from residents, for whom the neighbourhood is a 'place to live'.

In modern cities, Logan and Molotch point out, large financial and business firms continually try to intensify land use in specific areas. The more they can do so, the more there are opportunities for land speculation and for the profitable construction of new buildings. These companies have little concern with the social and physical effects of their activities on a given neighbourhood – whether or not, for example, attractive older residences are destroyed to make room for large new office blocks. The growth processes fostered by big firms involved in property development often go against the interests of local businesses or residents, who may attempt actively to resist them. People come together in neighbourhood groups in order to defend their interests as residents. Such local associations may campaign for the extension of zoning restrictions, block new building in green belt areas or on parkland, or press for more favourable rent regulations.

Post-war patterns of Western urban development

Far more research on urban processes has been carried out in the United States than in Britain, but generally patterns of urban development in the UK in the post-war period have mirrored those that occurred somewhat earlier in the USA. We shall therefore look at the American experience before discussing urban problems and issues in the UK.

Urbanism in the United States

Suburbanization

One of the clearest developments in US cities since the war has been the expansion of *suburbia*. The word 'suburb' has its origins in the Latin term *sub urbe*, meaning 'under city control'. Throughout most of the history of urbanism, this meaning of the term was an appropriate one. Suburbs were small pockets of dwellings dependent on urban centres for their amenities and livelihood. In current times, the word has come to be used to refer to any built-up area adjoining a large city.

In the United States, the process of **suburbanization** reached its peak in the 1950s and 1960s. Central cities during those decades had a 10 per cent growth rate, while that of the suburban areas was 48 per cent. Most of the movement to the suburbs involved white families. The enforcement of racial mixing in schools contributed to the decamping of whites from inner-city areas, many of whom wished to put their children in all-white schools. Of course, there were other reasons too. People moved to escape the pollution, congestion and higher crime-rates of the central city areas; they were also attracted by lower property taxes and the prospect of more spacious houses, or having homes with gardens rather than apartments. At the same time, an extensive road-building programme made previously far-flung areas more accessible to places of work, and led to the establishment of industries and services in suburban areas themselves. Many suburban areas became themselves essentially separate cities, connected by rapid highways to others around them. From the 1960s onwards the proportion of those commuting between suburbs increased faster than those commuting to cities (a pattern found today in the UK).

Inner-city decay

The inner-city decay which has marked all large American cities over the past few decades is a direct consequence of the growth of the suburbs. (This is also a phenomenon emerging clearly in Britain.) The movement of high-income groups away from the city means a loss of their local tax revenues. Since those that remain, or replace them, include many living in poverty, there is little scope for replacing that lost income. If rates are raised in the central city, wealthier groups and businesses tend to move further out.

This situation is worsened by the fact that the building stock in central cities becomes more run-down than in the suburbs, crime rates rise, and there is higher unemployment. More therefore must be spent upon welfare services, schools, the upkeep of buildings, police and fire services. A cycle of deterioration develops, in which the more suburbia expands, the greater become the problems of the city centres. In many American urban areas, the effect has been horrifying – particularly in the older cities, such as New York, Boston or Washington DC. In some neighbourhoods in these cities, the deterioration of property is probably worse than in large urban areas anywhere else in the industrialized world. Decaying tenement blocks and boarded-up and burnt-out buildings alternate with empty areas of land covered in rubble.

Financial crises

In the 1970s and early 1980s several cities in the United States came close to bankruptcy, and virtually all were compelled to cut back many of their services. The city of Cleveland defaulted on its debts in 1979, unable to pay off debts equivalent to about a fifth of its annual budget, and Chicago and San Francisco have also faced deficits of many millions of dollars which they were unable to pay. But the most well-known recent crisis affected New York.

In common with most other older industrial cities, New York has suffered a major decline in manufacturing jobs since the Second World War. Expansion in finance and insurance was not sufficient to compensate for this; the net result was a steady decline in the city's revenue. From the 1950s onwards, New York also attracted large numbers of blacks, Puerto Ricans and other low-income groups. Between 1950 and 1970, when poverty rates were declining in the United States as a whole, the number of people living below the poverty line in New York increased from a third to a half of the city's population. By 1974, the city had accumulated debts of 1.2 billion dollars. There was a general economic downturn in 1974 and 1975, and the banks refused to extend their loans to the city, while Congress and the state legislature reduced their assistance.

New York City avoided bankruptcy only when the city government made major cuts in expenditure. Some 50,000 public jobs were eliminated and the municipal payroll cut by nearly 20 per cent. Schools, sanitation services, police and fire departments were all drastically affected. Some social welfare programmes were more or less completely abandoned. On the other hand, new tax benefits were given to businesses. The policies pursued since 1975 have been called a 'tale of two cities' by critics. Manhattan has experienced a boom in office and hotel construction, attracting large-scale new capital investment. The majority of the urban population, on the other hand, is made up of low-income residents whose needs have been largely ignored by policy-makers (Tabb, 1982).

New York today has a huge population of homeless people. They are visible even to a casual traveller through the city, not only occupying park benches for the night, but making homes of bus and train stations and even airports. Official shelters have been opened in various neighbourhoods, but many of the homeless reject them as being run in as authoritarian a way as prisons. The New York State Supreme Court ruled in 1987 that the thousands of single homeless people in the city are entitled to medical care and welfare grants – which previously had been denied to them. These provide for some basic needs which most of the homeless have been unable to meet, but also have created great pressure on the resources available to fund other welfare services.

Urbanism in Britain

Suburbanization and inner-city decay

Most of the main patterns of urban change found in post-war America also appear in Britain. Over the past thirty years, the population of all the major central city areas in the UK has declined, largely through movement to outlying suburbs and *dormitory towns* (towns outside the city boundaries lived in mainly by people who work in the city) or villages. The population of Greater London dropped by about a half a million over the period 1970–85, while that of many smaller cities and towns has grown over that time – for example, Cambridge, Ipswich, Norwich, Oxford or Leicester. The inner cities have experienced a rapid loss of manufacturing industry, especially in the North.

With some exceptions, the 'flight to the suburbs' has not been as pronounced as in the USA, and the resulting central city decay has been less marked. Yet some inner city areas – for instance, in Liverpool – are as dilapidated as many neighbourhoods in American cities. The Church of England report of 1985, *Faith in the City*, describes the inner city areas in bleak terms: 'Grey walls, littered streets, boarded-up windows, graffiti, demolition and debris are the drearily standard features of the districts and parishes with which we are concerned . . . the dwellings in the inner cities are older than elsewhere. Roughly one-quarter of England's houses were built before 1919, but the proportion in the inner areas ranged from 40 to 60 per cent in 1977' (Church of England, 1985, p. 18).

As in the United States, new industry is largely being established away from the inner-city areas, either around the outer rim of the cities, or in smaller towns. This process has in some part been deliberately reinforced by the creation of planned *new towns*, like Milton Keynes in Buckinghamshire. A range of national schemes – involving, for example, grants for the owner-rehabilitation of houses, or tax incentives to attract businesses – has been introduced to try to revive the fortunes of the inner cities, but for the most part these have met with little success. The Scarman Report of 1982, the result of an official enquiry into the Brixton riots in London a year earlier, noted that there was no co-ordinated approach to inner-city problems (Scarman, 1982). Rioting occurred in several areas again in 1985 (including in Brixton once more, and at the Broadwater Farm estate at Tottenham, North London, where a policeman was murdered). In response to this, the government appointed an inner-city task force, which in 1986 outlined plans to spend £1 million on each of eight deprived inner-city areas, in London, Leeds, Manchester and elsewhere. Critics pointed out, however, that these funds were lower, in real terms, than the rates of spending on inner-city areas fifteen years earlier.

Financial crises in British cities

The relation between central and local taxation in Britain differs from that of the USA, so no city in the UK has become bankrupt. But similar forms of financial crisis have affected many inner city areas in Britain. The Local Government Act of 1972 set up six new 'metropolitan counties' – Merseyside, Greater Manchester, South Yorkshire, West Midlands, West Yorkshire and Tyne and Wear. The county councils of these areas were given responsibility for the overall planning of the urban regions, with smaller district councils providing education, some social services, housing and other amenities. London had a different system. For a period of twenty-one years, it was administered by the Greater London Council (GLC), established in 1965. About half of the income on which the metropolitan counties depend, as well as the GLC prior to its abolition in 1985, come from central government sources.

From the mid-1970s onwards, very strong pressure was put on the local authorities to limit their budgets, and cut local services, even in inner-city areas most subject to decay. A bill passed through Parliament in 1980 introduced penalties for authorities which exceeded expenditure levels set by the national government. Some of the councils running the most distressed inner-city areas were not able to meet their set budget levels, and this led to intense conflicts between the government and a number of metropolitan councils, especially those controlled by the Labour party – such as in Liverpool or Sheffield. Some initially refused to accept the limits drawn up in Whitehall, eighty councillors in Liverpool and Lambeth being personally fined in March 1986 for their lack of co-operation.

An official government publication, called *Streamlining the Cities*, published by the Conservative government in the same year, proposed abolishing the six metropolitan county councils. As had happened in London, their tasks were to be redistributed to the smaller district councils.

Gentrification or 'urban recycling'

Again following a model applied in some American cities, emphasis is currently being put on the use of financial incentives to encourage private enterprise to redevelop inner-city areas. **Urban recycling** – the refurbishing of old buildings to put them to new uses – has become fairly common in large cities. Occasionally this has been attempted as part of planning programmes, but more often it is the result of the renovation of buildings in dilapidated city neighbourhoods for use by those in higher income groups, plus the provision of amenities, like shops and restaurants to serve them. The prime example is the renovation of the Docklands area in London. Recycling has been widely welcomed as injecting resources back into central city areas. The Docklands project, however, almost exclusively benefits affluent groups, putting up prices of houses well beyond the means of those who used to live in the area.

Urbanism and international influences

In urban analysis today – as in many areas of sociology – we must be prepared to link global and local issues. Some of the factors which influence the inner cities originate in changes happening well beyond the borders of Britain. For example, the problems suffered by Liverpool, or Teesside, originate largely in the decline of some of the major industries previously centred there, in the face of international competition.

Discussing the ways in which urban areas are increasingly tied to an international system of economic relations, Logan and Molotch have distinguished five emerging forms of city (Logan and Molotch, 1987, chapter 7). One is the **headquarters city**. Cities of this type are the centres in which the large, transnational corporations house their key activities, and are oriented to global concerns. London, for example, has become one of the world's leading headquarters cities – the centre of financial and industrial transactions, as well as networks of communication and transportation which stretch world-wide.

A second type of city is the **innovation centre**. This is an urban area in which research and development industries become concentrated, developing technical and scientific processes used to make goods produced elsewhere. Cambridge is an example, in which the university has connections with a large 'Science Park'. The most influential world centre is the Silicon Valley area of Northern California. Innovation centres in the United States, and to a lesser degree in Britain, are often directly connected to military production needs. The research and development budget of the Defense Department makes up about a third of all research and development expenditure in the United States; where major contracts are placed strongly influences the level of prosperity of innovation centres.

The third type of city is the **module production place**. In the complex international division of labour that now exists, goods are made and assembled in regions distant from one another across the world. Some urban areas become the sites for production processes in which parts of products are made, final assembly being carried out in other regions or countries. A number of transnational companies, for example, have set up plants in Belfast, making parts utilized in final production elsewhere.

A fourth form is the **Third World entrepôt,** related even more directly than the other types to international influences. Cities of this kind are border centres, with substantial new immigrant populations drawn from Third World countries. An example would be Marseilles, a major point of entry for North Africans coming into France. In the United States, the clearest examples are the cities linked to the South American societies, like Miami with its large Cuban population, or Los Angeles with its ever-growing Mexican areas.

Finally, there are cities developing as **retirement centres**. Retired people now move in considerable numbers to places with good climates. This is partly internal migration; for example people go to live in south coast resorts like Bournemouth or Worthing. Retirement areas also have a strongly international flavour: British people who have holiday houses in Spain may move to these when they retire.

Third World urbanization

In 1960, the New York and New Jersey region combined was the world's largest urban agglomeration, having a population of 15.4 million. In that year, eight of the ten largest urban areas in the world were in First World countries, together with Shanghai and Buenos Aires from the Third World. If current trends continue, however, by the year 2000 Mexico City will be easily the world's largest urban area, having more than thirty million people. By that date, eight out of the ten biggest cities will be in Asia or South America (Hughes, 1985, pp. 60–1).

The urban areas now developing rapidly in Third World countries differ dramatically from cities in the industrialized countries. People are drawn to cities in the Third World either because their traditional systems of rural production have disintegrated, or because the urban areas offer superior job opportunities. They may intend to migrate to the city only for a relatively short time, aiming to return to their villages once they have earned enough money. Some actually do return, but most find themselves forced to stay, having for one reason or another lost their position in their previous communities. Migrants crowd into squatters' zones mushrooming around the edges of cities. In Western urban areas, newcomers are most likely to settle close to the central parts of the city, but the reverse tends to happen in Third World countries, where migrants populate what has been called the 'septic fringe' of the urban areas. Many live in conditions which are almost unbelievable to someone accustomed to Western conditions of life, even in slum neighbourhoods.

As illustrations we can take cities in India and Latin America. The Indian population is still growing very rapidly, and the increasing numbers cannot be accommodated within the traditional economy of the rural areas. The rate of migration to cities, even by Third World standards, is exceptionally high. Delhi, the capital, has been the fastest growing of all, but Calcutta, Bombay and Madras all have several million inhabitants. These cities are massively congested. In many areas, large numbers of individuals wander the streets during the day and sleep on the streets at night. They have no homes of any kind.

Others exist in shanty dwellings made of hessian or cardboard, set up around the edges of the city wherever there is a little space. Even if some of the immigrants do find jobs, the rate of urban immigration is much too high for the provision of permanent housing. The shanty dwellers in Indian cities have virtually no personal possessions, but there are often strongly developed forms of community and self-help organizations.

Delhi

To show how different patterns of neighbourhood organization are from Western cities, we shall look at the example of Delhi, the capital city of India (Breese, 1966). The Delhi urban area incorporates an ancient 'old city' and New Delhi, a section built much later in which government buildings are concentrated. As in the case of other large Indian cities, some areas have an extremely high population density in relatively small neighbourhoods, with quite low density population in other areas. The old city is a convoluted maze of small streets, while some adjoining neighbourhoods have broad avenues. Most of the population move about on foot or by bicycle, rather than by motorized transport.

There is no distinct business district on the model of Western cities; banks and offices are mostly out of the centre. In the old city, there are innumerable small businesses, mainly devoted to commerce, many of the shops being no more than a few feet wide. It is common to find the manufacture and sale of articles combined in these establishments. There are large numbers of street sellers and hawkers. The New Delhi sections of the city are relatively open and quiet. Those who work in them tend to live in comparatively affluent suburbs situated several miles away towards the edge of the urban area. Makeshift squatter housing surrounds the outer edges of the city, however, and is found along many access routes. Squatter housing tends to spring up in any cleared or undeveloped area, including public parks, and sometimes in neighbourhoods which in the past have been affluent. Squatter dwellings are sometimes found in small clumps or, more often, in clusters of many thousands. The city authorities periodically clear some of the squatter areas, only to see the makeshift huts reappear elsewhere.

Mexico City

The major Latin American cities are similarly surrounded by large-scale shanty neighbourhoods, whose occupants include both recent migrants and families displaced from other sections by urban renewal and highway construction. In Mexico City, over a third of the population live in dwellings or neighbourhoods without running water, and nearly a quarter of these buildings lack sewerage. The city contains an old centre, business and entertainment districts, and affluent housing areas (which are all most tourists see). Almost all the outer perimeter, however, is occupied by shanty or slum dwellings. There is a large amount of state-subsidized housing, but this demands a level of income that no more than 40 per cent of the city's population can afford. Only about 10 per cent of the inhabitants are able to buy or rent on the private housing market. The majority of the city's population, therefore, are excluded from access to available housing (Castells, 1983, p. 188). Most housing is provided by the occupants themselves, who have cleared the land and built their own homes. The majority of these housing settlements are in fact illegal, but tolerated by the city authorities.

Three types of 'popular housing' areas are found in Mexico City. The *colonias proletarias* are composed of self-constructed shanty dwellings, mainly put up illegally, on the edges of the city. Over half the population of the metropolitan area of Mexico City lives in such housing. Most of these areas were not spontaneously colonized by squatters, but were organized with the connivance of local authorities and illegal private developers. The developers have their local network of organizers, to whom regular payments have to be made by those living there. Most of the land occupied by the *colonias* was in fact originally public or communal, supposedly protected by the Mexican constitution from being sold or transferred.

A second type of housing is the *vecindadas* or slums. These are mostly in the older sections of the city, and are characterized by the multi-family occupation of dilapidated rental units. Two million people live in such slums, in conditions which are at least as deprived as those in the squatters' areas. The third type is the *ciudades perdidas*, or shanty towns. These are similar to the *colonias proletarias*, but put up in the middle of the city rather than on the periphery. Some of these settlements have been demolished by city authorities in recent years and their inhabitants have moved to the outer areas.

Ninety-four per cent of the federal district of Mexico City consists of built-up areas, with only 6 per cent of land being open space. The level of 'green spaces' – parks and open stretches of green land – is far below that found in even the most densely populated North American or European cities (Ward, 1981). Pollution is a major problem, coming mostly from the cars, buses and trucks which pack the inadequate roads of the city, the rest deriving from industrial pollutants (Fox, 1972). The photochemical smog is far worse than in notorious areas of the United States, such as the Los Angeles basin. It has been estimated that living in Mexico City is equivalent to smoking forty cigarettes a day.

Cities in Eastern Europe

If cities in the Third World contrast with those of Western countries, so do those of Eastern Europe – although not so markedly. In most Western countries, private land and industrial development, and private housing markets, have dominated urban patterns. Planning and financial controls operated by central and local authorities have taken second place. This situation is reversed in Eastern Europe, where city planning has been much more widespread. In the Soviet Union, the designing of urban environments is integrated with the overall planning of the economy.

Soviet planners believe that urban areas should not grow too large, that the length of daily journeys should be kept to a minimum, and that public transport should be the main source of mobility (Bater, 1977). The organization of urban space is determined by considerations of social welfare (as determined by government authorities), rather than by market values as in Western cities (French, 1979). Rents, for example, are not directly related to quality of dwellings. They are fixed by the government to make up only a small element of household expenditure – much less than in Western countries. Families (not individuals) have a right to housing independently of their ability to pay particular rents.

Contrasts with the West

On the basis of research in Hungary, and comparisons drawn with some other East European countries, Ivan Szelenyi was able to document some of the resulting differences between urbanism West and East (Szelenyi, 1983). In Eastern Europe, dwellings built by private contractors, and bought and sold on the market, form a small proportion of the total housing stock. Privately owned housing is largely held by people in lower-income groups, in direct contrast to most Western cities.

Those of higher status, such as government officials or professionals, live in apartments owned and maintained by the state. These are greatly superior to dwellings in which the majority of the population live.

City zoning is influenced primarily by administrative decisions; there are deteriorating areas, but these do not cluster around the city centres as is usually the case in the West. Most central land is owned by the government, and in the city centres there are often areas with superior housing stock, the transitional zones lying further out. Neighbourhoods tend to be more homogeneous in terms both of the character of ownership and the style of housing than in Western cities (Szelenyi, 1983).

Rates of urban growth in Eastern Europe since the Second World War have for the most part not been as high as in most other regions of the world. Until the 1950s, Moscow and Leningrad were the only cities in the Soviet Union with over a million inhabitants – a situation unchanged since before the Russian Revolution of 1917. Today there are twenty cities with more than a million inhabitants. Since residents' permits are needed by Soviet citizens wherever they live, however, population migration has been much more strictly controlled than in the West.

Up to 1917, the major Soviet cities resembled their counterparts in the United States. Moscow and Leningrad possessed central business districts, and the patterning of poorer and higher income group areas was clearly established. Pre-revolutionary Soviet cities, however, were much more crowded, and housing was in far shorter supply than in large Western cities of the same period. Large-scale programmes of government sponsored housing construction in the post-war period altered this situation. Most of the dwellings built were apartment blocks, and these are still over-crowded by Western standards: whole families live in flats of only two or three rooms. Many families in older buildings still live in one-room apartments, sharing communal kitchens and bathrooms.

The planned nature of city growth, together with the standardization of housing blocks, mean that population density tends to remain the same in all neighbourhoods. Rather than more and more space being given over to each home as the outer suburbs are approached, as is characteristic of Western cities, the outer suburbs usually have the largest number of high-rise, high-density buildings, because these are the most recently built. Soviet cities do not tend to 'fade away' towards the outskirts, but end suddenly, with built-up areas of apartment blocks facing open forest and farmland. Thus attempts to fit Western ecological models of zones to Eastern European cities meet with little success.

Moscow, for example, has a historic core within which shopping and entertainment facilities are located. But these are much less concentrated than in the average Western city, and are not surrounded by dilapidated areas. There are no ethnically distinct areas like those of Britain or the United States. Industry and commerce are much more scattered over different areas of the city than in the West, where residential and industrial areas are usually quite distinct. Moscow is divided for planning purposes into sixty-five zones; the aim is to distribute industry evenly across these, so as to reduce the length of journeys to work.

The study of urban areas in the Soviet Union and Eastern Europe drives home the point made by Harvey and Castells – that urban environments are strongly influenced by the nature of the wider society in which they exist.

Likely future developments

What does the future hold for cities and city-dwellers? The patterns analysed in this chapter form a complicated mosaic, and no single overall trend emerges from them. In the industrialized countries, it is likely that tendencies towards the 'spreading' of urban life will continue. Improved systems of communication allow people to live further from their places of work than before. At the same time, their places of work are coming to them, as new industries are located away from city centres. Some older cities, particularly those based on the older manufacturing industries, will continue to decline in population, as people are drawn away to other areas altogether. Yet these same circumstances will stimulate further gentrification. The more dilapidated central cities become, in fact, the more opportunities there are for gentrification; property becomes so cheap that renovation can be undertaken at reasonable cost.

While cities in the industrialized countries remain stable, or diminish, in population, those in Third World societies will continue to expand. Conditions of life in Third World cities seem likely to decline even further, at least for the urban poor. The problems that exist in First and Second World cities, important as they are, pale almost into insignificance when compared to those faced in the Third World.

Summary

1   Traditional cities differed in many ways from modern urban areas. They were mostly very small by modern standards, were surrounded by walls, and dominated in the centre by religious buildings and palaces.

2   In traditional societies, only a small minority of the population lived in urban areas. In the industrialized countries today, between 60 and 90 per cent do so. *Urbanism* is developing very rapidly in Third World societies too.

3   Early approaches to urban sociology were dominated by the work of the 'Chicago School', the members of which saw urban processes in terms of ecological models derived from biology. Louis Wirth developed the concept of *urbanism as a way of life*, arguing that city life

breeds impersonality and social distance. These approaches have been challenged, without being discarded altogether.

4   The more recent work of David Harvey and Manuel Castells connects patterns of urbanism to the wider society, rather than treating urban processes as self-contained. The modes of life people develop in cities, as well as the physical lay-out of different neighbourhoods, express broad features of the development of industrial capitalism.

5   The expansion of *suburbs* and *dormitory towns* has contributed to inner-city decay. Wealthier groups and businesses tend to move out of the central city to take advantage of lower local tax-rates. A cycle of deterioration is set under way, in which the more suburbia expands, the greater the problems faced by those living in the central cities. *Urban recycling* – the refurbishing of old buildings to put them to new uses – has become common in many large cities, but there currently seems little sign of reversing the trend towards inner-city decay.

6   Urban analysis today must be prepared to link global and local issues. Factors which influence urban development locally are sometimes part of much more far-reaching processes. The structure of local neighbourhoods, and their patterns of growth and decline, often reflect changes in industrial production internationally.

7   Massive processes of urban development are occurring in Third World countries. Cities in these societies differ in major respects from those of the West, and are often dominated by makeshift illegal housing, in which conditions of life are extremely impoverished.

8   Urbanism in the communist countries, in contrast to the West, is part of the planned economy. Cities are planned in conjunction with the overall development of industry and the realization of egalitarian ideals. Rates of urban growth in Eastern Europe since the Second World War have been comparatively low, largely because of government rules restricting the movement of citizens.

Basic concepts

inner city	the created environment
urban ecology	

Important terms

urbanization	collective consumption
conurbation	suburbanization
megalopolis	urban recycling
ecological approach	headquarters city

urbanism	innovation centre
competition	module production place
invasion	Third World entrepôt
succession	retirement centre

Further reading

Albert N. Cousins et al., *Urban Life: the Sociology of Cities and Urban Society* (New York: Wiley, 1979) — presents an overall view of urban sociology today with reference to modern American cities.

A. Gilbert et al., *Cities, Poverty and Development: Urbanization in the Third World* (Oxford: Oxford University Press, 1982) — an account of Third World urbanization as part of global social and economic development.

Peter Hall, *The World Cities*, 3rd edition (New York: St Martin's Press, 1984) — an examination of the growth of some of the world's cities and the problems connected with this growth.

Kenneth T. Jackson, *Crabgrass Frontier: The Suburbanization of the United States* (Oxford: Oxford University Press, 1985) — presents a history of suburban America, referring also to the European situation.

Jiri Musil, *Urbanization in Socialist Countries* (White Plains, New York: M. E. Sharpe Inc., 1980) — addresses the complexities of urban development in the socialist countries of Europe during the past twenty years.

B. Roberts, *Cities of Peasants: The Political Economy of Urbanization in the Third World* (Beverly Hills: Sage, 1978) — studies the expansion of capitalism in the Third World, linking urbanization to the way these countries have become part of the world economy.

18

Population, Health and Ageing

Writing of his first visit to India, the noted biologist Paul R. Ehrlich commented:

I have understood the population explosion intellectually for a long time. I came to understand it emotionally one stinking hot night in Delhi a few years ago. My wife and daughter and I were returning to our hotel in an ancient taxi. The seats were hopping with fleas. The only functional gear was third. As we crawled through the city, we entered a crowded slum area. The temperature was well over a 100° Fahrenheit; the air was a haze of dust and smoke. The streets seemed alive with people. People eating, people washing, people sleeping. People visiting, arguing, and screaming. People thrusting their hands through the taxi window, begging. People defecating and urinating. People clinging to buses. People herding animals. People, people, people, people. As we moved slowly, through the mob, hand-horn squawking, the dust, noise, heat, and cooking fires gave the scene a hellish aspect. Would we ever get to our hotel? All three of us were, frankly, frightened. It seemed that anything could happen – but, of course, nothing did. Old India hands will laugh at our reaction. We were just some over-privileged tourists, unaccustomed to the sights and sounds of India. Perhaps since that night I've known the *feel* of over-population. (Ehrlich, 1971, p. 1)

With the exception of the spread of nuclear weaponry and threats to global ecological systems (although these are problems enough!), population growth is the most pressing and urgent issue currently faced by humanity. The affluent countries have more food than they need for themselves, and in most of them levels of population growth are low or declining. In much of the remainder of the world, population growth is quite staggering and the pressure on available resources immense.

Those of us who live in the industrialized countries might feel Third World population expansion is not 'our' problem, and that the societies concerned should be left to deal with their swelling populations as best they can. But such a view cannot be justified, quite apart from the immorality of being unconcerned about the fate of three-quarters of the world's human beings. If it continues at the present rate, world population growth carries the risk of global catastrophe. The pressure on the world's resources may lead to bitter conflict, which could end in major wars. At this point, the three great issues with which humanity must deal over the next few decades – the possibility of nuclear conflict, ecological dangers and population growth – merge with one another.

Why has world population increased so dramatically? What are the main consequences of this increase? In this chapter, we shall try to answer these questions, connecting our analysis with two related issues: the study of health and illness, and the consequences of the *ageing* of populations in the industrialized countries.

World population growth

There are currently just over five billion (five thousand million) people in the world. It is estimated that 'baby number five billion' was born on 11 July 1987, although of course no one can know when and where this event happened! Ehrlich calculated in the 1960s that, if the rate of population growth at that period continued, 900 years from now (not a long period in world history as a whole) there would be 60,000,000,000,000,000,000 people on the face of the earth. There would be a hundred people for every square yard of the earth's surface, including both sea and land. The physicist J. H. Fremlin worked out that housing such a population would need a continuous 2,000-storey building covering the complete planet. Even in such a stupendous structure there would only be three or four yards of floor-space per person (Fremlin, 1964).

Such a picture, of course, is nothing more than a nightmare fiction, designed to drive home how cataclysmic the consequences of continued population growth would be. The real issue is what will happen over the next thirty or forty years, because if current trends are not reversed during this period the world's population will already have grown to intolerable levels. Perhaps partly because governments and other agencies heeded the warnings of Ehrlich and others twenty years ago, introducing population control programmes, there are grounds for supposing that world population growth is beginning to tail off. Estimates produced in the 1960s of the likely world population by the year 2000 have recently been reduced. The World Bank estimates the probable world population by that year at 6.5 billion, compared to some earlier estimates of over 8 billion. Nevertheless, considering that a century ago there were only 1.5 billion people in the world, this still represents growth of staggering proportions. Moreover, the factors underlying population growth are by no means completely predictable, and all estimates have to be interpreted with caution.

Population analysis: demography

The study of population is referred to as **demography.** The term was invented about a century and a half ago, at a time when states were beginning to keep official statistics on the nature and distribution of their populations. Demography is concerned with measuring the size of populations and explaining their rise or decline. Population patterns are governed by three factors: births, deaths and migrations. Demography is customarily treated as a branch of sociology because the factors which influence the level of births and deaths in a given grouping or society, as well as migrations of population, are largely social and cultural.

Much demographic work tends to be statistical. All the industrialized states today gather and analyse basic statistics about their populations by carrying out censuses (systematic surveys designed to find out about the whole population of a given country). Rigorous as the modes of data collection now are, even in these nations demographic statistics are not wholly accurate. In the United Kingdom a comprehensive population census is taken every ten years, and sample studies conducted more frequently. Yet many people are not registered in the official population statistics – perhaps as many as half a million. These are illegal immigrants, tramps, vagrants and others who for one reason or another avoid registration.

In many Third World countries, particularly those with very high rates of recent population growth, demographic statistics are much more unreliable and partial. For instance, some demographers have estimated that registered births and deaths in India may represent only about three-quarters of the true totals (Cox, 1976), and the accuracy of official statistics is even lower in parts of Central Africa.

Governments find it difficult to acquire an accurate picture of their populations in such countries; and many of the inhabitants themselves lack personal information that virtually everyone in the industrialized world possesses. We all know our dates of birth, and hence our ages. This was not the case before literacy became common; and in Third World countries today many people do not know how old they are. 'Age' is usually measured in traditional communities by reference to life experiences. A person is a 'young adult', or 'married with young children', or a 'grandparent' – rather than twenty-one, thirty or sixty years old.

Basic demographic concepts

Among the basic concepts used by demographers, the most important are *crude birth-rates, fertility, fecundity*, and *crude death-rates*. **Crude birth-rates** are usually expressed as the number of live births per year per 1,000 of the population. They are called *crude* rates because of their very general character. Crude birth-rates, for example, do not tell us what proportion of a population is male or female, or what the *age-distribution* of a population is (the relative proportion of young and older people in that population). Where statistics are collected that relate birth- or death-rates to such categories, demographers speak of *specific* rather than crude rates. For instance, age-specific death-rates specify the proportions of a population dying per year in each age-group.

If we wish to understand population patterns in any detail, the information provided by specific birth-rates is normally necessary. Crude birth-rates, however, are useful for making overall comparisons between different groups, societies and regions. Thus the crude birth-rate in Britain was 13.1 per 1,000 in 1985. Other industrialized countries range from a low of 10 per 1,000 (West Germany and Denmark) to a high of 20 per 1,000 (USSR, Poland and Ireland). In many other parts of the world, crude birth-rates are much higher still. In India, for instance, the crude birth-rate in 1985 was 33 per 1,000; in Kenya it is 54 per 1,000 (World Bank, 1987).

Birth-rates are an expression of the **fertility** of women. 'Fertility' refers to how many live-born children the average woman has. A fertility rate is quite a complex calculation. It is the number of children that would be born to an average woman in a given population if she were to live to the end of her child-bearing years, and bear children at the same rate as those currently in the age-group who have just passed the age of child-bearing. The fertility rate in the UK in 1985 was 1.8, which is fairly typical of the industrialized countries. Using the previously mentioned countries as a basis of comparison, in India the rate was 4.5 and in Kenya 7.8. Since these are average figures, many families in these societies are considerably larger (although not every live-born child survives).

Fertility is distinguished from **fecundity**, which means the number of children women are *able* to have in biological terms. It is physically possible for a normal woman to bear a child every year during the period at which she is capable of conception. There are variations in fecundity according to age of puberty and menopause (both of which differ on average between countries as well as among individuals). While there may be families in which a woman bears twenty or more children, fertility rates in practice are always much lower than fecundity, because social and cultural factors limit breeding.

Crude death-rates (also called *mortality rates*) are calculated in the same way as birth-rates – the number of deaths per 1,000 of population per year. Again there are major variations between countries; but death-rates in many Third World societies are falling to levels comparable to those of the West. The death-rate in the United Kingdom in 1985 was 12 per 1,000. In India it is also 12 per 1,000; in Kenya it is 13 per 1,000. A few states have much higher death-rates. In Sierra Leone, for example, the death-rate is 25 per 1,000. Like crude birth-rates, crude death-rates only provide a very general index of *mortality* (the number of deaths in a population); *specific* death-rates give more precise information. A particularly important aspect of death-rates in general is the **infant mortality rate.** The infant mortality rate is the number of babies per 1,000 live births in any year who die before reaching the age of one. One of the key factors underlying the population explosion has been the reduction in infant mortality rates.

Declining rates of infant mortality are the most important influence on increasing **life expectancy** – that is, the number of years the average person can expect to live. In 1900, life expectancy in Britain was about forty years. Today it has increased to nearly seventy-four (seventy-two for men and seventy-seven for women). This does not mean, however, that most people at the turn of the century died when they were about forty years of age. Where large numbers of infants die, average life expectancy – which is of course a statistical average – is brought down. Taking the life expectancy of people surviving the first year of life, in 1900 the average person could expect to live to be fifty-eight. Illness, nutrition, and the effects of natural disasters, are the other factors influencing life expectancy, which has to be distinguished from **life span**, which is the maximum period of time that a member of a species can live. While life expectancy has increased in most societies in the world, life span has remained unaltered. Only a tiny proportion of people live to be a hundred or more.

The dynamics of population change

Rates of population growth or decline are measured by subtracting the number of deaths over a given period from the number of births – this is usually also calculated as an annual rate. Some European countries have negative growth-rates – in other words, their populations are declining – and virtually all the industrialized countries have growth-rates of below 0.7 per cent. Rates of population growth were high in the eighteenth and nineteenth centuries in Europe and the United States, but have since levelled off. Many Third World countries today have rates of between 2 to 3 per cent, which may not seem a significant difference from the rates of the industrialized countries; in fact, the difference is enormous.

Growth in population is **exponential;** that is it occurs in an accelerating way. There is an ancient Persian myth which helps to illustrate this. A courtier asked a ruler to reward him for his services by giving him twice as many grains of rice as before, for each service. Starting with a single grain on the first square of a chess-board, and believing himself to be on to a good thing, the king commanded grain to be brought up from his storehouse. By the twenty-first square, the storehouse was empty; the fortieth square required ten billion rice grains (Meadows et al., 1972). In other words, starting from one item and doubling it, doubling the result, and so on, rapidly leads to huge figures: 1:2:4:8:16:32:64:128, etc. In seven operations, the figure has risen by 128 per cent. Exactly the same principle applies to population growth. We can measure this effect by means of the **doubling time**, the period of time it takes for the population to double. One per cent population growth in a year will produce a doubling of numbers in seventy years. At 2 per cent growth, a population will double in thirty-five years, while at 3 per cent it will double in twenty-three years.

Malthusianism

Various attempts have been made to interpret demographic patterns in the world, and the changes which have taken place within societies, so as to be able to predict future trends and possibly influence them. One of the first was that developed by Thomas Malthus some two centuries ago. In ancient societies, birth-rates were very high by the standards of the industrialized world today. None the less, population growth remained low until the eighteenth century, because there was a rough overall balance between births and deaths. The general trend of numbers was upwards, and there were sometimes periods of more marked population increase, but these were followed by increases in death-rates. In mediaeval Europe, for example, when harvests were bad marriages tended to be postponed and the number of conceptions fell, while deaths increased. These complementary trends reduced the number of mouths to be fed. No pre-industrial society was able to escape from this self-regulating rhythm (Wrigley, 1969).

During the rise of industrialism, many looked forward to a new age in which scarcity would be a phenomenon of the past. The development of modern industry, it was widely supposed, would create a new era of abundance. In his work *Essay on the Principles of Population,* published in 1798, Thomas Malthus set out to criticize these ideas. In so doing, he initiated a debate about the connection between population and food resources which continues to this day. When Malthus wrote, the population in Europe was growing rapidly.

He pointed out that, while population increase is exponential, food supply depends on fixed resources which can only be expanded by developing new land for cultivation. Population growth therefore tends to outstrip the means of support available, and the inevitable outcome is famine, which, combined with the influence of war and plagues, acts as a natural limit to population increase. It is the fate of human beings always to live in circumstances of misery and starvation, unless they practise what Malthus called 'moral restraint' – by which he meant accepting strict limitations on the frequency of sexual intercourse. (The use of contraception he claimed was a 'vice'.)

For a while, **Malthusianism** was ignored, since the population development of the Western countries followed quite a different pattern from that which he anticipated. Rates of population growth tailed off in the nineteenth and twentieth centuries. Indeed, in the 1930s there were major worries about population *decline* in many industrialized countries. Some experts at the time forecast that the population of the United Kingdom might be reduced to no more than thirty-five million people within fifty years (Simon, 1981).

The upsurge in world population growth in the current century has again lent some credence to Malthus's views, although few support them in their original version. Population expansion in Third World countries seems to be outstripping the resources which these countries can generate.

Population growth in the Third World

Virtually all the industrialized countries today have low birth- and death-rates, as compared both with their history and with Third World nations. In the majority of Third World countries, death-rates have fallen but birth-rates remain high. Because of the relatively sudden introduction of modern medicine and methods of hygiene, demographic changes that took more than 200 years in the West have occurred within less than half a century in the Third World.

Population growth in Asia, Africa and Latin America severely limits possibilities of economic development in these regions. In a population with zero growth (as in most Western countries) between 3 to 5 per cent of national income has to be invested to produce a 1 per cent increase in income per head. Where a population grows by 3 per cent per year, up to 20 per cent of national income has to be invested in order to create a similar increase in living standards. As the regions in which population is growing rapidly include most of the poorest countries in the world, such a level of investment cannot possibly be met; so these countries fall further and further behind the industrialized sectors of the globe (see chapter 16: 'The Globalizing of Social Life').

The rapid drop in mortality, with little or no decline in fertility, has produced a completely different age structure in Third World countries compared to the industrialized ones. In Mexico, for example,

45 per cent of the population is less than fifteen years old. In the industrialized countries, on the other hand, only about a quarter of the population is in this age-group. The 'elongated pyramid' age-distribution in the non-industrialized countries adds to their social and economic difficulties. A youthful population needs support and education, during which period its members are not economically productive. In fact, in many Third World countries large numbers of children are either employed in full-time work or scratch a living as 'street children', begging for whatever they can. When such children mature, most become unemployed, homeless, or both (Davis, 1976; Ennew, 1986).

A population which has a very large proportion of young people will continue to grow even if the birth-rate suddenly should fall. If fertility declined to 'replacement level' – one birth for every living person in a population – it would still take seventy-five years before that population stopped increasing (Duncan, 1971).

The demographic transition

Demographers often refer to the changes in the ratio of births to deaths in the industrialized countries from the nineteenth century onwards as the **demographic transition**. The term was first coined by Warren S. Thompson, who described a three-stage process, through which one type of population stability is eventually replaced by another (Thompson, 1929).

Stage one refers to the conditions characteristic of most traditional societies, in which both birth- and death-rates are high, and the infant mortality rate is especially large. Population grows little if at all, as the high number of births is more or less balanced by the level of deaths. Stage two, which began in Europe and United States in the early part of the nineteenth century – with wide regional variations – occurs when death-rates fall, while fertility remains high. This is therefore a phase of marked population growth. It is subsequently replaced by stage three, in which, with industrial development, birth-rates drop to a level such that population is again fairly stable.

Demographers are not agreed as to how this sequence should be interpreted, or how long-lasting the third stage is likely to be. Fertility in the Western countries has not been completely stable over the past century or so; and there remain considerable differences in fertility between the industrialized nations, as well as between classes or regions within them. Nevertheless, it is generally agreed that the sequence of stages accurately describes a major transformation in the demographic character of modern societies.

Likely prospects for the Third World

Will the demographic transition be repeated in the Third World? The answer to this question is not yet clear. Fertility remains high in many Third World societies because traditional attitudes to family size have been maintained. Large families are often still regarded as desirable, providing a source of labour. Some religions influential in areas where population growth is high are either opposed to birth control, or positively affirm the desirability of having many children. Contraception is opposed by Islamic leaders in several countries, and by the Catholic Church, whose influence is especially marked in Latin America. The motivation to reduce fertility has not always been forthcoming even from political authorities. Thus in 1974 contraceptives were banned in Argentina as part of a programme to double the population of the country as fast as possible; this was seen as a means of developing its economic and military strength.

Yet it does seem that the phenomenal rate of population increase of the past few decades is at least slowing. A decline in fertility levels has occurred in at least some large Third World countries. An example is China, which currently has a population of nearly a billion people – almost a fifth of the world's inhabitants as a whole. The Chinese government established one of the most far-reaching programmes of population control that any country has undertaken, with the object of stabilizing the country's numbers at close to their current level. Government policy is that every couple should have no more than *one* child. A range of incentives has been established to promote single-child families (such as better housing, free health care and education), while families who have more than one child face special hardships (wages are cut for those who have a third child).

There is evidence that these policies have had a substantial impact (Mirsky, 1982), although they have come up against people's reluctance to regard 'parents and one child' as a proper 'family'. In addition, the programme demands a degree of centralized government control that is either unacceptable, or unavailable, in most other developing countries. In India, for instance, many schemes for promoting family planning and the use of contraceptives have been tried, but with relatively small success. India in 1985 had a population of 765 million. Its average annual growth of population from 1975 to 1985 was 2.3 per cent; this is projected to decline to 1.8 per cent over the twenty years from 1980 to 2000. By 2000, however, there will be 1 billion people in the country. Even if its growth-rate does diminish as projected, the increase in population remains enormous.

Technological advance is unpredictable, so no one can be sure how large a population the world might eventually be able to support. Yet even at current population levels, global resources may already be well below those required to create living standards in the Third World comparable to those of the industrialized countries. The consumption of energy, raw materials and other goods is vastly higher in the Western countries than in other areas of the world. These levels partly depend, moreover, on resources transferred from Third World regions (Ehrlich and Ehrlich, 1979). Thirty-two times as much energy is consumed per person in the United States as in an average African country. Unless there are major changes in patterns of world energy consumption – such as the large-scale harnessing of solar energy or wind power – there is no possibility of extending this level of energy consumption to everyone in the world. There are simply not enough known energy resources to go round (McHale et al., 1979; Gupte, 1984).

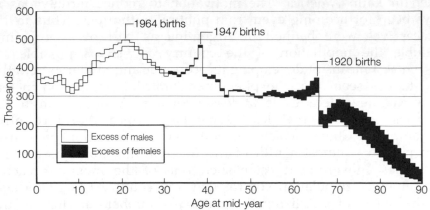

Figure 23   The United Kingdom population by age and sex in 1985
Source: Social Trends (London: HMSO, 1987), p. 35.

Population in the United Kingdom

The population of the United Kingdom has been increasing slightly in recent years. Between 1981 and 1986 the population increased by 441,100 to 50,075,400, although in 1981–2 there was actually a fall of 32,000 (*Social Trends*, 1987). Between 1985 and 2001, a rising curve of population growth is projected, but one of the most important changes of this century is in the age-distribution of the population. The number of people aged sixty-five or over is four times greater today than it was in 1901, representing 18 per cent of the population compared to less than 6 per cent at the earlier date.

Another important change since the 1900s has been an overall decline in fertility. However, there have been fluctuations over this period. A marked, but temporary, rise in fertility occurred after the Second World War – the so-called 'baby boom'. The birth-rate rose from a low of 17 per 1,000 during the early 1930s to 22 per 1,000 in the late 1950s. The baby boom was not a consequence of a tendency to form larger families – there was little increase in the proportion of families with three or more children. Rather, there was a marked *decline* in the proportion of childless or one-child families.

Demographers did not anticipate the baby boom; nor did they foresee the return to the lower levels of fertility in the early 1970s. In spite of this reversion, the overall population of the country continues to increase. The baby boom, to change metaphors, has produced a 'bulge' in the age-distribution of the population. Those of the baby boom generation are now adults, having children of their own. Since the proportion of people of child-bearing age will remain high for the next twenty years or so, the number of people born each year will still be greater than those who die.

As the baby boom generation gets still older, if the present low fertility rate is maintained, the result will be a situation of zero population growth. In such a circumstance, those who are born each year (plus those who immigrate) would be equal in numbers to those who die or emigrate. Many demographers believe that zero population growth is likely to be characteristic of some forty countries by the end of the 1980s. If this proves to be the case, there will be an even larger proportion of older people in their populations than at present. However, since demographers have not been particularly accurate in predicting trends in the past, especially in the short term, it cannot be assumed that such a pattern of development will inevitably occur.

The institutional impact of fluctuations in fertility for a society is evidenced by the consequences of the baby boom. In their early years, this generation created the need to expand child-based medical services and the production of child-care goods and welfare provisions. As the baby boomers moved into the school system, they strained existing personnel and resources. Now they have entered the labour market, they have added to the pressure on employment opportunities. When they come to retirement age, a particular burden will be placed upon welfare and medical services for the elderly. Since the baby boom was followed by the 'birth dearth' of the 1970s, the succeeding generation is considerably smaller in size. This has already brought about a need for restructuring school resources, with much lower demand for elementary school teachers, and will create similar imbalances of resources as this succeeding generation itself ages.

Health and illness

Population issues are intimately connected to problems of health and illness. How many children are born, the proportion that live beyond infancy, the ages to which people survive, and the major causes of death, are all bound up with states of health. Health and illness, in turn, are strongly influenced by aspects of social structure. Social factors affect not simply life expectancy, but the chances individuals have of contracting major types of disease and the nature of the health care they receive.

Treatment of illness in the past

All cultures have concepts of physical health and illness, but most of what we now recognize as *medicine* derives from developments in

Western society over the past two or three centuries. Before then, the family or kinship unit was the main institution coping with sickness or affliction. There have always been individuals who specialized as 'healers', using a mixture of physical and magical remedies, and many traditional systems of medical treatment survive today in non-Western cultures throughout the world. Ayurvedic medicine (traditional healing) has been practised in India, for instance, for nearly 2,000 years. It is founded on a theory of the equilibrium of psychological and physical aspects of the personality, imbalances of which are treated by nutritional means and herbal remedies. Chinese folk medicine is similarly based on a concept of the overall harmony of the personality, involving the use of herbs and other remedies, together with acupuncture.

It is common in traditional cultures for illness to be seen as one aspect of the overall psychological and social well-being of the individual, and similar views survived in Europe until the eighteenth century. Most schools of European medicine had their origins in Greek systems of treatment, which sought to explain illness in terms of the general mental and physical disposition of the individual (Patrick and Scambler, 1982; Porter, 1986). Physicians did not belong to a defined 'profession', but were usually employed as healers by aristocrats or gentry. As was mentioned in chapter 5 ('Conformity and Deviance'), hospitals in the modern sense have only come into being in large numbers since the early nineteenth century. Up to that time, and in some areas until even later, treatment of illness depended almost wholly on a mixture of folk remedies, prayer and magic.

The development of modern medicine

Modern medicine introduced a view of illness which sees its origins as physical, and as explicable in scientific terms. The application of science to medical diagnosis and cure is a major feature of modern health systems. Others are the acceptance of hospitals as the settings within which more serious illnesses are coped with or cured; and the development of the medical profession as a body having recognized codes of ethics and significant social power. These three aspects of medicine were closely related developments. The scientific view of disease was linked to the requirement that medical training be systematic and long-term – with self-taught healers being excluded. Although professional medical practice is not limited to hospitals, the hospital provided an environment in which doctors for the first time were able to treat and study large numbers of patients, in circumstances permitting the concentration of medical technology.

In mediaeval times the major diseases were above all infectious illnesses such as tuberculosis, cholera, malaria and plague. In 1348, the Black Death, a plague spread by fleas carried by black rats, killed a quarter of the population of England, and devastated large areas of Europe. Infectious diseases have now become relatively minor causes of death in the industrialized countries, and several have also been substantially eradicated from other parts of the world. In the industrialized countries today, the most common causes of death are non-infectious illnesses such as cancer or heart disease. Whereas in previous centuries the highest rates of mortality were among infants and young children, today mortality rates rise with increasing age.

In spite of the prestige which modern medicine has acquired, improvements in medical care account only for a relatively minor part of the decline in mortality rates before the present century. Effective sanitation, better nutrition, control of sewage and improved hygiene generally were the dominant factors. Their effects were felt particularly in reductions in the infant mortality rate and deaths of young children. Drugs, advances in surgery and antibiotics did not influence mortality rates in a significant way until several decades into the present century. Antibiotics used to treat bacterial infections first became available in the 1930s and 1940s, while immunization (against diseases such as polio) was developed still later.

The Third World

Colonialism and the spread of disease

The expansion of the West in the colonial era took certain diseases into parts of the world where they had not previously existed. Smallpox, measles and typhus were unknown to the indigenous populations of Central and South America before the Spanish conquest, and English and French colonists brought the same diseases to North America (Dubos, 1959). Some of these illnesses produced epidemics that ravaged local populations which had little or no resistance to them. There is good evidence that the hunting and gathering communities of the Americas had not been as subject to infectious disease as the European societies of the period. Many infectious organisms only thrive when human populations are living above a density characteristic of hunting and gathering life. Permanently settled communities risk contamination of water supplies by waste products, which hunters and gatherers, moving across the countryside, avoid.

Studies also indicate that, in spite of their low material level of technology, the diet of hunters and gatherers in favourable environments tended to be superior to that of people living in larger societies. Reliance upon cereals as a major source of food (which came about with the fixed cultivation of land) reduced the variety and quality of diet, as compared to the range of foods eaten by hunters and gatherers (Patrick and Scambler, 1982, p. 20).

In Africa and sub-tropical parts of Asia, infectious diseases have almost certainly been rife for a long time. Tropical and sub-tropical conditions are especially conducive to diseases such as malaria, carried by mosquitoes, and sleeping sickness, carried by the tsetse fly. Yet it seems probable that, before contact with the Europeans, levels of risk from infectious diseases were lower than they subsequently became. There was always the threat of epidemics, drought or natural disaster, but colonialism led to major changes in the relation between populations and their environments, producing harmful effects on health patterns. The Europeans introduced new farming methods, upsetting the ecology of whole regions. For example, large tracts of East Africa today are completely devoid of cattle as a result of the uncontrolled spread of the tsetse fly. Before the arrival of the Westerners, Africans successfully maintained large herds in these same areas (Kjekshus, 1977, pp. 51–68).

The most significant consequence of the colonial system was its effect upon nutrition, and therefore levels of resistance to illness, as a result of the changed economic conditions involved in producing for world markets. In many parts of Africa in particular, the nutritional quality of diets fell as cash-crop production took over (Hughes and Hunter, 1971).

This was not simply a one-way process, however. The early development of colonialism also radically changed Western diets, having a paradoxical impact so far as health is concerned. On the one side, Western diets were improved by the addition of a range of new foods previously either completely unknown or very rare, like bananas, pineapples or grapefruit. On the other hand, the importation of tobacco and coffee, together with raw sugar, which began increasingly to be used in all manner of foods, has had harmful consequences. The high level of sugar in Western diets, together with the effects of the smoking of tobacco, are linked to the prevalence of cancer and heart disease.

The infectious diseases today

Although major strides have been made in reducing, and in some cases virtually eliminating, infectious diseases in the Third World, they remain far more widespread there than in the West. The most important example of a disease that has almost disappeared is smallpox, in earlier times a scourge of Europe as well as many other parts of the world. Campaigns against malaria have been much less successful. When the insecticide DDT was first produced, it raised hopes that the mosquito, the prime carrier of malaria, could be eradicated, and indeed at first considerable progress was made. This has slowed down because some strains of mosquito have become resistant to DDT.

Basic medical resources are still lacking in the vast majority of Third World countries. Hospitals which do exist, together with trained doctors, tend to be heavily concentrated in urban areas, and their services are largely monopolized by the affluent minority. Most Third World countries have introduced some form of National Health Service organized by central government, but the medical services available are usually very limited. The small section of the wealthy utilize private health care, sometimes travelling to the West when sophisticated medical treatment is needed. Conditions in many cities, particularly in the shanty towns, make the control of infectious diseases very difficult: in many shanty areas there is an almost complete lack of basic services such as water, sewage and rubbish disposal.

Studies carried out by the World Health Organization suggest that more than two-thirds of people living in urban areas in Third World countries draw their water from sources which fail to meet minimal health needs. It has been estimated that seventeen out of the twenty-five main water-related diseases rife in Third World nations could either be cut by half, or eradicated altogether, simply by the provision of ready supplies of safe water (Doyal and Pennell, 1979, pp. 131–2). Only about a quarter of the city dwellers in Third World countries have water-borne sewage facilities; some 30 per cent have no sanitation at all. These conditions provide breeding grounds for diseases such as cholera (*Lancet*, 1974; Dwyer, 1975).

Health and illness in the developed countries

The distribution and main types of disease

Within the industrialized societies, there are striking differences in the distribution of the major diseases. Around 70 per cent of deaths in Western countries are attributable to four major types of illness: cancer, heart disease, strokes and lung disease. Some progress has been made in understanding the origins of these, and in controlling their effects in individual cases, but none can be effectively cured. Since their distribution varies between countries, regions and classes, it seems evident that they are related to diet and life-style. Individuals from higher socio-economic positions are on average healthier, taller and stronger, and live longer, than those lower down the social scale. Differences are greatest in infant mortality and child death, but lower-class people are at greater risk of dying *at all ages* than more affluent people (see figure 24).

Why is this? People in wealthier sectors of society tend to have superior diets; but they also usually have more ready access to medical care, and are more likely to take advantage of that access by frequent self-referral. Proneness to disease and the likelihood of death are also directly influenced by working conditions. Those who work in offices, or in domestic settings, escape various sorts of potentially injurious influences. The extent of industrial disease is difficult to calculate, because it is not always possible to determine how far illnesses are picked up from working conditions rather than from other sources. However, some work-related diseases are well documented, such as lung disease, widespread in mining owing to the inhaling of dust. Working in environments involving the use of asbestos increases the risk of suffering certain types of cancer.

It is generally accepted that propensity to heart ailments is increased by a diet rich in animal fats, lack of exercise and habitual smoking. Most of the evidence about this is indirect, inferred from correlational studies linking the rate of heart disease with different dietary habits and the tendency to take exercise. Twenty years ago, the United States had the highest rate of death from heart disease in the world, but over the past two decades the level has dropped. This seems to be the result of changes in diet, a higher proportion of the population than before engaging in regular exercise, together with improved means of providing quick response to those who suffer heart attacks.

No such drop has occurred in the UK, which has a very high rate of death from heart disease. Campaigns against smoking, however, have been effective to some degree. When the first reports were issued, documenting a close correlation between cigarette smoking and cancer, in the early 1960s, over 50 per cent of the male population smoked regularly. That proportion has now declined to well under 30 per cent, yet there has been little change in the proportion of young people who smoke, while the proportion of women smoking

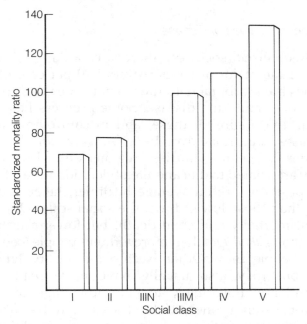

Figure 24 Mortality of married women aged 20–59 by husband's social class in Great Britain, 1979–80 and 1982–3. The standardized mortality ratio (SMR) is the ratio of the death-rate in a particular occupational class compared to the average for the whole population, after allowing for the difference between their age-structures. The SMR for all men and women would be 100: SMRs below 100 indicate lower than average death-rates; those above 100 higher than average. Unskilled workers run at least twice the risk of dying at any particular time than do professionals. Social class I is the richest and V the poorest section of the community.
Source: B. D. Cox et al., *The Health and Lifestyle Survey* (London: Office of Population Censuses and Surveys, 1986), p. 12.

on a regular basis has actually increased. Smoking is an even more widespread habit in many other Western countries than in Britain. It has been estimated that 20 per cent of deaths from cancer world-wide could be prevented if cigarette smoking ceased completely.

Health care in the United Kingdom

Health-care systems differ widely within the industrialized world. In the Soviet Union and the East European societies, for instance, there are very extensive systems of **public health care**. Most medical services are free, although the available facilities are often too few to prevent long waiting-lists for many types of medical treatment. Virtually all other industrialized countries, with the exception of the United States, have comprehensive systems of publicly provided medical services. The National Health Service (NHS) in Britain, for example, was set up in 1948. The stated principle underlying its founding was that access to health care should depend on medical need rather than ability to pay (Eckstein, 1958).

The NHS is funded from central government revenues, collected as part of income tax. Access to general practitioner (GP) and hospital treatment is free to all users. Drugs obtained by prescriptions given by doctors were originally supplied without charge, but legislation by recent governments has introduced a system of partial payments. When the NHS was first established, pressure from the medical profession, among other influences, ensured that there would remain **private health care**, operating alongside the publicly provided facilities. While the majority of general practitioners work exclusively for the NHS, a high proportion of consultants also maintain private practices. Some purely private hospitals and health-care facilities exist, together with medical personnel working exclusively in the private sector. Only a small minority of the population, however, are members of private health insurance schemes.

General practitioners have a basic role in filtering the access patients have to more specialized medical treatments. The average British citizen sees a GP about four times a year (Klein, 1983). GPs deal directly with some 90 per cent of all illness, every GP having a 'list' of patients registered with them (up to a maximum number set by the NHS). Patients who see GPs have no intrinsic right to be referred to specialists; this is a matter for the judgement of the practitioner. Since specialists are not able to advertise, even self-referral to private consultants may not be easy if a GP disapproves.

Among the criticisms often offered of the NHS is that there are long waiting-lists for those recommended by GPs to see specialists and receive appropriate treatment. A survey carried out by a royal commission appointed to study the health service, however, found that on the whole this was not the case. Twenty-six per cent of patients were seen in seven days or less, while 60 per cent waited less than three weeks (Royal Commission on the National Health Service, 1979, para. 10.5). But since the study was carried out, the average waiting time has risen considerably. The ineffective nature of consumer feedback into the NHS, moreover, has been repeatedly demonstrated. Where patients cannot 'shop around', it is hard for them to gain effective response to complaints they might have about the nature of the service (Richman, 1987).

Health care in the United States

A higher proportion of total output is spent on health care in the USA than in any other nation. American medical services are based primarily on private insurance, supplemented by public provision for the elderly and poor, and the system is much more fragmented and diverse than in most other countries. For example, hospitals are owned by federal and state governments, by city and county authorities, by private organizations and by voluntary non-profit-making groups. There are far fewer general practitioners in the United States than there are in Britain. People seeking health care usually contact specialists directly. Hospital charges represent a higher proportion of health costs in the United States than in Britain – or indeed in most other Western countries.

The American health-care system has changed markedly over the past twenty years (Starr, 1982; Light, 1986, 1987). In 1968, the first hospital chain explicitly seeking to make a profit was set up by Thomas F. Frist, a Nashville doctor, and Jack C. Massey, a businessman who was responsible for turning Kentucky Fried Chicken into a national chain. Frist's hospital, Park View, was provided with capital for expansion by the Hospital Corporation of America (HCA) which the two had founded. Subsequently HCA began acquiring other hospitals, and has today become the largest hospital chain of its type in the country. Before this development, most privately owned medical facilities were non-profit-making and run by local community associations or religious orders. Profit-making organizations have also been established in many other areas of health care, including diverse clinics, consultancies and specialized medical centres.

Medicine has traditionally been associated with an imagery of care, service and charity. Has the development of for-profit organizations served to extend, or to damage, these ideals? Can medicine be run in a similar way to fast-food chains? Several studies have been undertaken on these questions, including a major investigation by the Institute of Medicine of the National Academy of Science (Krause, 1977; Fein, 1986). These researches do not support the claim of the for-profit chains that their hospitals are more efficient, and provide better value, than the non-profit ones. On average, charges are significantly higher in the for-profit hospitals.

Comparing quality of medical care is more difficult. The facilities of for-profit organizations seem to match those of others in terms of services available for people who can pay. However, the for-profit hospitals have few patients who are uninsured, or only covered by welfare benefits, so the effect of such organizations is to shift much of the burden of health care on to other sectors of the system. Their overall impact seems to be to drive up the general cost of health care, reduce the proportion of income spent on teaching and research, and produce a pressure towards 'cost-cutting' which can lead to economizing on essential services (Waitzkin, 1986; Califano, 1986).

In spite of the country's high level of wealth, and the vast sums spent on health-care industries, the United States is not the healthiest country in the world. It ranks quite low in terms of the two common measures of the physical well-being of a population – average life expectancy and the rate of infant mortality. There are estimated to be nearly twenty million people in the United States who do not have private health insurance, and have virtually no access to public health care.

The logic of the health-care system in the United States is based on the idea that competition will produce the cheapest services, allowing consumers to pick and choose. The weaknesses in this position are well known. First, consumers cannot readily shop around when they are ill, and are usually unable technically to judge the services they are offered. Secondly, those with inadequate resources have very limited access to medical services, while affluent sections of the population are able to buy far superior medical provision. Thirdly, people who are fully covered by medical insurance have little incentive to seek lower prices for services. The general result is a system which is very expensive to run in proportion to the health levels achieved, and in which there are serious gaps in provision for the population.

The American experience is directly relevant to current British debates about the provision of health care. Private medical organizations

Table 15   The proportion of doctors in the populations of twenty-two countries, 1984

Doctors per 100,000 people		Doctors per 100,000 people	
USSR	357	France	172
Italy	294	United Kingdom	154
Israel	270	Japan	128
Hungary	250	Singapore	87
Switzerland	244	Bahamas	66
West Germany	222	Saudi Arabia	61
Spain	217	Brazil	59
Sweden	204	China	52
USA	192	India	27
Canada	182	Sri Lanka	14
Australia	179	Kenya	9

Source: Leslie Watkins and Robert M. Worcester, *Private Opinions, Public Polls* (London: Thames and Hudson, 1986), p. 123.

have expanded considerably in the UK over the past ten years, and many people see the National Health Service as inefficient, bureaucratic, and insensitive to the needs of individual patients. These critics want a more extensively privatized system, like that of the United States. Yet, as we have seen, there is good reason to view such proposals with caution. Assessing the comparative efficiency of different national health-care systems is very difficult, but the evidence suggests that a substantial dismantling of the NHS would cause more problems than it would resolve, and would almost certainly accentuate existing inequalities in access to health care.

Reproductive technologies

Among the most important phenomena upon which modern medicine has had considerable impact are conception and child-bearing. Four types of medical intervention in human reproduction can be distinguished (Stanworth, 1987).

1 *The prevention of conception.* Contraceptives have been widely available in Western countries for many years. Their introduction and increased efficiency has put parenthood under the direct control of the couple involved in a way unknown in previous times.
2 *The extension of obstetrical services back into pregnancy.* In recent years, increasingly sophisticated means of measuring and screening foetal development in the early stages have been devised, and thus earlier treatment made possible.
3 *The 'managing' of labour and childbirth.* Over the past century or so, this has changed from being a home-based activity, carried out mainly by relatives, friends and amateur midwives, to one undertaken by medical professionals.
4 *Influencing the manner of conception.* New techniques have been developed for bypassing sexual conception and overcoming infertility. These began with the introduction of *artificial insemination* in the 1930s, followed some thirty years later by the discovery of 'fertility drugs'. Such drugs made it possible for some women to have children who had previously been unable to conceive. However, the drugs also frequently gave rise to multiple births.

Some of the most important recent developments in **reproductive technologies** have been in the fourth category. There have been major advances in techniques of *in vitro* fertilization (artificial fertilization of the woman's egg, whether inside or outside the body), including egg or embryo donation (from one woman to another) and low-temperature storage of gametes and embryo. The most important method, however – because it is the simplest – is **surrogate parenthood.** In surrogacy, a woman agrees to be artificially implanted with the sperm of a male from another couple, to whom custody of the child is transferred when it is born.

One general consequence of the development of reproductive technologies is the fact that women bearing children forfeit control over their bodies to gynaecologists and obstetricians – who are mostly male. Until relatively recently, births normally took place in the home, and most aspects of pregnancy and after-birth care were dealt with by midwives. Today most births occur in hospital, and the male-dominated medical profession has moved into the central position in these areas.

The complexity of reproductive technologies presents many social problems and dilemmas, whose importance can only increase as intervention in the reproductive process becomes more and more far-reaching. One major issue concerns the emergence of complicated legal tangles over the definition of parenthood. When a couple has paid a surrogate mother to bear the husband's child, for example, who should have custody of the child if the mother decides she wishes to keep it? The courts in numerous countries are still debating this issue, and commercial surrogacy has been made illegal in several countries.

Age and ageing in the West

Demographic trends

Population trends discussed earlier in the chapter have brought about a very large increase in the proportion of older people in the industrialized countries (Jorgensen, 1980; Zopf, 1986). Yet, at the same time, the social position of older people in modern societies is much more insecure than was the case in many earlier cultures, where old age often brought prestige, wealth and power. Not only did older people usually have a secure position in the community, they retained important duties within the family. Much of this has disappeared in modern societies today (Riley, 1987).

The average age of Britons has been rising for more than a century and a half. In 1800, the average (median) age of the population was probably as low as sixteen. At the turn of the present century, it had risen to twenty-three. By 1970, it was twenty-eight, and today has reached over thirty. The median age of the population will go on rising for some while yet, given that no major changes in current demographic trends occur. It is likely to be thirty-five by 2000, and may climb to thirty-seven by 2030. By the latter year there may be as many as eleven million people over sixty-five in the population. There has also been a large expansion in the numbers of the very old. According to some estimates, the number of those over eighty-five will be 60 per cent above present levels by the year 2000, composing over 1.5 per cent of the whole population (Acheson et al., 1981, p. 7).

There are two main reasons for the growth in the proportion of older people in the population. One is that, on average, people live longer than they used to. Average life expectancy at age one has increased by twelve years for men, and fourteen years for women, since 1900. The other is the effect of the baby boom, as that enlarged generation 'works its way through' the population structure.

What is 'old age'?

As measured purely in terms of years, *old age* is as much a construction of modern times as is *childhood* (see chapter 3: 'Socialization and the Life-Cycle'). Becoming old used to be associated with changes in appearance and physical abilities rather than with chronological age – which in any case was generally unknown. Old age today has a legal definition, in the sense that it refers to the age at which most people retire from work and claims for particular kinds of welfare benefit, such as pensions, can be made.

Retirement

Ages set for retirement and qualification for welfare benefits in fact vary widely both within and between countries. Only a half-century ago it was usual in Britain to regard retirement from work as dependent on ill-health or failing physical abilities. In the late 1920s, more than half of all men over sixty-five were in paid employment. This situation, oddly enough, persists only in certain spheres of social responsibility: leading figures in politics, law, the arts, and a few other fields, often carry on until advanced ages.

In Britain today, the age of compulsory retirement for most men is sixty-five, while for women it is sixty (despite the fact that women usually outlive men by several years). In the United States, a fixed age of retirement has recently been abolished altogether. Most European countries have been improving in the opposite direction, acting to reduce the age levels at which employees must retire. Some European countries oblige employees in government and industrial sectors to retire at sixty – although again this is most often applied to women rather than to male workers. Many countries have now outlawed this practice, however, as a result of legislation on equal rights.

Retirement creates social, economic and psychological problems for individuals and, quite often, for households; it signals a major transition even for those able to treat their new-found free time as an opportunity (Parnes, 1985). Retirement virtually always involves loss of income. The average income for families in which at least one member is sixty-five or older is only just above half the average wage for the UK as a whole. There are, of course, wide variations of income among the over sixty-fives, since this now includes such a large segment of the population.

But many older people (15 per cent of those aged sixty-five or over) live in conditions of some poverty, since the state-provided old-age pension permits few luxuries. Women living alone are on average poorest of all.

The social and psychological consequences of retirement vary according to previous job experience and standards of living. In a society geared to the central value of work, retirement frequently means a loss of status, and the absence of routines that may have structured an individual's life for as much as half a century creates a void difficult to fill. Because of the pace of technological and other changes, knowledge and skills acquired over a lifetime no longer command the respect of the young, as was the case in most traditional cultures.

For housewives, of course, there is no such thing as retirement, and the presence of a husband in the house during the day may make extra work; it certainly needs adjusting to!

Social problems in old age

Old age is often a time of loss in terms of relationships. Retirement spells the loss not only of a job itself but also of contact with others at work. Children have normally moved to homes of their own, and relationships with relatives and friends are lost through death – or distance, since older people normally travel less frequently than the young (Matthews, 1979, p. 47). The proportion of women aged sixty-five or more living alone in the UK is considerably larger than in the age-group forty-five to sixty-five (32 per cent as compared to 15 per cent, in 1985). The ratio of men of sixty-five or more who live alone, however, is actually slightly lower, at 8 per cent, than those aged between forty-five and sixty-four (9 per cent). Fear of violence is a strong influence on the elderly, which may restrict their activities, especially in city areas.

The social situation of older women is usually more problematic than that of men. It is easier for a man, if widowed or divorced, to find a new regular female companion or wife than for a woman to find a male companion, because women live longer – there are more old women. In addition, it is 'socially acceptable' for men to go out with, or marry, much younger women. Older women, too, are generally less used to seeking companionship outside the home and family relationships. Most women respond to the death of their husband with shock, depression and guilt, often becoming physically ill themselves (Riley and Waring, 1976). On the other hand, a minority consider that their lives have improved after their husband's death. They may have been confined to the home as a result of his illness, or perhaps felt restricted by having to fit in with his wishes (Lopata, 1977).

The physical effects of ageing

Old age cannot as such be identified with ill health or disability, although advancing age tends to bring increased health problems. Only during the past twenty years or so have biologists made a systematic attempt to distinguish the physical effects of ageing from traits associated with disease. Precisely to what extent the body inevitably 'wears out' with advancing age is a matter of argument. Social and economic losses are also difficult to disentangle from the effects of physical deterioration as such. Loss of relatives and friends, separation from children where they have moved elsewhere, and loss of employment, may all take a physical toll. While there are many people over sixty-five who claim to have almost perfect health, a high proportion of people in this group in an American study reported 'poor health' and 'not enough medical care' as their most serious problems (Kart, 1985).

The future

In a society which places high value on youth, vitality and physical attractiveness, older people tend to become 'invisible'. Recent years, however, have seen some changes in attitudes towards old age. Older people are unlikely to recover the full authority and prestige that used to be accorded to 'elders' of the community in ancient societies. But as they become a larger and larger proportion of the population, older people acquire more political influence. They have already become a powerful political lobby in the USA, and similar developments are visible in Britain.

Activist groups have also started to fight against **ageism**, seeking to encourage a positive view of old age and older people. Ageism – discrimination against people on the basis of their age – is an ideology just as sexism and racism are. There are as many false stereotypes of older people as there are in other areas of prejudice. For instance, it is often believed that most of the over sixty-fives are in hospital or homes for the elderly; or that a high proportion are senile; or that older workers are less competent than younger ones. All these beliefs are erroneous. Ninety-five percent of people over sixty-five in Britain live in private dwellings; only about 7 per cent of those under the age of eighty show pronounced symptoms of senile decay; and the productivity and attendance records of workers over sixty are superior to those of younger age-groups (Atchley, 1985).

A redefinition of the value and contributions of older people would increase the general level of social tolerance. Benefits at the moment monopolized by the young and the middle-aged might perhaps become more evenly distributed in the future. At the moment, people in these age groups have a monopoly over education, work, power and material rewards. A more even distribution of these, from which older people can draw just as much profit as younger individuals, would be in the interests of social justice.

Summary

1   Population growth is one of the most significant global problems currently faced by humanity. About a quarter of the world's population suffer from malnutrition and over ten million people die of starvation each year. This misery is concentrated in the Third World countries.

2   The study of population is called *demography*. Much demographic work is statistical, but demographers are also concerned to try to explain why population patterns take the form they do. The most important concepts in population analysis are *birth-rates, death-rates, fertility* and *fecundity*.

3   The changes in population patterns which have occurred in the industrialized societies are usually analysed in terms of a process of *demographic transition*. Before industrialization, both birth- and death-rates were high. During the initial period, there was population growth, because death-rates were reduced while birth-rates took longer to decline. Finally there was a new equilibrium, with low birth-rates balancing low death-rates.

4   World resources are finite, even if the limits of what can be produced are continually revised in the light of technological developments. Energy consumption, consumption of raw materials and other goods, are vastly higher in the Western countries than in other areas of the world, and these consumption levels depend on resources transferred from Third World regions to the industrially developed nations. If resources were shared out equally, there would be a significant drop in Western living standards.

5   Population issues are intimately linked to problems of health and illness. All cultures have concepts of physical health and illness, but much of what we now understand as 'medicine' is relatively recent in origin – such as the existence of hospitals, and the application of science and technology to modes of medical treatment.

6   Susceptibility to the major illnesses in modern societies is strongly influenced by socio-economic status. People from more affluent backgrounds tend to be healthier, taller, stronger, and to live longer, than those from poorer backgrounds.

7   *Reproductive technologies* – affecting fertilization, the growth of the embryo, and the manner of birth – pose difficult and controversial ethical questions. Much debate now centres on the rights – of parents and children – involved in *surrogacy*.

8   Retirement creates social, economic and psychological problems for individuals (and often for households). For most people retirement is a major transition, usually signalling loss of income and often a change in status. It can be disorientating, since people must restructure much of their daily routine, and lonely.

9   In recent years, older people, who now make up a large proportion of the population of the industrialized countries, have started to press for

more recognition of their distinctive interests and needs. The struggle against 'ageism' (discrimination against people on grounds of their age) is an important aspect of this development.

Basic concepts

crude birth-rate	crude death-rate
fertility	demographic transition

Important terms

demography	Malthusianism
fecundity	health-care system
infant mortality rate	public health care
life expectancy	private health care
life span	reproductive technologies
exponential growth	surrogate parenthood
doubling time	ageism

Further reading

E. Boserup, *Population and Technological Change* (Chicago: Chicago University Press, 1981) — a useful discussion of population dynamics and technology.

Lesley Doyal and Imogen Pennell, *The Political Economy of Health* (London: Pluto Press, 1979) — discusses the role of economic factors in the treatment of illness.

D. Hobman (ed.), *The Social Challenge of Ageing* (London: Croom Helm, 1978) — an account of the problems posed by the ageing of modern populations.

Nathan Keyfitz, 'On future population', *Journal of the American Statistical Association*, 67 (1972) — an interpretation of population trends into the future.

M. Morgan et al., *Sociological Approaches to Health and Medicine* (London: Croom Helm, 1985) — a useful survey of the sociology of health and illness.

19

Revolutions and Social Movements

Revolutions have brought about some of the most momentous social changes in world history over the past two or three centuries. The American and French revolutions, of 1776 and 1789 respectively, were the most important eighteenth-century revolutions. Some of their leaders' ideas were subsequently very influential. The ideals of liberty, citizenship and equality, in the name of which the two revolutions were fought, have become fundamental modern political values. The announcement of these as goals – and the supposition that they could be realized through mass action – was a profound historical innovation. In previous eras, only the most idealistic dreamers had ventured to suggest that human beings could establish a social order in which political participation would be open to everyone.

The term **revolution** came to be employed in its modern sense at about the same time as the term **democracy**. It was not widely used until the success of the American and French struggles made it clear that something new was afoot in the world. The European observer who wrote with more insight than anyone else about the United States and France at that period, Alexis de Tocqueville, observed: 'What, to start with, had seemed to European monarchs and statesmen a mere passing phase, a not unusual symptom of a nation's growing pains, was now discovered to be something absolutely new, quite unlike any previous movement, and so widespread, extraordinary, and incalculable as to baffle human understanding' (Tocqueville, 1966, p. 35).

At that time, 'revolution' still carried a strong remnant of its previous meaning, which had been to 'move in a circle' (the sense in which we still speak of the revolution of a wheel when a vehicle is in motion). The American and French revolutionary leaders, in fact, believed that they were 'turning back' to a natural order of things. They declared that human beings are born free and equal, but have been oppressed by the rule of kings and other self-appointed authorities; revolution was the means of restoring their happy natural condition. In some respects, therefore, the truly innovative nature of the American and French revolutions was not apparent even to those who had played the greatest part in bringing them about.

As it became more and more obvious that at least some of the resulting changes were permanent, and as the influence of the ideals for which the revolutionaries had fought spread, 'revolution' came increasingly to refer to mass action taken with the objective of bringing about fundamental social reconstruction (Abrams, 1982). Although some revolutions since then have been prompted by a concern to restore a pre-existing form of society (such as the Islamic revolution in contemporary Iran), the idea of revolution has been overwhelmingly associated with *progress* – representing a break with the past in order to establish a new order for the future (Arendt, 1963).

What is a revolution? What are the social conditions that lead to revolutionary change? How should we best analyse movements of protest or rebellion? These are the main questions to be addressed in this chapter. First, we must define our terms. It is not possible to understand revolution in general without knowing about the conditions under which major processes of revolutionary change have occurred. So we shall look at several revolutions in some detail before discussing various thinkers' attempts to generalize about radical political change and the impact of social movements.

Defining revolution

As a first step, we need to define the concept of revolution in as precise a fashion as possible. Everyday uses of the term vary widely. A **coup d'état**, involving simply the replacement of one set of leaders by others with no change in the political institutions and overall authority system, for example, would not be a revolution in sociological terms. For a set of events to constitute a revolution, they have to have several characteristics.

1 A series of events is not a revolution unless a *mass social movement* is involved. This condition serves to exclude instances in which either a party comes to power through electoral processes, or a small group, such as army leaders, seize power.
2 A revolution leads to *major processes of reform or change* (Skocpol, 1979, pp. 4–5). John Dunn has pointed out that this means that those who take power must genuinely be more capable of governing the society over which they assume control than those who have been overthrown; the leadership must be capable of achieving at least some of its targets (Dunn, 1972, pp. 15–16). A society in which a movement succeeds in gaining the formal trappings of power, but is then unable to rule effectively, cannot be said to have experienced a revolution; it is likely rather to be a society in chaos, or threatened with disintegration.
3 Revolution involves the *threat or use of violence* on the part of those participating in the mass movement. Revolutions are political changes brought about in the face of opposition from the pre-existing authorities, who cannot be persuaded to relinquish their power without the threatened or actual use of violent means.

Assembling the three criteria together, we can define a revolution as the seizure of state power through violent means by the leaders of a mass movement, where that power is subsequently used to initiate major processes of social reform.

Revolutions differ from armed **rebellions**, which involve the threat or use of violence, but do not lead to substantial change. Until around three hundred years ago, the majority of uprisings were rebellions rather than revolutions. In mediaeval Europe, for example, serfs or peasants sometimes rose up in protest against the policies of their masters (Scott, 1986; Zagorin, 1982). However, their objective almost invariably was to secure more favourable treatment from them, or to replace a particularly tyrannical individual by someone less harsh. The idea of action taken to alter radically the existing political structure of society was virtually unknown.

Revolutions in the twentieth century

Almost all twentieth-century revolutions have happened in developing societies, not in the industrial nations (Moore, 1965). The episodes of revolutionary activity that have had the most profound consequences for the world as a whole were the Russian Revolution of 1917 and the Chinese Revolution of 1949. Both took place in heavily rural, peasant societies, although the Soviet Union has since attained a high level of industrialization. Many Third World countries have also experienced revolutions in this century – for example, Mexico, Turkey, Egypt, Vietnam, Cuba and Nicaragua.

The Russian Revolution

Before 1917, Russia was an economically backward society ruled in an autocratic way by the tsars (emperors or kings). Most of the population lived in rural poverty and the tsarist regime was for the most part a dictatorial one, involving the extensive use of secret police and informers to keep dissidents powerless. Serfdom (or slavery) was not abolished in Russia until after 1860. The decision of the government to free the serfs was part of an attempt to modernize a society no longer able to compete militarily with the leading European powers. Russia was the loser in the Crimean War of 1854–5, and again in a war with the Japanese, fought in 1905. Largely in response to these defeats, programmes of investment in industrial development, including the building of many new roads and railways, were instituted. While some economic success was achieved, the tsarist government was too traditionalist to permit the thorough social reforms that were taking place in the European countries.

Russia by 1905 was already a society under considerable strain. The beginnings of rapid industrialization had produced a developing class of industrial workers, whose conditions of life were sometimes as miserable as those of most of the peasantry. Prevented from organizing effective trade unions, and completely excluded from political influence, the industrial workers became increasingly hostile to the government. For a far longer period, there had been growing hostility to the tsars among some of the peasantry. During the Russo-Japanese war of 1905, an uprising had been led by factory workers and members of the armed forces disillusioned with the progress of the war. It was only quelled because the government rapidly signed a peace treaty with the Japanese, disciplining the dissident troops and bringing them back to crush the rebels. The tsar, Nicholas II, introduced a few reforms, such as the establishing of a representative parliament, but retracted them all once he felt his power was again secure.

Between 1905 and 1917 there was considerable discontent among industrial workers and peasants, expressed in many strikes. Some of these were led by the Bolsheviks, one among a number of parties professing allegiance to socialism or Marxism. The influence of such parties increased during the early years of the First World War (1914–18), a conflict in which Russia again fared badly – with much more serious consequences than in earlier wars, because of the huge numbers of people involved. Russia had fifteen million men in its armies, but could not afford to equip them well enough to defeat the Germans. Several million men were killed, wounded or taken prisoner, and a high proportion of the officers were killed.

Shortages of food and fuel caused considerable suffering among civilians as most resources were devoted to the war effort. The wealthier groups, as well as the poor, started to turn decisively against the government. The Tsar, maintaining his right to absolute rule, and guided by his strange adviser Rasputin, became more and more isolated from other groups in the country. In March 1917, workers and soldiers in Petrograd initiated a series of strikes and riots which rapidly spread throughout Western Russia. The Tsar was forced to abdicate and a new provisional government was set up.

The army, meanwhile, had more or less disintegrated, most of the soldiers returning to their home villages, towns and cities. Peasants began forcibly to take over land from the major landowners, and the provisional government was unable to contain continuing unrest and violence among workers and demobilized soldiers. Lenin, the leader of the Bolsheviks, determined to seize power, using as his slogan 'Peace and Bread, Peace and Land' – an appeal to both the urban workers and the peasantry. In October 1917 the Bolsheviks forcibly dismissed the provisional government. Reorganizing and remobilizing the armed forces in the new Red Army, and successfully emerging from a period of bitter civil war, the new Soviet government set about implementing fundamental social changes. The basis for what has now become the second most mighty industrial and military power in the world was laid (Carr, 1970).

The Russian Revolution was unusual in certain ways. The uprisings which initially undermined the tsarist regime were more spontaneous, and occurred on a larger scale, than those which happened in most other revolutions this century. At the beginning of 1917, not even the Bolsheviks anticipated that a successful revolution would be brought about within such a short time. Yet the Russian experience teaches us a good deal about modern revolutions in general:

1 Many revolutions have taken place against the background of a war. Prolonged war puts strain on accepted institutions and, if conducted ineptly, is likely to result in a sharply declining level of support for the government. Disaffection within the armed forces removes a regime's major instrument for suppressing those who oppose it.
2 The peasants played an important role. Before the Russian Revolution, many people (including Lenin) believed peasants to be an almost completely conservative force, wedded to traditional ways of life, and unlikely to join any movement for radical social change. This assumption was shown to be false: in the majority of twentieth-century revolutions, in fact, peasants have been directly involved.

Revolution in China

China was remote from the West until the development of steel-built passenger and cargo ships in the nineteenth century. The historical continuity of the Chinese imperial state, stretching back at least two thousand years, remained unbroken until after the turn of the present century. Indeed, although some processes of modernization had been promoted within government circles, much of Chinese society on the eve of the 1949 revolution still followed long-established, traditional ways of life.

While China was too large for any Western power to colonize, the extensive trading activities which the European states maintained in the country in the nineteenth century undermined the established economy. Largely because of the unfavourable conditions of trade imposed on China, the imperial government in the late nineteenth century found itself increasingly impoverished. Unable to repay debts to European creditors, the government increased its taxation of the peasantry. As a consequence, riots and rebellions among peasants became frequent. In many parts of the enormous country, particularly where central political control had always been weak, local lords and bandits more or less did as they pleased.

Although the Chinese believed deeply in the superiority of their civilization to all others, they were regularly humiliated both by the European states and by the Japanese. China lost various territories over which it had previously held sway in Central and South East Asia, and was also defeated in successive military encounters with the British, French and Japanese.

In 1911 a large-scale uprising forced the Emperor to abdicate. Although they are sometimes spoken of as a 'revolution', the events of 1911 and 1912 did not establish a government capable of unifying the country and promoting effective reforms. A Chinese Republic was set up, but local military leaders also established their own kingdoms and some of the provinces declared their independence. For the next few years there was effectively a prolonged civil war, during which the mass of the peasant population suffered as much as those actually involved in the fighting.

This was followed by a period of relative stability, when one war leader, Chiang Kai-Shek, won control over much of the country, hunting down and massacring members of the Communist Party wherever he could find them. As a result the Communists, who had previously established themselves in the cities, moved out to remote peasant areas. Mao Tse-tung, at the head of the surviving elements of the Communist movement, attempted to adapt Marx's ideas to the Chinese context, giving particular importance to the peasantry as a revolutionary force. The movement Mao led also had strong nationalist overtones, emphasizing the need to rebuild Chinese society in the face of the inroads made both by Western influences and by the Japanese.

The Communists became the main group resisting the Japanese invasion which occurred during the Second World War, doing so primarily by the use of guerrilla tactics. The Japanese occupation during this period threw the country back again into a state of almost complete disintegration. Following the war, the battles between the Communists and Chiang Kai-Shek's followers resumed, ending in victory in 1949 for Mao's Red Army. The remnants of Chiang Kai-Shek's forces were moved with the aid of the American fleet to Formosa (now Taiwan).

When the new government came to power in 1949, China could hardly be said to be a political unity. If the Communists had not been as successful as they were in reforging national unity, 'China' as it is today might not exist. The country could well have been broken up into several states, as indeed had happened to most traditional empires. (There are several states in North Africa and the Middle East, for example, where the Ottoman empire used to be (Dunn, 1972, p. 74).) The Communist government was able to build up a broad base of support by combining appeals to nationalism with very extensive rural reconstruction. Three years after the revolution, 45 per cent of the cultivated land had been removed from the control of traditional land-lords and distributed among 300 million peasants (Carrier, 1976, p. 140).

The Cuban experience

As a contrast to the cases of Russia and China, it is worth looking at the Cuban Revolution. Cuba, of course, is not a massive land-locked country, but a small island with a population of only some eight million people. Unlike most of the less-developed countries, over half of Cuba's population before the revolution lived in urban areas, the majority in Havana, the capital. The country was originally a colony of Spain, but the Spanish settlers treated the existing Indian population brutally; the islanders were virtually wiped out by the colonists and the ravages of epidemics they brought. Slaves were therefore fetched from Africa in the eighteenth and early nineteenth centuries to work in the sugar, coffee and tobacco fields.

As a result of a war in 1898 with the United States (from which the Americans emerged also controlling the Philippines, Puerto Rico and Guam), Spain relinquished its control over Cuba. The island was occupied by the American army, following the Spanish withdrawal, and a treaty was signed with the new government that gave the United States extensive rights to intervene in Cuba's internal affairs. (The US Marines were in fact called into Cuba on several occasions.) Commercial enter-prises owned by firms in the United States came to dominate the econo-my of the island; Americans owned 75 per cent of the cultivated land, 63 per cent of the sugar industry and all the railways. Over three-quarters of Cuba's exports were of sugar, most of it shipped to the United States (Boorstein, 1967). Cuba was thus extremely dependent economically on the United States, which was able to keep the price of sugar artificially low. It has been said that 'even though a Cuban flag flew over the island, the real power sign was the American dollar' (Carrier, 1976, p. 299).

By the 1930s Cuba had a history of unrest and unstable govern-ment, which culminated in a series of uprisings across the island.

Eventually, Cuban army officers led by Fulgencio Batista took control, banning elections. Batista pursued policies favourable to United States business interests, while accumulating a vast fortune for himself. A system of elections was reintroduced, as a result of which Batista lost power in 1944. (He moved then for a while to Florida, enjoying the fruits of his personal fortune.) In 1952, he returned to power by means of a military *coup d'état*.

Batista was in turn overthrown by a band of revolutionaries led by Fidel Castro – although initially it was far from obvious that Castro would become a successful military leader. Castro raised a small guerrilla force in Mexico, consisting of eighty-two individuals, which landed in Cuba late in 1956. They were soon spotted by Batista's air force, and attacked by the army. Only twenty-two survived, ten of whom were captured. The other twelve, including Castro, managed to reach the Sierra Mountains in Oriente, where they started a new guerrilla group, attracting several hundred peasants to join them.

Although Batista sent 12,000 soldiers into the area to crush the guerrillas, they were not successful; the guerrilla movement grew, and gained a following in the urban areas as well as among rural workers. Castro's aims were patriotic, and included the introduction of democracy and reform of ownership of land. He was not at that time closely associated with Marxism, and the Communist-led Popular Socialist Party did not give him active encouragement until it became clear that the movement was gaining more and more public approval.

The guerrilla forces never exceeded more than 2,000 in number, deployed against an army of over 40,000, plus an air force, yet the revolution was successful. The crumbling of support for Batista among the population at large, and defections in the armed forces themselves, made it possible for Castro to enter Havana without a shot being fired. Batista left the island in January 1959, and the army surrendered to the guerrillas.

The proximity of Cuba to the American mainland, combined with the history of US intervention on the island, made the new revolutionary state very vulnerable to US invasion. Its dependence upon sugar exports to the United States was a further brake on the new government's ability to control the island. Castro dealt with this problem by acquiring support from the Soviet Union, which was only too willing to acquire a political, and possibly a military, presence so near the American mainland. An agreement was made to sell sugar to the USSR in exchange for oil, but in 1960 the United States government cancelled orders for the balance of Cuba's sugar imports that year. The Cubans responded by nationalizing all American-owned sugar fields, together with some other industries, services and railways. Cuba to some extent exchanged one form of dependence for another: trade, and inflows of material support, from the Soviet Union became as essential to the economy as sugar exports to the United States had been before. Yet the very rivalry between the

United States and the Soviet Union over the fate of the island allowed Castro space for the creation of a strong and effective government.

Looking at the origins and nature of the Cuban Revolution, we can see that caution is needed in generalizing from the examples of Russia and China. The Cuban Revolution did not take place against a background of general war, as in the other two cases. The ideas that originally prompted the guerrilla movement which Castro led were not primarily derived from Marxism. Yet the Cuban example does allow us to identify some factors probably characteristic of most revolutions, certainly twentieth-century ones. These include the influence of nationalism; the role of intellectuals as leaders; the important part played by the peasantry; and the fact that, at some point, the pre-existing regime loses effective control of at least a large part of the military.

Theories of revolution

Since revolutions have been so important in world history over the past two centuries, it is not surprising that a diversity of theories exists to try to account for them. Some such theories were formulated early in the history of the social sciences; the most important approach here is that of Marx. Marx lived well before any of the revolutions undertaken in the name of his ideas took place, yet he intended his views to be taken not just as an analysis of the conditions of revolutionary change, but as a means of furthering such change. Whatever their intrinsic validity, Marx's ideas have had immense practical impact on twentieth-century social change.

Other influential theories date from much later, and have tried to explain both the 'original' revolutions (such as the American or French) and subsequent ones. Some have cast the net even more widely, trying to analyse revolutionary activity in conjunction with other forms of rebellion or protest. We shall look at four frameworks for the study of revolution: Marx's view; the theory of political violence suggested by Chalmers Johnson; the account of revolution and rising economic expectations put forward by James Davies; and the interpretation of collective protest proposed by the historical sociologist Charles Tilly.

Marx's theory

Marx's view of revolution is based on his interpretation of human history in general. According to him, the development of societies is marked by periodic class conflicts which, when they become acute, tend to end in a process of revolutionary change. Class struggles derive from the **contradictions** – unresolvable tensions – which societies embody.

The main sources of contradiction are to be traced to economic changes, changes in the *forces of production*. In any fairly stable society, there is a balance between the economic structure, social relationships and the political system. As the forces of production alter, contradiction is intensified, leading to open clashes between classes – and ultimately to revolution.

Marx applies this model both to the past development of feudalism and to what he sees as the probable future evolution of industrial capitalism. The traditional, feudal societies of Europe were based on peasant production, the producers being serfs ruled by a class of landed aristocrats and gentry. Economic changes within these societies gave rise to towns and cities, in which trade and manufacture developed. This new economic system, created *within* feudal society, threatened its very basis. Rather than being founded upon the traditional lord–serf relationship, the emerging economic order encouraged industrialists to produce goods for sale on open markets. The contradictions between the old feudal economy and the newly emerging capitalist one eventually became acute, taking the form of violent conflicts between the rising capitalist class and the feudal landowners. Revolution was the outcome of this process, the most important example being the French Revolution of 1789. Through such revolutions, and revolutionary changes occurring in other European societies, Marx argues, the capitalist class managed to achieve dominance.

The coming of capitalism, however, according to Marx, set up new contradictions, which would eventually lead to a further series of revolutions prompted by ideals of **socialism** or **communism**. *Industrial capitalism* is an economic order based on the private pursuit of profit and on competition between firms to sell their products. This system creates a gulf between a rich minority, who control the industrial resources, and an impoverished majority of wage-workers. Workers and capitalists come into more and more intense conflict with one another. Labour movements and political parties, representing the mass of the working population, eventually mount a challenge to the rule of the capitalist class and overthrow the existing political system. Where the position of a dominant class is particularly entrenched, Marx believes, violence is needed to bring about the required transition. In other circumstances, this process might happen peacefully through parliamentary action – a *revolution* (in the sense in which it was defined above) would not be necessary.

Marx expected revolutions to occur in some Western countries during his life-time. Towards the end of his life, when it became clear that this was not to be, he turned his attention elsewhere. Interestingly, he looked particularly towards Russia. Russia, he argued, was an economically retarded society within which new forms of commerce and manufacture, borrowed from Western Europe, were being adopted. He thought that this was likely to create contradictions more severe than those developing within the European countries themselves, because introduction of novel types of production and technology into a backward society led to a highly explosive mixture of the old and the new. In correspondence with Russian radicals, Marx claimed that these conditions might lead to a revolution in their country, but he added that the revolution would only be successful if it spread to other Western states. In these circumstances, a post-revolutionary government in Russia could take advantage of the more developed economic circumstances of the rest of Europe to push forward a rapid process of modernization.

Evaluation

Revolutions have failed to occur, contrary to Marx's expectation, in the advanced, industrialized societies of the West. In most Western countries (the United States being a notable exception) there are political parties regarding themselves as socialist or communist, many of which claim to be following Marx's ideas. Where they have come to power, however, they have generally become less, rather than more, radical. It is possible, of course, that Marx simply got the time-scale wrong, and that the revolutions he anticipated will one day take place in Europe, the United States and elsewhere. It is much more plausible to suppose that Marx's diagnosis was at fault. The development of industrial capitalism does not lead, as Marx supposed, to more and more intense clashes between workers and capitalists.

It does not follow from this that Marx's theory is irrelevant to the contemporary world. There is an important sense in which it *cannot* be irrelevant, because it has become part of the ideals and values held both by revolutionary movements and by established governments. Moreover, some of Marx's views can be adapted to make sense of Third World revolutions. The thesis he applied to Russia seems relevant to events in many peasant countries affected by the spread of industrial capitalism. Tensions are set up at the points of contact between the expansion of modern industry and traditional systems. As the traditional modes of life dissolve, those affected become a source of potentially revolutionary opposition to governments which try to preserve the old order.

Chalmers Johnson: revolution as 'disequilibrium'

Marx had only few cases of revolution on which to base his analyses. Those trying to understand revolution today have a much wider range of historical examples to study. They can also see what impact Marx's ideas themselves have had in helping generate the momentum of revolutionary change.

The work of Chalmers Johnson is based on notions drawn from Talcott Parsons (Johnson, 1964, 1966). According to Parsons, societies are *self-regulating systems*. A self-regulating system is one which adjusts to change by a reordering of its institutions, so as to maintain a balance between them and keep the system working effectively. The best way to understand this idea is by an analogy with the physiology of the body. When the bodily system is in working order, it is able to respond successfully to changes in its environment. If external temperature rises, for example, the body mobilizes certain mechanisms, such as the sweat glands, to keep its own temperature stable. It may happen, however, that conditions change so drastically that the whole system is thrown into disarray. If, say, outside temperature rises too high, the body's mechanisms would not be able to cope, and there would be major disturbance in the functioning of the physiological system. The bodily system at this point is in disequilibrium.

In Johnson's theory, the **disequilibrium** of societies is a necessary condition for the occurrence of revolution. The main source of disequilibrium, according to him, is dislocation between the major cultural values of the society and the system of economic production. This can happen as a result of either internal or major external changes, but usually involves both. In nineteenth- and early twentieth-century China, for example, the traditional values of Chinese culture came under increasing strain from the impact of changes in the economic system brought about by Western trade and commerce. The old system of production, involving landlords and bonded peasants, began to disintegrate – producing disequilibrium.

Once such disequilibrium has occurred, according to Johnson, many people become disorientated and willing to look to new leaders who promise social transformation. The existing authorities start to lose the support of an increasing proportion of the population. Revolution does not happen automatically at this point. If the political authorities react effectively to the situation, initiating policies that will restore equilibrium, they can avoid being overthrown. A stubborn ruling elite might dig in its heels, and deploy whatever armed force it has at its command to crush sources of protest, and if this is successful, a coercive regime or 'police state' may come into being. Military force might be used ruthlessly to stamp out opposition, moving the whole society back from the changes that were beginning to occur.

No society can be governed for long, however, purely by the use of force. If the regime cannot persuade most of the population to readopt their traditional habits and attitudes, it will not last. When it is clear that the society is in fundamental disarray, the armed forces themselves start to lose their loyalty to the rulers. Several factors may hasten this process, the most important of which is defeat in war (as occurred in Russia before the 1917 revolution), which demoralizes the military, as well as inherently weakening them. At this point there will be either a collapse into chaos and civil war, or a revolution. A new regime comes to power, initiating reforms that bring the society back into (a new form of) equilibrium.

Evaluation

Johnson's theory is clear and comprehensive. What he refers to as 'disequilibrium' is plainly similar to Marx's notion of contradiction. While it is not obvious that Johnson's notion is superior to Marx's, the idea that social change sets up dislocations that cannot be handled by existing institutions without their radical restructuring, does seem to make sense.

A limitation of Johnson's view is the idea that societies normally exist in some kind of natural condition of harmony or equilibrium. This is surely not so: most societies, particularly in the modern world, include many sources of tension or dislocation, without becoming prone to revolution. Moreover, Johnson pays little attention to the actual *content* of the ideas which revolutionaries pursue. People do not become revolutionaries merely because a social system is undergoing strain. We cannot understand modern revolutions without seeing the distinctive effect of calls for freedom, democracy and equality on impulses to create new forms of social order (Smith, 1973, pp. 115–29). Finally, Johnson's theory cannot easily explain why revolution has become quite common in the modern era, but was previously virtually unknown.

James Davies: why do revolutions occur?

One clue as to why revolution has become relatively common has been suggested by James Davies. Davies points out that we find innumerable periods of history at which people have lived in dire poverty, or subject to extreme oppression, but have not risen up in protest. Constant poverty or deprivation does not make people into revolutionaries; rather, they usually endure such conditions with resignation or mute despair. Revolutions are more likely to occur when there is an *improvement* in people's living conditions. Once standards of living have started to rise, people's levels of expectation also go up. If improvement in actual conditions subsequently slows down, propensities to revolt are created because rising expectations are frustrated.

Thus social protest, and ultimately revolution, tend to occur in circumstances in which there is some improvement in people's conditions of life. It is not *absolute deprivation* that leads to protest, but **relative deprivation** – what matters is the discrepancy between the lives people are forced to lead and what they think could realistically be achieved.

Assessment

This thesis is useful in understanding the connections between revolution and modern social and economic development. The influence of ideals of progress, together with expectations of economic growth, tend to induce rising expectations, which, if then frustrated, spark protest.

Such protest gains further strength from the spread of ideas of equality and democratic political participation (Davies, 1962; Brinton, 1965).

As Charles Tilly has pointed out, however, Davies's theory does not show how and why different groups *mobilize* to seek revolutionary change. Protest might well often occur against a backdrop of rising expectations; to understand how protest is transformed into revolutionary action, we need to identify how groups become collectively organized to make effective political challenges.

Charles Tilly's theory of protest

In his *From Mobilization to Revolution*, Charles Tilly concentrates on this issue, attempting to analyse processes of revolutionary change in the context of an interpretation of broader forms of protest and violence (Tilly, 1978). He distinguishes four main components of **collective action** – action taken to contest or try to overthrow an existing social order.

1 The **organization** of the group or groups involved. Protest movements are organized in many ways, varying from spontaneous formation of crowds to tightly disciplined revolutionary groups. The movement Castro led, for example, began as a small guerrilla band.
2 **Mobilization.** This involves the ways in which a group acquires control over sufficient resources to make collective action possible. Such resources may include supplies of material goods, political support or weaponry. Castro was able to acquire material and moral support from a sympathetic peasantry, together with many townspeople.
3 The *common interests* of those engaging in collective action, what they see as the gains and losses likely to be achieved by their policies or tactics. Some common interests always underlie mobilization to collective action. Castro managed to weld together a broad coalition of support because many people had, or thought they had, a common interest in removing the existing government.
4 *Opportunity*. Obviously chance events may occur that provide opportunities to pursue revolutionary aims. Many forms of collective action, including revolution, are greatly influenced by such incidental happenings. There was no inevitability to Castro's success, which depended on a number of contingent factors – in the early stages, Castro's 'invasion' was almost a complete fiasco. If he had been one of the seventy captured or killed, would there have been a revolution?

Collective action itself can simply be defined as people acting together in pursuit of interests they share – for example, gathering to demonstrate in support of their cause. There may be various levels of activism among those who engage in such behaviour, some being intensely involved, others lending more passive or irregular support. Effective collective action, such as that which culminates in revolution, usually moves from (1) organization, to (2) mobilization, to (3) the perceiving of shared interests, and finally to (4) the occurrence of concrete opportunities to act effectively (Tilly, 1978, pp. 7–10).

Social movements, in Tilly's view, tend to develop as means of mobilizing group resources either when people have no institutionalized means of making their voices heard, or where their needs are directly repressed by the state authorities. How far groups can secure active and effective representation within an existing political system is of key importance in determining whether their members turn to violence to achieve their ends. Collective action at some point involves open confrontation with the political authorities – 'taking to the streets'. However, only where such activity is backed by groups who are systematically organized is it likely to have much impact on established patterns of power.

Typical modes of collective action and protest vary with historical and cultural circumstances. In Britain today, for example, most people know how groups get together to represent their demands, and are familiar with forms of demonstration like mass marches, large assemblies and street riots – whether or not they have participated in any such activities. There are many other types of collective protest, however, which have become less common or have disappeared altogether in most modern societies (such as fights between villages, machine-breaking or lynching). Those who form protest movements can also build on examples taken from elsewhere, modifying their own practice. For instance, guerrilla movements proliferated in various parts of the world once disaffected groups learned how successful guerrilla actions can be against regular armies.

When and why does collective action become violent? After studying a large number of different incidents occurring in Western Europe since 1800, Tilly concludes that most collective violence develops from action which is not itself initially violent. Whether violence occurs depends not so much on the nature of the activity, as on other forces – in particular, how the authorities respond. A good instance is the street demonstration. The vast majority of such demonstrations pass off without damage either to people or to property. A minority lead to violence, and are then labelled in a different way – as 'riots'. Sometimes, of course, the authorities step in when violence has already come about; more often, the historical record shows, they are the originators of violent reaction. In Tilly's words, 'in the modern European experience repressive forces are themselves the most consistent initiators and performers of collective violence' (1978, p. 177). Moreover, where violent confrontations do occur, the agents of authority are responsible for the largest share of deaths and injuries. This is not surprising given the special access they have to arms and military discipline. The groups they are attempting to control, conversely, do a greater range of damage to objects or property (Tilly, 1978, pp. 176–7).

Revolutionary movements, according to Tilly, are a type of collective action that occurs in situations of what he calls **multiple sovereignty** – conditions in which a government for some reason lacks full control over the areas it is supposed to administer. Multiple sovereignty can arise as a result of external war, internal political clashes, or the two combined. Whether a revolutionary take-over of power is accomplished depends on how far the ruling authorities maintain control over the armed forces, the existence of conflicts within ruling groups, and the level of organization of the protest movements trying to seize power.

Assessment

Tilly's work represents one of the most sophisticated attempts to ana-lyse collective violence and revolutionary struggles. The concepts he develops seem to have wide application, and his use of them is sensitive to the variabilities of historical time and place. Questions of the nature of the organization of social movements, the resources they are able to mobilize, and the relation between groups contending for power, are all important aspects of circumstances of revolutionary transformation.

Tilly says little, however, about the circumstances that *lead* to 'multiple sovereignty'. This is such a fundamental part of explaining revolution that it represents a serious omission. According to Theda Skocpol, Tilly assumes that revolutionary movements are guided by the conscious and deliberate pursuit of interests, successful pro-cesses of revolutionary change occurring when people manage to realize these. Skocpol, by contrast, sees revolutionary movements as more ambiguous and indecisive in their objectives. Revolutions, she emphasizes, largely emerge as unintended consequences of more partial aims towards which groups and movements strive. She writes:

> The purposive image is just as misleading about the process and outcome of historical revolutions as it is about their causes. For the image strongly suggests that revolutionary processes and outcomes can be understood in terms of the activity and intentions or interests of the key group(s) who launch the revolution in the first place. . . such notions are much too simple. In fact, in historical revolutions, differently situated and motivated groups have become participants in complex unfoldings of multiple conflicts. These conflicts have been powerfully shaped and limited by existing social, economic and international conditions. And they have proceeded in different ways depending upon how each revolutionary situation emerged in the first place. (Skocpol, 1979, p. 17; Dunn, 1985)

The consequences of revolution

Investigating the outcome of revolutions is every bit as complex as analysing their origins. What happens *after* a revolution is partly influenced by the very events that led up to it. After a period of revolutionary struggle, a country may be impoverished and bitterly divided. Remnants of the defeated regime, or other groups contending for power, may regroup their forces and reinvade. If surrounding states are hostile to the new government (as was the case after the 1917 Russian Revolution, for example), its success in achieving social reconstruction may be much more limited than where they are sympathetic and prepared to lend active support. There are also major differences between the objectives of revolutionary governments themselves – some have much more radical aims than others. Finally, although revolutions may have long-term consequences for the society in which they occur, it is extremely difficult to disentangle these from other factors involved in that society's subsequent development.

Short-term consequences

Many revolutions are followed by a period of civil war, during which the incoming regime must defeat the opposing groups. Revolutions usually occur in circumstances in which the authority of a pre-existing government has been radically undermined, and several movements may be competing to replace it. Some of these might be militarily strong enough to continue the fight against the new government, or receive funding from other nations supporting their cause. This was the case in the Russian, Chinese and Cuban revolutions, although the degree of opposition they faced varied – Russia was actually invaded by forces sent by Western countries to assist those loyal to the old regime.

Revolutions are made in the name of freedom, but they are often succeeded by a period in which there is severe social repression. This was not true of the American revolution, and there are other exceptions too. In Cuba, for instance, although some of the more affluent residents fled the country, there were few imprisonments or arbitrary killings by the new authorities. More commonly, however, revolutions have been succeeded by periods of widespread arbitrary imprisonment, executions and rigid censorship. Some have been followed by extensive violence. The use of the term **revolutionary terror** to mean the systematic application of violence to enforce obedience to the new authorities first developed to describe the aftermath of the French Revolution of 1789 (see chapter 10: 'Politics, Government and the State'). Large numbers of people deemed to be supporters of the old regime, or enemies of the revolution, were hunted down and publicly executed.

Where they occur, such episodes tend to happen some years after the assumption of power by the new regime, rather than immediately, because there is usually a 'settling down' period before a revolutionary government starts to try to implement its radical new programme. At this point, existing resistance either from supporters of the old regime, or from other dissident groups, is likely to combine with opposition generated by the new policies. In the Soviet Union, for example, Stalin pursued a vigorous policy of setting up collective farms, in the face of widespread resistance from the peasants. In this process, and in the purges of dissident groups, very many people lost their lives or were transported to labour-camps; it has been estimated that 5 per cent of the Soviet population were arrested during this period (Kesselman et al., 1987). These events happened, however, more than a decade after the revolution itself.

Long-term consequences

We can attempt to assess the longer-term impact of revolution by comparing societies which resemble one another save for the fact that some have experienced revolutions while others have not. For example, we can compare the development of China over the past forty years with that of India. Both countries freed themselves from direct Western influence at about the same time, shortly after the Second World War, but whereas China experienced a revolution, India did not. In India, although strong movements of protest against British rule caused much disruption, the British withdrew without being overthrown in a revolutionary process.

The lines of development the two societies have taken since the 1940s differ significantly. In China, the Communist Party established a strong, centralized government apparatus, imposing strict censorship on the press and other media. India, by contrast, has a parliament on the Western model, with multi-party elections. The level of political freedom in China is well below that of India, as measured in terms of the diversity of views which can be publicly expressed, and types of political organization that can be legally formed. On the other hand, China has made far more progress in reducing extreme poverty, eliminating official corruption, and in providing health and welfare facilities. The level of literacy is much higher in China than in India. Given the frequent violence of the years before the revolution, a remarkable feature of the period of Chinese Communist rule has been the relative absence of violent repression by the state. There were few mass killings or internments such as characterized the Stalinist period in the Soviet Union.

Estimates of Chinese economic development vary widely, but it is generally agreed that the growth-rate in China in the fifteen years after the revolution was high – much higher than that of India. The growth-rate during this period, and for most years since, was well ahead of population expansion – again, unlike India. Chinese agrarian reform was also much more successful, with the power of the rich landlords being broken and land redistributed to the poorer peasantry (Bergmann, 1977).

Neither India nor China has experienced a particularly stable process of development. In India, the central government has struggled to maintain control in a country in which regional divisions are pronounced. Between 1966 and 1968 the 'Cultural Revolution' threw

China into turmoil. During this period, millions of mostly young people sought to reimpose 'proletarian values' upon professional and managerial workers, and party officials whom they believed were ignoring the teachings of the revolution. Today, this process has been replaced by one which is in some ways its opposite. The Chinese government is currently emphasizing the need for the use of 'capitalist' mechanisms of personal incentive and profit in an effort to improve the efficiency of agricultural and industrial production.

Riots, crowds and other forms of collective action

All revolutions involve collective action. But, as Tilly's theory indicates, collective action is found in many other circumstances besides those of revolutionary change, and can occur wherever there is the chance of large numbers of people gathering together. The 'urban rabble' constituted a potential danger to political authorities since the first development of cities. In urban neighbourhoods, in contrast to rural areas, many people live in close proximity to one another, and can relatively easily 'take to the streets' to demonstrate support for causes or express grievances.

The actions of urban groups are one example of **crowd activities**. A crowd is any relatively sizeable collection of people who are in direct interaction with one another in a public place. Crowds are an everyday part of urban life in one sense. We speak of a 'crowded' shopping street, or a 'crowded' theatre or amusement park, for instance, meaning that many people are jostling together in a physically confined space. These are individuals in circumstances of *unfocused interaction* (see chapter 4: 'Social Interaction and Everyday Life'). They are physically present in the same setting, and aware of one another's presence, but are pursuing, in small groups or as individuals, their own aims, going their own separate ways. However, in some situations – in a demonstration, riot or panic – everyone's actions become bound up with those of all the others. The situation suddenly becomes one of *focused interaction*, because, however temporarily, the crowd starts acting as a single unit. Crowd action in this sense has stimulated the interests of sociologists and historians for many years – in fact, ever since the French Revolution of 1789.

Le Bon's theory of crowd action

One of the most influential early studies of crowd action was Gustave Le Bon's book *The Crowd*, published in 1895. Le Bon's work was stimulated by his studies of the revolutionary mob during the French Revolution. In his view, people's behaviour when caught up in the collective emotion of a crowd differs significantly from their actions in smaller groups. Under the influence of a **focused crowd**, individuals are capable of acts of barbarism, and of heroism, which they would not contemplate alone. The revolutionary mobs that stormed the Bastille, for example, did so apparently regardless of the casualties they suffered, and street crowds in 1789 perpetrated numerous savageries.

What happens to produce this effect? According to Le Bon, when involved in the collective excitement generated by crowds, people temporarily lose some of the critical reasoning faculties they usually display in day-to-day life. They become highly suggestible, and easily swayed by the exhortations of mob leaders or demagogues. Under the influence of the crowd, individuals regress to more 'primitive' types of reaction. As Le Bon wrote, 'Isolated, a person may be a cultivated individual; in a crowd, he is a barbarian – that is, a creature acting by instinct. He possesses the spontaneity, the violence, the ferocity, and also the enthusiasm and heroism of primitive beings' (Le Bon, 1960, p. 12).

Although many subsequent authors have drawn on them, Le Bon's ideas have to be treated with some reserve. Le Bon wrote as a conservative critic of democracy, seeing the French Revolution as the start of an era in which 'crowds' – i.e., the mass of the ordinary population – would dominate their rightful rulers. Large groups, including parliamentary assemblies in Le Bon's eyes, cannot make rational decisions as individuals can. They are liable to be swayed by mass emotion, fashion or whim, as street crowds are. Le Bon was concerned to demonstrate that democracy will call out the more primitive reactions of human beings, swamping the higher, more civilized faculties.

Some of Le Bon's ideas, however, at least about street crowds, do seem valid. It does appear to be the case that the massing of large numbers of people together, in some circumstances, can generate a collective emotionalism which leads to unusual types of activity. Audiences sometimes 'go wild' at pop concerts or riot at sports events; when gripped by panic, people will sometimes rush helter-skelter for safety, even if others are crushed or trampled to death. Mobs will on occasion rampage through the streets, beating up or killing those they see as their enemies – as happened, for example, in attacks on the Jews in Nazi Germany.

Rational aspects of crowd action

Yet most forms of crowd behaviour are more discriminating and 'rational' than Le Bon believed. Those engaging in such collective action are often more clearly aware of their aims than Le Bon supposed. Nor do such crowds always consist mainly of people already prone to behave irresponsibly – the criminal riff-raff – as Le Bon suggested. George Rudé's studies of the French Revolution show that most of the people in the mob that stormed the Bastille were 'respectable' individuals in orthodox occupations, not criminals or vagabonds (Rudé, 1959). Research into the urban riots of the 1960s in black neighbourhoods in the United States showed that most rioters were not drawn from criminal elements, or even from people on social welfare. The average rioter was a man holding a blue-collar job, more likely to be well informed about social and political issues and to be involved in civil rights activities than other urban blacks. Moreover, although the rioting appeared haphazard, virtually all the property attacked or looted was white-owned (US Riot Commission, 1968).

Some authors have suggested that most crowd activities become intelligible if a quite opposite interpretation is put on them to that given by Le Bon. Thus Richard Berk has argued that the activities of individuals in crowds are best understood as logical responses to specific situations (Berk, 1974). The gathering of crowds often offers opportunities to achieve aims at little personal cost. In crowd situations, individuals are relatively anonymous, and can escape detection for acts that would otherwise result in punishment – for instance, looting a shop to get consumer goods. When acting as a crowd, individuals temporarily have far more power than they have as isolated citizens (Turner and Killian, 1972).

Could this interpretation be applied to situations in which extreme violence towards innocent people is involved – say, to actions by lynch mobs in the American South? The lynching (non-judicial hanging) of blacks was at one time a frequent occurrence. After the Civil War, 'nigger hunts' were regularly undertaken, in which freed slaves were sought out and killed. Between 1889 and 1899, over 1,800 lynchings were reported, and since some no doubt went unrecorded, the actual number was probably considerably higher (Cantril, 1963). The burning of blacks' homes, torture and mutilation, were also practised by the mobs. It might seem as though only the type of view offered by Le Bon can make sense of such actions, and no doubt some of the features of mob violence he identified are relevant. But there were some 'rational' aspects to the lynchings. Those involved were usually semi-organized vigilante groups, who saw themselves as having a righteous cause. Taking action as a mob reduced their individual responsibility for the events, while publicly proclaiming their fury at the freeing of the slaves. The violence also served as a means of social control over blacks, emphasizing to the black population as a whole that the passing of a law in the North did not change the reality of white power in the South. It could be argued that people are to some extent able to overcome the usual forms of social control when in focused crowds; the power and anonymity of the crowd allows them to act as they might normally wish to, but feel unable to.

Mob action and rioting – as Tilly emphasizes – characteristically express the frustrations of people who cannot gain access to orthodox channels to express grievances or press for reforms they think necessary. Ruling authorities of all types have always feared mob activity, not just because of the direct threat it poses, but because it gives a public and tangible form to felt social injustices. Crowd action in the context of revolutions helps bring about momentous social changes, but even riots that may on the face of things seem negative, giving rise to wanton destruction and loss of life, may stimulate change and produce at least some desired benefits. The spate of riots in black areas of the USA in the 1960s forced the white community to pay attention to the deprivations blacks suffered, leading to the setting up of new reform programmes.

Social movements

Besides those engaged in revolutionary activity, a wide variety of other social movements, some long-enduring, some highly transient, have existed in modern societies. Social movements are as evident a feature of the contemporary world as are the formal, bureaucratic organizations they often oppose. Studying their nature and impact forms an area of major interest in sociology.

Definition

A **social movement** may be defined as a collective attempt to further a common interest, or secure a common goal, through collective action outside the sphere of established institutions. The definition has to be a broad one, precisely because of the variations between different types of movement. Many social movements are very small, numbering perhaps no more than a few dozen members; others might include thousands or even millions of people. Some movements carry on their activities within the laws of the society or societies in which they exist, while others operate as illegal or underground groups. Often, of course, laws are altered partly or wholly as a result of the action of social movements. For example, groups of workers that called their members out on strike used to be engaging in illegal activity, punished with varying degrees of severity in different countries. Eventually, however, the laws were amended, making the strike a permissible tactic of industrial conflict. Other modes of economic protest, by contrast, still remain outside the law in most countries – such as sit-ins in factories or workplaces.

The dividing lines between social movements and formal organizations are sometimes blurred, because movements which become well established usually take on bureaucratic characteristics. Social movements may thus gradually become formal organizations, while – less frequently – organizations may devolve into social movements. The Salvation Army, for example, began as a social movement, but has now taken on most of the characteristics of a more permanent organization. An example of the opposite process would be the case of a political party which is banned, and forced to go underground, perhaps becoming a guerrilla movement.

Similarly, it is not always easy to separate social movements from **interest groups** – associations set up to influence policy-makers in ways that will favour their members. An example of an interest group would be the Automobile Association, which lobbies Parliament to defend the interests of motorists. But is the Campaign for Nuclear Disarmament, which regularly lobbies Parliament about matters to do with nuclear weapons, an interest group or part of a more wide-ranging mass movement? No clear-cut answer can be given in such cases; social movements often actively promote their causes through organized channels while also engaging in more unorthodox forms of activity.

Classifying social movements

Many different ways of classifying social movements have been proposed. Perhaps the neatest and most comprehensive classification is that developed by David Aberle, who distinguishes four types of movement (Aberle, 1966).

1 **Transformative movements** aim at far-reaching change in the society or societies of which they are a part. The changes their members anticipate are cataclysmic, all-embracing, and often violent. Examples are revolutionary movements, or some radical religious movements. Many millenarian movements, for instance, have foreseen a more or less complete restructuring of society when the era of salvation arrives.
2 **Reformative movements** have more limited objectives, aspiring to alter only some aspects of the existing social order. They concern themselves with specific kinds of inequality or injustice. Cases in point are the Women's Christian Temperance Union or anti-abortion groups.

Transformative and reformative movements both are concerned primarily with securing changes in society. Aberle's other two types are each mainly aimed at changing the habits or outlook of individuals.

3 **Redemptive movements** seek to rescue people from ways of life seen as corrupting. Many religious movements belong in this category, in so far as they concentrate on personal salvation. Examples are the Pentecostal sects, which believe that individuals' spiritual development is the true indication of their worth (Schwartz, 1970).
4 Finally, there are the somewhat clumsily titled **alterative movements**, which aim at securing partial change in individuals. They do not seek to achieve a complete alteration in people's habits, but are concerned with changing certain specific traits. An illustration is Alcoholics Anonymous.

Theories of social movements

Theories of revolution inevitably tend to overlap with those of social movements. Tilly's emphasis on 'resource mobilization', for example, is intended to have wide application, and has been employed by students of social movements. Davies's interpretation of rising expectations

and protest has also been influential in the analysis of social movements. Two theoretical perspectives have been particularly important,
however, in terms of both their theoretical sophistication and the
amount of empirical research they have helped to generate. These
are the approaches of Neil Smelser and Alain Touraine.

Neil Smelser: six conditions for social movements

Smelser distinguishes six conditions underlying the origins of collective
action in general, and social movements in particular (Smelser, 1963).
Structural conduciveness refers to the general social conditions promoting
or inhibiting the formation of social movements of different types. For
example, in Smelser's view the socio-political system of the United
States leaves open certain avenues of mobilization because of the
relative absence of state regulation in those areas. Thus there is no
official state-sponsored religion, for example, people being free to
choose the religious groups to which they wish to be affiliated, if any.
Social movements based on religious ideals are tolerated by the political
authorities, so long as they do not transgress criminal or civil laws.

Such conditions are favourable for the development of some sorts of
social movement; they do not as such bring them into being. *Structural
strain* refers to tensions – in Marx's terminology, contradictions – which
produce conflicting interests within societies. Uncertainties, anxieties,
ambiguities or direct clashes of goals, are expressions of such strains.
Sources of strain may be quite general, or specific to particular
situations. Thus sustained inequalities between ethnic groups give rise to
overall tensions; these may become focused in the shape of specific conflicts when, say, blacks begin to move into a previously all-white area.

The third condition Smelser outlines is the spread of *generalized
beliefs*. Social movements do not develop simply as responses to vaguely
felt anxieties or hostilities. They are shaped by the influence of definite
ideologies, which crystallize grievances and suggest courses of action
that might be pursued to remedy them. Revolutionary movements, for
instance, are based on ideas about why injustice occurs and how it
can be alleviated by political struggle. *Precipitating factors* are events
or incidents that actually trigger direct action by those who become
involved in the movement. The incident when Rosa Parks refused to
move to the part of the bus reserved for blacks in Montgomery, Alabama, in 1955, helped to spark off the American civil rights movement.

These four sets of factors combined, Smelser argues, might occasionally lead to street disturbances or outbreaks of violence, but such
incidents do not lead to the development of social movements unless
there is a *co-ordinated group* which is mobilized to act. Leadership
and some kind of means of regular communication between participants, together with a supply of funding and material resources,
are necessary for a social movement to exist.

Finally, the manner in which a social movement develops is strongly influenced by the *operation of social control*. The governing authorities may respond to the challenge by intervening in the conditions of conduciveness and strain which stimulated the emergence of the movement. For instance, in a situation of ethnic tension steps might be taken to reduce some of the worst aspects of ethnic inequality that had generated resentment and conflict. Another important aspect of social control concerns the response of the police or armed forces. As we have seen, for example, the extent of divisions within the police and military can be crucial in deciding the outcome of confrontations between revolutionary movements and the authorities.

Smelser's model is useful for analysing sequences in the development of social movements, and collective action in general. According to him, we can understand each stage in the sequence as 'adding value' to the overall outcome, each stage being a condition for the occurrence of the subsequent ones. But there are some problems with his theory. A social movement may become strong without any particular precipitating incidents – in the sense of public confrontations – being involved in its growth. Conversely, a series of incidents might bring home the need to establish a movement to change the circumstances which gave rise to them. The movement may *open up* strains, rather than just developing as a response to them. For example, the women's movement has actively sought to identify and combat gender inequalities where before these had been unquestioned. Smelser's theory treats all social movements as 'responses' to situations, rather than allowing that their members might spontaneously organize to achieve desired social changes. In this respect his ideas contrast with the approach developed by Alain Touraine.

Alain Touraine: historicity

Touraine emphasizes that social movements reflect the stress placed in modern societies on *activism* in the achievement of goals (Touraine, 1977, 1981). Modern societies are marked by what Touraine calls **historicity** – an outlook in which knowledge of social processes is used to reshape the social conditions of our existence. For instance, identifying the nature and distribution of inequalities in schooling was one of the factors that promoted the rise of the civil rights movement in the United States. Touraine has been less interested in the background conditions that give rise to social movements than in understanding the *objectives* social movements pursue. Social movements do not just come about as irrational responses to social divisions or injustices; they develop with views and strategies as to how these can be overcome.

Social movements, Touraine suggests, cannot be understood as isolated forms of association. They develop in deliberate antagonism with other groups – usually with established organizations, but sometimes with rival movements. All social movements have interests or aims which they are *for;* all have views and ideas they are *against.* In Touraine's view, other theories of social movements (including that of Smelser) have given insufficient consideration to how their objectives are shaped by their encounters with others who hold divergent ideas – as well as the ways in which they themselves influence the outlooks and action of their opponents. For instance, the objectives and outlook of the women's movement have been shaped in opposition to the male-dominated institutions which it seeks to alter, and have shifted in relation to its successes and failures. They have also influenced the perspectives of men. These changed perspectives in turn have stimulated a re-orientation in the women's movement – and so the process continues.

Touraine argues that social movements should be studied in the context of what he calls **fields of action**. The term refers to the connections between a social movement and the forces or influences against which it is ranged. The process of mutual 'negotiation' involved in a field of action may lead to a change in the circumstances the movement sought to contest, but also to a merging of the perspectives held by each side. Either way the movement may evaporate – or become institutionalized as a permanent organization. Trade unions became formal organizations, for example, when the right to strike and modes of bargaining acceptable to both workers and employers were achieved. These were forged out of earlier processes of confrontation involving considerable violence on both sides. Where there are continuing sources of conflict (as in the relationships between employees and employers), new movements still tend sporadically to re-emerge.

Evaluation

Touraine's approach lacks the clarity of Smelser's. Yet it is illuminating to stress that social movements develop through a process of mutual shaping and redefinition alongside opposing groups or organizations. Such an analysis can also be applied to movements concerned primarily with individual change – Aberle's redemptive and alterative categories – even though Touraine himself says little about them. For instance, Alcoholics Anonymous is a movement based on medical findings about the effects of alcohol on people's health and social activities. The movement has been shaped by its opposition to advertising designed to encourage alcohol consumption, and its attempt to confront the pressures alcoholics face in a society in which drinking is seen in a tolerant light.

Social movements and sociology

Social movements have a double interest for the sociologist. They provide a subject-matter for study but, more than this, they may help shift the ways in which sociologists *look at* the areas of behaviour they try to analyse. The women's movement, for instance, is not just relevant to sociology because it provides material for research. It has identified weaknesses in established frameworks of sociological thought, and developed concepts (such as that of patriarchy) which help us to understand issues of gender and power. There is a continuing dialogue not only between social movements and the organizations they confront, but between social movements and sociology itself.

Summary

1   Revolutions have occurred in many areas of the world over the past two centuries. The American Revolution of 1776, and the French Revolution of 1789, introduced ideals and aspirations which have come to be very widespread in political life. In the twentieth century, most revolutions have been inspired by socialist or Marxist aspirations.

2   *Revolution* is a slippery concept to define. To count as a revolution, a process of political change must involve the influence of a mass social movement which is prepared to use violence to achieve its ends and able both to seize power and subsequently to initiate reform.

3   Various different theories of revolution have been advanced. Marx's interpretation of revolution is particularly significant, not just because of its intellectual contribution – which can be questioned in various ways – but because it has served in some part to shape actual processes of revolution in the current century.

4   Since revolution is such a complex phenomenon, generalizing about the conditions leading to revolutionary change is difficult. Most revolutions occur in circumstances where governmental power has become fragmented (for instance, as a result of war), and where an oppressed group is able to create and sustain a mass movement. Revolutions are usually unintended consequences of more partial aims towards which such movements initially strive.

5   Post-revolutionary regimes are often authoritarian, imposing censorship and other controls. Revolutions normally have long-term consequences for the societies in which they occur, although it is difficult to disentangle these from other factors that affect the subsequent development of those societies.

6   Crowd activities occur not only in revolutions, but in many other circumstances of less dramatic social change – as in urban riots. The actions of rioting mobs might seem wholly destructive and haphazard, but often serve definite purposes for those involved.

7   Many types of social movement are found in modern societies. Social movements involve a collective attempt to further common interests

through collaborative action outside the sphere of established institutions. Sociology not only studies such movements but also responds to the issues they raise.

Basic concepts

revolution	collective action
rebellion	social movement

Important terms

democracy	revolutionary terror
coup d'état	crowd activity
contradiction	focused crowd
socialism	interest groups
communism	transformative movement
disequilibrium	reformative movement
relative deprivation	redemptive movement
organization	alterative movement
mobilization	historicity
multiple sovereignty	field of action

Further reading

John Dunn, 'Understanding revolutions' in his *Rethinking Modern Political Theory* (Cambridge: Cambridge University Press, 1985) — a discussion of the problems of understanding modern revolutions.

J. Goldstone, 'The comparative and historical study of revolutions', *Annual Review of Sociology*, 8 (1982) — a useful critical survey of work concerned with the comparative analysis of revolutions.

Roy Porter and M. Teich (eds), *Revolution in History* (Cambridge: Cambridge University Press, 1986) — readings in revolutionary history by Eric Hobsbawm, M. I. Finley, Victor Kiernan and others.

John Wilson, *Introduction to Social Movements* (New York: Basic Books, 1973) — a general discussion of the major types of social movement, together with an interpretation of relevant theoretical approaches.

20

Social Change – Past, Present and Future

Human beings have existed on earth for about a half a million years. Agriculture, the necessary basis of fixed settlements, is only about twelve thousand years old. Civilizations date back no more than some six thousand years or so. If we were to think of the entire span of human existence as a day, agriculture would have been invented at 11.56 p.m., and civilizations would have come into being at 11.57. The development of modern societies would get under way only at 11.59.30! Yet perhaps as much change has gone on in the last thirty seconds of this 'human day' than in the whole of the time leading up to it.

The pace of change in the modern era is easily demonstrated by reference to rates of technological development. As the economic historian David Landes has observed:

> Modern technology produces not only more, faster; it turns out objects that could not have been produced under any circumstances by the craft

methods of yesterday. The best Indian hand-spinner could not turn out yarn so fine and regular as that of the mule; all the forges in eighteenth century Christendom could not have produced steel sheets so large, smooth and homogeneous as those of a modern strip mill. Most important, modern technology has created things that could scarcely have been conceived in the pre-industrial era; the camera, the motor car, the aeroplane, the whole array of electronic devices from the radio to the high-speed computer, the nuclear power plant, and so on almost *ad infinitum*. . . The result has been an enormous increase in the output and variety of goods and services, and this alone has changed man's way of life more than anything since the discovery of fire: the Englishman [and, we might add, the Englishwoman] of 1750 was closer in material things to Caesar's legionnaires than to his own great-grandchildren. (Landes, 1969, p. 5)

The modes of life and social institutions characteristic of the modern world are radically different from those of even the relatively recent past. During a period of only some two or three centuries – a minute sliver of time in the context of human history – human social life has been wrenched away from the types of social order in which people lived for thousands of years.

Over the past half-century or so, the pace of change has accelerated rather than slackened, and far more than any generation before us, we face an uncertain future. Conditions of life for previous generations were always insecure: people were at the mercy of natural disasters, plagues and famines. In the industrialized countries today we are largely immune from these insecurities; our uncertainties about the future derive from the social forces we ourselves have unleashed.

Defining change

How should we define **social change?** There is a sense in which everything changes, all of the time. Every day is a new day; every moment is a new instant in time. The Greek philosopher, Heraclitus, pointed out that a person cannot step into the same river twice. On the second occasion, the river is different, since water has flowed along it and the person has changed in subtle ways too. While this observation is in a sense correct, we *do* of course normally want to say that it is the same river and the same person stepping into it on two occasions. There is sufficient continuity in the shape or form of the river, and in the physique and personality of the person with wet feet, to say that each remains 'the same' through the changes that occur.

Identifying significant change involves showing how far there are alterations in the *underlying structure* of an object or situation over a period of time. In the case of human societies, to decide how far, and in what ways, a system is in a process of change, we have to show to what degree there is any modification of *basic institutions* during a specific period. All accounts of change also involve showing what remains stable, as a baseline against which to measure alterations. Even in the rapidly moving world of today there are continuities with the long-distant past. Major religious systems, for example, like Christianity or Islam, retain their ties with ideas and practices initiated some 2,000 years ago. Yet most institutions in modern societies clearly change much more rapidly than did institutions of the traditional world.

In this chapter, we shall look at attempts to interpret patterns of change affecting human history as a whole; we shall then consider why the modern period should be associated with such especially profound and rapid social change. This will be followed by discussion of where the major lines of development in modern societies seem at the moment to be leading.

Theories of social change

Two general approaches have probably been more influential than any others in the attempt to understand the general mechanisms of change through human history. One is the approach suggested by **social evolutionism,** which tries to connect biological and social change. The second standpoint is that associated with **historical materialism** – originally worked out by Marx, but elaborated subsequently by a diversity of writers.

Evolutionary theories

Evolutionary approaches to social change start from a rather obvious fact. If we compare different types of human society in history, it seems clear that there is a movement towards increasing complexity (see chapter 2: 'Culture and Society'.) Hunting and gathering societies, found at the earliest stages of human development (although some still exist) seem to be relatively simple in structure as compared to the agricultural societies which emerged at a later period in history. For instance, in hunting and gathering societies there were no separate ruling groups or political authorities, such as normally exist in agrarian societies. Traditional states were even larger and more complicated: in these societies, there were clearly distinct classes, plus separate political, legal and cultural institutions. Finally, industrialized societies are more complex than any preceding types: they involve many separate institutions and organizations.

The development of increasing complexity has often been analysed using the concept of **differentiation**. As societies become more complex, areas of social life that once were mingled become clearly differentiated – that is to say, separate from one another. Increasing differentiation and complexity in human society, evolutionary thinkers argue, can be compared to processes involved in the biological development of species. The trend of biological evolution also moves from simple to more complex. Organisms right at the bottom of the evolutionary scale, like the amoeba, are very simple in structure compared to the higher animals.

In biological evolution, development from simple to more complex organisms is explained in terms of adaptation to the environment – how well animals adjust to their material milieu (see chapter 2: 'Culture and Society'). More complex organisms have a greater capacity to adapt to, and survive in, their environments than simpler ones. According to evolutionary theorists, therefore, there are direct parallels between biological development and the succession of human societies in history. The more complex a society is, the greater its 'survival value' as compared with simpler types.

Social Darwinism

Early theories of social evolution, in the nineteenth century, frequently associated evolutionism with progress – with a movement towards morally superior forms of society. One version of this view, which became very popular just before the present century, was **social Darwinism**. As its name suggests, social Darwinism drew its inspiration from Charles Darwin's writings on biological evolution. It was argued that, like biological organisms, human societies struggle with one another for survival. The modern societies of the West have come out on top in this struggle, and so represent the highest stage of social progress yet achieved. Some authors used social Darwinist ideas to justify the supremacy of whites over blacks, working out 'scientific' justifications for racism, and the theory was used to support the dominant position of the West. It was at its most popular during the time of the 'scramble for Africa' among the European powers – before the rise of modern field-work anthropology, which documented the diversity of human culture and served to redress the 'Eurocentric' outlook involved in social Darwinist thought. By the late 1920s, social Darwinism was thoroughly discredited – and in fact the popularity of social evolutionism as a whole declined.

Unilinear and multilinear evolution

Nineteenth-century theories of social evolution often tended to be **unilinear**, asserting that there is a single line of development in human society, from simple to more complex. To ascend the evolutionary path, each society must pass through the same stages of development. Over the past few decades, however, evolutionary theory in sociology has undergone something of a revival, but emphasizes

multilinear rather than unilinear evolution (Sahlins and Service, 1960; Lenski, 1966; Lenski and Lenski, 1982). Multilinear theories recognize that there may be various lines of development leading from one type of society to another. According to this view, different types of society can be categorized in terms of their level of complexity and differentiation, but no single path of change is followed by all.

Multilinear evolutionists still see the main mechanism of change as increasing adaptation to the environment. They regard each succeeding type of society as more effective in adapting to its environment than more simple types. Thus, for example, agrarian societies are more effective in generating consistent sources of food supply than hunting and gathering cultures. Contemporary evolutionists, however, are careful not to identify such increases in adaptive capacity as 'progress'.

Parsons's theory of evolution

One of the most influential theories today was put forward by Talcott Parsons. He suggests that social evolution is an extension of biological evolution, although the actual mechanisms of development are different. Both types of evolution can be understood in terms of what Parsons calls *evolutionary universals*, which are any types of development which crop up on more than one occasion in different conditions, and have great survival value. Vision is an example of an evolutionary universal in the natural world; it emerged not just in one part of the animal kingdom, but developed independently in several species. The ability to see allows for a much wider range of co-ordinated responses to the environment than is possible for unsighted organisms, and hence has great adaptive value. Vision is necessary to all animals at the higher stages of biological evolution.

Communication, as Parsons points out, is fundamental in all human culture, and language is the basis of communication. Language is thus the first and most significant evolutionary universal; there is no known human society that does not possess a language. Three other evolutionary universals found even in the earliest forms of society are religion, kinship and technology. These four universals concern such essential aspects of any human society that no process of social evolution could get under way without them.

Parsons claims that social evolution can be analysed as a process of progressive differentiation of social institutions, as societies move from the simple to the more complex. The earliest forms of society show only a very low level of differentiation, and are characterized by what Parsons calls *constitutive symbolism*. This means the existence of a set of symbols, largely religious in character, which permeate virtually all aspects of social life. As an example of a culture at the lowest stage of social evolution, Parsons takes the case (as Durkheim did) of the aboriginal societies of Australia. These societies are structured almost wholly in terms of kinship relations, which in turn express religious beliefs, and are integrated with economic activities. There is very little property; no distinct forms of chiefdom; and no productive economy, since hunting and gathering is the means of subsistence.

The next level of evolution is that of 'advanced primitive society'. In this type, a stratification system replaces the more egalitarian character of the simpler cultures. Advanced primitive societies often involve ethnic as well as class divisions. They develop a definite productive system, involving agricultural or pastoral production, and settled places of residence. Religion becomes more separated from other aspects of social life, and is organized and developed by a distinct priesthood.

Further up the scale we find what Parsons calls 'intermediate societies'. Intermediate societies are what most other writers have termed civilizations or traditional states – such as ancient Egypt, Rome or China. They are associated with the emergence of writing and literacy. Religion undergoes a further elaboration, with the development of systematic theologies, and emerges as a clearly distinct sphere from political, economic and familial relationships. Political leadership develops in the shape of government administrations headed by aristocratic rulers. Several new evolutionary universals come into being at this stage, including specialized forms of political legitimacy, bureaucratic organization, monetary exchange and a specialized system of law. Each of these, Parsons claims, greatly increases the ability of a society to integrate large numbers of people within an overall community.

Industrialized societies stand at the highest point in Parsons's evolutionary scheme. They are far more internally differentiated than societies of the intermediate type. In industrialized societies, the economic and political systems become clearly separated from one another, and both are distinct from the legal system, as well as from religion. The development of mass democracy provides a means of involving the whole population within the political order. Industrialized societies have a much higher territorial unity than earlier types, being distinguished by well-defined borders. The superior survival value generated by the institutions of industrialized societies is well demonstrated by the spread of industrialism world-wide, leading to the more or less complete disappearance of the earlier types of society.

Assessment

Even in their more recent and sophisticated forms, evolutionary theories face considerable difficulties (Gellner, 1964; Giddens, 1984). It is not at all clear that the development of human societies closely resembles evolution in the natural world, and the concept of adaptation is probably of little value in sociology. In biology, **adaptation** has a fairly precise meaning, referring to the way in which the randomly generated characteristics of some organisms promote their survival, thereby influencing the genes transmitted from one generation to another (Alland, 1967, 1970). No such clearly designated meaning exists in the case of social evolutionism.

It is not even certain that we can usefully classify societies, as we can biological organisms, in terms of ascending levels of complexity. Hunting and gathering societies, for example, in some respects are *more* complex than industrialized ones, even if they are much smaller: most hunting and gathering communities have kinship systems considerably more complicated than those of most industrialized societies.

More recent evolutionary theories are clearly more sophisticated than those developed earlier, but although we can say that there is an overall *direction* of human social development, from smaller societies to larger ones, it is not clear whether this can be explained in terms of adaptation and survival value. The nature of social and cultural change seems altogether more complicated than evolutionary theories suggest.

Historical materialism

Marx's interpretation of social change has something in common with evolutionary theories; both regard the major patterns of change as being brought about by interaction with the material environment. According to Marx, every society rests on an economic base or *infrastructure*, changes in which tend to govern alterations in the *superstructure* – political, legal and cultural institutions. Marx does not use the concept of 'adaptation', which would have seemed to him too mechanical. In his view, human beings actively relate to the material world, seeking to master it and subordinate it to their purposes; they do not merely 'adapt to' or 'fit into' their environment.

Social change, Marx argues, can be understood through the ways in which, in developing more sophisticated systems of production, human beings progressively come to control the material world and subordinate it to their purposes. He refers to this process as one of the expansion of the **forces of production**, in other words the level of economic advancement a society has reached. According to Marx, social change does not occur only as a process of slow development, but in the shape of revolutionary transformations. Periods of gradual alteration in the forces of production and other institutions alternate with phases of more dramatic revolutionary change. This has often been referred to as a **dialectical interpretation of change**. The most significant changes come about through tensions, clashes and struggles.

Changes that occur in the forces of production set up tensions in other institutions in the superstructure; the more acute these tensions become, the more there is a pressure towards an overall transformation of society. Struggles between classes become more and more acute, ultimately producing either the disintegration of existing institutions or the transition to a new type of social order through a process of political revolution.

As an illustration of Marx's theory, we might take the changes involved in the replacement of feudalism by industrial capitalism in European history. The feudal economic system was based on small-scale agricultural production, the two principal classes being aristocrats and serfs. According to Marx, as trade and technology (the forces of production) developed, major changes began to occur in the infrastructure. These led to a new set of economic relations, centred on capitalist manufacture and industry in the towns and cities. A series of tensions developed between the old land-based, agricultural economic order and the newly emerging capitalist manufacturing system. The more acute these tensions became, the greater were the strains on other institutions. Conflict between aristocrats and the newly developing capitalist class ultimately led to a process of revolution, signalling the consolidation of a new type of society. In other words, industrial capitalism had come to replace feudalism.

Criticisms

Marx's ideas certainly help make sense of some major transitions in history, and many historians and sociologists who would not see themselves as 'Marxists' have accepted much of Marx's interpretation of the decline of feudalism and the origin of modern capitalism. Yet as a general framework for analysing social change, Marx's views have notable limitations. It is not clear how far other historical transitions fit into Marx's scheme; for instance, some archaeologists have drawn on aspects of Marx's theory to explain the early development of civilizations (Childe, 1956, 1979). They argue that civilizations began when the forces of production had developed far enough to allow a class-based society to emerge. At best, this is an oversimplified view, since traditional states were more commonly formed as a result of military expansion and conquest. Political and military power was often a *means* of accumulating wealth, rather than the result of it. Moreover, Marx's theory has never been able to deal satisfactorily with the development of the large Eastern civilizations of India, China and Japan.

The limitations of theories: Weber's interpretation of change

Max Weber criticized both evolutionary theories and Marx's historical materialism. Attempts to interpret historical change as a whole in terms of adaptation to the material world, or economic factors, he argues, are doomed to failure. Although such influences are undoubtedly important, there is no sense in which they ultimately *control* overall processes of development. No 'single factor' theory of social change has a chance of accounting for the diversity of human social development. Other factors besides the economic – including military power, modes of government, and ideologies – are often equally or more important.

If Weber's view is correct, as most would agree it is, no single theory can explain the nature of all social change. In analysing such change, we can at most accomplish two things. First, we can identify some of the factors which have a consistent and general influence on social change in many contexts. Second, we can develop theories which account for certain phases or 'episodes' of change – for instance, the early emergence of traditional states. Evolutionist and Marxist thinkers were not *wrong* to emphasize the importance of environmental and economic factors on patterns of social change – they simply gave undue weight to these as compared to other influences.

Influences on change

The main influences on social change can be summarized under three headings: the *physical environment, political organization*, and *cultural factors*.

The physical environment

As evolutionists have emphasized, the physical environment often does have an effect upon the development of human social organization. This is clearest in more extreme environmental conditions, where people have to organize their modes of life in relation to weather conditions. Peoples in polar regions necessarily develop different habits and practices from those of others living in sub-tropical areas.

Less extreme physical conditions also often affect society. The native population of Australia never stopped being hunters and gatherers, since the continent contained hardly any indigenous plants suitable for regular cultivation, or animals which could be domesticated to develop pastoral production. The world's early civilizations mostly originated in areas in which there was rich agricultural land – for instance, in river deltas. Other factors such as ease of communications across land, or the availability of sea routes, are also important: societies cut off from others by mountain ranges, impassable jungles or deserts, often remain relatively unchanged over long periods of time.

Yet the direct influence of the environment on social change is less than might be supposed. Even peoples who only have simple technology sometimes develop considerable productive wealth in relatively inhospitable areas. Conversely, hunting and gathering cultures have frequently lived in highly fertile regions without moving to pastoral or agricultural production. There is little direct or constant relation between the environment and the types of productive system which develop. The evolutionists' emphasis on adaptation to the environment is thus less illuminating than Marx's stress on the importance of productive relations in influencing social development. There is no doubt that types of production system strongly influence the level and nature of change which goes on in a society, although they do not have the overriding impact Marx attributed to them.

Political organization

A second factor strongly influencing social change is the mode of political organization. In hunting and gathering societies, this influence is at a minimum, since there are no separate political authorities capable of mobilizing the community. In all other types of society, however, the existence of distinct political agencies – chiefs, lords, kings and governments – strongly affects the course of development a society takes.

Political systems are not, as Marx argues, expressions of underlying economic organization; quite different types of political order may exist in societies which have similar production systems. For instance, forms of production in small, non-state pastoral societies are not particularly different to those of large, state-based civilizations, and rulers may initiate processes of territorial expansion which greatly increase the economic wealth of the societies over which they hold sway. On the other hand, a monarch who tries, but fails to take over other lands may bring a society to economic disruption or ruin.

Military strength is an important aspect of political influences over social change. As was mentioned above, military power played a fundamental part in the establishing of most traditional states – and influenced their subsequent survival or expansion in an equally basic way. The connections between the level of production and military strength are again fairly indirect. A ruler may choose to channel resources into building up the military, for example, even where this impoverishes most of the rest of the population.

Cultural factors

These include the effects of religion, styles of thought and consciousness. As we have previously seen (in chapter 14: 'Religion'), religion may be either a conservative or an innovative force in social life. Many forms of religious belief and practice have acted as a brake on change, emphasizing above all the need to adhere to traditional values and rituals. Yet, as Weber emphasizes, religious convictions frequently play a mobilizing role in pressures for social change.

A particularly important cultural influence that affects the character and pace of change is the nature of communication systems. The invention of writing, for instance, influenced social change in several ways. It allowed for the keeping of records, making possible increased control of material resources and the development of large-scale organizations. In addition, writing altered people's perception of the relation between past, present and future. Societies that possess writing have a record of past events and know themselves to have a 'history'. Understanding history can serve to develop a sense of the overall 'movement' or 'line of development' a society is following, which groups can then actively seek to promote further.

Under the general heading of cultural factors we should also refer to the influence of *leadership*. Individual leaders have had an enormous influence on some phases and aspects of world history – one only has to think of such people as the great religious figures (like Jesus), individual political and military leaders (like Julius Caesar), or innovators in science and philosophy (like Newton), to see that this is the case. A leader capable of pursuing dynamic policies, and able to generate a mass following, or someone who can radically alter pre-existing modes of thought, can overturn a previously established order of things.

However, individuals can only reach positions of leadership, and become effective in what they do, if favourable social conditions exist. Hitler was able to seize power in Germany in the 1930s, for instance, partly as a result of the tensions and crises which beset the country at that time. If those circumstances had not existed, he would no doubt have remained an obscure figure within a minor political faction.

Analysing episodes of change

The impact of the various factors just listed varies according to time and place. We cannot single out one as the determining influence over the whole of human social development; but we can develop theories about more specific passages or **episodes of change**. To illustrate this, we shall take Robert Carneiro's interpretation of the initial development of traditional states or civilizations (Carneiro, 1970). Carneiro accepts that warfare played a major part in the origin of traditional states, but points out that warfare is commonplace among societies at a certain level of development, and therefore cannot itself account for state formation.

War tends to lead to the emergence of states, in Carneiro's view, when the peoples involved possess only physically limited areas of agricultural land – such as was the case in ancient Egypt (the Nile delta), the Valley of Mexico, or the mountain coastal valleys of Peru, among other examples. In such circumstances, war puts great pressure on scarce resources. Migration out of the area is difficult, because of its physically confined character. The result is great strain on established ways of life, inducing some groups to seek military ascendancy over others, and encouraging attempts to centralize control over production. An entire valley eventually becomes unified under a single chief-dom, which is then able to concentrate administrative resources to become a governing apparatus or state.

The theory is an interesting and important one, which helps illuminate a substantial number of cases of state development. Yet not all early states did develop in the physically circumscribed areas Carneiro iden-tifies (Claessen and Skalnik, 1978), and later forms of traditional state often emerged in quite different circumstances. Once states actually exist, they stimulate further developments elsewhere; other peoples are able to follow their example in forming their own political systems. The fact that Carneiro's theory only helps explain a limited number of instances of the formation of traditional states is no reason to condemn or reject it. It has sufficient generality to be a good and useful theory; and it is implausible to suppose that single theories can be developed that will explain much broader phases of social transformation than it covers.

Change in the recent past

What explains why the last two hundred years, the period of modernity, have seen such a tremendous acceleration in the speed of social change? This is of course a very complex issue, but it is not difficult to indicate some of the factors involved. Not surprisingly, they can be categorized along similar lines to those involved in influencing social change throughout history. In analysing them, we shall subsume the impact of the physical environment within the overall importance of economic factors more generally.

Economic influences

On the level of the economy, the most far-reaching influence is the impact of *industrial capitalism*. Capitalism differs in a fundamental way from pre-existing production systems, because it involves the constant expansion of production and ever-increasing accumulation of wealth. In traditional production systems, levels of production were fairly static, being geared to habitual, customary needs. Capitalist develop-ment promotes the constant revision of the technology of production, a process into which science is increasingly drawn. The rate of technological innovation fostered in modern industry is vastly greater than in any previous type of economic order.

Take as an example the motor-car industry today: almost every year, the major manufacturers bring out new models, and they constantly seek to improve and modify their existing ones. Or consider the current development of information technology. Over the past fifteen years, the power of computers has increased by 10,000 times. A large computer in the mid-sixties required several tens of thousands of hand-made connectors; an equivalent device today is not only very much smaller, but needs only ten elements in an integrated circuit.

In traditional societies, most production was local. Merchants may quite often have journeyed far and wide, engaging in various kinds of long-distance trade, but most such trade was confined to luxury goods, consumed by the few. The development of modern industry did away with the localized character of traditional production, integrating producers and consumers in a division of labour which today has become truly global in scope. Marx described this process very accurately, pointing out that modern capitalism:

> has given a cosmopolitan character to production and consumption in every country. . . It has drawn from under the feet of industry the national ground on which it stood. All old-fashioned national industries have been destroyed or are daily being destroyed. They are dislodged by new industries, whose introduction becomes a life and death question for all civilised nations, by industries that no longer only work upon indigenous raw materials, but raw materials drawn from the remotest zones; industries whose products are consumed, not only at home, but in every quarter of the globe. (Marx and Engels, 1968, pp. 38–9)

The development of industrial capitalism fundamentally altered people's ways of life; for example, most people in modern societies now live in cities rather than in rural communities, and work in factories and offices rather than in agricultural production. We tend to take these conditions of life for granted today, not realizing how unqiue they are in human history. Ours is the first type of society in which the large majority of the population do not either live in small rural communities, or gain their livelihood from the land. The changes associated with urbanism and the development of new work environments have affected – as well as been affected by – most other institutions.

Political influences

The second major type of influence on change in the modern period consists of novel political developments. The struggle between nations to expand their power, develop their wealth, and triumph militarily over their competitors, has been an energizing source of change over the past two or three centuries. Political change in traditional civilizations was normally confined to elites. One aristocratic family, for example, would replace another as rulers, while for the majority of the population life would go on relatively unchanged. This is not true of modern political systems, in which the activities of political leaders and government officials constantly affect the lives of the mass of the population. Both externally and internally, political decision-making promotes and directs social change far more than in previous times.

Political development in the last two or three centuries has certainly influenced economic change as much as economic change has influenced politics. Governments now play a major role in stimulating (and sometimes retarding) rates of economic growth, and in all industrial societies there is a high level of state intervention in production, the government being far and away the largest employer.

Military power and war have also been of far-reaching importance (Aron, 1954; Marwick, 1974; Howard, 1976; Giddens, 1985). The military strength of the Western nations from the seventeenth century onwards allowed them to influence all quarters of the world – and provided an essential backing to the global spread of Western life-styles. In the twentieth century, the effects of the two world wars have been profound – the devastation of many countries, which led to processes of rebuilding that brought about major institutional changes, for example, in Germany and Japan after the Second World War. Even those states which were the victors – like the USA – experienced major internal changes as a result of the impact of the war on the economy.

Cultural influences

Cultural factors have also greatly affected processes of social change in modern times. The development of science, and the secularization of thought, have been primarily influences here. Each has contributed to the *critical* and *innovative* character of the modern outlook. We no longer assume that customs or habits are acceptable merely because they have the authority of tradition. On the contrary, our modes of life in modern societies are increasingly required to have a 'rational' basis. That is to say, they have to be defended, and if necessary changed, according to whether or not they can be justified on the basis of persuasive arguments and evidence. For instance, a design for building a hospital would not be based mainly upon previous tastes, but upon its ability to serve the purposes to which a hospital is put – effectively caring for the sick.

It is not merely alterations in *how* we think that have influenced processes of change in the modern world; the *content* of ideas has also changed. Ideals of self-betterment, freedom, equality and democratic participation are very largely creations of the past two or three centuries; and such ideals have served to mobilize far-reaching processes of social and political change, including revolutions. These are again not notions which can be tied to tradition, but rather suggest the constant revision of modes of life in the pursuit of human betterment. Although they were initially developed in the West, such ideals have become genuinely universal in their application, promoting change in most regions of the world.

Current change and future prospects

Where is social change leading us today? What are the main developments likely to affect our lives as the twenty-first century opens?

Sociologists are not agreed about the answers to these questions, which obviously involve an element of speculation. We shall look at three varying perspectives on the issues involved.

Convergence theory

One view about current processes of development has been offered by Clark Kerr and his colleagues, whose standpoint has come to be known as **convergence theory**. According to Kerr, 'the world is entering a new age – the age of total industrialization. Some countries are far along the road; many are just beginning the journey. But everywhere, at a faster or slower pace, the peoples of the world are on the march towards industrialism' (Kerr et al., 1960, p. 29). In Kerr's view, there is a 'logic of industrialism' which ensures that social development produces a definite set of changes in social institutions. All industrialized societies tend to become alike; moreover, the rest of the world faces an industrial future, because only through industrialization can Third World societies break free from poverty.

Kerr cites several social and economic processes fostered by industrialization, which he asserts will become features of all countries. The industrialized countries are already far along the road which they signpost.

1 Modern large-scale production systems demand a wide range of technical skills and professional competence, producing a highly complex *division of labour*. Work in factories and offices, the predominant work settings in an industrialized society, follows regular and disciplined patterns – quite different to the more irregular types of labour characteristic of pre-industrial economies. People accept that they have to work certain hours on certain days each week, for example.

2 Industrialized societies are more open than their predecessors, with a high degree of *lateral and vertical social mobility*. There are strong tendencies towards equality of opportunity in the educational and occupational systems. Unlike in traditional societies, work roles are not generally allocated on the basis of inheritance or kinship position.

3 A large educational sector develops to transmit the skills and knowledge required to do the many different tasks involved in an industrial economy. Not only is there a high level of literacy and basic educational achievement among the population at large; specialized education for technical, managerial and professional tasks becomes more and more important.

4 Industrialized societies necessarily become highly urbanized, with the majority of the population living in cities. Developed communications systems are also required – road, rail and air systems, together with media of printed and electronic communication.

5 General agreement is reached over cultural values, involving the

secularization of belief, acceptance of the usefulness of science and technology, opposition to tradition and acceptance of a work ethic.
6 As industrialized societies become increasingly alike, and develop extensive networks of economic interdependence, the risks of war diminish. Wars derive from cultural clashes, or from divisions of economic interest; as societies become more and more locked into an industrialized world, a common outlook and shared interests outweigh divisive influences.

Since first setting out his views, in the 1960s, Kerr has developed and elaborated them. He later came to see convergence as less of a 'blanket' process than he had before. The industrialized societies, he now argues, tend to converge more closely in some aspects than in others. Convergence is most marked in the means and methods of production – e.g. in the use of similar technologies – and in terms of the daily lives led by the mass of the population. Forms of economic organization, political systems and patterns of belief and ideology remain much more variable. For instance, although car-production, and the lives of those working in the industry, are much the same in the USA and the Soviet Union, the political systems and ideologies of the two societies remain very different. 'The process of convergence', in Kerr's words, 'that has taken place thus far in history may be compared to a series of lines that approach one another at different but also at generally slower and slower rates, and that may at some point stop approaching one another at all' (Kerr, 1983, p. 75).

Convergence will probably continue to advance, Kerr claims, in economic structures. As more Third World countries industrialize, they will reproduce patterns of life already found in the more developed societies. There is likely to be some movement towards political convergence between the two largest industrialized societies, the United States and the Soviet Union. But many other differences will remain, because of their contrasting political orders.

Kerr's analysis stops short of endorsing convergence as helping humanity resolve some of its major problems, but others of rather similar views have not been so reluctant. Andrei Sakharov, a prominent Soviet dissident who won the Nobel Peace Prize, has accepted that convergence is occurring, and has proposed that it should actively be furthered. The greater the similarities which develop between the United States and the Soviet Union, Sakharov argues, the greater will be the reduction in global tension. The Soviet Union has to become more liberalized (as seems to be happening under Mikhail Gorbachev), as the pre-requisite of more flexible and rapid economic development. At present the USSR lags behind the West because of its bureaucratic, repressive style of government and economic management. On the other hand, the greater affluence of the Western countries is associated with pronounced inequalities between wealthier groups and the poor, and Sakharov argues that the governments of these countries should spread the wealth more equally. According to Sakharov, both systems 'are capable of long-term development, borrowing positive elements from each other' (Sakharov, 1974, p. 97; see also Galbraith, 1971).

Assessment

No one can dispute that industrialism has had a major effect on world social development over the past two centuries. Industrialization brings about major changes in the social institutions of any society, and there are basic similarities between societies that have achieved a high level of industrial organization. The United States has a capitalist economy and liberal democratic political institutions, while in the Soviet Union the Communist Party maintains centralized control over economic life; yet there are parallels between the two societies in many spheres (Brzezinski and Huntington, 1982). Each resembles the other more closely than either resembles the types of society of the traditional world.

Nevertheless, the convergence hypothesis has marked limitations, which have been identified by critics since its first formulation (Meyer, 1970; Goldthorpe, 1971; Ellman, 1980), and can be summarized as follows.

1 Pervasive as its influence is, industrialization is only one among other major sets of factors – such as political or cultural influences – shaping the development of modern societies.
2 Similarities between the industrialized countries do not necessarily stem directly from industrialism itself. They may derive, for example, from the competition of states to secure higher levels of economic development, or from the 'borrowing' by one society of aspects of the institutions of another.
3 Industrialization is a complicated phenomenon, having a less unified character than Kerr seems to believe – at least in the first formulation of his ideas. For instance, there are major variations between industrialized countries in terms of the type of manufacturing industries that exist, the relation between manufacture and services, and the relative proportion of large corporations and smaller firms.
4 Even if it were the case that the United States and Soviet Union were converging, it would not follow that military conflicts necessarily diminish. So far, at least, the intensity of military conflict in the present century has grown, rather than decreased. If the threat of major military confrontation recedes, it will not be because of increasing similarities between the United States and the Soviet Union, but rather because the imperatives which previously drove states to warfare are of reduced importance in an interdependent world (Cooper, 1986).

Towards a post-industrial society?

Many observers have suggested that what is occurring today is a transition to a new society no longer primarily based on industrialism. We are entering, they claim, a phase of development *beyond the industrial era altogether*. Alvin Toffler has argued that 'what is occurring now is, in all likelihood, bigger, deeper, and more important than the Industrial Revolution. . . The present moment represents nothing less than the second great divide in human history' (Toffler, 1970, p. 21).

A variety of terms have been coined to describe the new social order supposedly coming into being, such as the *information society*, *service society* or *knowledge society*. The sense that we are moving beyond the old forms of industrial development has led many to introduce terms including the word *post* (meaning 'after') to refer to the changes. Authors have spoken of *post-modern* or *post-scarcity* society, for example. The term which has come into most common usage, however – apparently first employed by Daniel Bell, writing in the United States, and Alain Touraine, working in France – is **post-industrial society** (Bell, 1973; Touraine, 1974).

The diversity of names is one indication of the many ideas put forward to interpret current social changes. But one theme that consistently appears is the significance of the use of *information* or *knowledge* in the society of the future. Our way of life, based on the manufacture of material goods, centred on the power machine and the factory, is being displaced by one in which information is becoming the main basis of the productive system.

The clearest and most comprehensive portrayal of the post-industrial society is provided by Daniel Bell in his work *The Coming of the Post-industrial Society* (Bell, 1973). The post-industrial order, Bell argues, is distinguished by a growth of service occupations at the expense of those producing material goods. The blue-collar worker, employed in a factory or workshop, is no longer the most essential type of employee. White-collar (clerical and professional) workers come to outnumber those in blue-collar jobs, with professional and technical occupations growing fastest of all.

People working in higher-level white-collar occupations specialize in the production of information and knowledge. The production and control of what Bell calls *codified knowledge* – systematic, co-ordinated information – is the main strategic resource on which the society depends. Those who are concerned with its creation and distribution – scientists, computer specialists, economists, engineers and professionals of all kinds – increasingly become the leading social groups, replacing the industrialists and entrepreneurs of the old system. On the level of culture, there is a shift away from the 'work ethic' towards an emphasis on a freer and more pleasure-seeking life-style. The work-discipline characteristic of industrialism relaxes in the post-industrial order; people are freer to innovate in both their work and their domestic lives.

Critical evaluation

How valid is the view that the old industrial order is being superseded by a post-industrial society? While the thesis has been widely accepted, there are good reasons to treat it with some caution (Kumar, 1978; Williams, 1985). The empirical assertions on which the notion depends are suspect in several ways.

1 The idea that information is becoming the main basis of the economic system is based on a questionable interpretation of the shift towards service occupations. This trend, accompanied by a decline in employment in other production sectors, dates back almost to the beginning of industrialism itself; it is not simply a recent phenomenon. From the early 1800s onwards manufacture and services *both* expanded at the expense of agriculture, with the service sector consistently showing a faster rate of increase than manufacture. The blue-collar worker never really was the most common type of employee; a higher proportion of paid employees has *always* worked in agriculture and services, with the service sector increasing proportionally as the numbers in agriculture dwindled. Easily the most important change has not been from industrial to service work, but from farm employment to all other types of occupation.
2 The service sector is very heterogeneous. 'Service occupations' cannot be simply treated as identical to 'white-collar jobs'; many jobs in services (such as that of petrol-station attendant) are blue-collar, in the sense that they are manual. Most white-collar positions involve very little specialized knowledge – and have become substantially mechanized. This is true of most lower-level office work, such as secretarial or clerical duties.
3 Many 'service' jobs contribute to a process which in the end produces material goods – and therefore should really be counted as part of manufacture. Thus a computer-programmer working for an industrial firm, designing and monitoring the operation of machine tools, is directly involved in a process of making material goods. Analysing service occupations, Jonathan Gershuny concludes that more than half are concerned with manufacturing production in such a way (Gershuny, 1978).
4 Bell proposes that the United States has advanced further than any other country towards becoming a post-industrial society – it is the furthest along a course of development that others will increasingly follow. Yet the American economy has long been different from that of other industrialized countries: throughout this century, a higher

relative proportion of workers has been in service occupations in the United States. There remain today wide variations in the ratio between service and manufacturing occupations in different countries, and it is not clear that other countries will ever become as 'service-based' as the USA. What some see as general trends might really be specific characteristics of American society.

5 No one can be sure what the long-term impact of the spreading use of microprocessing and electronic communications systems will be. At the moment, these are integrated *within* manufacturing production, rather than *displacing* it. It seems certain that such technologies will continue to show very high rates of innovation, and will permeate more areas of social life. But any assessment of their impact still has to be speculative. How far we yet live in a society in which 'codified knowledge' is the main resource is very unclear (Gill, 1985; Lyon, 1987).

6 Like convergence theory, the post-industrial society thesis tends to exaggerate the importance of economic factors in producing social change. Such a society is described as the outcome of developments in the economy which lead to changes in other institutions. Most of those advancing the post-industrial hypothesis have been little influenced by, or are directly critical of, Marx; but their position is a quasi-Marxist one in the sense that economic factors are held to dominate social change.

Some of the developments cited by the post-industrial theorists are important features of the current era, but it is not obvious that the concept of 'post-industrial society' is the best way to come to terms with them. Moreover, the forces behind the changes going on today are political and cultural as well as economic.

Capitalism and socialism

Neither convergence theory, nor the post-industrial society hypothesis, cast much light on political differences between societies. The clearest differences among the industrialized societies today are between the liberal democratic states of the West and the communist societies of Eastern Europe, the ideological battles between these two blocs being a major source of antagonism in international relations. What does the future hold for the relationship of capitalism and socialism? Political organizations and parties calling themselves 'socialist' believe that a new type of society, which overcomes many of the shortcomings of both West and East, can be created. How realistic are these aspirations? Will socialist ideals continue to mobilize social movements in the future? ('Socialism', as usually understood, is a much broader concept than 'Communism', which refers to movements and ideas associated with Marx and Lenin, such as became established in the USSR.)

Socialism is held by its advocates to be a stage 'beyond' the liberal democratic political systems and capitalist economies of Western societies. They believe that Western societies cannot realize the goals of equality and democracy they themselves proclaim because of their capitalist framework. Rights of political participation are supposed to be open to all citizens, but in practice most of the population have little or no influence over the decisions which affect their lives. The economic system is supposedly based on 'free enterprise', but this is almost meaningless, socialists argue, for the majority of the labour-force. Workers have no choice but to contract themselves to employers in order to obtain a living. Given the lack of industrial democracy, they have very little control over the work settings in which they are involved.

The system of capitalist production may generate considerable wealth, but, socialists claim, this is distributed highly unequally; large-scale poverty continues to exist in the midst of general affluence. Moreover, in a market economy there are continual fluctuations of economic life, with periods of boom succeeded by long phases of recession. At such times, there is large-scale unemployment, and many productive resources lie idle.

In a socialist society, it is held, these problems can be overcome, creating a more just and participatory social order. Although models of socialism vary considerably, most hold that a socialist society involves a combination of industrial democracy and central direction of economic enterprise. Government control of economic life is needed to control economic fluctuation and redistribute wealth. More extensive democracy, covering industry as well as the political sphere, is necessary to make sure that government power is not used to suppress individual liberties.

Socialism: the twentieth-century record

Until well into the twentieth century, socialism was a concept – a dream, or a nightmare, according to different points of view – rather than a reality. There were then no parties in power which claimed to be implementing socialist ideals, but over the past half-century or so, the situation has changed greatly. Governments adhering to socialist ideals have come to power in most regions of the world. These include communist parties, but also many others, such as the democratic socialist parties of Western European countries. Self-professedly socialist governments have also been involved in some of the most barbaric events of twentieth-century history, for instance the mass killings and deportations under Stalin in the Soviet Union. In the light of this half-century of experience, we can be clearer about both the promise and the limitations of socialist thought.

Industrialized countries that have experienced central political and economic control – in particular the societies of Eastern Europe – do not show up well either in terms of their level of economic development or the degree of liberalism of their political systems. The attempt to supersede market mechanisms by strongly defined state planning has in most respects not been successful; it seems impossible effectively to organize a complex modern economy centrally. Market mechanisms appear to have a key role to play in efficiently allocating goods and resources. Moreover, the evidence is that strongly centralized economic planning tends to be associated with a high degree of authoritarianism in the political system.

Some Third World socialist countries have been more effective in promoting the social and economic welfare of their citizens than their non-socialist counterparts. Cuba, for example, has higher standards of literacy, general education, medical care and other welfare provisions, than comparable non-socialist countries in South America. But although many Western socialists at one point saw Cuba as pioneering new modes of socialist organization, few would today hold that Cuban socialism presents a model that industrialized countries might profitably follow. Cuba remains at a low level of economic development, depending upon extensive subsidies from the Soviet Union, and freedom of political expression is limited.

Democratic socialist parties in Western countries have usually found their more radical aspirations frustrated, either by electorates unwilling to endorse their views, or by the opposition of business interests, but their impact has still been considerable. Such parties have played a leading part in establishing welfare institutions, and in limiting the inequalities which unchecked market forces tend to bring about. In some societies where socialist or labour parties have achieved power for lengthy periods, the results have been notable. Sweden is a good example, where there is now a higher average income per head of the population than in the United States, and poverty has virtually been eradicated. None the less, Sweden remains a capitalist society in its basic economic institutions. It is not clear how such a society might become more fully socialist without being authoritarian and overly centralized in the manner of the East European countries (Himmelstrand et al., 1981). Its combination of economic prosperity, liberalism and social justice seems to derive from an effective compromise between socialist ideals and capitalistic mechanisms.

Alternatives to socialism

Socialist thought has been seriously compromised by twentieth-century developments, and in recent years there has been a major challenge from Rightist political thought. Authors on this side of the political spectrum have not only attacked socialist doctrines as denying individual liberties, but have increasingly sought to develop positive alternatives of their own. According to such writers, expanding the realm of market operations is the key to a just and free social and political order – the very reverse of traditional socialist arguments. In the light of the dilemmas posed for socialism, together with the sorts of changes highlighted by the theorists of post-industrial society, many now argue that socialist ideas have become largely irrelevant to the fundamental problems of our age. Those putting forward .such arguments include Left-wing as well as Right-wing authors.

What are we to make of such views? Certainly socialist parties and movements are unlikely to disappear, or even diminish in importance, in the near future. Socialism is a fundamental part of the Western political heritage, and the number of countries in the world ruled by governments proclaiming themselves to be either communist or socialist will probably grow rather than decline in the future. But it also seems certain that socialist ideas will be increasingly challenged in future years, not only by traditional opponents on the political Right, but from others associated with liberal views. New groups and movements are likely to have a notable place in political debates and struggles. They are already raising issues and questions which do not fit readily into traditional debates about the relative merits of socialism and free-market capitalism.

One such set of issues concerns **environmental ecology**. Those on both Left and Right used to hold that economic growth could go on more or less indefinitely, even if they disagreed about the best means of achieving it. It has become increasingly apparent, however, that the earth's resources are finite; what may amount to irreparable damage to the environment has already been brought about by the spread of industrial production. Ecological questions do not only concern how we can best cope with and contain environmental damage, but are bound up with the very ways of life fostered within the industrialized societies. If the goal of continuous economic growth has to be abandoned, new social institutions will probably have to be pioneered. Technological progress is unpredictable, and it may be that the earth will in fact yield sufficient resources for Kerr's global process of industrialization. At the moment, however, this does not seem feasible, and if the Third World countries are to achieve living standards even moderately comparable to those currently enjoyed in the West, global readjustments will be necessary.

Other fundamental issues are to do with *gender divisions* and with *violence*. Inequalities between men and women are deeply ingrained in all cultures, and the establishing of greater equality between the sexes is likely to demand major changes in our existing social institutions. Although there are many debates about this, there is no obvious sense in which a concern with issues of gender fits particularly closely with the established aspirations of socialism. Much the same is true of attempts to meet the threat posed by the accelerating development of weaponry and military power. The problem of how to limit – and possibly eventually eliminate altogether – the risks of nuclear confrontation, is by any token the most urgent task facing humanity in the 1990s and beyond. The issues posed here do not fit readily into established contrasts between a 'capitalist' and a 'socialist' outlook. Indeed, the clash between these rival ideologies is at the very core of the militarized world in which we now live.

Social change: looking into the future

We may or may not be moving into a post-industrial order, but we do seem to be living through a period of social change which is dramatic even by the standards of the past two centuries. We know what the major dimensions of such change are, even if their interpretation remains problematic. They include the influences mentioned by the post-industrial society theorists and others:

1 exceptionally rapid rates of technological innovation, coupled with the impact of information technology and micro-electronics;
2 an erosion of the established manufacturing industries of Western economies, associated with a transfer of basic industrial production Eastwards;
3 the deepening involvement of all the industrialized societies in integrated global connections;
4 major transitions within the domestic and cultural spheres, associated with changes in gender relations;
5 the persistence of marked divisions of wealth and power between the industrialized and the poorer Third World countries;
6 in the background to everything, a delicate balance between the possibility of long-lasting global peace and a nuclear conflict that could wipe out most of the earth's population.

As we peer over the edge of our century into the next, we cannot foresee whether the coming hundred years will be marked by peaceful social and economic development, or by a multiplication of global problems – perhaps beyond humanity's ability to solve. Unlike the early sociologists, writing two hundred years ago, we see very clearly that modern industry, technology and science are by no means wholly beneficial in their consequences. Our world is much more populous and wealthy than ever before; we have possibilities to control our destiny, and shape our lives for the better, quite unimaginable to previous generations – yet the world hovers close to nuclear and ecological disaster. To say this is not in any way to counsel an attitude of resigned despair. If there is one thing which sociology offers us, it is a profound consciousness of the human authorship of social institutions. As human beings, aware of our achievements and limitations, we make our own history. Our understanding of the dark side of modern social change need not prevent us from sustaining a realistic and hopeful outlook towards the future.

Summary

1   The modern period – from about the eighteenth century to the present day – has seen an extraordinary acceleration in processes of change. Probably more profound changes have occurred in this period, which is a tiny segment of time in human history, than in the whole previous existence of humankind.

2   The two most prominent general attempts to interpret social change are *evolutionism* and *historical materialism*. Both see change as deriving mainly from the ways in which human beings relate to the material environment; major criticisms can be made of both.

3   No 'single factor' theory can explain all social change. A number of major influences on change can be distinguished, of which adaptation to the material environment is one. Others include political, military and cultural influences.

4   It is possible to develop theories of particular episodes of change. An example is Robert Carneiro's theory of the development of traditional states.

5   Among the important factors in modern social change are the expansion of industrial capitalism; the development of centralized nation-states; the industrialization of war; and the emergence of science and 'rational' or critical modes of thought.

6   According to *convergence theory*, industrialization is the main force shaping the modern world; as they industrialize, societies tend to become more alike in certain basic respects. Although the convergence thesis helps us understand some features of change today, it has marked limitations centred on the prime causative role it gives to industrialization.

7   Another view is associated with the idea of the 'post-industrial' society. In this view, the old industrial order is being left behind in the development of a new social order based on knowledge and information. These ideas underestimate the extent to which service work is embedded within manufacture, and also give too much emphasis to economic factors.

8   Traditional debates between the advocates of *free market capitalism* and *socialism* may be becoming outdated. New issues are coming to the fore which cannot easily be grasped or responded to within the framework of established positions in political theory.

Basic concepts

social change	post-industrial society
social evolutionism	

Important terms

historical materialism	forces of production
differentiation	dialectical interpretation of change
social Darwinism	episodes of change
unilinear evolution	convergence
multilinear evolution	environmental ecology
adaptation	

Further reading

Daniel Bell, *The Coming of the Post-industrial Society* (London: Heinemann, 1974) — one of the first and most influential books to propose the new post-industrial order.

Raymond Boudon, *Theories of Social Change* (Cambridge: Polity Press, 1986) — an analysis and critique of some dominant approaches to the understanding of social change.

Boris Frankel, *The Post-industrial Utopians* (Cambridge: Polity Press, 1987) — a discussion of some of the main problems posed by debates about the 'end of industrialism' today.

Krishan Kumar, *Prophecy and Progress: The Sociology of Industrial and Post-industrial Society* (Harmondsworth: Penguin, 1978) — a discussion of older and more recent theories of the impact of industrialism in modern society.

Harley Shaiken, *Work Transformed: Automation and Labour in the Computer Age* (Lexington, Mass.: Heath, 1986) — an analysis of the major changes which may be looming as a result of recent technological developments.

PART VI

Methods and Theories in Sociology

The first chapter in this concluding part considers how sociologists set about doing research. A number of basic methods of investigation are available to help us find out what is going on in the social world, and we have to make sure that the information on which sociological reasoning is based is as reliable and accurate as possible. The chapter examines the problems involved, indicating how they can best be dealt with.

In the final chapter of the book we analyse some of the main theoretical approaches in sociology. Sociology is not a subject based on a body of theories whose validity is generally agreed. In this chapter, differing theoretical traditions are compared and contrasted.

21

Working with Sociology: Methods of Research

The issues with which sociologists are concerned, both in their theorizing and in their research, are often similar to those that worry many other people. How can mass starvation exist in a world that is far wealthier than it has ever been before? What effects will the increasing use of information technology have on our lives? Is the family beginning to disintegrate as an institution? Do films and television encourage violent crime?

Sociologists try to provide answers to these and many other problems. Their findings are by no means necessarily conclusive. Nevertheless it is always the aim of sociological theorizing and research to break away from the speculative or ill-informed manner in which the ordinary person usually considers such questions. Good sociological work tries to make the questions asked as precise as possible, and seeks to assess factual evidence before coming to conclusions. To achieve these aims, we must utilize sound research procedures and be able accurately to analyse the material. We have to know the most useful forms of **research method** to apply in a given study, and how we should best analyse the results.

Several aspects are involved in sociological research. Research procedure or *strategy* relates to how research is planned and carried out. This means choosing the appropriate method of research and working out how to apply it to the area of study. Research *methodology* is to do with the logic of interpreting results and analysing findings. Research *methods* are the actual *techniques* of investigation used to study the social world (Bulmer, 1984). They include the use of questionnaires, interviews, 'participant observation' or field-work within a community being studied, together with the interpretation of official statistics and historical documents – plus other techniques not so widely used.

In this chapter, we shall begin by outlining the stages involved in sociological research, together with the main principles used in interpreting findings. We shall then compare the most widely used research methods, considering some actual projects and investigations. There are often large differences between the way research should ideally be carried out and real-life studies!

Research strategy

The research problem

All research starts from a *research problem*. This may sometimes be mainly an area of factual ignorance: we may simply wish to improve our knowledge about certain institutions, social processes or cultures. The researcher might set out to answer questions like: what proportion of the population holds strong religious beliefs? Are people today really disaffected with 'big government'? How far does the economic position of women lag behind that of men? The answers would be mainly *descriptive*. The best sociological research, however, starts from problems which are also *puzzles*. A puzzle is not just a lack of information, but a *gap in our understanding*. A large part of the skill of producing worthwhile sociological research consists in correctly identifying puzzles. Descriptive research simply answers the question: 'What is going on here?' Puzzle-solving research tries to contribute to our understanding of *why* events happen as they do, rather than simply accepting them at their face value. Thus we might ask, why are patterns of religious belief changing? What accounts for the rise of the 'New Right' in politics in recent years? Why are women so poorly represented in high-status jobs?

No piece of research stands alone. Research problems come up as part of on-going work; one research project may easily lead to another, because it raises issues which the researcher had not previously considered. Puzzles may also be suggested by reading the work of other researchers in books and professional journals, or by an awareness of specific trends in society. For example, as was mentioned in chapter 5 ('Conformity and Deviance'), over recent years there have been an increasing number of programmes that seek to treat the mentally ill in the community rather than confining them in asylums. Sociologists might be prompted to ask: 'what has given rise to this shift in attitude towards the mentally ill?'; 'what are the likely consequences both for the patients themselves and for the rest of the community?'.

Reviewing the evidence

The first step taken in the research process is usually that of *reviewing the available evidence in the field*. It might be that previous research has already satisfactorily clarified the problem, so the would-be researcher must read other sociologists' work in the area. If the problem has not been clarified, the researcher will need to sift through whatever related research does exist to see how useful it is for the purpose at hand. Have previous researchers spotted the same puzzle? How have they tried to resolve it? What aspects of the problem has their research left unanalysed? Drawing upon others' ideas helps the researcher to clarify the issues which might be raised in a possible project, and the methods that might be used in the research.

Making the research problem precise

The next stage involves working out a *clear formulation of the research problem*. If relevant research literature already exists, the researcher might return from the library with a good notion of how the research problem should be approached. Hunches about the nature of the problem can usefully be turned into definite **hypotheses** at this stage. A hypothesis is a guess about the relationship between the phenomena in which the researcher is interested. If the research is to be effective, a hypothesis must be set out in such a way that the factual material gathered provides the opportunity to test it.

Working out a research design

We must now decide just *how* we are going to collect the material (information) we need. A range of different research methods exists, and which is chosen depends on the overall objectives of the study, as well as the aspects of behaviour to be analysed. For some purposes, a survey (in which questionnaires are normally used) might be suitable. In other circumstances interviews, or an observational study, might be appropriate. None of these methods, of course, can be employed if we are studying a problem in historical sociology. Here we must use documents relating to the period we wish to study.

Carrying out the research

At the point of actually doing the research, unforeseen practical difficulties can easily crop up. It might prove impossible to contact some of those to whom questionnaires are due to be sent, or whom the researcher wishes to interview. A business firm or government agency, for example, might be unwilling to let the researcher carry out the work planned. Documentary materials might prove much harder to trace than was originally envisaged.

Interpreting the results

The material gathered has to be analysed and brought to bear on the problem which prompted the study. The researcher's troubles are not over – they may be just beginning! Working out the implications of the data collected, and relating these back to the research problem, is rarely easy. While it may be possible to reach a clear answer to the questions with which the research was concerned, many investigations are in the end less than fully conclusive.

Reporting research findings

The research report, usually published as a journal article or book, provides an account of the nature of the research, and justifies whatever conclusions are drawn. This is a 'final stage' only in terms of the individual research project. Most reports indicate the questions which remain unanswered and suggest further research that might profitably be done in the future. All individual research investigations are part of the continuing process of research going on within the sociological community.

The overall process

The preceding sequence of steps is a simplified version of what happens in actual research projects. In real sociological research, these stages rarely if ever succeed each other so neatly, and there may be a certain amount of sheer 'muddling through' (Bell and Newby, 1977). The difference is a bit like that between the procedures outlined in a recipe book and the actual process of cooking a meal. People who are experienced cooks might not work from recipe books at all, and their work is often much more creative than those who do. Following fixed schemes can be unduly restricting; much of the most outstanding sociological research could not readily be fitted into the sequence just mentioned (Orenstein and Phillips, 1984).

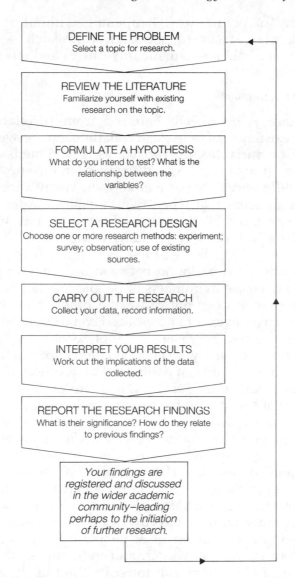

Figure 25   Steps in the research process

General methodology

One of the main problems to be tackled in research *methodology* (the study of logical problems involved in research) is the analysis of cause and effect. A **causal relationship** between two events or situations is one in which one event or situation produces another. If I release the handbrake in a car facing down a hill, it will roll down, gathering speed as it goes. Taking the brake off *caused* this to happen; and the reasons for this can readily be understood by reference to the physical principles involved. Like natural science, sociology depends on the assumption that all events have causes. Social life is not a random array of occurrences, happening without rhyme or reason. One of the main tasks of sociological research – in combination with theoretical thinking – is to identify causes and effects.

Causation and correlation

Causation cannot be directly inferred from **correlation**. Correlation means the existence of a regular relationship between two sets of occurrences or **variables**. A variable is any dimension along which individuals or groups vary. Age, differences in income, crime-rates, and social class differences are some among the many variables sociologists study. It might seem that when two variables are found to be closely correlated, one must be the cause of another, but such is often not the case. There are many correlations without any causal relationship between the variables. For example, since the Second World War, a strong correlation can be found between a decline in pipe-smoking in Britain and a decrease in numbers of people regularly going to cinemas. Clearly one change does not cause the other, and we would find it difficult to discover even a remote causal connection between them.

In many instances, however, it is not so obvious that an observed correlation does not imply a causal relationship. Such correlations are traps for the unwary and can easily lead to questionable or false conclusions. In his classic work *Suicide*, Emile Durkheim found a correlation between rates of suicide and the seasons of the year (Durkheim, 1952). In the societies he studied, levels of suicide increased progressively from January up to around June or July, before declining towards the end of the year. It might be supposed that this demonstrates that temperature or climatic change is causally related to the propensity of individuals to kill themselves. Perhaps as temperatures increase, people become more impulsive and hot-headed? However, the causal relation involved here is almost certainly nothing directly to do with temperature or climate at all. In spring and summer most people engage in a more intensive social life than they do in winter, and individuals who are isolated or unhappy tend to experience an intensification of these feelings as the activity level of other people rises. Hence they are more likely to experience acute suicidal tendencies in spring and summer than in autumn and winter, when the pace of social activity slackens. We always have to be on our guard in assessing whether correlation involves causation, and deciding in which direction causal relations run.

Causal mechanisms

Working out the causal connections involved in correlations is often a difficult process. There is a strong correlation, for instance, between level of educational achievement and occupational success in modern societies. The better the marks an individual gets in school, the more well-paid the job he or she is likely eventually to obtain. What explains this correlation? Research tends to show that it is not mainly school experience itself; levels of school attainment are influenced much more by the home from which the person comes. Children from better-off homes, whose parents take a strong interest in their learning skills and where books are abundant, are more likely to do well in both school and work than those from homes where these qualities are lacking. The causal mechanisms here are the attitudes of parents towards their children, together with the facilities for learning which a home provides. (For further discussion of home and school, see chapter 13: 'Education, Communication and Media'.)

Causal connections in sociology should not be understood in too mechanical a way. The attitudes people have, and their subjective reasons for acting as they do, are causal factors in the relationships between variables in social life.

Controls

In assessing the cause or causes which explain a correlation, we need to distinguish **independent variables** from **dependent variables**. An independent variable is one which produces an effect upon another variable; the variable affected is the dependent one. In the example just mentioned, academic achievement is the independent variable and occupational income the dependent variable. The distinction is one which refers to the *direction* of the causal relationship we are investigating. The same factor may be an independent variable in one study, and a dependent variable in another, depending on what causal processes are being analysed. If we were looking at the effects of differences in occupational income on lifestyles, occupational income would then be the independent variable rather than the dependent one.

Finding out whether a correlation between variables is a causal connection involves using **controls**, which means holding some variables constant in order to look at the effects of others. By doing this, we are able to judge between explanations of observed correlations, separating causal from non-causal relationships. For example, researchers studying child development have claimed that there is a causal connection between maternal deprivation in infancy and serious personality problems in adulthood. ('Maternal deprivation involves a child being separated from its mother for a long period – several months or more – during the early years of its life.') How might we test whether there really is a causal relationship between maternal deprivation and later personality disorders? We would do so by trying to control, or 'screen out', other possible influences that might explain the correlation.

One source of maternal deprivation is the admission of a child to hospital for a lengthy period, during which it is separated from

Statistical Terms

Research in sociology often makes use of statistical techniques in the analysis of findings. Some of these techniques are highly sophisticated and complex, but those used most commonly are easy to understand. The most widely employed are *measures of central tendency* – ways of calculating averages – and *correlation coefficients* (measures of the degree to which one variable relates consistently to another).

There are three methods of calculating averages, each of which has certain advantages and certain shortcomings. Take as a working example the amount of personal wealth (including all assets, such as houses, cars, bank accounts and investments) owned by thirteen individuals. Suppose the thirteen own amounts as follows:

1	£000 (zero)	8	£80,000
2	£5,000	9	£100,000
3	£10,000	10	£150,000
4	£20,000	11	£200,000
5	£40,000	12	£400,000
6	£40,000	13	£10,000,000
7	£40,000		

The **mean** corresponds to the *average* as it is usually understood, arrived at by adding together the personal wealth of all thirteen people, and dividing the result by the total number of people, i.e. 13. The total is £11,085,000; dividing this by thirteen, we reach a mean of £852,692. The mean is often a useful calculation because it is based on the whole range of data provided. However, it can be misleading where one, or a small number, of cases are very different from the majority. In the above example, the mean is not in fact a very appropriate measure of *central tendency*, because the presence of one very large figure, £10,000,000, skews all the rest. One might get the impression that most of the people own far more than they actually do.

In such instances, one of two other measures may be used. The **mode** is the figure which occurs *most frequently* in a given set of data. In the example given here, it is £40,000. The problem with the mode is that it does not take into account the *overall distribution* of the data, i.e. the range of figures covered. The most frequently occurring case in a particular set of figures is not necessarily representative of their distribution as a whole, and thus may not be a very useful 'average'. In this case £40,000 does not give a very accurate idea of central tendency, because it is too close to the lower end of the figures.

The third measure is the **median**, which is the figure in the *middle* of any set of figures. In the example given here, this would be the seventh figure, £40,000. An odd set of figures has been given in our example. If there had been an even number – for instance, twelve instead of thirteen – the median would be calculated by taking the mean of the two middle cases, figures six and seven. Like the mode, the median gives no idea of the actual *range* of the data measured.

Sometimes a researcher will use more than one measure of central tendency, in order not to provide a deceptive picture of the average. More often, he or she will calculate the **standard deviation** for the data in question. This is a way of calculating the *degree of dispersal*, or the range, of a set of figures – which in this case goes from zero to £10,000,000.

Correlation coefficients offer a useful way of expressing how closely connected two (or more) variables are with one another. Where two variables correlate completely, we can speak of a perfect positive correlation – expressed as a coefficient of 1.0. Where no relation is found between two variables (they simply have no consistent connection at all) the coefficient is zero. A perfect *negative* correlation, expressed as −1.0, exists when two variables are in a completely *inverse* relation to one another. Perfect correlations are never found in the social sciences. Correlations of the order of 0.6 or more, whether positive or negative, are usually regarded as indicating a strong degree of connection between whatever variables are being analysed. Positive correlations of this level, for example, might be found between, say, social class background and voting behaviour. The higher a British person is on the socio-economic scale, the more likely he or she is to vote Conservative rather than Labour.

its parents. Is it really attachment to the *mother*, however, that really matters? Perhaps if a child receives love and attention from other people during infancy, he or she might subsequently be a stable person? To investigate these possible causal connections, we would have to compare cases where children were deprived of regular care from anyone, with other instances in which children were separated from their mothers, but received love and care from someone else. If the first group developed severe personality difficulties, but the second group did not, we would suspect that regular care from *someone* in infancy is what matters, regardless of whether or not it is the mother. (In fact, children do normally seem to prosper as long as they have a loving, stable relationship with someone looking after them – this does not have to be the mother herself.)

Identifying causes

Many possible causes could be invoked to explain any given correlation. How can we ever be sure that we have covered them all? We cannot. We would never be able to carry out, and interpret the results of, a piece of sociological research satisfactorily if we were compelled to test for the possible influence of every causal factor we could imagine as potentially relevant. Identifying causal relationships is normally guided by previous research into the area. If we have no reasonable idea beforehand of the likely causal mechanisms involved in a correlation we would probably find it very difficult to discover what the real causal connections are. We wouldn't know what to test *for*.

A good example of the problems involved in correctly assessing the causal relations involved in a correlation is given by the long history of studies of smoking and lung cancer. Research has consistently demonstrated a strong correlation between the two. Smokers are more likely to contract lung cancer than non-smokers, and very heavy smokers more likely to do so than light smokers. The correlation can also be expressed the other way around. A high proportion of those who have lung cancer are smokers, or have smoked for long periods in their past. There have been so many studies confirming these correlations that it is generally accepted that a causal link must be involved. The exact causal mechanisms, however, are so far largely unknown.

However much correlational work is done on any issue, there always remains some doubt about possible causal relationships; other interpretations of the correlation are possible. It has been proposed, for instance, that people who are predisposed to get lung cancer are also predisposed to smoke. In this view it is not smoking which causes lung cancer; both smoking and lung cancer are produced through dispositions which some individuals have built into their biological make-up.

Research methods

Field-work

Various different methods of research are used in sociology. In **participant observation** or **field-work** (the two terms can be used interchangeably), the investigator lives with a group or community being studied, and perhaps takes a direct part in their activities. An example of field-work research is Erving Goffman's celebrated study of behaviour in an asylum (Goffman, 1961). Goffman spent several months in a mental hospital, working as an assistant athletic director. One or two of the staff knew him to be a sociological researcher, but the inmates did not. Hence Goffman was able to mix easily and informally with them, and made contact even with the most severely ill patients in the 'back wards'. In this way he was able to build up a detailed picture of the life of the organization, together with the attitudes and views of those living and working in it. His research materials were the daily descriptions he wrote about life on the wards, together with accounts of conversations or contacts with the patients and staff.

He found, for example, that on the back wards, where many of the patients were resistant to ordinary social communication, the ward orderlies had one or two 'working patients' from other wards, who helped them with their work. The working patients usually received a steady flow of favours as rewards for their efforts in this way. This practice was not officially approved of by the hospital authorities, but was in fact essential for the smooth working of the organization. An example comes from the field notes which Goffman kept, recording each day's activities:

Am eating with a patient-friend in one of the large patient cafeterias. He says, 'the food is good here but I don't like canned salmon.' He then excuses himself, dumps his plateful of food into the waste-bucket, and goes to the dietary section of the steamtray line, coming back with a plate of eggs. He smiles in a mocking conspiratorial way and says: 'I play pool with the attendant who looks after that.' (Goffman, 1961, pp. 257–8)

Goffman managed to see the asylum from the patients' point of view rather than in terms of the medical categories applied to them by psychiatrists. 'It is my belief', he wrote, 'that any group of persons, primitives, pilots or patients, develop a life of their own that becomes meaningful, reasonable, and normal once you get close to it . . .' (Goffman, 1961, p. 7). Goffman's work indicates that what looks 'insane' to an outside observer is not quite so irrational when seen in the context of the hospital. Asylums involve forms of discipline, dress and behaviour that make it almost impossible for inmates to behave like people in the outside world. When they were admitted to the hospital, patients' personal possessions were mostly taken away from them; they were undressed, bathed and disinfected and issued with institutional clothing. From then on, virtually all their behaviour occurred under the gaze of staff; they had very little privacy; and staff often treated patients as though they were children. As a consequence, they developed patterns of behaviour which seem bizarre to the outsider, but were understandable attempts to cope with the unusual demands of their environment.

The demands of field-work

A field-worker cannot just *be present* in a community, but must explain and justify her or his presence to its members. She or he must gain the confidence and co-operation of the community or group, and sustain it over a period of time, if any worthwhile results are to be achieved. This may involve living in conditions, especially when studying cultures very different from their own, that are difficult to adjust to.

For a long while it was usual for research based on participant observation to exclude any account of the hazards or problems which had to be overcome, but more recently, the published reminiscences and diaries of field-workers have been more open about them. Frequently, feelings of loneliness have to be coped with – it is not easy to 'fit into' a community to which a person does not really belong. The researcher may be constantly frustrated because the members of the group or community refuse to talk frankly about themselves; direct queries may be welcomed in some cultural contexts, but meet with a chilly silence in others. Some types of field-work may even be physically dangerous – for instance, a researcher studying a delinquent gang might be seen as police informer, or might become unwittingly embroiled in conflicts with rival groups.

Like most types of social research, field-work is normally a one-sided endeavour, so far as those whose behaviour is studied are concerned.

The selection of a group for study is usually decided solely by the researcher; its members are rarely consulted in advance or involved in the design of the project (Georges and Jones, 1980). It is not surprising that field-workers sometimes meet with suspicion, or that attempts at field research sometimes have to be abandoned at the very beginning.

One of the very first anthropological field-workers, Frank Hamilton Cushing, who studied the Zuñi Indians of New Mexico in the 1870s, wrote an account of the problems he experienced (as well as the rewards he obtained) (Cushing, 1967; originally published 1882–3). When he first arrived, Cushing took numerous small gifts, and made various attempts to ingratiate himself with the community. The Zuñi were reasonably friendly to him, but strenuously refused to let him study their religious ceremonials. Their leader tried to compel him to leave, but eventually allowed him to stay on condition that he adopt some of the Indian ways – to show that he did not regard their beliefs and practices as foolish. He was obliged to wear Zuñi clothing, which he found ill-fitting and uncomfortable; he had to eat Zuñi food; his hammock was torn down, and he was made to sleep on sheepskins on the floor like the Zuñi themselves. One of his most difficult experiences came when he was told that he must take a wife, and a woman was sent to live with him. At first he tried to ignore her attentions, but without success. Eventually he sent her away, although this brought dishonour on her in the eyes of the Zuñi.

Since then, the Zuñi – like many other American Indian groups – have become used to visiting researchers, but their relationship with them has frequently been tense. The archaeologist F. W. Hodge aroused their enmity in the 1920s by starting excavations in one of their ancient religious shrines (Pandey, 1972, pp. 331–2); he was made to leave, and the cameras of his expedition's photographer were smashed.

The celebrated anthropologist Ruth Benedict was better received among the Zuñi when she arrived not long afterwards. A Zuñi interpreter afterwards said that she was polite and distributed money generously, but that her published descriptions of Zuñi life were poorly founded, as she had not taken an active part in many aspects of Zuñi life. On various occasions since then other field-workers have been expelled from the Zuñi community. One man asked a visiting researcher recently, 'Are we still so primitive that you anthropologists have to come to study us every summer?' (Pandey, 1975, p. 203).

The advantages and limitations of field-work

Field-work – where it is successful – provides much richer information about social life than most other research methods. Once we understand how things look 'from the inside' of a given group, we are likely to have a much better understanding than before of why those involved act as they do. Field-work is virtually the only method available when the researcher is studying a group whose culture is largely unknown to outsiders, and has to be 'learned' before their activities become fully comprehensible. For this reason, it is the main research method used in anthropology, which is concerned to document and understand non-Western cultures.

Field-work gives the investigator more flexibility than other methods (such as questionnaires). The researcher in the field is able to adjust to novel or unexpected circumstances and follow up leads that develop in the process of the research itself. Field-work is probably more likely to turn up unexpected results than most other methods of investigation, as the researcher may discover with a jolt that his or her preconceived ideas about the group or community in question were completely wrong. Field-work also has its limitations: only fairly small groups or communities can be studied; and much depends on the skill of the researcher in gaining the confidence of the individuals involved. Without this, the research is unlikely to get off the ground at all.

Surveys

Interpreting field studies usually involves problems of generalization. How can we be sure that what is found in one context will apply in other situations? This is usually less of a problem in **survey** research, although, of course, such work has shortcomings of its own. In a survey, questionnaires are either sent, or given directly in interviews, to a selected group of people – sometimes as many as several thousand. Field-work is best suited for in-depth studies of social life; survey research tends to produce information that is less detailed, but which we can be fairly confident applies over a broad area.

Standardized and open-ended questionnaires

Two sorts of questionnaire are used in surveys. Some have a *standardized* set of questions, to which only a fixed range of responses is possible. Either the respondents or the researcher mark certain categories of reply to the questions asked – for instance, 'Yes/No/Don't know', or 'Very likely/Likely/Unlikely/Very unlikely'. Fixed-choice surveys have the advantage that responses are easy to compare and tabulate, since only a small number of categories are involved. On the other hand, because they do not allow for subtleties of opinion or verbal expression, the information they yield is likely to be restricted in scope. Other types of questionnaire are *open-ended*, giving opportunities for respondents to express their views in their own words: they are not limited to ticking fixed-choice responses. Open-ended questionnaires are more flexible, and provide richer information than standardized ones. The researcher can follow up answers to probe more deeply into what the respondent thinks. On the other hand, the lack of standardization means that responses may be more difficult to compare.

Survey questions have to be carefully constructed if the results are to be useful. A question like 'What do you think of the government?' is worthless because it is much too vague. If they were able to answer it at all, respondents would interpret what the researcher was trying to get at in many different ways. Survey researchers also have to take care to avoid *leading* questions – questions expressed in such a way as to encourage a definite response. A question that begins: 'Do you agree that . . .?' is leading, since it *invites* agreement from the respondent. A more neutral question would begin: 'What is your opinion of . . .?' There are many other sources of possible distortion or ambiguity in the framing of questions. For instance, a question may state a double choice: 'Is your health better or worse now than it was a year ago?' The double choice is between 'better–worse' and 'now–then'. A clearer formulation would be 'Is your health better now than it was a year ago?' (Smith, 1975, p. 175). Respondents might well answer 'yes' or 'no' to both questions; in the former case, the researcher could not interpret this. Questions should be as simple as possible so as to avoid ambiguous responses.

Questionnaire items are normally laid out so that a team of interviewers can ask the questions in the same predetermined order, recording responses in the same way. All the items have to be readily understandable to interviewer and interviewees alike. In the large national surveys undertaken regularly by government agencies and research organizations, interviews are carried out more or less simultaneously across the whole country by many interviewers. Those who conduct the interviews, and whoever analyses the results, could not do their work effectively if they constantly had to be contacting each other to check ambiguities in the questions or answers.

Schedules have to be carefully designed in relation to the characteristics of respondents. Will they see the point which the researcher has in mind in asking a particular question? Have they enough information to answer usefully? *Will* they answer? The terms with which the researcher may be working might be unfamiliar to the respondents: for instance, the question 'What is your marital status?' might be received with some bafflement. It would be more appropriate to ask, 'Are you single, married or divorced?' Most surveys are preceded by *pilot studies* in order to pick up problems not anticipated by the investigator. A pilot study is a trial run in which a questionnaire is completed by just a few people. Any difficulties found can be ironed out before the main survey is done.

Sampling

Often sociologists are interested in the characteristics of large numbers of individuals – for example, the political attitudes of the British electorate. It would be impossible to study all these people directly, so in such situations, the research concentrates on a small proportion of the overall group – a *sample* of the total. One can usually be fairly confident that results deriving from a survey of a population sample can be generalized to the whole of that population. Studies of only some two to three thousand British voters, for instance, can give a very accurate indication of the attitudes and voting intentions of the whole population. But to achieve such accuracy, a sample must be representative. *Representative sampling* involves ensuring that the group of individuals studied is typical of the population as a whole. **Sampling** is more complex than it might seem, and statisticians have developed various rules for working out the correct size and nature of samples.

A particularly important procedure is *random sampling*, in which a sample is chosen so that every member of the population concerned has the same probability of being included. The most sophisticated way of obtaining a random sample is to give each member of the population a number, and then use a computer to generate random numbers, from which the sample is derived – for instance by picking every tenth number in a random series.

Example: The People's Choice?

One of the most famous early examples of survey research was *The People's Choice?*, a study carried out by Paul Lazarsfeld and a number of colleagues about half a century ago (Lazarsfeld, Berelson and Gaudet, 1948). The study pioneered several of the main techniques of survey research in use to this day. At the same time, however, its shortcomings show rather clearly the limitations of the survey research method. *The People's Choice?* was based on an investigation into the voting intentions of residents of Erie County, Ohio, during the 1940 campaign for the US presidency, and it influenced the design of many subsequent political polls, not just those conducted by academic researchers (Clemens, 1983). In order to probe a little more deeply than a single questionnaire would do, the investigators interviewed each member of a sample of voters on seven separate occasions. The aim was to trace, and understand the reasons for, alterations in voting intentions.

The research was set up with a number of definite hypotheses in view. One was that relationships and events *close* to voters in a community influence voting intentions more than distant world affairs, and the findings on the whole confirmed this. The researchers developed sophisticated measurement techniques for analysing political attitudes; yet their work was also strongly influenced by theoretical ideas, and made significant contributions to theoretical thinking. Among the concepts they helped to introduce were those of 'opinion leaders' and the 'two-step flow of communication'. Some individuals – opinion leaders – tend to shape the political opinions of those around them. They take the lead in influencing responses to political events, by interpreting them to those around them. People's views on the political system are not just formed in a direct fashion, but in a 'two-step' process: the views expressed by opinion leaders, filtered through personal relationships, influence the responses of other individuals towards political issues of the day.

The study was admired by many, but has also been widely criticized. Lazarsfeld and his colleagues claimed they were 'interested in all the conditions which determine the political behaviour of people'. As critics pointed out, their research in fact only illuminated certain aspects of political behaviour. The study contained little discussion of the actual institutions of the political system and how they work, concentrating instead on political attitudes. The use of repeat interviewing – or what has come to be called a *panel study* – meant the findings were less superficial than many forms of survey research. But by their very nature surveys normally only find out what people *say* about themselves – not what they really think or do.

Assessment

Surveys continue to be very widely used in sociological research for several reasons (C. Marsh, 1982; Miller, 1983). Questionnaire responses can more easily be quantified and analysed than material generated by most other research methods; large numbers of people can be studied; and, given sufficient funds, researchers can employ a research agency specializing in survey work to collect the material they need.

Many sociologists are critical, however, of what they see as over-reliance on the survey method. The results of surveys can often be easily quantified and analysed statistically; but critics argue that such quantification gives an appearance of precision to findings whose accuracy may be dubious, given the relatively shallow nature of most survey responses. There are other drawbacks too. Levels of non-response are sometimes high, especially where questionnaires are sent and returned through the mail. It is not uncommon for studies to be published that are based on results derived from little over half of those in a sample – although normally an effort is made to recontact non-respondents, or to substitute others for them. Little is known about those who choose not to respond to surveys, or refuse to be interviewed when the researcher turns up on the door-step, but survey research is often experienced as obtrusive and time-consuming by those approached (Converse and Schuman, 1974; Fitzgerald and Fuller, 1982; Goyder, 1987).

The conditions under which surveys are administered, and the language usually employed to describe the results, often distance survey research from the complexities of the flesh-and-blood individuals who react to the questions posed. Where mailed questionnaires are used, the investigator is so far removed from those concerned in the research that it may be difficult to remember that living people read and return the material that arrives through their letter-boxes. Telephone surveys – used with increasing frequency in polling where immediate analysis is needed of opinions on a topical issue – are almost as anonymous. The language in which survey results are discussed, involving 'subjects', 'respondents' or 'interviewees', expresses an abstract and impersonal concept of the people involved. Treating human beings as essentially passive and reactive in this way is probably more than just a convenient means of analysing survey answers – it often expresses a limited and limiting view of human reasoning processes.

Two people may hold an apparently similar attitude as measured by a questionnaire item, for example, but have quite different reasons for holding that view. Thus both might respond to a question on foreign policy by saying they believe 'very strongly' that Britain should decrease the range of its military commitments abroad – and each would be counted as having the same view. But their real orientations might be utterly different from one another. One might believe in a 'fortress Britain' – in reducing overseas commitments because of an isolationist view that foreigners should be left to deal with their own problems; while the other might have a strong commitment to global disarmament, holding that Britain should use the influence it has in the world in other ways than by means of the deployment of force.

When interviewers have some flexibility in pursuing answers in some depth, they can sometimes cope with such problems. In general, the more intensive and direct the encounter between researcher and those involved in a study, the more informative and well-founded the conclusions which can be drawn from it. Survey research findings need wherever possible to be complemented by in-depth material of the sort provided by field research.

Documentary research

Most discussions of research in sociology put their main emphasis on field-work, survey research, or a combination of the two. **Documentary research** – the systematic use of printed or written materials for investigation – is often regarded as an also-ran. Yet there are very few pieces of field-work or survey research which do not involve some scrutiny of documentary material. For example, in *The People's Choice?* newspapers and other materials were used extensively both in preparing and in writing up the research. Documentary research, in one guise or another, is in fact one of the most widely used of all methods of gathering sociological data.

Some of the documents most often consulted in sociological research are public and private records (usually termed *archival* sources; an archive being simply a place in which written records are deposited); for example, government documents, church records, letters or judicial records. The documents used in research virtually always also include information and findings produced by previous writers in the field in question. Many investigations are as much concerned with collecting together and analysing materials from the work of others as with generating wholly new data.

An example of the use of historical documents is Anthony Ashworth's study of the sociology of trench warfare during the First World War (Ashworth, 1980). Ashworth was interested in analysing what life was like for the men who had to endure being under constant fire, crammed in close proximity with one another for weeks on end. In studying the social relations they developed he drew upon a diversity of documentary sources: official histories of the war, including those written of different divisions and battalions, archival materials, the notes and records kept informally by individual soldiers, personal accounts of war experiences and other memoirs.

Although these materials were obviously in some respects very different from one another, by drawing on such a diversity of sources Ashworth was able to develop a rich and detailed description of life in the trenches. He discovered, for instance, that some groups of soldiers developed their own norms about how often they would engage in combat with the enemy, often effectively ignoring the commands of their officers. For example, on Christmas day the soldiers on both sides, the Germans and the Allies, suspended hostilities, and in one place even staged an impromptu soccer match with one another.

A major sub-type of documentary research consists of the reanalysis of *data sets* – recorded research findings – generated by other investigators. Governments and other organizations regularly publish 'official statistics' on a multitude of social phenomena: population, crime, marriage and divorce, suicide, rates of unemployment, and so forth. From the early development of sociology these have been used as a basis for sociological research. Researchers can utilize or reanalyse data derived from such statistics, applying that material to help resolve a given research problem.

The data produced by governments is extremely extensive, and includes several major types of resource material. Population censuses, for example, are taken at regular intervals, and provide data on many social and economic issues. Since response is obligatory, the material available from censuses is unusually comprehensive. Governments also carry out other surveys to provide more continuous information than that generated by the periodic censuses (Carley, 1981; Hakim, 1982).

Pitfalls in documentary research

Of course, documentary sources vary widely in terms of their accuracy, and a researcher making use of them has to evaluate their authenticity. Newspaper reports, for example, are notoriously casual in their standards of accuracy, particularly the more 'popular' papers and magazines. Some years ago a letter was published in the *Guardian*. The letter-writer, who called herself or himself 'Student of the Press', had collected eight different newspaper accounts of the much-publicized wedding in Venice of a young socialite, Ira von Fürstenberg. The letter-writer reported that the press 'has shown its enterprise and sturdy individuality. It refuses to conform to any agreed standard even when simple facts are in question.' The bride was reported as being anywhere from 30 to 70 minutes late for the ceremony. Someone fell in the Grand Canal, but there were four different versions of who that was. The number of photographers said to be present varied from 50 to 250, and the guests from 250 to 600 (Mann, 1985, p. 75).

Officially published statistics are of course more reliable than newspaper reports. However, even such statistics must always be *interpreted* by the researcher, who has to be aware of the many limitations they can have. For example, all countries keep official statistics of rates of different types of crime, but these reveal rather little about the real distribution of criminal behaviour, because the crimes registered are only those reported to the police. In the case of crimes like theft, these include only a small proportion of offences which actually occur; many simply never come to the notice of police. Large stores, for instance, report to the police only a fraction of the cases of shoplifting which occur each week – usually only when the store detective actually catches someone in the act. (For further discussion of crime statistics, see chapter 5: 'Conformity and Deviance'.)

Experiments

In one respect, experiments offer major advantages over other research procedures. In an experimental situation, the researcher directly controls the relevant variables. An **experiment** can in fact be defined as an attempt, within artificial conditions established by an investigator, to test the influence of one or more variables upon others. Experiments are widely used in the natural sciences, but the scope for experimentation in sociology is restricted (Silverman, 1982). We can only bring small groups of individuals into a laboratory setting, and in such experiments, people know that they are being studied and may behave differently from normal.

None the less, experimental methods can sometimes usefully be applied in a helpful way in sociology. An example is the ingenious experiment carried out by Philip Zimbardo (Zimbardo, 1972), who set up a make-believe gaol, allocating student volunteers to the roles of guards and prisoners. His aim was to see how far playing these different roles led to changes in attitude and behaviour. The results shocked the investigators, even though they were to some degree expecting them. Those who played the guards quickly assumed an authoritarian manner, displaying real hostility towards the 'prisoners'. They started to order the 'prisoners' around, verbally abuse and bully them. The

Reading a Table

You will often come across tables in reading sociological and statistical literature. They sometimes look complex, but are actually nearly always easy to decipher if a few basic principles are followed; with practice, these will become automatic. *Do not* succumb to the temptation to skip over tables; they contain information in concentrated form, which can be 'read off' more quickly than would be possible if the same material were expressed in words. By becoming skilled in the interpretation of tables you will also be able to check how far the conclusions a writer draws from the material in question actually seem justified.

The steps to follow in grasping the content of a table are these.

1   Read the title in full. Tables frequently have longish titles, which represent an attempt by the researcher or statistician to state accurately the nature of the information conveyed. The title of the table given in this box gives first the *subject* of the material in the table, second the fact that it provides material for *comparison* and third, the fact that material is offered only for a limited number of countries.

2   See if there are explanatory comments or *notes* about the data. A note at the foot of the example table linked to the column heading points out that the data only cover licensed cars. This is important because in some countries the proportion of vehicles properly licensed may be less than in others. Notes may say how the material was collected, or why it is displayed in a particular way. If the data in the table have not been gathered by the researcher, but are based on findings originally reported elsewhere, a *source* will be given. The source sometimes gives you some insight into how reliable the information is likely to be, as well as showing where you would have to look to find the original data on which the table is based. In our table, the source note makes clear that the data have been taken from more than one source.

3   Read the *headings* along the top and left-hand side of the table. (Sometimes tables are arranged with 'headings' at the foot rather than the top.) These tell you what type of information is contained in each row and column. In reading the table, each set of headings has to be kept in mind as you scan the figures. In our example, the headings on the left give the countries involved, while those at the top refer to the particular years for which levels of car ownership are given.

4   Identify the *units* used – the figures in the body of the table may represent a number of cases, percentages, averages, or other measures. Sometimes it may be useful to convert the figures given in a table to a form more useful to you: if percentages are not provided, for example, it may be worth calculating them. In the case given here, no percentages are provided, but it would be easy to work them out.

5   Consider the conclusions that might be reached from the information in the table. Most tables are discussed by the author presenting them, and what she or he has to say should of course be borne in mind when you assess the tabulated material yourself. You should also consider what further issues or questions could be suggested by the data.

Car ownership: international comparisons of several selected countries

	Number of cars per 1,000 of the adult population[a]		
	1971	1981	1984
Brazil	12	78	84
Chile	19	45	56
Eire	141	202	226
France	261	348	360
Greece	30	94	116
Italy	210	322	359
Japan	100	209	227
Sweden	291	348	445
United Kingdom	224	317	343
USA	448	536	540
West Germany	247	385	412
Yugoslavia	43	114	125

[a]Includes all licensed cars.
Source: United Nations Annual Bulletin of Transport Statistics; World Road Statistics, International Road Federation, reported in *Social Trends* (London: HMSO, 1987), p. 68.

Several interesting trends can be seen in the figures in our table. First the level of car ownership varies very considerably between different countries: the number of cars per 1,000 people is nearly ten times greater in the USA than in Chile. Second, the table reveals clear connections between car ownership and the level of affluence of a country. In fact, we could probably use car-ownership ratios as a rough indicator of differential prosperity. Third, in all countries represented, the level of car ownership has increased between 1971 and 1984, but in some, the rate of increase is higher than in others – probably indicating differences in the degree to which countries have successfully generated economic growth.

others, by contrast, showed a mixture of apathy and rebelliousness often noted among inmates in real prison situations. These effects were so marked, and the level of tension so high, that the experiment had to be called off at an early stage. The researcher concluded that behaviour in prisons is more influenced by the nature of the prison situation than by the individual characteristics of those involved.

Other methods: interviews, life histories, diaries and conversation analysis

Interviews

There is no clear distinction between the survey method and interviews, since where questionnaires are directly administered, the researcher effectively interviews the respondents. Interviewing with a question-naire is sometimes called 'formal' or 'controlled', to distinguish it from less structured interviews, in which the interviewee is allowed to talk freely about various aspects of a topic. Some interview studies do not utilize a questionnaire at all: people may sometimes be interviewed at considerable length; and where the objective is to develop in-depth information only a few respondents may be involved. Extended interviews provide richer material than is usually available from surveys, but the disadvantages are that the influence of the interviewer may be greater, possibly affecting the results; and it is more difficult to compare responses in a rigorous way (Brenner, 1978).

Life histories

Life histories consist of biographical material assembled about particular individuals – usually as recounted by themselves. No other method of research can give us as much detail about the development of people's beliefs and attitudes over time. Life histories are particularly valuable when research is concerned with connections between psychological development and social processes. Such studies rarely rely wholly on the memories of the people involved, however. Normally documentary sources – such as letters, contemporary reports or newspaper descriptions – are used to expand upon and check the validity of information provided. Views differ about the value of life history material. Some feel the method is too unreliable to provide useful information; but others believe that life histories offer sources of insight that few other sociological research methods can match.

Life histories have been successfully employed in studies of major importance and are widely used in anthropology as well as sociology (Bertaux, 1981). A celebrated early study which made extensive use of such material was *The Polish Peasant in Europe and America*, by W. I. Thomas and Florian Znaniecki, the five volumes of which were first published between 1918 and 1920 (Thomas and Znaniecki, 1966). Thomas and Znaniecki were able to provide a much more sensitive and subtle account of the experience of migration than would have been possible without the life-history materials they collected. A more recent work, which became a best-seller, was Studs Terkel's book, *Working* (Terkel, 1977). It was subtitled 'People talk about what they do all day and how they feel about what they do', and provided a rich and moving account of the views of Americans about their daily work routines.

Life histories do not necessarily cover the whole span of an individual's life, or all of its main aspects. For instance, Edwin H. Sutherland published a study based on the life history of Chic Conwell, a professional thief; the material presented was largely limited to Conwell's criminal activities (Sutherland and Conwell, 1937). Life histories shade over into *oral history* more generally – verbal accounts of the past supplied by those who lived through the events.

Four of the Main Methods Used in Sociological Research

Research method	Strengths	Limitations
Field-work	1 Usually generates richer and more 'in-depth' information than other methods. 2 Provides flexibility for the researcher to alter strategies and follow up new leads that arise.	1 Can only be used to study relatively small groups or communities. 2 Findings might only apply to the groups or communities studied; it is not easy to generalize on the basis of a single field-work study.
Surveys	1 Make possible the efficient collection of data on large numbers of individuals. 2 Allows for precise comparisons to be made between the answers of respondents.	1 The material gathered may be superficial; where a questionnaire is highly standardized, important differences between respondents' viewpoints may be glossed over. 2 Responses may be what people profess to believe rather than what they actually believe.
Documentary research	1 Can provide sources of 'in-depth' materials as well as data on large numbers – according to the type of documents studied. 2 Is often essential when a study is either wholly historical, or has a defined historical dimension.	1 The researcher is dependent on the sources that exist, which may be partial. 2 The sources may be difficult to interpret in terms of how far they represent real tendencies – as in the case of some kinds of official statistics.
Experiments	1 The influence of specific variables can be controlled by the investigator. 2 Experiments are usually easier for subsequent researchers to repeat.	1 Many aspects of social life cannot be brought into the laboratory. 2 The responses of those studied may be affected by their experimental situation.

Diaries

Diaries are sometimes used when sociologists want to keep track of the day-to-day activities of individuals in a particular social environment. Field-work and surveys may not give us enough information about the regular round of people's lives, so if we want to build up a picture of what they do at various parts of the day, and at different times of the day or month, it is often helpful to get them to keep their own records. Once again, there are very few studies which rely upon such information alone; it is nearly always used alongside material gleaned by other methods.

Conversation analysis

Tape-recorders and videos are increasingly employed in sociological research. Both are frequently used in **conversation analysis**, the study of how conversations are carried on in real-life settings. Using a tape-recorder, all the audible characteristics of a conversation between two or more people can be put on record. Since when we talk to one another we also use facial expressions and gestures to convey meaning, video-recordings provide an even more complete register of the unfolding of a conversational exchange. Although much of the richness of the original context is lost, by the use of appropriate notation recorded conversations can then be transcribed on to the printed page. (For an illustration, see chapter 4: 'Social Interaction and Everyday Life'.)

Many studies involving conversational analysis have been published over the past few years, offering a variety of insights into the nature of human interaction. An example is William B. Sanders's study of a very special type of conversation: police interrogations. Interrogation involves conversation, but not 'just any talk' – as is indicated in one of the favourite phrases of police melodramas, 'I'll ask the questions!' Sanders was able to analyse the distinctive character of interrogation so as to highlight features that might otherwise escape notice. For instance, interrogators often do not actually say very much at all, stimulating the victim to talk by grunts and deliberately prolonged pauses (Sanders, 1974).

Conversation analysis can only be utilized in small-group settings, and frequently covers what might seem to be purely trivial aspects of day-to-day life, but its importance in sociology is much greater than might appear. Conversation and talk, after all, are universal features of social activity in both informal and more structured settings of interaction (see chapter 4: 'Social Interaction and Everyday Life').

Triangulation

All research methods have their advantages and their limitations. Hence it is common to combine several methods in a single piece of research, using each to supplement and check upon the others, a process known as **triangulation**. We can see the value of combining methods – and, more generally, the problems and pitfalls of real sociological research – by looking at a specific research study.

An example: Wallis and Scientology

Roy Wallis set out to investigate the movement known as Scientology. The founder of Scientology, L. Ron Hubbard, developed various religious doctrines which came to form the basis of a church. According to Scientology, we are all spiritual beings – Thetans – but we have neglected our spiritual nature. We can recover forgotten supernatural powers through processes of training, which make us aware of our real spiritual capacities. Wallis admitted that he was first drawn to do the research because of the 'exotic' nature of Scientology. How could people believe in such apparently bizarre ideas? (Wallis, 1976). Scientology was very controversial, but had attracted a large following. Why had this particular movement, one of many new religious groups, become so prominent?

Initiating the research presented problems. Wallis knew that the leaders of the movement were likely to be unwilling to co-operate in sociological research because they had already been 'investigated' by various government agencies. However, while reading about the movement's history he came across a book by one of its former members. He contacted that person, and was eventually put in touch with a number of his acquaintances who had also mostly severed their ties with Scientology. Many of these people agreed to be interviewed, and some still maintained contact with believers. These early interviewees provided Wallis with a range of documents and literature arising from their involvement with the movement, which included the mailing list of a Scientology organization. Wallis drew up and sent off a questionnaire to a sample of the names on the list. It proved to be so out of date that a large proportion of the sample had moved from the address on the list. Some others had got onto the list merely because they had bought a single book on Scientology, and had no real connections with the movement.

The survey thus proved of limited value as a sample of Scientologists in general, although certain conclusions could be drawn from it. Yet it provided Wallis with a few further contacts. Some respondents to the questionnaires indicated that they would be willing to be interviewed. Wallis therefore travelled around the United States and Britain conducting interviews and collecting more documentary information at the same time. He began with a fixed schedule of questions, but soon found it more profitable to adopt a looser and more flexible style, allowing respondents to talk at length on matters they regarded as important. Some respondents were willing to be tape-recorded; others were not.

Wallis soon came to believe that he needed to understand more about the doctrines of Scientology, so he applied to follow an introductory 'communications' course put on by a Scientology group. He thus began participant observation, but did not reveal his identity as a researcher. Staying at the Scientology lodging house during the course, Wallis found the role of covert participant observer difficult to sustain. Conversation with other members, and progress on the course, required a display of commitment to ideas which he did not share. Expressing disagreement with these views led to such difficulties that it became clear he could not continue without publicly assenting to some of the main principles of Scientology. He therefore slipped away quietly without finishing the course.

Later he wrote to the leaders of the movement, saying he was a sociologist engaged in research into Scientology. Pointing out that the movement had been under much attack, he suggested that his own research would provide a more balanced view. He subsequently visited the headquarters of the sect in Britain, and spoke to one of the officials there. This person was concerned about his having dropped out of the communications course, and knew about the questionnaires sent to the list of Scientologists. None the less he gave Wallis permission to interview some staff members and students, supplying addresses to be contacted in the United States. Eventually Wallis felt he had enough material to publish a book on the Scientologists (Wallis, 1976).

Wallis faced particular difficulties because his research was about an organization jealous of its secrecy; in other respects, the problems he encountered, together with the need to use a combination of research methods, are typical of much sociological research. All of the material he gathered was partial, but combined together the various methods he used produced a worthwhile study which became important and influential.

Ethical problems of research: the respondents answer back

All research concerned with human beings, not only sociology, can pose ethical dilemmas (Barnes, 1979). Medical experiments are routinely carried out on human subjects, sometimes on the sick and the dying, and it is not easy to say how far such experiments are ethically justifiable. In order to be effective, experiments in medicine may involve misleading patients. In testing a new drug, one group of patients might actually be given the drug; others are told they are receiving it, but are not in fact doing so. Believing that one is being given a healing drug might itself lead to positive effects on health; this can be controlled for by only giving the real drug to half the patients involved in the experimental trials. But is this ethical? It surely approaches the limits of what can be justified, if there is a possibility that the real drug can have beneficial results or save lives. On the other hand, if such procedures are not followed, it may be difficult or impossible to find out how effective the drug actually is.

Similar problems arise in sociological research wherever any deception is practised on those involved. An example is the celebrated, and highly controversial, series of experiments carried out by Stanley Milgram. Milgram wished to see how far people would be prepared to hurt others if they received commands from an authoritative source to do so (Milgram, 1973). An electric-shock machine was rigged up, by means of which volunteers in the experiment were required to administer shocks to people who failed to respond correctly in a memory test. The experiments involved systematically deceiving those who volunteered to participate: they were not told the true purpose of the study, believing it to be an investigation into memory. Although they imagined they were delivering real shocks to other experimental subjects, in fact these were accomplices of the researcher, feigning their reactions because the 'shock machine' was in fact a fake.

Was such deception ethical, particularly since the people studied found the experience extremely unsettling? The general consensus of critics is that this investigation 'went too far', the deception involved being potentially psychologically harmful to the volunteers. But it is not at all clear where a line can be drawn in research between 'excusable' and 'inexcusable' deception. Milgram's research has become very well known, not just because of the deception, but because of the striking nature of the results he obtained. For the research indicated that many people are prepared to act brutally towards others if they are 'under orders' to do so.

Wallis was less than truthful to those whose behaviour he studied, because he did not disclose his identity as a sociologist when registering for the Scientology course. Moreover, he apparently gave his written agreement to conditions he did not observe – for he wanted to publish his work. He tried to avoid any direct lies, but he did not disclose the real reason for his participation; was this unethical? The answer is not obvious (Dingwall, 1980). Had Wallis been completely frank at every stage, the research might not have got as far as it did, and it could be argued that it is in society's interest to know what goes on inside secretive organizations. On these grounds, we might consider his strategy justified.

Ethical issues are also often posed in sociology, however, by the potential consequences of the publication or utilization of research findings. The subjects of a particular study might find its results offensive, either because they are portrayed in a light they find unappealing, or because attitudes and modes of behaviour they would prefer to keep private are made public. In most settings of social life some people engage in practices which they do not want to become public knowledge. For instance, some people working in factories and

offices regularly pilfer materials; hospital nurses sometimes wrap terminally ill patients in morgue sheets before they die, and give them little
care; prison guards may accept bribes from inmates, and recognize
certain prisoners as 'trustees', allowing them to do tasks they should take
care of themselves.

In most circumstances, notwithstanding possible hostile reactions
from those involved, or from others, it is the obligation of the sociologist
to make findings public. Indeed, this is one of the main contributions
sociological research can make to the fostering of a free and open
society. 'A good study', it has been said, 'will make somebody angry'
(Becker, 1976, p. 113). There seems no reason for the sociological
researcher to fear this, if the research work was done competently and
the conclusions drawn are backed by good arguments. But sociological
investigators do have to consider carefully the possible consequences
of the publication of findings, and the *form* in which these should be
announced. Often the researcher will wish to discuss the issues directly
with those affected before deciding on a final form for publication.

Problems in publication: Wallis's experience

Before publishing his book, Wallis sent his manuscript to the Scientology
headquarters. He made some alterations to meet some of their objections, and then later they sent more detailed comments. Although he
made further changes, the Scientologists sent the manuscript to a
lawyer experienced in libel cases. On his advice, further deletions
were made. A commentary on the book, highly critical of Wallis's
research methods and conclusions, was prepared by a sociologist who
was also a practising Scientologist, which was eventually incorporated
into the published work as an appendix. The Scientologists also
published an article analysing his research in one of their own
periodicals. In their discussion they quoted the Panel on Privacy and
Behavioral Research set up by the US President's Office of Science and
Technology, which had stressed that 'informed consent' should be
obtained by researchers engaged in work on human subjects. Informed
consent, they emphasized, had not been secured, and they added that
Wallis's published work was based on information gained from only a
small circle of people, mostly hostile to the Church of Scientology.

Wallis later became involved in further entanglements arising from
his research. In 1984, he was named as a potential witness in an
extended legal battle between the Church of Scientology and the
author of another book on Scientology. Wallis had contacted that
author while carrying out his own work, and she had provided him
with documents and information about the Scientologists and her own
contacts with them. As a result of a Californian court order in the case,
he was obliged to release some of this material – which he had in fact

received in confidence. Fortunately, the information in question was of no great significance to any of the parties concerned, but if it had been more damaging, Wallis would have had a difficult decision to make – to break a confidence, or resist the law (Wallis, 1987).

Wallis was dealing with a powerful and articulate group, who were able to persuade him to modify early versions of his research reports, but many individuals or groups studied by sociologists and other social scientists do not have similar influence. If they did, the difficulties in which Wallis found himself might be much more common than they actually are.

It surely should be usual for researchers to secure informed consent in all but a minority of research studies. Yet there are bound to be some circumstances in which this principle cannot be fully followed. If we wished to study police brutality, there would be little chance of doing so effectively if we were open with police authorities and officers about our aim. The purpose of the research would have to be disguised to some degree to achieve any degree of co-operation, and this might be justified given the potential importance of the results to the wider community.

The over-riding obligation of the sociologist, and every other social scientist, is to promote free and open discussion of social issues. Occasionally deception – paradoxically – can be the means of achieving this, by bringing to light facts that would otherwise be hidden from the general public.

The influence of sociology

Sociological research is rarely of interest only to the intellectual community of sociologists. Its results are often either read about, or in other ways disseminated to, many others in society. This fact has far-reaching implications. Sociology is not just *about* the study of modern societies; it has itself become a significant element in the continuing life of those societies.

Take the example mentioned in chapter 1 ('Sociology: Problems and Perspectives'): the nature of the transformations going on in marriage, divorce and the family. Very few people living in a modern society do not have some knowledge of these, as a result of the 'filtering down' of research. Our thinking and behaviour are affected by sociological knowledge in complex and often subtle ways, thus reshaping the very field of sociological investigation. One way of describing this phenomenon is to say that sociology stands in a *reflexive* relation to the human beings whose behaviour is studied. 'Reflexive' describes the interchange between sociological research and human behaviour. We should not be surprised that, while they sometimes contradict our common-sense beliefs, sociological findings often correlate quite closely with common sense. The reason is not simply that sociology comes up with findings which we knew already; it is rather that sociological research continually influences what our common-sense knowledge of society actually is.

Summary

1   All research begins from a *research problem*, which worries or puzzles the investigator. Research problems may be suggested by gaps in the existing literature, theoretical debates or practical issues in the social world. A number of clear steps can be distinguished in the development of research strategies – although these are rarely followed precisely in actual research.

2   Sound sociological research involves the use of a reliable approach for analysing a particular social phenomenon. Three aspects of sociological enquiry can be distinguished: *research strategy* concerns the planning of any particular piece of research; *research methodology* deals with the overall logic and principles of research; *research methods* concern how research is carried out, e.g. by means of field-work, surveys etc.

3   Various statistical techniques are used in the analysis of research that generates quantitative data. The most important are *measures of central tendency* and *correlation coefficients*. Measures of central tendency are ways of calculating averages from a given set of figures; correlation coefficients measure the degree to which one variable consistently relates to another.

4   In field-work, or *participant observation*, the researcher spends lengthy periods of time with the group or community being studied. A second method, *survey research*, involves sending or administering question-naires to sample groups from larger populations. *Documentary research* means using printed materials, from archives or elsewhere, as a source for information. Other methods include *experiments*, *in-depth interviews*, the use of *life histories* and *diaries*, and *conversation analysis*.

5   Each of the various methods of research has its limitations. For this reason, researchers will often combine two or more methods in their work, each being used to check or supplement the material obtained from the others. This process is called *triangulation*.

6   Sociological research often presents the investigator with ethical dilem-mas. These may arise either where the subjects of the research are deceived by the researcher, or where the publication of research findings might adversely affect the feelings or lives of those studied. There is no entirely satisfactory way to deal with these issues, but all researchers have to be sensitive to the dilemmas they pose.

Basic concepts

research methods   correlation
causation

Important terms

hypothesis   correlation coefficient
causal relationship   participant observation (field-work)
variable   survey
independent variable   sampling
dependent variable   documentary research
control   experiment
mean   life histories
mode   conversation analysis
median   triangulation
standard deviation

Further reading

John A. Barnes, *Who Should Know What? Social Science, Privacy and Ethics* (Harmondsworth: Penguin, 1979) — a discussion of the ethical issues involved in research in the social sciences.

J. Irvine, I. Miles and J. Evans (eds), *Demystifying Social Statistics* (London: Pluto Press, 1979) — a deliberately provocative attempt at revealing the uses and abuses of statistical data.

Peter H. Mann, *Methods of Social Investigation* (Oxford: Basil Blackwell, 1985) — a valuable simple survey of the methods of research used in sociology.

Catherine Marsh, *Exploring Data* (Cambridge: Polity Press, 1988) — an excellent introduction to data analysis, concentrating on the study of real issues to illustrate statistical techniques.

Gerry Rose, *Demystifying Social Research* (London: Macmillan, 1981) — a discussion of research methods based on the critical analysis of well-known sociological studies.

22

The Development of Sociological Theory

When they first start studying sociology, many people are puzzled by the diversity of perspectives they encounter. Sociologists do not have an agreed theoretical standpoint; they quite often argue among themselves about how we should go about studying human behaviour, and how research results might best be interpreted. Why should this be? Why can't sociologists agree with one another more consistently, as natural scientists seem able to do?

The answer to these questions is bound up with the very nature of sociology itself. It is about our own lives and our own behaviour, and studying ourselves is the most complex and difficult endeavour we can undertake. In all academic disciplines – including the natural sciences – there is far more disagreement over theoretical approaches than over empirical research, because empirical work can be directly checked, and repeated if there are varying views about its factual

findings. Theoretical disputes are always partly dependent on interpretation, and can rarely be decisively settled in the same way. In
sociology, the difficulties inherent in subjecting our own behaviour to
study further complicate this problem. Hence theoretical controversies
and debates occupy a central place in the discipline.

In this chapter, we shall analyse the development of the major
theoretical approaches in sociology, identifying the dilemmas to which
they point. We shall start by looking at the views of some of the
founders of modern sociology – for many of the ideas they pioneered
are still influential – before considering the theoretical approaches
which dominate the discipline today, going on to discuss some of
the problems they raise.

Early origins

Human beings have always been curious about the sources of their
own behaviour, but for thousands of years our attempts to understand
ourselves relied on ways of thinking passed down from generation to
generation, expressed in religious terms. The systematic study of human
behaviour and human society is a relatively recent development, whose
beginnings can be found in the late eighteenth century. The background
to the new approach was the series of sweeping changes referred to
many times in the book associated with industrialization and urbanism.
The shattering of traditional ways of life prompted the attempt to develop
a new understanding of both the social and the natural worlds.

Auguste Comte

No single individual, of course, can found a whole discipline, and there
were many contributors to early sociological thinking. Pride of place is
usually given to the French author, Auguste Comte (1789–1857), if only
because he actually coined the word 'sociology'. Comte originally used
the term 'social physics' to refer to the new field of study, but other
writers were also beginning to use that term and he wanted to distinguish
his views from theirs, so he invented a new word to describe the subject
he wished to establish. Comte regarded sociology as the last science to
develop, but as the most significant and complex of all sciences. He
believed it should contribute to the welfare of humanity; in the later
part of his career, he drew up ambitious plans for the reconstruction
of French society in particular and human societies in general.

Emile Durkheim

Comte's work had a direct influence on another French writer, Emile
Durkheim (1858–1917). Although he drew on aspects of Comte's writings,
Durkheim thought much of his work too speculative and vague,

believing that Comte had not successfully carried out his programme – to establish sociology on a scientific basis. To become scientific, according to Durkheim, sociology must study 'social facts'. That is to say, it must pursue the analysis of social institutions with the same objectivity as scientists study nature. Durkheim's famous first principle of sociology is: 'study social facts as *things*!' By this he means that social life can be analysed as rigorously as objects or events in nature.

Like all the major founders of sociology, Durkheim was preoccupied with the changes transforming society. He tried to understand these changes in terms of the development of the **division of labour** (the growth of ever more complex distinctions between different occupations), as part of industrialization. Durkheim argues that the division of labour gradually replaces religion as the main basis of social cohesion. As the division of labour expands, people become more and more dependent on one another, because each person needs goods and services that those in other occupations supply. According to Durkheim, processes of change in the modern world are so rapid and intense that they give rise to major social difficulties, which he linked to **anomie**. Anomie is the feeling of aimlessness or purposelessness provoked by certain social conditions. Traditional moral controls and standards, which used to be supplied by religion, are largely broken down by modern social development, and this leaves many individuals in modern societies with the feeling that their day-to-day lives lack meaning.

One of Durkheim's most famous studies is concerned with the analysis of suicide (Durkheim, 1952; originally published 1897). Suicide seems to be a purely personal act; it appears to be entirely the outcome of extreme personal unhappiness. Durkheim shows, however, that social factors have a fundamental influence on suicidal behaviour – anomie being one of these influences. Suicide rates show regular patterns from year to year, and these patterns have to be explained sociologically. Many objections can be raised against aspects of Durkheim's study, but it remains a classic work whose relevance to sociology today is by no means exhausted.

Karl Marx

The ideas of Karl Marx contrast quite sharply with those of Comte and Durkheim. Marx was born in Germany in 1818, and died in England in 1883. Although originally trained in German traditions of thought, he spent much of his life in Britain and produced his major works there. Marx was not able to pursue a university career, since as a young man his political activities had brought him into conflict with the German authorities. After a brief stay in France he settled permanently in exile in Britain.

Marx's writings cover a diversity of areas. Even his sternest critics regard his work as of significance to the development of sociology, but Marx did not see himself as a 'sociologist'. Much of his writing concentrates on economic issues, but since he is always concerned to connect economic problems to social institutions, his work is rich in sociological insights.

Marx's viewpoint is founded upon what he calls the **materialist conception of history**. According to him, it is not the ideas or values which human beings hold that are the main sources of social change. Rather, social change is prompted primarily by economic influences. These are linked to the conflicts between classes that provide the motive power of historical development. In Marx's words: 'All human history thus far is the history of class struggles' (Marx and Engels, 1968, p. 35).

Though he writes about various phases of history, Marx concentrates his attention on change in modern times. For him, the most important changes involved in the modern period are bound up with the development of **capitalism**. Capitalism is a system of production that contrasts radically with previous economic orders in history, involving as it does the production of goods and services sold to a wide range of consumers. Those who own capital – factories, machines and large sums of money – form a ruling class. The mass of the population make up a class of wage-workers, or working class, who do not own the means of their own livelihood, but have to find employment provided by the owners of capital. Capitalism is thus a class system, in which conflict between classes is a common occurrence.

According to Marx, capitalism will in future be supplanted by socialism or communism (he used these words interchangeably), and in socialist society there will be no classes. Marx does not mean by this that all inequalities between individuals will disappear; rather, societies will no longer be split into a small class which monopolizes economic and political power and the large mass of people who benefit little from the wealth their labour creates. The economic system will come under communal ownership, and a more egalitarian and participatory social order be established.

For Marx, the study of the development and likely future of capitalism was to provide the means of actively transforming it through political action. Marx's sociological observations were thus closely related to a political programme. However valid Marx's writings themselves may or may not be, this programme has had a far-reaching effect upon the twentieth-century world. More than a third of the world's population live in societies whose governments claim to derive their inspiration from Marx's ideas.

It is important to try to approach the study of Marx's work in an unprejudiced way. This is not easy, because the widespread influence of Marx's writings has produced major differences of opinion about their value. Even those strongly influenced by Marx have used them in widely varying ways – there are large differences between the views of those who call themselves 'Marxists'. Many Marxists living in the West today, for example, are extremely critical of the Soviet Union and other communist countries, where Marx's ideas supposedly form the basis of the social system.

Max Weber

Like Marx, Max Weber (1864–1920) cannot simply be labelled as a 'sociologist' – his interests and concerns ranged across many disciplines. He was born in Germany and spent the whole of his academic career there. Weber was somewhat depressive in character, and for much of his life was unable to sustain a full-time teaching post in a university; a private income allowed him to devote himself to scholarship. He was an individual of quite extraordinarily wide learning. His writings covered the fields of economics, law, philosophy and comparative history as well as sociology, and much of his work was concerned with the development of modern capitalism. He was influenced by Marx, but was also strongly critical of some of Marx's major views. He rejected the materialist conception of history and saw class conflict as less significant than Marx. In Weber's view, ideas and values have as much impact as economic conditions on social change.

Some of Weber's most important writings are concerned with analysing the distinctiveness of Western society and culture, as compared to those of other major civilizations. He produced extensive studies of the traditional Chinese empire, India and the Near East (Weber, 1951; 1958; 1952), and in the course of these researches made major contributions to the sociology of religion. Comparing the leading religious systems in China and India with those of the West, Weber concludes that certain aspects of Christian beliefs strongly influenced the rise of capitalism. (See chapter 14: 'Religion'.)

One of the most persistent concerns of Weber's work is the study of **bureaucracy**. A bureaucracy is a large-scale organization divided into offices and staffed by officials of varying ranks; large industrial firms, government organizations, hospitals and schools are all examples. Weber believes the advance of bureaucracy to be an inevitable feature of our era. It makes possible the efficient running of large-scale organizations, but poses problems for effective democratic participation in modern societies. Bureaucracy involves the rule of experts, whose decisions are taken without much reference to those affected by them.

Weber's contributions range over many other areas, including the study of the development of cities, systems of law, types of economy and the nature of classes. He also wrote extensively on the overall character of sociology itself. Weber is more cautious than either Durkheim or Marx in claiming sociology to be a science. According to him, it is misleading to imagine that we can study people using the same procedures as are applied to investigating the physical world. Humans are thinking, reasoning beings; we attach meaning and significance to most of what we do, and any discipline that deals with human behaviour must acknowledge this.

Later developments

While the origins of sociology were mainly European, this century the subject has become firmly established world-wide, and some of the most important developments have taken place in the United States. The work of George Herbert Mead (1863–1931), a philosopher teaching at the University of Chicago, has had an important influence on the development of sociological theory. Mead emphasizes the centrality of language, and of symbols as a whole, in human social life. The perspective he developed later came to be called **symbolic interactionism**. Mead gave more attention to studying small-scale social processes than overall societies.

Talcott Parsons (1902–79) was the most prominent American sociological theorist of the post-war period. He was a prolific author, who wrote on many empirical areas of sociology as well as theory. He made contributions to the study of the family, bureaucracy, the professions and the study of politics among other areas. He was one of the main contributors to the development of **functionalism**, a theoretical approach originally pioneered by Durkheim and Comte. According to the functionalist viewpoint, in studying any given society we should look at how its various 'parts', or institutions, combine to give that society continuity over time.

European thinkers continue to be prominent in the latter-day development of sociological theory, however. An approach which has achieved particular prominence there is **structuralism**, which links sociological analysis closely to the study of language. Structuralist thought was originally pioneered in linguistics, and imported into the social sciences by the anthropologist Claude Lévi-Strauss (1908–). But its origins can also be traced back to Durkheim and Marx.

Present-day approaches

The main theoretical divisions in sociology today reflect the different approaches established in earlier periods, the most important currently being *functionalism, structuralism, symbolic interactionism*, and *Marxism*.

Functionalism

Functionalist thought, as was pointed out, was originally pioneered by Comte, who saw it as closely bound up with his overall view of sociology. Durkheim also regarded functional analysis as a key part of his formulation of the tasks of sociological theorizing and research. The development of functionalism in its modern guise, however, was strongly influenced by the work of anthropologists. Until early this century, anthropology was based mainly on reports and documents produced by colonial administrators, missionaries and travellers. Nineteenth-century anthropology therefore used to be rather speculative and inadequately documented. Writers would produce books collecting examples from all over the world, without bothering too much about either how authentic they were, or the particular cultural context from which they came. For instance, religion would be analysed by comparing numerous examples of belief and practice drawn from the most diverse cultures.

Modern anthropology dates from the time at which researchers became dissatisfied with this approach, and started to spend long periods of field-study in different cultures around the world. Two of the originators of anthropological field-work were a British author strongly influenced by Durkheim, A. R. Radcliffe-Brown (1881–1955), and Bronislaw Malinowski (1884–1942), a Pole who spent much of his career in Britain. Malinowski produced some of the most celebrated anthropological studies ever written, as a result of spending a lengthy period in the Trobriand Islands in the Pacific. Radcliffe-Brown studied the Andaman Islanders, who lived on an archipelago just off the coast of Burma.

Radcliffe-Brown and Malinowski both assert that we must study a society or a culture as a whole if we are to understand its major institutions and explain why its members behave as they do. We can analyse the religious beliefs and customs of a society, for example, only by showing how they relate to other institutions within it, for the different parts of a society develop in close relation to one another.

To study the *function* of a social practice or institution is to analyse the contribution which that practice or institution makes to the continuation of the society as a whole. The best way to understand this is by analogy to the human body, a comparison which Comte, Durkheim and many subsequent functionalist authors make. To study a bodily organ, like the heart, we need to show how it relates to other parts of the body. By pumping blood around the body, the heart plays a vital role in the continuation of the life of the organism. Similarly, analysing the function of a social item means showing the part it plays in the continued existence of a society. According to Durkheim, for instance, religion reaffirms people's adherence to core social values, thereby contributing to the maintenance of social cohesion. (For more detail on Durkheim's theory of religion, see chapter 14: 'Religion'.)

Merton's version of functionalism

Functionalism 'moved back' into sociology through the writings of Talcott Parsons and Robert K. Merton, each of whom saw functionalist analysis as providing the key to the development of sociological theory and research. Merton's version of functionalism has been particularly influential, serving to focus the work of a whole generation of American sociologists in particular, but also being widely used elsewhere. Merton produced a more sophisticated account of functionalist analysis than was offered by either Radcliffe-Brown or Malinowski. At the same time, he re-adapted it to the study of industrialized societies, which differ in certain basic ways from the simpler cultures studied by anthropologists.

Merton distinguishes between **manifest** and **latent functions**. Manifest functions are those known to, and intended by, the participants in a specific type of social activity. Latent functions are consequences of that activity of which participants are unaware (Merton, 1957). To illustrate this distinction, Merton uses the example of a rain dance performed by the Hopi Indians of New Mexico. The Hopi believe that the ceremonial will bring the rain they need for their crops (manifest function). This is the reason why they organize and participate in it. But the rain dance, Merton argues, using Durkheim's theory of religion, also has the effect of promoting the cohesion of the society (latent function). A major part of sociological explanation, according to Merton, consists of uncovering the latent functions of social activities and institutions.

Merton also distinguishes between functions and *dysfunctions*. The small cultures anthropologists study, he points out, tend to be more inte-grated and solidary than the large-scale, industrialized societies which are the main concern of sociology. Radcliffe-Brown and Malinowski could concentrate solely on identifying functions, because the cultures they analysed were stable and integrated. In studying the modern world, however we must be aware of disintegrative tendencies. 'Dys-function' refers to aspects of social activity which tend to produce change because they *threaten* social cohesion.

To look for the dysfunctional aspects of social behaviour means focusing on features of social life which challenge the existing order of things. For example, it is mistaken to suppose that religion is always functional – that it contributes only to social cohesion. When two groups support different religions, or even different versions of the same religion, the result can be major social conflicts, causing widespread social disruption. Thus wars have often been fought between religious communities – as in the struggles between Protestants and Catholics in European history.

Recent developments

For a long while functionalist thought was probably the leading theoretical tradition in sociology, particularly in the United States. In recent years its popularity has begun to wane, as its limitations have become apparent – although it still has articulate defenders (Alexander, 1985). While this was not true of Merton, many functionalist thinkers

(Talcott Parsons was an example) unduly stress factors leading to social cohesion, at the expense of those producing division and conflict. In addition, it has seemed to many critics that functional analysis gives societies qualities they do not have. Functionalists often write as though societies have 'needs' and 'purposes', even though these concepts make sense only when applied to individual human beings. Take, for instance, Merton's analysis of the Hopi rain dance. Merton writes as though, if we can show that the ceremonial helps integrate Hopi culture, we have explained why it 'really' exists – because, after all, we know that the dance does not actually bring rain. This is not so, unless we imagine that somehow Hopi society 'propels' its members to act in ways which it 'needs' to hold it together. But this cannot be the case, for societies are not endowed with will-power or purposes; only human individuals have these.

Structuralism

Like functionalism, structuralism has been influenced by Durkheim's writings, although the main impetus to its development lies in linguistics. The work of the Swiss linguist Ferdinand de Saussure (1857–1913) was the most important early source of structuralist ideas. Although Saussure only wrote about language, the views he developed were subsequently incorporated into numerous disciplines in the social sciences as well as the humanities.

Before Saussure's work, the study of language was concerned mainly with tracing detailed changes in the way words were used. According to Saussure, this procedure omits the central feature of language. We can never identify the basic characteristics – or *structures* – of language if we look only at the words people use when they speak (Saussure, 1974). Language consists of rules of grammar and meaning that 'lie behind' the words, but are not stated in them. To take a simple example: in English we usually add '-ed' to a verb when we want to signal that we are referring to an event in the past. This is one grammatical rule among thousands of others which every speaker of the language knows, and which is used to *construct* what we say. According to Saussure, analysing the structures of language means looking for the rules which underlie our speech. Most of these rules are known to us only implicitly: we could not easily state what they are. The task of linguistics, in fact, is to uncover what we implicitly *know*, but only on the level of being able to use language in practice.

Language and meaning

Saussure argues that the meaning of words derives from the structures of language, not the objects to which the words refer. We might naïvely imagine that the meaning of the word 'tree' is the leafy object to which the term refers. According to Saussure, however, this is not so. We can see this by the fact that there are plenty of words in language which do not refer to anything – like 'and', 'but' or 'nevertheless'. Moreover, there are perfectly meaningful words which refer to mythical objects and have no existence in reality at all – like 'unicorn'. If the meaning of a word does not derive from the object to which it refers, where does it come from? Saussure's answer is that meaning is created by the *differences* between related concepts which the rules of a language recognize. The meaning of the word 'tree' comes from the fact that we distinguish 'tree' from 'bush', 'shrub', 'forest' and a host of words which have similar – but distinct – meanings. Meanings are created internally within language, not by the objects in the world which we refer to by means of them.

Structuralism and semiotics

To this analysis, Saussure adds the important observation that it is not only sounds (speaking) or marks on paper (writing) that can create meaning. Any objects which we can systematically distinguish can be used to *make meanings*. An example is a traffic light. We use the contrast between green and red to mean 'go' and 'stop' (yellow means 'get ready to start' or 'get ready to stop'). Notice that it is the *difference* that creates the meaning, not the actual colours themselves. It would not matter if we used green to mean 'stop' and red to mean 'go' – so long as we were consistent in recognizing the difference. Saussure calls the study of non-linguistic meanings *semiology*, but the term most often used today is **semiotics**.

Semiotic studies can be made of many different aspects of human culture. One example is clothing and fashion. What makes a certain style of clothing fashionable at a given time? It is certainly not the actual clothes that are worn, for short skirts might be fashionable one year, and unfashionable the next. What makes something fashionable is again the *difference* between what is worn by those who are 'in the know', and those who lag behind. Another example from the sphere of clothing is the wearing of mourning dress. In our culture, we show we are in mourning by wearing black. In some other cultures, on the other hand, people who are in mourning wear white. What matters is not the colour itself, but the fact that people in mourning dress differently from their normal style.

The structuralist approach has been used more widely in anthropology than in sociology, particularly in the United States. Following the lead of Lévi-Strauss – who popularized the term *structuralism* – structuralist analysis has been employed in the study of kinship, myth, religion and other areas. However, many writers on sociological theory have been influenced by notions drawn from structuralism. Structuralist concepts have been applied to the study of the media (newspapers, magazines, television), ideology and culture in general.

Structuralist thought has weaknesses which limit its appeal as a general theoretical framework in sociology. Structuralism originated in the study of language, and has proved more relevant to analysing certain aspects of human behaviour than others. It is useful for exploring communication and culture, but has less application to more practical concerns of social life, such as economic or political activity.

Symbolic interactionism

Symbolic interactionism gives more weight to the active, creative individual than either of the other theoretical approaches. Since Mead's time it has been further developed by many other writers, and in the United States has been the principal rival to the functionalist standpoint. As in the case of structuralism, symbolic interactionism springs from a concern with language; but Mead develops this in a different direction.

Symbols

Mead claims that language allows us to become self-conscious beings – aware of our own individuality, and the key to this view is the **symbol**. A symbol is something which *stands for* something else. Pursuing the example used by Saussure, the word 'tree' is a symbol by means of which we represent the object, tree. Once we have mastered such a concept, Mead argues, we can think of a tree even if none is visible. We have learned to think of the object symbolically. Symbolic thought frees us from being limited in our experience to what we actually see, hear or feel.

Unlike the lower animals, human beings live in a richly symbolic universe. This applies to our very sense of self. (Animals do not have a sense of self as human beings do.) Each of us is a self-conscious being, because we learn to be able to 'look at' ourselves as if from the outside – seeing ourselves as others see us. When a child begins to use 'I' to refer to that object (himself or herself) which others call 'you', she or he is exhibiting the beginnings of self-consciousness. (Further discussion of Mead's theory of the development of self can be found in chapter 3: 'Socialization and the Life-Cycle'.)

Virtually all interaction between human individuals, symbolic interactionists reason, involves an exchange of symbols. When we interact with others, we constantly look for 'clues' about what type of behaviour is appropriate in the context, and about how to interpret what others intend. Symbolic interactionism directs our attention to the detail of interpersonal interaction, and how that detail is used to make sense of what others say and do. For instance, suppose a man and a woman are out on a date for the first time. Each is likely to spend a good part of the evening sizing the other up, and assessing how the relationship is likely to develop – if at all. Neither wishes to be seen doing this too openly, although each recognizes that it is going on. Both individuals are careful about their own behaviour, being anxious to present themselves in a favourable light, but, knowing this, each is likely to be looking for aspects of the other's behaviour which would reveal their true opinions. A complex and subtle process of symbolic interpretation shapes the interaction between the two.

Sociologists influenced by symbolic interactionism usually focus on face-to-face interaction in the contexts of everyday life. Erving Goffman, whose work is discussed in chapter 4 ('Social Interaction and Everyday Life') has made particularly illuminating contributions to this type of study, introducing wit and verve into what in the hands of Mead was a drier, abstract theoretical approach. In the hands of Goffman and others, symbolic interactionism yields many insights into the nature of our actions in the course of day-to-day social life. But symbolic interactionism is open to the criticism that it concentrates too much on the small-scale. Symbolic interactionists have always found difficulty in dealing with more large-scale structures and processes – the very phenomena which the other two traditions most strongly emphasize.

Marxism

Functionalism, structuralism and symbolic interactionism are not the only theoretical traditions of any importance in sociology, nor is this three-fold division the only way in which we can classify theoretical approaches. One influential type of approach which straddles this division is **Marxism**. Marxists, of course, all trace their views back in some way to the writings of Marx, but numerous interpretations of Marx's major ideas are possible, and there are today schools of Marxist thought which take very different theoretical positions.

Broadly speaking, Marxism can be sub-divided along lines that correspond to the boundaries between the three theoretical traditions previously described. Many Marxists have implicitly or openly adopted a functionalist approach to historical materialism (Cohen, 1978). Their version of Marxism is quite different from that of Marxists influenced by structuralism, the most well-known writer developing such a standpoint being the French author Louis Althusser (Althusser, 1969). Both these types of Marxist thought differ from that of Marxists who have laid stress on the active, creative character of human behaviour. Few such writers have been directly influenced by symbolic interactionism, but they have adopted a perspective quite close to it (Fromm, 1967; Marcuse, 1968).

In all of its versions, Marxism differs from non-Marxist traditions of sociology. Most Marxist authors see Marxism as part of a 'package' of sociological analysis and political reform. Marxism is supposed to generate a programme of radical political change. Moreover, Marxists put more emphasis on class divisions, conflict, power and ideology than many non-Marxist sociologists, especially most of those influenced by functionalism. It is best to see Marxism not as a type of approach within sociology, but as a body of writing existing alongside sociology, each overlapping and quite frequently being influenced by the other. Non-Marxist sociology and Marxism have always existed in a relationship of mutual influence and opposition.

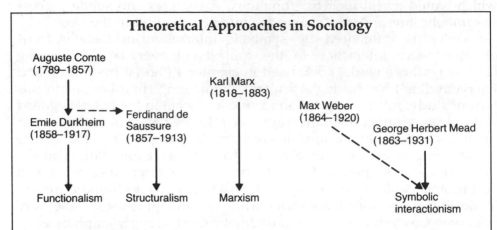

Theoretical Approaches in Sociology

The unbroken lines indicate direct influence, the dotted lines an indirect connection. It is not certain that Saussure owed many of his ideas directly to Durkheim, but there are several major areas of overlap. Mead is not indebted to Weber, but Weber's views – stressing the meaningful, purposive nature of human action – have affinities with the themes of symbolic interactionism.

Theoretical dilemmas

How should we assess the relative value of these four theoretical approaches? Although each has its committed advocates, there are obvious respects in which they are complementary to one another. Functionalism, and most versions of Marxism, concentrate on the more large-scale properties of social groups or societies. They are principally concerned with the 'grand questions' – like 'How do societies hold together?', or 'What are the main conditions producing social change?' Symbolic interaction is, by contrast, more concentrated on face-to-face contexts of social life. Structuralism differs from the other approaches by being focused mainly on cultural features of social activity.

To some extent, therefore, we can draw selectively on all the theories in discussing specific sociological problems; but in certain respects they clearly do clash. There are several basic **theoretical dilemmas** – matters of continuing controversy or dispute – which these clashes of viewpoint bring to our attention, some of which concern very general matters to do with how we should interpret human activities and social institutions. We shall discuss four such dilemmas here.

1 One dilemma concerns *human action* and *social structure*. It is: how far are we creative human actors, actively controlling the conditions of our own lives? Or is most of what we do the result of general social forces outside our control? This issue has always divided, and continues to divide, sociologists. Symbolic interactionism stresses the active, creative components of human behaviour. The other three approaches (with the exception of some variants of Marxism) emphasize the constraining nature of social influences on our actions.

2 A second theoretical dilemma concerns *consensus* and *conflict* in society. Some standpoints in sociology – including many linked to functionalism – emphasize the inherent order and harmony of human societies. Those taking this view – such as Talcott Parsons – regard continuity and **consensus** as the most evident characteristics of societies, however much they may change over time. Other sociologists, on the other hand – particularly those strongly influenced by Marx or Weber – accentuate the pervasiveness of social **conflict** (Collins, 1974). They see societies as plagued with divisions, tensions and struggles. To them, it is illusory to claim that people tend to live amicably with one another most of the time – even when there are no open confrontations, they say, there remain deep divisions of interest which at some point are liable to break out into active conflicts.

3 A third dilemma concerns not so much the general characteristics of human behaviour or of societies as a whole, as features of *modern social development*. It is to do with the determining influences affecting the origins and nature of modern societies, and derives from the differences between non-Marxist and Marxist approaches. This dilemma centres on the following issue: how far has the modern world been shaped by the economic factors which Marx singled out – in particular, the mechanisms of capitalist economic enterprise? How far, alternatively, have other influences (such as social, political or cultural factors) shaped social development in the modern era?

4 There is a fourth basic problem of theory which hardly figures at all in orthodox traditions of sociology, but which can no longer be ignored. This is the problem of how we are to incorporate a satisfactory understanding of *gender* within sociological analysis. All the major figures in the past development of sociological theory were men, and in their writings they gave virtually no attention to the fact that human beings are gendered (Sydie, 1987). In their works, human individuals appear as if they were 'neuter' – they are abstract 'actors', rather than differentiated women and men. Since we have very little to build upon in relating issues of gender to the more established forms of theoretical thinking in sociology, this is perhaps at the current time the most acutely difficult problem of the four to grapple with.

One of the main theoretical dilemmas associated with gender is the following. Shall we build 'gender' as general category into our sociological thinking? Or, alternatively, do we need to analyse gender issues by breaking them down into more specific influences affecting the behaviour of women and men in different contexts? Put in another way: are there characteristics that separate men and women, in terms of their identities and social behaviour, in all cultures? Or are gender differences always to be explained mainly in terms of other differences which divide societies (such as class divisions)?

We shall look at each of these dilemmas in turn.

Structure and action

A major theme pursued by Durkheim, and by many other sociological authors since, is that the societies of which we are members exert **social constraint** over our actions. Durkheim argued that society has primacy over the individual person. Society is far more than the sum of individual acts; when we analyse social structure, we are studying characteristics that have a 'firmness' or 'solidity' comparable to structures in the material environment. Think of a person standing in a room with several doors. The structure of the room constrains the range of her or his possible activities. The siting of the walls and the doors, for example, defines the routes of exit and entry. Social structure, according to Durkheim, constrains our activities in a parallel way, setting limits to what we can do as individuals. It is 'external' to us, just as the walls of the room are.

This point of view is expressed by Durkheim in a famous statement:

> When I perform my duties as a brother, a husband or a citizen and carry out the commitments I have entered into, I fulfil obligations which are defined in law and custom and which are external to myself and my actions. . . . Similarly, the believer has discovered from birth, ready fashioned, the beliefs and practices of his religious life; if they existed before he did, it follows that they exist outside him. The system of signs that I employ to express my thoughts, the monetary system I use to pay my debts, the credit instruments I utilise in my commercial relationships, the practices I follow in my profession, etc. – all function independently of the use I make of them. Considering in turn each member of society, the following remarks could be made for each single one of them. (Durkheim, 1982, pp. 50–1)

Although the type of view Durkheim expresses has many adherents, it has also met with sharp criticism. What is 'society', the critics ask, if it is not the composite of many individual actions? If we study a group, we do not see a collective entity, only individuals interacting with one another in various ways. 'Society' *is* only many individuals behaving in regular ways in relation to each other. According to the critics (who include most sociologists influenced by symbolic interactionism), as human beings we have reasons for what we do, and we inhabit a social world permeated by cultural meanings. Social phenomena, according to them, are precisely *not* like 'things', but depend on the symbolic meanings with which we invest what we do. We are not the *creatures* of society, but its *creators*.

Assessment

It is unlikely that this controversy will ever be fully resolved, since it has existed since modern thinkers first started systematically to try to explain human behaviour. Moreover, it is a debate which is not just confined to sociology, but preoccupies scholars in all fields of the social sciences. You must decide, in the light of your reading of this book, which position you think more nearly correct.

Yet the differences between the two views can be exaggerated. While both cannot be wholly right, we can fairly easily see connections between them. Durkheim's view is clearly in some respects valid. Social institutions do precede the existence of any given individual; it is also evident that they exert constraint over us. Thus, for example, I did not invent the monetary system which exists in Britain. Nor do I have a choice about whether I want to use it or not, if I wish to have the goods and services which money can buy. The system of money, like all other established institutions, does exist independently of any individual member of society, and constrains that individual's activities.

On the other hand, it is obviously mistaken to suppose that society is 'external' to us in the same way as the physical world is. For the physical world would go on existing whether or not any human beings were alive, whereas it would plainly be nonsensical to say this of society. While society is external to each individual taken singly, by definition it cannot be external to *all* individuals taken together.

Moreover, although what Durkheim calls 'social facts' might constrain what we do, they do not *determine* what we do. I could choose to live without using money, should I be firmly resolved to do so, even if it might prove very difficult to eke out an existence from day to day. As human beings, we do make choices, and we do not simply respond passively to events around us. The way forward in bridging the gap between 'structural' and 'action' approaches is to recognize that we *actively make and remake* social structure during the course of our everyday activities. For example, the fact that I use the monetary system contributes in a minor, yet necessary, way to the very existence of that system. If everyone, or even the majority of people, at some point decided to avoid using money, the monetary system would dissolve.

Consensus and conflict

It is also useful to begin with Durkheim when contrasting the *consensus* and *conflict* viewpoints. Durkheim sees society as a set of interdependent parts. For most functionalist thinkers, in fact, society is treated as an *integrated whole*, composed of structures which mesh closely with one another. This is very much in accord with Durkheim's emphasis on the constraining, 'external' character of 'social facts'. However, the analogy here is not that of the walls of a building, but of the physiology of the body.

A body consists of various specialized parts (such as the brain, heart, lungs, liver, and so forth), each of which contributes to sustaining the continuing life of the organism. These necessarily work in harmony with one another; if they do not, the life of the organism is under threat. So it is, according to Durkheim (and Parsons), with society. For a society to have a continuing existence over time, its specialized institutions (such as the political system, religion, the family, and the educational system) must work in harmony with one another. The continuation of a society thus depends upon co-operation, which in turn presumes a general consensus, or agreement, among its members over basic values.

Those who focus mainly on conflict have a very different outlook. Their guiding assumptions can easily be outlined using Marx's account of class conflict as an example. According to Marx, societies are divided into classes with unequal resources. Since such marked inequalities exist, there are divisions of interest which are 'built into' the social system. These conflicts of interest at some point break out into active struggle between classes – which can generate processes of radical change. Not all of those influenced by this viewpoint concentrate on classes to the degree which Marx did; other divisions are regarded as important in promoting conflict – for example, divisions between racial groups or political factions. Whatever the conflict groups on which most emphasis is put, society is seen as essentially *full of tension* – even the most stable social system represents an uneasy balance of antagonistic groupings.

Assessment

As with the case of structure or action, it is not likely that this theoretical debate can be completely brought to a close. Yet, once more, the difference between the consensus and conflict standpoints seems wider than it is. The two positions are by no means wholly incompatible. All societies probably involve some kind of general agreement over values, and all certainly involve conflict.

Moreover, as a general rule of sociological analysis we have always to examine the connections *between* consensus and conflict within social systems. The values different groups hold, and the goals their members pursue, often reflect a mixture of common and opposed interests. For instance, even in Marx's portrayal of class conflict, different classes share some common interests as well as being pitted against one another. Thus capitalists depend on a labour-force to work in their enterprises, just as workers depend on them to provide their wages. Open conflict is not continuous in such circumstances; rather, sometimes what both sides have in common tends to override their differences, while in other situations the reverse is the case.

A useful concept which helps analyse the interrelations of conflict and consensus is that of *ideology* – values and beliefs which help secure the position of more powerful groups at the expense of less powerful ones. Power, ideology and conflict are always closely connected. Many conflicts are *about* power, because of the rewards it can bring. Those who hold most power may depend mainly on the influence of ideology to retain their dominance, but are usually able also to use force if necessary. For instance, in feudal times aristocratic rule was supported by the idea that a minority of people were 'born to govern', but the aristocratic rulers often also resorted to the use of violence against those who dared to oppose their power.

The shaping of the modern world

The Marxist perspective

Marx's writings throw down a powerful challenge to sociological analysis; one which has not been ignored. From his own time to the present day many sociological debates have centred on Marx's ideas about the development of modern societies. As was mentioned earlier, Marx sees modern societies as *capitalistic*. The driving impulse behind social change in the modern era is the pressure towards constant economic transformation which is an integral part of capitalist production. Capitalism is a vastly more dynamic economic system than any preceding one. Capitalists compete with one another to sell their goods to consumers and, to survive in a competitive market, firms have to produce their wares as cheaply and efficiently as possible. This leads to constant technological innovation, because increasing the effectiveness of the technology used in a particular production process is one way in which companies can secure an edge over their rivals.

There are also strong incentives to seek out new markets in which to sell goods, acquire cheap raw materials, and make use of cheap labour-power. Capitalism, therefore, according to Marx, is a restlessly expanding system, pushing outwards across the world. This is how Marx explains the spread of Western industry globally.

Marx's interpretation of the influence of capitalism has found many supporters, and subsequent Marxist authors have considerably refined Marx's own portrayal. On the other hand, numerous critics have set out to rebut Marx's view, offering alternative analyses of the influences shaping the modern world. Virtually everyone accepts that capitalism *has* played a major part in creating the world in which we live today. But other sociologists have argued both that Marx exaggerated the impact of purely *economic* factors in producing change, and that capitalism is *less central* to modern social development than he claimed. Most of these writers have also been sceptical of Marx's belief that a socialist system would eventually replace capitalism.

Weber's view

One of Marx's earliest, and most acute, critics was Max Weber. Weber's writings, in fact, have been described as involving a life-long struggle with 'the ghost of Marx' – with the intellectual legacy that Marx left. The alternative position which Weber worked out remains important today. According to him, non-economic factors have played a key role in modern social development. Weber's celebrated and much discussed work, *The Protestant Ethic and the Spirit of Capitalism*, argues that religious values – especially those associated with Puritanism – were of fundamental importance in creating a capitalistic outlook. This outlook did not emerge, as Marx supposed, from economic changes as such.

Weber's understanding of the nature of modern societies, and the reasons for the spread of Western modes of life across the world, contrasts substantially with that of Marx. According to Weber, capitalism – a distinct way of organizing economic enterprise – is one among other major factors shaping social development in the modern period. Underlying capitalistic economic mechanisms, and in some ways more fundamental than them, is the impact of *science* and *bureaucracy*. Science has shaped modern technology – and will presumably continue to do so in any future socialist society. Bureaucracy is the only way of organizing large numbers of people effectively, and therefore inevitably expands with economic and political growth. The development of science, modern technology and bureaucracy, Weber refers to collectively as **rationalization**. Rationalization means the organization of social and economic life according to principles of efficiency, on the basis of technical knowledge.

Evaluation

Which type of interpretation of modern societies, that deriving from Marx, or that coming from Weber, is correct? Again, scholars are divided on the issue. The box lists some of these differences. (It must be remembered that within each camp there are variations, so not every theorist will agree with all the points.)

The contrasts between Marxist and Weberian standpoints inform many areas of sociology. They influence not only how we analyse the nature of the industrialized societies, but our view of Third World societies also. In addition, the two perspectives are linked to differing political positions, Leftist authors on the whole adopting views on side A, Liberals and Conservatives those on side B. Yet the factors with which this particular dilemma are concerned are more of a more directly empirical nature than those involved in

A Broadly Marxist Ideas	**B Broadly Weberian Ideas**
1 The main dynamic of modern development is the expansion of capitalistic economic mechanisms.	1 The main dynamic of modern development is the rationalization of production.
2 Modern societies are riven with class inequalities, which are basic to their very nature.	2 Class is one type of inequality among others – such as inequalities between men and women – in modern societies.
3 Major divisions of power, like those affecting the differential position of men and women, derive ultimately from economic inequalities.	3 Power in the economic system is separable from other sources. For instance, male–female inequalities cannot be explained in economic terms.
4 Modern societies as we know them today (capitalist societies) are of a transitional type – we may expect them to become radically reorganized in the future. Socialism, of one type or another, will eventually replace capitalism.	4 Rationalization is bound to progress further in the future, in all spheres of social life. This explains why societies like the Soviet Union, which are supposedly 'socialist', closely resemble Western countries. All modern societies are dependent on the same basic modes of social and economic organization.
5 The spread of Western influence across the world is mainly a result of the expansionist tendencies of capitalist economic enterprise.	5 The global impact of the West comes from its command over industrial resources, together with superior military power.

the other dilemmas. Factual studies of the paths of development of modern societies, and Third World countries, help us assess how far patterns of change conform to one side or the other.

The problem of gender

Issues of gender are scarcely central in the writings of the major figures who established the framework of modern sociology. The few passages in which they did touch upon gender questions, however, allow us at least to specify the outlines of a basic theoretical dilemma – even if there is little in their works to help us try to resolve it. We can best describe this dilemma by contrasting a theme which occasionally occurs in Durkheim's writings with one that appears in those of Marx. Durkheim notes at one point, in the course of his discussion of suicide, that man is 'almost entirely the product of society', while woman is 'to a far greater extent the product of nature'. Expanding on these observations, he says of man: 'his tastes, aspirations and humour have in large part a collective origin, while his companion's are more directly influenced by her organism. His needs, therefore, are quite different from hers . . .' (Durkheim, 1952, p. 385). In other words, women and men have different identities, tastes and inclinations because women are less socialized, and are 'closer to nature' than men.

No one today would accept a view stated in quite this manner. Female identity is as much shaped by socialization as that of males. Yet, when modified somewhat, Durkheim's claim does represent one possible view of the formation and nature of gender. This is that gender differences rest fundamentally on biologically given variations between men and women. Such a view does not necessarily mean believing that gender differences are mostly inborn. Rather, it presumes that women's social position and identity is mainly shaped (as Chodorow suggests; see chapter 6: 'Gender and Sexuality') by their involvement in reproduction and child-rearing. If this standpoint is correct, differences of gender are deeply embedded in all societies. The discrepancies in power between women and men reflect the fact that women bear children, and are their primary caretakers, whereas men are active in the 'public' spheres of politics, work and war.

Marx's view is substantially at odds with this. For Marx, gender differences in power and status between men and women mainly reflect other divisions – in his eyes, especially class divisions. According to him, in the earliest forms of human society, neither gender nor class divisions are present. The power of men over women only comes about as class divisions appear. Women come to be a form of 'private property' owned by men, through the institution of marriage. Women will be freed from their situation of bondage when class divisions are overcome. Again, few if any would accept this analysis today, but we can make it a much more plausible view by generalizing it further. Class is not the only factor shaping social divisions which affect the behaviour of men and women. Other factors include ethnicity and cultural background. For instance, it might be argued that women in a minority group (say, blacks in the United States), have more in common with men in that minority group than they do with women in the majority (that is, white women). Or it may be the case that women from a particular culture (like a small hunting and gathering culture) share more common characteristics with the males of that culture than they do with women from an industrial society.

Evaluation

The issues involved in this fourth dilemma are highly important, and bear directly on the challenge which feminist authors have thrown down to sociology. No one can seriously dispute that a great deal of sociological analysis in the past has either ignored women, or has operated with interpretations of female identity and behaviour that are drastically inadequate. In spite of all the new research on women carried out in sociology over the past twenty years, there still are many areas in which the distinctive activities and concerns of women have been insufficiently studied. But 'bringing the study of women into sociology' is not in and of itself the same as coping with problems of gender, because gender concerns the relations between the identities and behaviour of women *and* men. For the moment it has to be left as an open question how far gender differences can be illuminated by means of other sociological concepts (class, ethnicity, cultural background and so forth), or how far, on the contrary, other social divisions need to be explained in terms of gender. Certainly some of the major explanatory tasks of sociology in the future will depend on tackling this dilemma effectively.

Theories

We can draw a distinction between *theoretical approaches* and **theories**. So far in this chapter, we have been concerned with theoretical approaches, which are broad overall orientations to the subject-matter of sociology. Theories are more narrowly focused, and represent attempts to explain particular sets of social conditions or types of occurrence. They are usually formed as part of the process of research, and in turn suggest problems to which research investigations should be devoted. An example would be Durkheim's theory of suicide.

Innumerable theories have been developed in the many different areas of research in which sociologists work. Some are very precisely set out, and even occasionally expressed in mathematical form – although this is more common in other social sciences (especially economics) than in sociology.

Some types of theory attempt to explain much more than others, and opinions vary about how far it is desirable or useful for sociologists to concern themselves with very wide-ranging theoretical efforts. Robert Merton, for example, argues forcefully that sociologists should concentrate their attention on what he calls *theories of the middle range* (Merton, 1957). Rather than attempting to create grand theoretical schemes (in the manner of Parsons, for instance), we should be more modest.

Middle-range theories are specific enough to be able to be directly tested by empirical research, yet sufficiently general to cover a range of different phenomena. A case in point is the theory of **relative deprivation**. This theory holds that how people evaluate their circumstances depends on whom they compare themselves to. Thus feelings of deprivation do not conform directly to the level of material poverty individuals experience. A family living in a small home in a poor area, where everyone is in more or less similar circumstances, is likely to feel less deprived than one living in a similar house in a neighbourhood where the majority of homes are much larger and more affluent.

It is indeed true that the more wide-ranging and ambitious a theory is, the more difficult it is to test it empirically. Yet there seems no obvious reason why theoretical thinking in sociology should be confined to the 'middle range'. To see why this is so, let us take as an example the theory that Weber advances in *The Protestant Ethic and the Spirit of Capitalism*.

An example: the Protestant ethic

In *The Protestant Ethic* (1976; originally published 1904–5), Weber sets out to tackle an extremely major problem: why capitalism developed in the West and nowhere else. For some fifteen centuries after the fall of ancient Rome, other civilizations were much more prominent in world history than the West. Europe in fact was a rather insignificant area of the globe, while China, India and the Ottoman Empire in the Near East were all major powers. The Chinese in particular were a long way ahead of the West in terms of their level of technological and economic development. What happened to bring about a surge in economic development in Europe from the seventeenth century onwards?

To answer this question, Weber reasons, we must show what separates modern industry from earlier types of economic activity. We find the desire to accumulate wealth in many different civilizations, and this is not difficult to explain; people have valued wealth for the comforts, security, power and enjoyment it can bring. They wish to be free of want, and having accumulated wealth, they use it to make themselves comfortable.

If we look at the economic development of the West, Weber argues, we find something quite different. According to him, there was an attitude towards the accumulation of wealth found nowhere else in history. This attitude is what Weber calls the *spirit of capitalism* – a set of beliefs and values held by the first capitalist merchants and industrialists. These people had a strong drive to accumulate personal wealth. Yet, quite unlike the wealthy elsewhere, they did not seek to use their accumulated riches to follow a luxurious life-style. Their way of life was in fact self-denying and frugal; they lived soberly and quietly, shunning the ordinary manifestations of affluence. This very unusual combination of characteristics, Weber tries to show, was vital to early Western economic development. For unlike the wealthy in previous ages, and in other cultures, these groups did not dissipate their wealth. Instead, they reinvested it to promote the further expansion of the enterprises they headed.

The core of Weber's theory is that the attitudes involved in the spirit of capitalism derived from religion. Christianity in general played a part in fostering such an outlook, but the essential motive force was provided by the impact of Protestantism – and especially one variety of Protestantism, *Puritanism*. The early capitalists were mostly Puritans, and many subscribed to Calvinist views. Weber argues that certain Calvinistic doctrines were the direct source of the spirit of capitalism. One was the idea that human beings are God's instruments on earth, required by the Almighty to work in a *vocation* – an occupation – for the greater glory of God.

A second important aspect of Calvinism was the notion of *predestination*, according to which only certain predestined individuals are to be among the 'elect' – to enter heaven in the after-life. In Calvin's original doctrine, nothing a person does on this earth can alter whether he or she happens to be one of the elect; this is predetermined by God. However, this belief caused such anxiety among his followers that it was modified to allow believers to recognize certain signs of election. Success in working in a vocation, indicated by material prosperity, became the main sign that a person was truly one of the elect. A tremendous impulse towards economic success was created among groups influenced by these ideas. Yet this was accompanied by the believer's need to live a sober and frugal life. The Puritans believed luxury to be an evil, so the drive to accumulate wealth became joined to a severe and unadorned life-style.

The early entrepreneurs had little awareness that they were helping to produce momentous changes in society; they were impelled above all by religious motives. The ascetic – that is, self-denying – life-style of the Puritans has subsequently become an intrinsic part of modern civilization. As Weber says:

> The Puritan wanted to work in a calling; we are forced to do so. For when asceticism was carried out of the monastic cells into everyday life, and began to dominate worldly morality, it did its part in building the tremendous cosmos of the modern economic order. . . . Since asceticism undertook to remodel the world and to work out its ideals in the world,

material goods have gained an increasingly and finally an inexorable power over the lives of men as at no previous period in history. . . . The idea of duty in one's calling prowls about in our lives like the ghost of dead religious beliefs. Where the fulfilment of the calling cannot directly be related to the highest spiritual and cultural values, or when, on the other hand, it need not be felt simply as economic compulsion, the individual generally abandons the attempt to justify it at all. In the field of its highest development, in the United States, the pursuit of wealth, stripped of its religious and ethical meaning, tends to become associated with purely mundane passions . . . (Weber, 1976, pp. 181–2)

Weber's theory has been criticized from many angles. Some have argued, for example, that the outlook he called 'the spirit of capitalism' can be discerned in the early Italian merchant cities long before Calvinism was ever heard of. Others have claimed that the key notion of 'working in a vocation', which Weber associated with Protestantism, already existed in Catholic beliefs. Yet the essentials of Weber's account are still accepted by many, and the thesis he advanced remains as bold and illuminating as it did when first formulated. If Weber's thesis is valid, modern economic and social development has been decisively influenced by something that seems at first sight utterly distant from it – a set of religious ideals.

Weber's theory meets several criteria important in theoretical thinking in sociology.

1 It is **counter-intuitive** – it suggests an interpretation that breaks with what common sense would suggest. The theory thus develops a fresh perspective on the issues which it covers. Most authors before Weber gave little thought to the possibility that religious ideals could have played a fundamental role in the origins of capitalism.
2 The theory is neither a purely 'structural' nor a purely 'individual' account. The early development of capitalism was an unintended consequence of what the Puritan businessmen aspired to – to live virtuously according to God's will.
3 The theory makes sense of something that is otherwise puzzling: why individuals would want to live frugally while making great efforts to accumulate wealth.
4 The theory is capable of illuminating circumstances beyond those it was originally developed to understand. Weber emphasized that he was trying only to understand the early origins of modern capitalism. None the less, it seems reasonable to suppose that parallel values to those instilled by Puritanism might be involved in other situations of successful capitalist development.
5 A good theory is not just one that happens to be valid. It is also one that is *fruitful* in terms of how far it generates new ideas and stimulates further research work. Weber's theory has certainly been highly successful in these respects, providing the springboard for a vast amount of subsequent research and theory.

Theoretical thinking in sociology

Assessing theories, and especially theoretical approaches, in sociology is a challenging and formidable task. Theoretical debates are by definition more abstract than controversies of a more empirical kind. The fact that there is not a single theoretical approach which dominates the whole of sociology might seem to be a sign of weakness in the subject. But this is not the case at all. On the contrary, the jostling of rival theoretical approaches and theories is an expression of the vitality of the sociological enterprise. In studying human beings – ourselves – theoretical variety rescues us from dogma. Human behaviour is complicated and many-sided, and it is very unlikely that a single theoretical perspective could cover all of its aspects. Diversity in theoretical thinking provides a rich source of ideas that can be drawn upon in research, and stimulates the imaginative capacities so essential to progress in sociological work.

Summary

1   A diversity of theoretical approaches is found in sociology (and also in the other social sciences). The reason for this is not particularly puzzling: theoretical disputes are difficult to resolve even in the natural sciences, and in sociology we face special difficulties because of the complex problems involved in subjecting our own behaviour to study.

2   Important figures in the early development of sociological theory include Auguste Comte (1789–1857), Emile Durkheim (1858–1917), Karl Marx (1818–83) and Max Weber (1864–1920). Many of their ideas remain important in sociology today.

3   The main theoretical approaches in sociology are *functionalism, structuralism, symbolic interactionism* and *Marxism*. To some extent, these approaches are complementary to one another. However, there are also major contrasts between them which influence the ways in which theoretical issues are handled by authors following different approaches.

4   One main theoretical dilemma in sociology concerns how we should relate human action to social structure. Are we the creators of society, or created by it? The choice between these alternatives is not as stark as may initially appear, and the real problem is how to *relate* the two aspects of social life together.

5   A second dilemma concerns whether societies should be pictured as harmonious and orderly, or whether they should be seen as marked by persistent conflict. Again, the two views are not completely opposed, and we need to show how *consensus* and *conflict* interrelate. The concepts of *ideology* and *power* are useful in undertaking this task.

6   A third focus of continuing debate in sociology is to do with the analysis of modern social development. Are processes of change in the modern world mainly shaped by capitalist economic development, or by other factors, including non-economic ones? Positions taken in this debate to some extent are influenced by the political beliefs and attitudes held by different sociologists.

7   A fourth dilemma concerns how we should cope with issues of gender in sociological analysis. Feminists have thrown down a challenge to sociology which is slowly being met on the level of empirical research: far more studies of the concerns and outlooks of women are being carried out than used to be done. But these do not in and of themselves resolve the question of how we should best analyse gender in relation to the existing approaches and concepts of sociological theory.

8   Weber's thesis about the influence of Puritanism on modern economic development provides a useful example in thinking about what makes a theory valuable. Weber's ideas remain controversial, but in several respects his theory broke new ground, stimulating much subsequent research.

Basic concepts

theoretical approach	conflict
consensus	theory

Important terms

division of labour	semiotics
anomie	symbol
materialist conception of history	Marxism
capitalism	theoretical dilemma
bureaucracy	social constraint
symbolic interactionism	rationalization
functionalism	relative deprivation
structuralism	counter-intuitive thinking
manifest functions	
latent functions	

Further reading

Richard J. Bernstein, *The Restructuring of Social and Political Theory* (Oxford: Basil Blackwell, 1976) — a survey of some of the main changes taking place in theoretical approaches in the social sciences today.

Anthony Giddens, *Capitalism and Modern Social Theory* (Cambridge: Cambridge University Press, 1971) — a discussion of the writings of Marx, Durkheim and Max Weber.

C. Wright Mills, *The Sociological Imagination* (Harmondsworth: Penguin, 1979) — a classic analysis of the themes which should inform theoretical thinking in sociology.

Quentin Skinner (ed.), *The Return of Grand Theory* (Cambridge: Cambridge University Press, 1986) — a collection of articles dealing with leading traditions of theory.

Jonathan Turner, *The Structure of Sociological Theory* (Holmewood: Dorsey, 1986) — covers several major theoretical approaches in sociology.

PART VII

Appendix and Glossaries

Appendix: How to Use Libraries

Libraries, especially large ones, can seem daunting places. Many people feel rather lost when confronted with the apparently innumerable sources of information which libraries contain. They may therefore end up using only a small proportion of what they have to offer, perhaps with damaging effects on their academic work. It is a good idea to get to know – at the beginning of your course – the range of resources libraries have. If you do this early on, the 'lost' feeling won't last long!

All the information available in the library is stored and catalogued in a systematic way, in order to make finding things easy. Most smaller libraries operate with *open stacks* – the books can be visibly inspected on the shelves, and the user can select whichever volume he or she wants directly. Most larger collections keep only a proportion of their books on open shelves, and store others in vaults where less space is required to keep them. In these libraries, anyone who wishes to use or borrow a book must ask for it, or fill in a request slip. Some libraries have some books in each system.

If you are looking for a particular book, you'll be able to look it up under author or title in the index or catalogue. This may be a computerized list, drawerfuls of index cards, or a microfiche – or all three! Once you find its catalogue number, you can then either order it from library staff quoting that number, or find it on the open shelves which are always arranged by catalogue numbers. All – or most – sociology books will be in one area. Any librarian will be able to explain how the cataloguing system works.

Finding books on a particular topic when you don't know any names or titles involves using a subject index (again, this may be computerized or on cards). A subject index lists books by topics – such as 'class', 'bureaucracy' etc.

Many of the larger libraries today have computer-trace systems, which are very easy to operate, and are normally available to all library-users. You simply key in the area or areas about which you require bibliographical information, and the computer will display a list of titles relevant to them.

Most libraries provide very similar services, but different libraries do have their own ways of doing things, and there are variations in cataloguing systems. Never be afraid to ask the librarian or assistants for their help, if there is any aspect of library procedure which puzzles you, or about which you need guidance. You should not be worried about bothering them; librarians are trained professionals, committed to making sure that the library resources are available to everyone who wants to make use of them. They are usually highly knowledgeable about the range of material the library contains, and only too willing to provide guidance if asked.

Sources of general information in sociology

If you are beginning the study of a particular topic in sociology, and want to find some general information about it, there are a number of useful sources. Several dictionaries of sociology are available. These provide brief discussions of the major concepts in the subject, and also accounts of the ideas of some of the leading contributors to the discipline. The major encyclopaedias – like the *Encyclopaedia Britannica* – contain many entries relevant to sociological topics. The entries in dictionaries and encyclopaedias virtually always provide short lists of books or articles as a guide to further reading.

There are various other ways in which books and articles relevant to a given problem or issue can be traced. The *International Bibliography of the Social Sciences*, published annually by Unesco, offers a comprehensive listing of works that have appeared in different social science subjects over the course of any year. Thus, for example, you can look up the heading 'sociology of education', and find a range of up-to-date materials in that field. An equally useful source is *Sociological Abstracts*, which not only lists books and articles in the different areas of sociology, but gives a short description of the contents of each of them.

Sociological journals

It is worth familiarizing yourself with the main journals in sociology. Journals usually appear three or four times a year. The information and debates they contain are often more up-to-date than those in books, which take longer to write and publish. Journal articles are sometimes quite technical, and a person fairly new to sociology may well not find them readily understandable. But all the leading journals regularly publish articles of general interest, accessible to those with only limited knowledge of the subject.

The most important journals include *Sociology* (the official journal of the British Sociological Association), the *British Journal of Sociology*, the *Sociological Review* and the *American Journal of Sociology*.

Research for dissertations or longer projects

On some occasions you may wish to use the library to pursue a particular research project, perhaps in the course of writing a dissertation. Such a task might involve carrying out a more 'in-depth' search of relevant sources than is required for normal study.

If you require statistical information concerning Britain, a good place at which to start is *Social Trends*, a book published each year by the government (HMSO). *Social Trends* contains selected statistical information on many aspects of British social life. Further information is contained in *The General Household Survey*; more detailed statistical information is contained in the *Annual Abstract of Statistics*, both of these also being government publications.

Newspaper articles provide a mine of valuable information for the sociological researcher. A few newspapers are what are sometimes called 'journals of record'. That is to say, they not only carry news stories, but also record sections from parliamentary speeches, government reports and other official sources. *The Times* and the *Guardian* are the most important examples, and each produces an index of topics and names that have appeared in its pages.

Once you start using a library regularly, you are likely to find that it is more common to feel overwhelmed by the number of works available in a particular area than to experience difficulty in tracing relevant literature. One way of dealing with this problem, of course, is to base your selection of books or articles on reading-lists provided by lecturers and tutors. Where such lists are not available, or are inadequate, the best procedure to follow is to define the information you require as precisely as possible. This will allow you to narrow the range of choice to feasible limits. If your library is an open-stack one, it is worth looking through a number of potentially relevant books or articles before selecting those you decide to work with. In making the decision, apart obviously from considerations of the subject-matter, bear in mind *when* the book was written. New developments are constantly taking place in sociology, and in the other social sciences, and obviously older books won't cover these.

Glossary of Basic Concepts

Words in bold type within entries refer to concepts or terms found elsewhere in the glossaries.

ALIENATION. The sense that our own abilities, as human beings, are taken over by other entities. The term was originally used by Marx to refer to the projection of human powers on to gods. Subsequently he employed the term to refer to the loss of control on the part of workers over the nature of the labour task, and over the products of their labour.

CAUSATION. The causal influence of one factor or **variable** upon another. A 'cause and effect' relationship exists wherever a particular event or state of affairs (the effect) is produced by the existence of another (the cause). Causal factors in sociology include the reasons individuals have for what they do, as well as many external influences on their behaviour.

CLASS. Although it is one of the most frequently used concepts in sociology, there is no clear agreement about how the notion should best be defined. However, most sociologists use the term to refer to socio-economic differences between groups of individuals which create differences in their material prosperity and power.

COLLECTIVE ACTION. Action undertaken in a relatively spontaneous way by a large number of people assembled together in a particular place or area. One of the most important forms of collective action is crowd behaviour. In crowds, individuals can seek to achieve objectives which in ordinary circumstances are denied to them.

COMMUNICATION. The transmission of information from one individual or group to another. Communication is the necessary basis of all social interaction. In face-to-face contexts, communication is carried on by the use of language, but also by many bodily cues which individuals interpret in understanding what others say and do. With the development of writing, and electronic media, like radio, television, or computer transmission systems, communication becomes in some part detached from immediate contexts of face-to-face social relationships.

CONFLICT. Antagonism between individuals or groups in society. Conflict may take two forms. One occurs where there is a clash of interests between two or more individuals or groups; the other happens where people or collectivities engage in active struggle with one another. Interest conflict does not always lead to open struggle, while active conflicts may sometimes occur between parties who mistakenly believe their interests are opposed.

CONFORMITY.   Behaviour which follows the established norms of a group or society. People do not always conform to social norms because they accept the **values** that underlie them. They may behave in the approved ways simply because it is expedient to do so, or because of **sanctions**.

CONSENSUS.   Agreement over basic social values by the members of a group, community or society. Some thinkers in sociology strongly emphasize the importance of consensus as a basis for social stability. These writers believe that all societies which endure over any substantial period of time involve a 'common value system' of consensual beliefs held by the majority of the population.

CORRELATION.   The regular relationship between two dimensions or **variables**, often expressed in statistical terms. Correlations may be positive or negative. A positive correlation between two variables exists where a high rank on one variable is associated with a high rank on the other. A negative correlation is where a high rank on one variable is associated with a low rank on the other.

THE CREATED ENVIRONMENT.   Those aspects of the physical world which derive from the use of humanly created **technology**. The created environment refers to constructions established by human beings to serve their needs – including, for example, roads, railways, factories, offices, private homes and other buildings.

CRIME.   Any action which contravenes the laws established by a political authority. Although we may tend to think of 'criminals' as a distinct sub-section of the population, there are few people who have not broken the law in one way or another during the course of their lives. While laws are formulated by state authorities, it is by no means unknown for those authorities to engage in criminal behaviour in certain contexts.

CRUDE BIRTH-RATE.   A statistical measure representing the number of births within a given population per year. Crude birth-rates are normally calculated in terms of the number of births per thousand members of a population. Although the crude birth-rate is a useful index for many purposes, it is only a general measure, because it does not specify numbers of births in relation to the age distribution of the society in question.

CRUDE DEATH-RATE.   A statistical measure representing the number of deaths that occur annually in a given population. Crude death-rates are normally calculated as the ratio of deaths to every thousand members of a population in a particular year. Crude death-rates give a general indication of the mortality levels of a community or society, but are limited in their usefulness because they do not take into account the age distribution of the population in question.

CULTURAL REPRODUCTION.   The transmission of cultural **values** and **norms** from generation to generation. Cultural reproduction refers to the mechanisms by which continuity of cultural experience is sustained across time. The processes of schooling in modern societies are among the main mechanisms of cultural reproduction, and do not operate solely through what is taught in courses of formal instruction. Cultural reproduction occurs in a more profound way through the **hidden curriculum** – aspects of behaviour which individuals learn in an informal way while at school.

CULTURE.   The **values**, **norms** and material goods characteristic of a given group. Like the concept of **society**, the notion of culture is very widely used in sociology, as well as in the other social sciences (particularly anthropology). Culture is one of the most distinctive properties of human social association.

DEMOGRAPHIC TRANSITION. An interpretation of population change which holds that a stable ratio of births to deaths is achieved once a certain level of economic prosperity has been reached. According to this notion, in pre-industrial societies there is a rough balance between births and deaths, because population increase is kept in check by a lack of available food, and by disease or war. In modern societies, by contrast, population equilibrium is achieved because families are moved by economic incentives to limit numbers of children.

DEVIANCE. Modes of action which do not conform to the **norms** or **values** held by most of the members of a group or society. What is regarded as 'deviant' is as widely variable as the norms and values that distinguish different cultures and sub-cultures from one another. Many forms of behaviour which are highly esteemed in one context, or by one group, are regarded negatively by others.

DISCRIMINATION. Activities that deny to the members of a particular group resources or rewards which can be obtained by others. Discrimination has to be distinguished from prejudice, although the two are usually quite closely associated. It can be the case that individuals who are prejudiced against others do not engage in discriminatory practices against them; conversely, people may act in a discriminatory fashion even though they are not prejudiced against those subject to such discrimination.

DIVISION OF LABOUR. The specialization of work tasks, by means of which different occupations are combined within a production system. All societies have at least some rudimentary form of division of labour, especially between the tasks allocated to men and those performed by women. With the development of industrialism, however, the division of labour becomes vastly more complex than in any prior type of production system. In the modern world, the division of labour is international in scope.

THE ECONOMY. The system of production and exchange which provides for the material needs of individuals living in a given society. Economic institutions are of key importance in all social orders. What goes on in the economy usually influences many other aspects of social life. Modern economies differ very substantially from traditional ones, because the majority of the population is no longer engaged in agricultural production.

EDUCATION. The transmission of knowledge from one generation to another by means of direct instruction. Although educational processes exist in all societies, it is only in the modern period that mass education takes the form of schooling – that is, instruction in specialized educational environments in which individuals spend several years of their lives.

ENCOUNTER. A meeting between two or more individuals in a situation of face-to-face interaction. Our day-to-day lives can be seen as a series of different encounters strung out across the course of the day. In modern societies, many of the encounters we have with others involve strangers rather than people we know well.

ETHNICITY. Cultural **values** and **norms** which distinguish the members of a given group from others. An ethnic group is one whose members share a distinct awareness of a common cultural identity, separating them from other groups around them. In virtually all societies ethnic differences are associated with variations in power and material wealth. Where ethnic differences are also racial, such divisions are sometimes especially pronounced.

FAMILY. A group of individuals related to one another by blood ties,

marriage or adoption, who form an economic unit, the adult members of which are responsible for the upbringing of children. All known societies involve some form of family system, although the nature of family relationships is widely variable. While in modern societies the main family form is the **nuclear family**, a variety of **extended family** relationships are also often found.

FEMINISM. Advocacy of the rights of women to equality with men in all spheres of life. Feminism dates from the late eighteenth century in Europe, and feminist movements exist in most countries of the world today.

FERTILITY. The average number of liveborn children produced by women of childbearing age in a particular society. Fertility has to be distinguished from **fecundity**, which refers to the potential numbers of births of which women in a given population are capable. Fertility always falls well short of fecundity.

FORMAL RELATIONS. Relations which exist in groups and organizations laid down by the **norms** or rules of the 'official' system of authority.

GENDER. Social expectations about behaviour regarded as appropriate for the members of each sex. Gender does not refer to the physical attributes in terms of which men and women differ, but to socially formed traits of masculinity and femininity. The study of gender relations has become one of the most important areas of sociology in recent years, although for a long time it received little attention.

GLOBALIZATION. The development of social and economic relationships stretching world-wide. In current times, many aspects of people's lives are influenced by organizations and social networks located thousands of miles away from the societies in which they live. A key aspect of the study of globalization is the emergence of a **world system** – that is to say, for some purposes we have to regard the world as forming a single social order.

GOVERNMENT. The process of the enacting of policies and decisions on the part of **officials** within a political apparatus. We can speak of 'government' as a process, or *the* government to refer to the officialdom responsible for the taking of binding political decisions. While in the past virtually all governments were headed by monarchs or emperors, in most modern societies governments are run by officials, who do not inherit their positions of power, but are elected or appointed on the basis of expertise and qualifications.

IDEOLOGY. Shared ideas or beliefs which serve to justify the interests of dominant groups. Ideologies are found in all societies in which there are systematic and engrained inequalities between groups. The concept of ideology connects closely with that of **power**, since ideological systems serve to legitimize the differential power which groups hold.

IMPERIALISM. The establishing of empires during the period of colonialism.

INDUSTRIALIZATION OF WAR. The application of modes of industrial production to weaponry, coupled with the organization of fighting forces as 'military machines'. The industrialization of war is as fundamental an aspect of the development of modern societies as is industry evolved for peaceful purposes. It is closely associated with the emergence of **total war** in the twentieth century – warfare involving hundreds of thousands or millions of soldiers, plus the overall mobilizing of the **economy** for war-related needs.

INFORMAL RELATIONS. Relations which exist in groups and organizations developed on the basis of personal connections; ways of doing things that depart from formally recognized modes of procedure.

INNER CITY. The areas composing the central neighbourhoods of a city, which normally have distinct characteristics from the **suburbs**. In many modern urban settings in the First World, inner-city areas are subject to dilapidation and decay, the more affluent residents having moved to outlying areas.

KINSHIP. A relation which links individuals through blood ties, **marriage**, or adoption. Kinship relations are by definition involved in marriage and the **family**, but extend much more broadly than these institutions. While in most modern societies few social obligations are involved in kinship relations extending beyond the immediate family, in many other cultures kinship is of vital importance for most aspects of social life.

MAGIC. Rites which attempt to influence spirits or supernatural beings in order to achieve human aims. In most societies, magic exists in a relation of some tension with religion. In contrast to religion, magic tends to be more of an 'individual' activity, practised by a sorcerer or **Shaman**.

MARRIAGE. A socially approved sexual relationship between two individuals. Marriage almost always involves two persons of opposite sexes, but in some cultures types of homosexual marriage are tolerated. Marriage normally forms the basis of a **family of procreation** – that is, it is expected that the married couple will produce and bring up children. Many societies permit **polygamous** marriage, in which an individual may have several spouses at the same time.

MENTAL ILLNESS. Disorder of the personality or mental processes. Psychiatrists recognize two general types of mental disorder, neuroses (milder forms of illness, such as anxiety states) and psychoses (more serious forms of disturbance, in which individuals lose touch with reality as defined by the majority of the population). How far mental illness has an organic basis – and how far it should be regarded as an 'illness' at all – are disputed matters.

MILITARY RULE. Government by military leaders, rather than by elected officials. Military governments have existed in many parts of the world in the current century. There are several types of military rule; in some instances the military tends to govern in a direct way, while in others government is conducted by officials appointed by, and directly responsible to, military leaders.

NATION-STATE. A particular type of **state**, characteristic of the modern world, in which a government has sovereign power within a defined territorial area, and the mass of the population are **citizens** who know themselves to be part of a single nation. Nation-states are closely associated with the rise of **nationalism**, although nationalist loyalties do not always conform to the boundaries of specific states that exist today. Nation-states developed as part of an emerging nation-state system, originating in Europe, but in current times spanning the whole globe.

NORMS. Rules of conduct which specify appropriate behaviour in a given range of social contexts. A norm either prescribes a given type of behaviour, or forbids it. All human groups follow definite types of norm, which are always backed by sanctions of one kind or another – varying from informal disapproval to physical punishment or execution.

OBJECTIVITY. In common with those working in the natural sciences, sociologists seek to be objective in assessing the results of studies of the social world. Objectivity means giving rival interpretations a 'fair hearing' – that is, striving as far as possible to reduce or eliminate bias in the interpretation of findings. A crucial dimension of objectivity, however, is that the conclusions drawn by any particular author are open to critical assessment by other members of the social scientific community.

ORGANIZATION. A large group of individuals, involving a definite set of authority relations. Many types of organization exist in industrial societies, influencing most aspects of our lives. While not all organizations are bureaucratic, there are quite close links between the development of organizations and bureaucratic tendencies.

PATRIARCHY. The dominance of men over women. All known societies are patriarchal, although there are many variations in the degree and nature of the power men exercise, as compared to women. One of the prime objectives of women's movements in modern societies is to combat existing patriarchal institutions.

POLITICS. The means by which power is employed to influence the nature and content of governmental activities. The sphere of the 'political' includes the activities of those in **government**, but also the actions of many other groups and individuals. There are many ways in which people outside the governmental apparatus seek to influence it.

POST-INDUSTRIAL SOCIETY. A notion advocated by those who believe that processes of social change are taking us beyond the industrialized order. A post-industrial society is one based on the production of information, rather than on the production of material goods. According to those who favour this concept, we are currently experiencing a series of social changes as profound as those which initiated the industrial era some two hundred years ago.

POWER. The ability of individuals, or the members of a group, to achieve aims or further the interests they hold. Power is a pervasive aspect of all human relationships. Many **conflicts** in society are struggles over power, because how much power an individual or group is able to achieve governs how far they are able to put their wishes into practice at the expense of those of others.

PREJUDICE. The holding of preconceived ideas about an individual or group, ideas that are resistant to change even in the face of new information. Prejudice may be either positive or negative.

RACISM. The attributing of characteristics of superiority or inferiority to a population sharing certain physically inherited characteristics. Racism is one specific form of prejudice, focusing on physical variations between people. Racist attitudes became entrenched during the period of Western colonial expansion, but seem also to rest on mechanisms of prejudice and discrimination found in very many contexts of human societies.

REBELLION. A revolt against the political authorities, involving the use, or threat, of force. Rebellions, unlike **revolutions**, are mainly aimed at removing particular rulers or regimes, rather than bringing about structural change in a society.

RELIGION. A set of beliefs adhered to by the members of a community, involving **symbols** regarded with a sense of awe or wonder, together with **ritual** practices in which members of the community engage. Religions do not universally involve a belief in supernatural entities. Although distinctions between religion and **magic** are difficult to draw, it is often held that magic is primarily practised by individuals rather than being the focus of community ritual.

RESEARCH METHODS. The diverse methods of investigation used to gather empirical (factual) material. Numerous different research methods exist in sociology, but perhaps the most commonly used are field-work (or **participant observation**) and **survey** methods. For many purposes it is useful to combine two or more methods within a single research project.

REVOLUTION. A process of political change, involving the mobilizing of a mass **social movement**, which by the use of violence successfully overthrows an existing regime and forms a new government. A revolution is distinguished from a *coup d'état* because it involves a mass movement and the occurrence of major change in the political system as a whole. A *coup d'état* refers to the seizure of power through the use of arms by individuals who then replace the existing political leaders, but without otherwise radically transforming the governmental system. Revolutions can also be distinguished from **rebellions**, which involve challenges to the existing political authorities, but again aim at the replacement of personnel rather than the transformation of the political structure as such.

RITUAL. Formalized modes of behaviour in which the members of a group or community regularly engage. **Religion** represents one of the main contexts in which rituals are practised, but the scope of ritual behaviour extends well beyond this particular sphere. Most groups have ritual practices of some kind or another.

SCIENCE. Science, in the sense of physical science, is the systematic study of the physical world. Science involves the disciplined marshalling of empirical data, combined with the construction of **theoretical approaches** and **theories** which illuminate or explain those data. Scientific activity combines the creation of boldly new modes of thought with the careful testing of **hypotheses** and ideas. One major feature which helps distinguish science from other types of idea system (such as that involved in religion) is the assumption that *all* scientific ideas are open to mutual criticism and revision on the part of the members of the scientific community.

SECULARIZATION. A process of decline in the influence of religion. Although modern societies have become increasingly secularized, tracing the extent of secularization is a complex matter. Secularization can refer to levels of involvement with religious organizations (such as rates of church attendance), the social and material influence wielded by religious organizations, and the degree to which people hold religious beliefs.

SELF-CONSCIOUSNESS. Awareness of one's distinct social identity, as a person separate from others. Human beings are not born with self-consciousness, but acquire an awareness of self as a result of early **socialization**. The learning of language is of vital importance to the processes by which the child learns to become a self-conscious being.

SOCIAL CHANGE. Alteration in basic structures of social group or society. Social change is an ever-present phenomenon in social life, but has become especially intense in the modern era. The origins of modern **sociology** can be traced to attempts to understand the dramatic changes shattering the traditional world and promoting new forms of **social order**.

SOCIAL EVOLUTIONISM. An approach to social change which draws upon concepts and ideas from evolutionary theory in biology. Although evolutionary thought was particularly influential in sociology in the nineteenth century, evolutionary ideas have continued to exert some influence in contemporary sociology. There are many versions of sociological evolutionism, but most such theories hold that human societies move progressively from simple to more complex forms of association.

SOCIAL GROUPS. Collections of individuals who interact in systematic ways with one another. Groups may range from very small associations to large-scale **organizations** or **societies**. Whatever their size, it is a defining feature of a group that its members have an awareness of a common identity. Most of our lives are spent in group contact; in modern societies, most people belong to numerous different types of group.

SOCIAL INSTITUTION. Basic modes of social activity followed by the majority of the members of a given society. Institutions involve **norms** and **values** to which large numbers of individuals conform, and all institutionalized modes of behaviour are protected by strong sanctions. Institutions form the 'bedrock' of a society, because they represent relatively fixed modes of behaviour which endure over time.

SOCIAL MOBILITY. Movement of individuals or groups between different social positions. **Vertical mobility** refers to movement up or down a hierarchy in a stratification system. **Lateral mobility** is physical movement of individuals or groups from one region to another. When analysing vertical mobility, sociologists distinguish between how far an individual is mobile in the course of his or her own career, and how far the position which the person reaches differs from that of his or her parents.

SOCIAL MOVEMENT. A large grouping of people who have become involved in seeking to accomplish, or to block, a process of **social change**. Social movements normally exist in relations of **conflict** with **organizations**, whose objectives and outlook they frequently oppose. However, movements which successfully challenge for power, once they become institutionalized, can develop into organizations.

SOCIAL POSITION. The social identity an individual has in a given group or society. Social positions may be very general in nature (such as those associated with **gender** roles) or may be much more specific (as in the case of occupational positions).

SOCIAL ROLE. The expected behaviour of an individual occupying a particular **social position**. The idea of social role originally comes from the theatre, referring to the parts which actors play in a stage production. In every society individuals play a number of different social roles, according to the varying contexts of their activities.

SOCIAL STRATIFICATION. The existence of structured inequalities between groups in society, in terms of their access to material or symbolic rewards. While all societies involve some forms of stratification, only with the development of state-based systems do wide differences in wealth and power arise. The most distinctive form of stratification in modern societies involves **class** divisions.

SOCIAL STRUCTURE. Social structure refers to the fact that societies do not consist of random actions, but have a stable, organized character. The structure of a society refers to the underlying regularities, or patternings, of the social relationships in which people engage. Social structure can be pictured like the girders of a building, or the skeleton of the body, but we have to be very careful about pushing this kind of analogy too far. Societies only have distinct patterns of organization in so far as people regularly repeat activities in the different contexts of social life. Structural features of society strongly influence our behaviour as individuals; at the same time, in our actions we recreate – and also to some extent alter – those structural characteristics.

dozen people. Others are very large, involving many millions – modern Chinese society, for instance, has a population of more than a billion individuals.

SOCIOLOGY.   The study of human groups and societies, giving particular emphasis to the analysis of the industrialized world. Sociology is one of a group of social sciences, which include also anthropology, economics, political science and human geography. The divisions between the various social sciences are not clear-cut, and all share a certain range of common interests, concepts and methods.

THE STATE.   A **political apparatus** (**government** institutions, plus civil service **officials**) ruling over a given territorial order, whose authority is backed by **law** and the ability to use **force**. Not all societies are characterized by the existence of a state. Hunting and gathering cultures, and smaller agrarian societies, lack state institutions. The emergence of the state marks a distinctive transition in human history, because the centralization of political power involved in state formation introduces new dynamics into processes of **social change**.

STATUS.   The social honour or prestige which a particular group is accorded by other members of a society. Status groups normally involve distinct styles of life – patterns of behaviour which the members of a group follow. Status privilege may be positive or negative. 'Pariah' status groups are regarded with disdain, or treated as outcasts, by the majority of the population.

THEORETICAL APPROACH.   A perspective on social life derived from a particular theoretical tradition. Some of the major theoretical traditions in sociology include **functionalism, structuralism, symbolic interactionism** and **Marxism**. Theoretical approaches supply overall 'perspectives' within which sociologists work, and influence the areas of their research as well as the modes in which research problems are identified and tackled.

THEORY.   An attempt to identify general properties which explain regularly observed events. The construction of theories forms an essential element of all sociological work. While theories tend to be linked to broader **theoretical approaches**, they are also strongly influenced by the research results they help generate.

THE UNCONSCIOUS.   Motives and ideas unavailable to the conscious mind of the individual. A key psychological mechanism involved in the unconscious is repression – parts of the mind are 'blocked off' from an individual's direct awareness. According to Freud's theory, unconscious wishes and impulses established in childhood continue to play a major part in the life of the adult.

URBAN ECOLOGY.   An approach to the study of urban life based on an analogy with the adjustment of plants and organisms to the physical environment. According to ecological theorists, the various neighbourhoods and zones within cities are formed as a result of natural processes of adjustment on the part of urban populations as they compete for resources.

VALUES.   Ideas held by human individuals or groups about what is desirable, proper, good or bad. Differing values represent key aspects of variations in human **culture**. What individuals value is strongly influenced by the specific culture in which they happen to live.

WORK.   The activity by which human beings produce from the natural world and so ensure their survival. Work should not be thought of exclusively as paid employment. In traditional cultures, there was only a rudimentary monetary system, and very few people worked for money payments. In modern societies, there remain many types of work which do and zones within cities are formed as a result of natural processes of adjustment on the part of urban populations as they compete for resources.

VALUES.   Ideas held by human individuals or groups about what is desirable, proper, good or bad. Differing values represent key aspects of variations in human **culture**. What individuals value is strongly influenced by the specific culture in which they happen to live.

WORK.   The activity by which human beings produce from the natural world and so ensure their survival. Work should not be thought of exclusively as paid employment. In traditional cultures, there was only a rudimentary monetary system, and very few people worked for money payments. In modern societies, there remain many types of work which do not involve direct payment of wages or salary (such as housework).

WORLD SYSTEM.   A social system of global dimensions, linking all societies within a world social order. The world system may most easily be thought of as a 'single global society'. The world system has only come into being since the period of the expansion of the West from about the seventeenth century onwards. Today, however, the existence of an increasingly integrated world system is one of the most important features affecting the lives of most individuals.

Glossary of Important Terms

Words in bold type within entries refer to concepts or terms found elsewhere in the glossaries.

ABSOLUTE POVERTY. Poverty as defined in terms of the minimal requirements necessary to sustain a healthy existence.

ACTION-REACTION. An aspect of the arms race, in which each side develops its defence strategy and spending in relation to the anticipated response of the others.

ADAPTATION. Refers to the ability of a biological organism to survive within a given environment.

AFFECTIVE INDIVIDUALISM. The belief in romantic attachment as a basis for contracting **marriage** ties.

AFFIRMATIVE ACTION. Reforms designed to reduce inequalities by the taking of positive steps to ensure the representation of minorities in educational and other organizations.

AGE-GRADES. The system found in many small, traditional cultures, according to which individuals belonging to a similar age-group are categorized together, and hold similar rights and obligations.

AGEISM. **Discrimination** or prejudice against a person on the grounds of age.

AGENCIES OF SOCIALIZATION. Groups or social contexts within which significant processes of **socialization** take place.

AGGREGATE. A collection of people present in a public setting, all going their separate ways rather than composing a solidary group.

AGRARIAN SOCIETIES. Societies whose means of subsistence is based on agricultural production (crop-growing).

AGRIBUSINESS. The mass production of agricultural goods on the basis of mechanized agriculture.

AIDS. A disease that attacks the auto-immune system of the body.

ALIENATION. The sense that our own abilities, as human beings, are taken over by other entities. The term was originally used by Marx to refer to the projection of human powers on to gods. Subsequently he employed the term to refer to the loss of control on the part of workers over the nature of the labour task, and over the products of their labour.

ALTERATIVE MOVEMENT. A movement concerned to alter individuals' behaviour or consciousness.

ANDROGENITAL SYNDROME. An endocrinal abnormality which produces male-like genitals in individuals who have female hormonal make-up.

ANIMISM. A belief that events in the world are mobilized by the activities of spirits.

ANOMIE. A concept first brought into wide usage in sociology by Durkheim, referring to a situation in which social **norms** lose their hold over individual behaviour.

ANTHROPOLOGY. A social science, closely linked to sociology, which concentrates on the study of traditional cultures and on the **evolution** of the human species.

APARTHEID. The system of racial segregation established in South Africa.

ARMS RACE. A competition between two or more nations to achieve military superiority over the other or others.

ARMS TRADE. The selling of armaments for profit, whether carried on by **governments** or by private contractors.

ASSIMILATION. The acceptance of a minority group by a majority population, in which the group takes over the values and norms of the dominant **culture**.

AUTHORITARIAN PERSONALITY. A set of specific personality characteristics, involving a rigid and intolerant outlook and an inability to accept ambiguity.

AUTHORITARIAN PRAETORIANISM. A type of military rule in which the armed forces share leadership with non-military political officials.

AUTOCRATIC MILITARY RULE. Rule by a specific military leader, who concentrates power in his own hands.

AUTOMATION. Production processes monitored and controlled by machines with only minimal supervision from human beings.

BACK REGION. An area away from 'front region' performances, as specified by Erving Goffman, in which individuals are able to relax and behave in an informal way.

BUREAUCRACY. A type of **organization** marked by a clear hierarchy of authority, the existence of written rules of procedure, and staffed by full-time, salaried **officials**.

CAPITALISM. An economic system based on the private ownership of wealth, which is invested and reinvested in order to produce profit.

CAPITALISTS. Those who own companies, land or stocks and shares, using these to generate economic returns.

CARCERAL ORGANIZATION. An **organization** in which individuals are shut away for long periods of time from the outside world – such as a prison, mental hospital, army barrack or boarding school.

CASH-CROP PRODUCTION. Production of crops sold on world markets, rather than being consumed by the local population.

CASTE. A form of stratification in which an individual's social position is fixed at birth and cannot be changed. There is virtually no inter-marriage between the members of different caste groups.

CAUSAL RELATIONSHIP. A relationship whereby one state of affairs (the effect) is brought about by another (the cause).

CHURCH. A large body of people belonging to an established religious organization. The term is also used to refer to the place in which religious ceremonials are carried on.

CITIZEN. A member of a political community, having both rights and duties associated with that membership.

CIVIL INATTENTION. The process whereby individuals who are in the same physical setting of interaction demonstrate to one another that they are aware of each other's presence.

CIVIL RELIGION. Forms of ritual and belief similar to those involved in **religion**, but concerning secular activities – such as political parades or ceremonials.

CIVIL RIGHTS. Legal rights held by all **citizens** in a given national community.

CLAN. A kin group stretching more broadly than the family, found in many pre-industrial societies.

CLASS CONSCIOUSNESS. Awareness of the class system, including the class an individual believes him- or herself to be in, together with the imagery of the class system he or she possesses.

CLIENTSHIP. A system of patronage, in which services are available to specific individuals in positions of influence or power. Those 'patrons' tie others to them by means of the rewards they control.

CLOCK TIME. Time as measured by the clock – that is, assessed in terms of hours, minutes or seconds. Before the invention of clocks, time-reckoning was based on events in the natural world, such as the rising and setting of the sun.

CLOSED DOMESTICATED NUCLEAR FAMILY. The **nuclear family** system characteristic of modern West, in which the domestic unit is largely separate from the surrounding community.

COGNITION. Human thought processes involving perception, reasoning and remembering.

COHABITATION. Two people living together in a sexual relationship of some permanence, without being married to one another.

COLLECTIVE CONSUMPTION. A concept used by Manuel Castells to refer to processes of urban consumption – such as the buying and selling of property.

COLONIALISM. The process whereby Western nations established their rule in parts of the world away from their home territories.

COMMON-SENSE BELIEFS. Widely shared beliefs about the social or natural worlds held by lay members of society.

COMMUNISM. A set of political ideas associated with Marx, as developed particularly by Lenin, and institutionalized in the Soviet Union, Eastern Europe and in some Third World countries.

COMPARATIVE QUESTIONS. Questions concerned with the drawing of comparisons between different human societies for the purposes of sociological **theory** or research.

COMPETITION. A concept used in ecology to refer to the struggle of different species to occupy the most advantageous locations in a given territory.

CONCESSION COMPANIES. European companies which established themselves in colonial areas on the basis of exclusive rights of production in a given area or industry.

CONCRETE OPERATIONAL STAGE. A stage of cognitive development, as formulated by Piaget, in which the child's thinking is based primarily upon physical perception of the world. In this phase, the child is not yet capable of dealing with abstract concepts or hypothetical situations.

CONGLOMERATES. Corporations made up of companies producing or trading in a variety of different products and services.

CONSTITUTIONAL MONARCH. A king or queen who is largely a 'figurehead', real power resting in the hands of other political leaders.

CONTRADICTION. A term used by Marx to refer to mutually antagonistic tendencies in a society.

CONTRADICTORY CLASS LOCATIONS. Positions in the class structure, particularly involving routine white-collar and lower managerial jobs, which share characteristics of the class positions both above and below them.

CONTROL. A statistical or experimental means of holding some **variables** constant in order to examine the causal influence of others.

CONURBATION. An agglomeration of towns or cities into an unbroken urban environment.

CONVERGENCE. The term for the thesis that the more economically developed a society becomes, the more it resembles other industrialized countries.

CONVERSATION. Verbal communication between two or more individuals.

CONVERSATION ANALYSIS. The empirical study of conversations, employing techniques drawn from **ethnomethodology**.

CORE. The core countries in the world economy are those which occupy a central position as a result of being most fully industrialized (they include primarily the USA, Western Europe and Japan).

CORPORATENESS. A sense of belonging to a body of people having a similar outlook to one's own.

CORPORATIONS. Business firms or companies.

CORRELATION COEFFICIENT. A measure of the degree of correlation between variables.

COUNTER-INTUITIVE THINKING. Thinking which suggests ideas contrary to common-sense assumptions.

COUP D'ÉTAT. An armed takeover of **government**. Unlike in the case of **revolutions**, no mass **social movement** is involved.

CRIMES OF THE POWERFUL. Criminal activity carried out by those in positions of power.

CRIMINAL NETWORK. A network of social relations between individuals engaging in criminal activities.

CRITICAL SITUATIONS. Social circumstances in which individuals are compelled to cope with radically new demands, which put a strain upon their existing behaviour and attitudes.

CROWD ACTIVITY. Actions carried on by individuals when associated together as a crowd.

CULT. A fragmentary religious grouping, to which individuals are loosely affiliated, but which lacks any permanent structure.

CULTURAL PLURALISM. The coexistence of several sub-cultures within a given society on equal terms.

CULTURAL UNIVERSALS. **Values** or modes of behaviour shared by all human cultures.

DECARCERATION. The release of large numbers of individuals from mental hospitals and prisons to live in the outside world.

DEMOCRACY. A political system that allows the citizens to participate in political decision-making, or to elect representatives to government bodies.

DEMOCRATIC CENTRALISM. A mode of political organization characteristic of Eastern Europe and the Soviet Union, which takes the form of a pyramid of electoral bodies. Those in groups at each level elect representatives to groups at higher levels, who in turn elect representatives to yet higher-level organizations.

DEMOCRATIC ELITISM.   A theory of the limits of **democracy**, which holds that democratic participation in large-scale societies is necessarily limited to the regular election of political leaders.

DEMOGRAPHY.   The study of population

DENOMINATION.   A religious **sect** which has lost its revivalist dynamism, and has become an institutionalized body, commanding the adherence of significant numbers of people.

DEPENDENCY THEORY.   The term for the thesis that a range of countries, particularly in the **Third World**, lack the ability to control major aspects of their economic life, because of the dominance of the industrialized societies in the world economy.

DEPENDENT VARIABLE.   A **variable** or factor causally influenced by another (the **independent variable**).

DETERRENCE.   The prevention of military conflict on the basis of ensuring that an aggressor would suffer too many losses to make the initiation of hostilities worthwhile.

DEVIANT SUB-CULTURE.   A sub-culture the values of whose members differ substantially from those of the majority in a society.

DEVELOPMENTAL QUESTIONS.   Questions which sociologists pose when looking at the origins and path of development of **social institutions** from the past to the present.

DIALECTICAL INTERPRETATION OF CHANGE.   An interpretation of change emphasizing the clash of opposing influences or groups as the motor of social transformation.

DIFFERENTIAL ASSOCIATION.   An interpretation of the development of criminal behaviour proposed by Edwin H. Sutherland. According to him, criminal behaviour is learnt through association with others who regularly engage in crime.

DIFFERENTIATION.   The development of increasing complexity within organic systems or societies.

DISEQUILIBRIUM.   The break-down of social equilibrium or **consensus**.

DISPLACEMENT.   The transferring of ideas or emotions from their true source to another object.

DIVISION OF LABOUR.   The specialization of work tasks, by means of which different occupations are combined within a production system. All societies have at least some rudimentary form of division of labour, especially between the tasks allocated to men and those performed by women. With the development of industrialism, however, the division of labour becomes vastly more complex than in any prior type of production system. In the modern world, the division of labour is international in scope.

DOCUMENTARY RESEARCH.   Research based on evidence drawn from the study of documents, such as archives or official statistics.

DOMESTIC VIOLENCE.   Violent behaviour directed by one member of a household against another. Most serious domestic violence is carried out by males against females.

DOUBLING TIME.   The time it takes for a particular level of population to double.

DRAMATURGICAL MODEL. An approach to the study of social interaction based on the use of metaphors derived from the theatre.

ECOLOGICAL APPROACH. A perspective on urban analysis emphasizing the 'natural' distribution of city neighbourhoods into areas having contrasting characteristics.

ECONOMIC INTERDEPENDENCE. Refers to the fact that, in the **division of labour**, individuals depend on others to produce many or most of the goods they need to sustain their lives.

EDUCATIONAL SYSTEM. The system of educational provision operating within a given society.

EGOCENTRISM. The characteristic outlook of a child, according to Piaget, during the early years of its life. Egocentric thinking involves understanding objects and events in the environment solely in terms of the child's own position.

ELABORATED CODE. A form of speech involving the deliberate and constructed use of words to designate precise meanings.

EMPIRICAL INVESTIGATION. Factual enquiry carried out in any given area of sociological study.

ENDOGAMY. A system in which an individual may only marry another person from within the same kin group as herself or himself.

ENTREPRENEUR. The owner of a business firm.

ENVIRONMENTAL ECOLOGY. The term refers to a concern with preserving the integrity of the physical environment in the face of the impact of modern industry and technology.

EPISODES OF CHANGE. Sequences of **social change** occurring in a similar way in several societies.

ESTATE. A form of stratification involving inequalities between groups of individuals established by law.

ETHICAL RELIGIONS. Religions which depend on the ethical appeal of a 'great teacher' (like Buddha or Confucius), rather than on a belief in supernatural beings.

ETHNOCENTRIC TRANSNATIONALS. **Transnational companies** largely run directly from the headquarters of the parent company.

ETHNOCENTRISM. The tendency to look at other cultures through the eyes of one's own culture, and thereby misrepresent them.

ETHNOMETHODOLOGY. The study of how people make sense of what others say and do in the course of day-to-day social interaction. Ethnomethodology is concerned with the 'ethno-methods' by means of which human beings sustain meaningful interchanges with one another.

EVOLUTION. The development of biological organisms by means of the adaptation of species to the demands of the physical environment.

EXOGAMY. A system in which individuals may only marry a spouse from a kinship group different from their own.

EXPERIMENT. A research method in which **variables** can be analysed in a controlled and systematic way, either in an artificial situation constructed by the researcher, or in naturally occurring settings.

EXPONENTIAL GROWTH. A geometric, rather than linear, rate of progression, producing a very fast rise in the numbers of a population experiencing such growth.

EXTENDED FAMILY. A family group consisting of more than two generations of relatives living either within the same household or very close to one another.

EXTERNAL ARENA. Countries which remain outside the world economy at any particular period of time.

FACTUAL QUESTIONS. Questions which raise issues concerning matters of fact (rather than theoretical or moral issues).

FAMILY. A group of individuals related to one another by blood ties, **marriage** or adoption, who form an economic unit, the adult members of which are responsible for the upbringing of children. All known societies involve some form of family system, although the nature of family relationships is widely variable. While in modern societies the main family form is the **nuclear family**, a variety of **extended family** relationships are also often found.

FAMILY CAPITALISM. Capitalistic enterprise owned and administered by entrepreneurial families.

FAMILY OF ORIENTATION. The family into which an individual is born.

FAMILY OF PROCREATION. The family an individual initiates through marriage or by having children.

FASCISM. A set of political ideas, or an actual political system, based on notions of the superiority of some races over others.

FECUNDITY. A measure of the number of children which it is biologically possible for a woman to produce.

FEMININITY. The characteristic forms of behaviour expected of women in any given culture.

FIELD OF ACTION. The arena within which **social movements** interact with established **organizations**, the ideas and outlook of the members of both thereby often becoming modified.

FIRST WORLD. The group of nation-states that possesses mature industrialized economies, based upon capitalistic production.

FOCUSED CROWD. A crowd of people acting in pursuit of common objectives.

FOCUSED INTERACTION. Interaction between individuals engaged in a common activity or a direct conversation with one another.

FORCE. Compulsion, based on the threat or actual use of violence.

FORCES OF PRODUCTION. A term used by Marx to refer to the factors promoting economic growth in a society.

FORDISM. The system of production pioneered by Henry Ford, involving the introduction of the assembly-line.

FORMAL OPERATIONAL PERIOD. A stage of cognitive development, according to Piaget's theory, at which the growing child becomes capable of handling abstract concepts and hypothetical situations.

FRONT REGION. A setting of social activity in which individuals seek to put on a definite 'performance' for others.

FUNCTIONALISM. A theoretical perspective based on the notion that social events can best be explained in terms of the functions they perform – that is, the contributions they make to the continuity of a society.

FUNDAMENTALISM. A belief in returning to the literal meanings of scriptural texts.

GANG. An informal group of individuals meeting regularly to engage in common activities, which may be outside the framework of the law.

GENERALIZED OTHER. A concept in the theory of G. H. Mead, according to which the individual takes over the general **values** of a given group or society during the **socialization** process.

GEOCENTRIC TRANSNATIONALS. Transnational companies whose administrative structure is global, rather than organized from any particular country.

GROSS NATIONAL PRODUCT (GNP). The amount of wealth produced in a country per year, usually measured as the average per head of population.

GROUP PRODUCTION. Production organized by means of small groups rather than individuals.

GUERRILLA MOVEMENT. A non-governmental military **organization**.

HEADQUARTERS CITY. A city which has a co-ordinating role in the international **division of labour** – a headquarters of world finance or commerce.

HEALTH-CARE SYSTEM. The organization of medical services in a given country.

HETEROSEXUALITY. An orientation in sexual activity or feelings towards people of the opposite sex.

HIDDEN CURRICULUM. Traits of behaviour or attitudes that are learned at school, but which are not included within the formal curriculum. The hidden curriculum is the 'unstated agenda' involved in schooling – teaching, for example, aspects of gender differences.

HIGH-TRUST SYSTEMS. Organizations, or work settings, in which individuals are permitted a great deal of autonomy and control over the work task.

HIGHER EDUCATION. Education beyond school level, in colleges or universities.

HISTORICAL MATERIALISM. Marx's interpretation of **social change** in history, according to which processes of change are determined primarily by economic factors.

HISTORICITY. The use of an understanding of history as a basis for trying to change history – that is, producing informed processes of **social change**.

HOMOSEXUALITY. An orientation of sexual activities or feelings towards others of the same sex.

HOUSEWORK (domestic labour). Unpaid work carried on, usually by women, in the home, concerned with day-to-day domestic chores such as cooking, cleaning and shopping.

HUNTING AND GATHERING SOCIETIES. Societies whose mode of sub-sistence is gained from hunting animals, fishing and gathering edible plants.

HYPOTHESIS. An idea, or a guess, about a given state of affairs, put forward as a basis for empirical testing.

IDEAL TYPE. A 'pure type', constructed by emphasizing certain traits of a given social item which do not necessarily exist anywhere in reality. An example is Max Weber's ideal type of bureaucratic **organization**.

INCOME. Payment, usually derived from wages, salaries or investments.

INDEPENDENT VARIABLE. A **variable** or factor which causally affects another (the **dependent variable**).

INDUSTRIAL DEMOCRACY. Modes of democratic participation or representation in the workplace.

INFANT MORTALITY RATE. The number of infants who die during the first year of life, per thousand live births.

THE INFORMAL ECONOMY. Economic transactions carried on outside the sphere of orthodox paid employment.

INFORMATION TECHNOLOGY. Forms of technology based on information processing and involving micro-electronic circuitry.

INNOVATION CENTRE. A city or town whose prosperity depends on being a centre of technological innovation or creativity.

INSTINCT. A fixed pattern of behaviour which has genetic origins and which appears in all normal animals within a given species.

INSTITUTIONAL CAPITALISM. Capitalistic enterprise organized on the basis of institutional shareholding.

INTELLIGENCE. Level of intellectual ability, particularly as measured by IQ (Intelligence Quotient) tests.

INTEREST GROUPS. Groups organized to pursue specific interests in the political arena, operating primarily by lobbying the members of legislative bodies.

INTERGENERATIONAL MOBILITY. Movement up or down a social stratification hierarchy from one generation to another.

INTERNATIONAL DIVISION OF LABOUR. The phrase refers to the interdependence of countries or regions which trade on global markets.

INTRAGENERATIONAL MOBILITY. Movement up or down a social stratification hierarchy within the course of a personal career.

INVASION. A notion used in ecology to refer to the intrusion of a new species into an area previously dominated by others.

IQ (Intelligence Quotient). A score attained on tests of symbolic or reasoning abilities.

KIBBUTZIM. Communities established in Israel in which production is carried on co-operatively and inequalities of wealth and income are kept to a minimum.

LABELLING THEORY. An approach to the study of **deviance** which suggests that people become 'deviant' because certain labels are attached to their behaviour by political authorities and others.

LATENT FUNCTIONS. Functional consequences which are not intended or recognized by the members of a social system in which they occur.

LATERAL MOBILITY. Movement of individuals from one region of a country to another, or across countries.

LAW. A rule of behaviour established by a political authority and backed by state power.

LEGITIMACY. The belief that a particular political order is just and valid.

LEGITIMATION CRISIS. The failure of a political order to generate a sufficient level of commitment and involvement on the part of its **citizens** to be able properly to govern.

LESBIANISM. Homosexual activities or attachment between women.

LIBERAL DEMOCRACY. A system of **democracy** based on parliamentary institutions, coupled to the free market system in the area of economic production.

LIFE EXPECTANCY. The number of further years which people at any given age can on average expect to live.

LIFE HISTORIES. Studies of the overall lives of individuals, often based both on self-reporting and documents such as letters.

LIFE SPAN. The maximum length of life that is biologically possible for a member of a given species.

LIMITED WAR. Warfare involving relatively small numbers of the population, and fought principally by soldiers.

LITERACY. The ability of individuals to read and write.

LOCAL KNOWLEDGE. Knowledge of a local community, or context of action, possessed by individuals who spend long periods of their lives in them.

LOW-TRUST SYSTEMS. An **organizational** or work setting in which individuals are allowed little responsibility for, or control over, the work task.

MACHINE PRODUCTION. Economic production carried on through the use of machinery driven by inanimate sources of power.

MACROSEGREGATION. Segregation between very large numbers of the members of different racial groups, separated territorially.

MACROSOCIOLOGY. The study of large-scale groups, **organizations** or social systems.

MALE INEXPRESSIVENESS. The difficulties men have in expressing, or talking about, their feelings to others.

MALTHUSIANISM. A doctrine about population dynamics developed by Thomas Malthus, according to which population increase comes up against 'natural limits', represented by famine and war.

MANAGEMENT OF VIOLENCE. The mode in which the military, together with armaments, are organized within a given society, in respect of their relation to the civil authorities.

MANAGERIAL CAPITALISM. Capitalistic enterprises administered by managerial executives, rather than by owners.

MANIFEST FUNCTIONS. The functions of an aspect or type of social activity which are known to, and intended by, the individuals involved in a given situation of social life.

MARXISM. A body of thought deriving its main elements from Marx's ideas.

MASCULINITY. The characteristic forms of behaviour expected of men in any given culture.

MASS CIRCULATION. The large-scale audiences reached by modern media of communication, such as newspapers or television.

MASS MEDIA. Forms of communication, such as newspapers, magazines, radio or television designed to reach mass audiences.

MATERIALIST CONCEPTION OF HISTORY. The view developed by Marx, according to which 'material' or economic factors have a prime role in determining historical change.

MATERNAL DEPRIVATION. The situation in which infants or very young children are deprived of close contact with the mother for a period of several weeks or longer.

MATRILINEAL INHERITANCE. The inheritance of property or titles through the female line.

MATRILOCAL FAMILY. A family system in which the husband is expected to live near to the wife's parents.

MEAN. A statistical measure of 'central tendency' or average based on dividing a total by the number of individual cases involved.

MEANINGFUL ACTIVITIES. Human action which is carried out for definite reasons, and with specific purposes in mind. The vast bulk of human behaviour is composed of meaningful activities, this being one of the main characteristics which separates human conduct from the movement of objects and events in the natural world.

MEANS OF PRODUCTION.   The means whereby the production of material goods is carried on in a society, including not just technology but the social relations between producers.

MEDIAN.   The number that falls halfway in a range of numbers – a way of calculating 'central tendency' which is sometimes more useful than calculating a **mean**.

MEGALOPOLIS.   The 'city of all cities' in ancient Greece – used in modern times to refer to very large **conurbations**.

MELTING POT.   The idea that ethnic differences can be combined to create new patterns of behaviour drawing on diverse cultural sources.

MEZZOSEGREGATION.   Segregation between racial groups in terms of areas of neighbourhood residence.

MICROSEGREGATION.   Segregation between racial groups enforced in the details of daily life – for example separate waiting rooms in bus or railway stations.

MICROSOCIOLOGY.   The study of human behaviour in contexts of face-to-face interaction.

MIDDLE CLASS.   A social class composed broadly of those working in white-collar and lower managerial occupations.

MILITARY–INDUSTRIAL COMPLEX.   A set of institutional connections between business firms and the armed forces, based upon common interests in weapons production.

MILITARY MIND.   A concept used by Samuel Huntington to refer to the typical outlook which the soldier has towards the world.

MILLENARIANISM.   Beliefs held by the members of certain types of religious movement, according to which cataclysmic changes will occur in the near future, heralding the arrival of a new epoch.

MINORITY GROUP (OR ETHNIC MINORITY).   A group of people, in a minority in a given society who, because of their distinct physical or cultural characteristics, find themselves in situations of inequality within that society.

MOBILIZATION.   The 'gearing up' of groups for collective action.

MODE.   The number that appears most often in a given set of data. This can sometimes be a helpful way of portraying central tendency.

MODULE PRODUCTION PLACE.   An urban area in which parts are made for products whose final assembly is carried out elsewhere.

MONOGAMY.   A form of marriage in which each married partner is allowed only one spouse at any given time.

MONOPOLY.   A situation in which a single firm dominates in a given industry.

MONOTHEISM.   Belief in a single god.

MULTILINEAR EVOLUTION.   An interpretation of social evolution which holds that there are varying 'paths' of evolutionary development followed by different societies.

MULTIPLE SOVEREIGNTY.   A situation in which there is no single sovereign power in a society.

MUTATION.   A process of random genetic change introducing an alteration in the physical characteristics of an animal or plant. The vast majority of mutations lead 'nowhere' in the course of **evolution** – that is the mutant organisms fail to survive. In a tiny proportion of cases, however, mutation produces characteristics which allow new species to flourish.

NATIONALISM. A set of beliefs and **symbols** expressing identification with a given national community.

NATION-STATE. A particular type of **state**, characteristic of the modern world, in which a government has sovereign power within a defined territorial area, and the mass of the population are **citizens** who know themselves to be part of a single nation. Nation-states are closely associated with the rise of **nationalism**, although nationalist loyalties do not always conform to the boundaries of specific states that exist today. Nation-states developed as part of an emerging nation-state system, originating in Europe, but in current times spanning the whole globe.

NEO-IMPERIALISM. The dominance of some nations over others by means of unequal conditions of economic exchange. Neo-imperialism, unlike older empires, is not founded upon the direct imposition of political power by one society upon another. The most important global context in which relations of neo-imperialism are established are between industrialized societies and the **Third World** countries.

NEO-LOCAL RESIDENCE. A family pattern in which the married couple sets up home away from the place of residence of either the bride's or the husband's parents.

NEUROTIC. An individual suffering from a relatively mild form of mental disorder, such as an anxiety state.

NEWLY INDUSTRIALIZING COUNTRIES. **Third World** countries which over the past two or three decades have begun to develop a strong industrial base, such as Singapore or Hong Kong.

NON-STATE ACTORS. International agencies, other than states, which play a part in the world system.

NON-VERBAL COMMUNICATION. Communication between individuals based on facial expression or bodily gesture, rather than on the use of language.

NUCLEAR FAMILY. A family group consisting of wife, husband (or one of these) and dependent children.

OCCUPATION. Any form of paid employment in which an individual works in a regular way.

OEDIPUS COMPLEX. A phase of early human psychological development, according to Freud, in which the child experiences intense feeling of love for the mother, together with hatred for the father. The overcoming of the Oedipus complex marks a key transition, in Freud's view, in the development of the child as an autonomous being.

OFFICIALS. Individuals who occupy formal positions in large-scale **organizations**.

OLIGARCHIC MILITARY RULE. **Government** headed by a small group of top officers in the armed forces.

OLIGARCHY. Rule by a small minority within an organization or society.

OLIGOPOLY. A situation in which a small number of firms dominates in a given industry.

OPEN LINEAGE FAMILY. A family system found in traditional Europe, in which domestic relationships are closely intertwined with the local community.

ORGANIZATION. A large group of individuals, involving a definite set of authority relations. Many types of organization exist in industrial societies, influencing most aspects of our lives. While not all organizations are bureaucratic, there are quite close links between the development of organizations and bureaucratic tendencies.

ORGANIZED CRIME. Criminal activities carried out by organizations established as businesses.

PACIFISM.   The belief that war is morally wrong.

PARIAH GROUPS.   Groups who suffer from negative **status discrimination** – in other words, are 'looked down on' by most other members of society. The Jews have been a pariah group throughout much of European history.

PARTICIPANT OBSERVATION (field-work).   A method of research widely used in sociology and anthropology, in which the researcher takes part in the activities of a group or community being studied.

PARTICIPATORY DEMOCRACY.   A system of democracy in which all members of a group or community participate collectively in the taking of major decisions.

PASTORAL SOCIETIES.   Societies whose subsistence derives from the rearing of domesticated animals.

PATRILINEAL INHERITANCE.   The inheritance of property or titles through the male line.

PATRILOCAL FAMILY.   A family system in which the wife is expected to live near to the husband's parents.

PEASANTS.   People who produce food from the land, using traditional farming methods.

PEER GROUP.   A friendship group composed of individuals of similar age and social status.

PERIPHERY.   The term refers to countries which have a marginal role in the world economy, and are thus dependent on the 'core' producing societies for their trading relationships.

PERSONAL DISTANCE.   The physical space individuals maintain between themselves and others when they know them on a personal basis.

PLURAL SOCIETY.   A society in which several ethnic groupings coexist, each living in communities or regions largely separate from the others.

PLURALIST THEORIES OF DEMOCRACY.   Theories which emphasize the role of diverse and competing interest groups in preventing too much power being accumulated in the hands of political leaders.

POLITICAL APPARATUS.   A set of governmental **organizations** making possible the regular political administration of a given territorial area.

POLITICAL PARTY.   An organization established with the aim of achieving governmental power and using that power to pursue a specific programme.

POLITICAL RIGHTS.   Rights of political participation, such as the right to vote in local and national elections, held by **citizens** of a given national community.

POLYANDRY.   A form of **marriage** in which a woman may simultaneously have two or more husbands.

POLYCENTRIC TRANSNATIONALS.   **Transnational corporations** run from two or several main administrative centres in different countries.

POLYGAMY.   A form of **marriage** in which a person may have two or more spouses simultaneously.

POLYGYNY.   A form of **marriage** in which a man may have more than one wife at the same time.

POLYTHEISM.   Belief in two or more gods.

POSITIVISM. A philosophical position according to which there are close ties between the social and natural sciences, which share a common logical framework.

POWER ELITE. Small networks of individuals who, according to the interpretation of C. Wright Mills, hold concentrated power in modern societies.

PRE-OPERATIONAL STAGE. A stage of cognitive development, in Piaget's theory, in which the child has advanced sufficiently to master basic modes of logical thought.

PRESTIGE. The respect accorded to an individual or group in virtue of their **status**.

PRIMARY GROUP. A group of individuals standing in a personal relationship to one another.

PRIMARY LABOUR MARKET. The term refers to the economic position of groups of individuals who have secure jobs and good conditions of work.

PRIMARY SECTOR. That part of a modern economy based on the gathering or extraction of natural resources (including agricultural production).

PRIVATE HEALTH CARE. Health-care services available only to those who pay the full cost of them.

PROFANE. That which belongs to the mundane, everyday world.

PROFESSIONALS. Occupants of jobs requiring high-level educational qualifications, whose behaviour is subject to codes of conduct laid down by central bodies (or professional associations).

PROJECTION. The attributing to others of feelings that one actually has oneself.

PROPHETS. Religious leaders who mobilize followers through their interpretation of sacred texts.

PROSTITUTION. The sale of sexual favours.

PSYCHOANALYSIS. The technique of psychotherapy invented by Sigmund Freud. The word 'psychoanalysis' has also come to be used for the intellectual system of psychological theory that Freud constructed.

PSYCHOPATH. A specific personality type; such individuals lack the moral sense and concern for others held by most normal people.

PSYCHOTIC. An individual suffering from a serious mental disorder.

PUBLIC DISTANCE. The physical space individuals maintain between themselves and others when engaged in a public performance, such as giving a lecture.

PUBLIC HEALTH CARE. Health-care services available to all members of the population, supported by government funding.

RACE. Differences in human physical stock regarded as categorizing large numbers of individuals together.

RAPE. The threat, or use, of force to compel one individual to engage in a sexual act with another.

RATIONALIZATION. A concept used by Weber to refer to the process by which modes of precise calculation and organization, involving abstract rules and procedures, increasingly come to dominate the social world.

REDEMPTIVE MOVEMENT. A **social movement** aiming to produce a return to a past state of affairs believed to be superior to the current one.

REFORMATIVE MOVEMENT. A **social movement** concerned to implement a practical, but limited programme of **social change**.

REGIONALIZATION. The division of social life into different regional settings or zones.

RELATIVE DEPRIVATION. Feelings of deprivation relative to a group with which an individual compares him- or herself.

RELATIVE POVERTY. Poverty defined by reference to the living standards of the majority in any given society.

REPRESENTATIVE MULTI-PARTY DEMOCRACY. A democratic system based on the existence of two or more political parties, in which voters elect political leaders to represent them.

REPRESENTATIVE ONE-PARTY DEMOCRACY. A democratic system involving a single party, in which voters elect candidates from the party to represent them in government.

REPRODUCTIVE TECHNOLOGIES. Techniques of influencing the human reproductive process.

RESIDUAL RULE-BREAKING. The transgressing of **norms** which control basic aspects of day-to-day **social interaction**.

RESOCIALIZATION. A pattern of personality change whereby a mature individual adopts modes of behaviour distinct from those he or she previously accepted.

RESPONSE CRIES. Seemingly involuntary exclamations individuals make when, for example, being taken by surprise, dropping something inadvertently, or expressing pleasure.

RESTRICTED CODE. A mode of speech which rests on strongly developed cultural understandings, such that many ideas do not need to be put into words.

RESTRICTED PATRIARCHAL FAMILY. A transitional **family** type found in Europe from the late seventeenth to the mid-nineteenth centuries, in which the domestic unit becomes largely separated from the external community and where the power of the father within the family circle is stressed.

RETIREMENT CENTRE. A city or town, normally having a favourable climate, to which many people move when they retire.

REVOLUTIONARY TERROR. The use of violence, or threat of its use, by revolutionary leaders to induce a compliant attitude towards their policies.

RIOT. An outbreak of illegal violence, directed against persons, property or both.

SACRED. Something which inspires attitudes of awe or reverence among believers in a given set of religious ideas.

SAMPLING. Taking a proportion of individuals or cases from a larger population, studied as representative of that population as a whole.

SANCTION. A mode of reward or punishment that reinforces socially expected forms of behaviour.

SCAPEGOATING. Blaming an individual or group for wrongs that were not of their doing.

SCHIZOPHRENIA. A serious form of **mental illness** in which an individual's sense of reality is distorted.

SCIENCE. The application of systematic methods of research, and careful logical analysis, to the study of objects, events or people; and the body of knowledge produced by such means.

SECOND WORLD. The industrialized, communist societies of Eastern Europe and the Soviet Union.

SECONDARY GROUP. A group of individuals who do not know one another intimately on a personal level.

SECONDARY LABOUR MARKET. Refers to the economic position of individuals who have insecure jobs and poor conditions of work.

SECONDARY SECTOR. That part of an economy devoted to the manufacture of goods.

SECT. A religious movement which breaks away from orthodoxy.

SELF-ENLIGHTENMENT. The increased understanding which sociology can provide for people to understand the circumstances of their own actions.

SEMI-PERIPHERY. Countries which supply sources of labour and raw materials to the core industrial countries and the world economy, but are not themselves fully industrialized.

SEMIOTICS. The study of the ways in which non-linguistic phenomena can generate meaning – as in the example of a traffic light.

SENSORIMOTOR STAGE. A stage of human cognitive development, according to Piaget, in which the child's awareness of its environment is dominated by perception and touch.

SERIAL MONOGAMY. The practice of a person contracting several marriages in succession, but not having more than one spouse at any one time.

SERVICE INDUSTRIES. Industries concerned with the production of services rather than manufactured goods, such as the travel industry.

SEX. The biological and anatomical differences distinguishing females from males.

SEXISM. Attitudes or beliefs which falsely attribute, or deny, certain capacities to the members of one of the sexes, thereby justifying sexual inequalities.

SEXUAL ACTIVITY. Activity engaged in for the purpose of sexual gratification.

SEXUAL HARASSMENT. The making of unwanted sexual advances by one individual towards another, in which the first individual persists even though it is made clear that the other party is resistant.

SHAMAN. An individual believed to have special magical powers; a sorcerer or witch doctor.

SLAVERY. A form of social stratification in which some individuals are literally owned by others as their property.

SOCIAL CATEGORY. A statistical grouping of individuals who share a common trait – such as all the individuals in a given society earning a certain level of income.

SOCIAL CLOSURE. Practices by which groups separate themselves off from other groups.

SOCIAL CONSTRAINT. The term refers to the fact that the groups and societies of which we are a part exert a conditioning influence on our behaviour. Social constraint was regarded by Durkheim as one of the distinctive properties of 'social facts'.

SOCIAL DARWINISM. A view of social evolution emphasizing the importance of struggle or warfare between groups or societies as the motor of development.

SOCIAL DISTANCE. The level of spatial separation maintained when individuals interact with others whom they do not know well.

SOCIAL REPRODUCTION. The processes which sustain or perpetuate characteristics of social structure over periods of time.

SOCIAL RIGHTS. Rights of social and welfare provision held by all **citizens** in a given national community involving, for example, the right to claim unemployment benefit or sickness payments provided by the state.

SOCIAL SELF. The basis of self-consciousness in human individuals, according to the theory of G. H. Mead. The social self is the identity conferred upon an individual by the reactions of others. A person achieves self-consciousness by becoming aware of this social identity.

SOCIAL TRANSFORMATION. Processes of change in 'societies' or social systems.

SOCIALISM. A set of political ideas emphasizing the co-operative nature of modern industrial production and stressing the need to achieve an egalitarian social community.

SOCIOBIOLOGY. An approach which attempts to explain the behaviour of both animals and human beings in terms of biological principles.

THE SOCIOLOGICAL IMAGINATION. The application of imaginative thought to the asking and answering of sociological questions. The sociological imagination involves the individual in 'thinking herself or himself away' from the familiar routines of day-to-day life.

SOVEREIGNTY. The undisputed political rule of a **state** over a given territorial area.

STANDARD DEVIATION. A way of calculating the spread of a group of figures.

STANDING ARMY. A full-time, professional army having a relatively permanent existence.

STATE OVERLOAD. A **theory** which holds that modern states face major difficulties as a result of being overburdened with complex administrative decisions.

STATE SOCIETY. A **society** which possesses a formal apparatus of **government**.

STATELESS SOCIETY. A **society** which lacks formal institutions of **government**.

STEP-FAMILIES. Families in which at least one partner has children from a previous marriage, either living in the home or nearby.

STEREOTYPICAL THINKING. Thought-processes involving rigid and inflexible categories.

STRIKE. A temporary stoppage of work by a group of employees in order to express a grievance or enforce a demand.

STRUCTURALISM. A **theoretical approach**, derived originally from the study of language, concerned with the identification of structures in social or cultural systems.

SUB-CULTURE. **Values** and **norms** distinct from those of the majority, held by a group within a wider society.

SUBURBANIZATION. The development of suburbia, areas of housing outside inner cities.

SUCCESSION. An ecological term referring to the replacement of one dominant type of species in a particular environment by another.

SUFFRAGISTS. Members of early women's movements who pressed for equal voting rights for women and men.

SURPLUS VALUE. The value of an individual's labour-power, in Marxist theory, which is 'left over' when an employer has repaid the cost involved in hiring a worker.

SURROGATE PARENTHOOD. A situation in which a woman bears a child on behalf of a couple of which the female partner is unable to reproduce.

SURVEILLANCE. The supervising of the activities of some individuals or groups by others in order to ensure compliant behaviour.

SURVEY. A method of sociological research involving the administration of questionnaires to a population being studied.

SYMBOL. One item used to stand for or represent another – as in the case of a flag which symbolizes a nation.

SYMBOLIC INTERACTIONISM. A **theoretical approach** in sociology developed by George Herbert Mead, which places strong emphasis on the role of symbols and language as core elements of all human interaction.

TALK. The carrying on of conversations or verbal exchanges in the course of day-to-day social life.

TAYLORISM. A set of ideas, also referred to as 'scientific management', developed by Frederick Winslow Taylor, involving simple, co-ordinated operations in industry.

TECHNOLOGY. The application of knowledge to production from the material world. Technology involves the creation of material instruments (such as machines) used in human interaction with nature.

TERRORISM. The use of violence on the part of non-governmental groups to achieve political ends.

TERTIARY SECTOR. That part of an economy concerned with the provision of services.

TESTICULAR FEMINIZATION SYNDROME. An endrocrinal abnormality which produces physically female genitals in individuals who are male in terms of their chromosomal make-up.

THEORETICAL DILEMMA. A basic theoretical problem that forms the focus of long-standing debates in sociology.

THEORETICAL QUESTIONS. Questions posed by the sociologist when seeking to explain a particular range of observed events. The asking of theoretical questions is crucial to allowing us to generalize about the nature of social life.

THIRD WORLD. The less-developed societies, in which industrial production is either virtually non-existent or only developed to a limited degree. The majority of the world's population live in Third World countries.

THIRD WORLD ENTREPÔT. A city serving as an entry point for migration from less developed countries to a more developed one.

TIME GEOGRAPHY. An approach to the study of human behaviour, pioneered by the Swedish geographer Torsten Hägerstrand, which emphasizes the movement of individuals simultaneously across time and space.

TIME–SPACE CONVERGENCE. The process whereby distances become 'shortened in time', as the speed of modes of transportation increases.

TOTAL WAR. Warfare in which large numbers of the population are involved, directly or indirectly, and in which hundreds of thousands or millions of soldiers are deployed.

TOTALITARIANISM. A form of political administration in which power is concentrated in the hands of a dictator, who operates through a mixture of cultivating a devoted following and terrorizing those who do not agree with his policies.

TOTEMISM.   A system of religious belief which attributes divine properties to a particular type of animal or plant.

TRADING NETWORKS.   Networks of economic exchange linking companies or countries.

TRADITIONAL STATES.   State-based societies in which the main basis of production is agriculture or pastoralism. Traditional states are also often referred to as 'early civilizations'.

TRANSFORMATIVE MOVEMENT.   A **social movement** aiming to produce major processes of **social change**.

TRANSITIONAL CLASSES.   A term used by Marx to refer to classes belonging to a declining type of society which linger on in a new one – such as peasants or large landowners in a system which has become capitalist.

TRANSNATIONAL COMPANIES.   Business corporations located in two or more countries.

TRIANGULATION.   The use of multiple research methods as a way of producing more reliable empirical data than is available from any single method used in isolation.

UNDERCLASS.   A class of individuals situated right at the bottom of the class system, normally composed of people from ethnic minority backgrounds.

UNFOCUSED INTERACTION.   Interaction occurring among people present in a particular setting, but where they are not engaged in direct face-to-face communication.

UNILINEAR EVOLUTION.   An account of social evolution according to which all societies must pass through the same sequence of stages in order to develop.

UNINTENDED CONSEQUENCES.   Consequences which result from behaviour initiated for other purposes. Many of the major features of social activity are unintended by those who participate in it.

UNION.   A body of people set up to represent workers' interests in an industrial setting.

UNIVERSAL CONSCRIPTION.   A system of national service, under which every individual of a certain age (or, more commonly, all males of a certain age) have to undergo a period of military training.

UPPER CLASS.   A social class broadly composed of the more affluent members of society, especially those who have inherited wealth, own businesses or hold large numbers of stocks and shares.

URBAN RECYCLING.   The process of renovating deteriorating neighbourhoods by encouraging the renewal of old buildings and the construction of new ones.

URBANISM.   A term used by Louis Wirth to denote distinctive characteristics of urban social life, such as its impersonality.

URBANIZATION.   The development of towns and cities.

VARIABLE.   A dimension along which an object, individual, or group may be categorized, such as income or height.

VERTICAL INTEGRATION.   The centralized co-ordination of the worldwide activities of **transnational companies**.

VERTICAL MOBILITY.   Movement up or down a hierarchy of positions in a social stratification system.

VICTIMLESS CRIME.   An activity in which an individual engages, which is defined as criminal, but where no other person is directly involved, such as drug-taking or illegal gambling.

WEALTH. Money and material possessions held by an individual or group.

WELFARE STATE. A political system which provides a wide range of welfare benefits for its citizens.

WHITE-COLLAR CRIME. Criminal activities carried out by those in white-collar or professional jobs.

WORKING CLASS. A social class broadly composed of people involved in blue-collar or manual occupations.

WORLD INFORMATION ORDER. A global system of communications, operating through satellite links, radio and TV transmission, telephone and computer links

WORLD SYSTEM THEORY. A **theoretical approach** associated particularly with the writings of Immanuel Wallerstein which analyses the development of particular societies in terms of their position within global social systems.

Bibliography

Aberle, David 1966: *The Peyote Religion Among the Navaho* (Chicago: Aldine Press)

Abrams, Philip 1978: *Work, Urbanism and Inequality: UK Society Today* (London: Weidenfeld and Nicolson)

Abrams, Philip 1982: *Historical Sociology* (Ithaca, NY: Cornell University Press)

Acheson, E. D. et al. 1981: *The Impending Crisis of Old Age: A Challenge to Ingenuity* (Oxford: Oxford University Press)

Acquaviva, S. S. 1979: *The Decline of the Sacred in Industrial Society* (Oxford: Basil Blackwell)

Adorno, Theodor W. 1974: 'The stars down to earth: the *Los Angeles Times* astrology column', *Telos*, 19

Adorno, Theodor W. et al. 1950: *The Authoritarian Personality* (New York: Harper and Row)

Agell, Anders 1980: 'Co-habitation without marriage in Swedish Law', in John M. Eekelaar et al. (eds), *Marriage and Cohabitation in Contemporary Societies* (Toronto: Butterworths)

Ainsworth, M. D. S. 1977: *Infancy in Uganda* (Baltimore, Md: Johns Hopkins University Press)

Alavi, H. 1983: 'Colonial and post-colonial societies', in T. B. Bottomore (ed.), *A Dictionary of Marxist Thought* (Oxford: Basil Blackwell)

Alba, Richard 1985: *Italian Americans: Into the Twilight of Ethnicity* (Englewood Cliffs, NJ: Prentice-Hall)

Albrow, Martin 1970: *Bureaucracy* (London: Pall Mall Press)

Aldridge, Alan 1987: 'In the absence of the minister: structures of subordination in the role of deaconess in the Church of England', *Sociology*, 21

Alexander, Jeffrey C. (ed.) 1985: *Neofunctionalism* (London: Sage)

Alland, Alexander 1967: *Evolution and Human Behaviour* (Garden City, NY: Natural History Press)

Alland, Alexander 1970: *Adaptation in Cultural Evolution* (New York: Columbia University Press)

Allen, Michael P. 1981: 'Managerial power and tenure in the large corporation', *Social Forces*, 60

Allen, Robert L. 1970: *A Guide to Black Power in America: A Historical Analysis* (London: Gollancz)

Allmän/månad statistik 1987: *Sveriges Officiella Statistik* (Stockholm: Statistika Centralbyrån)

Althusser, Louis 1969: *For Marx* (London: Allen Lane)

Altman, Dennis 1986: *AIDS and the New Puritanism* (London: Pluto Press)

Amir, Menachem 1971: *Patterns in Forcible Rape* (Chicago: University of Chicago Press)

Anderson, F. S. 1977: 'TV violence and viewer aggression: accumulation of study results 1956–1976', *Public Opinion Quarterly*, 41

Anderson, Michael 1980: *Approaches to the History of the Western Family* (London: Macmillan)

Anderson, Michael 1981: *Family Structure in Nineteenth Century Lancashire* (Cambridge: Cambridge University Press)

Annett, T. S. 1976: *The Many Ways of Being: A Guide to Spiritual Groups and Growth Centres in Britain* (London: Abacus)

Anyon, Jean 1987: 'Intersections of gender and class: accommodation and resistance by working class and affluent females to contradictory sex-role ideologies', in Stephen Walker and Len Barton (eds), *Gender, Class and Education* (New York: International Publications Service)

Archibald, Katherine 1947: *Wartime Shipyard* (Berkeley: University of California Press)

Arendt, Hannah 1963: *On Revolution* (London: Faber and Faber)

Arendt, Hannah 1977: *Eichmann in Jerusalem* (revised edn, Harmondsworth: Penguin)

Ariès, Philippe 1973: *Centuries of Childhood* (Harmondsworth: Penguin)

Aron, Raymond 1954: *The Century of Total War* (London: Verschoyle)

Ashford, Douglas E. 1987: *The Emergence of Welfare States* (Oxford: Basil Blackwell)

Ashworth, A. E. 1980: *Trench Warfare, 1914–1918* (London: Macmillan)

Atchley, Robert C. 1985: *Social Forces and Ageing* (4th edn, Belmont: Wadsworth)

Atholl, Justin 1954: *Shadow of the Gallows* (London: Hutchinson)

Attwood, Lynne and Maggie McAndrew 1984: 'Women at work in the USSR', in Marilyn J. Davidson and Cary L. Cooper, *Working Women: An International Survey* (Chichester: Wiley)

Ayres, Robert and Steven Miller 1983: *Robotics: Applications and Social Implications* (Cambridge, Mass.: Ballinger Press)

Ayres, Robert and Steven Miller 1985: 'Industrial robots on the line', in Tom Forrester (ed.), *The Information Technology Revolution* (Oxford: Basil Blackwell)

Babbage, Charles 1835: *On the Economy of Machinery and Manufactures* (London: Charles Knight)

Bach, R. 1980: 'The new Cuban immigrants: their background and prospects', *Monthly Labour Review*, 103, October

Bailyn, Bernard 1960: *Education in the Forming of American Society* (New York: Random House)

Bakal, Donald A. 1979: *Psychology and Medicine: Psychobiological Dimensions of Health and Illness* (London: Tavistock)

Ballard, Roger 1982: 'South Asian families', in R. N. Rapoport et al., *Families in Britain* (London: Routledge and Kegan Paul)

Balswick, J. O. 1983: 'Male inexpressiveness', in Kenneth Solomon and Norman B. Levy, *Men in Transition: Theory and Therapy* (New York: Plenum Press)

Barghoorn, Frederick C. and Thomas Remington 1986: *Politics in the USSR* (3rd edn, Boston: Little, Brown)

Barker, Eileen 1984: *The Making of a Moonie* (Oxford: Basil Blackwell)

Barker, Sheila and Diana Allen (eds) 1976: *Dependence and Exploitation in Work and Marriage* (New York: Longman)

Barnes, John A. 1979: *Who Should Know What? Social Science, Privacy and Ethics* (Harmondsworth: Penguin)

Barnouw, Eric 1975: *Tube of Plenty: The Evolution of American Television* (Oxford: Oxford University Press)

Barth, Frederick 1969: *Ethnic Groups and Boundaries* (London: Allen and Unwin)

Bartolle, K. et al. 1980: *Integrated Co-operatives in the Industrial Society: The Example of the Kibbutz* (Amsterdam: Van Gorum)

Barton, S. E. et al. 1985: 'HTLV–III antibody in prostitutes', *Lancet*, 1424

Bastide, Roger 1967: 'Colour, racism and Christianity', *Daedalus*, Spring

Bastide, Roger 1978: *The African Religions of Brazil* (Baltimore, Md: Johns Hopkins University Press)

Bate, J. St John 1985: *The Automated Office: Information Technology and Its Effect on Management and Office Staff* (London: Collins)

Bater, James H. 1977: 'Soviet town planning: theory and practice in the 1970s', *Progress in Human Geography*, 1

Baumrind, D. 1964: 'Some thoughts on ethics of research: after reading Milgram's "Behavioural study of obedience"', *American Psychologist*, 19

Baxter, Sandra and Marjorie Lansing 1983: *Women and Politics: The Visible Majority* (Ann Arbor: University of Michigan Press)

Beattie, John 1964: *Other Cultures* (London: Routledge and Kegan Paul)

Beauvoir, Simone de 1972: *The Second Sex* (Harmondsworth: Penguin)

Becker, Howard 1950: *Through Values to Social Interpretation* (Durham, NC: Duke University Press)

Becker, Howard S. 1967: 'Whose side are we on?', *Social Problems*, 14

Becker, Howard S. 1974: 'Labelling theory reconsidered', in P. Rock and M. McIntosh, *Deviance and Social Control* (London: Tavistock)

Becker, Howard S. 1976: 'Problems in the publication of field studies', in *Sociological Work* (New Brunswick, NJ: Transaction Books)

Bell, Colin and Howard Newby 1977: *Doing Sociological Research* (London: Allen and Unwin)

Bell, Daniel 1953: 'Crime as an American way of life', *Antioch Review*, 13

Bell, Daniel 1973: *The Coming of Post-Industrial Society: A Venture in Social Forecasting* (London: Heinemann)

Bellah, Robert N. 1970: *Beyond Belief* (New York: Harper and Row)

Bennett, Jon and Susan George 1987: *The Hunger Machine* (Cambridge: Polity Press)

Bennett, Lerone 1967: *Black Power USA: The Human Side of Reconstruction* (Chicago: Johnson Publishing)

Benson, Ian and John Lloyd 1983: *New Technology and Industrial Change* (New York: Nichols Publishing)

Bentham, Jeremy 1791: *Panopticon: or, The Inspection House*

Bequai, A. 1980: *Organized Crime: The Fifth Estate* (Lexington, Mass.: D. C. Heath)

Berger, John 1977: *Ways of Seeing* (Harmondsworth: Penguin)

Berghe, Pierre L. van den 1970: *Race and Ethnicity: Essays in Comparative Sociology* (New York: Basic Books)

Bergmann, Theodor 1977: *The Development Models of India, the Soviet Union and China* (Amsterdam: Van Gorum)

Berk, Richard A. 1974: 'A gaming approach to crowd behaviour', *American Sociological Review*, 37

Berle, Adolf and Gardiner C. Means 1967: *The Modern Corporation and Private Property* (reprinted edn, New York: Harcourt, Brace and World)

Berman, L. V. 1982: 'The United States of America: a cooperative model for worker management', in F. H. Stephen (ed.), *The Performance of Labour-Managed Firms* (New York: Macmillan)

Bernstein, Basil 1975: *Class, Codes and Control* (3 vols, London: Routledge and Kegan Paul)

Berry, Brewton and Henry L. Tischler 1978: *Race and Ethnic Relations* (Boston: Houghton Mifflin)

Bertaux, Daniel 1981: *Biography and Society: The Life History Approach in the Social Sciences* (London: Sage)

Bertelson, David 1986: *Snowflakes and Snowdrifts: Individualism and Sexuality in America* (Lanham: University Press of America)

Bettelheim, Bruno 1986: *The Informed Heart* (Harmondsworth: Penguin)

Beynon, Hugh 1975: *Working for Ford* (England: EP Publishing)

Bicchieri, M. G. (ed.) 1972: *Hunters and Gatherers Today* (New York: Holt, Rinehart and Winston)

Binder, A. and P. Scharf 1982: 'Deadly force in law enforcement', *Crime and Delinquency*, 28

Birdwhistell, Ray L. 1971: *Kinesics and Context* (Philadelphia: Pennsylvania University Press)

Blackstone, Tessa and O. Fulton 1975: 'Sex discrimination among university teachers: a British–American comparison', *British Journal of Sociology*, 26

Blau, Peter M. 1963: *The Dynamics of Bureaucracy* (Chicago: University of Chicago Press)

Blau, Peter M. and Otis Dudley Duncan 1967: *The American Occupational Structure* (New York: Wiley)

Blauner, Robert 1964: *Alienation and Freedom* (Chicago: University of Chicago Press)

Bloch, S. and P. Reddaway 1977: *Russia's Political Hospitals* (London: Victor Gollancz)

Blomstrom, Magnus and Bjorn Hettne 1984: *Development Theory in Transition. The Dependency Debate and Beyond: Third World Responses* (London: Zed Books)

Blumberg, Paul 1968: *Industrial Democracy: The Sociology of Participation* (London: Constable)

Blumberg, Paul 1987: *Inequality in an Age of Decline* (New York: Oxford University Press)

Blyton, Paul 1985: *Changes in Working Time: An International Review* (London: Croom Helm)

Bobbio, Norberto 1987: *The Future of Democracy* (Cambridge: Polity Press)

Boden, Deirdre 1987: 'Temporal frames: time, talk and organizations' (mimeo, Department of Sociology, Washington University, St Louis)

Bogart, Leo 1975: 'The future of the metropolitan daily', *Journal of Communication*, 25

Bohannan, Paul (ed.) 1960: *African Homicide and Suicide* (Princeton, NJ: Princeton University Press)

Bohannan, Paul 1970: 'The six stations of divorce', in Paul Bohannan (ed.), *Divorce and After* (New York: Doubleday)

Boorstein, Edward 1967: *The Economic Transformation of Cuba* (New York: Monthly Review Press)

Booth, Alan 1977: 'Food riots in the North-West of England, 1770–1801', *Past and Present*, 77

Booth, Charles 1889: *Labour and Life of the People*. Vol. I of *Life and Labour of the People in London* (London: Williams and Norgate)

Booth, William 1970: *In Darkest England and the Way Out* (London: Macmillan. First pub. 1890)

Bottomley, A. K. and K. Pease 1986: *Crime and Punishment: Interpreting the Data* (Milton Keynes: Open University Press)

Bourdieu, Pierre 1986: *Distinction: A Social Critique of Judgements of Taste* (London: Routledge and Kegan Paul)

Bourdieu, Pierre 1988: *Language and Symbolic Power* (Cambridge: Polity Press)

Bourdieu, Pierre and Jean-Claude Passeron 1977: *Reproduction: In Education, Society and Culture* (London: Sage)

Bowlby, John 1951: *Maternal Care and Mental Health* (Geneva: World Health Organization)

Bowlby, John 1958: 'The nature of the child's tie to its mother', *International Journal of Psychoanalysis*, 39

Bowles, Samuel and Herbert Gintis 1976: *Schooling in Capitalist America* (London: Routledge and Kegan Paul)

Box, Steven 1983: *Power, Crime and Mystification* (London: Tavistock)

Brandt Commission 1983: *Common Crisis North–South: Co-operation for World Recovery* (Cambridge, Mass.: MIT Press)

Braun, Ernest 1984: *Wayward Technology* (London: Frances Pinter)

Braverman, Harry 1974: *Labour and Monopoly Capital: The Degradation of Work in the Twentieth Century* (New York: Monthly Review Press)

Breese, Gerald 1966: *Urbanization in Newly Developing Countries* (Englewood Cliffs, NJ: Prentice-Hall)

Brekke, Toril et al. 1985: *Women: A World Report* (London: Methuen)

Brennan, Teresa 1988: 'Controversial discussions and feminist debate', in Naomi Segal and Edward Timms, *The Origins and Evolution of Psychoanalysis* (New Haven, Conn.: Yale University Press)

Brenner, Michael 1978: 'Interviewing: the social phenomenology of a research instrument', in Michael Brenner, Peter Marsh and Marilyn Brenner, *The Social Contexts of Method* (London: Croom Helm)

Brenner, Robert 1977: 'The origins of capitalist development: a critique of neo-Smithian Marxism', *New Left Review*, 105

Breuilly, John 1982: *Nationalism and the State* (Manchester: Manchester University Press)

Brinton, Crane 1965: *The Anatomy of Revolution* (New York: Knopf)

Brittan, Samuel 1975: 'The economic contradictions of democracy', *British Journal of Political Science*, 15

Broch, T. et al. 1966: 'Belligerence among the primitives', *Journal of Peace Research*, 3

Brothers, Joan 1971: *Religious Institutions* (London: Longman)

Brown, Judith K. 1977: 'A note on the division of labour by sex', in Nona Glazer and Helen Youngelson Waehrer (eds), *Woman in a Man-Made World* (Chicago: Rand McNally)

Brown, Lester R. et al. 1974: *By Bread Alone* (Washington DC: Overseas Development Council)

Brownmiller, Susan 1975: *Against Our Will: Men, Women and Rape* (London: Secker and Warburg)

Brummer, Alex 1987: 'San Francisco gives the Pope a rough ride', *Guardian*, 19 September

Bryan, Beverley, Stella Dadzie and Suzanne Scafe 1987: 'Learning to resist: black women and education', in Gaby Weiner and Madeleine Arnot, *Gender Under Scrutiny: New Inquiries in Education* (London: Hutchinson)

Brzezinski, Zbigniew and Samuel P. Huntington 1982: *Political Power: USA/USSR* (London: Greenwood)

Buckle, Abigail and David P. Farrington 1984: 'An observational study of shoplifting', *British Journal of Criminology*, 24

Buckley, P. J. and M. Casson 1976: *The Future of Multinational Enterprise* (London: Macmillan)

Bulkeley, Rip and Graham Spinardi 1986: *Space Weapons: Deterrence or Delusion?* (Cambridge: Polity Press)

Bull, Peter 1983: *Body Movement and Interpersonal Communication* (New York: Wiley)

Bulmer, Martin (ed.) 1975: *Working Class Images of Society* (London: Routledge and Kegan Paul)

Bulmer, Martin 1984: *Sociological Research Methods* (London: Macmillan)

Burawoy, Michael 1979: *Manufacturing Consent* (Chicago: University of Chicago Press)

Burns, E. M. and P. L. Ralph 1974: *World Civilizations* (New York: Norton)

Burridge, Kenneth 1971: *New Heaven, New Earth: A Study of Millenarian Activities* (Oxford: Basil Blackwell)

Burt, Cyril 1977: *The Subnormal Mind* (3rd edn, Oxford: Oxford University Press)

Bynum, Caroline Walker, Steven Harrell and Paula Richman (eds) 1986: *Gender and Religion: On the Complexity of Symbols* (Boston, Mass.: Beacon Press)

Byrd, Max 1978: *London Transformed: Images of the City in the Eighteenth Century* (New Haven, Conn.: Yale University Press)

Califano, Joseph A. 1986: *America's Health Care Revolution: Who Lives? Who Dies? Who Pays?* (New York: Random House)

Campagna, David 1985: 'The economics of juvenile prostitution in the USA', *International Children's Rights Monitor*, 2

Campbell, Anne 1986a: *The Girls in the Gang* (Oxford: Basil Blackwell)

Campbell, Anne 1986b: 'Self-reporting of fighting by females', *British Journal of Criminology*, 26

Campbell, Anne and John T. Gibbs (eds) 1986: *Violent Transactions* (Oxford: Basil Blackwell)

Campbell, Duncan 1982: *War Plan UK: The Truth about Civil Defence in Britain* (London: Burnett Books)

Campbell-Jones, Suzanne 1979: *In Habit: An Anthropological Study of Working Nuns* (London: Faber and Faber)

Camporesi, Piero 1988: *Bread of Dreams* (Cambridge: Polity Press)

Cancian, Francesca M. 1987: *Love in America: Gender and Self-Development* (New York: Cambridge University Press)

Cannon, Geoffrey 1987: *The Politics of Food* (London: Century)

Cantril, Hadley 1963: *The Psychology of Social Movements* (New York: Wiley)

Caplan, Arthur L. (ed.) 1978: *The Sociobiology Debate: Readings on Ethical and Scientific Issues* (New York: Harper and Row)

Caplan, Pat 1987: *The Cultural Construction of Sexuality* (London: Tavistock)

Caplin, L. and D. Kessler 1976: *An Economic Analysis of Crime* (Springfield, Ill.: Charles Thomas)

Cardoso, F. H. 1972: 'Dependency and under-development in Latin America', *New Left Review*, 74

Cardoso, G. 1983: *Negro Slavery in the Sugar Plantations of Veracruz and Pernambuco, 1550–1680* (Washington DC: University Press of America)

Carlen, Pat et al. 1985: *Criminal Women: Autobiographical Accounts* (Cambridge: Polity Press)

Carley, Michael 1981: *Social Measurement and Social Indicators* (London: Allen and Unwin)

Carlstein, Tommy 1983: *Time Resources, Society and Ecology*. Vol. I: *Preindustrial Societies* (London: Allen and Unwin)

Carlstein, Tommy, Don Parkes and Nigel Thrift (eds) 1978: *Making Sense of Time* (3 vols, New York: Wiley)

Carmichael, Stokeley and C. Hamilton 1968: *Black Power: The Politics of Liberation in America* (London: Jonathan Cape)

Carneiro, Robert L. 1970: 'A theory of the origin of the state', *Science*, 169

Carr, Edward Hallett 1970: *The October Revolution: Before and After* (London: Macmillan)

Carrier, Fred J. 1976: *The Third World Revolution* (Amsterdam: B. R. Gruner)

Carrington Goodrich, L. 1946: 'The early development of firearms in China', *Isis*, 36 (2)

Carswell, John 1985: *Government and the Universities in Britain: Progress and Performance 1960–1980* (Cambridge: Cambridge University Press)

Castells, Manuel 1977: *The Urban Question: A Marxist Approach* (London: Edward Arnold)

Castells, Manuel 1983: *The City and the Grass Roots: A Cross-cultural Theory of Urban Social Movements* (London: Edward Arnold)

Castles, Stephen with Heather Booth and Tina Wallace 1984: *Here for Good: Western Europe's New Ethnic Minorities* (London: Pluto Press)

Centers, Richard 1949: *The Psychology of Social Classes* (Princeton, NJ: Princeton University Press)

Chafe, William H. 1972: *The American Woman: Her Changing Social, Economic and Political Roles, 1920–1970* (Oxford: Oxford University Press)

Chafe, William H. 1977: *Women and Equality: Changing Patterns in American Culture* (Oxford: Oxford University Press)

Chalfant, Paul H., Robert E. Beckley and C. Eddie Palmer 1986: *Religion in Contemporary Society* (2nd edn, Palo Alto, Ca.: Mayfield)

Challener, R. D. 1965: *The French Theory of the Nation in Arms, 1866–1939* (New York: Russell and Russell)

Chapman, Karen 1986: *The Sociology of Schools* (London: Tavistock)

Cherlin, Andrew J. 1981: *Marriage, Divorce, Re-Marriage* (Cambridge, Mass.: Harvard University Press)

Childe, V. Gordon 1956: *Man Makes Himself* (London: Watts)

Childe, V. Gordon 1979: 'Prehistory and Marxism', *Antiquity*, 53

Chodorow, Nancy 1978: *The Reproduction of Mothering* (Berkeley: University of California Press)

Chodorow, Nancy 1988: *Psychoanalytic Theory and Feminism* (Cambridge: Polity Press)

Chomsky, Noam 1976: *Reflections on Language* (New York: Pantheon)

Christie, Bruce (ed.) 1985: *Human Factors of Information Technology in the Office* (Chichester: Wiley)

Church of England 1985: *Faith in the City: The Report of the Archbishop of Canterbury's Commission on Urban Priority Areas* (London: Christian Action)

CIBA Foundation 1984: *Child Sexual Abuse Within the Family* (London: Tavistock)

Cipolla, Carlo M. 1965: *Guns and Sails in the Early Phase of European Expansion 1400–1700* (London: Collins)

Claessen, Henri J. M. and Peter Skalnik 1978: *The Early State* (The Hague: Mouton)

Clark, Burton R. 1985: *The School and the University: An International Perspective* (Berkeley: University of California Press)

Clark, K. and M. Clark 1963: *Prejudice and Your Child* (2nd edn, Boston, Mass.: Beacon Press)

Clark, Lorenne M. G. and Debra J. Lewis 1977: *Rape: The Price of Coercive Sexuality* (Toronto: The Women's Press)

Clausewitz, Karl M. von 1908: *On War* (London: Routledge and Kegan Paul), vol. 1

Clayton, Richard R. and Harwin L. Voss 1977: 'Shacking up: cohabitation in the 1970s', *Journal of Marriage and the Family*, 39

Clemens, John 1983: *Polls, Politics and Populism* (Aldershot: Gower)

Clinard, Marshall 1978: *Cities with Little Crime: The Case of Switzerland* (Cambridge: Cambridge University Press)

Cloward, R. and L. Ohlin 1960: *Delinquency and Opportunity* (New York: Free Press)

Clyne, P. 1973: *Guilty But Insane* (London: Thomas Nelson and Sons)

Cockerham, William C. 1986: *Medical Sociology* (3rd edn, Englewood Cliffs, NJ: Prentice-Hall)

Cohen, Albert 1955: *Delinquent Boys* (New York: Free Press)

Cohen, G. A. 1978: *Karl Marx's Theory of History: A Defence* (Oxford: Clarendon Press)

Cohen, Stanley 1985: *Visions of Social Control: Crime, Punishment and Classification* (Oxford: Basil Blackwell)

Cohn, Norman 1970a: *The Pursuit of the Millennium* (London: Paladin)

Cohn, Norman 1970b: 'Mediaeval millenarianism', in Sylvia L. Thrupp (ed.), *Millennial Dreams in Action: Studies in Revolutionary Religious Movements* (New York: Shocken Books)

Coleman, James S. et al. 1966: *Equality of Educational Opportunity* (Washington DC: US Government Printing Office)

Coleman, James S., Thomas Hoffer and Sally Kilgore 1981: *Public and Private Schools* (Chicago: National Opinion Research Centre)

Collins, Randall 1974: *Conflict Sociology: Toward an Explanatory Science* (New York: Academic Press)

Collins, Randall 1979: *The Credential Society: An Historical Sociology of Education* (New York: Academic Press)

Collins, Randall 1981: 'On the micro-foundations of macro-sociology', *American Journal of Sociology*, 86

Cone, James H. 1984: *For My People: Black Theology and the Black Church* (Braamfontein: Skotaville Publishers)

Connelly, Mark Thomas 1980: *The Response to Prostitution in the Progressive Era* (Chapel Hill: University of North Carolina Press)

Converse, Jean M. and Howard Schuman 1974: *Conversations at Random: Survey Research as Interviewers See It* (New York: Wiley)

Cook, Alice and Gwyn Kirk 1983: *Greenham Women Everywhere: Dreams, Ideas and Actions from the Women's Peace Movement* (London: Pluto Press)

Cook P. J. 1982: 'The role of firearms in violent crime', in Marvin E. Wolfgang and Neil Alan Wiener, *Criminal Violence* (London: Sage)

Cook, Thomas D. et al. 1975: *Sesame Street Revisited* (New York: Russell Sage)

Cook, Thomas D. and Donald T. Campbell 1979: *Quasi-Experimentation. Design and Analysis Issues for Field Settings* (Chicago: Rand McNally)

Cooley, Charles 1969: *Sociological Theory and Social Research* (New York: Wiley)

Coombs, Philip H. 1985: *The World Crisis in Education* (New York: Oxford University Press, Inc.)

Cooper, R. 1986: *The Economics of Interdependence* (New York: McGraw-Hill)

Corcoran, P. E. 1983: 'The limits of democratic theory', in G. Duncan (ed.), *Democratic Theory and Practice* (Cambridge: Cambridge University Press)

Cornish, Derek B. and Ronald V. Clarke 1986: *The Reasoning Criminal: Rational Choice Perspectives on Offending* (New York: Springer-Verlag)

Cottam, Jean 1980: 'Soviet women in combat in World War 2: the ground forces and the navy', *International Journal of Women's Studies*, 3

Cowan, Ruth Schwartz 1985: 'The Industrial Revolution in the home', in Donald MacKenzie and Judy Wajcman, *The Social Shaping of Technology* (Milton Keynes: Open University Press)

Coward, Rosalind 1984: *Female Desire: Women's Sexuality Today* (London: Paladin)

Cowen, P. 1979: 'An XYY Man', *British Journal of Psychiatry*, 135

Cox, Oliver C. 1948: *Caste, Class and Race* (New York: Doubleday)

Cox, Oliver C. 1964: 'The pre-industrial city reconsidered', *Sociological Quarterly*, 5

Cox, Peter R. 1976: *Demography* (5th edn, Cambridge: Cambridge University Press)

Craft, M. and A. 1985: 'The participation of ethnic minority pupils in further and higher education', *Education Research*, 25

Crenshaw, Martha (ed.) 1983: *Terrorism, Legitimacy, and Power: The Consequences of Political Violence* (Middletown, Conn.: Wesleyan University Press)

Crewe, Ivor 1987: 'The campaign of confusion', *New Society*, 8 May

Crozier, Michel 1964: *The Bureaucratic Phenomenon* (London: Tavistock)

Cruickshank, Margaret (ed.) 1982: *Lesbian Studies, Present and Future* (Old Westbury, NY: The Feminist Press)

Currell, Melville E. 1974: *Political Woman* (London: Croom Helm)

Curtiss, Susan 1977: *Genie* (New York: Academic Press)

Cushing, Frank H. 1967: *My Adventures in Zuni* (Palmer Lake: Filter Press. First pub. 1882–3)

Dahl, Robert 1985a: *Polyarchy: Participation and Opposition* (New Haven, Conn.: Yale University Press)

Dahl, Robert 1985b: *A Preface to Economic Democracy* (Cambridge: Polity Press)

Davenport, W. 1965: 'Sexual patterns and their regulation in a society of the South West Pacific', in F. Beach (ed.), *Sex and Behaviour* (New York: Wiley)

Davidson, Basil 1974: *Africa in History: Themes and Outlines* (London: Macmillan)

Davies, D. 1986: *Information Technology at Work* (London: Heinemann)

Davies, James C. 1962: 'Towards a theory of revolution', *American Sociological Review*, 27

Davies, R. 1979: *Capital, State and White Labour in South Africa, 1900–1960* (Brighton: Harvester Press)

Davis, Angela 1971: 'Reflections on black woman's role in the community of slaves', *Black Scholar*, 3

Davis, Kingsley 1940: 'Extreme social isolation of a child', *American Journal of Sociology*, 45

Davis, Kingsley 1976: 'The world's population crisis', in Robert K. Merton and Robert Nisbet, *Contemporary Social Problems* (4th edn, New York: Harcourt Brace Jovanovich)

Davis, Mike et al. (ed.) 1987: *The Year Left 2: Toward a Rainbow Socialism. Essays on Race, Ethnicity, Class and Gender* (London: Verso)

Dear, Michael and Jennifer Wolch 1987: *Landscapes of Despair* (Princeton, NJ: Princeton University Press)

Delamont, Sarah 1976: *Interaction in the Classroom* (London: Methuen)

Delgard, P. and E. Kringlen 1976: 'A Norwegian twin study of criminality', *British Journal of Criminology*, 29

Demars, O. 1974: *Dirty Business* (New York: Harper and Row)

Diamond, Stanley 1974: *In Search of the Primitive* (New Brunswick, NJ: Transaction Press)

Dicken, Peter 1986: *Global Shift: Industrial Change in a Turbulent World* (New York: Harper and Row)

Dingwall, Robert 1980: 'Ethics and ethnography', *Sociological Review*, 28

Dinham, Barbara and Colin Hines 1983: *Agribusiness in Africa* (London: Earth

Resources Research)

Ditton, Jason 1977: *Part-time Crime: An Ethnography of Fiddling and Pilferage* (London: Macmillan)

Dizard, W. 1982: *The Coming Information Age: An Overview of Technology, Economics and Politics* (New York: Longman)

Djilas, Milovan 1967: *The New Class: An Analysis of the Communist System* (New York: Praeger)

Dobash, Russell P., R. Emerson Dobash and Sue Gutteridge 1986: *The Imprisonment of Women* (Oxford: Basil Blackwell)

Doerner, Klaus 1981: *Madmen and the Bourgeoisie* (Oxford: Basil Blackwell)

Dolbeare, Kenneth M. and Murray J. Edlelman 1974: *American Politics: Policies, Power and Change* (Lexington, Mass.: D. C. Heath)

Domhoff, G. William 1967: *Who Rules America?* (Englewood Cliffs, NJ: Prentice-Hall)

Domhoff, G. William 1970: *The Higher Circles: The Governing Class in America* (New York: Random House)

Domhoff, G. William 1979: *The Powers That Be: Processes of Ruling Class Domination in America* (New York: Random House)

Donaldson, Margaret 1979: *Children's Minds* (New York: Norton)

Dore, Ronald 1973: *British Factory, Japanese Factory: The Origins of National Diversity in Industrial Relations* (London: Allen and Unwin)

Dore, Ronald and K. Aoyagi 1965: 'The Burakumin minority in urban Japan', in A. Rose and C. Rose (eds), *Minority Problems* (New York: Harper and Row)

Dowling, Cowlette 1984: *The Cinderella Complex* (London: Fontana)

Doyal, Lesley and Imogen Pennell 1979: *The Political Economy of Health* (London: Pluto Press)

Drew, Paul and Tony Wootton 1988: *Erving Goffman and the Interaction Order* (Cambridge: Polity Press)

Dubos, René 1959: *Mirage of Health* (New York: Doubleday Anchor)

Duchen, Claire 1986: *Feminism in France* (London: Routledge and Kegan Paul)

Dugdale, R. 1877: *The Dukes: A Study in Crime, Pauperism and Heredity* (New York: Putnam)

Dumont, Louis 1970: *Homo Hierarchicus: The Caste System and Its Implications* (London: Weidenfeld and Nicolson)

Duncan, Otis Dudley 1971: 'Observations on population', *New Physician*, 20 April

Dunn, John 1972: *Modern Revolutions: An introduction to the Analysis of a Political Phenomenon* (Cambridge: Cambridge University Press)

Dunn, John 1985: 'Understanding revolutions', in Dunn (ed.), *Rethinking Modern Political Theory* (Cambridge: Cambridge University Press)

Durie, Sheila and R. Edwards 1982: *Fuelling the Nuclear Arms Race: The Links Between Nuclear Power and Nuclear Weapons* (London: Pluto Press)

Durkheim, Emile 1952: *Suicide: A Study in Sociology* (London: Routledge and Kegan Paul. First pub. 1897)

Durkheim, Emile 1976: *The Elementary Forms of the Religious Life* (London: Allen and Unwin. First pub. 1912)

Durkheim, Emile 1982: *The Rules of Sociological Method* (London: Macmillan. First pub. 1895)

Duverger, Maurice 1954: *Political Parties* (New York: Wiley)

Dwyer, D. J. 1975: *People and Housing in Third World Cities* (London: Longman)

Dye, Thomas R. 1986: *Who's Running America?* (4th edn, Englewood Cliffs, NJ: Prentice-Hall)

Dyer, Gwynne 1985: *War* (London: Bodley Head)

Eberhard, Wolfram 1966: *Conquerors and Rulers* (Leiden: Brill)

Eckstein, Harry 1958: *The English Health Service* (Cambridge, Mass.: Harvard University Press)

Edgell, Stephen R. 1980: *Middle-Class Couples* (London: Allen and Unwin)

Edwards, Richard and Michael Podgursky 1986: 'The unravelling accord: American unions in crisis', in Richard Edwards, Paolo Garonna and Franz Todtling, *Unions in Crisis and Beyond: Perspectives from Six Countries* (Dover, Mass.: Auburn House)

Ehrlich, Paul R. 1971: *The Population Bomb* (London: Pan)

Ehrlich, Paul R. and Anne H. Ehrlich 1979: 'What happened to the population bomb?', *Human Nature*, 2

Ehrenreich, Barbara 1983: *The Hearts of Men: The American Dream and the Flight from Commitment* (Garden City, NY: Doubleday)

Eibl-Eibesfeldt, I. 1972: 'Similarities and differences between cultures in expressive movements', in Robert A. Hinde (ed.), *Non-verbal Communication* (Cambridge: Cambridge University Press)

Eibl-Eibesfeldt, I. 1973: 'The expressive behaviour of the deaf-and-blind born', in M. von Cranach and I. Vine (eds), *Social Communication and Movement* (New York: Academic Press)

Eisenstadt, S. N. 1963: *The Political System of Empires* (Glencoe: Free Press)

Ekman, Paul and W. V. Friesen 1971: 'Constants across culture in the face and emotion', *Journal of Personality and Social Psychology*, 17

Ekman, Paul and W. V. Friesen 1978: *Facial Action Coding System* (New York: Consulting Psychologists Press)

Elkind, David 1984: *All Grown Up and No Place to Go: Teenagers in Crisis* (Reading, Mass.: Addison-Wesley)

Ellman, Michael 1980: 'Against convergence', *Cambridge Journal of Economics*, 4

Ellwood, Robert S. 1979: *Alternative Altars: Unconventional and Eastern Spirituality in America* (Chicago: University of Chicago Press)

Elshtain, Jean Bethke 1981: *Public Man, Private Woman* (Princeton, NJ: Princeton University Press)

Elshtain, Jean Bethke 1987: *Women and War* (New York: Basic Books)

Elston, M. 1980: 'Medicine: half our future doctors?', in R. Silverstone and A. Ward (eds), *Careers of Professional Women* (London: Croom Helm)

Engerman, Stanley L. 1977: 'Black fertility and family structure in the United States, 1880–1940', *Journal of Family History*, 2

England, Paula and George Farkas 1986: *Households, Employment and Gender: A Social, Economic and Democratic View* (New York: Aldine)

Ennew, Judith 1986: *The Sexual Exploitation of Children* (Cambridge: Polity Press)

Epstein, Cynthia Fuchs and Rose Laub Coser (eds) 1981: *Access to Power: Cross-National Studies of Women and Elites* (London: Allen and Unwin)

Erickson, John 1974: 'Some military and political aspects of the "Militia Army" controversy, 1919–1920', in C. Abramsky et al. (eds), *Essays in Honour of E. H. Carr* (Hamden: Shoe String Press)

Erikson, Erik H. 1963: *Childhood and Society* (2nd edn, New York: Norton)

Erikson, Robert and John J. Goldthorpe 1986: 'National variation in social fluidity', CASMIN Project Working Paper, no. 9

Ermann, David and Richard Lundman 1982: *Corporate and Governmental Deviance* (Oxford: Oxford University Press)

Estabrook, A. 1916: *The Dukes in 1915* (Washington DC: Carnegie Institution)

Estrich, Susan 1987: *Real Rape* (Cambridge, Mass.: Harvard University Press)

Etzioni-Halévy, Eva 1983: *Bureaucracy and Democracy: A Political Dilemma* (London: Routledge and Kegan Paul)

Evans, R. 1982: *The Fabrication of Virtue: English Prison Architecture, 1750–1840* (Cambridge: Cambridge University Press)

Evans, Richard J. 1977: *The Feminists: Women's Emancipation Movements in Europe, America and Australasia, 1840–1920* (New York: Barnes and Noble)

Evans-Pritchard, E. E. 1940: *The Nuer: A Description of the Modes of Livelihood and Political Institutions of a Nilotic People* (Oxford: Clarendon Press)

Evans-Pritchard, E. E. 1950: *Witchcraft, Oracles and Magic Among the Azande* (Oxford: Oxford University Press)

Evans-Pritchard, E. E. 1956: *Nuer Religion* (Oxford: Oxford University Press)

Eysenck, Hans 1977: *Crime and Personality* (St Albans: Paladin)

Fagan, Jeffrey A., Douglas K. Stewart and Karen V. Hansen 1983: 'Violent men or violent husbands? Background factors and situational correlates', in David Finkelhor et al., *The Dark Side of Families: Current Family Violence Research* (Beverly Hills, Ca.: Sage)

Farley, R. 1985: 'Three steps forward and two back? Recent changes in the social and economic status of blacks', in R. Alba, *Ethnicity and Race in the U.S.A.: Toward the 21st Century* (London: Routledge and Kegan Paul)

Farrington, David and R. Kidd 1980: 'Stealing from a "lost" letter: effects of victim characteristics', *Criminal Justice and Behaviour*, 7

Farrington, David and J. Gunn (eds) 1985: *Aggression and Dangerousness* (New York: Wiley)

Farrington, David, Lloyd E. Ohlin and James Q. Wilson 1986: *Understanding and Controlling Crime: Toward a New Research Strategy* (New York: Springer-Verlag)

Fausto-Sterling, Anne 1985: *Myths of Gender: Biological Theories about Men and Women* (New York: Basic Books)

Feeney, F. 1986: 'Robbers as decision-makers', in Derek B. Cornish and Ronald V. Clarke (eds), *The Reasoning Criminal: Rational Choice Perspectives on Offending* (New York: Springer-Verlag)

Feige, L. 1981: *The Theory and Measurement of the Unobserved Sector of the US Economy* (Leiden: Reidel)

Fein, Rashi 1986: *Medical Care, Medical Costs* (Cambridge, Mass.: Harvard University Press)

Feld, Maury de 1977: *The Structure of Violence: Armed Forces as Social Systems* (Washington DC: Seven Locks Press)

Feldberg, Roslyn and Evelyn Nakano Glenn 1984: 'Male and female: job versus gender models in the sociology of work', in Janet Siltannan and Michelle Stanworth, *Women and the Public Sphere: A Critique of Sociology and Politics* (London: Hutchinson)

Feldman, Philip and Malcolm MacCulloch 1980: *Human Sexual Behaviour* (Chichester: Wiley)

Fenstermaker Berk, Sarah 1985: *The Gender Factory: The Apportionment of Work in American Households* (New York: Plenum Press)

Fettner, Ann G. and William A. Check 1984: *The Truth About AIDS: Evolution of an Epidemic* (New York: Holt, Rinehart and Winston)

Feuerbach, Ludwig 1957: *The Essence of Christianity* (New York: Harper and Row)

Finch, M. 1981: *The NAACP: Its Fight for Justice* (London: Methuen)

Fine, B. 1977: 'Labelling theory', in *Economy and Society*, 4

Fineman, Stephen et al. 1987: *Unemployment: Personal and Social Consequences* (London: Tavistock)

Finer, Samuel E. 1962: *The Man on Horseback: The Role of the Military in Politics* (London: Pall Mall Press)

Finer, Samuel E. 1975: 'State and nation-building in Europe: the role of the military', in Charles Tilly (ed.): *The Formation of National States in Europe* (Princeton, NJ: Princeton University Press)

Finkelhor, David and K. Yllo 1982: 'Forced sex in marriage: a preliminary report', *Crime and Delinquency*, 28

Finkelhor, David 1984: *Child Sexual Abuse: New Theory and Research* (New York: Free Press)

Finley, Moses I. (ed.) 1968: *Slavery in Classical Antiquity* (Cambridge: Heffer)

Finley, Moses I. 1980: *Ancient Slavery and Modern Ideology* (London: Chatto and Windus)

Firestone, Shulamith 1971: *The Dialectic of Sex* (London: Paladin)

Fischer, Claude S. 1975: 'Toward a subcultural theory of urbanism', *American Journal of Sociology*, 80

Fischer, Claude S. 1984: *The Urban Experience* (2nd edn, New York: Harcourt Brace Jovanovich)

Fisher, B. 1972: *The Gay Mystique: The Myth and Reality of Male Homosexuality* (New York: Stein and Day)

Fitzgerald, R. and L. Fuller 1982: '"I hear you knocking but you can't come in": the effects of reluctant respondents and refusers on sample survey estimates', *Sociological Methods and Research*, 2

Fitzpatrick, J. 1971: *Puerto Rican Americans: The Meaning of Migration to the Mainland* (Englewood Cliffs, NJ: Prentice-Hall)

Flake, Carol 1984: *Redemptorama: Culture, Politics and the New Evangelicalism* (Garden City, NY: Anchor)

Flanz, Gisbert H. 1983: *Comparative Women's Rights and Political Participation in Europe* (Epping: Bowker)

Flowers, Ronald Barri 1987: *Women and Criminality: The Woman as Victim, Offender and Practitioner* (New York: Greenwood Press)

Fogel, Robert W. and Stanley L. Engerman 1974: *Time on the Cross* (2 vols, Burton: University Press of America)

Ford, Clellan S. and Frank A. Beach 1951: *Patterns of Sexual Behaviour* (New York: Harper and Row)

Form, William 1985: *Divided We Stand: Working Class Stratification in America* (Urbana: University of Illinois Press)

Forrester, Tom (ed.) 1985: *The Information Technology Revolution* (Oxford: Basil Blackwell)

Foucault, Michel 1971: *Madness and Civilization: A History of Insanity in the Age of Reason* (London: Tavistock)

Foucault, Michel 1979: *Discipline and Punish* (Harmondsworth: Penguin)

Fox, Alan 1974: *Beyond Contract: Work, Power and Trust Relations* (London: Faber and Faber)

Fox, D. J. 1972: 'Patterns of morbidity and mortality in Mexico City', *Geographical Review*, 62

Fraiberg, Selma, 1959: *The Magic Years: Understanding and Handling the Problems of Early Childhood* (New York: Scribner's)

Francis, Arthur 1980: 'Company objectives, managerial motivation and the behaviour of large firms: an empirical test of the theory of "managerial" capitalism', *Cambridge Journal of Economics*, 4

Frank, André Gunder 1969: *Capitalism and Under-development in Latin America* (New York: Monthly Review Press)

Frank, André Gunder 1981: *Crisis: In the Third World* (New York: Holmes and Meier)

Frazier, Franklin 1939: *The Negro Family in the United States* (Chicago: University of

Chicago Press)

Frazier, Nancy and Myra Sadker 1973: *Sexes in School and Society* (New York: Harper and Row)

Freeman, R. B. and D. A. Wise 1982: *The Youth Labour Market Problem: Its Nature, Causes and Consequences* (Chicago: University of Chicago Press)

Freidson, Eliot 1980: *Doctoring Together: A Study of Professional Social Control* (Chicago: University of Chicago Press)

Freidson, Eliot 1986: *Professional Powers: A Study of the Institutionalization of Formal Knowledge* (Chicago: University of Chicago Press)

Fremlin, J. H. 1964: 'How many people can the world support?', *New Scientist*, 19 October

French, R. A. 1979: 'The individuality of the Soviet city', in R. A. French and F. E. I. Hamilton (eds), *The Socialist City: Spatial Structure and Urban Policy* (New York: Wiley)

Freud, Sigmund 1975: *The Psychopathology of Everyday Life* (Harmondsworth: Penguin)

Friedan, Betty 1981: *The Second Stage* (New York: Summit)

Friedl, John 1981: *The Human Portrait: Introduction to Cultural Anthropology* (Englewood Cliffs, NJ: Prentice-Hall)

Friedrich, Carl 1954: *Totalitarianism* (Cambridge, Mass.: Harvard University Press)

Friedrich, Carl 1969: *Totalitarianism in Perspective: Three Views* (London: Pall Mall Press)

Fröbel, Folker et al. 1980: *The New International Division of Labour* (Cambridge: Cambridge University Press)

Fromm, Erich (ed.) 1967: *Socialist Humanism* (London: Allen Lane)

Fryer, David and Stephen McKenna 1987: 'The laying off of hands – unemployment and the experience of time', in Stephen Fineman (ed.), *Unemployment: Personal and Social Consequences* (London: Tavistock)

Fryer, Peter 1984: *Staying Power: The History of Black People in Britain* (London: Pluto Press)

Furnivall, J. 1956: *Colonial Policy and Practice: A Comparative Study of Burma and Netherlands India* (New York: New York University Press)

Furstenberg, Frank F. Jr., Theodore Hershberg and John Modell 1975: 'The origins of the female-headed black family: the impact of the urban experience', *Journal of Interdisciplinary History*, 6

Furtado, C. 1984: *The Economic Growth of Brazil: A Survey from Colonial to Modern Times* (Westport, Ont.: Greenwood Press)

Gaertner, W. and A. Wenig (eds) 1985: *The Economics of the Shadow Economy* (Berlin: Springer-Verlag)

Gage, Matilda Joslyn 1980: *Women, Church and State* (Watertown, Mass.: Persephone Press. First pub. 1893)

Gailey, H. A. 1970/72: *A History of Africa: 1800 to the Present* (2 vols, New York: Houghton-Mifflin)

Galbraith, John Kenneth 1971: *The New Industrial State* (2nd edn, Harmondsworth: Penguin)

Galbraith, John Kenneth 1974: *Economics and the Public Purpose* (London: André Deutsch)

Gallup Opinion Index 1976: 'Religion in America', Report no. 130

Gans, Herbert J. 1962: *The Urban Villagers: Group and Class in the Life of Italian-Americans* (2nd edn, New York: Free Press)

Gans, Herbert J. 1968: *People and Plans: Essays on Urban Problems and Solutions* (New York: Basic Books)

Gansler, Jacques 1980: *The Defence Industry* (Cambridge, Mass.: MIT Press)

Gardner, Beatrice and Allen Gardner 1969: 'Teaching sign language to a chimpanzee', *Science*, 165

Gardner, Beatrice and Allen Gardner 1975: 'Evidence for sentence constituents in the early utterances of child and chimpanzee', *Journal of Experimental Psychology*, 104

Garfinkel, Harold 1963: 'A conception of, and experiments with, "trust" as a condition of stable concerted actions', in O. J. Harvey (ed.), *Motivation and Social Interaction* (New York: Ronald Press)

Garfinkel, Harold 1984: *Studies in Ethnomethodology* (Oxford: Basil Blackwell)

Geary, Dick 1982: *European Labour Protest, 1848–1939* (London: Croom Helm)

Geertz, Clifford 1983: *Local Knowledge: Further Essays in Interpretative Anthropology* (New York: Basic Books)

Geis, G. 1972: *Not the Law's Business?* (Rockeville: National Institute of Mental Health)

Geis, G. and Stottland, E. (eds) 1980: *White Collar Crime: Theory and Research* (London: Sage)

Gelb, I. J. 1952: *A Study of Writing* (Chicago: University of Chicago Press)

Gellner, Ernest 1964: *Thought and Change* (London: Weidenfeld and Nicolson)

Gellner, Ernest 1983: *Nations and Nationalism* (Oxford: Basil Blackwell)

Georges, Robert A. and Michael O. Jones 1980: *People Studying People: The Human Element in Fieldwork* (Berkeley: University of California Press)

Gerbner, George et al. 1979: 'The demonstration of power: violence profile no. 10', *Journal of Communication*, 29

Gerbner, George et al. 1980: 'The "mainstreaming" of America: violence profile no. 11', *Journal of Communication*, 30

Gershuny, J. I. 1978: *After Industrial Society?* (London: Macmillan)

Gershuny, J. I. and I. D. Miles 1983: *The New Service Economy: The Transformation of Employment in Industrial Societies* (London: Frances Pinter)

Gerson, Kathleen 1985: *Hard Choices: How Women Decide About Work, Career and Motherhood* (Berkeley: University of California Press)

Gibbons, Don 1979: *The Criminological Enterprise: Theories and Perspectives* (Englewood Cliffs, NJ: Prentice-Hall)

Giddens, Anthony 1976: *New Rules of Sociological Method* (London: Hutchinson)

Giddens, Anthony 1984: *The Constitution of Society* (Cambridge: Polity Press)

Giddens, Anthony 1985: *The Nation-State and Violence* (Cambridge: Polity Press)

Giliomee, Hermann and Lawrence Schlemmer (eds) 1985: *Up Against the Fences. Poverty, Passes and Privilege in South Africa* (Cape Town: Philip)

Gill, Colin 1985: *Work, Unemployment and the New Technology* (Cambridge: Polity Press)

Gillen, R. 1978: 'A study of women shoplifters', *Excerpta Medica Psychiatrica*, 123

Gilligan, Carol 1982: *In a Different Voice: Psychological Theory and Women's Development* (Cambridge, Mass.: Harvard University Press)

Gilroy, Paul 1987: *'There Ain't no Black in the Union Jack'* (London: Hutchinson)

Ginzburg, Carlo 1980: *The Cheese and the Worms* (London: Routledge and Kegan Paul)

Gissing, George 1973: *Demos* (Brighton: Harvester. First pub. 1892)

Glass, David (ed.) 1954: *Social Mobility in Britain* (London: Routledge and Kegan Paul)

Gleitman, Henry 1986: *Psychology* (New York: Norton)

Glenn, Norval D. and Charles N. Weaver 1956: 'The marital happiness of re-married divorced persons', *Journal of Marriage and the Family*, 39

Glueck, Sheldon W. et al. 1949: *Varieties of Delinquent Youth* (New York: Harper and Row)

Glueck, Sheldon W. and Eleanor Glueck 1956: *Physique and Delinquency* (New York: Harper and Row)

Goffman, Erving 1961: *Asylums: Essays on the Social Situation of Mental Patients and Other Inmates* (Harmondsworth: Penguin)

Goffman, Erving 1963: *Behaviour in Public Places* (New York: Free Press)

Goffman, Erving 1967: *Interaction Ritual* (New York: Doubleday Anchor)

Goffman, Erving 1969: *The Presentation of Self in Everyday Life* (Harmondsworth: Penguin)

Goffman, Erving 1970: *Stigma: Notes on the Management of Spoiled Identity* (Harmondsworth: Penguin)

Goffman, Erving 1971: *Relations in Public: Microstudies of the Public Order* (London: Allen Lane)

Goffman, Erving 1974: *Frame Analysis* (New York: Harper and Row)

Goffman, Erving 1979: *Gender Advertisements* (London: Macmillan)

Goffman, Erving 1981: *Forms of Talk* (Philadelphia: University of Pennsylvania Press)

Goldfield, Michael 1987: *The Decline of Organized Labour in the United States* (Chicago: University of Chicago Press)

Golding, Peter and Sue Middleton 1982: *Images of Welfare: Press and Public Attitudes to Poverty* (Oxford: Martin Robertson)

Goldstein, Paul J. 1979: *Prostitution and Drugs* (Lexington, Mass.: D. C. Heath)

Goldthorpe, J. E. 1984: *The Sociology of the Third World: Disparity and Development* (2nd edn, Cambridge: Cambridge University Press)

Goldthorpe, John H. 1971: 'Theories of industrial society', *Archives Européennes de Sociologie*, 12

Goldthorpe, John H. 1983: 'Women and class analysis: in defence of the conventional view', *Sociology*, 17

Goldthorpe, John H. et al. 1968–9: *The Affluent Worker in the Class Structure* (3 vols, Cambridge: Cambridge University Press)

Goldthorpe, John H., C. Llewellyn and C. Payne 1980: *Social Mobility and Class Structure in Modern Britain* (Oxford: Oxford University Press)

Goldthorpe, John H. and C. Payne 1986: 'Trends in intergenerational class mobility in England and Wales 1972–1983', *Sociology*, 20

Goode, E. 1972: *Drugs in American Society* (New York: Alfred Knopf)

Goode, William J. 1963: *World Revolution in Family Patterns* (New York: Free Press)

Goodhardt, G. J., A. S. C. Ehrenberg and M. A. Collins 1987: *The Television Audience: Patterns of Voting* (2nd edn, London: Gower)

Goodwin, Charles 1981: *Conversational Organization: Interaction Between Speakers and Hearers* (New York: Academic Press)

Goodwin, Jean 1982: *Sexual Abuse, Incest Victims and Their Families* (Boston, England: John Wright)

Goody, Jack 1977: *The Domestication of the Savage Mind* (Cambridge: Cambridge University Press)

Gordon, Milton 1964: *Assimilation in American Life: The Role of Race, Religion and National Origins* (Oxford: Oxford University Press)

Gordon, Milton 1978: *Human Nature, Class and Ethnicity* (Oxford: Oxford University Press)

Gorz, André 1982: *Farewell to the Working Class* (London: Pluto)

Gossett, Thomas F. 1963: *Race: The History of an Idea in America* (Dallas: Southern Methodist University Press)

Gottman, Jean 1961: *Megalopolis: The Urbanized Northeastern Seaboard of the United States* (New York: Twentieth Century Fund)

Gouldner, Alvin 1979: *The Future of Intellectuals and the Rise of the New Class* (London: Macmillan)

Goyder, John 1987: *The Silent Minority: Non-respondents on Sample Surveys* (Cambridge: Polity Press)

Greeley, Andrew 1977: *The American Catholic: A Social Portrait* (New York: Basic Books)

Greenbaum, Joan 1979: *In the Name of Efficiency: Management Theory and Shopfloor Practice in Data-Processing Work* (Philadelphia: Temple University Press)

Greenberg, David F. and Marcia H. Bystryn 1984: 'Capitalism, bureaucracy and male homosexuality', *Contemporary Crises*, 8

Greenberg, Martin S., Chauncey E. Wilson and Michael K. Mills 1978: 'Victim decision-making: an experimental approach', in D. Walsh, *Shoplifting: Controlling a Major Crime* (London: Macmillan)

Greenblat, Cathy Stein 1983: 'A hit is a hit . . . or is it? Approval and tolerance of the use of physical force by spouses', in David Finkelhor et al., *The Dark Side of Families: Current Family Violence Research* (Beverly Hills, Ca.: Sage)

Greenfield, P. M. and J. H. Smith 1976: *The Structure of Communication in Early Language Development* (New York: Academic Press)

Gregory, Derek and John Urry 1985: *Social Relations and Spatial Structures* (London: Macmillan)

Griffin, Susan 1978: *Rape. The Power of Consciousness* (New York: Harper and Row)

Grinker, Roy and P. Spiegel 1945: *Men under Stress* (Philadelphia: Balkiston)

Grusky, David B. and Robert M. Hauser 1984: 'Comparative social mobility revisited: models of convergence and divergence in 16 countries', *American Sociological Review*, 49

Gunter, Barrie 1985: *Dimensions of Television Violence* (London: Gower)

Gupte, Pranay 1984: *The Crowded Earth: People and the Politics of Population* (New York: Norton)

Gutman, Herbert G. 1975: 'Extended review of "Time on the Cross"', *Journal of Negro History*, 60

Gutman, Herbert G. 1976: *The Black Family in Slavery and Freedom, 1750–1925* (New York: Pantheon)

Habermas, Jürgen 1976: *Legitimation Crisis* (Cambridge: Polity Press)

Habermas, Jürgen 1979: *Communication and the Evolution of Society* (Cambridge: Polity Press)

Habermas, Jürgen 1984: *Theory of Communicative Action*, vol. 1 (Cambridge: Polity Press)

Hagen, John 1988: *Structural Criminology* (Cambridge: Polity Press)

Hägerstrand, Torsten 1973: 'The domain of human geography', in R. J. Chorley (ed.), *Directions in Geography* (London: Methuen)

Hakim, Catherine C. 1982: *Secondary Analysis in Social Research* (London: Allen and Unwin)

Hale, Robert B. 1971: *The Strengths of Black Families* (New York: Emerson Hall)

Hall, Edward T. 1959: *The Silent Language* (New York: Doubleday)

Hall, Edward T. 1966: *The Hidden Dimension* (New York: Doubleday)

Hall, Ruth 1985: *Ask Any Woman: A London Enquiry into Rape and Sexual Assault* (Bristol: Falling Wall Press)

Hall, Ruth, Selma James and Judith Kertesz 1984: *The Rapist who Pays the Rent* (2nd edn, Bristol: Falling Wall Press)

Hall, Stuart and Martin Jacques (eds) 1983: *The Politics of Thatcherism* (London: Lawrence and Wishart)

Halle, David 1984: *America's Working Man: Work, Home and Politics Among Blue Collar Property Owners* (Chicago: University of Chicago Press)

Halsey, A. H., A. F. Heath and J. M. Ridge 1980: *Origins and Destinations* (Oxford: Oxford University Press)

Hammond, Phillip E. (ed.) 1985: *The Sacred in a Secular Age: Toward Revision in the Scientific Study of Religion* (Berkeley: University of California Press)

Handy, Charles 1984: *The Future of Work: A Guide to a Changing Society* (Oxford: Basil Blackwell)

Hansen, I. 1980: 'Sex education for young children', quoted in J. Scanzoni and G. L. Fox, 'Sex role, family and society', *Journal of Marriage and the Family*, 42

Harder, Mary White et al. 1972: 'Jesus people', *Psychology Today*, 6

Harding, Vincent 1980: *The Other American Revolution* (Los Angeles: University of California Center for Afro-American Studies, Culture and Society Monograph Series, vol. 4)

Hardyment, Christina 1987: *Labour Saved?* (Cambridge: Polity Press)

Harlow, Harry F. and Margaret K. Harlow 1962: 'Social deprivation in monkeys', *Scientific American*, 207

Harlow, Harry F. and R. R. Zimmerman 1959: 'Affectional responses in the infant monkey', *Science*, 130

Harrington, Michael 1963: *The Other America* (New York: Firethorn)

Harrington, Michael 1984: *The New American Poverty* (New York: Firethorn)

Harris, Christopher 1983: *The Family and Industrial Society* (London: Allen and Unwin)

Harris, Marvin 1978: *Cannibals and Kings: The Origins of Cultures* (London: Fontana)

Harris, Nigel 1987: *The End of the Third World: Newly Industrializing Countries and the Decline of an Ideology* (Harmondsworth: Penguin)

Hartley, E. 1946: *Problems in Prejudice* (New York: Kings Crown Press)

Hartman, Mary and Lois Banner (eds) 1974: *Clio's Consciousness Raised: New Perspectives on the History of Women* (New York: Norton)

Hartmann, Heidi 1981: 'The family as the locus of class, gender and political struggle: the example of housework', *Signs*, 6

Harvey, David 1973: *Social Justice and the City* (Oxford: Basil Blackwell)

Harvey, David 1982: *The Limits to Capital* (Oxford: Basil Blackwell)

Harvey, David 1985: *Consciousness and the Urban Experience: Studies in the History and Theory of Capitalist Urbanization* (Oxford: Basil Blackwell)

Hatch, S. and R. Kickbusch 1983: *Self-Help and Health in Europe* (Geneva: World Health Organization)

Hausson, Carola and Karin Linden 1984: *Moscow Women* (London: Allison and Busby)

Hawkes, Terence 1977: *Structuralism and Semiotics* (London: Methuen)

Hawley, Amos H. 1950: *Human Ecology: A Theory of Community Structure* (New York: Ronald Press Company)

Hawley, Amos 1968: 'Human ecology', *International Encyclopaedia of Social Science*, vol. 4 (Glencoe: Free Press)

Heath, Anthony 1981: *Social Mobility* (London: Fontana)

Heath, Anthony et al. 1986: *How Britain Votes* (Oxford: Pergamon Press)

Heitlinger, Alena 1979: *Women and State Socialism: Sex Inequality in the Soviet Union and Czechoslovakia* (London: Macmillan)

Held, David 1987: *Models of Democracy* (Cambridge: Polity Press)

Hemming, John 1987: *Amazon Frontier: The Defeat of the Brazilian Indians* (London: Macmillan)

Hennig, Margaret and Anne Jardin 1977: *The Managerial Woman* (Garden City, NY: Doubleday Anchor)

Henriques, Fernando 1963: *Prostitution and Society*, vol. 2 (London: MacGibbon and Kee)

Henry, S. 1978: *The Hidden Economy* (Oxford: Martin Robertson)

Henslin, James M. and Mae A. Briggs 1971: 'Dramaturgical desexualization: The sociology of the vaginal examination', in Henslin (ed.), *Studies in the Sociology of Sex* (New York: Appleton-Century-Crofts)

Heritage, John 1984: *Garfinkel and Ethnomethodology* (Cambridge: Polity Press)

Hiebert, Paul G. 1976: *Cultural Anthropology* (Philadelphia: Lippincott)

Hill, Richard C. 1984: 'Economic crisis and political response in the motor city', in Larry Sawer and William K. Tabb (eds), *Sunbelt/Snowbelt: Urban Development and Regional Restructuring* (Oxford: Oxford University Press)

Hill, Richard C. 1984: 'Transnational capitalism and urban crisis: The case of the auto industry and Detroit', in Ivan Szelenyi (ed.), *Cities in Recession: Critical Responses to the Urban Policies of the New Right* (London: Sage)

Hill, Ronald J. and Peter Frank 1983: *The Soviet Communist Party* (London: Allen and Unwin)

Himmelstrand, Ulf et al. 1981: *Beyond Welfare Capitalism* (London: Heinemann)

Hindelang, Michael J. et al. 1978: *Violence of Personal Crime* (Cambridge: Ballinger)

Hirst, Paul and Penny Woolley 1982: *Social Relations and Human Attributes* (London: Tavistock)

Hobson, John A. 1965: *Imperialism: A Study* (Ann Arbor: University of Michigan Press)

Hodge, Robert and David Tripp 1986: *Children and Television: A Semiotic Approach* (Cambridge: Polity Press)

Holloway, David 1984: *The Soviet Union and the Arms Race* (2nd edn, New Haven, Conn.: Yale University Press)

Holman, Robert 1978: *Poverty: Explanations of Social Deprivation* (Oxford: Martin Robertson)

Holmes, Leslie 1986: *Politics in the Communist World* (Oxford: Oxford University Press)

Holton, Robert J. 1978: 'The crowd in history: some problems of theory and method', *Social History*, 3

Homans, Hilary 1987: 'Man-made myth: the reality of being a woman scientist in the NHS', in Anne Spencer and David Podmore (eds), *In a Man's World: Essays on Women in Male-Dominated Professions* (London: Tavistock)

Hooks, Bell 1986: *Ain't I a Woman: Black Women and Feminism* (London: Pluto Press)

Hooper, Judith O. and Frank H. Hooper 1985: 'Family and individual development theories: conceptual analysis and speculations', in J. A. Meacham, *Family and Individual Development* (Basel: Karger)

Hopkins, A. 1980: 'Controlling corporate deviance', *Criminology*, 18

Hopkins, Mark W. 1970: *Mass Media in the Soviet Union* (New York: Pegasus)

Hopper, Earl 1981: *Social Mobility: A Study of Control and Instability* (Oxford: Basil Blackwell)

Hough, Jerry W. F. and Merle Fainsod 1979: *How the Soviet Union is Governed* (Cambridge, Mass.: Harvard University Press)

Hounshell, David A. 1984: *From the American System to Mass Production, 1800–1932: The Development of Manufacturing Technology in the United States* (Baltimore, Md:

Johns Hopkins University Press)

Howard, Michael 1976: *War in European History* (Oxford: Oxford University Press)

Hoy Steele, C. 1975: 'Urban Indian identity in Kansas: some implications for research', in J. Bennett (ed.), *The New Ethnicity: Perspectives from Ethnology* (St Paul, Minn.: West Publishing)

Hughes, Barry 1985: *World Futures: A Critical Analysis of Alternatives* (Baltimore, Md: Johns Hopkins University Press)

Hughes, C. C. and J. M. Hunter 1971: 'Disease and "development" in Africa', in H. P. Dreitzel (ed.), *The Social Organization of Health* (New York: Collier-Macmillan)

Humphries, Judith 1983: *Part-time Work* (London: Kogan Page)

Hundley, N. (ed.) 1975: *The Chicano* (Santa Barbara, Ca.: Clio Press)

Huntington, Samuel P. 1981: *The Soldier and the State: The Theory and Politics of Civil–Military Relations* (Cambridge, Mass.: Harvard University Press)

Hutchinson, E. 1981: *Legislative History of American Immigration Policy, 1785–1965* (Philadelphia: University of Pennsylvania Press)

Huttenback, Robert A. 1976: *Racism and Empire: White Settlers v. Coloured Immigrants in British Self-Governing Colonies, 1830–1910* (Ithaca, NY: Cornell University Press)

Hyde, H. M. 1970: *The Other Love: An Historical and Contemporary Survey of Homosexuality in Britain* (London: Heinemann)

Hyde, Janet Shibley 1986: *Understanding Human Sexuality* (New York: McGraw-Hill)

Hyman, Richard 1984: *Strikes* (2nd edn, London: Fontana)

Ianni, Francis A. J. 1974: *Black Mafia* (New York: Simon and Schuster)

Ianni, Francis A. J. and Elizabeth Reuss-Ianni 1973: *A Family Business: Kinship and Social Control in Organized Crime* (New York: Mentor)

ICS Newsletter 1987: 'The US economy: who owns the wealth, who needs welfare, who saves, and why' (Institute for Social Research, Michigan: University of Michigan, Winter 1986–7)

Idell, Albert 1956: *The Bernal Diaz Chronicles* (New York: Doubleday)

Ignatieff, Michael 1978: *A Just Measure of Pain: The Penitentiary in the Industrial Revolution 1750–1850* (London: Macmillan)

Illich, Ivan D. 1973: *Deschooling Society* (Harmondsworth: Penguin)

Ingham, Geoffrey 1984: *Capitalism Divided? The City and Industry in British Social Development* (London: Macmillan)

IISS (International Institute for Strategic Studies) 1987: *Strategic Survey, 1986–1987* (London)

Issel, William 1985: *Social Change in the United States, 1945–1983* (London: Macmillan)

Jackman, Mary R. and Robert W. Jackman 1983: *Class Awareness in the United States* (Berkeley: University of California Press)

Jackson, K. 1967: *The Ku Klux Klan in the City, 1915–1930* (Oxford: Oxford University Press)

Jackson, Kenneth T. 1981: 'The spatial dimensions of social control: race, ethnicity and government housing policy in the United States, 1918–1968', in Bruce N. Stave (ed.), *Modern Industrial Cities: History, Policy and Survival* (Beverly Hills, Ca.: Sage)

Jackson, Kenneth T. 1985: *Crabgrass Frontier: The Suburbanization of the United States* (New York: Oxford University Press)

Jackson, Michael P. 1986: *Industrial Relations* (3rd edn, London: Croom Helm)

Jacobs, Jane 1961: *The Death and Life of Great American Cities* (Harmondsworth: Penguin)

Jaher, Frederic Cople (ed.) 1973: *The Rich, the Well Born and the Powerful* (Urbana: University of Illinois Press)

Jaher, Frederic Cople 1980: 'The gilded elite: American multimillionaires, 1865 to the present', in William D. Rubinstein (ed.), *Wealth and the Wealthy in the Modern World* (London: Croom Helm)

James, William 1890: *Principles of Psychology* (New York: Holt, Rinehart and Winston)

Janelle, D. G. 1968: 'Central place development in a time–space framework', *Professional Geographer*, 20

Janowitz, Morris 1977: *Military Institutions and Coercion in the Developing Nations: An Essay in Comparative Analysis* (Chicago: University of Chicago Press)

Janus, S. S. and D. H. Heid Bracey 1980: 'Runaways: pornography and prostitution' (New York: mimeo)

Jencks, Christopher et al. 1972: *Inequality: A Reassessment of the Effects of Family and School in America* (New York: Basic Books)

Jenkins, Simon 1986: *The Market for Glory: Fleet Street Ownership in the Twentieth Century* (London: Faber and Faber)

Jenkins, Simon 1987: 'Eve versus the Adams of the Church', *Sunday Times*, 6 September

Jensen, Arthur 1967: 'How much can we boost IQ and scholastic achievement?', *Harvard Educational Review*, 29

Jensen, Arthur 1979: *Bias in Mental Testing* (New York: Free Press)

Johnson, Chalmers 1964: *Revolution and the Social System* (Stanford, Ca.: Stanford University Press)

Johnson, Chalmers 1966: *Revolutionary Change* (Boston, Mass.: Little, Brown)

Jones, Barry 1982: *Sleepers Awake! Technology and the Future of Work* (Brighton: Wheatsheaf)

Jones, R. and Schneider, P. 1984: 'Self-help production cooperatives: government-administered cooperatives during the depression', in R. Jackall and H. Levin, (eds), *Worker Cooperatives in America* (Berkeley: University of California Press)

Jordan, Winthrop 1968; *White Over Black* (Chapel Hill: University of North Carolina Press)

Jorgensen, James 1980: *The Graying of America* (New York: Dial Press)

Jowell, Roger et al. (eds) 1986: *British Social Attitudes: The Nineteen Eighty-Six Report* (Aldershot: Gower)

Kahn, R. N. 1986: 'Multinational companies and the world economy: economic and technological impact', *Impact of Science on Society*, 36

Kaldor, Mary 1982: *The Baroque Arsenal* (New York: Hill and Wang)

Kamata, Satoshi 1982: *Japan in the Passing Lane* (London: Allen and Unwin)

Kamin, Leon J. 1977: *The Science and Politics of IQ* (Harmondsworth: Penguin)

Karabel, Jerome and A. H. Halsey (eds) 1977: *Power and Ideology in Education* (Oxford: Oxford University Press)

Kart, Gary S. 1985: *The Social Realities of Ageing* (Boston, Mass.: Allyn and Bacon)

Kasarda, John D. and Morris Janowitz 1974: 'Community attachment in mass society', *American Sociological Review*, 39

Katz, Elihu et al. 1978: *Broadcasting in the Third World: Promise and Performance* (London: Macmillan)

Katz, G. 1976: *Gay American History: Lesbians and Gay Men in the USA* (New York: Thomas Y. Crowell)

Katz, Sedelle and Mary Ann Mazur 1979: *Understanding the Rape Victim: A Synthesis of Research Findings* (London: Wiley)

Kautsky, John J. 1982: *The Politics of Aristocratic Empires* (Chapel Hill: University of North Carolina Press)

Kavanagh, Dennis A. 1987: *Thatcherism and British Politics* (Oxford: Oxford University Press)

Kelly, J. E. 1982: *Scientific Management: Job Re-design and Work Performance* (New York: Academic Press)

Kelso, W. 1984: *Kingsmill Plantations, 1619–1800: Archaeology of Country Life in Colonial Virginia* (Orlando: Academic Press)

Kennedy, Gavin 1983: *Defence Economics* (New York: St Martin's Press)

Keohane, Robert 1984: *After Hegemony* (Princeton, NJ: Princeton University Press)

Kern, Steven 1983: *The Culture of Time and Space: 1880–1918* (Cambridge, Mass.: Harvard University Press)

Kerner Commission 1968: *Report of the National Advisory Commission on Civil Disorders* (New York: Bantam)

Kerr, Clark 1983: *The Future of Industrialized Societies* (Cambridge, Mass.: Harvard University Press)

Kerr, Clark et al. 1960: *Industrialism and Industrial Man: The Problems of Labour and Management in Economic Growth* (Cambridge, Mass.: Harvard University Press)

Kesselman, Mark et al. 1987: *European Politics in Transition* (Lexington, Mass.: D. C. Heath)

King, D. (ed.) 1979: *The Cherokee Indian Nation* (Knoxville: University of Tennessee Press)

Kinsey, Alfred C. et al. 1948: *Sexual Behaviour in the Human Male* (Philadelphia: W. B. Saunders)

Kinsey, Alfred C. et al. 1953: *Sexual Behaviour in the Human Female* (Philadelphia: W. B. Saunders)

Kitcher, Philip 1985: *Vaulting Ambition: Sociobiology and the Quest for Human Nature* (Cambridge, Mass.: MIT Press)

Kjekshus, H. 1977: *Ecology, Control and Economic Development in East African History* (London: Heinemann)

Klein, Rudolph 1974: 'Accountability in the National Health Service', *Political Quarterly*, 41

Klein, Rudolf 1983: *The Politics of the National Health Service* (London: Longman)

Knorr-Cetina, Karen and Aaron V. Cicourel (eds) 1981: *Advances in Social Theory and Methodology: Towards an Interpretation of Micro- and Macro-Sociologies* (London: Routledge and Kegan Paul)

Koestler, Arthur 1976: *The Act of Creation* (London: Hutchinson)

Kogan, Maurice, with David Kogan 1988: *The Attack on Higher Education* (London: Kogan Page)

Kohn, Melvin 1969: *Class and Conformity* (Homeward, Ill.: Dorsey Press)

Komarovsky, Mirra 1976: *Dilemmas of Masculinity* (New York: Norton)

Kosa, John and Irving Kenneth Zola (eds) 1975: *Poverty and Health: A Sociological Analysis* (Cambridge, Mass.: Harvard University Press)

Kovel, Joel 1970: *White Racism: A Psychohistory* (New York: Random House)

Kramer, S. N. 1959: *History Begins at Sumer* (New York: Anchor)

Krause, Elliot A. 1977: *Power and Illness: The Political Sociology of Health and Health Care* (New York: Elsevier)

Krieger, Joel 1986: *Reagan, Thatcher, and the Politics of Decline* (Cambridge: Polity Press)

Krupat, Edward 1985: *People in Cities: The Urban Environment and Its Effects* (Cambridge: Cambridge University Press)

Kubalkova, V. and A. A. Cruickshank 1981: *International Inequality* (London: Croom Helm)

Kübler-Ross, Elisabeth 1975: *Death: The Final Stage of Growth* (Englewood Cliffs, NJ: Prentice-Hall)

Kübler-Ross, Elisabeth 1987: *Living with Death and Dying* (London: Souvenir Press)

Kumar, Krishan 1978: *Prophecy and Progress: The Sociology of Industrial and Post-Industrial Society* (London: Penguin)

Labov, William 1978: *Sociolinguistic Patterns* (Oxford: Basil Blackwell)

Lake, R. 1981: *The New Suburbanites: Race and Housing in the Suburbs* (New Brunswick, NJ: Center for Urban Policy Research, Rutgers University Press)

Lancet 1974: 'World Health Losing Ground', *The Lancet*, 18 May

Landes, David S. 1969: *The Unbound Prometheus* (Cambridge: Cambridge University Press)

Lane, Harlan 1976: *The Wild Boy of Aveyron* (Cambridge, Mass.: Harvard University Press)

Lane, James B. 1974: *Jacob A. Riis and the American City* (London: Kennikat Press)

Landry, Bart 1987: *The New Black Middle Class* (Berkeley: University of California Press)

Lantenari, Vittorio 1963: *The Religions of the Oppressed: A Study of Modern Messianic Cults* (New York: Knopf)

Lantz, Herman, Martin Shultz and Mary O'Hara 1977: 'The changing American family from the pre-industrial to the industrial period: a final report', *American Sociological Review*, 42

Lappé, Frances Moore and Joseph Collins 1980: *Aid as an Obstacle* (San Francisco: Institute for Food and Development Policy)

Lapping, Brian 1986: *Apartheid: A History* (London: Grafton Books)

Laqueur, Walter 1976: *Guerrilla: A Historical and Critical Study* (Boston, Mass.: Little, Brown)

Large, Peter 1984: *The Micro Revolution Revisited* (Totowa: Rowan and Littlefield)

Laslett, Peter 1977: *Family Life and Illicit Love in Earlier Generations* (Cambridge: Cambridge University Press)

Laslett, Peter 1979: *The World We Have Lost* (London: Methuen)

Latane, B. and J. Darley 1970: *The Unresponsive Bystander: Why Doesn't He Help?* (New York: Appleton Century Crofts)

Lazarsfeld, Paul F., Bernard Berelson and Hazel Gaudet 1948: *The People's Choice* (New York: Columbia University Press)

Le Bon, Gustave 1960: *The Crowd* (New York: Viking. First pub. 1895)

Leach, Edmund 1976: *Culture and Communication: The Logic by which Symbols are Connected* (Cambridge: Cambridge University Press)

Lee, Laurie 1965: *Cider with Rosie* (London: Hogarth Press)

Lee, R. 1960: *The Chinese in the United States of America* (Oxford: Oxford University Press)

Lee, R. B. 1968: 'What hunters do for a living or, how to make out on scarce resources', in R. B. Lee and I. Devore (eds), *Man the Hunter* (Chicago: Aldine)

Lee, R. B. 1969: '¡Kung Bushman subsistence: an input–output analysis', in A. P. Vayda (ed.), *Environment and Cultural Behaviour* (New York: Natural History Press)

Lees, Andrew 1985: *Cities Perceived: Urban Society in European and American Thought, 1820–1940* (New York: Columbia University Press)

Leiuffsrud, Hakon and Alison Woodward 1987: 'Women at class crossroads: repudiating conventional theories of family class', *Sociology*, 21

Lemert, Edwin 1972: *Human Deviance, Social Problems and Social Control* (Englewood Cliffs, NJ: Prentice-Hall)

Lenski, Gerhard 1966: *Power and Privilege* (New York: McGraw-Hill)

Lenski, Gerhard and Jean Lenski 1982: *Human Societies* (4th edn, New York: McGraw-Hill)

Lerner, Barbara 1982: 'American education: how are we doing?', *Public Interest*, 69

Leslie, Gerald R. 1982: *The Family in Social Context* (5th edn, Oxford: Oxford University Press)

Levison, Andrew 1974: *The Working Class Majority* (New York: Coward, McGann and Geoghegan)

Lewontin, Richard 1982: *Human Diversity* (London: W. H. Freeman)

Liazos, A. 1972: 'The poverty of the sociology of deviance: nuts, sluts and perverts', in *Social Problems*, 20

Lieberson, Stanley 1972: 'An empirical study of military–industrial linkages', in Sam C. Sarkesian (ed.), *The Military–Industrial Complex: A Re-assessment* (Washington DC: Seven Locks Press)

Lieberman, M. 1978: *Power for the Poor – The Family Centre Project: An Experiment in Self-Help* (London: Allen and Unwin)

Lieberson, Stanley 1963: *Ethnic Patterns in American Cities* (New York: Free Press)

Liebert, Robert M., Joyce N. Sprafkin and M. A. S. Davidson 1982: *The Early Window: Effects of Television on Children and Youth* (London: Pergamon Press)

Liederman, P. Herbert, Stephen R. Tulkin and Ann Rosenfeld 1977: *Culture and Infancy: Variations in the Human Experience* (New York: Academic Press)

Lifton, Robert J. et al. 1982: *Indefensible Weapons: The Political and Psychological Case against Nuclearism* (New York: Basic Books)

Light, Donald W. 1986: 'Corporate medicine for profit', *Scientific American*, 255

Light, Donald W. 1987: 'Social control and the American health care system', in Howard E. Freeman and Sol Levine (eds), *Handbook of Medical Sociology* (4th edn, Englewood Cliffs, NJ: Prentice-Hall)

Lindblom, Charles E. 1977: *Politics and Markets* (New York: Basic Books)

Linden, E. 1976: *Apes, Men and Language* (Harmondsworth: Penguin)

Linhart, R. 1981: *The Assembly Line* (London: John Calder)

Linton, Ralph 1937: 'One hundred percent American', *American Mercury*, 40

Lipset, Seymour Martin (ed.) 1981: *Party Coalitions in the 1980s* (San Francisco: Institute for Contemporary Affairs)

Lipset, Seymour Martin and Reinhard Bendix 1959: *Social Mobility in Industrial Society* (Berkeley: University of California Press)

Lipton, M. 1986: *Capitalism and Apartheid* (Aldershot: Wildwood House)

Littlejohn, James 1972: *Social Stratification* (London: Allen and Unwin)

Littler, Craig and Graeme Salaman 1984: *Class at Work: The Design, Allocation and Control of Jobs* (London: Batsford)

Lockwood, David 1966: *The Blackcoated Worker: A Study in Class Consciousness* (London: Unwin)

Lodge, Juliet (ed.) 1981: *Terrorism: A Challenge to the State* (New York: St Martin's Press)

Lofland, John 1977: 'The dramaturgy of state executions', in Horace Bleackley and John Lofland, *State Executions, Viewed Historically and Sociologically* (Montclair, NJ: Patterson Smith)

Logan, John R. and Harvey L. Molotch 1987: *Urban Fortunes: The Political Economy of Place* (Berkeley: University of California Press)

Lombroso, Cesare 1911: *Crime: Its Causes and Remedies* (Boston, Mass.: Little, Brown)

Lopata, Helena 1977: 'Widows and widowers', *Humanist*, 37

Lowe, Stuart 1986: *Urban Social Movements: The City after Castells* (London: Macmillan)

Luard, E. 1977: *International Agencies: The Emerging Framework of Interdependence* (New York: Oceana)

Lueptow, L. B. 1975: 'Parental status and influence on the achievement orientations of high school seniors', *Sociology of Education*, 48

Luft, Harold S. 1978: *Poverty and Health: Economic Causes and Consequences of Health Problems* (Cambridge, Mass.: Ballinger Press)

Luia, Z. 1974: 'Recent women college graduates: a study of rising expectations', *American Journal of Ortho Psychiatry*, 44.

Lynch, K. 1976: *Making Sense of a Region* (Cambridge, Mass.: MIT Press)

Lyon, David 1987: *The Information Society: Issues and Illusions* (Cambridge: Polity Press)

Lystad, Mary (ed.) 1986: *Violence in the Home: Interdisciplinary Perspectives* (New York: Brunner and Mazel)

McConville, Sean 1981: *A History of English Prison Administration*, vol. I (London: Routledge and Kegan Paul)

McGill, Peter 1987: 'Sunset in the East', *Observer*, 2 August

McGoldrick, Ann 1973: 'Early retirement: a new leisure opportunity?', Leisure Studies Association Conference Paper No. 15 (London: Continued Education Centre, Polytechnic of Central London)

McHale, Magda Cordell et al. 1979: *Children in the World* (Washington DC: Population Reference Bureau)

McKay, David 1983: *American Politics and Society* (Oxford: Martin Robertson)

Mackenzie, Donald and Judy Wajcman 1985: *The Social Shaping of Technology* (Milton Keynes: Open University Press)

Mackenzie, Gavin 1973: *The Aristocracy of Labour: The Position of Skilled Craftsmen in the American Class Structure* (Cambridge: Cambridge University Press)

McKenzie, R. D. 1933: *The Metropolitan Community* (New York: Russell and Russell)

MacKinnon, Catherine A. 1979: *Sexual Harassment of Working Women: A Case of Sex Discrimination* (New Haven, Conn.: Yale University Press)

Macklin, Eleanore D. 1978: 'Non-marital heterosexual co-habitation', *Marriage and Family Review*, 1

McLean, Charles 1978: *The Wolf Children* (New York: Hill and Wang)

McNeill, William H. 1983: *The Pursuit of Power: Technology, Armed Force and Society since AD 1000* (Oxford: Basil Blackwell)

McPhail, Thomas L. 1987: *Electronic Communication: The Future of International Broadcasting and Communication* (2nd edn, Beverly Hills, Ca.: Sage)

Macquet, Jacques 1961: *The Premise of Inequality in Ruanda. A Study of Political Relations in a Central African Kingdom* (London: International African Institute)

Maddox, Brenda 1975: *The Half Parent* (New York: Evans)

Mair, Lucy 1974: *African Societies* (Cambridge: Cambridge University Press)

Malinowski, Bronislaw 1982: *'Magic, Science and Religion', and Other Essays* (London: Souvenir Press)

Mallier, A. T. and M. J. Rosser 1987: *Women and the Economy: A Comparative Study of Britain and the USA* (London: Macmillan)

Mann, Michael 1986: *The Sources of Social Power*. Vol. I: *A History of Power from the Beginning to 1760* (Cambridge: Cambridge University Press)

Mann, Peter H. 1965: *An Approach to Urban Sociology* (London: Routledge and Kegan Paul)

Mann, Peter H. 1985: *Methods of Social Investigation* (Oxford: Basil Blackwell)

Mansbridge, J. J. 1983: *Beyond Adversary Democracy* (Chicago: University of Chicago Press)

Manwaring, T. and S. Sigler (eds) 1985: *Breaking the Nation* (London: Pluto Press)

Marcuse, Herbert 1968: *Reason and Revolution* (London: Routledge and Kegan Paul)

Marsh, Catherine 1982: *The Survey Method: The Contribution of Surveys to Sociological Explanation* (London: Allen and Unwin)

Marsh, Peter 1982: *The Robot Age* (London: Sphere)

Marshall, S. L. A. 1947: *Men Against Fire* (New York: Marrow)

Marshall, T. H. 1973: *Class, Citizenship and Social Development* (Westport: Greenwood Press)

Marty, Martin E. 1970: *The Righteous Empire* (New York: Dial Press)

Marwick, Arthur 1974: *War and Social Change in the Twentieth Century* (London: Macmillan)

Marx, Karl 1963a: 'Alienated labour', in T. B. Bottomore (ed.), *Karl Marx: Early Writings* (Harmondsworth: Penguin)

Marx, Karl 1963b: 'Economic and philosophical manuscripts', in T. B. Bottomore (ed.), *Karl Marx: Early Writings* (Harmondsworth: Penguin)

Marx, Karl 1970: *Capital*, vol. I (London: Lawrence and Wishart. First pub. 1864)

Marx, Karl and Friedrich Engels 1968: 'Manifesto of the Communist Party', in *Karl Marx and Friedrich Engels: Selected Works in One Volume* (London: Lawrence and Wishart. First pub. 1848)

Mason, P. 1971: *Patterns of Dominance* (Oxford: Oxford University Press)

Massey, Doreen 1984: *Spatial Divisions of Labour: Social Structures and the Geography of Production* (London: Methuen)

Matteis, R. 1979: 'The New Bank Office on Customer Service', *Harvard Business Review*, March/April

Mattelart, A. 1979: *Multinational Corporations and the Control of Culture: The Ideological Apparatuses of Imperialism* (Atlantic Highlands, NJ: Humanities Press)

Matthews, Mervyn 1972: *Class and Society in Soviet Russia* (London: Allen and Unwin)

Matthews, Sarah H. 1979: *The Social World of Old Women: Management of Self-identity* (Beverly Hills, Ca.: Sage)

Maxwell Atkinson, J. and John Heritage (eds) 1984: *Structures of Social Action: Studies in Conversation Analysis* (New York: Cambridge University Press)

Mayo, Elton 1933: *The Human Problems of an Industrial Civilization* (London: Macmillan)

Mayo, Elton 1949: *The Social Problems of an Industrial Civilization* (London: Routledge and Kegan Paul)

Mead, George Herbert 1934: *Mind, Self and Society* (Chicago: University of Chicago Press)

Meadows, Donnella H. et al. 1972: *The Limits to Growth* (New York: Universe Books)

Mednick, S. et al. 1982: 'Biology and violence', in Martin E. Wolfgang and N. A. Wiener (eds), *Criminal Violence* (London: Sage)

Mednick, S. A. et al. 1987: *The Causes of Crime. New Biological Approaches* (Cambridge: Cambridge University Press)

Mednick, S. and T. Moffitt (eds) 1986: *The New Biocriminology* (Cambridge: Cambridge University Press)

Meier, August and Elliott Rudick 1973: *CORE: A Study in the Civil Rights Movement, 1945–1968* (Oxford: Oxford University Press)

Melbin, Murray 1978: 'The colonisation of time', in Tommy Carlstein, Don Parkes and Nigel Thrift: *Human Activity and Time Geography* (London: Edward Arnold)

Melbin, Murray 1987: *Night as Frontier: Colonising the World after Dark* (New York: Free Press)

Melton, J. Gordon 1978: *Encyclopaedia of American Religions* (2 vols, Wilmington: McGrath)

Merritt, Giles 1982: *World Out of Work* (London: Collins)

Merton, Robert K. 1949: 'Discrimination and the American creed', in R. M. McIver, *Discrimination and National Welfare* (New York: Harper and Row)

Merton, Robert K. 1957: *Social Theory and Social Structure* (revised edn, Glencoe:

Free Press)

Meyer, Alfred G. 1970: 'Theories of convergence', in Chalmers Johnson (ed.), *Change in Communist Systems* (Stanford, Ca.: Stanford University Press)

Meyr, S. 1981: *The Five Dollar Day: Labour Management and Social Control in the Ford Motor Company, 1908–1921* (New York: State University of New York Press)

Michels, Robert 1967: *Political Parties* (New York: Free Press. First pub. 1911)

Micklin, Michael and Harvey M. Choldin 1984: *Sociological Human Ecology: Contemporary Issues and Applications* (Boulder, Colo.: Westview)

Milgram, Stanley 1973: *Obedience to Authority: An Experimental View* (New York: Harper and Row)

Milgram, Stanley 1977: *The Individual in a Social World: Essays and Experiments* (Reading, Mass.: Addison-Wesley)

Miller, Eleanor M. 1986: *The Street Woman* (Philadelphia: Temple University Press)

Miller, S. M. 1960: 'Comparative social mobility', *Journal of Current Sociology*, 9

Miller, S. M. 1971: 'A comment: the future of social mobility studies', *American Journal of Sociology*, 77

Miller, William L. 1983: *The Survey Method in Social and Political Sciences: Achievements, Failures, Prospects* (New York: St Martin's Press)

Mills, C. Wright 1956: *The Power Elite* (Oxford: Oxford University Press)

Mills, C. Wright 1970: *The Sociological Imagination* (Harmondsworth: Penguin)

Mills, D. Quinn and Janice McCormick 1985: *Industrial Relations in Transition: Cases and Text* (New York: Wiley)

Milward, Alan S. 1984: *The Economic Effects of the World Wars on Britain* (London: Macmillan)

Miner, Horace 1956: 'Body ritual among the Nacirema', *American Anthropologist*, 58

Mintz, F. and Michael Schwartz 1985: *The Power Structure of American Business* (Chicago: University of Chicago Press)

Mirsky, Jonathan 1982: 'China and the one child family', *New Society*, 59, 18 February

Mitchell, Juliet 1973: *Psychoanalysis and Feminism* (London: Allen Lane)

Mitterauer, Michael and Reinhard Sider 1982: *The European Family: Patriarchy to Partnership from the Middle Ages to the Present* (Oxford: Basil Blackwell)

Molotch, Harvey, and Deirdre Boden 1985: 'Talking social structure: discourse, dominance and the Watergate hearings', *American Sociological Review*, 50

Mommsen, Wolfgang J. 1982: 'Violence and terrorism in Western industrial societies', in W. J. Mommsen et al., *Social Protest, Violence and Terror in Nineteenth and Twentieth-Century Europe* (New York: St Martin's Press)

Money, John and Anke A. Ehrhardt 1972: *Man and Woman/Boy and Girl* (Baltimore, Md.: Johns Hopkins University Press)

Montagu, Ashley 1980: *Sociobiology Examined* (Oxford: Oxford University Press)

Monter, E. William 1977: 'The pedestal and the stake: courtly love and witchcraft', in Renate Bridenthal and Claudia Koouz, *Becoming Visible: Women in European History* (Boston, Mass.: Houghton Mifflin)

Moore, Barrington 1965: *Political Power and Social Theory* (New York: Harper and Row)

Moquin, W. (ed.) 1974: *A Documentary History of the Italian Americans* (New York: Praeger)

Morawska, Eva 1985: *For Bread with Butter: Life-Worlds of the East Central Europeans in Johnstown, Pennsylvania, 1890–1940* (Cambridge: Cambridge University Press)

Morgan, Kevin and Andrew Sayer 1988: *Microcircuits of Capital: The Electronics Industry and Uneven Development* (Cambridge: Polity Press)

Morris, Allison 1987: *Women, Crime and Justice* (Oxford: Basil Blackwell)

Morris, Desmond 1977: *Manwatching: A Field Guide to Human Behavior* (New York:

Abrams)

Morris, Jan 1986: *Conundrum* (Oxford: Oxford University Press)

Mortimer, Edward 1982: *Faith and Power: The Politics of Islam* (London: Faber and Faber)

Moynihan, Daniel P. 1965: *The Negro Family: A Case for National Action* (Washington DC: US Government Printing Office)

Muller, Peter O. 1981: *Contemporary Suburban America* (Englewood Cliffs, NJ: Prentice-Hall)

Mumford, Lewis 1973: *Interpretations and Forecasts* (London: Secker and Warburg)

Munck, R. 1986: *Politics and Dependency in the Third World: The Case of Latin America* (London: Zed Books)

Murdock, George 1949: *Social Structure* (New York: Macmillan)

Murdock, George Peter 1945: 'The common denominator of cultures', in Ralph Linton (ed.), *The Science of Man in a World of Crisis* (New York: Columbia University Press)

Murray, Martin 1987: *South Africa: Time of Agony, Time of Destiny* (London: Verso)

Naipaul, V. S. 1976: *India: A Wounded Civilization* (Harmondsworth: Penguin)

Nairn, Tom 1977: *The Break-up of Britain* (London: New Left Books)

Naksase, T. 1981: 'Some characteristics of Japanese-type multi-national enterprises', *Capital and Class*, 13

Napes, G. 1970: 'Unequal justice: a growing disparity in criminal sentences troubles legal experts', *Wall Street Journal*, 9 September

Neary, Ian J. 1986: 'Socialist and communist party attitudes towards discrimination against Japan's Burakumin', *Political Studies*, 34

Needham, Joseph 1975: *The Development of Iron and Steel Technology in China* (Cambridge: Cambridge University Press)

Nelson, W. 1975: *Americanization of the Common Law: The Impact of Legal Change on Massachusetts Society, 1760–1830* (Cambridge, Mass.: Harvard University Press)

Newman, Philip L. 1965: *Knowing the Gururumba* (New York: Holt, Rinehart and Winston)

Newspaper Advertising Bureau 1978: *Seven Days in March: Major News Stories in the Press and on TV* (New York)

Nichols, Eve K. 1986: *Mobilizing Against Aids* (Cambridge, Mass.: Harvard University Press)

Nichols, Theo and Hugh Beynon 1977: *Living with Capitalism* (London: Routledge and Kegan Paul)

Nie, Norman H., Sidney Verba and John R. Petrocik 1976: *The Changing American Voter* (Cambridge, Mass.: Harvard University Press)

NORC 1981: *Social Survey* (Princeton, NJ: National Opinion Research Centre)

Noel, Gerard 1980: *The Anatomy of the Catholic Church* (London: Hodder and Stoughton)

Nordhaus, W. D. 1975: 'The political business cycle', *Review of Economic Studies*, 42

Novak, M. A. 1979: 'Social recovery of monkeys isolated for the first year of life: II. Long-term assessment', *Developmental Psychology*, 2

Nyilas, Jozsef 1982: *The World Economy and its Main Development Tendencies* (The Hague: Martinus Nijhoff)

Oakes, Jeannie 1985: *Keeping Track: How Schools Structure Inequality* (New Haven, Conn.: Yale University Press)

Oakley, Ann 1974: *The Sociology of Housework* (Oxford: Martin Robertson)

Oakley, Ann 1976: *Housewife* (Harmondsworth: Penguin)

Oakley, Ann 1982: *Subject Women* (London: Fontana)

Oberg, Jan 1980: 'The new international military order: a threat to human security', in Eide Asbjorn et al. (eds), *Problems of Contemporary Militarism* (New York: St Martin's Press)

Offe, Claus 1984: *Contradictions of the Welfare State* (Cambridge, Mass.: MIT Press)

Offe, Claus 1985: *Disorganized Capitalism* (Cambridge: Polity Press)

Oltman, Ruth 1970: 'Campus 1970 – Where do women stand?', *American Association of University Women Journal*, 64

Orenstein, Alan and William R. F. Phillips 1984: *Understanding Social Research: An Introduction* (Boston, Mass.: Allyn and Bacon)

Oswalt, Wendell Hillman 1972: *Other Peoples, Other Customs: World Ethnography and its History* (New York: Doubleday)

Otterbein, Keith F. 1985: *The Evolution of War: A Cross-Cultural Study* (New Haven, Conn.: Human Relations Area Files Press)

Ouchi, William G. 1979: 'A conceptual framework for the design of organizational control mechanisms', *Management Science*, 25

Ouchi, William G. 1981: *Theory Z: How American Business Can Meet the Japanese Challenge* (Reading, Mass.: Addison-Wesley)

Pagden, Anthony 1982: *The Fall of Natural Man* (Cambridge: Cambridge University Press)

Pahl, J. 1978: *A Refuge for Battered Women* (London: HMSO)

Pahl, R. E. 1977: 'Collective consumption and the state in capitalist and state socialist societies', in Richard Scase (ed.), *Industrial Society: Class, Cleavage and Control* (London: Tavistock)

Pahl, R. E. 1984: *Divisions of Labour* (Oxford: Basil Blackwell)

Pahl, R. E. 1987: 'A comparative approach to the study of the informal economy', paper presented at the 1987 Meeting of the American Sociological Association, August

Pahl, R. E. and P. A. Wilson 1987: 'The family as a hologram: first you see it then you don't', *Sociological Review*, 35

Pahl, R. E. and J. Winkler 1974: 'The economic elite: theory and practice', in Philip Stanworth and Anthony Giddens, *Elites and Power in British Society* (Cambridge: Cambridge University Press)

Pandey, Trikoli Nath 1972: 'Anthropologists at Zuñi', *Proceedings of the American Philosophical Society*, 166

Pandey, Trikoli Nath 1975: '"India man" among American Indians', in André Beteille and T. N. Madan (eds), *Encounter and Experience: Personal Accounts of Fieldwork* (Honolulu: University Press of Hawaii)

Park, Robert E. 1952: *Human Communities: The City and Human Ecology* (New York: Free Press)

Parkes, Don and Nigel Thrift 1980: *Times, Spaces and Places* (Chichester: Wiley)

Parkin, Frank 1971: *Class Inequality and Political Order* (London: McGibbon and Kee)

Parkin, Frank 1979: *Marxism and Class Theory: A Bourgeois Critique* (London: Tavistock)

Parkinson, C. Northcote 1957: *Parkinson's Law* (Boston, Mass.: Houghton Mifflin)

Parnes, Herbert S. 1985: *Retirement among American Men* (Lexington, Mass.: Lexington Books)

Parsons, Talcott 1952: *The Social System* (London: Tavistock)

Parsons, Talcott 1964: 'Evolutionary universals in society', *American Sociological Review*, 29

Parsons, Talcott 1966: *Societies: Evolutionary and Comparative Perspectives* (Englewood Cliffs, NJ: Prentice-Hall)

Parten, Mildred 1932: 'Social play among preschool children', *Journal of Abnormal and Social Psychology*, 27

Pascale, Richard T. and Anthony G. Athos 1982: *The Art of Japanese Management* (Harmondsworth: Penguin)

Patrick, Donald L. and Graham Scambler (eds) 1982: *Sociology as Applied to Medicine* (New York: Macmillan)

Paul, Diana Y. 1985: *Women in Buddhism: Images of the Feminine in the Mahayana Tradition* (Berkeley: University of California Press)

Payne, E. J. 1899: *History of the New World Called America* (2 vols, London: Oxford University Press)

Pearson, G. 1975: *The Deviant Imagination* (Basingstoke: Macmillan)

Pearton, Maurice 1984: *The Knowledgeable State: Diplomacy, War and Technology since 1830* (Kansas: University Press of Kansas)

Perlmutter, Amos 1977: *The Military and Politics in Modern Times: On Professionals, Praetorians, and Revolutionary Soldiers* (New Haven, Conn.: Yale University Press)

Perlmutter, H. V. 1972: 'Towards research on and development of nations, unions and firms as worldwide institutions', in H. Gunter (ed.), *Transnational Industrial Relations* (New York: St Martin's Press)

Pickvance, Chris 1985: 'The rise and fall of urban movements and the role of comparative analysis', *Society and Space*, 3

Pinkney, A. 1986: *The Myth of Black Progress* (Cambridge: Cambridge University Press)

Piven, Frances Fox and Richard A. Cloward 1977: *Poor People's Movements: Why They Succeed, How They Fail* (New York: Pantheon)

Platt, Anthony 1969: *The Child Savers* (Chicago: University of Chicago Press)

Plummer, Kenneth 1975: *Sexual Stigma: An Interactive Account* (London: Routledge and Kegan Paul)

Pollack, O. 1950: *The Criminality of Women* (Westport: Greenwood Press)

Porter, J. 1971: *Black Child, White Child: The Development of Racial Attitudes* (Cambridge, Mass.: Harvard University Press)

Porter, Roy 1986: *Patients and Practitioners: Lay Perceptions of Medicine in Pre-Industrial Society* (Cambridge: Cambridge University Press)

Pragnall, A. 1985: *Television in Europe* (Manchester: European Institute for the Media)

Pred, Allen 1986: *Place, Practice and Structure: Social and Spatial Transformation in Southern Sweden, 1750–1850* (Cambridge: Polity Press)

President's Commission on Organized Crime 1985 and 1986: *Records of Hearings, March 14, 1984 and June 24–26, 1985* (Washington DC: US Government Printing Office)

Prins, H. 1980: *Offenders, Deviants or Patients?* (London: Tavistock)

Ramirez, Francisco O. and John Boli 1987: 'The political construction of mass schooling: European origins and worldwide institutionalism', *Sociology of Education*, 60

Randall, Vicky 1982: *Women and Politics* (London: Macmillan)

Rapoport, Robert and Rhona 1982: 'British families in transition', in R. N. Rapoport et al., *Families in Britain* (London: Routledge and Kegan Paul)

Reitlinger, Gerald 1957: *The SS: Alibi of a Nation, 1922–1945* (New York: Viking)

Renninger, C. and J. Williams 1966: 'Black–White colour-connotations and race awareness in pre-school children', *Journal of Perceptual and Motor Skills*, 22

Rex, John 1986: *Race and Ethnicity* (Milton Keynes: Open University Press)

Richards, M. P. M. (ed.) 1974: *The Integration of a Child into a Social World* (Cambridge: Cambridge University Press)

Richards, Martin and Paul Light (eds) 1986: *Children of Social Worlds* (Cambridge: Polity Press)

Richards, Martin, Jacqueline Burgoyne and Roger Ormrod 1987: *Divorce Matters* (Harmondsworth: Pelican)

Richardson, James T. et al. 1979: *Organized Miracles* (New Brunswick, NJ: Transaction Books)

Richardson, Ken and David Spears 1972: *Race, Culture and Intelligence* (Harmondsworth: Penguin)

Richman, Joel 1987: *Medicine and Health* (London: Longman)

Riddell, Peter 1985: *The Thatcher Government* (Oxford: Basil Blackwell)

Rights of Women Lesbian Custody Group 1986: *Lesbian Mothers' Legal Handbook* (London: Women's Press)

Riis, Jacob A. 1957: *How the Other Half Lives: Studies Among the Tenements of New York* (New York: Dover. First pub. 1890)

Riley, Matilda White 1987: 'On the significance of age in sociology', *American Sociological Review*, 52

Riley, Matilda White and Joan Waring 1976: 'Age and ageing', in Robert K. Merton and Robert Nisbet (eds), *Contemporary Social Problems* (4th edn, New York: Harcourt Brace Jovanovich)

Robinson, D. 1977: *Self-Help and Health: Mutual Aid for Modern Problems* (London: Martin Robertson)

Robinson, D. 1979: *Talking Out of Alcholism: The Self-Help Process of AA* (London: Croom Helm)

Robinson, D. 1980: 'Self-help health groups', in P. Smith, *Small Groups and Personal Change* (London: Methuen)

Rockford, E. Burke 1985: *Hare Krishna in America* (New Brunswick, NJ: Rutgers University Press)

Rodgers, Harrell R. Jr 1986: *Poor Women, Poor Families: The Economic Plight of America's Female-Headed Households* (Armonk, NY: M. E. Sharpe)

Roper Organization 1977: *Changing Public Attitudes Towards Television and Other Mass Media, 1959–1976* (Washington DC: Television Information Office)

Ropp, T. 1959: *War in the Modern World* (Westport: Greenwood Press)

Rosecrance, Richard 1986: *The Rise of the Trading State: Commerce and Conquest in the Modern World* (New York: Basic Books)

Rosen, Ruth 1982: *The Lost Sisterhood: Prostitution in America, 1900–1918* (Baltimore, Md.: Johns Hopkins University Press)

Rosenhan, D. 1973: 'On being sane in an insane place', *Science*, 179

Rosenthau, J. N. 1980: *The Study of Global Interdependence* (London: Frances Pinter)

Rosner, Menachem and Arnold S. Tannenbaum 1987: 'Organisational efficiency and egalitarian democracy in an international communal society: the Kibbutz', *British Journal of Sociology*, 38

Ross, Arthur M. 1954: 'The natural history of the strike', in Arthur Kornhauser, Robert Dubin and Arthur M. Ross, *Industrial Conflict* (New York: McGraw-Hill)

Ross, Arthur M. and P. T. Hartman 1960: *Changing Patterns of Industrial Conflict* (New York: Wiley)

Ross, George, Stanley Hoffmann and Sylvia Malzacher 1987: *The Mitterrand Experiment: Continuity and Change in Modern France* (Cambridge: Polity Press)

Rossi, Alice S. and Ann Calderwood 1973: *Academic Women on the Move* (New York: Russell Sage)

Roth, Martin and Jerome Kroll 1986: *The Reality of Mental Illness* (Cambridge: Cambridge University Press)

Rothman, D. 1971: *The Discovery of the Asylum* (Boston, Mass.: Little, Brown)

Rowbotham, Sheila 1973: *Women's Consciousness, Man's World* (Harmondsworth: Penguin)

Royal Commission on the National Health Service 1979: *Report* (London: HMSO)

Rubenstein, E. A. et al. (eds) 1972: *Television in Day to Day Life: Patterns of Use* (Washington DC: US Government Printing Office)

Rubenstein, E. A. et al. (eds) 1972: *Television and Social Behaviour* (Washington DC: US Government Printing Office)

Rubinstein, W. D. 1980: *Wealth and Inequality in Britain* (London: Faber and Faber)

Rudé, George 1959: *The Crowd in the French Revolution* (Oxford: Oxford University Press)

Rudé, George 1985: *The Crowd in History* (London: Lawrence and Wishart)

Rumble, Greville 1985: *The Politics of Nuclear Defence: A Comprehensive Introduction* (Cambridge: Polity Press)

Russell, D. 1981: *Sexual Exploitation: Rape, Child Abuse and Sexual Harassment* (Beverly Hills, Ca.: Sage)

Rutherford, A. 1984: *Prisons and the Process of Justice* (London: Heinemann)

Rutter, M. and H. Giller 1983: *Juvenile Delinquency: Trends and Perspectives* (Harmondsworth: Penguin)

Ryan, Tom 1985: 'The roots of masculinity', in Andy Metcalf and Martin Humphries (eds), *Sexuality of Men* (London: Pluto)

Sabel, Charles F. 1982: *Work and Politics: The Division of Labour in Industry* (Cambridge: Cambridge University Press)

Sack, Robert David 1986: *Human Territoriality: Its Theory and History* (Cambridge: Cambridge University Press)

Sahlins, Marshall 1972: *Stone Age Economics* (Chicago: Aldine)

Sahlins, Marshall 1976: *The Use and Abuse of Biology* (Ann Arbor: University of Michigan Press)

Sahlins, Marshall and Elman R. Service 1960: *Evolution and Culture* (Ann Arbor: University of Michigan Press)

Said, Edward 1985: *Orientalism* (Harmondsworth: Penguin)

Sakharov, Andrei D. 1974: *Sakharov Speaks*, ed. Harrison E. Salisbury (New York: Vintage)

Salaman, Graeme 1981: *Class and the Corporation* (London: Fontana)

Salaman, Graeme 1986: *Working* (London: Tavistock)

Sampson, Anthony 1982: *The Changing Anatomy of Britain* (London: Hodder and Stoughton)

Sanders, William B. 1974: *The Sociologist as Detective: An Introduction to Research Methods* (New York: Praeger)

Sargant, William 1959: *Battle for the Mind* (London: Pan)

Sarsby, H. 1983: *Romantic Love and Society: Its Place in the Modern World* (Harmondsworth: Penguin)

Saul, J. and S. Gelb 1986: *The Crisis in South Africa* (2nd edn, London: Zed Books)

Saunders, Christopher 1981: *The Political Economy of the New and Old Industrial Countries* (London: Butterworths)

Saunders, Peter 1986: *Social Theory and the Urban Question* (2nd edn, London: Hutchinson)

Saussure, Ferdinand de 1974: *Course in General Linguistics* (London: Fontana)

Sayers, Janet 1986: *Sexual Contradiction. Psychology, Psychoanalysis and Feminism* (London: Tavistock)

Saywell, Shelley 1985: *Women in War* (New York: Viking)

Scarman, Leslie George 1982: *The Scarman Report* (Harmondsworth: Penguin)

Schafer, Kermit 1965: *Prize Bloopers* (Greenwich: Fawcett)

Schaffer, H. R. 1970: *The Growth of Sociability* (Harmondsworth: Penguin)

Schapiro, Leonard 1972: *Totalitarianism* (London: Pall Mall)

Scheff, T. 1966: *Being Mentally Ill* (Chicago: Aldine)

Schell, Jonathan 1982: *The Fate of the Earth* (London: Jonathan Cape)

Schiller, Herbert I. 1969: *Mass Communications and American Empire* (New York: Augustus M. Kelley)

Schiller, Herbert I. 1978: 'Computer systems: power for whom and for what?', in *Journal of Communication*, 28

Schmid, Alex P. 1982: *Violence as Communication: Insurgent Terrorism and the Western News Media* (London: Sage)

Schorske, Carl 1963: 'The idea of the city in European thought: Voltaire to Spengler', in Oscar Handlin and John Burchard (eds), *The Historian and the City* (Cambridge, Mass.: Harvard University Press)

Schrire, Carmel (ed.) 1984: *Past and Present in Hunter Gatherer Studies* (New York: Academic Press)

Schuman, Howard, Charlotte Steel and Lawrence Bobo 1985: *Racial Attitudes in America: Trends and Interpretations* (Cambridge, Mass.: Harvard University Press)

Schumpeter, Joseph 1976: *Capitalism, Socialism and Democracy* (London: Allen and Unwin. First pub. 1942)

Schur, Edwin 1965: *Crimes Without Victims* (Englewood Cliffs, NJ: Prentice-Hall)

Schwartz, Gary 1970: *Sect Ideologies and Social Status* (Chicago: University of Chicago Press)

Scott, J. 1969: *The White Poppy* (New York: Harper and Row)

Scott, James Brown 1918: *President Wilson's Foreign Policy: Messages, Addresses, Papers* (Oxford: Oxford University Press)

Scott, James C. 1986: *Weapons of the Weak: Everyday Forms of Peasant Resistance* (New Haven, Conn.: Yale University Press)

Scott, John 1981: *Corporations, Classes and Capitalism* (2nd edn, London: Hutchinson)

Scriven, Jeannie 1984: 'Women at work in Sweden', in Marilyn J. Davidson and Cary L. Cooper (eds), *Working Women: An International Survey* (New York: Wiley)

Scull, Andrew 1979: *Museums of Madness: The Social Organization of Insanity in Nineteenth-Century England* (London: Allen Lane)

Scull, Andrew 1984: *Decarceration: Community Treatment and the Deviant – A Radical View* (Cambridge: Polity Press)

Segal, Alexander 1976: 'The sick role concept: understanding illness behaviour', *Journal of Health and Social Behaviour*, 17

Seidenberg, M. S. et al. 1979: 'Signing behaviour in apes: a critical review', *Cognition*, 7

Sennett, Richard and Jonathan Cobb 1977: *The Hidden Injuries of Class* (Cambridge: Cambridge University Press)

Sereny, Gitta 1984: *The Invisible Children: Child Prostitution in America, West Germany and Great Britain* (London: Deutsch)

Sewell, William H. 1971: 'Inequality of opportunity for higher education', *American Sociological Review*, 36

Sharp, Sue 1976: *Just Like a Girl* (Harmondsworth: Penguin)

Shattuck, Roger 1980: *The Forbidden Experiment: The Story of the Wild Boy of Aveyron* (New York: Farrar, Straus and Giroux)

Shawcross, Tim and Kim Fletcher 1987: 'How crime is organized in London', *Illustrated London News*, October

Sheehan, Michael 1983: *The Arms Race* (Oxford: Martin Robertson)

Sheehy, Gail 1973: *Hustling: Prostitution in Our Wide Open Society* (New York: Delacorte)

Shepherd, Gill 1987: 'Rank, gender and homosexuality: Mombasa as a key to understanding sexual options', in Pat Caplan (ed.), *The Social Construction of Sexuality* (London: Tavistock)

Sieber, Sam 1981: *Fatal Remedies: The Ironies of Social Intervention* (New York: Plenum Press)

Silverman, David 1982: *Secondary Analysis in Social Research: A Guide to Data Sources and Methods with Examples* (London: Allen and Unwin)

Silverman, Irwin 1985: *Qualitative Methodology and Sociology* (Aldershot: Gower)

Simon, Julian L. 1981: *The Ultimate Resource* (Princeton, NJ: Princeton University Press)

Sinclair, Peter 1987: *Unemployment: Economic Theory and Evidence* (Oxford: Basil Blackwell)

Singh, J. A. L. and Robert M. Zingg 1942: *Wolf Children and Feral Man* (New York: Harper and Row)

SIPRI (Stockholm International Peace Research Institute) 1986: *World Armament and Disarmament: Yearbook 1986* (London: Taylor and Francis)

Sitkoff, Howard 1981: *The Struggle for Black Equality, 1954–1980* (New York: Hill and Wang)

Sjoberg, Gideon 1960: *The Pre-Industrial City: Past and Present* (Glencoe: Free Press)

Sjoberg, Gideon 1963: 'The rise and fall of cities: a theoretical perspective', *International Journal of Comparative Sociology*, 4

Skidmore, Thomas E. 1974: *Black into White: Race and Nationality in Brazilian Thought* (Oxford: Oxford University Press)

Skilling, H. Gordon and Franklyn Griffith (eds) 1971: *Interest Groups in Soviet Politics* (Princeton, NJ: Princeton University Press)

Skocpol, Theda 1977: 'Wallerstein's world capitalist system: a theoretical and historical critique', *American Journal of Sociology*, 82

Skocpol, Theda 1979: *States and Social Revolutions: A Comparative Analysis of France, Russia and China* (Cambridge: Cambridge University Press)

Smart, Carol 1977: *Women, Crime and Criminology* (London: Routledge and Kegan Paul)

Smelser, Neil J. 1963: *Theory of Collective Behaviour* (New York: Free Press)

Smith, Adam 1910: *The Wealth of Nations* (London: Dent)

Smith, Anthony D. 1973: *The Concept of Social Change: A Critique of the Functionalist Theory of Social Change* (London: Routledge and Kegan Paul)

Smith, Anthony D. 1979: *Nationalism in the Twentieth Century* (Oxford: Martin Robertson)

Smith, Anthony 1980a: *Goodbye Gutenberg: The Newspaper Revolution of the 1980s* (Oxford: Oxford University Press)

Smith, Anthony 1980b: *How Western Culture Dominates the World* (Oxford: Oxford University Press)

Smith, Dorothy E. 1978: 'K is mentally ill: the anatomy of a factual account', *Sociology*, 12

Smith, D. (ed.) 1982: *Living Under Apartheid* (London: Allen and Unwin)

Smith, H. W. 1975: *Strategies of Social Research: The Methodological Imagination* (Englewood Cliffs, NJ: Prentice-Hall)

Smith, R. 1981: *Moon of Popping Trees* (Lincoln: University of Nebraska Press)

Sommerville, I. 1983: *Information Unlimited: The Applications of Information Technology* (London: Addison-Wesley)

Sorokin, Pitrim A. 1927: *Social Mobility* (New York: Harper)

Soustelle, J. 1970: *Daily Life of the Aztecs on the Eve of the Spanish Conquest* (Stanford,

Ca.: Stanford University Press)

Spada, J. 1979: *The Spada Report: The Newest Survey of Gay Male Sexuality* (New York: New American Library)

Spitz, René A. 1945: 'Hospitalism: an enquiry into the genesis of psychiatric conditions in early childhood', in Anna Freud et al. (eds), *The Psychoanalytic Study of the Child* (New York: International Universities Press)

Stack, Carol B. 1974: *All Our Kin* (New York: Harper and Row)

Stampp, Kenneth 1956: *The Peculiar Institution* (New York: Knopf)

Stanton, Elizabeth Cady 1985: *The Woman's Bible: The Original Feminist Attack on the Bible* (Edinburgh: Polygon Books. First pub. 1895)

Stanton, Elizabeth Cady, Susan B. Anthony and Matilda Joslyn Gage (eds) 1889: *History of Woman Suffrage*, vol. I (Rochester, NY: Charles Mann)

Stanworth, Michelle 1984: 'Women and class analysis: a reply to John Goldthorpe', *Sociology*, 18

Stanworth, Michelle (ed.) 1987: *Reproductive Technologies* (Cambridge: Polity Press)

Stanworth, Philip and Anthony Giddens (eds) 1974: *Elites and Power in British Society* (Cambridge: Cambridge University Press)

Staples, Robert 1973: *The Black Woman in America* (Chicago: Nelson Hill)

Stark, Rodney and William Sims Bainbridge 1985: *The Future of Religion: Secularization, Revival and Cult Formation* (Berkeley: University of California Press)

Starr, Paul 1982: 'Medicine and the waning of professional sovereignty', *Daedalus*, 107

Statham, June 1986: *Daughters and Sons: Experiences of Non-Sexist Childraising* (Oxford: Basil Blackwell)

Stavrianos, L. S. 1981: *Global Rift: The Third World Comes of Age* (New York: Marrow)

Stein, Peter J. (ed.) 1980: *Single Life: Unmarried Adults in Social Context* (New York: St Martin's Press)

Steinberg, C. S. 1980: *TV Facts* (New York: Facts on File Inc.)

Steinson, Barbara J. 1980: '"The mother half of humanity": American women in peace and preparedness movements in World War I', in Carol R. Berkin and Clara M. Lovett, *Women, War and Revolution* (New York: Holmes and Meier)

Stinchcombe, Arthur 1982: 'The growth of the world system', *American Journal of Sociology*, 87

Stinner, William F. 1979: 'Modernization and the family extension in the Philippines: a social–demographic analysis', *Journal of Marriage and the Family*, 41

Stollman, Frans N., Rolf Ziegler and John Scott 1985: *Networks of Corporate Power: A Comparative Analysis of Ten Countries* (Cambridge: Polity Press)

Stone, John 1985: *Racial Conflict in Contemporary Society* (London: Fontana)

Stone, Lawrence 1977: *The Family, Sex and Marriage in England, 1500–1800* (London: Weidenfeld and Nicolson)

Straus, Murray A. 1978: 'Wife-beating: how common and why?', *Victimology*, 2

Straus, Murray A., Richard J. Gelles and Suzanne K. Steinmetz 1980: *Behind Closed Doors: Violence in the American Family* (Garden City, NY: Anchor)

Stromberg, A. H. and S. Harkness (eds) 1977: *Women Working, Theories and Facts in Perspective* (Palo Alto, Ca.: Mayfield)

Suransky, Valerie P. 1982: *The Erosion of Childhood* (Chicago: University of Chicago Press)

Surgeon General's Scientific Advisory Committee 1972: *Television and Social Behaviour* (Washington DC: US Government Printing Office)

Sussman, Marvin B. 1953: 'The help pattern in the middle class family', *American Sociological Review*, 18

Sutherland, Edwin H. 1949: *Principles of Criminology* (Chicago: Lippincott)
Sutherland, Edwin H. and C. Conwell 1937: *The Professional Thief* (Chicago: University of Chicago Press)
Suttles, Gerald 1968: *The Social Order of the Slum* (Chicago: University of Chicago Press)
Swann Report 1985: *Education for All* (London: HMSO)
Sydie, R. A. 1987: *Natural Women, Cultured Men: A Feminist Perspective on Sociological Theory* (New York: Methuen)
Szasz, Thomas 1971: *The Manufacture of Madness* (London: Routledge and Kegan Paul)
Szelenyi, Ivan 1983: *Urban Inequalities Under State Socialism* (Oxford: Oxford University Press)
Szreter, R. 1983: 'Opportunities for women as university teachers in England since the Robbins Report of 1963', *Studies in Higher Education*, 8
Tabb, William K. 1982: *The Long Default: New York City and the Urban Fiscal Crisis* (New York: Monthly Review Press)
Tannenbaum, A. et al. 1974: *Hierarchy in Organizations* (San Francisco: Jossey-Bass)
Task Force on Assessment 1967: 'Crime rates: impact and assessment': *Report to The President's Commission on Law Enforcement and the Administration of Justice* (Washington DC: US Government Printing Office)
Tatarian, Roger 1978: 'News flow in the Third World – an overview', in C. Horton (ed.), *The Third World and Press Freedom* (New York: Praeger)
Taylor, P. 1982: 'Schizophrenia and violence', in J. Gunn and D. Farrington (eds), *Abnormal Offenders, Delinquency and the Criminal Justice System* (Chichester: Wiley)
Terkel, Studs 1977: *Working: People Talk About What They Do All Day and How They Feel About What They Do* (Harmondsworth: Penguin)
Terkel, Studs 1984: *The Good War* (New York: Ballantine)
Thomas, Keith 1978: *Religion and the Decline of Magic* (Harmondsworth: Penguin)
Thomas, W. I. and Florian Znaniecki 1966: *The Polish Peasant in Europe and America* (New York: Dover. First pub. in 5 vols 1918–20)
Thompson, E. P. 1967: 'Time, work-discipline and industrial capitalism', *Past and Present*, 38
Thompson, E. P. 1971: 'The moral economy of the English crowd in the eighteenth century', *Past and Present*, 50
Thompson, P. 1983: *The Nature of Work* (London: Macmillan)
Thompson, Warren S. 1929: 'Population', *American Journal of Sociology*, 34
Thornley, Jenny 1981: *Workers' Co-operatives, Jobs and Dreams* (London: Heinemann)
Thrall, Charles 1970: 'Household technology and the division of labour in families', unpublished Ph.D. dissertation, Harvard University
Tilly, Charles 1975: 'Reflections on the history of European state making', in Charles Tilly (ed.), *The Formation of National States in Europe* (Princeton, NJ: Princeton University Press)
Tilly, Charles 1978: *From Mobilization to Revolution* (Reading, Mass.: Addison-Wesley)
Tilly, Louise A. and Joan W. Scott 1978: *Women, Work and Family* (New York: Holt, Rinehart and Winston)
Tinbergen, Niko 1974: *The Study of Instinct* (Oxford: Oxford University Press)
Tizard, Barbara and Martin Hughes 1984: *Young Children Learning, Talking and Thinking at Home and at School* (London: Fontana)
Tobias, J. 1967: *Crime and Industrial Society in the Nineteenth Century* (London: Batsford)
Tocqueville, Alexis de 1945: *Democracy in America*, vol. 1 (New York: Vintage. First

pub. 1835)

Tocqueville, Alexis de 1966: *The Ancien Régime and the French Revolution* (London: Collins/Fontana. First pub. 1856)

Toffler, Alvin 1970: *Future Shock* (London: Bodley Head)

Toffler, Alvin 1981: *The Third Wave* (London: Pan)

Tolliday, Steven and Jonathan Zeitlin (eds) 1986: *The Automobile Industry and Its Workers: Between Fordism and Flexibility* (Cambridge: Polity Press)

Tough, Joan 1976: *Listening to Children Talking* (London: Ward Lock Educational)

Touraine, Alain 1974: *The Post-Industrial Society* (London: Wildwood)

Touraine, Alain 1977: *The Self-Production of Society* (Chicago: University of Chicago Press)

Touraine, Alain 1981: *The Voice and the Eye: An Analysis of Social Movements* (Cambridge: Cambridge University Press)

Townsend, Peter 1979: *Poverty in the United Kingdom: A Survey of Household Resources and Standards of Living* (Harmondsworth: Penguin)

Troeltsch, Ernst 1981: *The Social Teaching of the Christian Churches* (2 vols, Chicago: University of Chicago Press)

Trow, Martin 1961: 'The second transformation of American secondary education', *Comparative Sociology*, 2

Truman, David B. 1982: *The Governmental Process* (London: Greenwood Press)

Tunstall, Jeremy 1977: *The Media are American: Anglo-American Media in the World* (London: Constable)

Turnbull, Colin 1983: *The Mbuti Pygmies: Change and Adaptation* (New York: Holt, Rinehart and Winston)

Turnbull, Colin M. 1984: *The Human Cycle* (London: Jonathan Cape)

Turner, A. 1981: 'The San José recall study', in R. Lehlen and W. Skogan (eds), *The National Crime Survey Working Papers*. Vol. I: *Current and Historical Perspectives* (Washington DC: Bureau of Justice Statistics)

Turner, John 1985: *Arms in the Eighties: New Developments in the Global Arms Race* (Cambridge: Cambridge University Press)

Turner, Ralph H. and Lewis M. Killian 1972: *Collective Behaviour* (Englewood Cliffs, NJ: Prentice-Hall)

Turowski, Jan 1977: 'Inadequacy of the theory of the nuclear family: the Polish experience', in Luis Lenero-Otero, *Beyond the Nuclear Family Model: Cross-Cultural Perspectives* (London: Sage)

Tuttle, Lisa 1986: *Encyclopedia of Feminism* (London: Longman)

Tyree, Andrea, Moshe Semyonov and Robert W. Hodge 1979: 'Gaps and glissandas: inequality, economic development and social mobility in 24 countries', *American Sociological Review*, 44

UNICEF 1987: *The State of the World's Children* (Oxford: Oxford University Press)

US Bureau of Statistics 1987: *Statistical Abstract of the United States* (Washington DC: US Government Printing Office)

US Dept of Health, Education and Welfare 1973: *Work in America: Report of a Special Task Force to the Secretary of Health, Education and Welfare* (Washington DC: US Government Printing Office)

US Riot Commission 1968: *Report of the National Advisory Commission on Civil Disorder* (New York: Bantam)

Useem, Michael 1984: *The Inner Circle: Large Corporations and the Rise of Business Political Activity in the US and the UK* (Oxford: Oxford University Press)

Van Gennep, Arnold 1977: *The Rites of Passage* (London: Routledge and Kegan Paul. First pub. 1908)

Vance, Carole S. 1984: *Pleasure and Danger: Exploring Female Sexuality* (London: Routledge and Kegan Paul)

Vanek, Joanne 1974: 'Time spent on housework', *Scientific American*, 231

Vanveley, T. et al. 1977: 'Trends in racial segregation 1960–70', *American Journal of Sociology*, 82

Vass, Anthony A. 1986: *Aids: A Plague in Us. A Social Perspective on the Condition and Its Social Consequences* (St Ives: Venus Academicus)

Vaughan, Diane 1986: *Uncoupling: Turning Points in Intimate Relationships* (Oxford: Oxford University Press)

Viorst, Judith 1987: 'And the prince knelt down and tried to put the glass slipper on Cinderella's foot', in Jack Zipes, *Don't Bet On The Prince: Contemporary Feminist Fairy Tales in North America and England* (London: Methuen)

Vischer, Emily B. and John S. Vischer 1979: *Step Families: A Guide to Working with Step-Parents and Step-Children* (Secaucus, NJ: Citadel Press)

Viteritti, Joseph P. 1979: *Bureaucracy and Social Justice: The Allocation of Jobs and Services to Minority Groups* (Port Washington, NY: Kennikat Press)

Vogel, Ezra F. 1979: *Japan as Number One: Lessons for America* (New York: Harper Colophon)

Wade, Wyn Craig 1987: *The Fiery Cross: The Ku Klux Klan in America* (New York: Simon and Schuster)

Waitzkin, Howard 1986: *The Second Sickness: Contradictions of Capitalist Health Care* (Chicago: University of Chicago Press)

Walby, Sylvia A. 1986: 'Gender, class and stratification: toward a new approach', in Rosemary Crompton and Michael Mann (eds), *Gender and Stratification* (Oxford: Basil Blackwell)

Walker, Martin 1986: *The Waking Giant: The Soviet Union Under Gorbachev* (London: Martin Joseph)

Walker, Stephen and Len Barton 1983: *Gender, Class and Education* (London: Falmer Press)

Wall, Richard, Jean Robin and Peter Laslett 1983: *Family Forms in Historic Europe* (Cambridge: Cambridge University Press)

Wallace, M. 1987: 'A caring community?', *Sunday Times*, 3 May

Wallace, Michelle 1982: 'A black feminist's search for sisterhood', in Gloria T. Hull, Patricia Bell Scott and Barbara Smith, *All the Women Are White, All the Blacks Are Men, But Some of Us Are Brave*, Black Women's Studies (Old Westbury, NY: Feminist Press)

Wallerstein, Immanuel 1974: *The Modern World System* (New York: Academic Press)

Wallerstein, Immanuel 1979: *The Capitalist World Economy* (Cambridge: Cambridge University Press)

Wallerstein, Judith S. and Joan Berlin Kelly 1980: *Surviving the Break-Up: How Children and Parents Cope with Divorce* (New York: Basic Books)

Wallis, Roy 1976: *The Road to Total Freedom: A Sociological Analysis of Scientology* (London: Heinemann)

Wallis, Roy 1987: 'My secret life: dilemmas of integrity in the conduct of field research', in Ragnhild Kristensen and Ole Riis, *Religiose Minoriteter* (Aarhus: Aarhus Universitetsfarlag)

Walsh, Dermot 1986: *Heavy Business: Commercial Burglary and Robbery* (London: Routledge and Kegan Paul)

Walum, Laurel Richardson 1977: *The Dynamics of Sex and Gender: A Sociological Perspective* (Chicago: Rand McNally)

Walvin, James 1984: *Passage to Britain: Immigration in British History and Politics*

(Harmondsworth: Penguin)

Ward, Peter M. 1981: 'Mexico City', in Michael Pacione, *Problems and Planning in Third World Cities* (London: Croom Helm)

Wardlaw, Grant 1983: *Political Terrorism: Theory, Tactics and Counter-Measures* (Cambridge: Cambridge University Press)

Warner, W. Lloyd et al. 1949: *Social Class in America* (Chicago: Science Research Associates)

Warner, W. L. and Paul Lunt 1942: *The Status System of a Modern Community* (New Haven, Conn.: Yale University Press)

Warner, W. Lloyd and P. S. Lunt 1947: *The Status System of a Modern Community* (New Haven, Conn.: Yale University Press)

Warren, Bill 1981: *Imperialism: Pioneer of Capitalism* (London: Verso)

Warren, Robert Penn 1965: *Who Speaks for the Negro?* (New York: Macmillan)

Watson, K. 1982: *Education in the Third World* (London: Croom Helm)

Weatherby, Joseph et al. 1987: *The Other World: Issues and Politics in the Third World* (New York: Macmillan)

Weber, Max 1948: *From Max Weber*, trans. and ed. by H. Gerth and C. Wright Mills (London: Routledge and Kegan Paul)

Weber, Max 1951: *The Religion of China* (New York: Free Press)

Weber, Max 1952: *Ancient Judaism* (New York: Free Press)

Weber, Max 1958: *The Religion of India* (New York: Free Press)

Weber, Max 1963: *The Sociology of Religion* (Boston, Mass.: Beacon)

Weber, Max 1976: *The Protestant Ethic and the Spirit of Capitalism* (London: Allen and Unwin. First pub. 1904–5)

Weber, Max 1978: *Economy and Society: An Outline of Interpretive Sociology* (2 vols, Berkeley: University of California Press)

Weeks, Jeffrey 1986: *Sexuality* (London: Methuen)

Weinstein, Fred 1980: *The Dynamics of Nazism: Leadership, Ideology and the Holocaust* (New York: Academic Press)

Weiss, Robert 1975: *Marital Separation* (New York: Basic Books)

Weiss, Robert 1976: *Going it Alone* (New York: Basic Books)

Weitzman, Lenore 1985: *Divorce Revolution: The Unexpected Social and Economic Consequences for Women and Children in America* (New York: Free Press)

Wellford, C. 1975: 'Labelling theory and criminology: an assessment', *Social Problems*, 22

Wellman, David T. 1987: *Portraits of White Racism* (Cambridge: Cambridge University Press)

Wells, Alan 1972: *Picture Tube Imperialism? The Impact of US Television on Latin America* (Maryknoll, NY: Orbis Books)

Western, J. 1981: *Outcast Cape Town* (London: Allen and Unwin)

Wesson, R. G. 1967: *The Imperial Order* (Berkeley: University of California Press)

Wheatley, Paul 1971: *The Pivot of the Four Quarters* (Edinburgh: Edinburgh University Press)

White, Michael and Malcolm Trevor 1983: *Under Japanese Management: The Experience of British Workers* (London: Heinemann)

Widom, Cathy Spatz and Joseph P. Newman 1985: 'Characteristics of non-institutionalized psychopaths', in David P. Farrington and John Gunn, *Aggression and Dangerousness* (Chichester: Wiley)

Wiegele, Thomas C. (ed.) 1982: *Biology and the Social Sciences: An Emerging Revolution* (Boulder, Colo.: Westview)

Wilkinson, Paul 1974: *Political Terrorism* (London: Macmillan)

Wilkinson, Paul 1986: *Terrorism and the Liberal State* (London: Macmillan)

Will, J., P. Self and N. Datan 1976: 'Maternal behaviour and perceived sex of infant', *American Journal of Orthopsychiatry*, 46

Williams, Philip M. et al. 1979: *De Gaulle's Republic* (London: Greenwood Press)

Williams, Raymond 1985: *Towards 2000* (Harmondsworth: Penguin)

Williams, Robin 1983: 'Sociological tropes: a tribute to Erving Goffman', *Theory, Culture and Society*, 2

Williams, W. M. 1956: *Gosforth: The Sociology of an English Village* (London: Routledge and Kegan Paul)

Willis, Paul 1977: *Learning to Labour: How Working Class Kids Get Working Class Jobs* (London: Saxon House)

Wilson, Bryan 1982: *Religion in Sociological Perspective* (Oxford: Oxford University Press)

Wilson, Edward O. 1975: *Sociobiology: The New Synthesis* (Cambridge, Mass.: Harvard University Press)

Wilson, Edward O. 1978: *On Human Nature* (Cambridge, Mass.: Harvard University Press)

Wilson, J. 1946: 'Egypt', in J. Frankfort et al., *The Intellectual Adventure of Ancient Man* (Chicago: University of Chicago Press)

Wilson, John 1972: *Religion* (London: Heinemann)

Wilson, M. 1951: *Good Company* (London: Routledge and Kegan Paul)

Wilson, Trevor 1986: *The Myriad Faces of War* (Cambridge: Polity Press)

Wilson, William Junius 1978: *The Declining Significance of Race: Blacks and Changing American Institutions* (Chicago: University of Chicago Press)

Wilson, William Junius et al. 1987: 'The changing structure of urban poverty', paper presented at the annual meeting of the American Sociological Association

Wiltsher, Anne 1985: *Most Dangerous Women: Feminist Peace Campaigners of the Great War* (London: Pandora)

Winch, G. (ed.) 1983: *Information Technology in Manufacturing Processes: Case Studies in Technological Change* (London: Rossendale)

Winick, Charles and Paul M. Kinsie 1971: *The Lively Commerce* (Chicago: Quadrangle)

Winn, Marie 1983: *Children Without Childhood* (New York: Pantheon)

Wirth, Louis 1938: 'Urbanism as a way of life', *American Journal of Sociology*, 44

Wistrand, Birgitta 1981: *Swedish Women on the Move*, ed. and trans. by Jeanne Rosen (Stockholm: Swedish Institute)

Wittke, Carl 1956: *The Irish in America* (Baton Rouge: Louisiana State University Press)

Wolf, Eric R. 1983: *Europe and the People Without History* (Berkeley: University of California Press)

Wolfgang, Marvin 1958: *Patterns of Homicide* (Philadelphia: University of Pennsylvania Press)

Wollstonecraft, Mary 1985: *A Vindication of the Rights of Women* (Harmondsworth: Penguin. First pub. 1792)

Wood, Stephen (ed.) 1982: *The Degradation of Work* (London: Hutchinson)

World Bank 1987: *World Development Report* (Oxford: Oxford University Press)

World Council of Churches 1980: *Programme to Combat Racism* (London: Institute for the Study of Conflict)

Worsley, Peter 1967: *The Third World* (London: Weidenfeld and Nicolson)

Worsley, Peter 1970: *The Trumpet Shall Sound: A Study of 'Cargo Cults' in Melanesia* (London: Paladin)

Worsley, Peter 1984: *The Three Worlds: Culture and World Development* (London: Weidenfeld and Nicolson)

Wright, Erik Olin 1978: *Class, Crisis and the State* (London: New Left Books)

Wright, Erik Olin 1985: *Classes* (London: Verso)

Wright, Lawrence 1968: *Clockwork Man* (London: Elek)

Wrigley, E. A. 1969: *Population and History* (London: Weidenfeld and Nicolson)

Wuthnow, Robert 1986: 'Religious movements in North America', in James A. Beckford (ed.), *New Religious Movements and Rapid Social Change* (London: Sage)

Yoffie, D. B. 1983: *Power and Protectionism: Strategies of the Newly Industrializing Countries* (New York: Columbia University Press)

Young, Allen 1972: 'Out of the closets into the streets', in Karla Jay and Allen Young (eds), *Out of the Closets: Voices of Gay Liberation* (New York: Douglas)

Zagorin, Perez 1982: *Rebels and Rulers 1550–1660*. Vol. I: *Society, States and Early Modern Revolution: Agrarian and Urban Rebellions* (Cambridge: Cambridge University Press)

Zammuner, Vanda Lucia 1987: 'Children's sex-role stereotypes: a cross-cultural analysis', in Phillip Shaver and Clyde Hendrick, *Sex and Gender* (London: Sage)

Zangrando, R. 1980: *The NAACP Crusade against Lynching, 1909–1950* (Philadelphia: Temple University Press)

Zeitlin, Irving 1984: *Ancient Judaism: Biblical Criticism from Max Weber to the Present* (Cambridge: Polity Press)

Zeitlin, Irving 1988: *The Historical Jesus* (Cambridge: Polity Press)

Zerubavel, Eviatar 1979: *Patterns of Time in Hospital Life* (Chicago: University of Chicago Press)

Zerubavel, Eviatar 1982: 'The standardization of time: a sociohistorical perspective', *American Journal of Sociology*, 88

Zimbardo, Philip 1972: 'Pathology of imprisonment', *Society*, 9

Zimblast, A. (ed.) 1979: *Case Studies in the Labour Process* (New York: Monthly Review Press)

Zola, Irving Kenneth and J. Kosa (eds) 1975: *Poverty and Health: A Sociological Analysis* (revised edn, Cambridge, Mass.: Commonwealth Fund)

Zopf, Paul E. 1986: *America's Older Population* (Houston, Texas: Cap and Gown Press)

Index

Index by Mandy Crook